LEMON-AID
NEW CARS
1999

LEMON-AID
NEW CARS
1999

PHIL EDMONSTON

Published in 1998 by
Stoddart Publishing Co. Limited
34 Lesmill Road
Toronto, Ontario
M3B 2T6

Canadian Cataloguing in Publication Data

The National Library of Canada has catalogued this publication as follows:

Edmonston, Louis-Philippe, 1944–
    Lemon-aid new cars

1998–
Annual.
Continues: Edmonston, Louis-Philippe, 1944–.
Lemon-aid new car guide, ISSN 0714-5861.
ISSN 1481-4188
ISBN 0-7737-5987-5 (1999)

1. Automobiles – Purchasing – Periodicals.
I. Title.

TL162.E3396   629.2'222'05   C98-901177-1

Cover design: Bill Douglas @ The Bang
Typesetting and text design: Wordstyle Productions
Editorial services: Greg Ioannou, Colborne Communications Centre

Printed and bound in Canada

CONTENTS

Part Three/NEW VEHICLE RATINGS
153

American Vehicles
162

Key Documents

The following photos, charts, documents, memos, and service bulletins are included in this index so that you can easily find and photocopy whichever document will prove helpful in your dealings with automakers, government agencies, dealers, or service managers. Most of the service bulletins outline repairs or replacements that should be done for free.

Part One

Part Two

Part Three

Appendices

Introduction
NASTY LITTLE SECRETS

Lemon-Aid New Cars 1999 is unlike any other auto book on the market. It's both a guide and a manifesto—with attitude. Its main objective, to inform and protect consumers dealing with an industry known for its dishonesty and exaggerated claims, remains unchanged. However, this guide also focuses on secret warranties and confidential service bulletins that automakers swear don't exist. The "Key Documents" list, found on the previous two pages, will help you find the exact bulletin, memo, or news clipping you need, reproduced from the original, so that neither the dealer nor automaker can weasel out of its obligations.

Lemon-Aid's information is culled mostly from Canadian and U.S. sources and is gathered throughout the year from owner complaints, whistle blowers, lawsuits, and judgments, as well as from confidential manufacturer service bulletins.

Each year, we also target abusive auto industry practices and lobby for changes. For example, last year we highlighted Chrysler's transmission, paint, and brake problems. Chrysler set up a telephone hot line (see Appendix V) to address owners' concerns. In addition, we called for airbag on-off switches to protect women and seniors from severe injuries caused by airbag deployment during fender-bender accidents. Following *Lemon-Aid's* urging, the government and automakers agreed to make the switches available and published the names of cooperating garages on the U.S. National Highway Traffic and Safety Administration (NHTSA) Internet site. This year, we expose the rising number of inadvertent airbag deployments, which maim thousands of drivers and passengers yearly (1 chance in 30), and we take Ford to task over its failure-prone automatic transmissions, a problem which pervades its entire product line, and over defective headgaskets on its Taurus, Sable, and Windstar 3.8L engines.

The 1999 guide makes a critical comparison of '98 and '99 cars and minivans. Safer, cheaper, and more reliable alternatives are given for each vehicle. Points are awarded for above-average crash test results and for the availability of essential safety features. Performance comparison tests and a list of essential accessories are only a sampling of the wealth of material you now have at your fingertips.

Lemon-Aid reader surveys form an essential part of a car or minivan's rating. Please fill out the questionnaire found at the end of this edition and rate the degree of satisfaction or dissatisfaction you've experienced with your new or used vehicle. The information will be compiled and used in *Lemon-Aid New Cars 2000.*

I wouldn't dare keep it a secret.

Phil Edmonston
November 1998

Part One
WHAT YOU DON'T KNOW *CAN* HURT YOU

"...The airbag knocks them silly. Then they have an accident..." (a forensic analysis as to why inadvertent airbag deployments can kill without anyone being the wiser).

Michael Lesner, Forensic Engineer
Automotive News
24 August 1995

"Out of 100 vehicles, we're apt to build 10 that are as good as any that Toyota has ever built, 80 that are okay and 10 that cause repeated problems for our customers."

Robert Lutz, President
Chrysler U.S.
Chrysler Times, 17 July 1995

That's right, Robert, and it's *Lemon-Aid*'s job to warn buyers to steer clear of that last 10 percent, and to reconsider that 80 percent that you deem to be "okay." Buyers need to know which vehicles pack an airbag "surprise" or are equipped with just "okay" transmissions and paint jobs.

It's hard to believe that I've been writing *Lemon-Aid* guides for almost 27 years. Imagine, when the first guides were written, Volkswagen had a monopoly on cold, slow (and unsold) Beetles and minivans, Ford was selling biodegradable pickups (and denying it had a secret J-67 warranty to cover rust repairs), and the average new car could be found for less than $3,000. The average price now tops $26,000.

Throughout the 1980s, the quality of imports improved dramatically, with Toyota, Nissan, and Honda leading the pack. American quality, on the other hand, improved at a snail's pace over the same period. Today, the Big Three automakers' quality control is about where the Japanese automakers' was in the mid-'80s. However, the gap hasn't narrowed (in fact, a case can be made that it's actually gotten wider) in powertrain reliability and fit and finish.

Chrysler owners' protests against paint peeling and powertrain failures led to the creation of CLOG (Chrysler Lemon Owners' Group) in British Columbia and New Brunswick. When faced with claims of paint peeling or discoloring, Chrysler usually blames its workers, bird droppings, or the sun, and then settles out of court. All automakers become more sensitive and generous when confronted with organized opposition.

Lower prices, safer products
This is the year to take the plunge and buy a new car or minivan, in spite of the persistent quality shortcomings that will likely afflict many 1999 Ford, Chrysler, and GM models. In light of GM's two-month, $3 billion strike earlier this year (guaranteed to provoke a rebate and price war in the coming months) and a plummeting yen, shoppers can expect to see more reasonable prices, a few promising new 1999 models, and a line-up of carried-over models with more standard conveniences and safety features than ever. For example, all vehicles *must* now be equipped with similar standard safety features, depowered airbags are used more extensively, child safety-seat tethers have been made more user-friendly, and overall crashworthiness has improved. All these factors mean that buyers can purchase a safer, upgraded new car or minivan this year for the same amount as—or even less than—a '98 model.

Know what you need (bring your better half along)
There are about 4,000 vehicle dealerships in Canada and they all want your money—over $26,139 for the average '97 model, according to the Automotive Industries Association of Canada. Before paying these big bucks, you should know how much you can afford to spend and what your real needs are. Don't confuse needs with styling (Do you transport the neighbourhood hockey team? Take long holiday trips?) or the trendy with the essential (Can you *really* fit into a Miata? Will you be towing a trailer?). Visiting the showroom with your spouse, a relative, or a friend

will help you steer a truer course among all the non-essential options you'll be offered. Keep in mind that most sales agents quail in front of shoppers who have done their homework and who pore over the fine print rather than be mesmerized by the many techno-toys available.

Did you spot the $475 "administration fee"?

Most car buyers don't have a clue as to what they really want and automakers are cashing in on their confusion by stuffing their cars and minivans with enough extra equipment to overwhelm most mortals—all in order to squeeze as many dollars as possible out of every sale. Dealers load up their vehicles with costly, complicated mechanical and electronic components that compromise the vehicle's original simplicity and easy reparability. Alternately, buyers are forced to purchase vehicles that are over-engineered for their driving requirements or equipped with expensive options needed only for hauling heavy cargo or for extended driving vacations. Don't fall for the dealer's "must have" song and dance. Instead, ask yourself the following questions about the kind of vehicle you want and at what price.

Can I afford it?

It makes good sense to determine how much money you can spend and *then* to decide on which vehicles interest you in that price range. Have several models in mind, so that you won't be tempted by one that may be overpriced. Use the ratings, alternative models, estimated purchase cost, and residual value figures shown in Part Three as your benchmarks. Remember, logic and prudence are the first casualties of showroom hype, so carefully consider your actual requirements and your budget before comparing models and prices at a dealership. Write down your first, second, and third choices relative to each model and the equipment offered (use the worksheet in Appendix III). To be assured of getting a sales agent's complete attention, call the dealership and ask for an appointment.

Keep in mind that car ownership is astoundingly expensive. The Canadian Automobile Association (CAA) publishes *Car Costs,* a free annual guide that pegs the annual cost of new vehicle ownership between $6,000 and $8,000. (To get a copy of the guide send a self-addressed, stamped business-size envelope to CAA at 1775 Courtwood Crescent, Ottawa, Ontario, K2C 3J2.) It breaks costs down into two categories: fixed costs and variable, or operating, costs. Fixed costs include the capital cost of the car, interest, depreciation, insurance, and licence and registration fees. Except for depreciation (the difference between the purchase price and the price your car could be sold for given its age, mileage, and condition), these costs don't vary with the amount and type of driving. Depreciation is the most important factor boosting fixed ownership costs, which is why it's a major factor in Part Three's ratings.

Variable costs are just that—variable. A lot depends on how and where you drive, the type of driving (highway or city), and the type and condition of the car. For example, Natural Resources Canada says that the difference between a car burning 13L of fuel every 100 km and one burning 10L every 100 km is about $1,200 over five years of ownership, given current gas prices and average driving patterns.

Canadian Car Operating Costs

Cost of operating a new 1996 all-equipped, 3.0L Ford Taurus
in major Canadian cities

Montreal	**$9,398**
Toronto	9,180
St. John's	9,161
Halifax	8,958
Moncton	8,696
Vancouver	8,503
Ottawa	8,406
Charlottetown	8,318
Regina	8,032
Winnipeg	7,783
Edmonton	**7,728**

*Runzheimer Canada puts out this annual analysis of what it costs to oper-
ate the average-sized car in Canada's major cities. For 1997, the firm
found that Montreal was the most expensive city in which to own a vehicle,
and Toronto came in second. The lowest cost region? Edmonton, Alberta.
Nothing beats having your own oil supply and no provincial sales tax.*

Will it suit my driving requirements?

In the city, a small wagon is more practical and less expensive than a
minivan. However, if you're going to be doing a lot of highway driving,
transporting small groups of people (especially kids), or loading up on
accessories, a medium-sized wagon or a minivan, like the Toyota
Sienna, could be the more logical choice for price, comfort, and reliability. You need an extended minivan or van only if you have to carry at
least seven occupants, haul supplies, or get a better view of the road.

Most families who travel less than 20,000 km per year should avoid the
smallest and largest engines available with a given model. Less driving
will be accommodated by a smaller engine that offers both economy and
performance. More than 20,000 km of driving per year demands the
cruising performance, extra power for additional accessories, and durability of a larger engine (a 6-cylinder, perhaps). If you spend lots of time
on the road—on business, for example—you'll definitely need an 8-
cylinder powerplant to handle the power-hungry accessories (like the AC)
essential to your driving comfort and convenience. Believe me, fuel savings will be the last thing on your mind if you buy an underpowered car.

What about short-term and long-term comfort?

The advantages of many sports cars and vans quickly pale in direct pro-
portion to your tolerance for a harsh ride, noise, a claustrophobic interior,
and limited visibility. Minivan and van owners often have to deal with a
high step-up, a cold interior, lots of buffeting from wind and passing
trucks, and limited rear visibility. With these drawbacks, many buyers find

that after falling in love with the showroom image, they end up hating their purchase. This is all the more reason to test-drive your choice over a period of several days to get a real feel for its positive and negative characteristics. Each year, I get a dozens of complaints from owners who didn't test-drive their choice sufficiently and must now trade in their almost-new vehicle because the seats are torture after a half-hour commute.

Does it respond to my special needs?

Auto designers have been more preoccupied with putting cupholders in their minivans than with designing the vans to be safer, more convenient to use, and more comfortable for women, families, and a rapidly aging population.

A survey of 2,400 women by *Chatelaine* magazine concluded that although 77 percent play a role in car buying, 52 percent feel that manufacturers don't adequately consider women's needs in designing vehicles. For example, some women remarked that if men wore skirts, it's doubtful that minivans and vans would have such a high step and that if more men hauled their children around, it's likely that standard seats would more easily accommodate child safety seats.

Will I have to change my driving habits?

Front-drive braking is quite different from braking with a rear drive, and braking efficiency on vehicles with an anti-lock brake system is compromised if you pump the brakes. As well, rear-drive minivans and vans handle like trucks and will scrub the right rear tire during sharp right-hand turns until you get the hang of making wider turns.

Which safety features do I want?

This is the year that anti-lock brakes and airbags have been proven to be of limited effectiveness in certain kinds of accidents and to be downright deadly for inexperienced drivers or occupants who aren't of "ideal" stature. If you're of small size, a senior, likely to carry someone small in the front seat, or have recently had upper torso surgery, airbags may pose a serious safety hazard. Since you can't buy a new car or minivan without a driver-side airbag, you'll want to choose a vehicle with an adjustable seat that can travel far enough backwards to keep you at a safe distance (about a foot) from the airbag's explosive 300 km/h deployment. (Some 1998–99 models come equipped with "Second Generation" airbags, which deploy with one-third less force.) Children's safety can be assured by getting a vehicle with an airbag shut-off switch or by having them sit in the rear-middle seat position. Just remember, it's a question of size, not age.

One safety feature that continues to be a lifesaver is a high crash-protection rating. Since some vehicles are more crashworthy than others and size doesn't always guarantee crash safety, it's important to buy the vehicle that gives you the best protection in a frontal collision. For example, the Chrysler Caravan and Ford Windstar minivans are similarly designed but your chances of surviving a high-speed collision in the Windstar are far

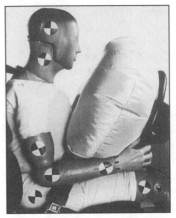

Don't be a dummy; sit at least a foot away from the airbag and make sure the tilt steering feature doesn't aim the bag at your head.

greater than if you were riding in a Caravan (or any other Chrysler minivan, for that matter). Furthermore, the latest redesigns don't translate into the *safest* redesigns, judging by the abysmal crash ratings the Insurance Institute for Highway Safety (IIHS) awarded GM's new Venture minivan. Before making a final decision on the vehicle you want, look up its crash rating in Part Three and compare that rating with similar vehicles in Appendix IV's Crash-test Summary.

Is new better than used?

Absolutely, with all the price-cutting clearance sales expected on the '98 models and with '99s holding the line on prices. This goes double for minivans, vans, pickups, or sport-utilities that, in addition to undergoing some price restraint, will also depreciate less rapidly than passenger cars. For example, depreciation will knock off less than one-third of your new minivan's value during the first three years of ownership, whereas the average new car will be worth only half its original value over the same period. Nevertheless, there is an easy way to reduce the depreciation "bite" on a new car—keep it five years or longer and choose a model predicted to last that long without requiring expensive repairs.

Keep in mind, however, that you begin to save money from the outset when purchasing any used vehicle, whether you keep it for a few months or a few years. Once you add federal and provincial taxes, financing costs, maintenance, and a host of other expenses, you'll find that the yearly outlay for a new car is about two times that of a used car.

Can I get the same vehicle for less, elsewhere?

Sure. You can shop on-line through the Internet and use one dealer's quotes as leverage to get a better deal elsewhere. (Hyundai dealers have quoted lower prices to cyber-shoppers than to walk-ins.) On the other hand, sometimes a cheaper twin or hybrid model will also fit the bill. Twins are those nameplates that are virtually identical in body design and mechanical components, like the Ford Sable/Taurus, GM Camaro/Firebird, and the Chrysler Caravan/Voyager.

If the Chevrolet Cavalier, shown above, costs too much, try a Pontiac Sunfire, shown below—they're practically identical.

Perhaps a hybrid or "captive import" will be more to your, and your pocketbook's, liking. American manufacturers have learned to join the Asian automakers instead of competing against them and vice versa. This has resulted in hybrids whose parentage is impossible to nail down but that incorporate a high degree of quality control. Suzuki builds the Chevrolet (formerly known as Geo) Tracker 4X4 in Ontario, Mazda and Ford churn out Probes in the U.S., and Ford's Villager/Quest minivan is a Nissan co-venture.

Sometimes choosing a higher trimline will cost you less when all the standard features are accounted for. (General Motors "special edition" vehicles, for example, could give you all the options you need for much less than if you ordered them separately on a cheaper model.) It's hard to compare value prices with the manufacturer's base price, however, because the base prices are inflated and can be negotiated downward, while value-priced cars are offered as a "take it or leave it" proposition.

Twins and hybrids are only two of the many alternatives. Minivans, for example, come in two versions: a base commercial version and a more luxurious model for private use. The commercial version doesn't have as many bells and whistles, but it's more likely to be in stock and will probably cost much less. If you're planning to convert it anyway, all the extras may just get in the way.

1998 Automotive Twins

Automotive "twins" are vehicles that have different nameplates but the same drivetrain and chassis. They may even come off the same assembly line. One twin may offer different equipment or a better deal in the marketplace than the other.

Small Cars
- Dodge Neon–Plymouth Neon
- Ford Escort–Mercury Tracer
- Geo Metro–Suzuki Swift
- Geo Prizm -Toyota Corolla
- Toyota Paseo–Toyota Tercel
- Volkswagen Golf–Volkswagen Jetta

Mid-Size Cars
- Audi A4–Volkswagen Passat
- Buick Skylark–Oldsmobile Achieva–Pontiac Grand Am
- Chevrolet Cavalier–Pontiac Sunfire
- Chevrolet Malibu–Oldsmobile Cutlass
- Chrysler Cirrus–Dodge Stratus–Plymouth Breeze
- Ford Contour–Mercury Mystique
- Hyundai Elantra–Hyundai Tiburon
- Infiniti I30–Nissan Maxima
- Lexus ES 300–Toyota Camry

Large Cars
- Buick LeSabre–Oldsmobile Eighty Eight–Oldsmobile LSS–Oldsmobile Regency–Pontiac Bonneville
- Buick Park Avenue–Buick Riviera–Oldsmobile Aurora
- Buick Regal–Pontiac Grand Prix
- Chevrolet Lumina–Chevrolet Monte Carlo–Oldsmobile Cutlass Supreme
- Chrysler Concorde–Dodge Intrepid–Eagle Vision

- Ford Crown Victoria–Mercury Grand Marquis
- Ford Taurus–Mercury Sable

Sporty Cars
- Chevrolet Camaro–Pontiac Firebird
- Chrysler Sebring–Dodge Avenger

Vans and Minivans
- Chevrolet Astro–GMC Safari
- Chevrolet Express–GMC Savana
- Chevrolet Venture–Oldsmobile Silhouette–Pontiac Trans Sport
- Chrysler Town & Country LX–Dodge Grand Caravan–Plymouth Grand Voyager
- Chrysler Town & Country SX–Dodge Caravan–Plymouth Voyager
- Mercury Villager–Nissan Quest

Trucks and Sport-Utility Vehicles
- Acura SLX–Isuzu Trooper
- Chevrolet Blazer–GMC Jimmy–Oldsmobile Bravada
- Chevrolet Silverado–GMC Sierra
- Chevrolet S10–GMC Sonoma–Isuzu Hombre
- Chevrolet Suburban–GMC Suburban
- Chevrolet Tahoe–GMC Yukon
- Ford Explorer–Mercury Mountaineer
- Ford Ranger–Mazda B-Series Pickup
- Geo Tracker–Suzuki Sidekick
- Lexus LX 430–Toyota Land Cruiser

Shhh! It's a secret! There's not a dime's worth of real difference between most of the above vehicles.

Leasing is an alternative often used to make vehicles appear to be more affordable but it's actually more expensive than buying; for most people, the pitfalls will far outweigh any advantages. If you have to lease, keep your losses to a minimum by leasing only for the shortest time possible and by making sure that the lease is closed-ended (meaning that you walk away from the vehicle when the lease period ends).

If long-term leasing looks to be too expensive, consider purchasing a three- to five-year-old vehicle with 60,000 to 100,000 km on the clock and some of the original warranty left. Such a vehicle will likely be just as reliable and will entail less than one-half the cost of one bought new. Parts will be easier to find, independent servicing should be a breeze, insurance premiums will come down from the stratosphere, and if you get a lemon, your financial risk is considerably lessened.

Hidden costs

There are a lot of hidden costs involved in owning a new car or mini-van. Automotive magazines don't provide many details about these costs because they don't want to anger their industry sponsors or direct buyers to used cars, thereby undercutting new car sales. Car columnists in particular don't want to offend the manufacturers who supply them with free test cars. This is why you don't see most of the motoring press including such important factors as crashworthiness, parts costs and availability, warranty complaints, and depreciation in their new car ratings. Yet this is precisely the information that most buyers want. The exceptions are *AutoWeek,* a spinoff of the fiercely independent *Automotive News; Mechanics Illustrated* and its quarterly spin-off *CarSmart,* both of which have always taken an independent line; and *Consumer Reports,* which spurns paid advertisements. Be wary of *Consumer Reports* knock-offs like *Consumer Guide* or *Consumer Digest,* which *do* carry advertising and aren't nearly as critical.

Don't be taken in by gas mileage figures trumpeted by the manufacturers, either. Because the vehicles are run under optimum conditions by automakers who must submit their test results to the government, these said results are exaggerated by about 10 percent. Sure, good fuel economy is important but it's hardly worth a harsh ride, highway noise, sidewind buffeting, anemic acceleration, and a cramped interior. You may end up with much worse gas mileage than advertised and a vehicle that's underpowered for your needs.

Tax advantages

Tax rules for cars and minivans are very complex. Nevertheless, whether you have a full-time job or are self-employed, there's a good chance that you can deduct some of your transportation expenses on your income tax return. It all hinges on the quality of your recordkeeping—*not* whether you buy or lease, as some sales people would lead you to believe.

"New" isn't always new

Sorry to burst your bubble, but it's quite probable that the vehicle you bought isn't really new. The odometer may have been disconnected or the vehicle could have been involved in an accident, as was the case with Chrysler cars sold in the late 1980s. Chrysler admitted to disconnecting the odometers on more than 60,000 vehicles. Some of these had been involved in serious accidents and were repaired and sold as new to unsuspecting Canadian and American buyers.

Alternately, the dealer may have disconnected the odometer and driven the car for several thousand kilometres as a demonstrator. Even if the vehicle hasn't been used, it may have been left outdoors for a considerable length of time, causing the deterioration of rubber components, premature body and chassis rusting, and rusting of internal mechanical parts (leading to brake malfunction and fuel line contamination, hard starting, and stalling).

You can check a vehicle's age by consulting the date of manufacture plate found on the driver's side door pillar. If the date of manufacture is 7/98, your car was one of the last 1998 models made before the September changeover to the 1999 models. Redesigned vehicles or those new to the market are exceptions to this rule. They arrive at dealerships in early spring or mid-summer and are considered to be next year's models. They also depreciate more quickly, owing to their earlier launching, but this difference narrows over time.

There's also the very real possibility that the new vehicle you've just purchased was damaged while being shipped to the dealer and was fixed by the dealer during the pre-delivery inspection. This happens to an estimated 10 percent of all new vehicles but there's no specific Canadian legislation allowing buyers of vehicles damaged in transit to cancel their contracts. In a more general sense, however, Canadian common law jurisprudence does allow for cancellation or compensation whenever the delivered product differs markedly from what the buyer expected to receive.

Carryover models from previous years generally have fewer problems than vehicles that have been significantly reworked or just introduced to the market. This fact is borne out by a recent J. D. Power study of 74 vehicles launched from 1989 to '96, which found that the Big Three's relaunched models suffered an 8 percent decline in quality, which turned into a 19 percent quality improvement in the second year. Among Japanese automakers, Honda, Toyota, and Nissan posted an average 17 percent decline in their first-year offerings and this decline was wiped out by an average 19 percent improvement in the next year.

Most vehicles assembled between September and February are called "first series" cars, because they were the first off the assembly line for that model year. Made between March and August, "second series" vehicles incorporate more assembly-line fixes and are better-built than the earlier models, which depend on ineffective "field fixes" that may only mask the symptoms until the warranty expires. Although both vehicles will sell for the same price, the post-February model is by far the better buy, since it benefits from assembly-line upgrades and rebates.

This is particularly true of GM's entire production output this year, which was delayed several months in the fall of '98 (during its model year changeover) due to strike action. Not only will first-series vehicle quality suffer due to the changeover, but the ensuing rushed production means dealers will be burdened with repairing assembly-line defects and replacing the sub-standard parts from suppliers who weren't "validated" through GM's quality control cycle. This gives car buyers all the more reason to let the fleet managers and rental car companies take their chances with GM's first six months of production.

Who Can You Trust?

Car columnists: hear no evil, see no evil
I find it hard to accept the passivity of Canadian automotive journalists, who by and large have been bought by the Canadian automobile industry through trips and trinkets or cowed by their editors and producers into believing that their job hinges on how well they kiss advertisers' butts. Unlike the American press, which boasts a number of principled investigative auto writers, few members of the Canadian automotive press corps will stand up for their constituents and expose the outrageously high cost of auto ownership; unsafe safety features, like airbags and anti-lock brakes, which are poorly designed, prone to malfunction, and capable of killing or maiming women, seniors, and other drivers or passengers of small stature; and national dealer/automaker sales scams—such as leasing—which bilk motorists out of millions annually. Their silence adds to their complicity.

Although car columnists claim that their integrity is not for sale, there's no doubt that it can be rented. Travel junkets, public relations, and advertising contracts all sweeten the honey pot for these pseudo-journalists. A few years ago, CTV's *W5* newsmagazine show ran an exposé of how Canadian car columnists and broadcasters ripped off automakers by demanding $3,000 in corporate membership fees to join their Automobile Journalists Association. (Individual memberships cost $100 at the time.) General Motors of Canada pulled out of the Association's "Car of the Year" competition (held shortly after the broadcast) but has since returned.

Additionally, the *Toronto Star* declared that henceforth its columnists would have to indicate in a footnote to their articles if their information came from a travel junket or if a manufacturer-supplied vehicle was used. Oddly enough, the CBC and *The Globe and Mail* don't accept automaker junkets or free loaners. Instead, these not-so-pristine news organs hire freelance automotive writers, who take the wheels and meals in their own name.

Nevertheless, there are some Canadian auto writers who have distinguished themselves by writing balanced investigative reports on the auto industry. These writers include John Terauds (the *Toronto Star* "Wheels" editor) and freelance writer Denyse O'Leary. Terauds, hired several years ago, writes in-depth profiles of the auto industry using a variety of consumer-based resources. Although he's been called on the carpet repeatedly for denouncing dealer sales scams and for his jaundiced eye for industry pap, he's made the "Wheels" section more consumer-friendly and still kept his job (keep your fingers crossed). O'Leary is a persistent freelance journalist who's quite resistant to government and corporate BS; she recently dug in her heels when the Ministry of Transport stonewalled her research into the dangers of airbags.

'Forget Paris,' GM Tells Journalists; Instead, They Get to Visit Detroit

By Robert L. Simison

Staff Reporter of The Wall Street Journal

DETROIT—The fallout from the recent strike at General Motors Corp. included a surprise victim: Cadillac's press junket to the Paris auto show next month.

To generate ink back home about their latest new cars and trucks, the Big Three auto makers routinely host expense-paid trips for U.S. journalists to foreign auto shows—most often in Paris, Frankfurt, Geneva and Tokyo. (Some news organizations, including this one, reimburse their reporters' hosts.)

So it was hardly surprising that GM's luxury division invited a score of auto writers and business reporters to join its executives on a five-day Paris fling in late September. After all, Cadillac is trying to position itself as GM's global luxury marque.

But two weeks after the invitations went out, GM management decreed deep cuts in all discretionary spending.

Cadillac won't say how much it had budgeted for plane fare, hotel rooms, meals, wine and its special briefings, but Detroit public-relations veterans say the tab would hit $10,000 to $12,000 per journalist pretty quickly.

All at once, what had seemed like a good idea started to look fiscally irresponsible, says J. Christopher Preuss, the Cadillac communications director. Cadillac decided its Paris activities could wait until January and the at-home Detroit auto show. The invitees who had accepted were quietly informed that because of the strike, the trip was off. "It's embarrassing," Mr. Preuss says.

GM cancelled its press junket to Paris for a score of auto writers during the UAW/CAW strike because the company felt it would look "fiscally irresponsible." In doing so, the automaker saved the earmarked $10,000 to $12,000—per journalist—for the planned five-day stay.

The *Montreal Gazette* and the *Windsor Star* stand as two examples of the pernicious effect advertisers can have on editorial slant. In a May 18, 1991, story on Chrysler's call for trade restraints on Japanese imports, the *Gazette* rightfully suggested that Chrysler Canada president Yves Landry was a hypocrite for supporting import quotas. The story pointed out that Chrysler, as a part owner of Mitsubishi, was a large-scale importer of Japanese-made vehicles, sold under Chrysler's name as the Colt, Eagle, Laser, and Talon. Chrysler claimed that the story was unfair and yanked all of its advertising from the paper. The *Gazette* stood its ground and Chrysler advertising in the paper has returned to normal.

Compare this with the *Windsor Star*'s strange, unnecessary, and exaggerated apology last year to car dealers made by that paper's publisher, James Bruce. Bruce ran a three-column apology to Windsor-area car dealers for having run a Canadian Press story criticizing Montreal car dealers (that's right, *Montreal* car dealers). The story, based on a survey done by Automobile Protection Association president George Iny, questioned the honesty of nine auto dealerships that were surveyed in Montreal. Bruce felt that the story might reflect badly on local dealers and insisted that the following apology be run.

Story Failed to Meet *Star's* Standards

...On rare occasions a story finds its way into the newspaper which does not meet the high ethical and journalistic standards of balance, fairness and factual accuracy which we set for ourselves at the *Windsor Star*.... Although the story did not involve any Essex County dealers, it may have by implication, cast aspersions on their business practices. The story was a discredit to the dealers and employees of members of the Windsor Essex County Dealers Association, who adhere to the highest of ethical standards and provide their customers with first rate standards of service....

Unreliable ratings

Once you've established a budget and selected some vehicles that interest you, the next step is to ascertain which ones have high reliability and safety ratings. Be wary of the ratings found in some enthusiast magazines—their supposedly independent tests are a lot of baloney. Their test car is supplied by the manufacturer and tuned to just the right specifications, servicing will be impeccable, and the manufacturer will probably load the car with an assortment of expensive options to compensate for any design faults.

Automakers can't lose with this rigged test. If the tester wants other free courtesy cars to drive, the published report had better gloss over the vehicle's defects and hype its mediocre features. Additionally, if the magazine or newspaper receives advertising from the manufacturer, any criticism that gets through the driver's own self-censorship will be muted by the editor. Another very important reason for discounting these tests is that they don't predict a car's vulnerability to rust or crash forces, or factor in poor servicing and inadequate parts distribution.

The Automobile Journalists Association of Canada (AJAC) 1997 Car of the Year Awards gave best marks to the Venture minivan (one of the worst-performing minivans ever crash-tested by the Insurance Institute for Highway Safety) and the '95 Car of the Year designation was given to the Chrysler Neon—one of Chrysler's worst performing vehicles, say CAA, APA, Consumer Reports, *and* Lemon-Aid. *Hmm...I wonder which car they'll judge Car of the Century at next year's Toronto Auto Show—the Bricklin, Delorean, or Vega?*

As mentioned earlier, don't look to the automakers or their dealers for helpful information relating to the crashworthiness of the vehicles they manufacture and sell. At Toronto's International Auto Show held in February 1995, Richard Martin, a TVOntario field producer, asked automaker representatives how well their vehicles fared in their own or government-run crash tests. With camera crew in tow, he was rebuffed by a half-dozen automakers who said crash information was unavailable or was given out only by head office. Even after calling each company's head office, no crash data was given out. Surprisingly, even Volvo and Saturn, two automakers who claim to put their car owners' interests first, refused to provide the requested crash-test information.

Handling information overload

Funny, as soon as they hear that you're shopping for a new car, everybody wants to tell you what to buy—relatives, co-workers, and friends all seem to know what's best for you. After a while, you'll get so many conflicting opinions that it'll seem as if any choice you make will be the wrong one. Before making your decision, remember that you should invest a month of research in your $26,000-plus new-car-buying project. This includes two weeks for basic research (see below) and another two weeks to actually bargain with dealers to get the right price and equipment. The following sources provide a variety of useful information that will help you ferret out the vehicle that best suits your needs and budget.

Online services/Internet

Anyone with access to a computer and a modem can now obtain useful information relating to the auto industry in a matter of minutes and at little cost. This is accomplished in two ways: by subscribing to one of the two American online services that offer everything from consumer forums to easy Internet access or by going directly to the Internet through a low-cost Canadian "server" and cruising the thousands of sites that summarize the subject matter or the services offered.

Online services
If you're new to cruising the Internet, try the two major American online services accessible to Canadians—America Online and CompuServe. The services are similar, barring minor differences in the way fees are collected. Without a doubt, the liveliest and most informative CompuServe sites are the forums on cars and consumer rights. Watched over, but not censored, by a volunteer system operator (sysop), members post hundreds of messages each week covering issues ranging from how to keep cats off your car (use an open box of mothballs) to the particulars of GM's secret paint warranty (a Chevrolet dealer's warranty administrator actually gave out all the details).

After only a few months, you will quickly acquire the skills to access the Internet on your own, browse the various forums, and shop the hundreds of auto-related services that simplify buying and owning a car. With the click of a button you can cruise consumer-advocacy message areas (called forums), download (receive data from a host computer via an electronic link) government auto-safety defect probes, recall campaigns, and crashworthiness ratings and find out what dealer incentives and customer rebates are being paid out by automakers. Subscribers can also access sites in order to shop for a new vehicle or accessories, read online versions of popular American auto magazines, including *Consumer Reports,* and get industry news and reviews.

Internet
After having their hand held by AOL or CompuServe for a few months, many online service subscribers jump ship and strike out on their own by switching to an Internet service provider that doesn't have all the razzle-dazzle of AOL and CompuServe but provides easier, quicker Internet access at more competitive prices.

To get on the Internet you must first find a "server," or service provider, who will give unlimited access to the Internet at an average cost of $25 a month. Most service providers provide test accounts so that you can try out the service before signing up. This allows you to check the number of phone lines your server has available and determine how accessible the phone-in technical support is.

Local newspapers or computer publications are a good place to comparison shop for servers in your area. Before signing up, however, talk to your local college, university, or library to find out if they offer free Internet connections to outsiders or if they can put you in touch with a "freenet" system (run largely by volunteers).

Surfing the Net requires software, such as Netscape Navigator, along with a "dial-up" program, both of which can be installed without much trouble. Your service provider (if it's a good one) will have a technical service line you can call for step-by-step help in downloading the software you need. There are also search engines that will list sites on the web according to subject or name. For example, if you want to find sites related to Chrysler cars, a web search using WebCrawler or Alta Vista will come up with hundreds of sites. Make your request as specific as possible. A search under "new cars," for example, would be useless.

Search Engines

Alta Vista
http://altavista.digital.com
Hotbot
http://www.hotbot.com
Lycos
http://www.lycos.com
Open Text
http://index.opentext.net
Yahoo.ca
http://www.yahoo.com

Excite
http://www.excite.com
Infoseek
http://guide.infoseek.com
Magellan
http://www.mckinley.com
WebCrawler
http://webCrawler.com

Helpful Automotive Web Sites

(All web site addresses are prefaced with *http://www* and most Canadian sites have the suffix *.ca*. Some sites may have changed or been dropped. If you have difficulty locating one of the following web sites, return to your search engine and try again, modifying the name slightly.)

Automakers

4adodge.com	*alfaromeo.com*	*audi.com*
bmw.ca	*cadillac.com*	*chryslercars.com*
ferrari.it	*fiat.nl*	*ford.ca*
gm.com	*hmc.co.kr (Hyundai)*	*honda.com*
infinitimotors.com	*jaguarvehicles.com*	*jeep_unpaved.com*
landrover.com	*lexuscanada.com*	*mazda.ca*
mercedesbenz.ca	*mitsubishi-motors.co.jp*	*nissancanada.com*
opel.com	*peugeot.com*	*plymouthcars.com*
pontiac.com	*porsche-usa.com*	*rolls-royce.com*
saabusa.com	*saturncars.com*	*subaru.ca*
suzuki.com	*toyota.com*	*vauxhall.co.uk*
volvocars.com	*vw.com*	

Purchasing and Information

All Things Automotive (*http://www.webcom.com/-autodir*)—Links to lots of other automotive sites.

autobytel.com—A bilingual service that gives out car specs and promises to give you price quotes from Canadian dealers within two days.

autocenter.com—One of the most comprehensive automotive web sites, with thousands of interesting links.

Auto Channel (*http://www.the-autochannel.com*)—Lots of substance and video glitz, and even reviews other automotive web sites.

autokey.com—A dealer site from B.C. with links to other general information sites.

automatch.com—More of the same, except it's not B.C.-based.

Automotive-Related Mailing Lists (*http://triumph.cs.utah.edu/othermail. html*)—Links to mailing lists for most makes of automobiles, as well as frequently asked questions (FAQ) for specific models.

autonet.ca—Another dealer-sponsored site with links to the *World of Wheels* and *Canadian Auto World* magazines.

autoshop-online.com—Everything you wanted to know about repair, maintenance, and operating your vehicle.

Autosite (*http://ias4.autosite.com*)—A site with an exhaustive compilation of car info.

autoweb.com—Looking for a rare collectible? Look no further.

CAA (*caa.ca*)—The CARP on wheels. See also CAA's *Autopinion* magazine (*magamall.com/mag/80698/profile.htm.*)

CAMVAP (*camvap.ca*)—Lots of fascinating statistics on who gets their car taken back through CAMVAP arbitration and who doesn't. Incidentally, Larry Johnson, Ford's former National Service Manager, is CAMVAP's chairman.

carcalulator.com—Rob Lo Presti's web site for prudent consumers who wish to look before they lease. Rob is an auto consumer advocate with over a decade's experience in helping motorists decipher leases and in defending consumer rights.

carpoint.msn.com—Microsoft's comprehensive auto information site.

Cartalk.com—Canadian radio show's comments about cars.

cybercar.com—Listings of Canadian used cars.

eauto.com—Mainly for racing fans and do-it-yourselfers.

edmunds.com—U.S. new car prices, specs, and comparisons.

findlinks.com—A comprehensive listing of auto industry web sites.

intellichoice.com—U.S. new car prices, specs, and comparisons.

kbb.com—U.S. new and used car prices, specs, and comparisons. A bit more thorough than Edmunds.

lynx.bc.ca.newcarprices—Gives out Canadian new car prices for a fee. Use it as an alternative to the Automobile Protection Association's dealer invoice price service (see Appendix V).

National Highway Traffic and Safety Administration (*nhtsa.dot.gov*)—The U.S. federal government's Department of Transportation site, with lots of info on crash tests, recalls, and safety information.

sover.net—Where have all the Firenzas gone? This Hemmings site lists all of the automotive clubs in Canada and the U.S.

Transport Canada (*tc.gc.ca*)—The NHTSA's weaker twin, posting a fuel consumption guide and Canadian recalls for the past three years.

Objective publications

The key word here is *objective.* Consumer groups and auto associations are your best bet for the most unbiased auto ratings. They're not perfect, however, so it's a good idea to consult several and look for ratings that agree. The following independent sources of new car buying information are available from your local library: the Automobile Protection Agency's *Magazine* (a quarterly publication also available for $12 from the APA, 292 St. Joseph Blvd. West, Montreal, Quebec, H2V 2N7) and the April auto edition of *Consumer Reports* (also sold at newsstands).

Neither the APA's *Magazine* nor *Consumer Reports* carries advertising. The former bases its evaluations on Canadian motorists' complaints, government probes, and reports from independent garages. *CR* rates vehicles from an American perspective through member surveys, government crash tests, and its own testing centre, where it road-tests vehicles purchased anonymously. All three publications list the MSRP (Manufacturer's Suggested Retail Price); however, Canadian dealers' higher markup isn't shown, and most prices have been boosted by the time these magazines hit the newsstands. Although the APA's list prices are too broad in range to be useful in negotiating a final price, the organization will fax the dealer's invoice price to subscribers for a small fee (fax your request to the APA at 514-273-0797 or call them at 514-APA-5555).

AutoWeek and *Automotive News* are the best trade and special-interest magazines for objective car-buying information. These publications accept automaker and engine "wonder drug" ads, but they remain relatively independent. Canadian Tire's *Autoroute* magazine is jam-packed with helpful do-it-yourself information and used car tips aimed at Canadian drivers. *Popular Mechanics* is a similar publication for Americans.

Consumer Reports ratings, extrapolated from Consumers Union's annual U.S. member survey, also accurately mirror the Canadian experience, with two exceptions. Components that are particularly vulnerable to our harsh climate usually perform less well than the *CR* reliability ratings indicate; and poor servicing, caused by a weak dealer body, can make some service-dependent vehicles a nightmare to own in Canada.

Based on 600,000-plus member responses, *CR* lists vehicles that vary from the industry average, according to owner reports. Statisticians agree that *CR*'s sampling method has some room for error, but the ratings are good, conservative guidelines for buying a new vehicle that hasn't changed much from year to year, and the ratings have stood up to court challenges from automakers. My only criticism is that many models—like Lada and Jaguar—are excluded from *CR*'s ratings, and its frequency-of-repair ratings for certain components aren't specific enough (a failing of CAA ratings, as well). For example, don't just tell me that there are problems with the fuel, or with the electrical system. Rather, let me know about specific components—is it the fuel pumps that are failure-prone, or the injectors that clog up, or the battery that suddenly dies?

There's also the Canadian Automobile Association's annual *Autopinion* magazine, published every January and available from CAA and newsstands for $6. Kind of like CARP on wheels, CAA is an efficient, competent organization that has reluctantly stuck its big toe into the hot water of consumer advocacy, mostly through promoting auto safety. The group spends much of its time starting and towing cars, selling vacations, preparing trip maps, and decrying gasoline taxes. Much like Canada's Better Business Bureaus, whose noble intentions were compromised early on by a mixture of business-led intimidation, threats of lawsuits, and the withdrawal of financial support, CAA has traditionally treated consumer advocacy with a mixture of fear and benign neglect.

That said, I must add that some provincial CAA-affiliated groups, such as the Alberta Automobile Motorists Association and Quebec's Club d'automobile du Québec take their consumer advocacy roles quite seriously, and have vigourously defended their members rights. Too bad they're the exception, not the rule.

Autopinion mostly contains general-interest articles from auto industry toadies, as well as a summary listing of new cars and trucks. It also offers used vehicle ratings, based on an owner sampling that's less than 5 percent of *CR*'s. *Autopinion* gives you a good general idea of those vehicles that have generated the most problems for CAA members, but its conclusions shouldn't be followed unless they're confirmed by the APA or *Consumer Reports*. CAA editors paint with too broad a stroke for vehicles and model years that have an insufficient number of responses. Just look at the Lada and Hyundai ratings and you'll see what I mean.

What about the APA's semi-annual ratings of new and used cars and my own *Lemon-Aid*'s auto ratings? Don't trust them either without checking other consumer publications. The APA's ratings are based on Canadian consumer complaints and independent garage reports. *Lemon-Aid* does tend to make technical mistakes because it concentrates more on driver feedback than manufacturers' press releases. I also tend to be very dismissive of auto industry hype and place perhaps too much emphasis on the thousands of consumer complaints and internal service bulletins I get each year. Nevertheless, I try to balance these shortcomings with a wide variety of objective data.

Look Before You Lease

Canadians are reluctant to buy new vehicles because they cost too darned much. Instead of doing the right thing—reducing prices—automakers are offering deceptive buy-back leases that hide padded list prices through longer monthly payments. And the tactic is working—leasing has never been more popular, or more lucrative for dealers and automakers alike.

Leasing costs more

Lessees pay the full manufacturer's suggested retail price on a vehicle loaded with costly options, plus hidden fees and interest charges that wouldn't be included if the vehicle were purchased instead. The dealer's MSRP markup for cars and minivans may scare you. DesRosiers Automotive Research Inc., a Toronto consulting firm that studies the leasing industry, found that cheaper cars often cost more to lease than some luxury models. This was confirmed by the Canadian Bankers Association (CBA) when it blasted dealers' leasing contracts for charging interest rates as high as 34 percent and called for consumer protection legislation to regulate the industry. In another survey, carried out five years ago by *Les Affaires,* a Montreal-based business weekly, mid-range cars and minivans were shown to cost about $3,000 more if leased rather than financed, and luxury cars about $7,000 to $9,000 more.

Sure, you get zero freight, PDI, air tax, and licence transfer—as long as you pay full MSRP and accept an annual limit of 18,000 km.

Rob Lo Presti, a Toronto-based consumer advocate and leasing consultant, has campaigned tirelessly for more disclosure in leasing contracts. He says a few provinces have legislation requiring disclosure and limiting contract cancellation penalties, but that it doesn't go far enough, and allows leasing agencies to get away with legalized highway robbery through outrageously excessive hidden leasing charges and usurious loan rates.

Most people don't have the time or patience to do the complex calculations that leasing contracts require. For them, Lo Presti has created CarCalculator, an easy-to-use program that runs on any computer with Windows 3.1 or 95. It takes the mystery out of leasing by giving you the annual interest rate you are paying, the total cost of the lease, and how it compares to financing—facts guaranteed to frustrate any fast-talking dealer or leasing agent. It costs $40 (including shipping and GST, for *Lemon-Aid* readers) from OrangeSoft Corp., P.O. Box 33518, 1277 York Mills Road, North York, Ontario M3A 1Z5. Callers may dial 1-800-647-8693 (toll free in Canada). OrangeSoft Corp. will also check a lease quote for $20 ($10 for each additional quote). For more information, call the 1-800 number or check out their Internet site at *www.carcalculator.com.*

The Obscure Language of Leasing

Acquisition fee: Frequently hidden in the body of the contract, this is a $300–$450 extra charge for what is essentially overhead covered in the monthly payment. It's 100 percent profit for the dealer. Save it as the last item to discuss and then refuse to pay it.

Closed-end lease: This lease protects you from a decline in the vehicle's value when the lease expires. Useful with some cars, but a waste of money with slow-depreciating MPVs.

Disposition fee: Another abusive "extra" for preparing the vehicle for resale at the end of the lease. Don't accept this charge.

Early termination penalty: The fee paid by the customer when the lease is broken (see previous comments).

Excess mileage charge: This fee is charged for mileage that exceeds the cap set in the contract. Try to get a cap of 20,000-30,000 km per lease year and a rate that's less than 6 cents per kilometre.

Open-end lease: This lease holds the customer responsible for the difference should a vehicle's value fall below the residual value pre-set when the contract was signed. Not a likely prospect with most sport-utilities, minivans, vans, and pickups that usually depreciate slowly over the years.

Residual value: Think of it as the pre-set trade-in value for a leased vehicle. The lower the residual value, the greater your chance of making money if you purchase the vehicle at the expiration of the lease and then sell it privately a year or two later.

Leasing advantages

Leasing can be worthwhile for people who frequently trade in their cars, since it's more convenient and results in less sales tax. (This advantage is wiped out, however, if you lease for longer than three years or buy back the car at the end of the lease.) In some cases, you may be paying too much if you don't lease, since leasing enables you to drive a new vehicle without tying up a bundle of money that you could otherwise invest or use to pay down more costly debts. Leasing may also offer some tax advantages if your car expenses are deductible from gross income. Unfortunately, the savings are often minimal. According to the accounting firm of Price Waterhouse, in 99 percent of the cases it examined, there wasn't much difference in the tax liability if the vehicle was bought or leased. Your chief consideration shouldn't be the tax savings, but rather the difference between the implicit interest rate in the lease and the financing charge.

Leasing disadvantages

Leased vehicles are usually overpriced, jam-packed with nonessential options, and accompanied by a hefty upfront fee. A leased vehicle's residual value gives the leasing agent another avenue to rip you off by setting the vehicle's buy-back value at much more than it's likely to be worth.

(Check the residual values section found in Part Three for a realistic buy-back price for the car or minivan you're thinking of leasing.) It's also a smart idea to buy additional "gap" insurance to cover the balance owed on the lease if the vehicle is stolen or written off in an accident, but most lessors charge too much for it (about $200 is fair). In some cases, the leasing company will throw in gap insurance at no extra cost.

Ask the leasing firm what it's prepared to do if the car turns out to be a lemon. Most companies accept that this happens from time to time, and will simply return the car to the manufacturer and get a replacement. That's not part of the standard agreement, however, so be sure that such a clause is included in your lease before you sign it.

Here are two other reasons why you may not wish to lease:
- If you drive more than 18,000–20,000 km a year (you may be charged from 6 to 15 cents per extra kilometre over that limit).
- If you always seem to have dents or scrapes on your car and can't be bothered getting regular maintenance. The vehicle's value at the end of the lease period is probably the single most important factor in computing whether leasing is to the driver's advantage or not. Responsible leasing firms allow for reasonable wear and tear on the vehicle during the leasing contract, but rip-off companies count every scratch, leaving you stuck with a grossly inflated repair bill.

Ford has recently responded to owner and dealer complaints about the definition of "normal" wear and tear with the following memo to dealers, which tells them exactly what should be considered "excessive wear" when a leased vehicle is returned.

Ford Defines "Normal" Wear and Tear

Normal Wear and Tear	Excess Wear and Tear
• Dings • Minor dents • Small scratches • Stone chips in the paint finish • Reduced tread on tires	• Broken or missing parts • Dented body panels or trim • Damaged fabric • Cracked or broken glass • Poor-quality repairs • Unsightly alterations • Tire/wheel damage or less than 1/8 inch of tread remaining • Mechanical and electrical malfunctions

Unfair lease restrictions
Make sure that the lease allows you to service the vehicle yourself at an independent repair facility. A maintenance lease that ties you to the

leasing firm's repair shop can lead to outrageous service charges. Use a less expensive independent repair shop for routine servicing and keep all your receipts to prove that proper maintenance (as required by the manufacturer) was carried out, should a warranty dispute arise.

Be wary of unfair restrictions, excessive penalties, and hidden damage charges. Excessive penalty charges for early cancellation of the contract are horrendous and usually require a payout of three to six months' lease payments. Sometimes lessors will put you on a leasing treadmill by waiving the penalty only if another vehicle is leased. Most impose a 20,000 km per year mileage limit and charge a whopping surcharge on the excess. Additionally, you may be restricted from driving your vehicle outside Canada or lending it to a third party.

Decoding leasing ads
Take a close look at the small print found in most leasing ads. Pay particular attention to the model year, kind of vehicle (demonstrator or used), equipment, warranty, interest rate, buy-back amount, down payment, security payment, monthly payment, transportation and preparation charges, administration fee ("acquisition" fee), insurance premium, number of free kilometres, and excess kilometre charge.

One final point about leasing. When you take your leased vehicle back at the end of an open lease, make sure that you get some written offers on your vehicle and tell the leasing company or dealer that you expect them to call these buyers. This could save you thousands of dollars by preventing the leasing agency from making a "lowball" bid and forcing you to make up the difference between the residual value and what the leasing company actually gets for the vehicle. (See "Leasing" jurisprudence in Part Two.)

When and Where to Buy

When to buy
The best time to buy a new truck or minivan is in the winter, between January and May, when you get the first series of rebates and dealer incentives, and when production quality begins to improve. Try not to buy during strike action—it will be especially tough to get a bargain because there's less product to sell and the dealer has to make as much profit as possible on each sale. Furthermore, work stoppages increase the chances that on-line defects will go uncorrected, and that the vehicle will be delivered as is to product-starved dealers. This is particularly true now that GM's two-month strike has been settled and the company is pumping out its redesigned, full-sized C/K pickups, the Silverado and Sierra. Production lines will be going full-blast, quality shortcuts will be the norm, and many of the trucks' new features will have been unproven or untested. Don't be GM's guinea pig.

Instead, lay low for about six months and then return in force in February or March, when you can double dip from additional automakers' dealer incentive and buyer rebate programs, which can average about a thousand dollars each. Remember too that vehicles made between March and August offer the most factory upgrades, based on field reports from those unfortunate owners who bought the vehicles when they first came out (fleet managers and rental car agencies fall in this category).

The driver-side doorplate tells you the month and year of manufacture; try to get an upgraded second-series car.

Since dealers have very few customers in the dead of winter, or in the month of August when most buyers are on vacation or moving, they will cut prices substantially during these times to keep their inventory and financing costs low. Some automakers cut special deals in December to boost year-end numbers for specific models—as Ford did with its Sable and Taurus, allowing Ford to proclaim them as outselling their closest competitor, Honda's Accord.

Allow yourself at least two weeks to finalize a deal if you're not trading in your vehicle, and longer if you sell your vehicle privately. Visit the dealer at the end of the month just before closing, when the salesperson will want to make that one last sale to meet the month's quota. If sales have been terrible, the sales manager may be willing to do some extra negotiating.

Where to buy
Good dealers aren't always the ones with the lowest prices. Dealing with someone who gives honest and reliable service is just as important as getting a good price. Check a dealer's honesty and reliability by talking with motorists who drive vehicles purchased from that dealer (identified by the nameplate on the trunk). If these customers have been treated fairly, they'll be glad to recommend him. You can also ascertain the quality of new car preparation and servicing by renting one of the dealer's cars or minivans for a weekend, or by having him service your trade-in.

How can you tell which dealers are the most honest and competent? Well, judging from the many reports I receive each year, dealerships in small suburban and rural communities are fairer than big city dealers, mainly because they're more vulnerable to negative word-of-mouth advertising and to poor sales—when their vehicles aren't selling, good service takes up the slack. Prices may also be more competitive, as overhead is often much lower than in metropolitan areas.

Dealers selling more than one manufacturer's product line present special problems. Overhead can be quite high, and cancellation of a dual dealership in favour of an exclusive franchise elsewhere is an ever-present threat. Parts availability may also be a problem, because a dealer with two separate car lines must split his inventory, and so may have an inadequate supply on hand.

The quality of new car service is linked directly to the number and competence of dealerships within the network. If the network is weak, parts are likely to be unavailable, repair costs can go through the roof, and the skill level of the mechanics may be questionable. Among foreign manufacturers, the Japanese automakers have the best overall dealer representation across Canada.

European automakers are almost all crowded into Quebec and Ontario, leaving car owners in the Maritimes and western Canada to fend for themselves. This is particularly troublesome, given that most European imports are highly dependent on dealers for parts and servicing.

Dealers offering top-quality repairs are able to keep their commercial fleet customers, so if a dealer has a large volume of commercial work, chances are he's giving good service at a reasonable price.

Patronize dealers that shun "shop supplies" charges and give you the choice of hourly rather than flat-rate time in calculating repair charges. Twenty-four-hour servicing, free loaner cars, and/or a downtown shuttle service make for more convenient servicing. (Make sure the free loaner car is spelled out in the sales contract.)

It's also a good idea to patronize dealerships that are accredited by auto clubs such as the Canadian Automobile Association affiliates, or consumer groups like the Automobile Protection Association (look for the accreditation symbol in their phone book ads, or affixed to the shop window). Auto club accreditation is no iron-clad guarantee of honest or competent business practices, but if you're cheated or fall victim to poor servicing from one of their recommended garages, the accreditor is one more place to which to take your complaint and apply additional mediation pressure. As you'll see under "Faulty Diagnosis" in Part Two, plaintiffs have won in court by pleading that the auto club is legally responsible for the consequences of the recommendations it makes.

Automobile brokers/vehicle-buying services

Throughout this book I've tried to give you all the key information you need to get a good deal when buying a new or used vehicle. Since I understand that this kind of negotiation isn't for everyone, I'm offering you the following alternative: an auto broker.

Brokers are independent agents who try to find the new or used vehicle you want at a price below what you'd pay at a dealership (including the extra cost of the broker's services). Broker services appeal to buyers who want to save time and money while simultaneously avoiding most of the stress and hassle associated with the dealership experience, which for many people is like a swim in shark-infested waters.

Brokers get new cars through dealers, while used cars may come from dealers, auctions, private sellers, and leasing companies. Basically, brokers find an appropriate vehicle to meet the client's expressed needs, and then negotiate the purchase (or lease) on behalf of their client. The majority of brokers tend to deal exclusively in new cars, with a small percentage dealing in both new and used vehicles. Ancillary services vary among brokers, and may include such things as comparative vehicle analysis and price research. One Willowdale, Ontario, broker (AutoBuy Advisory Services) even finds itself battling insurance adjusters on a regular basis to get fair settlements for clients.

The cost of hiring a broker ranges anywhere from a flat fee of a few hundred dollars to a percentage of the value of the car. Sometimes a car broker may offer his services for a nominal fee, or even tell the buyer that the service is "free." In such cases, it's best to remember that nothing is free in the car business. If the customer isn't paying the fee directly, then the broker's fee is being paid by the dealer, who simply buries that commission in the total price of the car. Ultimately, the customer pays either way. While it's not impossible to get a reasonable deal under such an arrangement, be aware that the broker may be unduly biased toward a certain dealer or manufacturer. Reputable brokers are not beholden to any particular dealership or make, and will immediately disclose their flat fee or the percentage amount they charge on a specific vehicle.

Finding the right broker
Buyers who are looking for a broker should first ask friends and acquaintances if they can recommend one. Word-of-mouth referrals are often the best, because people won't refer others to a service with which they were dissatisfied. Your local CAA representative is a good place to start looking for a good broker. For Toronto consumers, the APA has recommended AutoBuy Advisory Services, 107 Hendon Ave., Willowdale, Ontario M2M 1A6 (416-590-9902). I, too, have found them to be both efficient and professional.

Buying clubs
Be wary of buying clubs that aren't backed by a national organization. Except for Price Costco, the Internet's Auto-By-Tel, and some auto associations, buying clubs promising huge savings on purchases or claiming to get new vehicles at dealer's cost seldom survive close scrutiny. The savings they promote are often illusory, because the so-called wholesale or dealer's cost price is usually no different from the regular retail selling price suggested by the manufacturer.

Some union or credit union buying clubs do a very good job in cutting prices on all vehicles. They use their buying clout in a particular region to exact substantial concessions from local dealers. They generally charge minimal membership fees, and they don't get too "chummy" with the local dealers because they put their members' interests first.

Safety First

Two accidents per vehicle

According to the U.S. National Highway Traffic and Safety Administration (NHTSA), a new vehicle will be in an average of two accidents from the time it leaves the assembly line (10 percent of all new vehicles sustain some transport damage) to the day it's towed to the junkyard. Crash safety is therefore a major consideration when purchasing a new vehicle. NHTSA data show that 51 percent of deaths occur in head-on collisions, 27 percent in side impacts, and barely 4 percent in rear impacts. Sport-utilities, trucks, and vans protect passengers better than passenger cars in most collisions.

Traffic safety studies show that women are particularly vulnerable to traffic fatalities and injuries (and just wait until you read what airbags do to them). The number of women who die behind the wheel has increased 62 percent since 1975, while highway deaths among men are dropping. The reasons given for this difference include the fact that women are driving more, they drive smaller cars, drive more aggressively, are less tolerant of alcohol, and tend to drive on local roads where accident rates are higher. I would also add airbags as a factor.

Active and passive safety

How safe a vehicle is depends on its active and passive safety features. Active safety components, like radial tires and 4X4 capability, help drivers to avoid accidents. While professional drivers extol the virtues of active safety features, everyday drivers feel safer with passive safety protection. Interestingly, the anti-lock brake system (ABS), both an active and passive safety item, has been discredited of late—primarily because drivers use it improperly.

The theory of active safety has several drawbacks. First and foremost, there is no independent proof that safe driving can be successfully taught. Even if one learns how to master defensive driving techniques, there's still no assurance that this training will be of any use in an emergency situation, where panic reflexes kick in (look again at the disappointing ABS findings). And what about the NHTSA's 1994 study, which estimates that 41 percent of all fatal accidents are caused by drivers who are under the influence of alcohol or drugs? All the high-performance options and specialized driving courses in the world won't provide much protection for such drivers or their victims. That's why passive safety systems—like three-point seatbelts and a chassis designed to absorb crash forces and direct them away from a vehicle's occupants—are so effective: they work just as well with skilled and unskilled drivers. Incidentally, of all the passive safety features one can choose, traction control seems to be the least important, mainly because it's so rarely used and its advantages aren't apparent.

Airbags

I don't like airbags. I have read the stats and am unimpressed. True, there exist well-publicized American and Canadian safety studies which show convincingly that airbags save lives in high-speed collisions in excess of 39 km/h. However, equally thorough, though little-publicized, government-university studies show airbags can maim or kill through inadvertent deployment (1 chance in 30) or in low-speed collisions at speeds as low as 20–39 km/h, particularly if you're a woman, a senior, of smaller-than-average size, have had upper torso surgery, or use a tilt steering wheel. In fact, the dangers are so great that a recent Transport Canada and George Washington University study of 445 drivers and passengers concludes:

> While the initial findings of this study confirm that belted drivers are afforded added protection against head and facial injury in moderate to severe frontal collisions, the findings also suggest that these benefits are being negated by a high incidence of bag-induced injury....The incidence of bag-induced injury was greatest among female drivers...Furthermore, the intervention of the air bag can be expected to introduce a variety of new injury mechanisms such as facial injuries from "bag slap," upper extremity fractures, either directly from the deploying air bag module or from arm flailing, and thermal burns to the face and arms.

**AirBag Deployment Crashes
in Canada**

**Dainius J. Dalmotas
Jean Hurley
Alan German**
Transport Canada
Canada

Kennerly Digges
George Washington University
USA

Preprint

Paper Number 96-S1-O-05

**Fifteenth International Technical Conference
on the Enhanced Safety of Vehicles
Melbourne, Australia,
May 13–16, 1996**

I felt a deep sense of betrayal when I accessed the above document from the Internet. As I fit together all the recent accident reports and emergency room studies, it's obvious to me that for over two decades engineers, automakers, and government bureaucrats have lied to us about airbag dangers. Instead of the promised billowing protective cloud that would gently cushion us in an accident, we discover that the airbag's 300 km/h deployment is more like a Mike Tyson right cross. So far, 111 people have been killed by passenger airbags in low-speed or otherwise survivable accidents. All these deaths occurred in accidents at speeds as slow as 11 or 12 km/h, and three-quarters of the adults killed were women. Seven of the first 28 recorded deaths involved 1994–96 Chrysler minivans.

Sexist federal regulations governing automobile airbag design are the main reason why the safety devices put women, children, and the aged at risk. The auto industry and government engineers have set federal regulations that aim to protect the average-sized unbelted adult male in a 35-mph (57 km/h) frontal crash. Meeting that rule requires that the airbag inflate with a force sufficient to kill or seriously injure women, children, and seniors who don't fit the engineering norm. During the past year, automakers have phased in depowered "second generation" airbags—"Airbags Lite"—but there nevertheless remains a sizable number of new cars that use fully powered airbags.

A campaign of misinformation
The safety "establishment," composed of government, automakers, and safety advocates, hasn't levelled with the public about airbag dangers inherent in the 60 million airbag-equipped vehicles on North American highways. For example, their admonition that children under the age of 13 should sit in the rear is nonsense, since it's a question of size, not age—a small 18-year-old could be more vulnerable. Actually, no one who is of small stature, child or adult, should sit behind an airbag. The government also has yet to explain why airbags are of little benefit to seniors 70 and older, and why, according to the NHTSA, there have been over 25,000 recorded injuries from airbag deployment between 1988 and 1991. There have also been thousands of incidences of airbag malfunctions—causing late deployment or inadvertent deployment—reported to American federal safety regulators, resulting in the recall since 1993 of 2 million vehicles (one out of every 38 on the road). If the five ongoing investigations also result in recalls, one in thirty vehicles will be affected.

Most importantly, we have to stop blaming the victims of airbag deployment for sitting too close, not "buckling up," or allowing their children to ride in the front seat. The above-cited Canadian/American airbag study clearly demonstrates that most of the belted drivers and passengers who were injured did nothing to put themselves at risk— except, perhaps, being born the wrong gender and living in a country whose federal ministry of transport blindly follows Washington's lead.

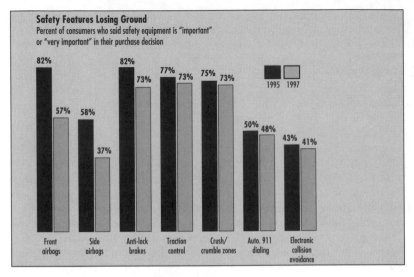

Safety Features Losing Ground
Percent of consumers who said safety equipment is "important" or "very important" in their purchase decision

Federal regulators' efforts to explain away airbag hazards represent a deliberate policy decision: they didn't want to damage their own credibility, alarm the public, or undermine the acceptance of airbags as a supplementary restraint. Well, guess what? The public is more than alarmed—in fact, it's clamouring for retrofitted cut-off switches and looking for new vehicles in which airbags aren't a standard feature. In fact, recent surveys show that the public's confidence in airbags has plummeted following the spate of news stories reporting airbag-induced deaths and injuries.

Despite government and industry promises to the contrary, substantial engineering improvements to airbags won't come online anytime soon. "Smart" airbags won't be generally available until well into the year 2000, and the use of "depowered" airbags may be curtailed due to the increased risk they pose for unbelted occupants.

How airbags do and don't work

Airbags *are* scary. Even the averaged-sized male driver, who is least at risk, doesn't like the idea of an explosive charge going off in the steering wheel a foot away from his face. On the other hand, as a former emergency medical technician, I prefer having my face smacked or hands scalded to my brains splattering on the windshield or wrapping myself around the wrap-around dash.

Despite the dangers they pose, airbags are here to stay. As a general rule, seatbelts alone reduce the risk of serious injury or death by 45 to 55 percent. Airbags increase that protection by an additional 11 percent when used with seatbelts. All North American passenger vehicles have had them since September 1997, and all light-duty vehicles (vans, pickups, etc.) will have them by September 1998. A few companies, including Volvo and Mercedes-Benz, have taken airbag protection a step further by installing standard side-impact airbags and dual airbags in their cars. Chrysler, Ford, and GM intend to put side-impact airbags in some of their cars and minivans prior to installing them in 4X4s, vans, and pickups the following year.

When an impact at a speed as low as 15 km/h is sensor-detected, a vehicle's front sensors send an electronic signal that almost instantaneously deploys an airbag or cushion from within the steering hub or underneath the dash. The airbag is designed to protect the head and upper torso from fatal injuries. Some studies show that airbags reduce the risk of a seatbelted occupant's death in an accident by 50 percent, compared to 45 percent for a seatbelted occupant with no airbag. That extra 5 percent margin has convinced governments, automakers, and insurance companies that airbags are a worthwhile investment. There is no proof, on the other hand, that *injuries* are reduced by airbags. In fact, one Virginia Commonwealth University study found that owners of cars equipped with airbags filed more personal injury claims than did owners of similar cars without airbags.

Airbags are designed to work best with people of "ideal proportions," in crashes at moderate speeds, and with occupants who have their seatbelt and shoulder harness fastened. All bets are off if you're seriously overweight or are involved in a collision at speeds of more than 57 km/h. If you have only your shoulder belt fastened, as is the case with many people who use automatic seatbelts, you risk decapitation.

Inadvertent airbag deployment
Airbags frequently go off for no apparent reason, due to what Ralph Hoar, a safety adviser to plaintiff's attorneys, calls "cheap sensors." Other causes of sudden deployment: passing over a bump in the road in your GM Cavalier or Sunfire, slamming the car door, having wet carpets in your Cadillac or, in some Chrysler minivans, simply putting the key in the ignition. This happens more often than you would imagine, judging by the frequent recalls and thousands of complaints recorded on the NHTSA web site (*http://www.nhtsa.dot.gov/cars/problems/complain/compmmy1.cfm*). Incidentally, insurers are refusing to pay for damage to the car or airbag replacements unless there has been a collision. Automakers deny responsibility on the grounds that the vehicle must have collided with "something." In the end, the driver is faced with a hefty repair bill and no means of proving the automaker's liability.

Airbag deployment for no apparent reason is bad enough if the vehicle is parked—if the airbag explodes while the vehicle is being driven, it will likely cause an accident, and then will be of no use during the ensuing impact, as it has already deflated. Says Michael Leshner, a U.S. forensic engineer, "The airbag knocks them silly. *Then* they have an accident."

Protect yourself
You should take the following steps to lessen the danger from airbag deployment:
• Make sure that seatbelts are buckled and all head restraints are properly adjusted (at about ear level).

• Insist that passengers who are frail, short, or have recently had surgery sit in the back.

• Make sure that the driver's seat can be adjusted for height and has tracks with sufficient rearward travel to allow short drivers to remain a safe distance away from the bag's deployment and still reach the accelerator and brake. Buy pedal extensions, if needed.

• Have a retrofitted cut-off switch installed by a dealer for your make of vehicle. Be patient—the American government has just sanctioned their use, and Canadian dealers and automakers haven't yet worked out the kind of legal waiver that motorists must sign. Canadian federal motor vehicle safety regulations don't specifically require the installation of airbags in motor vehicles. However, because the airbag is an integral part of the vehicle restraint system, provincial statutes in Nova Scotia, P.E.I., New Brunswick, and Alberta make airbag deactivation or removal illegal.

• If you feel at risk, don't want to wait, and live near the American border, you may have your airbag deactivated by an American dealer or independent garage, following factory-approved guidelines (in some cases, it may involve simply removing a fuse). An extensive listing of garages willing to perform this service is available from the NHTSA web site found in Appendix V. The cost averages about $100 (U.S.). Keep in mind, however, that you may be violating provincial statutes. On the other hand, inspectors can't easily check for compliance, and penalties for deactivation are practically nonexistent.

• Buy a 1998–99 car or minivan that comes with passenger-side airbag disablers.

• Buy a vehicle that uses sensors to detect the presence of an electronically tagged child safety seat in the passenger seat and disables the airbag for that seat (this is already a standard feature in the Mercedes SLK).

Childproof locks
Especially important in minivans, childproof locks consist of a special control that the driver can trip to prevent the rear doors from being unlocked from the inside while the vehicle is in motion. They offer extra safety and convenience.

Child restraint systems
Every year car accidents in Canada kill almost 70 youngsters under age five, and injure another 4,000. The tragedy of this statistic is that parents ignore it—half of the children riding in vehicles still aren't properly secured, compared to the 87 percent of adults who wear seatbelts. Seventy percent of these deaths and injuries could have been prevented if children had been properly belted into a safety seat. In recognition of this fact, safety authorities and the courts are cracking down on negligent parents. Provinces with seatbelt laws now require that children, especially infants, travel in an approved safety seat. Drivers who don't protect young passengers may face criminal charges and can be held liable for civil damages if a youngster is injured or killed.

Contrary to popular belief, carrying young children on laps in a moving vehicle is not safe. A 9-kg (20-pound) child will be pulled away with a force of over 270 kg (600 pounds) in a 48-km/h crash. Accident studies show that unrestrained adults can crush their children against the dashboard during a crash. Even in a relatively minor accident or panic stop, a child can be pulled away with surprising force and hit the dashboard or the floor hard enough to be seriously injured or killed.

There are three types of safety seats for children: infant-only carriers for newborns of up to about 9 kg (20 lbs.) or 0.69 m (27 in.) in height; convertible carriers for children from birth up to 18 kg (40 lbs.) or 1.02 m (40 in.) in height; and booster seats for kids weighing between 18 and 27 kg (40 to 60 lbs.). If you're not sure which seat fits your child's weight and height, check the Transport Canada compliance label affixed to the seat.

There are two sizes of infant carriers—those designed only for infants weighing up to 7.9 kg (17 lbs.), and others that can handle up to 9 kg (20 lbs.). Infant carriers often do double-duty as rockers and baby feeders. The typical carrier is lined with soft padding, has an internal safety harness, and is anchored by the vehicle's safety belt in the rear seat. Extra padding (a rolled-up towel or baby blanket) can be added between the legs or on the sides, as long as it's not placed under the harness straps. The baby faces backwards in a semi-reclining position. In an accident, the baby's back, rather than its delicate chest and abdomen, absorbs the crash forces. These rear-facing infant safety seats should never be used in the front seat of a vehicle equipped with a passenger-side airbag, unless the airbag has a disabler. The force of the airbag inflating is the equivalent of being hit by a vehicle travelling 300 km/h. Put the carrier in the rear outboard seats.

Forward-facing seats are anchored to the vehicle's frame by a tether strap, and they too should always be used in the rear seat. The U.S. Department of Transportation estimates that 80 percent of all child safety seats are improperly secured, so take the extra care needed to make sure that the seat is installed properly. Convertible models are bulky and much less portable than infant seats, but they can be used for a much longer time. Chrysler's built-in child safety seats are an innovative optional safety feature patented by Ontario-based Magna International Ltd., and are now offered by many other automakers. They're convenient to use and may spare you the expense of a convertible or booster seat. Since they can't be faced to the rear, don't use them to carry infants.

A booster seat bridges the gap between a forward-facing seat and the vehicle's standard seatbelt. It consists of a firm cushion that incorporates its own restraining system, which ensures that the lap belt doesn't ride up. Instead, the belt fits snugly over the child's lap and the shoulder harness doesn't touch the neck. Remember, booster seats used around the house cannot protect your child in a collision. You can discontinue use of the booster seat when the child's height or weight exceeds the compliance label's limits.

Tots who are almost, but not quite, large enough for regular seatbelts may be able to use the "Child Saver," a device that allows adjustment of a three-point seatbelt so that it fits a small child. It sells for
under $25 at most auto-parts stores.

A variety of child safety seats can be rented from hospitals and
provincial safety groups. If you decide to purchase one, be sure to ask
the retailer for a registration card. The manufacturer can then notify
you of a recall that you might not otherwise learn about.

Crashworthiness
All things being equal, a heavier vehicle—or some compacts and midsize sport-utilities—will fare better in a crash than a light one. GM's
recent two-car crash tests dramatically confirm this fact. Its engineers
concluded that if two cars collide, and one weighs half as much as the
other, the driver in the lighter car is ten times as likely to be killed as is
the driver in the heavier one.

*Ford's Windstar minivan provides excellent crash protection, says the
Washington-based Insurance Institute for Highway Safety. Now, if only
Ford would correct the Windstar's 3.8L engine headgasket failures and
automatic transmission glitches.*

The Washington-based IIHS says that vehicles in the midsize and
large car class are far safer than smaller ones when crashed at 40 mph
(64 km/h)—5 mph (8 km/h) more than in government tests. The
IIHS figures show that the fatality rate for the occupants in a small car
is roughly twice that of a midsize car, and three times as high as a big
car. What's the cutoff point? A wheelbase of at least 105 inches (2.67m).
Vehicles with wheelbases of 105 inches or more have 1.4 or fewer
deaths per 10,000 registered vehicles, while those with 104-inch wheelbases or less have 2.1 or more deaths for the same number of registered
vehicles.

Ergonomics
One of the new catchphrases used in rating vehicles is "ergonomics."
Simply put, it means making the vehicle's interior user-friendly. For

example, can you reach the controls you'll need without straining or taking your eyes off the road? Are the controls just as easy to operate by feel as they are by sight? Can rear-seat passengers enter or exit without becoming contortionists?

To answer these questions you need to drive the vehicle over a period of time to test how well it responds to the diversity of your driving needs. If this can't be done, you may find out too late that the climate control system leaves you cold in the winter and boiling in the summer, or that the handling is more truck-like than you'd wanted.

You can also conduct the following showroom test. Adjust the seat to a comfortable setting, buckle up, and settle in. When you look out the windshield and use the rear- and side-view mirrors, do you detect any serious blind spots? Will optional mirrors give you an unobstructed view? Does the seat feel comfortable enough for long trips? Can you reach important controls without moving off the seatback? If so, then your vehicle has been ergonomically designed. If not, shop for something that better suits your requirements.

Head restraints

Offered as a standard feature on all front and some rear seats, their main function is to prevent you from breaking your neck during a rear collision when the impact forces snap your head back. Your vehicle's head restraints may be either fixed or adjustable. Fixed restraints are preferable, but adjustable ones are acceptable as long as they're adjusted high enough (at ear level). Make sure that rear visibility isn't obstructed by the front or rear restraints.

Seats and seatbacks

Seat anchorages have to conform to government load regulations, but the regulations are so minimal that seats can easily collapse or tear loose from their anchorages, leaving drivers and passengers vulnerable in accidents.

Seatbelts

Seatbelts provide the best means of reducing the severity of injury arising from both low- and high-speed frontal collisions. In order to be effective, however, seatbelts must be adjusted properly and feel comfortably tight. Unfortunately, this is not always the case, and seatbelts rank high in customer complaints—they don't retract enough for a snug fit, are too tight, chafe the neck, or don't fit children properly. Some automakers have corrected this problem with adjustable shoulder-belt anchors that allow both tall and short drivers to raise or lower the belt for a snug, more comfortable fit.

Another important seatbelt innovation is front seatbelt pretensioners that instantly take up slack in a collision. They are found mostly among European imports and luxury cars. Among 1998 models, only the following vehicles came equipped with front seatbelt pretensioners. For the 1999 model year, other more moderately-priced vehicles will undoubtedly be so equipped; look for them in the dealer's showroom.

1998s with Seatbelt Pretensioners

Acura RL   Oldsmobile Silhouette
Audi A4   Pontiac Trans Sport
Audi A6   Porsche Boxster
BMW (all)   Saab 9-3
Cadillac Catera   Saab 9-5
Cadillac Seville   Toyota Avalon
Chevrolet Prizm   Toyota Camry
Honda CR-V   Toyota Corolla
Infiniti Q45   Toyota Land Cruiser
Jaguar XJ8   Toyota Sienna
Lexus (all)   VW (all)
Mercedes-Benz (all)   Volvo (all)

Vehicle size and safety
Insurance Institute for Highway Safety figures show that for every thousand pounds added to a car's mass, driver injury risk is lowered by 34 percent for the unrestrained driver and 25 percent for the restrained driver. This doesn't mean that motorists should drive cars and trucks built like army tanks. In fact, many small cars are so well engineered to absorb crash forces that they'll allow you to walk away from a frontal collision at 57 km/h (35 mph).

Choosing an Inexpensive Vehicle

Know your warranty
There's a big difference between warranty promise and warranty performance. All major automakers offer bumper-to-bumper warranties good for the first 3 years/60,000 kilometres. It's becoming an industry standard for car companies to also pay for roadside assistance, a loaner car, or hotel accommodations if your vehicle breaks down under warranty while you're away from home.

The auto industry's more comprehensive warranties have become an important marketing tool, and are featured heavily in advertising campaigns. But, like the performance ads you see on TV, what you think you see isn't always what you get. For example, bumper-to-bumper coverage usually excludes tires (GM vehicles are an exception, in that they allow you to claim a refund through the dealer), stereo components, brake pads, clutch disks, and many other expensive components. To really know what the warranty covers on your vehicle you have to read the fine print. Chrysler, for example, offers a fairly comprehensive powertrain warranty, but major items are excluded and Chrysler is very tightfisted in the interpretation of its obligations (exemplified by its frequent refusal to pay air conditioning, ABS brakes, automatic transmission, and paint delamination claims). Ford has also been less than generous in dealing with premature engine and transmission failures.

Automotive News   JUNE 24, 1996

Gripers get new Nissan engines

MARY CONNELLY
Staff Reporter

Nissan and Mercury are replacing engine blocks or entire engines in up to 125,000 1995 and 1996 vehicles because of engine knock in Nissan's 3.0-liter V-6.

Vehicles involved are the Nissan Quest, Pathfinder and pickup plus the Mercury Villager.

"Customers may drive the vehicles without causing damage to the engine."

Engines are being replaced because connecting rod designs are not interchangeable. Ford routinely replaces — rather than repairs — engines in new, low-mileage vehicles to increase customer satisfaction and to avoid creating new engine troubles.

Staff Reporter Mark Rechtin in Los Angeles contributed to this report.

Look for "secret" warranties

Automobile manufacturers are reluctant to publicize their secret warranty programs because they feel that such publicity would weaken consumer confidence in their products and increase their legal liability. The closest they come to an admission is to send out a "goodwill policy," "special policy," or "product update" service bulletin for dealers' eyes only. These bulletins admit liability and propose free repairs for defects running the gamut from fishy-smelling headliners on Chrysler sportutilities and minivans to transmission failures on Chrysler, Ford, and GM cars and minivans (see Part Three).

When faced with repairs for what is clearly a factory mistake, the only motorists who get compensated are the ones who yell the loudest or threaten to go to small claims court. Uninformed customers who hesitate to complain are forced to pay for the same repairs.

If you're refused compensation, keep in mind that secret warranty extensions are, first and foremost, an admission of manufacturing negligence. You can usually find them in the dealer service bulletins (DSBs), which automakers send to dealers daily. Your bottom-line position should be to accept a pro-rata adjustment from the manufacturer, whereby you share a third of the repair costs with the dealer and automaker. If polite negotiations fail, challenge the refusal in court on the grounds that you should not be penalized for failing to make a reimbursement claim under a secret warranty that you never knew existed!

Getting a DSB summary for your vehicle

If you want your own DSB summary, fill out the Bulletin Search Request found in Appendix VI. For a $15 fee (this includes computer time and mailing costs), you'll be faxed or mailed an exhaustive summary of all DSBs that concern your vehicle. For an additional $5 per DSB, you can then order any number of the DSBs listed in the summary that address your concerns. For example, one summary and one specific DSB would cost $20. Remember, there's no extra charge for fax replies. On the other hand, only VISA cards or cheques made out to DSB are accepted.

```
Article No.
98-4-9
03/02/98
COOLING SYSTEM—OVERHEATING AND/OR LOSS OF COOLANT—3.8L VEHICLES
FORD:
1988—95 TAURUS
LINCOLN-MARCURY:
1988—94 CONTINENTAL
1988—95 SABLE
LIGHT TRUCK:
1995 WINDSTAR
ISSUE:
Coolant may leak from the head gaskets and/or the vehicle may overheat. There may also be concerns of reduced heater
output due to low coolant levels. This may be caused by insufficient sealing of the head gastkets.
ACTION:
Replace the head gaskets and head bolts. The rwvised head gaskets and bolts provide improved sealing capability and high-
er clamping force between the cylinder head and block. Refer to the following Service Procedure for details.
PART NUMBER       PART NAME
F5PZ-6051-AA      Head Gasket and Bolt Kit (One Side)
OTHER APPLICABLE ARTICLES: 91-1-8, 94-10-10
WARRANTY STATUS: Eligible Under The provisions of Bumper to Bumper Warranty Coverage
OPERATION     DESCRIPTION          TIME
980409A       Verify Coolant Loss  0.3 Hr.
980409B       Replace Cylinder Head 8.0 Hrs.
              Gaskets—Taurus/Sable
980409C       Replace Cylinder Head 6.8 Hrs.
              Gaskets (Windstar)
980409D       Replace Cylinder Head 8.0 Hrs.
              Gaskets—Continental
```

Confidential dealer service bulletins pave the way to free repairs because they prove that a part failure is factory-related and not part of normal maintenance; hence, the above 3.8L engine repair should be paid by the dealer and Ford even if the normal warranty has expired.

Service bulletins are great guides for warranty inspections (especially the final one) and they're useful in helping you decide when it's best to trade in your car. They're written by automakers in "mechanic-speak," and are republished here unedited because service managers relate better to them that way, and manufacturers can't then weasel out of their obligations by claiming that they never wrote such a bulletin.

If your vehicle is out of warranty, show these bulletins to the less expensive independent garages to help them find the trouble quickly and order the most recent *upgraded* part, so that you don't replace one defective part with another.

Because these bulletins are sent out by U.S. automakers, Canadian service managers will sometimes deny, at first, that a bulletin exists. However, when they're shown a copy, they usually find the appropriate Canadian part number or DSB in their files. The problem and its solution don't change from one side of the border to another. (Imagine American and Canadian tourists being towed across the border because each country's technical bulletins were different.) Mechanical fixes do differ in cases where a bulletin is for California only or relates to a safety or emissions component used only in the U.S. But these cases are rare indeed.

The best way to get DSB-related repairs carried out is by visiting the dealer and showing him the specific DSB that covers your vehicle's problems. Direct his attention to all the techie-speak and codes and ask for the Canadian equivalent. If you're refused help:

• Fax the automaker in Canada a copy of the DSB and ask for the appropriate kit or upgraded part number for Canada.

• If the dealer and automaker say that Canadians are excluded, ask why Canadians don't have the same rights as Americans.

• Complain to Transport Canada and your provincial consumer affairs office about being refused corrective repairs that are given routinely to American customers.

• Finally, you could visit an American dealer to have the repair carried out during a regularly scheduled vacation trip. Once back in Canada, you can sue the Canadian automaker and its dealer for your costs (including DSB ordering costs) in small claims court, because they gave you the runaround in the first place.

Fuel economy fantasies
Fuel economy figures are published by Transport Canada (a free copy of its *Fuel Consumption Guide* can be obtained by calling 1-800-387-2000) and are based on data supplied by the automakers who follow U.S. Environmental Protection Administration testing guidelines. These figures can be off by 10 to 20 percent, depending on the testing method chosen. In fact, a recent Ford bulletin warns dealers that "very few people will drive in a way that is identical to the EPA tests (...) These [fuel economy] numbers are the result of test procedures that were originally developed to test emissions, not fuel economy."

If you never quite got the hang of metric fuel economy measurements (like me), use the fuel conversion table below to establish how many miles to a gallon of gas your vehicle provides.

Conversion Table

L./100 km	m.p.g.	L/100 km	m.p.g.	L/100 km	m.p.g.
5.0	56	7.4	38	12.5	23
5.2	54	7.6	37	13.0	22
5.4	52	7.8	36	13.5	21
5.6	50	8.0	35	14.0	20
5.8	48	8.5	33	15.0	19
6.0	47	9.0	31	15.0	18
6.2	46	9.5	30	17.0	17
6.4	44	10.0	28	18.0	16
6.7	43	10.5	27	19.0	15
6.8	42	11.0	26	20.0	14
7.0	40	11.5	25	21.0	13
7.2	39	12.0	24	23.0	12

Insurance costs
Insurance costs can vary between $500 and $5,000 per year, depending on the type of vehicle you own and your personal statistics and driving habits. Multipurpose vehicles are usually classed in the high-risk category (accident and theft) and therefore usually cost more than passenger cars to insure.

Now that banks are getting into the insurance business they're heating up the competition by offering lower premium payments through the independent agents whom they use as go-betweens. The Canadian Imperial Bank of Commerce, for example, says that it offers low insurance premiums by selling directly to the Ontario public, avoiding the 10–12 percent commission that most insurance brokers charge. During its first three and a half weeks of operation, the bank received more than 40,000 inquiries and signed up 1,000 customers. The Toronto Dominion Bank also jumped into the Ontario market several years ago.

You can cut insurance costs considerably by choosing a vehicle that has the best overall claims record. One good place to find this out is the Vehicle Information Centre of Canada, 175 Commerce Valley Dr. West, Suite 220, Markham, Ontario, L3T 7P6. This non-profit organization has free brochures that show which new and used vehicles have important safety features, and how well they perform in real-life accidents reported in Canada.

The dealer network
A weak dealer network drives up maintenance costs, adds to a vehicle's downtime, and makes it difficult for you to go elsewhere when servicing is poor. The more sophisticated and complicated a vehicle's engineering, and the farther away its manufacturing plant, the more important it is to have strong dealer service support. Ford Aerostar and GM Astro/Safari minivans, for example, use mostly old truck technology and so can often be repaired anywhere using parts from independent suppliers. The more complicated VW EuroVan, on the other hand, is severely handicapped by a lack of extensive dealer support.

Sometimes good parts availability exists within a weak dealer network. This occurs when a vehicle has sold quite well or has been on the market for a long time with few changes, thereby creating a good supply of replacement parts. Nissan/Mercury and dealerships are mutually supportive since they service the almost identical Quest and Villager minivans.

Parts and service
Parts for imports are generally no more expensive than parts sold by the major American automakers. But when it comes to captive imports, some American automakers have been known to charge twice as much for the same part as do their Japanese partners.

Here are a two tips that may help cut the high cost of repair parts:
• Try to find good-quality rebuilt parts whenever possible. Generally, rebuilt parts cost anywhere from one-third to one-half the price of

new parts and last just as long. A vehicle has to be on the market for at least two years before rebuilt or remanufactured parts become available in sufficient quantities.

• Before authorizing non-warranty repairs at an independent shop, ask the mechanic to compare the parts prices charged by different manufacturers selling the same basic vehicle. For example, a Villager part may be cheaper at a Nissan dealership under the Quest name than the same part bought from Ford.

Even when parts costs aren't deliberately "boosted" by American car manufacturers, prices are unacceptably high. For example, according to the Alliance of American Insurers, the price of original-equipment replacement parts needed to rebuild a vehicle is about 2.5 times the original retail price. In an annual study, a 1991 Jeep Cherokee Sport five-door retailing for $22,000 was rebuilt with Jeep-supplied replacement parts. Total cost? More than $52,000 for the parts alone. No labour was included in the estimate.

Consumers have found that, with the exception of Saturn, American automakers are more interested in sales than in ensuring that their dealers give honest, competent service. In fact, I can't recall a single occasion where an automaker terminated a dealership's franchise because of odometer tampering (for example), yet the RCMP reports dozens of odometer fraud convictions every year.

A vehicle can incorporate the best engineering in the world, but it will quickly deteriorate and fall into the lemon category if the servicing is lousy. The servicing problem is more acute with vehicles that are new on the market, and with European and South Korean imports. American manufacturers are generally weak in service support, and General Motors is the best example of this deficiency. Its own records show that 70 percent of its customers switch to other repair outlets when their vehicle warranty expires.

Servicing isn't much better among European importers, a fact recently confirmed by CAA's 1997 *Autopinion* membership survey. They get low ratings for mishandling customer complaints, inadequate service training, and hiring an insufficient number of service representatives—not to mention the abrasive, arrogant attitude typified by some automakers and service outlets.

Check servicing costs and the quality of repairs with owners who drive similar models, fleet administrators, and rental car counter attendants. They'll be glad to tell you about servicing problems they've encountered. Be sure to question consumer protection groups about which vehicles generate the most complaints, which mechanical components are the most failure-prone, and which are covered by secret warranties. Owner comments, found in online forums and through the owners' groups listed in collectors' publications and car buff magazines, will also give you a picture of the overall reliability, parts availability, servicing, and price range for specific models.

Finding a Reliable Vehicle

The elusive "American" car
A lot of controversy surrounds the relative quality control of North American and imported vehicles. Before deciding which manufacturer provides the best quality, forget all the popular mythology about what is made in North America and what is "foreign" made. The see-saw value of the dollar and the yen has led to a rush of foreign and American automakers moving production facilities to the U.S., Canada, and Mexico. Surprisingly, this has been accomplished without a corresponding drop in quality control. Toyota's Corolla assembly plant in Cambridge, Ontario, for example, has been rated by J. D. Power and Associates as the highest quality production facility in North America.

American or Japanese?
Despite improvements over the past several years, American vehicles still don't measure up to the Japanese in quality and technology, especially when it comes to body construction and paint. American firms have copied Japanese production methods and their team approach, but their vehicles haven't closed the reliability gap, except in co-ventures like the Ford/Mazda production of the Probe and Ranger, the Nissan/Mercury Villager, and the GM/Suzuki Sidekick, Tracker, and Vitara.

Japanese vehicles aren't made better or more quickly because of advanced robotics or overworked, underpaid workers, as American automakers would like us to believe. Actually, American production costs are now lower than what the Japanese and Europeans pay at home. High manufacturing costs in Japan and Europe (due mostly to high taxes and workers' benefits) are forcing European and Japanese automakers to locate plants in Canada and the U.S., where skilled workers are plentiful. The real reasons for the poor quality of American cars are the automakers' blind price-cutting at the expense of quality and their preference for style over substance.

European quality varies
Motorists' complaints, dealer service bulletins, and auto association membership surveys, like those sent out by CAA, confirm that the quality of European vehicles, such as those produced by Mercedes, BMW, VW, and Audi, remains quite high, while other European automakers, like Lada, Saab, and Jaguar, produce mediocre vehicles.

Nevertheless, European automakers are still doing quite well, mainly because of their cars' reputation for impressive driving performance and comfort. Volkswagen and Audi have managed to do relatively well by dramatically improving the quality of their vehicles over the past few years, offering comprehensive warranties, and by holding the line on prices in the mid-range, where Japanese imports are too pricey and American cars don't perform as well. Luxury and sports car importers, like BMW and Porsche, have also made a remarkable comeback through price cuts and attractive new products.

Other Buying Considerations

Front-wheel drive

Front-drives direct engine power to the front wheels, which pull the vehicle forward, while the rear wheels simply support the rear. The biggest benefit of front-wheel drive (FWD) is foul weather traction. With the engine and transmission up front, there's lots of extra weight pressing down on the front-drive wheels, increasing tire grip in snow and on wet pavement. But when you drive up a steep hill, or tow a boat or trailer, the weight shifts and you lose the traction advantage.

Although I recommend a number of FWD vehicles in this guide, I don't like them as much as rear-drives. Granted, front-drives provide a bit more interior room (no transmission hump), more car-like handling, and better fuel economy than do rear-drives, but damage from potholes and fender-benders is usually more extensive, and maintenance costs (especially premature front tire and brake wear) are much higher than with rear drives.

Servicing front-wheel drives can be a real nightmare—and a wallet-buster. Entire steering, suspension, and drivetrain assemblies have to be replaced when only one component is defective. Downtime is considerable, the cost of parts is far too high, and the drivetrain and its components aren't designed for the do-it-yourself mechanic. A new FWD transmission assembly (called a transaxle) can cost about $2,000 to repair, compared to $700 for a rear-drive transmission. And having to make such a repair isn't that remote a possibility, particularly if you own a 1989–96 Chrysler minivan or a Ford Taurus or Sable.

Accident repairs are a unique problem. Front-wheel-drive transmissions and steering and suspension components are easily damaged, and alignment difficulties abound. Repair shops need expensive, specialized equipment to align all four wheels and square up a badly smashed unibody chassis. Even if you manage to get all four wheels tracking true, the clutch and transaxle can still be misaligned. No wonder many insurance companies prefer to write off an FWD car rather than repair it. When that happens, you wind up eating the difference between what you paid for the vehicle and what the insurance company says your vehicle is worth—minus your deductible, of course.

Rear-wheel drive

Rear-drives direct engine power to the rear wheels, which push the vehicle forward. The front wheels steer and also support the front of the vehicle. With the engine up front, the transmission in the middle, and the drive axle in the rear, there's plenty of room for larger and more durable drivetrain components. This makes for less crash damage, lower maintenance costs, and higher towing capacities than front-drives.

On the other hand, rear-drives don't have as much weight over the rear wheels as do the front-drives (and no, putting cement blocks in the trunk is not a good idea—it will only void your transmission warranty), and therefore they can't provide as much traction on wet and icy roads unless they're equipped with an expensive traction-control system.

Rear-drives, however, have some of the highest payload and towing capabilities, usually slightly more than four-wheel drives.

Rear-drives are also scarcer than hens' teeth, so much of the foregoing dissertation may be of little practical value if all you have to pick from are front-wheel drives.

Four-wheel drive

Four-wheel drives direct engine power through a transfer case to all four wheels, which pull and push the vehicle forward, giving you twice as much traction. The system is activated with either a floor-mounted shift lever or a dashboard button. When the 4X4 drive isn't engaged, the vehicle is essentially a rear-drive truck. The large transfer case housing makes the vehicle sit higher, giving you additional ground clearance. The most fuel-efficient systems disengage the four-wheel drive when extra traction isn't needed.

Encouraged by the popularity of 4X4 vehicles in North America, many automakers now offer optional four-wheel drive or all-wheel drive on their more moderately priced family sedans, pickups, and minivans—at jacked-up prices.

All-wheel drive

Essentially, this is four-wheel drive *all* the time. Used mostly in minivans, AWD never needs to be deactivated when running over dry pavement and doesn't require a heavy transfer case that raises ground clearance and cuts fuel economy.

What Kind of 1999 Vehicle?

Approximately two-thirds of the vehicles driven on Canadian highways are cars—the rest are multipurpose vehicles, which include pickups, trucks, minivans, and vans. Whatever you choose, just remember that higher price doesn't guarantee higher quality. For example, although you might have your heart set on a luxury import, you may be surprised to learn that some American-built cars can provide as much performance, comfort, and reliability for much less money; or that the same Japanese automaker offers an almost identical vehicle for a third less under another name (Nissan and Toyota have been playing this game for years with their Infiniti and Lexus models).

Compare the advantages and disadvantages of the following vehicle classes, and consider the recommended models in each class to ensure that you get what best suits your driving needs at the lowest possible price.

Small cars

Small cars, also known as compacts or subcompacts, are designed for city dwellers who want fuel economy above all. Mostly front-wheel drives, they offer excellent gas economy (5 to 9.5L/100 km, or 30 to 56 mpg), easy manoeuvrability, and a low retail price. They can carry four passengers, but because rear seating is limited, only two can really ride in comfort. Engine and road noise are intrusive, small engines some-times can't supply enough power to adequately heat the interior or defrost the windshield, and luggage capacity is minimal. One of the more alarming characteristics of a small car's highway performance is its vulnerability to strong lateral winds.

Crash safety is compromised by the small size and weight of these vehicles. Nevertheless, careful engineering for better crashworthiness and the increased availability of airbags have made many small cars safer in collisions than some larger cars.

I recommend the following small cars:

Ford Escort/'98 Tracer   Subaru Impreza
Honda Civic   Toyota Corolla
Hyundai Accent   '98 Toyota Tercel
Mazda Protegé

Medium cars
This size car is a trade-off, providing more comfort and safety but a bit less fuel economy (9.6 to 11.5L/100 km, or 25 to 30 mpg) than a small car. These are excellent cars for city and highway driving, since they combine the advantages of a subcompact with those of a larger car, and manage to sustain lower-than-average depreciation. They provide ade-quate passenger space for five people (four in comfort), and most trunks are large enough to meet average baggage requirements. They also enhance safety through the use of anti-lock brake systems, airbags, transmission/brake interlocks, and three-point seatbelts. Crash protec-tion is well above average.

I recommend the following medium cars:

Audi A4   Subaru Legacy
Honda Accord   Toyota Camry
Mazda Millenia   Volvo S70/V70
Dodge Avenger, Sebring   VW Golf/Jetta

Large cars
The quintessential symbol of middle-class motoring, these cars are best suited for extensive highway driving by motorists who can write off rela-tively high gasoline consumption (19L/100 km, or 15 to 20 mpg), main-tenance, and insurance premiums. They fall into two groups: traditional, heavy, V8-equipped rear-wheel drives with mushy suspensions and sepa-rate body-on-frame construction; and the more recent, lighter, V6-equipped front-wheel drives with unit-body construction. Ford's Crown Victoria/Grand Marquis and GM's discontinued Caprice/Roadmaster and Fleetwood are examples of the former, while the Buick LeSabre/Oldsmobile Eighty-Eight and Chrysler LHS/New Yorker are typical of the more contemporary designs.

Owners have to pay a considerable amount of money for these roomy vehicles, but they do deliver comfort, trailer-towing capability (especially the rear-wheel drives), and stability at high speeds. They also depreciate slowly, can usually seat six adults in relative comfort, and incur less damage from front, rear, and side collisions—although recent U.S. government crash tests show that some smaller cars better absorb frontal crash forces. I recommend the following large four-door sedans:

Ford Crown Victoria	GM Olds Cutlass
/Grand Marquis	Toyota Avalon
GM Malibu	

Sports cars
Sports cars fall into four categories that I've set arbitrarily, based on cost and scarcity:
• Entry-level (Mustang, Camaro, and '98 Talon)
• Mid-level ('98 Honda del Sol and Mazda Miata)
• Upper-level (Chevrolet Corvette, Plymouth Prowler, and '98 Toyota Supra)
• Exotic-level (Acura NSX, Dodge Viper, Ferrari Testarossa, and Lamborghini DB132-Diablo)

Common characteristics of sports cars that you're not likely to find touted in brochures include cramped interiors (they can get very warm and there's very little cargo space), heavy steering in city traffic, hard riding, and difficult vehicle entry and exiting. As well, they burn lots of fuel, tend to overheat and stall, offer minimal visibility, are prone to leaks, rattles, and squeaks, are notoriously unreliable, and tend to be expensive to service and insure. The sports car market is currently drying up as a result of increased car and fuel prices—the shift in consumer tastes is toward sport-utility vehicles and family cocoons (best exemplified by soaring minivan sales), making practical family hauling a more important criterion than speed and wind blowing through your hair. Bucking the trends, I nevertheless recommend the following sports cars:

Ford Mustang	Mazda Miata
GM Camaro	'98 Nissan 240SX
GM Firebird	Toyota Celica
Honda Prelude	

Convertibles
Convertibles went underground for several decades while automakers worked out their crash-safety shortcomings and the motoring public put its love affair with topless cars on the back burner. They're now undergoing a resurgence, with attractive offerings in almost every marketing niche—on offer are the BMW 318i, Chevrolet Metro and Camaro Z28, Chrysler Sebring, Ford Mustang GT, Saab 900, and VW Cabrio, among others.

Of this group, the Chevrolet Metro, VW Cabrio, and Camaro lead the pack with their low initial cost and good reliability/warranty performance. From a safety perspective, the BMW stands out, featuring small rollover bars that deploy automatically if the car flips. Unfortunately, its small engine loses steam quickly when mated to an automatic transmission.

The VW and BMW are the most rattle-free ragtops, followed by Saab and Ford's Mustang, with Chevrolet's Camaro bringing up the rear. Although the Camaro takes top prize for a tacky interior, rattles, and water/wind leaks, its reasonable base price, powerful engine, superior handling, and in-your-face styling more than compensate for body shortcomings.

Luxury cars

Luxury cars fit into two classes, based primarily on price: entry-level models that range from $30,000 to $40,000, and high-end models that can cost a lot more. In the past, the luxury car niche has been a rear-wheel drive market dominated by the Cadillac DeVille and Fleetwood and the Lincoln Town Car and Continental. During the past two decades, however, buyers have gravitated toward Japanese and European front-wheel drive models. This shift in buyer preference has forced GM, Ford, and Chrysler to downsize and adopt front-wheel drive. Most American-made luxury cars aren't as reliable as Japanese models and depreciate more quickly, but they're generally safer in accidents than smaller vehicles, can be repaired almost anywhere, and are often sold for much less than list price.

In considering a luxury car, buy equipment and not a nameplate. Most luxury cars are overpriced, yet give you the same level of equipment found on other, less expensive, fully-equipped models sold by the same manufacturer. These cheaper versions offer other advantages: parts are more easily found and competitively priced, and mechanics are more familiar with cars they've been repairing for some time. This is the case with the Nissan Maxima and Toyota Camry. When fully loaded, they offer practically all the features provided by the Lexus and Infiniti, but for almost one-third less.

European luxury cars are on the upswing. Mercedes and BMW have been particularly successful in holding the line on or even lowering retail prices by cutting dealer profit margins and using North America as an export base. Audi has redesigned its offerings and overcome a reputation for poor quality and expensive parts. Infiniti and Lexus have maintained a higher degree of overall customer satisfaction and a much lower rate of depreciation. Remember, price is never an infallible indication of quality. Jaguar and Saab build some of the most problem-plagued vehicles on the planet, and even venerable Rolls-Royce has been hit by a number of lawsuits alleging serious factory-related defects.

European luxury cars are far more comfortable and driver-responsive than American vehicles, but their prices aren't discounted as often, they aren't easy to service, and parts are relatively rare. The Japanese midsize luxury models have the best overall record for reliability, and their interior ergonomics are outstanding from a comfort and convenience standpoint. I recommend the following luxury cars:

Audi A4, A6	'98 Lincoln Mark VIII
BMW 3-series	Lincoln Town Car
Infiniti series	Mercedes 300 series
Lexus series	Nissan Maxima

Multipurpose vehicles (minivans, vans, pickups, and sport-utilities)
Unlike passenger vehicle prices, MPV prices are deceptive—you're likely to spend a lot more money than you'd expect, since advertised prices don't include many of the must-have optional features that give these specialty vehicles their full utility. Expect to pay an additional 30 percent or more over the advertised price to make your new sport-utility, minivan, van, or truck as convenient and practical as the automakers promise. This means that a $20,000 base price for a bare-bones model can easily escalate to $27,000 for a model with essential—not lavish—performance and convenience features.

Take the phrase "car-like handling" with a large grain of salt. Since many of the rear-wheel drive models are built up on a modified truck chassis and use steering and suspension components from their truck divisions, they tend to handle more like trucks than cars, despite automakers' claims to the contrary. What you see is not necessarily what you get when you buy or lease a new minivan, 4X4, van, or pickup, because multipurpose vehicles seldom come with enough standard features to fully exploit their versatility.

Front-wheel drives handle better than rear-wheel drives, but their large size and extra weight still require a whole new set of driving skills when cornering under moderate speeds, parking, or turning. In a 4X4, a moment's inattention can easily lead to a deadly rollover, and the advent of ABS has made drivers so overconfident that they tend to exceed their driving skills or go way beyond their vehicle's safety/performance capabilities.

Other disadvantages: the heating-defrosting-AC is often inadequate and requires additional optional equipment, the ride can be quite rough without buying an optional suspension, and handling can be tricky. Fuel economy is atrocious with the full-size models.

Depreciation savings can be wiped out by higher insurance and maintenance costs (especially with full-size models) and by exorbitant fuel costs. ABS and 4X4 drivetrain components are particularly failure-prone, hard to troubleshoot, and expensive to replace. Consumers Union also confirms that body hardware (windows, locks, doors, trim, etc.), brakes, and shocks tend to fail or wear out sooner on minivans and sport-utility vehicles than on passenger vehicles. Your best protection is to make sure that you know what you need, and that you choose a minivan rated in Part Three of this guide as having the lowest rate of depreciation and highest quality/dependability. Ratings for sport-utilities, vans, and trucks can be found in the *Lemon-Aid New 4X4s, Vans and Trucks 1999*. This year, I recommend the following minivans:

Honda Odyssey	Nissan Quest
Mercury Villager	Toyota Sienna

Surviving the Options Jungle

Dealers make more than three times as much profit selling options as they do selling most cars (50 percent vs. 15 percent). No wonder their eyes light up when you start perusing their options list. If you must have some options, compare dealer prices with those of independent retailers, and buy where the price is lowest and the warranty is the most comprehensive. As a general rule, buy as few options as possible from the dealer, since you'll get faster service, more comprehensive guarantees, and lower prices from independent suppliers. Remember, extravagantly equipped vehicles hurt your pocketbook in three ways: they cost more to begin with, they cost more to maintain, and they often consume extra fuel.

Saver or spender? Know your options.

The options you choose in the showroom will affect your car's fuel efficiency for life.

Fuel-saving Options	Options with Little or No Effect on Fuel Economy	Options that Increase Fuel Consumption
• small engine	• space-saver spare tire	• high-performance engine
• small turbocharged engine	• exterior trim packages	• turbocharged V8 engine
• manual transmission	• tinted glass (on cars without air conditioning)	• 4-barrel carburetor on a V8 engine
• overdrive (manual or automatic)	• heavy-duty suspension	• four-wheel drive
• diesel engine		• power brakes
• cruise control		• power steering
• fuel injection		• air conditioning
• fuel economy reminders (shift indicator lights)		• power windows and seats
• block heater, preferably with timer		• heated seats
		• sun roof
		• roof rack

Before buying options separately, consider getting a vehicle in a higher trimline or in a "special edition" format, where the options package includes what you want for a lower price. Another possibility is "value pricing," where automakers like GM will offer a package of options on a bare-bones model. Whichever choice you make, don't buy any unnecessary options if the total cost of the package exceeds what you'd pay for separately purchased options.

A heavy-duty battery and suspension, and perhaps an upgraded sound system, will generally suffice for American-made vehicles; most imports already come well equipped. An engine block heater with a timer isn't a bad idea, either. It's an inexpensive investment that ensures winter starting and reduces fuel consumption by allowing you to start out with a semi-warm engine. Factory installed in-line heaters are also usually more efficient and durable.

It's hard to buy and even harder to lease a new vehicle that isn't loaded with unnecessary options. This is particularly evident with medium-size vehicles and minivans. If you're unsure as to what optional equipment like sound systems and anti-theft devices should cost, shop around and compare prices with independent suppliers like J. C. Whitney. Their mail order parts catalogue can be ordered by calling 312-431-6102 (Visa and Mastercard accepted).

Smart Options

Air conditioning

Whether or not you choose air conditioning should depend more on where you live and your comfort requirements than on saving money. In the same way that buying an underpowered car to save on fuel costs can leave you regretting its poor performance, your savings will be the last thing on your mind when you're sweltering in your vehicle some summer day.

Air conditioning costs between $800 and $1,650, plus a $100 federal excise tax, and may reduce fuel economy by as much as 10 percent in stop-and-go traffic. At highway speeds, air conditioning increases fuel consumption by three to four percent. It provides extra comfort, reduces wind noise (from not having to roll down the windows), and improves window defogging. But because air conditioning units aren't used year-round, they're failure-prone (expect repairs of about $1,500 around the five-year mark), easy prey for premature corrosion, and an excellent incubator for airborne bacteria and allergens. If you must have air conditioning, opt for a factory-installed unit. You'll get a longer warranty, and reduce the chance that other mechanical components will be damaged during installation.

Anti-lock brake system (ABS)

Although the jury is still out on the degree of ABS effectiveness, they're still a viable safety feature when used correctly and in harsh climatic conditions. For maximum effectiveness, it's important that you use the same size and type of tire on all four wheels; otherwise, the ABS computer can get confused.

Anti-lock brakes are impressive on the test track but not on the road, or for off-roading. In fact, the Insurance Institute for Highway Safety says that cars with anti-lock brakes are more likely to be in crashes in which a passenger is killed but where no other car is involved. Insurance claim statistics show that anti-lock brakes aren't producing the overall safety benefits that were predicted by the government and automakers. The latest IIHS study found that a passenger has a 45 percent greater chance of dying in a single-vehicle crash in a car with anti-lock brakes than in the same car with old-style brakes. On wet pavement, where ABS supposedly excels, the chance of being killed increased to 65 percent. In multi-vehicle crashes, ABS-equipped vehicles have a passenger death rate 6 percent higher than vehicles not equipped with ABS.

Essentially, ABS prevents a vehicle's wheels from locking when the brakes are applied in an emergency situation, thus reducing skidding and the loss of directional control. When braking on wet and dry roads, your stopping distance will be about the same as with conventional braking systems. But in gravel, slush, or snow, your stopping distance will be greater.

On dry pavement, a trained driver can outperform ABS using a technique called "threshold braking" in which you ease up on the brakes before reapplying them when you feel the brakes beginning to lock. On wet pavement, braking is so chancy that ABS will outperform threshold braking nearly every time.

Automakers have created the impression that cars equipped with ABS will stop on a dime, but they don't fully explain how ABS should be used. For example, many drivers don't know that anti-lock brakes require that they slam on the brakes in a skid—in other words, do exactly what driving schools have told them not to do.

A particularly important feature of ABS is that it preserves steering control. As you brake near the limit and turn the wheel, ABS will release the brakes if it senses steering-triggered lockup and reduce the percentage of time during which the brakes are applied. Braking distances will lengthen accordingly, but at least you'll have some steering control. On the other hand, if you start sliding on glare ice, don't expect ABS to help you out very much. The laws of physics—particularly the coefficient of friction—still apply, even on ABS-equipped vehicles. However, you can decrease your stopping distance by installing four snow tires that are the same make and size.

The high cost of ABS maintenance is one disadvantage that few safety advocates mention, so consider that original equipment parts costs can run five times higher than regular braking components, and that most manufacturers explicitly forbid the use of non-corrosive DOT-5 (silicone) brake fluids in ABS-equipped vehicles. Therefore, to prevent corrosion, the brake fluid needs to be replaced annually.

Insurance claims aren't very supportive of assertions that ABS prevents collisions. The Washington-based Highway Loss Data Institute's study of identical vehicles equipped and not equipped with ABS found that the frequency of collision claims and their cost were not reduced with ABS. Other studies do show a decrease in crashes, varying between

8 percent (the Markham, Ontario-based Vehicle Information Centre) and 3 percent (General Motors) depending on the road conditions. In view of these conflicting studies, insurance companies are backing away from premium reductions for ABS-equipped vehicles. Transport Canada is also concerned about the hype surrounding ABS effectiveness. Its tests indicate that the safety benefits may be compromised by drivers with ABS who are less cautious and who tend to drive more aggressively—they accelerate more quickly, drive faster, and apply the brakes later than do drivers using vehicles without anti-lock brakes. This contention was confirmed by a paper presented at the 1993 Multidisciplinary Road Safety Conference, which concluded that drivers of vehicles equipped with ABS drove up to 8 km/h faster than did people whose cars were not ABS-equipped.

Anti-theft systems
Car break-ins and thefts cost Canadians more than $400 million annually—there's a 1 in 130 chance that your car will be stolen and only a 60 percent chance that you'll ever get it back. No wonder that over one-third of new vehicles are equipped with standard or optional alarms, with a clear preference for fuel cut-off devices and electronic alarms among the four main types of security systems: active and passive units (either self-arming or armed by the driver), ignition disablers, parts identification, and security keys.

Some automakers have more effective standard alarm systems than others. Volkswagen, for example, was recently singled out for praise by the Canadian Crime Prevention Bureau after its new anti-theft devices and car-parts marking resulted in a 75 percent drop in VW thefts.

The most effective theft-deterrent systems aren't always the most expensive ones. Don't waste your money on costly anti-theft devices that depend solely upon your car's horn or lights to scare thieves away. They often go off at the wrong time and can be easily deactivated. Furthermore, they frighten the thief away only after the vehicle has been damaged. When it comes to stealing your car's contents, no alarm system can resist a brick through a side window. It takes just twelve minutes for thieves to strip a car seat, radio, and body parts, and few citizens are brave enough to personally stop a theft or testify in court. Your best protection is discretion: take your radio with you or lock it in the trunk, particularly if you own a Japanese or German car with an upgraded sound system.

Since most cars are stolen by amateurs, the best theft deterrent is a visible device that complicates the job while immobilizing the vehicle and sounding an alarm. For less than $150, you can install both a steering wheel lock and a hidden remote-controlled ignition disabler. Steering-wheel locks—clublike devices costing between $50 and $75—deter thieves by forcing them to carry a hacksaw and adding about a half-minute to the time it takes to steal the average car (they have to cut through the steering wheel or bust the lock). Ignition disablers are also inexpensive and very effective. They sell for $30 to $90, depending on their sophistication. The *Electronic Cop* sells for $89.95 and can be purchased from Sequel Security Systems, 853 Sanders Road, Box 278, Northbrook IL 60062 (1-800-215-4100).

Battery (heavy-duty)
The best battery for northern climates is the optional heavy-duty type offered for about $80 by many manufacturers. It's a worthwhile purchase, especially for vehicles equipped with lots of electrical options. Most standard batteries last only two winters; heavy-duty batteries give you an extra year or two for about 20 percent more than the cost of a standard battery.

Block heater
Costing about $75, a block heater is an inexpensive investment. Factory-installed in-line models are effective and durable. Cheaper ($40 installed) dipstick or freeze plug models are not recommended.

Cellular telephone
This is a recommended option mainly because it provides a greater degree of safety for drivers stuck on the side of the road or threatened by smash-and-grab artists. Buy the cheapest hands-free model available from an independent retailer.

Cellular phones are expensive to operate, due to the high rates charged by the phone companies to "carry" calls. Because calls are billed by the minute and according to the distance the caller or receiver is from a given site, charges can vary from $250 to $1,000-plus a month for a sales agent who uses it extensively. The temptation to use the car phone for nonessential calls is also hard to resist, and expensive in the long run. The average monthly cost for personal calls is about $125. And remember that what's said on a cellular phone can be heard by anyone.

Three independent studies have shown that car phones are a safety hazard. Drivers whose attention is distracted while talking on a cellular telephone have four times as high a risk of having an accident, according to a recent University of Toronto study of 699 car crashes, reported in the February 1997 issue of the *New England Journal of Medicine*. Drivers using hands-free phones were just as likely as people holding a receiver to be involved in an accident while on the phone or shortly after having used it. The American Automobile Association Foundation for Traffic Safety says that a road hazard is 20–30 percent more likely to go unnoticed by someone using a car phone than by a driver who gives full attention to driving. This warning is buttressed by another study done at the Rochester Institute of Technology in Rochester, New York, which found that drivers with cellular phones installed in their vehicles run a 34 percent greater risk of having an accident than other motorists.

If the possibility of crashing into someone isn't scary enough, how about cellular phones that are real heart-stoppers? The U.S. government is looking into allegations that people with heart pacemakers implanted in their chests may experience pacemaker malfunctions as a result of their cell phones. Safety researchers say that if the phone is placed in close proximity to the chest, it may cause the pacemaker to stop, restart, or recalibrate itself. The problem is more apparent with the new digital cellular phones than with the older analog models now most commonly used.

As well, cellular phones aren't particularly efficient in placing emergency calls through the 911 exchange. Rather than going to a central dispatch centre, where the caller's location is indicated on-screen, cell phone calls are often routed to other, distant places where staffers may be unfamiliar with the area from which the call originates.

Central locking control
Costing around $200, this option is most useful for families with small children, car-poolers, or minivan drivers who can't easily slide across the seat to lock the other doors. Look for a remote feature that provides automatic locking and then unlocking when the inside door handle is pulled.

Child safety seat (integrated)
One of the best child safety innovations to come along in decades, integrated safety seats are designed to accommodate any child more than one year old or weighing over 20 pounds. Since it's permanently integrated into the seatback, it takes the fuss out of installing and removing the safety seat and finding some place to store it. When not in use, it quickly folds away out of sight, becoming part of the seatback. Two other safety benefits: you know the seat has been properly installed (not the case with 80 percent of the bolt-ons), and your child gets used to having his or her "special" seat in back where it's safest to sit.

Courtesy lights
This option permits the car's lights to stay on a few seconds after the doors are closed. This is particularly convenient if the only outside source of illumination when entering your home is your car's headlights.

Engines
Choose the most powerful 6- or 8-cylinder engine available if you're going to be doing a lot of highway driving, plan to carry a full passenger load and luggage on a regular basis, or intend to load up the vehicle with convenience features like air conditioning. Keep in mind that multipurpose vehicles and cars with larger engines are easier to resell and retain their value the longest. For example, Honda's Odyssey minivan has been a sales dud in spite of its bulletproof reliability, mainly because buyers don't want a minivan with a four-cylinder powerplant. Some people underpower their vehicles in the mistaken belief that increased fuel economy is a good trade-off for decreased engine performance. It isn't.

Engine and transmission cooling system (heavy-duty)
This relatively inexpensive option provides extra cooling for the transmission and engine. It can extend the life of these components by preventing overheating when heavy towing is required.

Keyless entry (remote)
A safety and convenience option. You don't need to fiddle with the key in a dark parking lot or take off a glove in cold weather to unlock or lock the vehicle. Try to get a keyless entry system combined with such anti-theft measures as an ignition kill-switch or some other disabler.

Mirror options
Power mirrors are particularly convenient on vehicles that have a number of drivers, or on large sedans, wagons, or minivans.

Navigation aids
Both GM and Ford offer an optional navigation aid, called OnStar and RESCU respectively, which links a GPS satellite unit to the vehicle's cellular phone and electronics. For a monthly fee of about $25, GM's OnStar unit connects drivers to live operators who will help them with driving directions, give repair or emergency assistance, or relay messages. If the airbag deploys, or the car is stolen, satellite-transmitted signals are automatically sent from the car to operators who will notify the proper authorities of the vehicle's location.

Power-assisted windows and seats
Merely a convenience feature with cars, power-assisted windows and seats are a necessity with minivans—crawling across the front seat a few times to roll up the passenger-side window or to lock the doors will quickly convince you of their value. Power seats with memory are particularly useful if a vehicle is driven by more than one person. Automatic window and seat controls currently have few reliability problems, and they're fairly inexpensive to install, troubleshoot, and repair.

Running boards
Rather than returning you to '50s styling, running boards are practically essential for climbing into some minivans. They can be purchased from independent suppliers for $65–$200, which is much less than the $250–300 charged by the automakers.

Seats
Make sure the driver's seat has sufficient rearward travel to keep you out of harm's way (about a foot) should the airbag deploy. Also look for a height adjustment so that you can still see over the hood as the seat is pushed rearward. Make sure the head restraints are properly adjusted and don't block your rear vision. Finally, rent the vehicle overnight to determine if the seats are comfortable after an hour or two of driving.

Keep in mind that uncomfortable seats are one of the most frequent causes of complaints heard from new car buyers.

Sound system
Remember when it was just called a radio?

When buying a sound system, consider these three criteria: your overall budget, the make of car, and the kind of music that's likely to be played. A simple AM/FM stereo radio with a stereo cassette tape player is sold by GM for less than $500, but most independent aftermarket stores can easily beat GM's price. Sophisticated, personalized car stereos may cost between $500 and $1,000, and hi-fi fanatics can spend between $2,000 and $9,000 for a "total sound system" that'll likely get ripped off shortly after the car leaves the showroom. In addition to getting the best quality sound for the cheapest price, the stereo buyer should look for features that make it easy and safe to operate; for example, radios that automatically seek out stations, and cassette decks with automatic reverse, play, and eject.

In budgeting for a stereo sound system, allocate half the money for the speakers. Pare down the scores of available features to what's essential, like a strong FM receiver (under two decibels), separate controls for treble and bass, auto reverse, and a key-auto-eject to protect the tape when the ignition is turned on and off.

Factory-installed speakers are usually lousy performers, and options are outrageously priced by automakers. For example, an aftermarket CD player priced at $400 would cost about $1,200 if installed by the factory or dealer. Dealers often say that only the factory's original equipment can overcome electrical interference or provide the appropriate sound for a vehicle's particular interior configuration. This is baloney.

There are, however, some advantages to having a factory-installed sound system. It's usually guaranteed for a much longer period than an independently installed unit, and the dealer is better equipped than a retailer to remove, ship, and reinstall it. A factory unit will also be more cosmetically attractive and less prone to rattle, since it fits better when mounted in the dash and door panels.

Once a stereo system has been purchased, it must be protected from theft. Experts recommend the installation of a slider box for about $80 to $100. It's the size of a textbook and connects the cassette player and radio to the car's wiring when pushed into place. When the car is parked, the box and unit stereo can be removed from the vehicle.

CD players

Sales of car CD players exceed a million units annually, including at least 140 separate models. Mail-order discount houses offer them for less than $300. Improved vibration dampening has made the players impervious to potholes. Look for:

• repeat functions that allow you to select a mixture of tracks or repeat a particular track;
• anti-theft features that include removing the faceplate or unit; and
• a trunk-mounted CD changer, which allows you to play many different CDs.

Suspension (heavy-duty)

Always a good idea, this inexpensive option pays for itself by providing better handling, additional ride comfort (though a bit on the firm side), and extending shock life an extra year or two.

Tires

There are three rules to remember when purchasing tires. First, neither brand nor price is a reliable gauge of performance, quality, and durability. Second, choosing a tire recommended by the automaker may not be in your best interest, since traction and long tread life are often sacrificed for a softer ride and maximum EPA mileage ratings. And third, don't buy any new tire that's older than two years, since the rubber compound may have deteriorated due to poor handling and improper storage (near electrical motors). You can check the date of manufacture on the sidewall.

There are two types of tires: all-season and performance. Touring is just a fancier name for all-season tires. All-season radial tires cost between $90 and $150 per tire. They're a compromise, since according to Transport Canada they won't get you through winter with the same margin of safety as will snow tires, and they don't provide the same durability on dry surfaces as do regular summer tires. In low to moderate snowfall areas, however, these tires are adequate as long as they're not pushed beyond their limits.

Mud or snow tires provide the best traction on snowy surfaces, but traction on wet roads is actually decreased. Tread wear is also accelerated by the use of softer rubber compounds. Beware of using wide tires for winter driving; 70-series or wider give poor traction and tend to "float" over snow. Consumers report good performance from Nokia Hakkapellitas snow tires imported from Finland.

Performance tires have a low sidewall profile and a wider and shallower tread. They give good wet and dry traction, but do poorly on snow and ice. They also wear quickly and tend to give a hard ride. Remember, some sports cars can't be fitted with snow tires unless the rims are changed or a more expensive brand is chosen.

It's a good idea to purchase tires that provide a road hazard warranty. Under the terms of this guarantee, the tire dealer or manufacturer will provide compensation for any tire that's found to be defective. Additionally, don't pay full list for any tire; just as with cars, prices may vary by as much as 40 percent among retailers. Make sure, however, that the price includes mounting and balancing.

Tire dealers are the best place to find a wide selection of tire brands, models, and sizes, and their salespeople are usually more knowledgeable than they are at dealerships, discount houses, or gas stations. Mail order tire distributors are also quite price competitive and will often deliver your tires to the garage of your choice within a few days of purchase.

Which tires are best?
There is no independent Canadian agency that evaluates tire performance and durability. However, the NHTSA, a Washington-based government agency, rates treadwear, traction, and resistance to sustained high temperatures. It posts its findings on the Internet (just click on NHTSA after locating the Alta Vista search engine). The treadwear grade is fixed at a base 100 points and the tire's wear rate is measured after the tire is driven through a course that approximates most driving conditions. A tire rated at 300 will last three times as long as one rated 100.

Now, a word about run-flat tires: they can be unsafe if you drive a mini-van, van, sport-utility, or any vehicle that uses tires with an expect ratio of 60 or lower.

I've come up with the following tire ratings after researching government tests, consumer comments, and industry insiders.

Dunlop D65 and **D60 A2**: Treadwear rated 520, this tire is the bargain of the group. It corners well, and provides excellent wet braking and good steering response. Cost: $146 list; sells for $100. The SP40 A/S is an inexpensive, competent, all-season tire.
Goodyear Aquatred: Treadwear rated 340, this tire is a bit noisy and its higher-rolling resistance cuts fuel economy. Still, it's an exceptional performer on wet roads, and works especially well on front-drive cars where the weight is over the front tires. Average performance on dry pavement. Costs about $130; no discounts.
Goodyear Regatta: Treadwear rated 460, this $100 tire does everything well, including keeping tire noise to a minimum.
Michelin XM+S Alpin: Treadwear rated 320, this tire gives a smoother ride and a sharper steering response than the Aquatred. Cost: $144 list; often discounted to $100.
Pirelli Winter Ice Asimmetrico: Treadwear rating 460 and 420, these are two of the best all-around all-season tires. Cost: $173 list; sells for about $120.
Yokohama Guardex 600: With a treadwear rating of 300, this is another Aquatred knock-off that performs almost as well for half the price.

The following tires aren't recommended: Bridgestone Potenza RE 92, Cooper lifeline Classic II, Firestone Firehawk GTA, Firestone FR680, General XP2000 H4, Hydro 2000 and Ameri G4S, Goodyear Eagle GA and WeatherHandler, Goodrich Advantage, Michelin XGT H4, XW4, and MXV4 Green X, Pirelli P4000 Super Touring (not to be confused with the recommended P400), and the Toyo 800 Plus.

Trailer-towing equipment

Just because you need a vehicle with towing capability doesn't mean that you have to spend big bucks. The first thing you should do when choosing a towing option is determine if you really need a pickup or small van to do the job and if your tires will handle the extra burden. For most towing needs (up to 900 kg or 2,000 lbs.), a passenger vehicle, small pickup, or minivan will work just as well and cost much less than a full-size pickup or van. But if you're pulling a trailer that weighs more than 900 kg, most passenger vehicles won't handle the load unless they've been specially outfitted according to the automaker's specifications. Pulling a trailer that weighs more (up to 1,800 kg or 4,000 lbs.) will likely require a compact passenger van. A full-size van can handle up to 4,500 kg (10,000 lbs.), and may be cheaper and more versatile than a multipurpose vehicle, which would have to be equipped with a V8 engine and heavy-duty chassis components.

Don't trust the towing limit found in the owner's manual. Automakers publish tow ratings that are on the optimistic side, and sometimes they're outright wrong. As well, don't take the dealer's word that a vehicle is capable of pulling a particular trailer. Make the claim a condition of the sale by putting it in the sales contract. Check all claims with the trailer manufacturer for an independent assessment of your vehicle's capabilities.

Automakers reserve the right to change limits whenever they feel like it, so make any sales promise an integral part of your contract (see "Misrepresentation" in Part Three). A good rule of thumb is to reduce the promised tow rating by 20 percent. In assessing towing weight, consider the cargo, passengers, and equipment of both the trailer and the tow vehicle. Keep in mind that five people and luggage add 450 kg (1,000 lbs.) and that a full 227-litre (50 gallon) water tank adds another 225 kg (500 lbs.) to the load. The manufacturer's gross vehicle weight rating (GVWR) takes into account the anticipated average cargo and supplies that your vehicle is likely to carry.

Automatic transmissions are fine for trailering, although there's a slight fuel penalty to pay. Manual transmissions tend to have greater clutch wear from towing than do automatic transmissions. Both transmission choices are equally acceptable if the driver is competent. Ford and Chevrolet/GMC give higher tow ratings to their trucks with automatics than to those with manual transmissions—they know that drivers tend to ride the clutch and generally screw up shifting with a manual. Remember, the best compromise is to shift the automatic manually for maximum performance going uphill, and to maintain control while not overheating the brakes when descending mountains.

Unit-body vehicles (without a separate frame) can handle most trailering jobs as long as their limits aren't exceeded. Front-wheel drives aren't the best choice for pulling heavy loads in excess of 900 kg, since they lose some steering control and traction with all the weight concentrated in the rear.

Whatever vehicle you choose, keep in mind that the trailer hitch is crucial. It must have a tongue capacity of at least 10 percent of the trailer's weight, otherwise it may be unsafe to use. Hitches are chosen according to the type of tow vehicle and, to a lesser extent, the weight of the load. They fall into the following four classes, according to the weight they can pull:

• Class 1: loads up to 900 kg (2,000 lbs.); hooked to the frame or rear bumper of most passenger cars, small pickups, and small vans
• Class 2: loads up to 1,600 kg (3,500 lbs.); attached to a car or MPV frame
• Class 3: loads up to 3,400 kg (7,500 lbs.); also attached to a car or MPV frame
• Class 4: loads up to 4,500 kg (10,000 lbs.); attached to a pickup or MPV frame or incorporated as fifth-wheel hitches (used in the beds of large pickups)

Most hitches are factory installed, even though independents can put them on more cheaply. Expect to pay about $200 for a simple boat hitch and a minimum of $600 for a fifth-wheel version.

Equalizer bars and extra cooling systems for the radiator, transmission, engine oil, and steering are a prerequisite for towing anything heavier than 900 kg. Heavy-duty springs and brakes are a big help, too. Separate brakes for the trailer may be necessary to increase your vehicle's maximum towing capacity.

Transmission: automatic, manual, 5-speed, and overdrive automatic
A transmission with four or more forward speeds is usually more fuel efficient than one with three forward speeds, and manual transmissions are usually more efficient than automatics, although this isn't always the case. Nevertheless, most motorists prefer to pay extra to have a transmission that shifts by itself, even though this convenience saps the performance of small engines, requires expensive repairs, and makes you less alert to driving conditions. This last point is particularly important, because a manual transmission makes you aware of the traffic flow and requires that you shift gears in anticipation of changes.

If you want a stick shift, however, you'd better act quickly. The increasing popularity of cellular phones, aging knees, and cheap gasoline has led automakers to curtail their production of stick shift-equipped cars. In fact, J. D. Power & Associates says the percentage of cars and light trucks with manual transmissions has dropped from 17.5 percent in the 1989 model year to 13.6 percent in 1997. Even sports cars have been affected. Only 30 percent of GM's Corvettes carry a manual transmission, Ford's Taurus SHO only comes with an automatic, and both the Porsche 911 and Ferrari F1 are clutch-less. Industry experts predict that in the future, manual transmissions may only be offered in a small number of economy cars, trucks, and high-priced sports cars.

Dumb Options

Adjustable steering wheel
This option can be deadly in an airbag-equipped vehicle, since it can tilt the steering so that the deployed airbag could cause severe or fatal head and neck injuries. On the plus side, this option facilitates access to the driver's seat and permits a more comfortable driving position. It's particularly useful if a vehicle will be driven by more than one person.

Automatic level control
A useless option, unless you're planning to carry heavy loads or pull a trailer. It's expensive to repair and not easily adjusted.

Bumper strips and bumper guards
Merely decorative items that give very little real protection from fender-bender accidents.

Cruise control
Mainly a convenience feature, automakers provide this $250–$300 option to motorists who use their vehicles for long periods of high-speed driving. Some fuel is saved owing to the constant rate of speed and driver fatigue is lessened during long trips. Still, the system is particularly failure-prone and expensive to repair, and it can lead to driver inattention and make the vehicle hard to control on icy roadways. Malfunctioning cruise control units also are one of the major causes of sudden acceleration incidents. At other times, cruise control can be just plain annoying, as is the case with Chrysler's current crop, which often "hunt" for the right gear when traversing hilly terrain.

Electronic instrument read-out
If you've ever had trouble reading a digital watch face or re-setting your VCR, you'll feel right at home with this electronic gizmo. Gauges are presented in a series of moving digital patterns that are confusing, distracting, and unreadable in direct sunlight. It's often accompanied by a trip computer and a vehicle monitor that computes fuel use and kilometres to empty, indicates average speed, and signals component failures. Figures are frequently in error or slow to catch up.

Foglights
A pain in the eyes for other drivers, foglights aren't necessary for most drivers with well-aimed original-equipment headlights.

Leather upholstery
An expensive option that's too hot in summer, too cold in winter, too slippery, and tough to clean or repair.

Paint and fabric protectors
Paint protectors sold by auto dealers aren't just overpriced—they also don't work. The auto industry's equivalent of the "Emperor's New Clothes," I wouldn't give two cents for paint protector products sold by car dealers. This is said with the knowledge that Chrysler, Ford, and GM factory paint jobs have become less and less durable over the years. Selling for $200–$300, these "sealants" are a waste of money and add nothing to a vehicle's resale value. Although paint lustre may be temporarily heightened, this treatment is less effective and more costly than regular waxing, and may also invalidate the manufacturer's guarantee at a time when the automaker will look for any pretext at all to deny your paint claim.

According to tests carried out by the Consumers' Association of Canada and the Quebec Consumer Protection Bureau, waxing your vehicle regularly is a much better idea than investing in paint protectors. Certain waxes are better than others, as shown in CAC field tests; Nu Finish gave good paint protection for three to six months after each application and did very well in bringing out paint lustre. Surprisingly, Turtle Wax was one of the poorer performers in the CAC study.

Consumer Reports and the Automobile Protection Association claim that auto fabric protection products are nothing more than variations on Scotchguard, which can be bought in aerosol cans for a few dollars, instead of the $50–$75 charged by dealers. Still, if you want someone else to do the spraying, offer the dealer half of what he asks. Even at that, he should make a small profit.

Radar detectors and "stealth" devices
Another product that targets van vacationers and sports car enthusiasts, radar detectors are a dumb idea for two reasons: they're illegal in most provinces and most U.S. states and, like so-called paint protectors, they aren't always effective. The newest wrinkle is an electronic "stealth" cloaking device that claims to generate a frequency that confuses police radar and laser guns. Mounted on the front end of the vehicle, the $400 (tax and installation included) device failed every test carried out by the *Vancouver Province*. Even if it were effective, motorists would have to buy one for the rear end as well, since many laser guns are trained on vehicles after they've gone by.

"Rainsense" wiper system
A standard feature on the Cadillac STS, and soon to be offered as an option on other cars, this system automatically activates the wipers in inclement weather. Wipers accelerate, decelerate, pause, and return to Park automatically without driver interface. This is all done by an electronic controller module located on the windshield next to the inside

rear view mirror. It senses moisture on the windshield when the infrared beams emitted by the module are deflected by moisture on the windshield surface.

Two questions: Does this device solve a problem that doesn't exist? And, how long will it last against the squeegee-wielding windshield "cleaners" found at some traffic intersections?

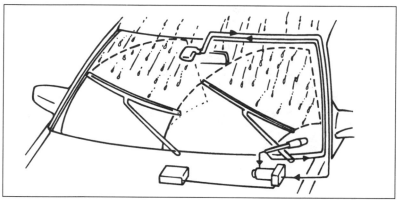

"Rainsense" is nonsense, in my opinion.

Roof-top carrier

Although this inexpensive option provides additional baggage space and may allow you to meet all your driving needs with a smaller vehicle, a loaded roof rack can increase fuel consumption by as much as 5 percent. An empty rack cuts fuel economy by about 1 percent.

Rustproofing

The high profits earned from rustproofing cars (over 75 percent in some cases) encourage dealers to sell aftermarket rustproofing, even though some automakers (like GM and Nissan) threaten to void the rust warranty if critical drain holes are plugged. Most automakers will reject all rust warranty claims where holes have been drilled into their cars by aftermarket rustproofers.

At any rate, rustproofing is no longer necessary now that the automakers have extended their own rust warranties. In fact, you have a greater chance of seeing your rustproofer go belly-up than having your untreated vehicle ravaged by premature rusting. Even if the rustproofer stays in business, you're likely to get a song and dance about why the warranty won't cover so-called "internal" rusting, or why repairs will be delayed until the sheet metal is actually rusted through.

If you live in an area where roads are heavily salted in winter, or in a coastal region, have your vehicle washed every few weeks and undercoated frequently—paying particular attention to rocker panels (door bottoms) and wheel wells. Also, keep your car away from a heated garage in winter; Canadian studies show that a heated garage will accelerate the damage caused by corrosion.

Sunroof

Unless you live in a temperate region, the advantages of a sunroof are far outweighed by its disadvantages. You're not going to get better ventilation than a good air-conditioning system would provide, and a sunroof will grace your highway trips with wind noises, water leaks, and road dust accumulation. Gas consumption is increased, night vision is reduced by overhead highway lights shining through the roof opening, and several inches of headroom can be lost, forcing tall drivers to adopt a hunched-over driving position. Flip-up styles are particularly leak-prone, while electronically-controlled sliding sunroofs often fall prey to short circuits. Without a manual override, your car will be vulnerable to theft and the weather.

Factory installation of a sunroof is far more costly than having it done by an independent—$1,000 vs. $250, with little difference in the quality of the job or the warranty.

Tinted glass

Tinting jeopardizes your safety by reducing night vision. On the other hand, it does keep the interior cool in hot weather, reduces glare, and hides the car's contents from prying eyes. Factory applications are worth the extra cost because cheaper aftermarket products (costing about $100) distort visibility and peel away after a few years. Some tinting done in the U.S. can run afoul of provincial highway codes that require more transparency.

Wheels (aluminum)

Standard equipment on many sporty models, alloy wheels are optional on other cars ($150–$300). They're fragile, frequently leak, corrode easily, and aren't always compatible with snow tires. Unpainted wheels require regular cleaning with acetone and an annual coating with a protective clear spray.

Cutting the Price

Buy by Internet or fax—no more "showroom shakedown"

Of the 15.1 million new vehicles sold last year in North America, 2 million were sold over the Internet. This figure isn't all that surprising, considering that hundreds of Internet-based new car shopping services (like Buy-By-Tel) have sprung up during the past several years. These services are for consumers who want a fair price, loathe haggling, or are just too busy to visit a number of showrooms. For a service fee, these firms encourage dealers to bid against each other for your business through electronic mail. In other cases, you can go directly to a number of dealer web sites and initiate the bidding process on your own. So far, shoppers report impressive savings, particularly in regions where there aren't that many dealers and the local dealer has a "take it or leave it" attitude.

If you don't have a computer or aren't Internet-savvy, don't despair. You can get the same results by using a fax machine. Simply fax an invitation (a cover letter with your company logo would help) for bids to area dealerships, asking them to give their bottom-line price for a specific make and model and clearly stating that all final bids must be faxed within a week. Because no salesperson is acting as a commission-paid intermediary, the dealers' first bids are likely to start off a few hundred dollars less than advertised. When all the bids are received, the lowest bid is faxed to the other dealers to give them a chance to beat that price. After a week of bidding, the lowest price gets your business.

Dozens of *Lemon-Aid* readers have told me how buying by fax kept the price down and averted the showroom song-and-dance routine between the sales agent and sales manager ("he said, she said, they said").

Here's how one Downsview, Ontario, *Lemon-Aid* reader got the bidding started and subsequently paid 18 percent, or $1,995.47, less than the list price of a 1994 Nissan Sentra.

FAX TRANSMISSION
Date: November 30, 1994
To: Joe Blow Motors
Att: President

Dear Sir,
    I have decided to buy a new car. What and from whom I buy depends on the responses to this fax.
    I have visited dealerships and have brochures for every car I am considering, and am sending this fax to other dealers. It is now a matter of finding the best deal.
    I will buy either a Nissan Sentra, Honda Civic, Toyota Corolla or Mazda Protegé. I would like the base model, and the only options that interest me are a full-size spare tire and a block heater. I will accept other features that are already installed, but my decision is going to be based on price. I want a manual transmission, will take either two or four doors, and will accept any color. I will pay by cheque and will not trade in my current car.
    Please fax me an offer. Include the price of the car, the price of all options, PDI, freight, GST, PST, all surtaxes (fuel, etc.), your administration fee and the license transfer fee. You should specify the total amount and include the name of the person I should contact if I accept the offer.
    Today is November 30, 1994. I will make my selection at the end of the business day on December 7th. When faxing your offer, please phone me first at 555-1212 so I may connect my modem.
    I want to buy a car. Do you want to sell one?

    Awaiting your earliest convenient response, I remain

                                  Sincerely,
                                  Jane Customer

    Several hours after sending this fax, our reader got her first quote. She also received additional bids by phone and mail, including one dealer's promise to beat the lowest price offered. That dealer gave the best price, drove the customer to his dealership, and sold the Sentra.

The myth of "no haggle" pricing
New cars and minivans have no "official" selling price, and most dealers will charge as much as the market will bear. If you let them they'll use any pretext they can to boost prices, including a "no dicker sticker" policy. They'll pretend to have abandoned negotiated prices and high-pressure sales tactics in favour of "no haggle prices," where they give the buyer a better deal.
    Don't believe dealers who say they won't negotiate the MSRP. In effect, all dealers bargain. They hang out the "NO DICKERING, ONE PRICE ONLY" sign simply as a means to discourage customers from asking for a better deal. Like parking lots and restaurants that claim they won't be responsible for lost or stolen property, they're bluffing. Still, you'd be surprised at how many people believe that if it's posted,

it's non-negotiable. Industry figures show that "no dicker" dealers average a 14 percent markup over their cost.

There are several price guidelines, however, and dealers use the one that will make the most profit on each transaction. Take, for example, the experience of one Vancouver shopper when he dealt with a major Chevrolet-Oldsmobile dealer in that city:

> ...Here's one to put in your "Things dealers do to sell cars" file (although you have probably seen this before): [this] Chev Olds [dealer] in Vancouver has been advertising that they are selling Chev Ventures at one dollar below invoice plus freight (which is in fine print). Seeing this, I decided to go down and check out what they are doing to maintain their profit margin. They gladly show you the invoice, which I looked at and confirmed that it was the factory price (based on the APA dealer prices). However, the "invoice price" includes the $840 freight charge and the $100 air conditioning levy. Then they take a dollar off that price and add freight and the levy AGAIN. When I pointed this out to them he said that this was their profit margin (he was quite candid about it). So I said it was a bit of stretching the truth about "a dollar below invoice," why didn't they just advertise that they would sell the vehicle at $840 above invoice? And why did he want to charge me a second air conditioning levy? I didn't get a straight answer on that one, so I left shaking my head at the things dealers do to sell cars...!

Two of the more common prices quoted are the Manufacturer's Suggested Retail Price (what the automaker advertises as a fair price) and the dealer's invoice cost, which is supposed to indicate how much the dealer paid for the vehicle. Both price indicators leave considerable room for the dealer's profit margin, along with some extra padding in the form of inflated transportation and preparation charges. If presented with both figures, go with the MSRP, since it can be verified by calling the manufacturer—any dealer can print up an invoice and swear to its veracity. If you want an invoice price from an independent source, contact the Automobile Protection Association (see Appendix V).

Buyers in rural and western Canada are often faced with grossly inflated car prices compared to those charged in major metropolitan areas. A good way to beat this scam without buying out of province is to buy a couple of out-of-town newspapers (the Saturday *Toronto Star* "Wheels" section is especially helpful) and demand that your dealer bring his selling price, preparation, and transportation fees into line with the costs as advertised.

Getting a Fair Price

What's the dealer's cut?
Most new car salespeople are reluctant to give out information on the amount of profit figured into the cost of each new car, but a few years

back *Automotive News* gave the following markups based on the Manufacturers' Suggested Retail Price. These percentages may vary a bit from year to year, but they're fairly accurate.

Dealer Markup (American Vehicles)
small cars: 10–15%
medium cars: 15–20%
large cars: 17–20+%
sports cars: 17–20+%
high-end sports cars: 20+%
luxury cars: 25+%
high-end luxury cars: 20+%
minivans: 15+%
high-end minivans: 20+%
base pickups: 15+%
vans and sport-utility vehicles: 25%
fully equipped top-of-the-line MPVs: 25%

Dealer Markup (Japanese Vehicles)
small cars: 8–12%
medium cars: 10–15%
large cars: 15–17%
sports cars: 15–17%
high-end sports cars: 20–25%
luxury cars: 20+%
high-end luxury cars: 20+%
minivans: 20%
high-end minivans: 20+%
base pickups: 15%
sport-utility vehicles: 15–20%
fully equipped top-of-the-line MPVs: 20%

In addition to the dealer's markup, some previous-year Big Three vehicles may also have a 3–5 percent carryover allowance paid out in a dealer incentive program and a holdback allowance of another 2–3 percent. The dealer's invoice price won't show these additional profits. Options are the icing on the cake with their average 35–65 percent markup.

What's a fair price?
To come up with a fair price, subtract one-half the dealer markup from the MSRP and trade the carryover and holdback allowance for a reduced delivery and transportation fee. Compute the options separately and sell your trade-in privately. Buyers can more easily knock $1,000 to $2,000 off a $20,000 base price if they wait until January or February (when sales are stagnant), choose a vehicle in stock, and forego unnecessary options.

Remember, the 7 percent GST and provincial sales tax must be paid on the *negotiated* price of a new vehicle, not on its suggested selling price. GST is calculated before subtracting the trade-in value from the purchase price. For example, if you buy a vehicle for $20,000 (plus $200 for transport and PDI), and you have a $5,000 trade-in, you must pay 7 percent GST on the $20,200. Taxes that have to be paid are a fuel conservation tax, a $100 federal excise tax on air conditioning, and provincial sales tax calculated on the $20,200 plus the GST but minus the price of the trade-in. If there's a $1,000 rebate, you deduct the amount from your total too. You only pay GST and provincial sales tax once, at the point of purchase. You don't pay it each time you make a loan payment.

Once again, *don't* overpay the sales tax. Make sure that each transaction is treated separately and that the trade-in amount is deducted from the new vehicle price *before* provincial tax is calculated. The federal 7 percent GST will be charged on the full price of the contract, including all options, and provincial tax is then charged only after the trade-in value has been deducted.

Once you and the dealer have settled on the vehicle's price, you aren't out of the woods yet. Like a tag-team wrestling match, you'll then be handed over to an F&I (financing and insurance) specialist, whose main goal is to convince you to buy additional financing, loan insurance, paint and seatcover protectors, rustproofing, and extended warranties. These items will be presented on a computer screen as costing only "a little bit more each month." Compare the dealer's insurance and financing charges with an independent agency that may offer better rates and better service. Often the dealer gets a kickback for selling insurance and financing, and guess who pays for it? Additionally, remember that if the financing rate looks too good to be true, you're probably paying too much for the vehicle. The F&I closer's hard-sell approach will take all your willpower and patience to resist, but when he gives up, your trials are over.

Add-on charges are the dealer's last chance to stick it to you before the contract is signed. Dealer preparation, PDI and transportation charges, "documentation" fees, and extra handling costs are ways that the dealer gets extra profits for nothing. Dealer preparation is a once-over-lightly affair, with a car seldom getting more than a wash job and a couple of dollars of gas in the tank. It's paid for by the factory in most cases and, when it's not, should cost no more than 2 percent of the car's selling price. Reasonable transportation charges are acceptable, although they're often inflated by dealers who claim that the manufacturer requires the payment.

One Estevan, Saskatchewan, Caravan owner recounts the following experience:

> ...In the *Lemon-Aid* book it lists the destination charge for a Chrysler Caravan at $350, yet when I was thinking of buying one at the first place they said $800, then in Regina it was $825, and here in Estevan it is $875...This appears to be a company

sponsored rip-off as there are other vehicles advertised with a destination charge of $400.

Wait until management has approved the vehicle's agreed-upon bottom-line price before rejecting these add-on charges; otherwise the dealership may try to pad the price to get its normal add-on profit. Negotiate delivery and preparation charges down to a strict minimum. Dealers are particularly adept at boosting these charges, but if you head for the door, they'll relent. Remember, the key to keeping costs down is to sell your trade-in privately (see "Selling Your Trade-In"), keep options to a minimum, and don't swallow a high markup for the sake of low interest rates or a rebate.

Dealer incentives and customer rebates

When vehicles are first introduced in the fall, they're generally overpriced. Later on, near the end of summer, automakers offer customer cash rebates of $750–$3,000, and increased dealer cash incentives for almost as much. Incentives are first offered during the winter months and boosted in late summer or early fall when dealer showroom traffic has fallen off. Smart shoppers who buy during these months can shave an additional 10 percent off a vehicle's list price by double-dipping from both of these automaker rebate programs.

In most cases, the manufacturer's rebate is straightforward and mailed directly to the buyer from the automaker. But there are other rebate programs that require a financial investment on the dealer's part, however, and these shared programs tempt dealers to offset losses by inflating the selling price or pocketing the manufacturer's rebate. Therefore, when the dealer participates in the rebate program, demand that the rebate be deducted from the suggested selling price and not from some inflated invoice price concocted by the dealer.

Some rebate ads will include the phrase "from dealer inventory only." If your dealer doesn't have the vehicle in stock, you won't get the rebate. Keep in mind that the manufacturer's rebate is considered to be part of the fair value and is not deductible from the purchase price prior to determining the payable retail sales tax.

Sometimes automakers will suddenly decide that a rebate no longer applies to a specific model, even though their ads continue to include it. When this happens, take all brochures and advertisements showing your eligibility for the rebate plan to provincial consumer protection officials. They can use false advertising statutes to force automakers to give rebates to every purchaser who was unjustly denied one.

When buying a heavily discounted vehicle, be wary of "option packaging" by dealers who push unwanted protection packages (rustproofing, paint sealants, and upholstery finishes) or levy excessive charges for preparation, filing fees, loan guarantee insurance, and credit life insurance.

Prevailing market value
Generally, vehicles are priced according to what the market will bear. Therefore, a vehicle's stylishness, scarcity, or general popularity can inflate its value considerably. For example, the Dodge Sebring convertible has a prevailing market value that's higher than its suggested selling price, mainly because it's part of a hot market segment and in short supply. Once sales slow down later in the new year, popular cars will sell at a discount. A good rule of thumb for vehicles that have a high prevailing market value is to wait for their popularity to subside, or to purchase the previous year's version. Don't try this with a Honda Accord or Toyota Camry, however. Their market value generally stays constant throughout the year. On the other hand, if a vehicle has an unusually low market value (like the Chevrolet Astro), find out why it's so unpopular before buying it. (In Chevrolet's case, the Astro has a no-longer-deserved reputation for being unreliable.)

Vehicles that don't sell because of their weird styling are no problem, but reports of poor quality control can send prices plummeting. Already, Ford Taurus and Sable owners are finding that dealers are reluctant to take their cars in trade due to reports of serious engine and transmission defects afflicting the 1991–95 models. This perceived lack of quality has carried over to the automaker's new models and resulted in lower-priced '98 models. If consumer confidence isn't restored, buyers will likely see these two Ford models drastically reduced in price this year through rebates and dealer incentives.

Accommodation sales
To carry out an accommodation sale, you must first find a buyer for your trade-in and obtain the cooperation of the dealer who'll be selling you your new vehicle. The dealer reduces the new car cost by deducting the selling price of the trade-in. This lowers the amount of sales tax you pay on the new car. The buyer of the trade-in pays you through the dealer, and the dealer ends up selling a new car plus receiving an additional small fee (usually $50) for permitting the transaction. The seller pays the dealer's fee and is responsible for any serious problems that the buyer may have with the trade-in.

Leftovers: false bargains?
In the fall, at the beginning of each new model year, most dealers still have a few of last year's cars left. Some are new, some are demonstrators. The factory gives the dealer a 3–5 percent rebate on late-season cars, and dealers will often pass on some of these savings to clients. But are these leftovers really bargains?

They might be, if you can amortize the first year's depreciation by keeping the vehicle for six to ten years. But if you're the kind of driver who trades every two or three years, you're likely to come out a loser by buying an end-of-the-season car. The simple reason is that, as far as trade-ins are concerned, a leftover is a used car that has depreciated at least 10–15 percent. The savings the dealer gives you may not equal that first year's depreciation (a cost you'll incur without getting any of the first year's driving benefits). If the dealer's discounted price matches or exceeds the depreciation, then you're getting a pretty good deal. But if the next year's model is only a bit more expensive and has been substantially improved, or is covered by a more extensive, comprehensive warranty, it could represent a better buy than a slightly cheaper leftover. Ask the dealer for all work orders relating to the car and make sure that the odometer readings follow in sequential order. Remember as well that most demonstrators should have less than 5,000 km on the ticker, and that the original warranty has been reduced from the day the vehicle was first put on the road. Have the dealer extend the warranty or lower the price accordingly—about $100 for each month of warranty that has expired. If the vehicle's file shows that it was registered to a leasing agency or any other third party, you're definitely buying a used vehicle disguised as a demo. You should walk away from the sale because you're dealing with a crook.

Mid-year models

Entirely new models often make their debut in mid-summer, and getting any kind of a discount from the dealer for mid-year models is like pulling teeth. Dealers know that a seller's market exists during the first few months of a model's launch, and they're not likely to sell their few sample cars for anything less than full price. Furthermore, you're likely to lose an extra year of depreciation since, over time, mid-year vehicles are depreciated back to the beginning of the model year in which they were introduced.

Paying Cash vs. Getting a Loan

The accounting firm of Price Waterhouse says that it may be smarter to borrow the money to purchase a new vehicle even if you can afford to pay cash, because if you use the vehicle for business a portion of the interest may be tax deductible. The cash that you free up can then be used to repay debts that aren't tax deductible (mortgages or credit card debt, for example).

Hidden loan costs

Decide how much you want to spend and then pre-arrange your loan before you buy the car, so that you'll know in advance if your credit is good enough to qualify for the amount you need. In your quest for an auto loan, remember that the Internet offers help for people who need an auto loan, want quick approval, but don't like to face a banker. The Bank of Montreal (*http:/www.bmo.com*) was the first Canadian bank that accepted loan applications on its web site, and claims to send a loan response within 20 seconds. Other banks, such as Royal Bank, are offering a similar service. Loans are available to any web surfer, including those who aren't current Montreal or Royal customers.

MONTHLY PAYMENTS ON A CAR LOAN

This table is provided to assist you in determining your costs in purchasing a car. It shows approximate monthly payments required for a car loan for amounts between $4000 and $8000 and for annual interest rates of 8 to 10 percent. It also shows the total interest which you would pay over the loan period of 2, 3 or 4 years. Figures have been rounded up or down to the nearest dollar.

Interest Rate	Loan Amount	2 YEARS Monthly Payment	2 YEARS Total Interest	3 YEARS Monthly Payment	3 YEARS Total Interest	4 YEARS Monthly Payment	4 YEARS Total Interest
8%	$4000	$181	$336	$125	$503	$97	$675
	5000	226	420	156	630	122	845
	6000	271	504	188	756	146	1013
	7000	316	588	219	882	170	1182
	8000	361	672	350	1008	195	1351
9%	$4000	$182	$379	$127	$568	$99	$763
	5000	228	473	159	710	124	953
	6000	274	568	190	852	149	1144
	7000	319	662	222	994	174	1335
	8000	365	757	254	1136	198	1525
10%	$4000	$185	$430	$129	$647	$101	$870
	5000	231	538	161	808	127	1087
	6000	277	645	194	970	152	1305
	7000	323	753	226	1131	178	1522
	8000	369	860	258	1293	203	1739

Be sure to call various financial institutions to find out:
- the annual percentage rate on the amount you want to borrow and for the duration of your repayment period;
- the minimum down payment that the institution requires;
- whether taxes and licence fees are considered part of the overall cost (and thus covered by part of the loan);
- whether lower rates are available for different loan periods or for a larger down payment; and
- whether discounts are available to depositors, and if so, how long you must be a depositor before qualifying.

When comparing loans, consider the annual rate and calculate the total cost of the loan offer; that is, how much you'll pay above and beyond the total price of the vehicle.

Don't dismiss dealer financing out of hand. Dealers can finance the cost of a new car at interest rates that are competitive with the banks because of the rebates they get from the manufacturers and some lending institutions. Some dealers, however, mislead their customers into thinking they can borrow money at as much as 5 percentage points below the prime rate. Actually, they're jacking up the retail price to more than make up for the lower interest charges. Sometimes, instead of boosting the price, dealers reduce the amount they pay for the trade-in. In either case, the savings are illusory.

When dealing with banks, keep in mind that the traditional 36-month loan has now been stretched to 48 and 60 months. Longer payment terms make each month's payment more affordable, but over the long run they increase the cost of the loan considerably. Therefore, take as short a term as possible.

Be wary of lending institutions or dealers that charge an "administration" or "document" fee ranging from $99 to $150. Sometimes consumers will be charged an extra 1–2 percent of the loan up front in order to cover servicing. This is similar to lending institutions adding "points" to mortgages, and it's totally unjustified.

TRADE IN DESCRIPTION & LIEN DISCLOSURE		TERMS OF SETTLEMENT	
☐ G.S.T. REGISTRANT	G.S.T. REGISTRANT NO.	TOTAL CASH SALE PRICE	10800 00
YEAR	MI / KM / ODOMETER READING		
MAKE	MODEL		
SERIAL		SUBTOTAL	10800 0.
YEAR	MI / KM / ODOMETER READING	TRADE-IN ALLOWANCE	
MAKE	MODEL	SUBTOTAL	
SERIAL		G.S.T.	756 00
I HEREWITH TRANSFER TO DEALER ALL MY RIGHTS, TITLE AND OWNERSHIP IN THE ABOVE MOTOR VEHICLE, AND I DECLARE I AM THE SOLE OWNER AND POSSESSOR OF SAME AND THAT THERE IS NO MORTGAGE, LIEN, NOTE OR CLAIM OF ANY KIND OR NATURE ADVERSE TO MY RIGHTS OF, UPON, OR AGAINST SAID VEHICLE OTHER THAN AS STATED BELOW		SUBTOTAL	11556 00
I HEREBY STATE THAT TO THE BEST OF MY KNOWLEDGE THE ODOMETER READING AS STATED ABOVE INDICATES THE TOTAL DISTANCE ACTUALLY TRAVELLED BY THE VEHICLE.			
CUSTOMER SIGNATURE X		ADMINISTRATION FEE	99 00
LIEN PAYABLE TO		PAYOUT LIEN ON TRADE-IN	
ADDRESS	$	BALANCE DUE	11655 00
		DEPOSIT CASH ☐ CHEQUE ☐ VISA	1000 00
		PAYABLE ON DELIVERY	10655 00
THIS AGREEMENT SUBJECT TO FOLLOWING ADDITIONAL PROVISIONS. ONLY THESE PROVISIONS WILL BE RECOGNIZED.			

Dealer greed knows no bounds. This buyer was charged a $99 "administration fee" for a used car!

Some banks will cut the interest rate if you're a member of an automobile owners association, or if loan payments are automatically deducted from your chequing account. This latter proposal may be costly, though, if the chequing account charges exceed the interest rate savings.

Finance companies affiliated with GM, Ford, and Chrysler have been offering low-interest loans many points below the prime rate. In many cases, this low rate is applicable only to hard-to-sell models or cars equipped with expensive options. The low rate frequently doesn't cover the entire loan period. If vehicles recommended in this book are covered by low-interest loans, however, then the automaker-affiliated finance companies become a useful alternative to regular banking institutions.

Loan protection
Credit insurance guarantees that the car loan will be paid if the borrower becomes disabled or dies. There are three basic types of insurance that can be written into an installment contract: credit life, accident and health, and comprehensive. Most bank and credit union loans are already covered by some kind of loan insurance, but dealers sell the protection separately at an extra cost to the borrower. For this service the dealer gets a hefty commission that may vary between 10 and 20 percent. The additional cost to the purchaser can be significant. The federal 7 percent GST is applied to loan insurance, but provincial sales tax is not applicable in some provinces (such as Ontario).

Collecting on these types of policies isn't easy. There's no payment if your illness is due to some condition that existed prior to your taking out the insurance. Nor will the policy cover strikes, layoffs, being fired, etc. Generally, credit insurance is unnecessary if you're in good health, have no dependents, and your job is secure.

The Royal Bank has two interesting loan programs. One protects motorists from depreciation losses arising from an accident. For example, if a vehicle is scrapped after an accident, the Royal Bank will reimburse its depreciated value. The other program keeps monthly payments low, except for a final balloon payment.

There are plenty of advantageous programs available elsewhere. Personal loans from financial institutions now offer lots of flexibility. Most offer 100 percent financing (with no down payment), fixed or variable interest rates, a choice of loan terms, and no penalties for prepayment. Precise conditions depend on your personal credit rating. Leasing contracts are less flexible. There's a penalty for any prepayment, and rates aren't necessarily competitive. Finally, credit unions can also underwrite new car loans that combine a flexible payment schedule with low rates.

Negotiating the Contract

Any document that requires your signature is a contract. Don't sign anything unless all the details are clear to you and all the blanks have been filled in. Don't accept any verbal promises. Remember, too, that your contract doesn't have to include all the clauses found in the dealer's preprinted form. You and the sales representative can agree to strike some clauses and add others. It's up to you to negotiate the best deal for yourself.

When the sales agent asks for a deposit, make sure that it's listed on the contract as a deposit, and try to keep it as small as possible (a couple of hundred dollars at the most). If you decide to back out of the deal on a vehicle taken from stock, let the seller have the deposit as an incentive to cancel the contract (believe me, it's cheaper than a lawyer and probably equal to his or her commission).

Scrutinize all references to prices and delivery dates. Delivery can sometimes be delayed three to five months, and you'll have to pay all price increases announced during the interim (3–5 percent) unless you specify a delivery date in the contract that protects the price.

Additional clauses

You can put things on a more equal footing by negotiating the inclusion of as many clauses as possible from the sample additional contract clauses found on page 79. To do this, write in a "Remarks" section on your contract, and add "See attached clauses, which form part of this agreement." Then attach a photocopy of the "Additional Contract Clauses" printed below and persuade the sales agent to initial as many of the clauses as possible. Although some clauses may be rejected, the inclusion of just a couple of them can have important legal ramifications later on if you want a full or partial refund. For example, as a result of GM's recent two-month strike, many GM dealers will experience two- and three-month delivery delays and may try to pass on to their customers any price increases announced in the interim. Clauses #2 and #4 will protect you from these delays and price increases.

Don't take the dealer's word that "we're not allowed to do that," heard most often in reference to your cancelling the sale or reducing the PDI/transportation fee. Sales are cancelled all the time. In fact, Saturn made a big deal of its money-back warranty where only a few dozen purchasers sought refunds over the several years the program was in effect. If Saturn dealers can do it, other dealers can, too. As far as PDI/transportation fees are concerned, some dealers have been telling *Lemon-Aid* readers that they are "obligated" by the automaker to charge a set fee and could lose their franchise if they charge less. This is pure hogwash. No dealer has ever had their franchise licence revoked for cutting prices, and the automakers clearly state that they don't set a bottom-line price, since that would violate Canada's Competition Act—that's why you always see them putting disclaimers in their ads saying the dealer can charge less.

The pre-delivery inspection

Many new vehicle orders are screwed up by the factory, so the pre-delivery inspection (PDI) is critical to making sure that corrections are made before taking delivery. Since about 10 percent of new vehicles are damaged in transit from the factory, the PDI can also spot this damage and determine the extent of repairs needed. If the repair costs are substantial, the dealer can be forced to exchange the vehicle or give the buyer a rebate. Every auto manufacturer expects the dealer to carry out a PDI on each vehicle sold.

Additional Contract Clauses

1. **Financing:** This agreement is subject to the purchaser obtaining financing at a rate of _____% or less within _____ days of the date below. Failing notification in writing confirming approval of this financing, the contract is automatically cancelled.

2. **Delivery:** The motor vehicle is to be delivered by _____.

3. **Cancellation: (a)** The purchaser retains the right to cancel this agreement without penalty at any time before delivery of the vehicle by sending a notice in writing to the vendor.
   (b) Following delivery of the vehicle, the purchaser shall have two days to return the vehicle and cancel the agreement in writing, without penalty. After two days and before thirty-one days, the purchaser shall pay the dealer $25 a day as compensation for depreciation on the returned vehicle.
   (c) Cancellation of contract can be refused where the vehicle has been subjected to abuse, negligence or unauthorized modifications after delivery.
   (d) The purchaser is responsible for accident damage and traffic violations while in possession of the said vehicle. The purchaser is also responsible for re-registering the vehicle traded in and obtaining reimbursement of the sales tax. If the traded vehicle has been resold, the vendor will remit the monetary value attributed to the vehicle when it was delivered to the vendor.

4. **Protected Price:** The vendor agrees not to alter the price of the new vehicle, the cost of preparation or the cost of shipping.

5. **Trade-in:** The vendor agrees that the value attributed to the vehicle offered in trade shall not be reduced. An exception may be made when the said vehicle has been significantly modified or has suffered from unreasonable and accelerated deterioration since the signing of the agreement.

6. **Courtesy Car: (a)** In the event the new vehicle is not delivered on the agreed-upon date, the vendor agrees to supply the purchaser with a courtesy car at no cost. If no courtesy vehicle is available, the vendor agrees to reimburse the purchaser the cost of renting a vehicle of equivalent or lesser value than the new car purchased.
   (b) If the vehicle is off the road for more than five days for warranty repairs, the purchaser is entitled to a free courtesy vehicle for the duration of the repair period. If no courtesy vehicle is available, the vendor agrees to reimburse the purchaser the cost of renting a vehicle of equivalent or lesser value.

7. **Work Orders:** The purchaser will receive duly completed copies of all work orders pertaining to the vehicle, including warranty repairs and the original pre-delivery inspection (PDI).

8. **Dealer Stickers:** The vendor will not affix any dealer advertising, in any form, on the purchaser's new vehicle.

Date   Vendor's Signature   Buyer's Signature

The PDI allowance is figured into the suggested retail price, so whatever you pay the dealer is profit. Dealers who don't get top dollar for a vehicle are tempted to skip the PDI. According to testimony before the U.S. Federal Trade Commission and the U.S. Senate Subcommittee on Antitrust and Monopoly, many dealers deliver vehicles straight from the factory to their customers with only a cursory inspection. This practice wouldn't have such serious consequences if vehicles were delivered from the factory in reasonably good shape. Unfortunately, they're not. The PDI serves as a last chance to catch the three or so major and minor defects that *Consumer Reports* estimates afflict most new vehicles. If they aren't corrected before delivery, there's a good chance the dealer will charge to fix them later, and if these minor defects aren't caught in time, they can quickly become major failures.

The best way to ensure that the PDI will be done is to write in the sales contract that you'll be given a copy of the completed PDI sheet when the vehicle is delivered to you. Then, with the PDI sheet in hand, verify some of the items that were to be checked. If any items appear to have been missed, refuse delivery of the vehicle. Once you get home, check out the vehicle more thoroughly and send a registered letter to the dealer if you discover multiple major defects.

Selling Your Trade-In

Buy, sell, or hold?
It doesn't take a genius to figure out that the longer one keeps a vehicle, the less it costs to own—up to a point. The Hertz Corporation has estimated that a small car equipped with standard options, driven 10,000 miles (16,000 km), and traded each year costs 9.6 cents more a mile (approximately 6 cents more a kilometre) than a comparable car traded after five years. That same car kept for ten years and run 10,000 miles a year would cost 10.8 cents less a mile (6.75 cents less a kilometre) than a similar vehicle kept for five years, and a whopping 20.38 cents less a mile (12.75 cents a kilometre) than a comparable compact traded in each year. That would amount to a savings of $20,380 over a ten-year period.

Shortly after your vehicle's fifth birthday (or whenever you start to think about trading it in), ask a mechanic to look at it to give you some idea of what repairs, replacement parts, and maintenance work it will need in the coming year. Find out if dealer service bulletins show that it will need extensive repairs in the near future. (See Appendix VI on how to order a bulletin summary.) If it's going to require expensive repairs, you should trade the car right away, but if expensive work isn't necessary you may want to keep your vehicle. Auto owner associations provide a good yardstick. They estimate that the annual cost of repairs and preventive maintenance for the average car is between $700 and $800. If your vehicle is five years old and you haven't spent anywhere near $3,000 in maintenance, it would pay to invest in your old car and continue using it for another few years.

Consider whether your car can still be serviced easily. If it's no longer on the market, the parts supply is likely to dry up and independent mechanics will be reluctant to repair it.

Don't trade for fuel economy alone. Most fuel-efficient vehicles, such as front-wheel drives, offset the savings through higher repair costs. Also, the more fuel-efficient cars may not be as comfortable to drive due to excessive engine noise, lightweight construction, and stiff suspension and torque steer.

Reassess your needs. Does your family growth require a different vehicle? Are you driving less? Are long trips taken less frequently? Let your car rust in peace and pocket the savings if its deteriorating condition doesn't pose a safety hazard or isn't too embarrassing. On the other hand, if you're in sales and are constantly on the road, it makes sense to trade every few years—in that case mechanical reliability becomes a prime consideration, and the increased depreciation costs are mostly tax deductible.

Getting the most for your trade-in
Even customers who are on guard against paying too much for a new car often sell their trade-ins for too little. Before agreeing to any trade-in amount, read Part Three of *Lemon-Aid Used Cars 1999* if your trade-in is a passenger car or minivan. For used pickup, van, or sport-utility prices, consult *Lemon-Aid Used 4X4s, Vans and Trucks 1999.* Both guides give your vehicle's dealer and private selling price, and offer a formula to figure out regional price fluctuations. For a small fee, you can also obtain new and used car prices by calling the Montreal or Toronto office of the Automobile Protection Association (514-273-1733 or 416-964-6774). Keep in mind, however, that the APA can't guarantee that you'll always get the best possible price. In fact, some buyers tell me that they've done better buying a new or used car on their own.

Once you've nailed down your trade in's approximate value, here are some tips on selling it with a minimum of stress:
• Never sign a new car sales contract unless your trade-in has been sold—you could end up with two cars.
• Negotiate the price from *retail* (dealer price) down to *wholesale* (private sales).
• If you haven't sold your trade-in after two weekends, you might be trying to sell it at the wrong time of year or have it priced too high.

Private sales
If you must sell your vehicle and want to make the most out of the deal, consider selling it yourself and putting the profits toward your next purchase. You'll likely come out hundreds or thousands of dollars ahead—buyers will pay more for your vehicle, since they won't have to pay the 7 percent GST on a private sale. The most important thing to remember is that there's a large market for used cars and minivans in good condition in the $7,000–$10,000 range. Although most people prefer buying from individuals rather than from used car lots, they may still be afraid that the vehicle is a lemon. The following suggestions should enable you to assuage that fear and to sell your vehicle quite easily:
1. Know its value. Study dealers' newspaper ads and compare them with the prices listed in this book. Undercut the dealer price by $300 to $800, and be ready to bargain down another 10 percent for a serious buyer. Remember, prices can fluctuate wildly depending on which models are trendy, so watch the want ads carefully.
2. Enlist the aid of the salesperson who's selling you your new car.

Offer him a few hundred dollars if he finds you a buyer. The fact that one sale hinges on the other, and the prospect of making two commissions, may work wonders.

3. Post notices on bulletin boards at your office or local supermarkets, and place a "For Sale" sign in the window of the car itself. Place a newspaper ad only as a last resort.

4. Don't give your address right away to a potential buyer responding to your ad. Instead, ask for the telephone number where you may call that person back.

5. Don't sell to friends or family members. Anything short of perfection, and you can forget Christmas dinner with the family.

6. Don't touch the odometer. You may get a few hundred dollars more—and a criminal record.

7. Paint the vehicle. Some specialty shops charge only $300 and give a guarantee that's transferable to subsequent owners.

8. Make minor repairs. This includes a minor tune-up and patching up the exhaust. Again, if any repair warranty is transferable, use it as a selling point.

9. Clean the vehicle. Go to a reconditioning firm or spend the weekend scrubbing the interior and exterior. First impressions are important. Clean the chrome, polish the body, and peel off old bumper stickers. Remove butts from the ashtrays and clean out the glove compartment. Make sure all tools and spare parts have been taken out of the trunk. Don't remove the radio or speakers—the gaping holes will lower the vehicle's worth by more than the cost of the radio or speakers. Replace missing or broken dash knobs and window cranks.

10. Change the tires. Recaps are good buys.

11. Let the buyer examine the vehicle. Insist that the vehicle be inspected by an independent garage, and accompany the prospective buyer to the garage.

12. Keep important documents handy. Show prospective buyers the sales contract, repair orders, owner's manual, and all other documents that show how the vehicle has been maintained. Authenticate your claims about fuel consumption.

13. Don't mislead the buyer. If the vehicle was in an accident, or some financing is still to be paid, admit it. Any misleading statements may be used later in court against you. It's also advisable to have someone witness the actual transaction in case of a future dispute.

14. Sell to a dealer who sells the same make. He'll give you more because he can easily sell your trade-in to customers who are interested only in that make of vehicle.

15. Write an effective ad.

Using the want ads

The most effective ads give all the basic information, including make, model, year, mileage, optional features, asking price, and whether the price is firm or negotiable. The ad should also give a number where the seller can be reached.

Don't use hyped-up or come-on advertising. An ad that screams in big, bold type "SHARP! MUST SEE TO BELIEVE!" does not inspire confidence. Stick with a more sober ad that gives all the needed information without the hoopla. Don't say anything that can be interpreted as a guarantee, and be cautious of such catch-all phrases as "mechanic's special," which is to a car buyer what a "handyman's special" is to a home buyer, and can mean anything. Another common error found in used car ads is the innocent misrepresentation of what the vehicle will do from a performance standpoint. Refrain from making fuel economy claims, even if you believe them to be true.

How to write a good want ad
• Begin your advertisement with the make of the vehicle you're selling. State the manufacturer, model name, and year.
• Give information clearly, including price. Readers react more quickly and favourably when given complete and definite information.
• Make it easy for the prospect to reach you. Always include your telephone number and state a preferred time for prospects to contact you.
• Use consecutive insertions for better exposure. A six-day order is best and costs less per insertion.
• Place yourself in the reader's position. Ask yourself what you would want to know if you were buying a used car.

Want ads that fail usually do so because they're carelessly worded and don't contain enough information to get prompt action. Even an interested reader may pass up an ad that doesn't include a telephone number where the seller can be reached, for example.

Selling to dealers
Selling to a dealer means that you're likely to get 20 percent less than if you sold your vehicle privately, unless the dealer agrees to participate in an accommodation sale. Most sellers will gladly pay some penalty to the dealer, however, for the peace of mind that comes with knowing that the eventual buyer won't lay a claim against them. This assumes that the dealer hasn't been cheated by the seller—if the car is stolen, isn't paid for, has had its odometer spun back (or forward to a lower setting), or is seriously defective, the buyer or dealer can sue the original owner for fraud.

Park and sell outlets
Private owners in some parts of Canada have been able to pay a rental fee to an intermediary agency that permits their vehicle to be parked on a public lot or at the corner gas station where prospective buyers can inspect it and arrange for purchase. This automotive flea-market idea comes from the U.S., where it's very popular—it eliminates the dealer's commission while affording the seller the freedom of not being disturbed at home.

Are these rented lots worth the extra expense? Judging by the comments already received, the answer is yes. Your vehicle is accessible, in constant public view, and you don't have to invest a lot of your own time. If you're a prospective buyer, make sure that the seller is really a private party, and that the vehicle is paid for (ask to see the original sales contract).

Drawing up the contract

Draw up a bill of sale in duplicate and date it (photocopy the preceding sample bill of sale). Identify the vehicle (including the serial number), its price, whether a warranty applies, and the nature of the examination made by the buyer. The buyer may ask you to put in a lower price than what was actually paid in order to reduce the sales tax. If you agree to this, don't be surprised when a Ministry of Revenue agent comes to your door. Although the purchaser is ultimately the responsible party, you're an accomplice in defrauding the government. Furthermore, if you turn to the courts for redress your own conduct may be put on trial.

Don't forget to take your licence plates off the car. They're your property and must remain with you once the vehicle has been sold. In most provinces, your vehicle's registration certificate will have a plate portion and a vehicle portion. When the car is sold, the vehicle portion of the permit must be signed by you and given to the buyer. The remaining portion and your plates must be turned in to your province's Ministry of Transportation if you don't intend to buy another vehicle. You'll get a refund for the unexpired time left on your plates. If you decide to buy another car, you may be able to put your old plates on it (if it's a similar class of vehicle), but it has to be re-registered within a short period (usually a week).

Sample Bill of Sale
Used Vehicles

1. The seller agrees to sell, and the buyer agrees to buy a:
   a) _____ , b) _____ .
         Year   Serial Number

2. The seller is selling the motor vehicle:
   ❑ without a warranty
   ❑ with the following warranty _____ .

3. The buyer:
   ❑ has test driven the motor vehicle
   ❑ has not test driven the motor vehicle.

4. The purchase price in full is $_____ .

5. The seller acknowledges receiving from the buyer a deposit in the amount of $_____ .

6. The seller warrants and guarantees that there are no liens, chattel mortgages, or security agreements outstanding with respect to the motor vehicle or any equipment and/or accessories, and that the motor vehicle and any equipment and/or accessories has/have not been given as collateral on any loan.

7. The seller and the buyer agree that the buyer was allowed to take the motor vehicle for an inspection by a mechanic before the signing of this agreement.

8. The seller warrants to the buyer that to the best of his knowledge:
   a) the odometer reading on the motor vehicle is accurate,
   b) the motor vehicle has not been damaged in a collision, and
   c) there are no outstanding traffic violations with respect to the motor vehicle.

_____   _____
    Date   City

_____   _____
   Buyer   Seller

Summary

Purchasing a used vehicle saves you the most money. Paying cash or with the biggest down payment you can afford, and piling up as many kilometres and years as possible on your trade-in, are the next best ways to save money. Remember, too, that safety is another consideration largely dependent on the type of vehicle you choose. Focus on the following objectives.

Buy smart

1. Buy the vehicle you need and can afford, not what someone wants you to buy, or one loaded with options that you'll probably never use. Take your time. Price comparisons and test drives may take a month, but you'll get a better car and price in the long run.
2. Buy in winter or later in the new year to double-dip from dealer incentive and customer rebate programs.
3. Sell your trade-in privately.
4. Arrange financing before buying your vehicle.
5. Test-drive your choice by renting it overnight or for several days.
6. Buy through the Internet, by fax, or use an auto broker if you're not confident in your own bargaining skills, lack the time to haggle, or want to avoid the "showroom shakedown."
7. Ask for at least a 5 percent discount off the MSRP and cut pre-delivery inspection and freight charges by at least 50 percent. Insist on a specific delivery date written in the contract as well as a protected price in case there's a price increase between the time the contract is signed and when the vehicle is delivered.
8. Order a minimum of options and seek a 30 percent discount on the entire option list. Try not to let the total option cost exceed 15 percent of the vehicle's MSRP.
9. Try to avoid leasing. If you must lease, choose the shortest time possible, drive down the MSRP, and refuse to pay an "acquisition" fee.
10. Japanese vehicles made in North America, co-ventures with American automakers, and rebadged imports often cost less than imports, and are just as reliable. However, some Asian and European imports aren't as reliable as you might imagine—Hyundai, Jaguar, and Saab are prime examples. Get extra warranty protection from the automaker if you're buying a model that has a poorer-than-average repair, quality control, or warranty performance history. Use auto club references to get honest, competent repairs at a reasonable price.

Buy safe

Look for:

1. a high crashworthiness rating and low rollover potential;
2. good quality radial tires; be wary of "all-season" tires;
3. three-point belts with belt pretensioners and adjustable shoulder belt anchorages;

4. integrated child safety seats and seat anchors;
5. depowered dual airbags with a cutoff switch and effective, unobtrusive head restraints;
6. front driver's seat with plenty of rearward travel and a height adjustment;
7. good all-around visibility; and
8. an ergonomic interior with an efficient heating and ventilation system.

Now that you know what the rules of the game are, Part Two will show you how to fight back when that dream car turns into a nightmare and your dealer tells you to get lost.

Part Two
THE ART OF COMPLAINING

Chrysler Battles Paint Blemishes by Banning Deodorant

"Paint-line workers at Chrysler Corp.'s Jeep plant were asked to stop using antiperspirant after the company discovered that falling flakes left costly blemishes on the new Jeep. General Motors officials contacted late yesterday said they didn't believe they had a similar problem. One woman filed a grievance last year after her supervisor asked to check her armpits."

Newsday, 1991

Ford Admits Its Paint Mistake

"...In June 1990, a field survey of about 1,000 F-series trucks (1985–1990 models) was conducted in three locations by Body and Chassis Engineering to assess paint durability. Results showed that about 13% of the F-series trucks displayed peeling paint, which would represent about 90,000 vehicles annually..."

Memo to Members of the Finance Committee from A. J. Trottman, Executive Vice President, Ford North American Automotive Operation

Both Chrysler and Runzhiemer Consultants estimate that one out of every ten American vehicles produced by the Big Three is a "lemon." If you've bought a lemon, or if you've been forced to pay for repairs that shouldn't be your responsibility, this section will help you get your money back—without going to court or getting frazzled by the broken promises or "benign neglect" of the dealer or private party who sold you the vehicle. But if going to court is your only recourse, you'll find the jurisprudence you need to get an out-of-court settlement or to win your case without spending a fortune on lawyers and research.

Subject: Re: defective Chrysler Transaxle
Date: Thu, 12 Feb 1998 19:14:36 –0500
From: "W. Sockovie" <wsockovi@niagara.com>
Reply-To: <@niagara.com>
To: <lemonaid@earthlink.net>

Hi Phil,

Just thought that I would let you know that I received a "goodwill" cheque from Chrysler Canada today in the amount of $1977.34 to cover the cost of transmission parts on my 91 Dodge Caravan. Thanks again for your advice-it sure was worthwhile pursuing the matter!!!

Sincerely,

Wayne Sockovie
Port Robinson, Ont. Canada.

Three Ways to Get Your Money Back

Remember the "money-back" guarantee? Well, with the exception of Saturn, automakers are reluctant to offer any warranty that requires them to take back a defective new car or minivan. Nevertheless, our provincial consumer protection laws have filled the gap so that now any sales contract for a new or used vehicle can be cancelled if the vehicle:

• is misrepresented;
• is unfit for the purpose for which it was purchased; or
• hasn't been reasonably durable, considering how well it was maintained, the mileage driven, and the type of driving done.

Here's what the three legal concepts enumerated above mean in real-life situations: if the seller says that a minivan can pull a 2,000-pound (900 kg) trailer and you discover that it can barely tow half that weight, you can cancel the contract for misrepresentation. The same principle applies to a seller's exaggerated claims concerning a vehicle's fuel economy or reliability; as well as to "demonstrators" that are in fact used cars with false (rolled back) odometer readings.

It's essential that printed evidence and/or witnesses (relatives are not excluded) are available to confirm that the false representation actually occurred. These misrepresentations must concern an important fact that substantially affects the vehicle's performance, reliability, or value.

When their products fail to live up to the advertised hype, automakers often blame the owner for having pushed the vehicle beyond its limits. Therefore, when you seek to set aside the contract by claiming that the vehicle is unfit for your needs, it's essential that you get the testimony of an independent mechanic and co-workers in order to prove that the vehicle's poor performance isn't caused by negligent maintenance or abusive driving.

The reasonable durability claim is probably the easiest allegation to prove, since all automakers have benchmarks as to how long body components, trim and finish, mechanical and electronic parts should last (see the durability chart on pages 105–106). Vehicles are expected to be reasonably durable and merchantable. What is reasonably durable depends on the price paid, miles driven, the purchaser's driving habits, and how well the vehicle was maintained by the owner. Judges carefully weigh all these factors in awarding compensation or cancelling a sale.

Whatever the reason you use to get your money back, don't forget to conform to the "reasonable diligence" rule that requires you to file suit within a reasonable time after purchase or after you've discovered the defect. If there have been no negotiations with the dealer or automaker, this delay cannot exceed a few months. If either the dealer or the automaker have been promising to correct the defects for some time, or have carried out repeated unsuccessful repairs, the delay for filing the lawsuit can be extended.

Consequential damages

It's a lot easier to get the automaker to pay to replace a defective part than it is to obtain compensation for a missed day of work or a ruined vacation. Manufacturers hate to pay for consequential expenses under the basic warranty, supplementary warranty, or extended warranty because they can't control the amount of the refund. (Towing expenses, however, are usually accepted.) Courts are more generous, having ruled that all expenses (damages) flowing from a problem covered by a warranty or service bulletin are the manufacturer's/dealer's responsibility under both common law (all provinces except Quebec) and Quebec civil law. Fortunately, when legal action is threatened—usually through small claims court—automakers quickly back down from their refusal to pay consequential damage claims.

Warranties

In addition to the automakers' and dealers' *expressed* warranty, every vehicle sold new or used in Canada is covered by an *implied* warranty— a collection of federal and provincial laws and regulations that protect you from misrepresentation and a host of other evils. Furthermore, Canadian law presumes that car dealers, unlike private sellers, are aware of the defects present in the vehicles they sell. That way, they just can't pass the ball to the automakers and walk away from the dispute.

The manufacturer's warranty is a legal promise that its product will perform in the normal and customary manner for which it was designed. Regardless of the number of subsequent owners, this promise remains in force as long as the warranty's original time/ kilometre limits haven't expired.

Tires and batteries aren't covered by most car manufacturers' warranties (except for GM's), and are warranted instead by the manufacturer on a pro-rated basis. Batteries are covered for at least a year against defects, and then usually pro-rated for another 24 months. This isn't such a good deal, because the manufacturer is making a profit by charging you the full list price. If you were to buy the same replacement battery from a discount store you'd likely pay less, even without the pro-rated rebate. The same principle applies to tires, because you're given a pro-rated rebate on the suggested list price, which almost nobody pays.

Safety restraints, such as airbags and safety belts, usually mirror the basic warranty, with coverage extended for the lifetime of the vehicle.

Aftermarket products and services—such as gas-saving gadgets, rustproofing, paint protectors, air conditioning, and van conversions—can render the manufacturer's warranty invalid, so be sure to check with your dealer before purchasing any optional equipment or services from an independent supplier.

1998 WARRANTIES

Manufacturer	Bumper-to-Bumper Yrs/Km	Powertrain Yrs/Km	Emission Components Yrs/Km	Rust Yrs/Km	Seatbelts & Airbags Yrs/Km
AUDI	3/80	3/80	5/80	Surf:3/80 10/unl	Belts:3/80 Airbags: 3/80
BMW	4/80	4/80	4/80 8/130 (A)	Surf: 4/80 Perf: 6/unl	Belts: 4/80 Airbags: 4/80
CHRYSLER, JEEP, EAGLE	3/60	3/60 (1)	3/60 8/130 (A)	Surf: 3/60 Perf: 5/160	Belts: 3/60 Airbags: 3/60
FORD	3/60	3/60 (2)	3/60 8/130 (A)	Surf: 3/60 Perf: 5/unl	Belts: 5/80 Airbags: 5/80
Lincoln	4/80	4/80	4/80 8/130 (A)	Surf: 4/80 Perf: 5/unl	Belts: 5/80 Airbags: 5/80
GENERAL MOTORS	3/60	3/60 (2)	3/60 8/130 (B-C)	Surf: 3/60 Perf: 6/160	Belts: 3/60 Airbags: 3/60
Cadillac/ Olds (Aurora)	4/80	4/80	4/80 8/130 (B-C)	Surf: 4/80 Perf: 6/160	Belts: 4/80 Airbags: 4/80
Saturn	3/60	3/60	3/60 8/130 (B-C)	Surf: 3/60 Perf: 6/160	Belts: 3/60 Airbags: 3/60
Saab	4/80	4/80	4/80 8/130 (B-C)	Surf: 4/80 Perf: 6/unl	Belts: 5/unl Airbags: 5/unl
Isuzu	3/60	5/100	3/60 8/130 (B-C)	Surf: 3/60 Perf: 6/160	Belts: 5/100 Airbags: 5/100
HONDA/ACURA	3/60	5/100 +M.C.	3/60 8/130 (A)	Surf: 3/unl Perf: 5/unl	Belts: 5/100 Airbags: 5/100
HYUNDAI*	3/60	5/100	3/60 8/130 (A)	Surf: 3/60 Perf: 5/unl	Belts: 3/60 Airbags: 3/60
INFINITI	4/100	6/100 +M.C.	6/100 8/130A	Surf: 4/100 Perf: 7/unl	Belts: Lifelong Airbags: 6/180
JAGUAR	4/80	4/80	4/80 8/130 (A)	Surf. 4/80 Perf: 6/unl	Belts. 4/80 Airbags: 4/80
LADA	3/60	3/60	3/60 5/80 (B-C)	Surf: 1/20 Perf: 5/unl	Belts: 3/60 Airbags: N/A
LEXUS	4/80	6/110 +M.C.	4/80 8/130 (A)	Surf: 4/80 Perf: 6/unl	Belts: 6/110 Airbags: 6/110
MAZDA	3/80	5/100	3/80 8/128 (A)	Surf: 3/80 Perf: 5/unl	Belts: 5/100 Airbags: 5/100
"B" Series Trucks	3/60	3/60	3/60 8/128 (A)	Serf: 3/60 Perf: 5/unl	Belts: 5/100 Airbags: 5/100
MERCEDES-BENZ C, E Class	4/80	4/80	4/80	Surf: 4/80	Belts: 4/80
S, SL Class	4/80	5/120	8/130 (A)	Perf: 5/unl	Airbags: 4/80
NISSAN	3/80	5/100 +M.C.	3/80 8/130(A)	Struc: 6/unl Surf: 3/80 Perf: 5/unl	Belts: Lifelong Airbags: 5/100
PORSCHE	2/unl	2/unl	2/40 8/130 (A)	Surf: 3/unl Perf: 10/unl	Belts: 2/unl Airbags: 2/unl
SUBARU	3/60	5/100 +M.C.	3/60 8/130 (A)	Surf: 3/unl Perf: 5/unl	Belts: 5/100 Airbags: 5/100
SUZUKI	3/80	3/80	3/80	Surf: 1/20 Perf: 5/unl	Belts: 3/unl Airbags: 3/unl
TOYOTA	3/60	5/100 +M.C.	3/60 8/130 (A-E)	Surf: 3/60 Perf: 5/unl	Belts: 5/100 Airbags: 5/100
VOLKSWAGEN	2/40 (D)	5/80	2/40 8/130 (A)	Surf: 2/40 Perf: 6/unl	Belts: 2/40 Airbags: 2/40
VOLVO	4/80	4/80	4/80 8/130 (A)	Surf: 1/unl Perf: 5/unl	Belts: 5/unl Airbags: 5/unl

M.C.:	Major Components	(A)	Catalytic converter; electronic control module and onboard emissions diagnostic device
Surf:	Surface		
Perf:	Perforation	(B)	Catalytic converter
unl:	Unlimited	(C)	Powertrain module
(1)	Diesel trucks: engine 5/160(D)	(D)	Includes free scheduled maintenance: 12,000 km,
(2)	Diesel trucks: 5/160– $100 deductible after 3/60(E)		24,000 km and 36,000 km (Audi 3/80)
		(E)	Includes EGR gas temperature sensor

Note: Warranties may vary: all may apply to subsequent owners
*A 5-year/100,000 km bumper-to-bumper and 10-year/200,000 km powertrain warranty is under study.

How fairly a warranty is applied is more important than how long it remains in effect. The new warranties are useful to consumers who are making claims before provincial small claims courts, because they prove that the technology exists to make powertrain components and rust resistance/paint adhesion last far longer than admitted in the past.

Once you know the normal wear rate for a mechanical component or body part, you can demand proportional compensation when you get less than normal durability—no matter what the original warranty said.

Some dealers tell customers that they need to have original equipment parts installed in order to maintain their warranty. A variation on this theme requires that routine servicing—including tune-ups and oil changes (with a certain brand of oil)—be done by the selling dealer, or the warranty is invalidated.

Nothing could be further from the truth.

Canadian law stipulates that whomever issues a warranty cannot make that warranty conditional on the use of any specific brand of motor oil, oil filter, or any other component, unless it's provided to the customer free of charge.

Sometimes dealers will do all sorts of minor repairs that don't correct the problem, and then, after the warranty runs out, they'll tell you that major repairs are needed. You can avoid this nasty surprise by repeatedly bringing in your vehicle to the dealership before the warranty ends. During each visit insist that a written work order include the specific nature of the problem, *as you see it*, and that it carries the notation that this is the second, third, or fourth time the same problem has been brought to the dealer's attention. Write it down yourself, if need be. This allows you to show a pattern of non-performance by the dealer during the warranty period and establishes that it's a serious and chronic problem. When the warranty expires, you have the legal right to demand that it be extended on those items consistently reappearing on your handful of work orders.

Extended (supplementary) warranties
Supplementary warranties providing extended coverage may be sold by the manufacturer, dealer, or an independent third party, and are automatically transferred when the vehicle is sold. They cost between $500 and $1,500, and should be purchased only if the vehicle you're buying is off its original warranty, has a poor repair history (see Part Three), or if you're reluctant to use the small claims courts when factory-related trouble arises. Don't let the dealer pressure you into deciding right away. Generally, you can purchase an extended warranty anytime during the period in which the manufacturer's warranty is in effect.

Because from one-third to one-half of the warranty's cost represents dealer markup, dealers love to sell extended warranties. Out of the remainder comes the sponsor's administration costs and profit margin, calculated at another 25 percent. What's left is a minuscule 25 percent of the original amount paid to the dealer. It's estimated that, of the car buyers who purchase an extended service contract, fewer than half actually use it.

It's often difficult to collect on supplementary warranties, because independent companies not tied to the automakers frequently go out of business. When this happens, and the company's insurance policy won't cover your claim, take the dealer to small claims court and ask for the repair cost and the refund of the original warranty payment. Your argument for holding the dealer responsible is a simple one: by accepting a commission for acting as an agent of the defunct company, the selling dealer took on the obligations of the company as well.

Emission control warranties
These little-publicized warranties can save you big bucks if major engine or exhaust components fail prematurely. They come with all new vehicles and cover the emission control system for up to 8 years/130,000 km. Unfortunately, although owners' manuals vaguely mention the emissions warranty, most don't specify which parts are covered (see the "1998 Warranties" chart above). Fortunately, the U. S. Environmental Protection Agency has intervened on several occasions with hefty fines against Chrysler and Ford and ruled that all major motor and fuel-system components are covered. These include fuel metering, ignition spark advance, restart, evaporative emissions, positive crankcase ventilation, engine electronics (computer modules), and catalytic converters, as well as hoses, clamps, brackets, pipes, gaskets, belts, seals, and connectors. Canada, however, has no government definition, and it's left up to each manufacturer and the small claims courts to decide which components are covered.

Many of the dealer service bulletins listed in Part Three under "Service Tips" show parts failures that are covered under the emissions warranty. A good example are these two recent bulletins, applicable to Ford's trucks, vans, and sport-utilities. It explicitly states that owners of these vehicles who experience hard starting, chronic stalling, or excessive exhaust noises will get free repairs under the basic warranty, and when it expires, the emissions warranty. Unfortunately, few owners will ever see these bulletins, and will end up paying for repairs that are really Ford's responsibility.

Article No.
97-9-5
04/28/97
LONG CRANK - STICKING IDLE AIR CONTROL (IAC) VALVE - VEHICLES BUILT FROM 11/1/94 THROUGH 3/30/96 STALL - AFTER STARTING WHEN ENGINE ALLOWED TO SOAK FROM 1-4 HOURS - STICKING IDLE AIR CONTROL (IAC) VALVE - VEHICLES BUILT FROM 1/11/94 THROUGH 3/30/96
1995–96 CONTOUR, CROWN VICTORIA, ESCORT, TAURUS, THUNDERBIRD
1996 MUSTANG
LINCOLN-MERCURY:
1995–96 CONTINENTAL, COUGAR, GRAND MARQUIS, MARK VIII, MYSTIQUE, SABLE, TOWN CAR, TRACER
LIGHT TRUCK:
1995–96 AEROSTAR, BRONCO, ECONOLINE, F-150-350 SERIES, RANGER, WINDSTAR
1996 EXPLORER
ISSUE:
After a 1–4 hour engine soak time, long crank times and/or long crank to start followed by a stall may occur on some vehicles. No further stalling or rough idle will occur after the engine is running. The long crank and/or stall may be due to the Idle Air Control (IAC) Valve sticking.
ACTION:
Replace the AC Valve with a revised AC Valve if no Diagnostic Trouble Codes (DTCs) are present. Refer to the following Service Procedure for details.
WARRANTY STATUS: Eligible Under The Provisions Of Bumper to bumper Warranty Coverage And Emissions Warranty

This fuel system repair would cost you several hundred dollars, if you didn't have this bulletin in your possession.

97-16-6
08/04/97
• EXHAUST SYSTEM - LOOSE CATALYST OR MUFFLER HEAT SHIELDS
• NOISE - "BUZZING" OR "RATTLING" - LOOSE CATALYST OR MUFFLER HEAT SHIELDS
FORD:

1985–94 TEMPO	1986-97 TAURUS
1985–97 CROWN VICTORIA, MUSTANG, THUNDERBIRD	1988-93 FESTIVA
1985–98 ESCORT	1989-97 PROBE

LINCOLN-MERCURY:

1985–92 MARK VII	1987-89 TRACER
1985–94 TOPAZ	1991-94 CAPRI
1985–97 CONTINENTAL, COUGAR, GRAND MARQUIS, TOWN CAR	1991-98 TRACER
1986–97 SABLE	

MERKUR:

1985–89 XR4TI	1988-89 SCORPIO

LIGHT TRUCK:

1985–90 BRONCO II	1986-97 AEROSTAR
1985–96 BRONCO	1988-97 F SUPER DUTY
1985–97 ECONOLINE, F-150, F-250, F-350, RANGER	1991-97 EXPLORER

This TSB article is being republished in its entirety to include vehicles built through the 1997 model year.
ISSUE:
A "buzzing or rattling" noise from the exhaust system may be caused by a loose heat shield attachment to the muffler or catalyst. The noise is noticeable during normal driving conditions or at engine idle.
ACTION:
Install worm clamps to secure the heat shield attachments. Refer to the following Service Procedure for details.
WARRANTY STATUS: Eligible Under Basic Warranty Coverage For 1991 And Prior Models, Bumper to bumper Warranty Coverage For 1992–97 Models, And Emissions Warranty Coverage For Catalytic Converters With Welded Heat Shields For All Model Years

Many problems related to the exhaust system are also covered by the emissions warranty.

Secret warranties

Secret warranties have been around since automobiles were first mass-produced. They're set up to provide free repairs of performance-related defects caused by substandard materials, faulty design, or assembly-line errors. In 1974, *Lemon-Aid* exposed Ford's secret J-67 seven-year rust warranty, which covered the company's 1970–74 models. After first denying that it had such a warranty, Ford admitted two years later that it was indeed in place, and negotiated a $2.8 million settlement with this author to compensate owners of rust-cankered Fords. And you know what? Twenty-five years later, hundreds of secret warranties continue to exist among most automakers and *Lemon-Aid* is still the only consumer publication blowing the whistle on hundreds of current programs that secretly allocate funds for the repair of engine, transmission, fuel pump, and paint defects on cars, sport-utilities, trucks, minivans and vans.

Even mundane little repairs that can still cost you a hundred bucks or more are covered. Take, for example, the elimination of foul, musty, or mildew odors emitted by your air conditioning unit. Despite what the dealer may say, it's covered by the base warranty. In fact, as you can see from the following GM, Ford, and Chrysler service bulletins, automakers have secret warranty policies that pay for AC service adjustments.

File In Section: 1 - HVAC
Bulletin No.: 53-12-12A
Date: December, 1996
Subject:
Air Conditioning Odor at Start Up in Humid Climates
(Disinfect Evaporator Core, Install Delayed Blower Control Package)

Models:
1993–96 Passenger Cars (Except GEO)
1993–96 Light Duty Models (Except Tracker)

Condition
Some owners may comment on odors emitted from the air conditioning system, primarily at start up in hot, humid climates.

Cause
This odor may be the result of microbial growth on the evaporator core. When the blower motor fan is turned on, the microbial growth may release an unpleasant musty odor into the passenger compartment.

Correction
To remove odors of this type, it is necessary to eliminate the microbial growth and prevent its recurrence- To accomplish this, these two procedures must be completed.
• Deodorize the evaporator core using Deodorizing Aerosol Kit, P/N 12377951 (AC Delco 15-102).
• Install the new A/C Delayed Blower Control Package, P/N 12370470, (AC Delco 15-8632).

Secret warranties leave their own foul odour.

Article No.
98-2-7
02/02/98
AIR CONDITIONING - MUSTY AND MILDEW TYPE ODORS - SERVICE PROCEDURE
FORD:
1992–93 FESTIVA
1992–94 TEMPO
1992–97 CROWN VICTORIA, ESCORT MUSTANG, PROBE, TAURUS, THUNDERBIRD
1994–96 ASPIRE
1995–97 CONTOUR
LINCOLN-MERCURY:
1992–94 TOPAZ
1992–97 CONTINENTAL, COUGAR, GRAND MARQUIS, SABLE, TOWN CAR, TRACER
1993–97 MARK VIII
1995–97 MYSTIQUE
LIGHT TRUCK:
1992–95 BRONCO
1992–97 AEROSTAR, ECONOLINE, EXPLORER, F SUPER DUTY F-l50, F-250 HD, F-250 LD, F-350, RANGER
1995–98 WINDSTAR
1997 MOUNTAINEER
1997–98 EXPEDITION
1998 NAVIGATOR
MEDIUM/HEAVY TRUCK:
1992–97 F & B SERIES

This TSB article is being republished in its entirety to include the Expedition, Navigator and 1998 Windstar.

ISSUE: Musty and mildew type odors may come from the air conditioner and heater system. This odor is caused by mildew-type fungi growth in the A/C evaporator. It is most noticeable when the A/C is first turned on.

ACTION: A new Disodorizer(R) which encapsulates the mildew is now available to reduce these odors. This is a seasonal repair. Engineering effort to provide a long term repair for A/C odors will continue. Apply the Ford A/C Disodorizer(R) product (F6AZ-19G210-AA or YN-18) to the A/C system as directed in the following A/C Odor Treatment Procedure.

WARRANTY STATUS: Eligible Under The Provisions Of Bumper to bumper Warranty Coverage

Ford's AC warranty service is a 20-minute job.

As mentioned in Part One, automakers are reluctant to make secret warranty extensions public because they feel it would weaken confidence in their product and increase their legal liability. The closest they come to an admission is sending a "goodwill policy," "product improvement program," or "special policy" service bulletin to dealers or first owners of record. Consequently, the only motorists who get compensated for repairs to defective parts are the ones who are the original owners, haven't moved or leased their vehicle, or who yell the loudest and present automaker service bulletins (see Appendix VI to order your own bulletins).

If you're refused compensation, keep in mind that secret warranty extensions are an admission of manufacturing negligence. Try to compromise with a pro rata adjustment from the manufacturer. If polite negotiations fail, challenge the refusal in court on the grounds that you should not be penalized for failing to make a reimbursement claim under a secret warranty you never knew existed!

NO: 24-11-97
GROUP: Heater & A/C
DATE: Jul. 11. 1997
SUBJECT:
A/C Evaporator Odor

MODELS:
1992–1995 (AA) Spirit/Acclaim/LeBaron Sedan
1994–1998 (AB) Ram Van/Wagon
1992–1993 (AC) Dynasty/New Yorker/New Yorker Salon
1992–1993 (AG) Daytona
1992–1995 (AJ) LeBaron Coupe/LeBaron Convertible
1992–1998 (AN) Dakota
1992–1994 (AP) Shadow/Shadow Convertible/Sundance
1992–1995 (AS) Town & Country/Caravan/Voyager
1992–1993 (AY) Imperial/New Yorker Fifth Avenue
1994–1998 (BR) Ram Pickup
1993–1995 (ES) Chrysler Voyager (European Market)
1996–1998 (GS) Chrysler Voyager (International Market)
1995–1998 (JA) Cirrus/Stratus/Breeze
1996–1998 (JX) Sebring Convertible
1993–1998 (LH) Concorde/Intrepid/LHS/New Yorker/Vision
1996–1998 (NS) Town & Country/Caravan/Voyager
1995–1998 (PL) Neon
1997–1998 (TJ) Wrangler
1992–1998 (XJ) Cherokee
1994–1998 (ZG) Grand Cherokee (International Market)
1993–1998 (ZJ) Grand Cherokee/Grand Wagoneer

SYMPTOM/CONDITION:
Some vehicle operators may experience a musty odor from the A/C system, primarily at start up in hot and humid climates. This odor may be the result of microbial growth on the evaporator core. During normal A/C system operation, condensation forms in and around the A/C evaporator. When airborne pollutants mix with this condensation, bacteria and fungi growth begins and odor results.

DIAGNOSIS:
Operate the A/C system, if a musty odor is experienced, perform the Repair Procedure.

PARTS REQUIRED:
1 04897625AA Cleaner, Aerosol Evaporator
POLICY: Reimbursable within the provisions of the warranty.

Chrysler's AC warranty service may take from 30 to 90 minutes and is classed: "Failure Code: XX–Service Adjustment."

Here are a few examples of the latest and most comprehensive secret warranties that have come across my desk this year. Keep in mind that an up-to-date listing of other secret warranties and service programs for every vehicle *Lemon-Aid* rates can be found in Part Three under the heading "Secret Warranties/Service Tips."

Chrysler
1991–96 cars, minivans, vans, sport-utilities, and trucks
• **Problem**: Defective automatic transmissions, air conditioners, and brakes; delaminated paint that turns a chalky colour and then peels off.
• **Warranty coverage**: Chrysler has offered full or partial refunds for claims that are within the durability guidelines set out on pages 105–106.

Chrysler set up a special Review Committee in February 1998 in response to the bad publicity and threats of court action coming from *Lemon-Aid* and the approximately six hundred Chrysler owners who helped form Chrysler Lemon Owners Groups (CLOG) in British Columbia and New Brunswick. These groups submitted the names of irate owners to Chrysler and have succeeded in getting sizable refunds for brake, transmission and paint repairs. If you have had any of these problems and want "goodwill" repairs (or a refund for repairs already carried out), go through Chrysler's regular customer relations hotline. If you're not satisfied by the response you get, then phone, fax, or email Mr. Bob Renaud, Vice President Parts, Service, and Engineering at: tel.: 519-973-2300; fax: 519-561-7005; email: *RAR17@CHRYSLER.COM*. He tells me the Review Committee will review all claims, including those that were previously rejected.

Three suggestions if you plan to contact the Review Committee: send Chrysler copies of all your repair bills or independent garage estimates; don't accept a refusal based on the fact that you're not the first owner, and finally, don't let Chrysler turn your claim down because the repairs were carried out by an independent repair facility (see below).

Dear Phil, I thought you might be interested to learn of the outcome of my troubles with a transmission failure on my 1993 Plymouth minivan. I requested a faxed dealer service bulletin summary from you on August 21 this year. You added a note that I should call a Bob Renaud at Chrysler and start the claim process.

We phoned this gentleman's office and spoke with Sharon McDonald, who assigned us a claim file number and asked that we fax her our bill and a covering letter outlining the circumstances. We sent that off on September 4, and heard nothing, until today the 25th of September. We were actually going through our copy of Lemon-Aid, reading up on our next step (threaten court action?) when the mail arrived containing a letter from Chrysler Canada and a cheque to reimburse us for our costs.

We were stunned! Surely it couldn't be this easy! We hadn't even trotted out our list of DSB numbers yet nor had we mentioned lawyers or Small Claims Court. Chrysler obviously knew they had a problem with the transmissions...

I hope my experiences can be used to help other motorists. They can be summarized thus:

1. Don't let the dealer brush you off (this is their job)—go to the factory.

2. Just because you chose the short-term warranty option doesn't mean you aren't covered by the long-term—if you fight for it.

Thank you very much for the excellent advice in your book: it gave us the determination to keep on at the problem when it would have been all too easy to let go. Thanks especially for the phone contact at Chrysler. I'm sure that one little piece of information saved us hours of time and many dollars in phone calls to

Ontario. Our local dealer certainly wasn't forthcoming with stuff like that. We are definitely a lot more satisfied with Chrysler now, thanks to their willingness to promptly settle a fair claim...

Yours sincerely,
Wally James & Barb Steele

CHRYSLER CANADA

September 12, 1998

Ms. Barbara Steele
166 Cleland Drive
Penticton, B.C.
V2A 7L7

Dear Ms. Steele:

We have received your letter of September 4, 1998 which is further to our previous telephone contact regarding your 1993 Plymouth Grand Voyager.

As a goodwill gesture, Chrysler Canada is enclosing a cheque in the amount of $2,685.73 to reimburse you for the transmission repairs performed by Honest "T" Repairs Inc. on July 13, 1998. We hope this cheque will convince you of our commitment to quality products and customer service.

The tie rod ends are not a powertrain component, and repairs are the owner's responsibility at the current date and metrage.

We apologize for the inconvenience you encountered, and we appreciate the opportunity to be of assistance.

Yours very truly,

CHRYSLER CANADA LTD.

V. Ryan

V. J. Ryan (Mrs.)
Customer Service Manager

CAIR #5119301

(Encl.)

Chrysler Canada Ltd.
P.O. Box 1621
Windsor, Ontario N9A 4H6

The transmission failed at 98,138 km.

Ford
1994–95 Taurus, Sable, and Windstar
- **Problem**: Defective 3.8L engine headgaskets may cause loss of engine coolant, engine overheating, or destruction of the engine.
- **Warranty coverage**: Ford will replace the defective components at no charge up to 5 years/100,000 km. Vehicles that have exceeded the kilometre limit will still be covered through December 31, 1998. Ford is also offering a full refund for repairs performed by independents prior to the issuing of its June 23,1998, letter.

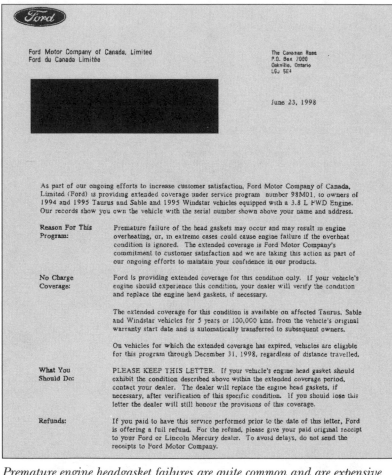

Ford Motor Company of Canada, Limited
Ford du Canada Limitée

The Canadian Road
P.O. Box 2000
Oakville, Ontario
L6J 5E4

June 23, 1998

As part of our ongoing efforts to increase customer satisfaction, Ford Motor Company of Canada, Limited (Ford) is providing extended coverage under service program number 98M01, to owners of 1994 and 1995 Taurus and Sable and 1995 Windstar vehicles equipped with a 3.8 L FWD Engine. Our records show you own the vehicle with the serial number shown above your name and address.

Reason For This Program: Premature failure of the head gaskets may occur and may result in engine overheating, or, in extreme cases could cause engine failure if the overheat condition is ignored. The extended coverage is Ford Motor Company's commitment to customer satisfaction and we are taking this action as part of our ongoing efforts to maintain your confidence in our products.

No Charge Coverage: Ford is providing extended coverage for this condition only. If your vehicle's engine should experience this condition, your dealer will verify the condition and replace the engine head gaskets, if necessary.

The extended coverage for this condition is available on affected Taurus, Sable and Windstar vehicles for 5 years or 100,000 kms. from the vehicle's original warranty start date and is automatically transferred to subsequent owners.

On vehicles for which the extended coverage has expired, vehicles are eligible for this program through December 31, 1998, regardless of distance travelled.

What You Should Do: PLEASE KEEP THIS LETTER. If your vehicle's engine head gasket should exhibit the condition described above within the extended coverage period, contact your dealer. The dealer will replace the engine head gaskets, if necessary, after verification of this specific condition. If you should lose this letter the dealer will still honour the provisions of this coverage.

Refunds: If you paid to have this service performed prior to the date of this letter, Ford is offering a full refund. For the refund, please give your paid original receipt to your Ford or Lincoln Mercury dealer. To avoid delays, do not send the receipts to Ford Motor Company.

Premature engine headgasket failures are quite common and are expensive to repair. At present, GM, Ford, and Toyota have "goodwill" programs in effect to pay for headgasket repairs. Symptoms indicating a faulty headgasket include overheating, poor fuel economy, reduced engine power, and coolant leaking into the engine, which then mixes with the ventilation system and causes a film to be deposited on the interior glass surfaces. (At night, the street lights will look blurry.)

Ford/Nissan

1995–96 Villager and Quest minivans equipped with 3.0L engines

• **Problem**: Excessive engine noise is caused by a poorly designed connecting rod that's insufficiently lubricated. The design on the VG30E was changed in January 1996 to provide a quieter operation; the new design should have worked its way into production by March of that same year (check the month of production on the doorplate).

• **Warranty coverage**: Ford will replace at no charge any 3.0L V6 engine block if customers complain of engine knock following a cold start. Ford is replacing the entire engine, including the cylinder head, and says it will issue an owner notification (not a recall) or set up a warranty extension program. Nissan, on the other hand, doesn't plan to notify customers of this free replacement program.

Both Ford and Nissan also have a serious problem with Villager, Quest, and Pathfinder engine exhaust manifold studs breaking, which costs over $3,000 to repair. Both companies will offer "goodwill" compensation if pressed, particularly if owners show up with service bulletins in hand.

General Motors

• **1992–93 Cavalier/Sunbird with 2.2L 4-cylinder engines**

• **Problem**: Faulty head gaskets may cause loss of engine coolant, engine overheating, or destruction of the engine.

• **Warranty coverage**: GM will replace the faulty head gasket or repair the engine damage caused by head gasket failure at no charge up to 7 years/160,000 km, as set out in its March 1996 letter to first owners. Second owners and repairs done by independent garages are included in this program. This warranty extension sets the benchmark at a new high for engine durability and can be used in claims against all automakers with similar engine problems.

Confidential service bulletins

These are special warranties confirmed by technical service bulletins (confidential, for the most part) sent to dealers by automakers to advise them of special warranties and to help them quickly diagnose and correct factory defects. These bulletins also disclose: a) how much of the repair the dealer can charge back to the manufacturer, and b) parts that are available free of charge. Armed with these bulletins, motorists can use less expensive independent garages to diagnose and repair their vehicles or to negotiate compensation for defects that the bulletins show are the manufacturer's fault.

The major problem with these bulletins is that they're difficult to get. Dealers and automakers are reluctant to provide this kind of detailed technical information because it allows customers to second-guess a mechanic's work or to buttress their demands for compensation. However, as long as their involvement isn't disclosed, some dealers will discreetly provide copies of service bulletins to help their customers fight for compensation from the auto manufacturer.

If needed, you can always order service bulletins from the author for $5 each (see Appendix VI for ordering instructions).

Recall campaigns

Safety- and emissions-recall campaigns confer warranty benefits on owners whereby the manufacturer and dealer are obligated to repair a defect at no charge, no matter how often the vehicle has been sold or what its mileage is. Furthermore, Transport Canada monitors how well automakers carry out recall campaigns and will intervene if any company stonewalls a legitimate request.

Recall repairs

Dealers learn of recall campaigns just like you and I—mostly from the media. It will therefore take several months for them to have the necessary parts and instructions to carry out the repairs. So don't expect to be welcomed with open arms when you stop by for recall repairs that have just been announced on television.

Let's say your vehicle develops a safety- or emissions-related problem that's not yet part of a recall campaign, yet you want it fixed for free. You will probably be charged for the repair. Automakers and dealers generally take a restrictive view of what constitutes a safety or emissions defect and, unless the customer strongly objects, frequently charge for repairs which should be free. To counter this tendency, look at the following list of typical safety-related defects, and if you experience similar problems, tell the dealer you expect your repair to be paid by the manufacturer:

• airbag malfunctions
• corrosion affecting safe operation
• disconnected or stuck accelerators
• electrical shorts
• faulty windshield wipers
• fuel leaks
• problems with original axles, drive shafts, seats, seat recliners, or defrosters
• seatbelt problems
• stalling or sudden acceleration
• sudden steering or brake loss
• suspension failures
• trailer coupling failures

Recall campaigns may be ordered by the U.S. Department of Transportation, or undertaken voluntarily in Canada. Voluntary recall campaigns are a real problem, though. They aren't as rigorously monitored as government-ordered recalls, and dealers and automakers routinely deny they exist. Additionally, the company's so-called "fix" may not correct the hazard, and the company may take its own sweet time in notifying owners. Take, for example, Chrysler's voluntary "service program" to strengthen the rear latches on as many as 4.5 million 1984–95 minivans. Almost 50 percent of affected owners were still waiting for Chrysler to fix their minivans nearly two years after the company volunteered to correct the defect without the government's involvement.

Getting free paint repairs
It may seem strange, talking about paint defects on new vehicles, but I've seen nothing in the 1999 model year lineup to indicate that automakers have taken steps to remedy what has been a decade-old problem: the paint whitens and takes on a chalky colour, or it peels away prematurely during the first six years of ownership.

Paint flaking (delamination, as it's called in the industry) occurs when the top coat of paint separates from the primer coat, mostly along horizontal surfaces, and often as a result of sunlight hitting paint that has insufficient UV protection. When the paint peels, the entire vehicle must be repainted after a new primer resurfacer has been added. For some vehicles, the labour alone can run about 20 hours, at a cost of $50 to $75 an hour.

Confidential GM dealer service bulletins and memos show us that GM expects its factory paint jobs to last at least six years. When they don't, the automaker pays dealers to repaint the entire car at no charge to the owner, regardless of whether it was bought new or used (see GM's Pontiac memo on the following page).

Ford is more generous than GM (judging by its service bulletins), although its dealers need Oakville's authorization first. Ford has been repainting 1983–93 cars, minivans, vans, F-series trucks, Explorers, Rangers, and Broncos for free under a little-known "Owner Dialogue" program. Ford says it discontinued the program several years ago, but owners who were never alerted to the program's existence and threaten small claims action are still getting compensation.

How long should parts/repairs last?
Let's say you can't find a service bulletin that says your problem is factory-related or covered by a special compensation program. Or a part lasts just a little longer than its guarantee, but not as long as is generally expected. Can you get a refund if the same problem reappears shortly after it has been repaired? Yes—if you can prove the part failed prematurely.

PONTIAC

PONTIAC DIVISION
GeneralMotors Corporation
One Pontiac Plaza
Pontiac, Michigan 48340-2952
October 16, 1992

TO: All Pontiac Dealers

SUBJECT: Partners in Satisfaction (PICS)
          Dealer Authorization

Pontiac continually reviews the Warranty Management System to ensure
that Warranty Administration achieves its purposes, including high levels of
customer satisfaction with after sale treatment.

Following a recent review, Pontiac has decided to provide dealers authorization for cases involving paint repairs for vehicles up to six (6) years
from the date of delivery, without regard for mileage. This is a change from
the current PICS dealer self-authorization which allows paint repair goodwill adjustments to be made up to 6 years/60,000 miles. Dealers who have
a deductible override capabilities may also waive deductibles as they see
appropriate on this type of repair.

Paint repairs are only to be authorized beyond the warranty period by the
Dealership Service Manager on a case-by-case basis as with any other
goodwill policy adjustment.

Assistance should only be considered for cases involving evidence of a
defect in materials or workmanship by the manufacturer. Assistance should
not be considered for conditions related to wear and tear and/or lack of
maintenance (such as fading, stone chips, scratches, environmental damage, etc.).

Please contact your Zone representative if you have specific questions.

Perry S. White
Director of Service/
Customer Satisfaction

GM says it has no secret paint warranty, so what's this?

   Automakers, mechanics, and the courts each have their own benchmarks as to what a reasonable period of time or amount of mileage is
during which one should expect a part or adjustment to last. The following table shows what most automakers consider reasonable durability, as expressed by their original warranties, secret warranties, and
"goodwill" or "special policy" programs.

GM Paint Program Overview

Group Ref: Body
Bulletin No: 331708
Date: November, 1993
SUBJECT:
CLEARCOAT DEGRADATION - CHALKING AND WHITENING
MODELS:
GM PASSENGER CARS WITH BASECOAT/CLEARCOAT
CONDITION:
The vehicle exterior surface may show large chalky or white patches in the clearcoat, usually but not limited to the horizontal surfaces.
Blacks, Dark Blues, Reds, may have potential for this condition. On rare occasions, other colors may be involved.
CAUSE:
The clearcoat (with sunlight and heat) may degrade and turn white or chalky.
IDENTIFICATION:
On a clean surface, at or above room temperature, firmly apply a 2" wide piece of masking tape to the chalky or white area of the clearcoat and pull upward quickly. The adhesive side of the tape WILL NOT HAVE THE PAINT COLOR ON IT. A light shine or reduced tackiness may be noticed on the tape adhesive surface, indication clearcoat transfer to the tape.
CORRECTION:
Refinish all horizontal surfaces using the following procedure.
- Remove the clearcoat layer from all horizontal surfaces and the top surfaces of fenders and quarter panels.
NOTE:
In some cases, it will be necessary to remove the clearcoat from the upper vertical surfaces of fenders, doors and quarters (approximately 3"), and the top areas directly above the front and rear wheelhouse openings.
- Lightly sand any previously exposed base color to remove chalky residue from the surface.
- The vertical surfaces should be sanded and colorcoated to the next lower breakline (typically the body side moldings) for color uniformity of the repair.

Estimated Part Durability

ACCESSORIES

Air conditioner	5 years
Cellular phone	5 years
Cruise control	5 years/ 100,000 km
Power antenna	5 years
Power doors, windows	5 years
Radio	5 years

BODY

Paint peeling	7 years
Rust (perforations)	7 years
Rust (surface)	5 years
Vinyl roof	5 years
Water/wind/ air leaks	5 years

BRAKE SYSTEM

Brake drum	120,000 km
Brake drum, turn	40,000 km
Brake drum linings	35,000 km
Disc brake calipers	30,000 km
Disc brake pads	30,000 km
Master cylinder, rebuild	100,000 km
Wheel cylinder, rebuild	80,000 km

ENGINE AND DRIVETRAIN

Constant velocity joint	5 years/ 100,000 km
Differential	7 years/ 150,000 km
Engine (gas)	7 years/ 160,000 km
Radiator	4 years/ 80,000 km
Transfer case	7 years/ 150,000 km
Transmission (auto.)	7 years/ 150,000 km
Transmission (man.)	7 years/ 200,000 km
Transmission oil cooler	5 years/ 100,000 km
Universal joint	5 years/ 100,000 km

EXHAUST SYSTEM

Catalytic converter	5 years/ 100,000 km or more
Muffler	2 years/ 40,000 km
Tailpipe	3 years/ 60,000 km

FUEL SYSTEM

Carburetor	5 years/ 120,000 km
Fuel filter	2 years/ 40,000 km
Fuel pump	5 years/ 80,000 km
Injectors	5 years/ 80,000 km

IGNITION SYSTEM

Cable set	60,000 km
Electronic module	5 years/ 80,000 km
Retiming	20,000 km
Spark plugs	20,000 km
Tune-up	20,000 km

SAFETY COMPONENTS

Airbags	life of vehicle
ABS brakes	7 years/ 150,000 km
ABS computer	7 years/ 150,000 km
Seatbelts	life of vehicle

STEERING AND SUSPENSION

Alignment	1 year/ 20,000 km
Ball joints	80,000 km
Power steering	5 years/ 80,000 km
Shock absorber	2 years/ 40,000 km
Struts	5 years/ 80,000 km
Tires (radial)	5 years/ 80,000 km
Wheel bearing	3 years/ 60,000 km

VISIBILITY

Aim headlights	20,000 km
Halogen/fog lights	3 years/ 60,000 km
Sealed beam	2 years/ 40,000 km
Windshield wiper motor	5 years/ 80,000 km

The above guidelines are extrapolated from Chrysler's payout to Chrysler Lemon Owner Group (CLOG) members in British Columbia and New Brunswick from December 1997 through June 1998, in addition to Chrysler's original 7-year/115,000 km powertrain warranty applicable from 1991–95. Other sources for this chart were the Ford and GM transmission warranties as outlined in their secret warranties, and GM, Mercury, Nissan, and Toyota engine "special programs," spelled out in their internal service bulletins.

Safety features generally have a lifetime warranty, with the exception of ABS brakes, which are a wear item. Nevertheless, the Chrysler 10-year "free service program" portion of its ABS recall announced last year can serve as a handy benchmark as to how long one can expect these components to last.

Airbags are a different matter. Those which deploy in an accident, and the personal injury and interior damage their deployment will likely have caused, are covered by your accident insurance policy. Insurance companies, however, won't cover damages caused by inadvertent airbag deployment resulting from passing over a bump in the road, slamming the car door, or, in the case of some Chrysler minivans, simply putting the key in the ignition.

Finally, the manufacturers' emission warranty serves as the primary guideline governing how long a vast array of electronic and mechanical components should last. Look first at your owner's manual for an indication of which parts are covered on your vehicle. If you come up with few specifics, use the EPA's guidelines along with GM's bulletins on the matter. Keep in mind that these durability benchmarks, secret warranties, and emissions warranties aren't limited to first owners.

Three Steps to a Settlement

Step 1: informal negotiations

If your vehicle was misrepresented, has major defects, or wasn't properly repaired under warranty, the first thing you should do is give the seller (the dealer or a private party) a written summary, by registered mail or fax, of the outstanding problems and stipulate a time period in which they will be corrected or your money will be refunded. Keep a copy for yourself along with all your repair records. At the beginning, try to work things out informally.

When negotiating with the seller, speak in a calm, polite manner and try to avoid polarizing the issue. Talk about how "we can work together" on the problem. Support your position with independent garage reports, service bulletins, and maintenance records. Let a compromise slowly emerge—don't come in with a hardline set of demands. Don't demand the settlement offer in writing, but make sure you're accompanied by a friend who can confirm the offer in court if it's not honoured (relatives can testify in court). Be prepared to act on the offer without delay, so that you won't be blamed for its withdrawal.

Dealers

Check all of the sales and warranty documents you were given to see if they conform to provincial laws. Any errors, omissions, or violations can be used to clinch a deal with the dealer in lieu of making a formal complaint, because the dealer could be fined if he's violated provincial protection laws.

If the dealer won't talk with you, write or call the nearest regional office or the manufacturer's head office. The address and telephone numbers can be found in the owner's manual. General Motors, for example, has a toll-free customer hotline (1-800-263-3777), which is Oshawa, Ontario-based and employs over 30 people (one-third of whom are bilingual) to answer customer inquiries. Don't expect miracles from these people. Each staffer has a guide book showing the appropriate, corporate-approved response for the most frequently asked consumer questions. If you dig too deeply, you'll likely get the cold shoulder or, as one GM owner wrote me, get the receiver hung up in your ear.

If there's a warranty dispute, or if you've found that your service manager can't correct a persistent problem, GM customer relations staff will intervene to set things right, if possible, at the dealership level. Once your name, vehicle identification number (VIN), and dealer's name are punched into the computer, the customer relations rep can tell you if you're eligible for free repairs under a special (i.e., secret) warranty or through a safety/emissions recall campaign. The telephone staff will never mention the phrase "secret warranty," nor will they ever pass you on to someone else who's in charge. Since they were hired to reduce the number of calls their bosses receive, every call that gets through their screening is a black mark against their job performance.

GM car owners tell me that the telephone staff have been told to "barter down" owners' requests for warranty compensation involving paint defects and other secret warranty-related problems. Callers are given a "Let's Make a Deal" spiel where the initial offer of 50 percent is often boosted to 75 percent compensation if the customer will agree— at that very moment—to pay 25 percent of the repair.

Factory reps
The factory rep is directly responsible to the manufacturer and has the last word on what work is covered under warranty. Not unlike the customer relations staff, he's paid to save the company money. Every time he says no, he does his job. When he says yes to warranty coverage, it's because you've convinced him he must. This can be done by personally presenting the facts in a confident, forthright manner with as many dealer service bulletins as you can find for support (see Appendix VI on how to order your own bulletins). Don't use your salesperson as a runner; he has less pull than you do, and the factory rep can promise him anything and later deny it. Should you see that you're getting nowhere with the factory rep, give him one last chance to make a reasonable offer. Don't threaten him or tip him off to your next move.

Step 2: send a registered letter or fax
This is the next step to take if your claim is refused. Send the dealer and manufacturer a polite registered letter or a fax that asks for compensation for repairs that have been done or need to be done, insurance costs while the vehicle is being repaired, towing charges, supplementary transportation costs like taxis and rented cars, and damages for inconvenience.

Specify five days (but allow ten) for either party to respond. If no satisfactory offer is made, file suit in small claims court. Make the manufacturer a party to the lawsuit, especially if the emissions warranty, a secret warranty extension, a safety-recall campaign, or extensive chassis rusting is involved. Use the sample claim letters on pages 110–112 as a guide for getting compensation. Include a reference in your letter to any court decisions you find in this section of the book that support your claim and add the sample fact sheet if you're seeking a "goodwill" payout from the automaker and dealer.

FILE IN SECTION: Warranty Administration
BULLETIN NO.: 57-05-01
DATE: April, 1995
SUBJECT:
Dealer/Retailer Administration of Case-by-Case individual Goodwill Adjustments
MODELS:
General Motors Passenger Cars and Trucks
All General Motors Marketing Divisions (**Except GM of Canada**)
ATTENTION: Service Manager/Warranty Claims Administrator
Listed below is the definition for goodwill adjustments, general administrative guidelines, identifying the facts and division claim authorization empowerment information.

DEFINITION:
Individual, case-by-case, goodwill adjustments are intended to recognize that circumstances, outside the parameters of the written warranty, may exist where special consideration is in order to enhance customer satisfaction and loyalty.

Such goodwill adjustments should not be confused with special policy adjustments provided to all involved owners through a special bulletin and direct mail. Case-by-case individual goodwill adjustments are not legal obligations like the terms of General Motors warranties.

GENERAL ADMINISTRATIVE GUIDELINES:
- Maximum dealer/retailer authorization empowerment, common to all GM divisions, is up to 2 years/24,000 miles for non-paint conditions and up to 2 years/unlimited mileage for paint, beyond the limits of the Bumper to bumper base new vehicle warranty. Maximum authorization empowerment regarding GMC and Chevrolet medium duty truck authorization empowerment will be 2 years unlimited mileage for both non-paint and paint due to the unlimited mileage base warranty.
- Some dealers/retailers may be empowered to limits less than the maximum while a few select dealers/retailers may not be empowered at all. Individual dealer/retailer authorization empowerment levels are subject to change upon divisional notification.
- Any claim involving "individual goodwill adjustments" submitted after the effective date of March 15, 1995, which exceeds the dealer/retailer goodwill adjustment authorization empowerment limit will require wholesale review and authorization. This includes work in process for which you may have already committed to perform.
- Bumper to bumper base new vehicle warranty coverage does not include current and past model year warranty coverages on specific components that carry warranty coverage longer than the base new vehicle warranty coverage, i.e., "Federal and California Emissions Warranties," "Sheet Metal Coverage" or "Diesel Engine Coverage."
- Paint Labor Operations excluded from authorization empowerment. See below:
  Dealer/retailer authorization empowerment for paint claims covers exterior body panels only.

IDENTIFYING THE FACTS:
Your authorization empowerment should be exercised when it appears that the condition could be the result of a defect in materials or workmanship rather than conditions occurring from aging, physical damage, lack of proper maintenance or owner abuse. Vehicle concerns should be assessed on their own merits within the con'ext of the current owner's reasonable expectations and with appropriate concern for the cost to General Motors.
In exercising your judgment in each case, the following questions are some which should be considered:
- Is the vehicle covered by other service or extended warranty contracts? If "YES," repairs must be performed under that contract.
- Does the vehicle show a lack of proper care and maintenance?
- Is the overall condition of the vehicle such that the cost to repair will approximate the vehicle's value?
- If the vehicle was purchased used by the current owner, is it likely the vehicle exhibited the condition before purchase?
- Did the condition occur while the vehicle was in the possession of a second or third owner and no vehicle history is available?
- Could the customer have done anything to prevent or cause the condition?
- Has the vehicle been used in ways for which it was not intended?
- Did the condition result from an after market conversion or alteration?
- Did the condition result from use of non-GM parts or accessories?
- Is there evidence of vehicle mileage alteration?
- Is the vehicle condition a normal operating characteristic?
- Is the condition largely a result of normal aging, wear, and usage?
- Is the condition a result of unusual localized environmental, geographical, or climate factors?
Additional Questions When Paint Condition Is the Concern:
- Is the condition largely the result of normal paint aging or environmental damage (fading, gloss loss, chalking, cracking, flaking, yellowing)?
- Is the condition only on a physically damaged panel that the customer declines to repair?
The above list is not intended to be all inclusive. However, if the answer to any of these or similar questions is "yes," then it probably is not a concern you should address at General Motors' expense.
PARTIAL PARTICIPATION:
In situations beyond the warranty period, but within your claim authorization empowerment, customers have received value from use of the vehicle. It would be reasonable to consider partial payment by the customer. The judgment belongs to you.
- Determine what the customer expects before making an offer to assist.
- Evaluate the reasonableness of the customer's expectations.
- Determine what offer would satisfy the customer as a fair and equitable adjustment.
- Make your evaluation of the situation through direct communication with the customer.
- Always strive for a mutually acceptable agreement.

Consumers are frequently given a "Let's Make a Deal" spiel where the initial offer of 50 percent is often boosted to 75 percent compensation if the customer will agree—at that very moment—to pay 25 percent of the repair.

New Car Complaint Letter/Fax

Without Prejudice

Date:
Name and address of dealer:
Name and address of manufacturer:

Please be advised that I am not satisfied with my _____
(indicate year, make, model and serial number of vehicle). The
vehicle was purchased on (indicate date) and currently indicates
_____ km on the odometer. The vehicle presently exhibits
the following defects:

    1. Premature rusting
    2. Paint peeling/discoloration
    3. Water leaks
    4. Other defects (explain)

(List previous attempts to repair the vehicle. Attach a copy of a
report from an independent garage, showing cost of estimated
repairs and confirming the manufacturer's responsibility.)

I hereby request that you correct these defects free of charge under
the terms of the implied warranty provisions of provincial consumer protection statutes as applied in Kravitz v. General Motors
(1979), I.S.C.R., and Chabot v. Ford (1983), 39 O.R. (2d).

If you do not correct the defects noted above to my satisfaction and
within a reasonable length of time, I will be obliged to ask an independent garage to _____ (choose [a] estimate or
[b] carry out) the repairs and claim the amount of $_____
(state the cost, if possible) by way of the courts without further
notice or delay.

I have dealt with your company because of its competence and
honesty. I close in the hope of hearing from you within five (5)
days of receiving this letter, failing which I will exercise the alternatives available to me. Please govern yourself accordingly.

Sincerely,

(signed with telephone number)

Misrepresentation Claim Letter/Fax

Without Prejudice

Date:
Name and address of dealer:
Name and address of manufacturer:

As you can see from the enclosed new car sales contract, I bought a new vehicle from your dealership with the understanding it was not a demonstrator. I have just learned it was, indeed, used as a demonstrator. You have misrepresented the vehicle to me, and as a consequence, I demand that you reimburse me $_____, representing the difference as to what a demonstrator would have cost, plus my claim costs and inconvenience.

I await your answer within the next five days, failing which I shall initiate a lawsuit in civil court seeking compensatory and punitive damages, as well as asking that fraud charges be laid by the appropriate justice officials.

Do govern yourselves accordingly.

Sincerely,

(signed with telephone number)

Secret Warranty Claim Letter/Fax

Without Prejudice

Date: _____
Name: _____

Please be advised that I am dissatisfied with my vehicle, a
_____, bought from you on _____.
It has had the following recurring problems that I believe are
factory-related defects confirmed by internal service bulletins
sent to dealers and covered by your "goodwill" policies:

1. _____

2. _____

3. _____

If your "goodwill" program has ended, I ask that my claim be
accepted, nevertheless, inasmuch as I was never informed of your
policy while it was in effect and should not be penalized for not
knowing it existed.

I hereby put you formally on notice under provincial consumer protection statutes that your refusal to apply this extended warranty
coverage in my case would be an unfair warranty practice within
the purview of the above cited laws.

I have enclosed several estimates (my bill) showing that this problem is factory-related and will (has) cost $_____to correct.
I would appreciate you refunding me the estimated (paid) amount,
failing which, I reserve the right to have the repair done elsewhere
and claim reimbursement, plus consequential and punitive damage
from you in court, without further delay.

A response by fax or phone within the next five (5) days would be
appreciated.

Sincerely,

Signed with telephone or fax number

"Goodwill" Claim Fact Sheet

Claimant: _____ Date: _____

Reference: Failure of _____ to last a reasonable period of time.

Dealer/Automaker: Request for "Goodwill" repair/refund for the following reasons:

VEHICLE
• Vehicle has NOT performed as represented by seller
• Vehicle isn't covered by any other warranty/service contract
• Vehicle shows no signs of mileage alteration or accident damage
• Vehicle has been properly maintained and driven
• Vehicle was NOT used for purposes for which it was not intended

PROBLEM
• Problem is recurring and seller has been given ample opportunity to fix it
• Problem is NOT a normal operating condition or part of normal maintenance
• Problem was NOT caused or worsened by owner's actions
• Problem was NOT caused by aftermarket conversion, use of non-GM parts, accessories, or servicing
• Problem is NOT the result of normal aging, wear, usage, or environmental factors
• Problem likely existed at the time of purchase

Signed with telephone or fax number

Step 3: mediation and arbitration

If you have a new or used vehicle complaint and the formality of a courtroom puts you off, or if you're not sure your claim is all that solid and don't want to pay legal costs to find out, consider using mediation or arbitration sponsored by the Better Business Bureau, the Automobile Protection Association, the Canadian Automobile Association, or provincial and territorial governments.

Except for Quebec, all provinces and the Northwest Territories have set up the Canadian Motor Vehicle Arbitration Plan (CAMVAP) to arbitrate disputes between consumers and automakers that result from alleged manufacturing defects.

CAMVAP offers its services free of charge to new and used car owners. There are few lawyers involved (so no awards need to be split); binding arbitration by a neutral third party can be arranged within a six- to eight-week period; and all negotiations are carried out informally.

CAMVAP won't consider personal injury claims, tire defects (except on GM's models), third-party rustproofing product claims, motorhomes, or vehicles used primarily for business purposes.

Nevertheless, based on its respectable Ontario predecessor's track record (verified by independent auditors), CAMVAP arbitration is worth serious consideration. Canadian residents who own or lease a defective 1994 or later model vehicle used for non-commercial purposes must first contact their dealer and automaker to settle the dispute before asking for arbitration. If this doesn't take care of the problem, ask the dealer for the regional CAMVAP phone number and call for an arbitration application form. If the dealer is uncooperative, call CAMVAP toll-free at 1-800-207-0685.

Stephen Moody, CAMVAP's general manager, says that 70 percent of the awards handed down by CAMVAP have been in favour of the consumer. Of course, this self-serving figure can't be checked because CAMVAP puts a gag order on all claimants, but the results of its first 1995–96 audit have been published on the Internet.

Getting outside help
Remember, it's not the mediator or arbitrator's fault if you lose your case due to poor preparation. Ask government and independent consumer protection agencies, like those listed below, to evaluate how well you're prepared before going to your first hearing.

Automobile Protection Association
292 St.-Joseph Blvd. West, Montreal, Quebec H2V 2N7
160 Pears Ave., Suite 322, Toronto, Ontario M5R 1T2
Attn.: George Iny, President

A non-profit Canadian motorist protection organization, the APA mediates thousands of complaints yearly, mostly for its own members. The group also negotiates class settlements on behalf of motorists across Canada after being alerted to common problems based on the complaints from both members and non-members.

Center for Auto Safety
2001 South St., NW, Washington, DC 20009
Tel: 202-328-7700
Attn.: Clarence Ditlow, Director
Founded by Ralph Nader, this group probes auto safety and consumer protection issues relating to the auto industry. The CFAS can give you full, independent reports on common vehicle defects reported by dissatisfied car owners, and put you in touch with lawyers in your area who have handled cases similar to yours.

Online services/Internet/web sites
America Online and CompuServe are two online service providers with active consumer forums that use experts to answer consumer queries

and to provide legal as well as technical advice. The Internet offers the same information, but uses a worldwide database. If you or someone you know is able to create a web site, you might consider using this site to attract attention to your plight and arm yourself for arbitration or court.

Several years ago, Debra and Edward Goldgehn's 1985 Ford Ranger caught fire and burned completely. The couple's suspicions that it was a factory-related defect were later confirmed by a TV show that reported a series of similar Ford fires. The couple created their own web site called Flaming Fords and began amassing a comprehensive database containing reports of similar fires, class action lawsuits, expert witnesses, and actions taken in other countries. Shortly thereafter, Ford USA recalled 8.7 million cars and trucks to fix the fire problem and the Flaming Ford site was taken down. Ford says that the Internet pressure was coincidental and not a factor in its decision to recall the vehicles in the States.

Right, and Elvis is building Fords in Oakville.

Michael Hos, a dissatisfied Acura owner, became fed up with what he felt was Acura's stonewalling of his complaints. Rather than get angry, he got organized and set up a web site called "Acura 1997 CL 3.0L: My Lemon" to collect other owners' comments and list some of the most common Acura problem areas. Within six months, Acura settled and, he too, took down his web page. Here's what Hos learned from his experience:

Phil,
Hi, remember me? I'm the guy that had the 1997 Acura CL lemon. Well, as it turns out, Acura settled with me. I got paid off on the car, my attorney fees taken care of, and I'm walking away with $4,000 in my pocket after the experience. I was so glad to get rid of this car you have no idea.

I have pulled down my "anti-Acura" website and washed my hands clean of the entire ordeal. I turned in the CL about 2 weeks ago, and my checks should be here next week...

...At any rate, I wanted to say thanks for all your input into the case and the encouragement to continue on. The last few months of driving the car were horrible, I'm glad it's done.

In a follow-up posting:

...As far as my website goes, I think it was a major part of them settling early. I had a counter placed on it which showed them how many people had visited the site. Anyone can set up a web site like mine pretty easily. I have web space on my university's computer, so it was free for me to use. Folks without space should expect to spend about $20 a month for space, or if they have their own email account, web space is usually provided for free. If they don't know how to set up their web site, paying someone to do it will be kinda pricey, a few hundred bucks should cover it. The main thing it needs to have is the counter, and it also needs to be slander free. I had only facts on my web site as I didn't want to get involved in a slander suit. They also need to register the site with all the major search engines so it comes up when looking for the manufacturer. Submitit.com offers such services for free. Putting in a <Meta> tag into the page also helps move it up the search engines' list of hits. Posting to newsgroups also is helpful. I also wrote to JD Power, NHTSA, Consumer Reports, and any other consumer oriented agency I could think of.

When we settled before going to court, I had to sign the settlement papers saying I would pull down my site. They would not settle with me until I did that. This shows how much power the site can have. I would also put the manufacture's phone number and address on it so viewers of the site can contact the manufacturer.

For the most part everyone who read my site took my side of the story and agreed that Acura should pay up. I did have a few folks that were mad I was slamming Acura, but I wasn't concerned with them. I have about 200 email responses that people have mailed to me over the last few months.

As a side note, I think the only real reason they settled with me, in addition to the page being up, was my attorney. I had 7 charges filed against them in Superior Court. Also keep in mind that I paid nothing for my attorney until after we settled. My bill for him is $1,500, but that's included in the settlement. Also, I'm only 23, so anyone can do this if they are persistent.

PROJECTS AND CAUSES

A BAD FIRE occured in our 1994 Jeep Cherokee because of driving with a compact spare tire while in 4WD (could not get out of 4WD). Compact spare is standard equipment but appropriate warning not in Owners Manual. No appropriate answers from Chrysler Canada yet. Seeking others with similar experience.

Classified ads
Use your local paper's classified section or *The Globe and Mail*'s "National Personals" column to gather data from others who may have experienced a problem similar to your own. This alerts others to the potential problem, helps build a core base for a class action or group meeting with the automaker, and puts pressure on the dealer or manufacturer to settle.

Federal and provincial consumer affairs
The wind left the sails of the consumer movement over a decade ago, leaving provincial consumer affairs offices understaffed and unsupported by the government. This has created a passive mindset among many staffers, who are tired of getting their heads kicked in by businesses and budget-cutters.

Consumer affairs offices can still help with investigation, mediation, and some litigation. Strong and effective consumer protection legislation has been left standing in most of the provinces, and resourceful consumers can use these laws in conjunction with media coverage to prod provincial consumer affairs offices into action. Furthermore, provincial bureaucrats aren't as well shielded from criticism as are their federal counterparts. A call to your MPP or MLA, or to the Minister's executive assistant, can often get things rolling.

Federal consumer protection is a government-created PR myth. Don't expect the reorganized Consumer and Corporate Affairs staffers to be very helpful—they've been de-fanged and de-gummed through budget cuts and a succession of ineffective ministers. Although the revised Competition Act has some bite concerning misleading advertising and a number of other illegal business practices, the federal government has downplayed the Act's usefulness to consumer groups and individual consumers.

Nevertheless, when used creatively the recently beefed-up Competition Act can be a powerful tool for forcing a formal government investigation and prosecution, attracting media attention, and obtaining individual and collective compensation. The Act costs little to use. Three years ago, the Ontario-based Consumer Action Group brought together six consumer complainants and successfully used the Competition Act to file a "six-citizen declaration" against a number of auto leasing companies that had allegedly misled the public by not disclosing various hidden fees. When word leaked out that the government was investigating auto leasing (it had no choice—the Act requires a formal inquiry), the major automakers and dealer organizations started scrambling over themselves to find ways to disclose the extra charges without losing customers.

This culminated in the drawing up of a provincial-government-approved and industry-adopted generic leasing contract that (more) specifically spells out leasing fees and obligations. This action would probably never have been taken if it weren't for the CAG filing its complaint under the Competition Act. This same approach can be used by other consumer groups to petition for a government probe of other deceptive business practices.

Launching a Lawsuit

If the dealer agrees to make things right, give him a deadline, then have the repairs checked by an independent garage. If no offer is made within ten working days, file suit in small claims court. Make the manufacturer a party to the lawsuit only if the original, unexpired warranty was transferred to you, if your claim falls under the emissions warranty, a secret warranty extension, or a safety recall campaign, or if extensive chassis rusting is involved.

There are small claims courts in most counties of each province, and you can make a claim either in the county where the problem occurred or in which the defendant lives and carries on business. The first step is to make sure that your claim doesn't exceed the dollar limit of the court. You should then go to the small claims court office and ask for a claim form. (The form includes instructions on how to properly fill it out.) Remember, you must identify the defendant correctly. It's a practice of some dishonest firms to change a company's name in order to escape liability. For example, it would be impossible to sue Joe's Garage (1991) if your contract is with Joe's Garage Inc. (1984).

You're entitled to bring any evidence to court that's relevant to the case, including such written documents as a bill of sale or receipt, a contract, or a letter. If your car has developed severe paint problems, take a photograph to court. Have the photographer sign and date the photo. You may also have witnesses testify in court (a family member may act as a witness). It's important to discuss a witness's testimony prior to the court date. If a witness can't attend the court date, he or she can write a report and sign it for representation in court. This situation usually applies to an expert witness, such as the independent mechanic who evaluated your car's problems.

Be sure to organize your evidence, prepare questions for the witnesses, and write down what you want to tell the court.

Choosing the Right Court

You must decide on the remedy to pursue—that is, whether you want to get a partial refund, or to have the sale cancelled. The amount of the refund is determined by estimating the cost of fixing existing mechanical defects plus the cost of prior repairs. Don't exaggerate your losses or claim for repairs that are considered routine maintenance.

Small claims court

Canadian small claims courts offer simple claim forms, and actions cost only about $50–$125 for a $6,000 claim and take only a few months to be heard. The beauty of a small claims action is that most provincial courts force the automaker into a mediation session with you before proceeding to trial. Many claims are settled through mediation for one-half to two-thirds of the amount demanded in the action.

Generally, if the cost of repairs or the sales contract falls within the small claims court limit (the limits differ from province to province), the case should be filed there to keep costs to a minimum and to obtain a speedy hearing. Small claims court judgments are not easily appealed. Lawyers aren't necessary, and trials are heard usually within a few months.

In some cases, small claims courts can be used creatively to get as much compensation as would be given by a higher court. For example, the hardship of owning a $6,000 lemon can be eased if the owner sues the dealer in small claims court for the maximum to cover repairs, insurance, rental cars, inconvenience, etc., which may total $3,000. If the court awards this amount, the car can then be sold without the repairs done for about $3,000. Thus, the customer gets back the $6,000 with few legal fees to pay after a delay of only a few months. Furthermore, the car can still be used during the lawsuit, because the plaintiff isn't seeking to set the sale aside.

If the damages exceed the small claims court limit and there is no way to reduce them, you'll have to go to a court with a higher claim limit. This will be costly. Before rushing off to file a lawsuit, consider the following ways in which you can win your case in a higher court and still wind up losing your shirt.

- For a simple case that comes to a short trial, lawyers' fees can vary between $500 and $1,000. These fees must be paid whether the case is won or lost. If you lose, you may have to pay court costs as well.
- The first trial isn't likely to take place for two or three years. Then, even if you win, the judgment is likely to be appealed, thus delaying final judgment for another two to four years, and boosting each side's legal fees.
- Once appeals are exhausted and you've won, the judgment will be paid in depreciated dollars supplemented by a low interest rate—if you can collect.
- Car dealers can avoid judgment by disappearing or closing down and reopening under a new name. It happens quite often, and the courts can do little to stop it.

There are also practical problems involved in a cancellation-of-sale suit. The court requires that the vehicle be "tendered" back to the seller at the time the lawsuit is filed. This means that the plaintiff is without transportation for as long as the case continues, unless the plaintiff purchases another car in the interim. If the plaintiff loses the case, he or she must take back the old car and pay storage fees. You could go from having no car to having two, one of which is a clunker.

For these reasons, try to stay out of the higher courts if at all possible and plead the case yourself (after getting a lawyer's advice).

Class actions
Class-action suits allow a single individual to sue a company, government, or other entity on behalf of hundreds or even thousands of others with similar claims. Although class-action suits have been used for three decades in the United States, they are a recent arrival in Canada. Quebec was the first province to adopt this legal remedy in the early '80s, and Ontario and British Columbia followed suit in 1992 and 1995, respectively.

Class actions allow for contingency fees, where consumers can enter into no-win-no-pay agreements with lawyers. If you lose, you usually pay your expenses and move on. However, Ontario judges can require that losing class-action plaintiffs pay the defendant's fees, as well. (B.C. legislation requires that both sides pay their own legal costs.)

One of the more recent successful class actions in Canada concerned the recovery of condo owner deposits in Toronto. In *Windisman v. Toronto College Park Ltd.*, 544 condominium residents recovered $2.6 million, representing the interest earned on their deposit payments for apartments, parking spaces, and storage lockers.

Other Canadian class actions presently wending their way through the courts involve breast-implant manufacturers, Red Lobster restaurants, appliance manufacturers, the Toronto Transit Commission, and Chrysler Canada.

How to file a class action
- Like any other lawsuit, a lawyer files the plaintiff's statement of claim against the defendant and the plaintiff applies to the court to certify the lawsuit as a class action.
- The presiding judge will then decide whether there is an "identifiable class of two or more persons," whether a class action is the "preferable procedure," and whether the plaintiff truly represents the class. If you meet all the above criteria, the judge will issue a certification order and designate you as the Class Representative.
- Other class members must be notified of the lawsuit. Small groups can be contacted by mail, but larger groups may require notification through newspaper ads backed up by a toll-free telephone line. Members of the class must then be given an opportunity to opt out of the lawsuit. If they don't, they remain part of the class.

If the class wins, individual cases may then be heard to assess damages, or a notification may be sent to each member to apply for their part of the settlement or award. It may take from three to five years before a final judgment is rendered, and appeals may double that time. Lawyers typically charge the class one-third of the amount obtained.

Trial conduct
Because the cost of defence would be prohibitive and the bad publicity could ruin the dealer's business, lawyers often tell their dealer-clients to settle a small-claims case out of court. Lawyers also know that urging their clients to settle out of court means they never lose a case.

Sometimes a dealer's lawyer will threaten to sue the plaintiff for libel or slander if the case is taken to court. This is a move designed to intimidate. No one can be sued for libel or slander merely for exercising his or her rights before the courts. The dealer, however, can be sued for harassment, and the lawyer can be cited for unprofessional conduct if the threat is carried out.

On the day of the trial, bring in a mechanic to confirm that the defects exist and to estimate the cost of repairing them. If the repairs have already been carried out, he can explain what caused the defects and justify his bill for repairing them. This should be done by presenting the defective parts, if possible. He must convince the judge that the defects were present at the time the car was sold, and that they were not caused by poor maintenance or abusive driving habits.

Before the dealer leaves the stand, get him to confirm any representations he or his salespeople made, either verbally or through a newspaper ad, extolling the vehicle's qualities. With witnesses excluded, it's quite likely that the dealer's witnesses will contradict him when their turn comes to testify. Your own co-workers or friends can testify as to how well you maintained the vehicle and how it was driven, as well as describe the seriousness of the defects.

Dos and don'ts

- Do complain to the provincial Transport and Consumer Affairs ministries about possible violations of provincial laws.
- Do contact local consumer groups and the Automobile Protection Association for recent jurisprudence and help in mediating the complaint.
- Do publicize any favourable court judgment as a warning to other dealers and as encouragement for other consumers.
- Don't sue a car dealer if he is bankrupt, or is willing to negotiate a settlement.
- Don't threaten or insult the dealer. This will only gain sympathy for him and hurt your own credibility.

Remember not to delay in filing a claim once it's obvious that no settlement is forthcoming. A lawsuit should be filed no later than three months after the final registered claim letter has been sent.

Collecting Your Winnings

Settlements

You may be asked to sign a document called a "release," which proves that a final settlement has been made. Generally, once you sign the release you can't sue the other person for that particular debt or injury. If you're the debtor, it's very important that you make sure the other person signs the release when you pay him or her. If you're the creditor collecting on the debt, you must sign the release, but don't do so until you've received the money or verified that the check is good. Also, don't give up any more rights than you have to. Release the debtor from that particular debt, but don't release him or her from all future debts.

I, John Doe, hereby acknowledge the receipt of $300 plus $10 interest from Jane Smith, in full and final satisfaction of all claims, which I may have against her arising from a sale of a used Ford Mustang by her to me on June 30th, 1996, and from all claims arising from a cheque for $300 dated November 30th, 1993, signed by her and payable to me, which was returned to me marked "Not Sufficient Funds."

_____   _____
Date   John Doe

Name of Witness: _____

Deadbeat defendants

If you're dealing with a professional crook, the real work begins once you win your case. You may have to garnishee (seize) part of the defendant's bank account or wages, or ask the sheriff to serve a writ of execution. This writ allows the sheriff to demand full settlement plus court costs and, failing that, to seize the defendant's goods to cover the amount of the judgment. Here's the catch. Property needed to earn a living (car, tools, machinery, etc.), household goods, and anything encumbered by a lien are all exempt from seizure.

Professional deadbeats can tell the sheriff that practically everything they own is exempt, and it will take another action before the regular courts, at the plaintiff's expense, to have the defendant questioned under oath. If he's found to be lying, he can then be sent to jail for perjury or contempt of court, and the small claims court judgment will remain unpaid.

Happily, a number of provinces are putting winning plaintiffs on a "fast-track" enforcement schedule that takes the time and cost out of collecting judgments.

Key Court Decisions

The following Canadian lawsuits and judgments cover typical problems that are likely to arise. Put any relevant case in your claim letter as leverage when negotiating a settlement, or as a reference should your claim go to trial. Legal principles are similarly applicable to Canadian and American law. Quebec court decisions, however, may be based on legal principles that don't apply outside that province. Therefore, do what most lawyers do: present all the court judgments that may be helpful and let the presiding judge or the defendant's lawyer sort out those that they feel may not apply.

Additional court judgments can be found in the legal reference section of your city's main public library or at a nearby university law library. Ask the librarian for help in choosing the legal phrases that best describe your claim.

Damages (Punitive)

Punitive damages (also known as exemplary damages) allow the plaintiff to get compensation that exceeds his or her losses. In Canada, judges sometimes award punitive damages as a deterrent to those who carry out dishonest or negligent practices; however, these kinds of judgments are more common in the U.S.

Bolduc v. Racicot, April 2, 1982, Quebec Provincial Court (Hauterive), No. 655-02-000364-817, Judge Cloutier. The plaintiff was given a verbal estimate of $500 for repairs, but the garage presented a bill for $1,255. The Court reduced the bill to $900 with the consent of the plaintiff, and then awarded another $300 as punitive damages against the garage for failing to provide a written estimate, doing more work than was requested, not guaranteeing the work, and not presenting a bill in conformance with the requirements of the Consumer Protection Act.

Vlchek v. Koshel (1988), 44 C.C.L.T. 314, B.C.S.C., No. B842974. The plaintiff was seriously injured when she was thrown from a Honda all-terrain cycle on which she had been riding as a passenger. The Court allowed for punitive damages because the manufacturer was well aware of the injuries likely to be caused by the cycle. Specifically, the Court ruled that there is no firm and inflexible principle of law stipulating that punitive or exemplary damages must be denied unless the defendant's acts are specifically directed against the plaintiff. The Court may apply punitive damages "where the defendant's conduct has been indiscriminate of focus, but reckless or malicious in its character. Intent to injure the plaintiff need not be present, so long as intent to do the injurious act can be shown."

See also:
- *Granek v. Reiter*, Ont. Ct. (Gen. Div.), No. 35/741.
- *Morrison v. Sharp*, Ont Ct. (Gen. Div.), No. 43/548.
- *Schryvers v. Richport Ford Sales*, May 18, 1993, B.C.S.C., No. C917060, Judge Tysoe.
- *Varleg v. Angeloni*, B.C.S.C., No. 41/301.

Furthermore, a slew of cases cover specifics in damage claims. Provincial business practices acts cover false, misleading, or deceptive representations, and allow for punitive damages should the unfair practice toward the consumer amount to an unconscionable representation. (See C. E. D. (3d) s. 76, pp. 140–45.) "Unconscionable" is defined as "where the consumer is not reasonably able to protect his or her interest because of physical infirmity, ignorance, illiteracy, or inability to understand the language of an agreement or similar factors."
- Exemplary damages are justified where compensatory damages are insufficient to deter and punish. See *Walker et al. v. CFTO Ltd. et al.* (1978), 59 O. R. (2nd), No. 104 (Ont. C.A.).
- Exemplary damages can be awarded in cases where the defendant's conduct was "cavalier." See *Ronald Elwyn Lister Ltd. et al. v. Dayton Tire Canada Ltd.* (1985), 52 O. R. (2nd), No. 89 (Ont. C.A.).
- The primary purpose of exemplary damages is to prevent the defendant and all others from doing similar wrongs. See *Fleming v. Spracklin* (1921).
- Disregard of the public's interest, lack of preventive measures, and a callous attitude all merit exemplary damages. See *Coughlin v. Kuntz* (1989), 2 C.C.L.T. (2nd) (B.C.C.A.).
- Punitive damages can be awarded for mental distress. See *Ribeiro v. Canadian Imperial Bank of Commerce* (1992), Ontario Reports 13 (3rd) and *Brown v. Waterloo Regional Board of Comissioners of Police* (1992), 37 O.R. (2nd).

Defects (Body/Performance Related)

What's a lemon?

The definitive description of a "lemon" is found in U.S. state law, in which it's defined as a vehicle with problems that can't be repaired after four attempts, keep the vehicle out of service for more than 30 days, or render it unfit for the purpose for which it was purchased.

When a vehicle no longer falls within the limits of the warranty expressed by the manufacturer or dealer, it doesn't necessarily mean that the manufacturer can't be held liable for damages caused by defective design. As mentioned before, the manufacturer is always liable for the replacement or repair of defective parts if independent testimony can show that the part was incorrectly manufactured or designed, and that this "mistake" affects its reliability or durability. The existence of a secret warranty extension or service bulletins indicating upgrades will usually help to prove that the part was poorly made (or the paint process was flawed).

Paint delamination or peeling, rusting

Although once a problem with early Hondas, Mazdas, and Nissans, premature paint delamination and peeling now mostly afflicts the Big Three American automakers. Chrysler, Ford, and GM 1984–96 models are equally affected. Each company, however, has responded differently to owners' requests for compensation. To help you prepare the best arguments for negotiations or court, read the following court judgments carefully and frame your claim accordingly.

Incidentally, Internet browsers will be pleased to learn that Ford and Chrysler owners have set up specific Internet sites with tips on getting refunds for paint delamination. Just click on the Alta Vista search engine and type in "paint delamination" after the automaker's name. GM owners also had a very helpful Internet site, but it has since been abandoned.

Chrysler

Because Chrysler has settled most of its paint claims out of court, there aren't any recent judgments against the company. There is, however, a 29-page class action lawsuit filed in the state of Washington which seeks damages for all Chrysler owners who have owned or leased paint-delaminated 1986–97 models: *Schurk, Chanes, Jansen, and Ricker v. Chrysler*, No. 97-2-04113-9-SEA, filed in the Superior Court of King County, Washington on October 2, 1997 (contact Steve Berman or Clyde Platt with the Seattle, Washington, law firm of Hagens and Berman at 206-623-7292).

Ford

Louisiana attorney Danny Becknel, along with other lawyers, has filed three separate class-action law suits against Chrysler, Ford, and GM. He's also filed suit against PPG Industries, a company out of Pittsburg that he says sold defective car paint to the three companies.

Becknel also claims in his suits that in the late '80s/early '90s, the Big Three bought a product from PPG Industries called "Uniprime" without thoroughly testing it. He says when the companies bought "Uniprime," they switched from a three-coat car painting process (bottom coat, spray primer, color coat) to a two-coat process which eliminated the middle coat. Mr. Becknel claims that eliminating the middle spray primer layer saved Ford anywhere from $6 to $16 a car: "This paint seems to be a minor cost, but when you multiply it by 10 to 15 million times a year, it's a big number."

Faced with an estimated 13 percent failure rate, Ford repainted its delaminated 1983–93 cars, minivans, vans, F-series trucks, Explorers, Rangers, and Broncos free of charge for five years under a secret "Owner Dialogue" program. Ford whistleblowers say the company discontinued the program in January '95 because it was proving to be too costly. Nevertheless, owners who cry foul and threaten small claims action are still routinely given initial offers of 50 percent compensation, and eventually complete refunds if they press further.

In your negotiations with Ford, be sure to refer to its admission of the delamination problem found in the Chrysler class action and quoted at the beginning of Part Two. The full text of the Chrysler class action can be found in Part Two of the *Lemon-Aid Used 4X4s, Vans and Trucks 1999*.

General Motors

Confidential U.S. dealer service bulletins and memos confirm the 6-year/unlimited mileage benchmark that GM uses to accept or reject secret warranty paint claims (see page 104). As with Ford and Chrysler, GM customers seeking paint compensation are thrust into a "Let's Make a Deal" scenario, where they're usually first offered a 50 percent refund—and then 100 percent, if they stand their ground.

Martin v. Honda Canada Inc., March 17, 1986, Ontario Small Claims Court (Scarborough), Judge Sigurdson. The original owner of a 1981 Honda Civic sought compensation for the premature "bubbling, pitting, cracking of the paint and rusting of the Civic after five years of ownership." Judge Sigurdson agreed and ordered Honda to pay the owner $1,163.95.

Perron v. Vincent Automobile Ltée. (1979), C.P., No. 166. The plaintiff had the dealer rustproof her new car at a cost of $115. This dealer's warranty said that any future rusting would be repaired up to a cost of $115, or the purchase price would be refunded. The dealer interpreted this to mean that $115 would be the total amount that could be claimed while the guarantee was in effect. However, the Court agreed with the plaintiff that she could claim up to $115 each time a warranty claim was made.

Prochera v. Sherwood Chevrolet, November 9, 1978, Saskatoon Small
Claims Court, Judge Clifford Peet. In this Blazer paint case, the plaintiff sued for the correction of a mismatched paint job carried out by the
dealer to repair delivery damage and the original mismatching of the
paint seen when the vehicle was first delivered. The plaintiff was awarded $75 plus court costs.

Rolland v. Chrysler, November 1979, Third Small Claims Court of Lanark
County, Ontario, No. 148/79, Judge Thorpe. After Chrysler admitted it
had a secret warranty that paid for the replacement of rusted-out front
fenders, Judge Thorpe awarded $896.17 to a couple who purchased a
used 1976 Chrysler Volaré from a relative in 1978.

Shields v. General Motors of Canada, July 24, 1997, Ontario Court
(General Division), Oshawa Small Claims Court, 33 King Street West,
Oshawa, Ontario L1H 1A1, No. 1398/96, Robert Zochodne, Deputy
Judge. Judgment rendered January 6, 1998.

Reasons for Judgment

The Plaintiff owns a 1991 Pontiac Grand Prix. This car was manufactured by General Motors. The Plaintiff did not buy the car
new but purchased it about one year after it was built and when
it had over 100,000 kilometres on its odometer.

Commencing in 1995 the paint on this car began to bubble
and then flake and eventually peel off. Exhibit 1 shows that the
problem is most evident on the front hood of the vehicle.

After the Plaintiff encountered this problem, he approached
General Motors of Canada Limited. After significant debate,
General Motors agreed to pay for one-half the cost of repairing
the three affected panels. The Plaintiff asked General Motors if
the rest of the car would peel and he advised that General
Motors' response was that they could not guarantee that that
would not occur. The Plaintiff rejected the proposal on the basis
that he believed that if the work was done, the car would look like
a 'checkerboard.'

The Plaintiff claims that there are thousands of people with
the same problem with General Motors' cars...

...What was the cause of the Plaintiff's difficulty?

Grant Greenwood is an engineer with General Motors. He
has worked for General Motors since 1963 and carries the title of
Senior Product Investigator. He testified that he checked the
vehicle history and confirmed that it went into service in
November 1990. He advised that the warranty on this vehicle is
three years or eighty thousand kilometres, whichever occurs first.
As Exhibit 13 is a copy of the warranty booklet.

He testified that the paint warranty was against defects and
workmanship. He also testified that the warranty excluded

consequential losses. He also stated that General Motors has not extended the warranty for paint.

Mr. Greenwood inspected the vehicle in March 1997 at Plaza Pontiac Buick. He stated that paint was coming off in three areas. He said that the cause was that the colourcoat, that is the coat visible to you and I, was separating from the primer. The cause of this was, in Mr. Greenwood's view, ultraviolet rays in the atmosphere. He stated that the ultraviolet rays were going through the colourcoat, attacking the primer and breaking down the bond between the primer and the colourcoat.

He said that ultraviolet rays have been increasing over the past decade and that since General Motors has become aware of this, they have been working on new paints that are more retardant to the effects of ultraviolet rays. He emphasized that the problem was not caused by the primer, which has been used by General Motors for decades, but rather by the ultraviolet rays. He stated that waxing a vehicle helps prevent delamination as well as storing the vehicle inside.

He said that light gray and light blue vehicles are more susceptible to this problem and appeared to be somewhat skeptical about the fact that this condition appeared with a white vehicle. At the time of his inspection the vehicle had travelled 156,000 kilometres. He noticed a scratch on the left front fender and chipping on the front hood.

As I indicated previously, he identified three areas on the vehicle where the paint was coming off. There is an extensive area on the hood as well as the trunk and left rear quarter-panel. He said that this was not typical paint delamination. He also found it odd that there was no paint peeling off of the roof of the car. He stated that if the vehicle was repaired and repainted, it would be difficult to tell that it had been repainted.

Exhibit 2 is a memo to all Pontiac dealers dated October 16, 1992, from Perry White, Director of Service/Customer Satisfaction with Pontiac Division of General Motors (U.S.). This letter states in part as:

> Following a recent review, Pontiac has decided to provide dealers' authorization for cases involving paint repairs for vehicles up to six years from the date of delivery, without regard to mileage.

Mr. Greenwood stated that this bulletin was not sent in Canada but only in the United States. He also stated that it did not deal with paint delamination, which was the Plaintiff's problem in this case.

Mr. Greenwood indicated that insofar as damages were concerned that the answer to the problem did not lie in removing the primer. He stated that the primer gives very good protection against rust and that if the primer was removed, the vehicle was more likely to rust even if it was replaced with primer.

Mr. Greenwood arranged for an estimate to be completed to strip the colourcoat and repaint the vehicle from the lower molding up. That repair estimate was marked as Exhibit 12 and is in the sum of $1,305.72.

In cross examination, Mr. Greenwood stated that delamination is a common condition. He also acknowledged that there were no warnings given to customers of such a problem.

Exhibit 8 is a Product Service Bulletin issued by General Motors of Canada. It is entitled "Service Procedures for Identification and Repair of Paint Colourcoat Delamination from ELPO Primer." Mr. Greenwood identified this document as being a valid Product Service Bulletin issued October 31, 1992, and revised on December 15, 1992.

> This bulletin is being issued to assure that the correct procedure is followed to repair a condition known as DELAMINATION
>
> This condition may occur on vehicles produced in plants where the paint process does not call for application of a primer surfacer. Under certain conditions, ultraviolet light can penetrate the colourcoat, sometimes causing a reaction and separation of portions of the colourcoat from the ELPO (electrocoat) primer
>
> CORRECTION:
>
> Refinish the ENTIRE BODY ABOVE THF BODY SIDE MOULDINGS using the following repair procedure

...Is the Defendant liable to the Plaintiff?

As the Plaintiff did not purchase this vehicle from General Motors, the Sale of Goods Act does not apply. In order to succeed, the Plaintiff must establish that General Motors of Canada's warranty covers this problem.

That warranty provides in part as follows:

> REPAIRS COVERED
>
> This warranty covers repairs or adjustments to correct any vehicle defect related to material or workmanship occurring during the WARRANTY PERIOD. New or remanufactured parts will be used. Adjustments refer to minor repairs not usually associated with the replacement of parts.

The warranty also provides as follows:

> The complete vehicle is covered for 3 years or 80,000 kilometres, whichever comes first.

It also states as follows:

> Warranty repairs and adjustments, including Towing, Parts and Labour, will be made at NO CHARGE (except for $100 deductible per repair visit after the first 12 months or 20,000 kilometres, whichever comes first).

The warranty also provided:

> This warranty is for GM vehicles registered in Canada and normally operated in Canada or the United States and is provided to the original and any subsequent owners of the vehicle during the WARRANTY PERIOD.

The Defendant did not seek to rely upon any exclusion within the warranty.

The questions to be decided therefore are as follows:

1. Did the vehicle have a "defect"?
2. If so, did the defect occur during the warranty period?

In my view, the vehicle did have a defect. While I acknowledge and accept Mr. Greenwood's evidence that the increase in ultraviolet rays has caused delamination, it is my view that the presence of ultraviolet light is an environmental condition to which the vehicle is subject. If it cannot withstand this environmental condition, it is defective, in my view. This is no different from a situation where a vehicle does not start in weather below 0° Celsius. Since motor vehicles are operated in such conditions on a regular basis, the failure of the vehicle to adequately operate in such temperatures is a defect, in my view. To be precise, the defect is the failure to ensure proper bonding between the colourcoat and primer. In reviewing the Product Service Bulletin and hearing the evidence of Mr. Greenwood, it is clear to me that the lack of a primer surfacer was a defect as defined by the warranty.

2. Did this defect occur during the warranty period?

The answer to this question is yes. General Motors contended that the problem was caused by ultraviolet light. A logical inference is that they contend that the problem did not arise until sufficient exposure to ultraviolet light, the result being that the warranty period would have expired.

I do not accept this contention.

The defect, which I have found, that is the lack of primer surfacer, occurred at the time that the vehicle was manufactured. At that point, however, the defect was latent. The defect became patent when the paint began to bubble, flake and then peel off of the vehicle.

Having decided that the warranty responds to this loss, I grant judgment in favour of the Plaintiff in the amount of $1,205.72 plus costs.

Thauberger v. Simon Fraser Sales and Mazda Motors, 3 B.C.L.R., No. 193. This Mazda owner sued for damages caused by the premature rusting of his 1977 Mazda GLC. The Court awarded him $1,000. Mr. Thauberger had previously sued General Motors for a prematurely rusted Blazer truck and was also awarded $1,000 in the same Court. Both judges ruled that the defects could not be excluded from the automaker's express warranty or from the implied warranty granted by ss. 20, 20(b) of the B.C. Sale of Goods Act.

Whittaker v. Ford Motor Company (1979), 24 O.R. (2nd), No. 344. A new Ford developed serious corrosion problems in spite of having been rustproofed by the dealer. The Court ruled that the dealer, not Ford, was liable for the damage for having sold the rustproofing product at the time of purchase. This is an important judgment to use when a rustproofer or paint protector goes out of business or refuses to pay a claim, since the decision holds the dealer jointly responsible.

Williams v. General Motors of Canada, October 27, 1997, British Columbia Provincial Small Claims Court, Nanaimo Registry, No. 15691, Presiding Judge J. D. Cowling.

Reasons for Judgment

...The claimants sought damages for the paint delamination of a blue 1988 Grand Am which they purchased new on October 1, 1988. They first noticed the paint chipping from their vehicle in September of 1994. They called GM's toll-free customer relations hot line and were told there were no known paint issues regarding their model of vehicle.

By 1995, the chipping problem had expanded into extensive delamination of paint on the upper horizontal surfaces of the car. The Plaintiffs' local dealer then admitted it was a common problem, but added that the "goodwill" program was discontinued as of August 1995. The Plaintiffs were quoted $1,939.60 to have their car repainted.

Subsequent inquiry by the claimants revealed that as of October 1992, the defendant GM had issued a product service bulletin that described the problem as follows:

> Blues, Grays, Silvers, and Black Metallics are the colours that have the highest potential for this condition...may have delamination (peeling) of the paint colourcoat from the ELPO primer depending upon variable factors including prolonged exposure to sunlight and humidity.

This condition may occur on vehicles produced in plants where the paint process does not call for application of a primer surfacer. Under certain conditions, ultraviolet light can penetrate the colourcoat, sometimes causing a reaction and separation of portions of the colourcoat from the ELPO (electrocoat primer).

Other product service bulletins from the U.S. branch of the defendant indicate the paint delamination problem was not unique to cars in Canada. In the U.S., the Center for Auto Safety negotiated an agreement with GM to implement a post-warranty adjustment program for paint problems described as follows in letter dated February 5, 1993:

- broad dealer discretion
- six years coverage from date of delivery
- unlimited mileage
- deductibles may be waived
- not just delamination

The nature of the delamination problem is such that once detected in a particular vehicle, spot repainting is not a viable remedy but rather the removal of the topcoat and primer surfaces is required.

The purchase of this car by the claimants is a sale by description within the meaning of s. 17 of the Sale of Goods Act. Pursuant to s. 18 (b) of the Act there is an "...implied condition that the goods are of merchantable quality..." and further by virtue of s. 18 (c) an "...implied condition that goods will be durable for a reasonable period of time."

I find that having regard to the type of car purchased by the claimants, the condition in which they have maintained it, the extent of the paint problem it suffers from and the reason for the problem that the claimants have established a breach of the section 18 (b) and (c) warranties. I consider the reasoning of O'Donnell, J, in *Thauberger v. Simon Fraser Sales Ltd. et al* (1977) 3 B.C.L.R. No. 193 with respect to what was then s. 20 (b) of the Act to be directly on point in this case. I acknowledge that the paint surface in Thauberger failed after 21 months and not six years as here, however, I consider that the buyer of a new car in 1988 may reasonably expect its paint surface not to delaminate under normal use within 6 years. I find that the settlement GM (U.S.) negotiated with the Center for Auto Safety supports that position although not determinative of it.

The claimants are entitled to judgment against the defendant in the sum of $1,229.70. They are entitled to Court Order interest on this amount from September 1, 1995, to the date of judgment to account for any increase in the present cost of a paint job from the date of the 1995 quote. The claimants will also have their costs in this matter for filing and service fees. The judgment is payable within 15 days from its entry."

See also:

• *Danson v. Chateau Ford* (1976) C.P., Quebec Small Claims Court, No. 32-00001898-757, Judge Lande.

• *Doyle v. Vital Automotive Systems*, May 16, 1977, Ontario Small Claims Court (Toronto), Judge Turner.

• *Lacroix v. Ford*, April 1980, Ontario Small Claims Court (Toronto), Judge Tierney.

• *Marinovich v. Riverside Chrysler*, April 1, 1987, District Court of Ontario, No. 1030/85, Judge Stortini.

Performance defects

Bagnell's Cleaners v. Eastern Automobile Ltd. (1991), 111 N.S.R. (2nd), No. 51, 303 A.P.R. 51 (T.D.). This Nova Scotia company found that the new van it purchased had serious engine, transmission, and radiator defects. The dealer pleaded unsuccessfully that the sales contract excluded all other warranties except for those contained in the contract. The Court held that there was a fundamental breach of the implied warranty and that the van's performance differed substantially from what the purchaser had been led to expect. An exclusionary clause could not protect the seller, who failed to live up to a fundamental term of the contract.

Burridge v. City Motor, 10 Nfld. & P.E.I.R., No. 451. This Newfoundland resident complained repeatedly of his new car's defects during the warranty period, and hadn't used his car for 204 days after spending almost $1,500 for repairs. The judge awarded all repair costs and cancelled the sale.

Davis v. Chrysler Canada Ltd. (1977), 26 N.S.R. (2nd), No. 410 (T.D.). The owner of a new $28,000 diesel truck found that a faulty steering assembly prevented him from carrying on his business. The Court ordered that the sale be cancelled and $10,000 in monthly payments be reimbursed. There was insufficient evidence to award compensation for business losses.

Fox v. Wilson Motors and GM, February 9, 1989, Court of Queen's Bench, New Brunswick, No. F/C/308/87. A trucker's new tractor-trailer had repeated engine malfunctions. He was awarded damages for loss of income, excessive fuel consumption, and telephone charges under the provincial Sale of Goods Act.

Gibbons v. Trapp Motors Ltd. (1970), 9 D.L.R. (3rd), No. 742 (B.C.S.C.). The Court ordered the dealer to take back a new car that had numerous defects that needed 32 hours of repairs. Refund was reduced by mileage driven.

Johnson v. Northway Chevrolet Oldsmobile (1993), 108 Sask. R. (Q.B.), No. 138. Two years after purchase, the buyer initiated a lawsuit for the purchase price of a new car that had been brought in for repairs on 14 different occasions and for general damages. The Court ordered the dealer to take back the car, and awarded general damages.

Julien v. GM of Canada (1991), 116 N.B.R. (2nd), No. 80. The plaintiff's new diesel truck produced excessive engine noise. The dealer claimed that the problem was caused by the owner's engine alterations. The plaintiff was awarded $5,000—the cost of having the engine repaired by an independent dealer.

Kravitz v. General Motors, January 1979, Supreme Court of Canada, I.R.C.S., No. 393. This owner of a new Oldsmobile was never able to have it properly repaired under warranty. When the warranty period was over, General Motors and the dealer refused to do further free work, or to give him another vehicle. The presiding judge awarded the car owner damages and a refund of the purchase price. This Quebec case is based on articles 1522 to 1530 of the Quebec Civil Code (hidden defects), but it applies in common-law provinces as well. The Supreme Court ruled that both the dealer and the manufacturer can be held jointly or separately responsible, and that the manufacturer's warranty does not negate the implied legal warranty of fitness.

Lowe v. Fairview Chrysler-Dodge Limited and Chrysler Canada Limited, May 14, 1996, Ontario Court (General Division), Burlington Small Claims Court, No.1224/95. This judgment raises the following important legal principles relative to Chrysler's chronic automatic transmission failures:
- Internal dealer service bulletins are admissible in court to prove that a problem exists and that certain parts should be checked out.
- If a problem is reported prior to a warranty's expiration, its warranty coverage is automatically carried over after the warranty ends.
- It's not up to the car owner to tell the dealer/automaker what the specific problem is.
- Repairs carried out by an independent garage can be refunded if the dealer/Chrysler unfairly refuses to apply the warranty.
- The dealer/Chrysler Canada cannot dispute the cost of the independent repair if they fail to cross-examine the independent mechanic.
- Auto owners can ask for and win compensation for their inconvenience, which in this judgment amounted to $150.
- Court awards aren't simply limited to a refund. The plaintiff was given $1,985.94 plus court costs and prejudgment interest—with costs of inconvenience fixed at $150, the final award amounted to $2,266.04.

MacDonald GMC v. Gillespie, June 3, 1986, New Brunswick Court of Appeal. Compensation of $7,148 was awarded to a new car buyer after the dealer failed to honour his salesman's verbal promises to repair certain defects at no charge.

Magna Management Ltd. v. Volkswagen Canada Inc., May 27, 1988, B.C.C.A., No. CA006037. This precedent-setting case allowed the plaintiff to keep his new $48,325 VW while awarding him $37,101—three years after the car was purchased. The problems were centred on poor engine performance. The jury accepted the plaintiff's view that the car was practically worthless with its inherent defects.

Maughan v. Silver's Garage Ltd., Nova Scotia Supreme Court, 6 B.L.R. 303, N.S.C. (2nd), No. 278. The plaintiff leased a defective backhoe. The manufacturer had to reimburse the plaintiff's losses because the warranty wasn't honoured. The Court rejected the manufacturer's contention that the contract's exclusion clause protected the company from lawsuits for damages resulting from a latent defect.

Murphy v. Penney Motors Ltd. (1979), 23 Nfld. & P.E.I.R., 152, 61 A.P.R., No. 152 (Nfld. T.D.). This Newfoundland trucker found that the repairing of engine problems took his new trailer off the road for 129 days during a seven-month period. The judge awarded all repair costs, as well as compensation for business losses, and cancelled the sale.

Murray v. Sperry Rand Corp., Ontario Supreme Court, 5 B.L.R., No. 284. The seller, dealer, and manufacturer were all held liable for breach of warranty when a forage harvester did not perform as advertised in the sales brochure or as promised by the sales agent. The plaintiff was given his money back and reimbursed for his economic loss based on what his harvesting usually earned. The Court held that the advertising was a warranty.

Oliver v. Courtesy Chrysler (1983) Ltd. (1992), 11 B.C.A.C., No. 169. This new car had numerous defects over a three-year period, which the dealer attempted to fix to no avail. The plaintiff put the car in storage and sued the dealer for the purchase price. The Court ruled that the car wasn't roadworthy and that the plaintiff couldn't be blamed for putting it in storage rather than selling it and purchasing another vehicle. The purchase price was refunded, minus $1,500 for each year the plaintiff used the car.

Olshaski Farms Ltd. v. Skene Farm Equipment Ltd., January 9, 1987, Alberta Court of Queen's Bench, 49 Alta. L.R. (2nd), No. 249. This Massey-Ferguson combine caught fire after the manufacturer had sent two notices to dealers informing them of a defect that could cause a fire. The judge ruled under the Sale of Goods Act that the balance of probabilities indicated that the manufacturing defect caused the fire, even though there was no direct evidence proving that the defect existed.

Western Pacific Tank Lines Ltd. v. Brentwood Dodge, June 2, 1975, B.C.S.C., No. 30945-74, Judge Meredith. The Court awarded the plaintiff $8,600 and cancelled the sale of a new Chrysler New Yorker with the following defects: badly adjusted doors, water leaks into the interior, and electrical short circuits.

Defects (Safety Related)

More than 250 million cars have been recalled since the late '60s to correct safety-related defects. Under Canadian federal legislation (Canadian Motor Vehicle Safety Act, 1971), car companies don't have to recall their cars, or fix them free of charge within a certain period of time. The law stipulates only that companies have to notify owners that their cars can kill them. American legislation requires notification and free correction unless the NHTSA's defect determination is challenged in the courts.

Airbags

The National Highway Traffic Safety Administration says that airbags have saved 2,500 lives and reduce moderate and severe injuries in auto accidents by 25 percent. Unfortunately, says the *Wall Street Journal*, these figures are shaky and not based on real-world experiences.

At least 25,000 people are estimated to have sustained injuries from airbag deployment between 1988 and 1991. As well, American federal safety regulators have received 3,000 reports of airbag malfunctions that have caused late or inadvertent deployment. All these injuries and deaths have led to hundreds of lawsuits wending their way through American courts. (Canadian court figures are unavailable.) Chrysler is the target of most of these lawsuits, because it was the first company to install airbags as a standard feature—Thiokol airbags, whose escaping gases cause first- or second-degree burns to the hands. Used on Chrysler's 1988–91 models, these airbags have vent holes that direct hot gases at the three o'clock and nine o'clock hand positions. In late 1990, the vent holes were relocated to the twelve o'clock position. A class-action lawsuit asking for damages arising from the earlier Thiokol design has been filed in the Court of Common Pleas in Philadelphia County. Coincidentally, the Insurance Institute for Highway Safety (IIHS) has backed airbag shut-off switches after completing an exhaustive investigation into reports that inflating airbags have seriously injured motorists.

Airbag burns
Collazo-Santiago v. Toyota, July 1998, 1st Circuit Court of Appeals. The driver of a 1994 Corolla suffered minor facial burns and abrasions when her airbag deployed as her car was rear-ended. The court concluded the airbag's design caused the injuries. Toyota maintained that the airbag deployed as it should, and that it couldn't change the design without reducing the airbag's effectiveness. The plaintiff was awarded $30,000 compensation.

Failure to deploy
Taylor v. Ford, Wayne County Circuit Court. American courts are taking a harder look at the automakers' liability when airbags fail to deploy, following a recent Michigan Court of Appeals decision to uphold a lower court's $292,000 verdict against Ford. Although the 1990 Lincoln Continental's driver-side airbag failed to deploy during a frontal collision, the jury found no design defect, but awarded damages against Ford for breach of an implied warranty based on defective manufacturing.

Inadvertent deployment
Trujillo v. Volvo, (*http://www.law.emory.edu/1circuit/mar98/97-1792.01a. html*).This lawsuit involves injuries suffered by a dockworker while parking a Volvo on the dock. The case has just been reinstated by a U. S. Appeals Court and provides an interesting, though lengthy, dissertation on the safety hazards that airbags pose and why automakers are ultimately responsible for the injuries and deaths caused by their deployment.

Axle
Fuller v. Ford of Canada Ltd. (1978), 2 O.R. (2nd), No. 764. This new 1974 Econoline truck had an axle failure that caused an accident. The Court held both the manufacturer and seller responsible.

Battery
Marin v. Varta Batteries Ltd. (1983), 28 Sask. R., No. 173; 5 D.L.R. (4th) (Q.B.), No. 427. An exploding battery caused serious injuries to the

plaintiff's face. The battery maker admitted liability, and the Court awarded the plaintiff $21,000 in damages.

Brakes

Chrysler and GM have both come under fire over the past several years for installing defective anti-lock brakes in their vehicles. GM has quietly bought back many of its vans and sport-utilities with ABS failures, while Chrysler has initiated a recall campaign and promised free servicing over a ten-year period.

Marton Properties v. Northbridge Chrysler Plymouth Ltd., March 2, 1979, B.C.S.C. The plaintiff's used Chrysler had serious brake defects that warranted cancellation of the sale contract. The Court ordered the vehicle returned and the purchase price refunded.

Phillips v. Ford of Canada and Elgin Motors (1970), 2 O.R., No. 714. Ford was held responsible for the injuries caused by a defect in the power brakes that would not have been apparent to the plaintiff. The dealer and Ford had a duty to warn the plaintiff that if the power-brake unit failed, the back-up brakes would be inadequate.

Santos v. Chrysler Corporation, February 1996, Suffolk County Superior Court. The plaintiff's wife and three children were killed when his 1988 Caravan's rear brakes locked as he applied them to avoid rear-ending another vehicle. The jury award for $19.2 million followed Paul Santos's pleadings that Chrysler "knowingly built the vehicle with a deadly defect that caused the rear brakes to lock before the front brakes." Chrysler's defence was that Santos drove the Caravan 100 miles with a broken windshield wiper and steered directly into oncoming traffic.

Fires

Brown v. Ford of Canada Ltd. (1979), 27 N.B.R. (2nd), No. 550. The plaintiff's 1977 van suddenly caught fire while under warranty. The Court held the manufacturer only partially negligent, because the plaintiff's son, who was a mechanic, should have spotted the defect.

Chabot v. Ford Motor Company of Canada Ltd. (1983), 39 O.R. (2nd), No. 162. This case contains an excellent and exhaustive review of a manufacturer's liability for defectively manufactured vehicles. It establishes liability for losses arising from a defect while the vehicle is being maintained by the dealer. Although the plaintiff couldn't prove that a defective part caused a fire, Judge Eberle's presumption that the 1979 F-250 truck ignited from some sort of manufacturing defect implied that the manufacturer was negligent *(re ipsa loquitur)*.

The Court also ruled that Ford breached a fundamental term of the sales contract by providing an unfit vehicle, and also failed to meet its obligations as set by the Manitoba Sale of Goods Act. In his decision, the judge made a number of interesting and critical observations about the motives and strategy of a large manufacturer like Ford when preparing for a case and presenting expert evidence.

In cases where companies try to avoid liability through their own limited warranties, or by invoking the exclusions expressed in the warranty, this decision confirms the *Kravitz v. General Motors* decision (which struck down these exclusions under Quebec law) from a common-law standpoint.

Delage v. Saab, November 1997, San Francisco Superior Court. A jury awarded Jean Delage $1.4 million for damages caused by an electrical fire in his 1988 Saab 9000, even though the car was never examined. The jury concluded that a defective fuse box caused the fire, after hearing testimony from eight other Saab owners whose cars had caught on fire. The *San Francisco Chronicle* had also published a Saab internal memo that indicated a main connection in the 9000 box (located behind the glove compartment) could loosen, overheat, and ignite the insulation.

La Paix v. Chrysler Canada, April 5, 1982, Quebec Provincial Court, No. 500-02-040677-796, Judge Prenouveau. A new 1976 Volaré suddenly caught fire while the owner tried to start the car. It had been in use for only 10 months. Chrysler Canada refused all liability, claiming that the fire was probably due to poor starting technique. The Court held Chrysler responsible for $4,039 in damages after it was proven that the fire was caused by unburned gasoline catching fire in the muffler.

Racine v. Durand Pontiac-Buick and General Motors, December 15, 1977, Quebec Provincial Court, No. 02-015218-774, Judge Lacoste. The plaintiff claimed $700 for a catalytic converter that exploded. General Motors and the dealer claimed that the explosion was due to poor maintenance and that the five-year/80,000 km emissions warranty on the converter didn't cover such maintenance-related defects. The judge disagreed, stating that the catalytic converter exploded due to a defective PCV valve for which General Motors and the dealer had to take responsibility. The fact that the converter could overheat and catch fire whenever the engine was badly tuned caused the judge to suggest that a warning be placed on all General Motors vehicles with the converter. The plaintiff was awarded $700.

See also:
• *CPR v. Kerr*, 49 S.C.R., 33 at 36.
• *Gougeon v. Peugeot Canada*, July 20, 1973, Quebec Superior Court, No. 12736, Judge Kaufman.
• *Lazanik v. Ford*, June 15, 1965, C.S.M., No. 623-664, Judge Challies.
• *Parent v. Lapointe* (1952), I S.C.R., No. 381.
• *Rioux v. General Motors*, March 9, 1970, C.S.M., No. 739-005, 6.
• *Touchette v. Pizzagalli* (1938), S.C.R., No. 433.

• *Zelezen v. Model Auto Sales Ltd.*, November 26, 1971, C.S.M., No. 722-487, Judge Nichols.

Minivan latches (Chrysler)

Jimenez v. Chrysler, October 8, 1997, South Carolina Federal Court. (For additional information contact the Jimenez family attorney, Garrick Grobler, at the Washington law firm of Ross, Dixon & Masback. He has another similar case against Chrysler scheduled to be heard in North Carolina.) Chrysler was hit by a $262.5 million South Carolina jury verdict arising from a lawsuit alleging that the plaintiff's son was killed after he was thrown out of a 1985 Caravan because the rear liftgate latch failed following a collision. Chrysler told the jury that its minivan latches aren't defective and that its recent retroactive "fix" of the latches on 4.3 million 1984–95 vehicles was simply a service campaign.

Then a subpoenaed Chrysler internal memo surfaced showing that top Chrysler officials knew all along that the latch problem was a safety defect. That memo, sent to Chairman Robert Eaton and Chrysler President Robert Lutz on December 9, 1994, confirmed that the latch problem "is a safety defect that involves children."

An incensed jury awarded $12.5 million in actual damages, plus another $250 million in punitive damages against Chrysler.

Parking gear slippage

General Motors v. Colton, October 17, 1980, Quebec Court of Appeal, No. 500-09-000692-772. A 1970 Oldsmobile parked on the plaintiff's inclined driveway rolled backwards and injured the owner. Judgment after appeal was against General Motors for $29,000.

Rusting undercarriage

McGouey v. Lawson Motors Ltd. (1982), 42 N.B.R. (2nd), No. 225. A used Fiat's frame collapsed from excessive corrosion seven weeks after purchase. The purchaser was awarded a complete refund of the purchase price and damages.

R. v. Ford Motor Company of Canada. The Federal Ministry of Transport successfully pleaded that rusting of the undercarriage of Ford's 1965–74 midsize cars was a safety defect.

Seatbelt design defects

Door-mounted seatbelts, motorized seatbelts, and lapbelts have come under fire during the past decade from safety advocates and the courts after insurance studies and trauma specialists showed that they increase the severity of accident injuries.

Door-mounted seatbelts

U.S. safety agencies are currently looking at the reliability and safety of door-mounted seatbelts in light of accident reports showing a high failure rate and an increased severity of injuries. GM, for example, is being

sued in the U.S. for $33 million over the inadequate performance of
the driver's door-mounted seatbelt on a 1990 Pontiac Sunbird. The dri
ver was killed when the car door opened, rendering the seatbelt inoperative. The suit claims that GM was negligent in the design of the belt,
and thus left the driver unprotected and unrestrained.

Motorized seatbelts
These front seat restraints run along a channel and cross the shoulder
when the ignition is turned on. A lapbelt has to be fastened separately.
These automatic belts are set so high above the door frame that they're
uncomfortable to wear and a nightmare to adjust. Their most serious
shortcoming, however, is that they give the driver a false sense of security, and the separate lapbelt often goes unfastened (the U.S. government says that only 29 percent of the people with motorized seatbelts
use the lap portion). This has resulted in a number of accidents in
which the driver or front passenger has been decapitated or paralyzed
by the shoulder belt. Ford was sued for $1.3 million in Akron, Ohio,
where the driver of a 1990 Escort was paralyzed in an accident in which
only the automatic shoulder belt was fastened *(Pflum v. Ford)*. Nissan
faces a $10-million suit in Newnan, Georgia, launched by the father of
a girl who did not have the lapbelt fastened and who was decapitated
by her 1989 Sentra's motorized shoulder harness *(Smith v. Nissan)*.

Three-point seatbelts
In *Garrett v. Ford*, a Baltimore, Maryland, Federal Court jury rendered
a $3.2-million verdict against Ford for installing a dangerously designed
lapbelt and for not including back seat shoulder harnesses in a 1985
Escort. The lapbelts were designed to cross at the waist instead of the
pelvis, an error that contributed to the passengers' paralysis. If shoulder harnesses had been installed, the lapbelts would not have aggra-
vated the injuries, says the Center for Auto Safety. Ford is involved in
another ongoing trial, under appeal, where the company is being sued
for compensatory and punitive damages arising from the death of a 72-
year-old nun, Sister Mary Margaret LeGlise. She was riding in the rear
seat of a 1987 Ford Tempo with her lapbelt fastened when the accident
occurred. At trial, California Superior Court judge Jeffrey Miller lit into
Ford for keeping its settlements in other cases secret (referring to a $6-
million payout to settle a San Diego case) in order to avoid embarrass-
ment and other lawsuits. Judge Miller further noted that Ford could
not claim that the technology to install three-point belts had not been
perfected when the company had, for years, put the safer three-point
belts in its European models. Judge Miller concluded:

> Ford knew that the rear seat lapbelt not only did not provide ade-
> quate protection but actually caused injury to its users. Ford
> also knew through its own internal engineering analysis and
> experimentation that the three-point restraint system was vastly
> superior and would save many lives.

Steering

Holley v. Ford of Canada, June 18, 1980, Nova Scotia Supreme Court, Judge Cowan. The plaintiff purchased a used 1976 Ford Custom 200 truck that was involved in an accident due to steering assembly failure. The plaintiff was awarded $4,100 in damages.

White v. International Harvester (1969), W.W.R., No. 235 (Alta. T.D.). This new truck's steering assembly had problems and was adjusted by the dealer, but 4,200 miles (6,720 km) later it suddenly veered out of control due to a defective steering component. The plaintiff was awarded both costs and damages.

Sudden acceleration

Willar v. Ford (1991), 118 N.B.R. (2nd), No. 323. The owner sued Ford after the throttle jammed open twice, causing several accidents. The Court held that Ford, not the dealer, was responsible for the plaintiff's damages.

Tires

Chase v. Goodyear Tire and Rubber Co. and Goodyear Canada Inc., New Brunswick Court of Queen's Bench, Trial Division, No. S/C/513/89, April 12, 1991. The plaintiff was injured when the tire he was inflating exploded. There was no evidence of a manufacturing defect on the original tire or with the retread. Goodyear was found negligent because it failed to warn its customer of the danger inherent in inflating a retreaded tire with worn-out and damaged radial cords, thereby breaching its duty to warn. The plaintiff was awarded $65,000 for his injuries.

Gagnon v. Canadian Tire (1979), C.P., No. 251. The plaintiff was awarded $1,310 as compensation for a radial tire that exploded when he was rocking his car out of a snowbank.

Murphy v. D. & B. Holdings (1979), 31 N.S.R. (2nd), No. 380; 52 A.P.R. (S.C.), No. 380. The Court held that the manufacturer was liable for damages for permitting a customer to use its tires in a dangerous manner.

Tire iron placement adding to collision injuries

Gallant v. Beitz (1983), 42 O.R. (2nd), No. 86. This judgment states clearly that automakers are presumed to know that their vehicles will be involved in accidents and must take reasonable steps to minimize injuries caused by flaws inherent in the design of their vehicles.

Transmissions jump from Park to Reverse

McEvoy v. Ford Motor Company et al., September 6, 1989, B.C.S.C., No. 3841989, Judge Hinds. Mr. McEvoy was killed when his new Ford pickup backed over him after the transmission jumped from Park to Reverse. He had left the engine running and was unloading cargo when the right front wheel crushed his chest.

Justice Hinds found Ford 65 percent negligent for the following reasons:
- The RCMP mechanic testified that the gearshift lever could easily be mispositioned into an "unstable Park" position.
- It was determined that Ford was aware of this defect as early as 1971, according to internal company documents presented during the trial.
- Ford had a duty to warn its customers of the hazard caused by the C-6 automatic transmission; the warning in the owner's manual was deemed insufficient to satisfy this duty.
- Ford and its Canadian distributor had breached their duty to the consumer.

Unger v. Ford. In this Bridgeport, Connecticut, out-of-court settlement, Ford paid $700,000 to the family of a man crushed to death when his 1988 F-series pickup went into Reverse while the gearshift lever was in Park. The plaintiff claimed that the automatic transmission and PRNDL indicator were defective. His lawyer also alleged that Ford had received 26,000 complaints about the transmission defect.

Wheels
Michel Beauregard v. Goyette Auto and General Motors, July 3, 1982, Quebec Provincial Court, No. 500-05-011478-763, Judge Aronovitch. One wheel on a new 1975 Ventura suddenly locked up, causing the vehicle to go out of control. The plaintiff was awarded $3,500.

Nason v. General Motors of Canada Ltd., November 1, 1995, British Columbia Provincial Court (Small Claims Division), No. C93-04200, Judge C. L. Bagnall. Judge Bagnall awarded the plaintiffs $5,416 plus interest for damages arising from an accident caused by their Reatta's faulty right rear wheel knuckle. Damages included $4,500 for the decrease in the car's value, and $916 for the loss of a safe driving discount offered by the Insurance Corporation of British Columbia.

Delay (In Bringing Lawsuit)

Bouchard v. Vaillancourt (1961), C.S., No. 171. If the seller has defrauded the consumer, delays for initiating a lawsuit are allowed to be longer than in cases where fraud isn't involved.

See also:
- *Ennis v. Klassen* 70 D.L.R. (4th), No. 325.
- *Ginn v. Canbec Auto* (1976), C.S., No. 1416.
- *Lemire v. Pelchat* (1957), R.C.S., No. 823.

False Advertising

False sales prices
R. v. Lanthier and Lalonde, Sessions Court (Montreal). A Montreal Ford dealer was fined $300 for placing ads showing tremendous reductions

to the manufacturer's suggested retail price on new cars. After criminal charges were laid, it was shown that the advertised savings were lies (judgment on file with Consumer and Corporate Affairs). Several dozen suburban Toronto Chrysler dealers were fined by the federal government for similar deceptions.

Odometer tampering
Odometer tampering is a criminal offence under the federal Weights and Measures Act. The Department of Consumer and Corporate Affairs uses the RCMP to investigate all such cases. Many violators have been caught and successfully prosecuted. Nevertheless, the federal law is weak because fines are so low that they practically represent a licence to operate illegally, and an individual can escape prosecution by pleading that the odometer was broken and had to be changed.

Bouchard v. South Park Mercury Sales (1978), 3 W.W.R., No. 78. The odometer figure written on the contract was incorrect. The dealer pleaded ignorance, but the judge ruled that the car's owner should receive damages to compensate for the extra mileage.

Used car sold as new (demonstrator)
Leblanc v. Frenette and Chrysler Credit, May 27, 1971, Quebec Provincial Court, No. 279-772, Judge Laurier. The plaintiff's "new" demonstrator was actually a used car with a rolled-back odometer. It had also been in an accident. The Court held the dealer responsible and ordered him to refund the purchase price.

Leasing

Although the state of Florida got a $4.2-million settlement from its Toyota dealers for leasing misrepresentation, no Canadian government has taken similar action, even though the same misleading practices are prevalent here among the major leasing agencies and dealers. Fortunately Canadian courts are more progressive than the government, and have made several significant rulings that give lessees added clout when seeking refunds for deceptive practices and defective vehicles.

Ford Motor Credit v. Bothwell, December 3, 1979, Ontario County Court (Middlesex), No. 9226-T, Judge Macnab. The defendant leased a 1977 Ford truck that had frequent engine problems, characterized by stalling and hard starting. After complaining for one year and driving 22,000 miles, the defendant cancelled the lease. Ford Credit sued for the money owing on the lease. Judge Macnab cancelled the lease and ordered Ford Credit to repay 70 percent of the amount paid during the leasing period. Ford Credit was also ordered to refund repair costs, even though the corporation claimed that it should not be held responsible for Ford's failure to honour its warranty.

Salvador v. Setay Motors/Queenstown Chev-Olds, Hamilton Small Claims Court, No.1621/95. Robert Salvador, an Ontario consumer advocate and founder of the Consumer Action Group (CAG), was awarded $2,000 plus costs from Queenstown Leasing. The Court found that the company should have tried harder to sell the leased vehicle, and for a higher price, when the "open lease" expired.

Salvador gave Queenstown a list of offers from independent buyers when he returned the vehicle, but they were never contacted. Instead, the leasing agency auctioned off the van to the highest bidder. You guessed it—Queenstown Leasing.

This judgment can also be helpful in cases where a repossessed vehicle is sold or auctioned off for far less than what it's worth, or where the seller is in a conflict of interest by being the buyer as well. Copies of this judgment can be obtained by calling the Ontario Consumer Action Group at 416-587-0070.

Schryvers v. Richport Ford Sales, May 18, 1993, B.C.S.C., No. C917060, Justice Tysoe. The Court awarded $17,578.47 (including $6,000 in punitive damages) plus costs to a couple who paid thousands of dollars over the purchase price for their Ford Explorer and Escort in unfair and hidden leasing charges. The Court found that this price difference constituted a deceptive, unconscionable act or practice in contravention of the Trade Practices Act, R.S.B.C. 1979, c. 406.

Judge Tysoe analyzed the price difference using the following method:

Explorer Purchase vs. Lease

The difference of these totals and the calculation of the tax consequences as follows:

$32,835.00	–	amount payable by lease method
(28,240.60)	–	amount payable by financing method
597.27	–	PST and GST on difference of above figures
(243.36)	–	saving on PST and GST under lease method
$4,948.31	–	total damages re Explorer

Escort Purchase vs. Lease

The difference of these totals and the calculation of the tax consequences are as follows:

$22,235.96	–	amount payable by lease method
(16,266.40)	–	amount payable by financing method
776.04	–	PST and GST on difference of above figures
(115.44)	–	saving on PST and GST under lease method
$6,630.16	–	total damages re Escort

The total of the general damages in respect of both vehicles is $6,630.16 + $4,948.16 – $11,578.47.

Judge Tysoe concluded that the total of the general damages awarded to the Schryvers' for both vehicles would be $11,578.47. He then proceeded to give the following reasons for awarding an additional $6,000 in punitive damages:

> Little wonder Richport Ford had a contest for the salesperson who could persuade the most customers to acquire their vehicles by way of a lease transaction. I consider the actions of Richport Ford to be sufficiently flagrant and high-handed to warrant an award of punitive damages.
>
> There must be a disincentive to suppliers in respect of intentionally deceptive trade practices. If no punitive damages are awarded for intentional violations of the legislation, suppliers will continue to conduct their businesses in a manner that involves deceptive trade practices because they will have nothing to lose. In this case I believe that the appropriate amount of punitive damages is the extra profit Richport Ford endeavoured to make as a result of its deceptive acts. I therefore award punitive damages against Richport Ford in the amount of $6,000...

See also:
- *Barber v. Inland Truck Sales*, 11 D.L.R. (3rd), No. 469.
- *Canadian-Dominion Leasing v. Suburban Super Drug Ltd.* (1966), 56 D.L.R. (2nd), No. 43.
- *Neilson v. Atlantic Rentals Ltd.* (1974), 8 N.B.R. (2nd), No. 594.
- *Volvo Canada v. Fox*, December 13, 1979, New Brunswick Court of Queen's Bench, No. 1698/77/C, Judge Stevenson.
- *Western Tractor v. Dyck*, 7 D.L.R. (3rd), No. 535.

Misrepresentation

Late delivery
When the delivery of a new car is delayed, the customer can either demand that the contract be cancelled or ask for special damages. If the delay was caused by the seller's or manufacturer's negligence, both the contract's cancellation and compensating damages can be claimed.

The seller can sometimes make a successful counter-argument that no specific delivery date was written on the contract, or that the delay was caused by elements beyond his control.

George Archer v. Metro Motor Sales, Quebec Small Claims Court, No. 32-006842-74. The plaintiff was not given his new vehicle at the promised time. He was awarded $300 as compensation for extra expenses, including the cost of an airplane ticket.

Manery v. Kampe (1943), 3 W.W.R., No. 687 (B.C.C.A.). The seller delivered the goods 18 days after the contracted delivery date. The buyer refused the merchandise and sued for cancellation of the contract. The Court ordered that the buyer's money be refunded.

"New" car really a used car
Bilodeau v. Sud Auto, Quebec Court of Appeal, No. 09-000751-73,
Judge Tremblay. This appellate Court cancelled the contract, and held
that a car can't be sold as new or as a demonstrator if it has ever been
rented, leased, sold, or titled to anyone other than the dealer.

Rourke v. Gilmore, January 16, 1928 (Ontario Weekly Notes, vol. XXXI-
II, p. 292). Before discovering that his new car was really used, the
plaintiff drove it for over a year. For this reason, the contract couldn't
be cancelled. However, the Appeals Court instead awarded damages for
$500, which was quite a sum in 1928!

Vehicle not as ordered
Whether you're buying a new or used vehicle, the seller can't misrep-
resent the vehicle. Anything that varies from what one would commonly expect, or from the seller's representation, must be disclosed
prior to signing the contract. Typical scenarios involve odometer turn-
backs, accident damage, used or leased cars sold as new, new vehicles
that are the wrong colour and the wrong model year, or vehicles that
lack promised options or standard features.

Chenel v. Bel Automobile (1981) Inc., August 27, 1976, Quebec Superior
Court (Quebec City), Judge Desmeules. The plaintiff didn't receive his
new Ford truck with the Jacob brakes essential for transporting sand in
hilly regions. The Court awarded the plaintiff $27,000, representing
the purchase price of the vehicle less the money he earned while using
the truck.

Lasky v. Royal City Chrysler Plymouth, February 18, 1987, Ontario High
Court of Justice, 59 O.R. (2nd), No. 323. The plaintiff bought a
4-cylinder 1983 Dodge 600 that was represented by the salesman as
being a 6-cylinder model. After putting 40,000 km on the vehicle over
a 22-month period, the buyer was given her money back, without interest, under the provincial Business Practices Act.

MacDonald v. Equilease Co. Ltd., January 18, 1979, Ontario Supreme
Court, Judge O'Driscoll. The plaintiff leased a truck that was misrepresented as having an axle stronger than it really was. The Court awarded
the plaintiff damages for repairs and set aside the lease.

White v. Munn Motors (1960), 45 M.P.R., No. 253 (Nfld. T.D.). The dealer misrepresented a half-ton truck as having a three-quarter-ton capacity. The buyer was given his money back because he didn't get what he
paid for.

Wrong model year
Adelaide Motors v. Alexander (1962), 48 M.P.R., No. 258 (Nfld. T.D.). The
customer bought a new 1960 car that was misrepresented as being a

1961 model. The Court ruled that the duped owner was entitled to damages.

Ginn v. Canbec Auto, Quebec Superior Court (Montreal), No. 500-05-014597-74-4. Relying on expert testimony provided by the APA, the Court awarded $10,000 to the purchaser of a new 1972 BMW that was fraudulently sold as a 1973 model. The case demonstrates beyond a doubt that car retailers are culpable for the misrepresentation of their products.

Woods v. Borstel (1962), 34 D.L.R. (2nd), No. 68 (Alta. C.A.). The customer bought a new 1958 car that was misrepresented as being a 1959 model. The Court ruled that the seller's model year representation was a warranty as defined under s. 2(1)(n) of the Alberta Sale of Goods Act. The plaintiff was entitled to all damages, but the contract remained in force.

In Ontario, two separate successful lawsuits claimed that Ford systematically cheated consumers by selling 1970 Cortinas as new 1971 models. Each purchaser received $400 in compensation from small claims court. In *Brosseau v. Lewis Motors,* Ottawa-Carleton, and *King v. Paddy Shanahan Ford,* Toronto, the Court pointed to deceptive and misleading sales tactics used to sell the Cortinas.

See also:
• *Ennis v. Klassen,* 70 D.L.R. (4th), No. 325.

Secret Warranties

It's common practice for manufacturers to extend their warranties secretly to cover components with a high failure rate. Customers who complain vigorously get extended warranty compensation in the form of "goodwill" adjustments.

François Chong v. Marine Drive Imported Cars Ltd. and Honda Canada Inc., May 17, 1994, British Columbia Provincial Court (Small Claims Division), No. 92-06760, Judge C. L. Bagnall. Mr. Chong is the first owner of a 1983 Honda Accord with 134,000 km on the odometer. He's had six engine camshafts replaced—four under Honda "goodwill" programs, one where he paid part of the repairs, and one via the small claims court judgment below.

In his ruling, Judge Bagnall ordered Honda and the dealer to each pay half of the $835.81 repair bill, for the following reasons:

The defendants assert that the warranty which was part of the contract for purchase of the car encompassed the entirety of their obligation to the claimant, and that it expired in February 1985. The replacements of the camshaft after that date were paid for wholly or in part by Honda as a "goodwill gesture." The time has come for these gestures to cease, according to the witness for Honda. As well, he pointed out to me that the most recent replacement of the camshaft was paid for by Honda and that, therefore, the work would not be covered by Honda's usual warranty of twelve months from date of repair. Mr. Wall, who testified for Honda, told me there was no question that this situation with Mr. Chong's engine was an unusual state of affairs. He said that a camshaft properly maintained can last anywhere from 24,000–500,000 km. He could not offer any suggestion as to why the car keeps having this problem.

The claimant has convinced me that the problems he is having with rapid breakdowns of camshafts in his car is due to a defect, which was present in the engine at the time that he purchased the car. The problem first arose during the warranty period and in my view has never been properly identified nor repaired.

Desjardins v. Canadian Honda and Du Portage Mercury, February 20, 1981, Quebec Small Claims Court (Hull), No. 550-32-000933-801, Judge Dagenais. The plaintiff bought a used Honda "as is" from a Ford dealership. One year later the headgasket blew and was repaired free of charge by a Honda dealer under a secret warranty extension and the emissions warranty. Ten months later the headgasket blew again and was repaired without charge. A few months later, the part failed again and was repaired a third time at Honda's expense.

The plaintiff brought suit 22 months after purchase for expenses relating to motor adjustments, rental cars, and general inconvenience. Judge Dagenais forced both Honda Canada and the Ford dealer to pay $281 in damages for having made and sold such a defect-ridden vehicle.

Marielle Signori v. Toyota Canada Ltée. and St.-Laurent Toyota Inc., February 18, 1985, Quebec Small Claims Court (Montreal), No. 505-32-002421-841, Judge Gilles Bélanger. In this case, a 1981 Tercel owner forced Toyota Canada to admit that the company had a secret warranty to cover premature brake wear for up to two years or 40,000 km. Judge Bélanger castigated Toyota and its dealer for keeping this warranty secret and awarded $286 to the plaintiff.

See also:
• *Crevier v. Fiat of Canada* (1979), No. 959.
• *Danis Mercury v. Société Sanitaire* (1979), C.S., No. 645.
• *Gascon v. Bonaventure Ford* (1974), C.S. (Hull), No. 550-05-000377-74.
• *Gerschicoff v. General Motors* (1979), C.S., No. 681.

Repairs

Faulty diagnosis

Let's say that before taking a holiday you have your van checked out and are assured that it's in good condition. While en route to your vacation spot, it dies on the highway and ruins your holiday. When the check-up is incorrect and leads to financial losses (damages), the garage owner is responsible for those losses, as well as for refunding the diagnostic costs. Of course, you'd better show that the defect that caused your troubles was present and detectable at the time the vehicle was checked.

Babcock v. Servacar (1970), 1 O.R., No. 125. A motorist took a car he was planning to buy to an Ottawa Esso Diagnostic Clinic to determine its condition. He did the recommended repairs, and then had serious problems with the car while on vacation. The judge ruled that the clinic would have to pay for the repairs and reimburse the diagnostic cost as well. The Court held that the garage's advertising claims gave rise to a contractual warranty that promised to root out the car's defects before it was purchased.

Chan v. W. Gordon Inc., October 15, 1981, Quebec Provincial Court, No. 02-000002-811, Judge Page. The plaintiff was awarded $300 to cover repairs to a 1973 Volvo that was taken to Gordon's Service Station prior to purchase. The garage mistakenly diagnosed the car as being sound and roadworthy.

Davies v. Alberta Motor Association, August 13, 1991, Alberta Provincial Court, Civil Division, No. P9090106097, Judge Moore. The plaintiff had a used 1985 Nissan Pulsar NX checked out by the AMA's Vehicle Inspection Service prior to buying it. The car passed with flying colours. A month later the clutch was replaced and numerous electrical problems ensued. At that time, another garage discovered that the car had been involved in a major accident, had a bent frame, a leaking radiator, and was unsafe to drive. The Court awarded the plaintiff $1,578.40 plus three years of interest. The judge held that the AMA set itself out as an expert and should have spotted the car's defects. The AMA's defence—that it was not responsible for errors—was thrown out. The Court held that a disclaimer clause could not protect the Association from a fundamental breach of contract.

McCormick v. Servacar and Esso, February 9, 1981, Quebec Small Claims Court, No. 500-32-008700-801, Judge Prevost. Before purchasing a used 1978 Ford Fairmont, the plaintiff had it checked out by an Esso Diagnostic Clinic. The clinic said that the car was in good condition except for dirty transmission fluid. Ten days after purchasing the car, the transmission was replaced. The Court ordered Servacar and Esso to pay the $300 for repairs, reasoning that were it not for the clinic's incompetence, negligence, or lack of experience, the defect could have been detected earlier.

See also:
• *Lowe v. Fairview Chrysler-Dodge Limited and Chrysler Canada Limited*, May 14, 1996, Ontario Court (General Division), Burlington Small Claims Court, No.1224/95.

Flat-rate abuses
Kesselman v. Chomedy Ford Sales Ltd., September 18, 1975, Quebec Provincial Court, No. 500-02-002113-756, Judge Decary. The plaintiff contested the flat-rate charges for 28.8 hours when the mechanic's clocked time was only 22.8 hours. The Ford dealership raised the defence that the mechanic was following a Ford Canada flat-rate manual and that this was a common practice. The Court didn't buy this argument. It held the dealer responsible for the excess charges because the customer was never told about the flat-rate method of computing repair time.

R. v. Birchcliff Lincoln Mercury Ltd., July 7, 1987, Ontario Court of Appeal, 60 O.R. (2nd), No. 610, 220; 220 A.C., No. 274. This new car dealer advertised a $38 hourly labour charge and then calculated the number of hours using a flat-rate guide that allowed more hours than those actually worked. This was held by the Appeal Court to be false advertising under the federal Combines Act (Competition Act).

See also:
• *Quebec Consumer Protection Bureau v. Canadian Tire.*

Fuel system fire
Lenz v. J. B.'s Automotive Service Center Ltd. (1987), 51 Alta. L.R. (2nd) (Q.B.), No. 16. The plaintiff's vehicle caught fire three weeks after the fuel system was worked on. The Court held the garage liable because the fire was in the same area that had been repaired.

Oil filter improperly installed
Proulx v. Salois Automobile, December 6, 1974, Quebec Provincial Court, No. 02-004322-74, Judge Lacourcière. The plaintiff was awarded damages to pay for motor repairs caused by an improperly installed oil filter. The dealer's mechanic was ordered to pay $1,000 in damages.

Repair misrepresentation
Smith v. Marc Patrick Motors and the Canadian Tire Corporation, September 20, 1984, Ontario Small Claims Court (Niagara North), Judge Kingstone. The plaintiff bought a used 1978 Honda Civic that was sold as having a "new" engine. It failed shortly thereafter—Canadian Tire hadn't installed a new engine. Judge Kingstone ordered both

defendants to split the cost of the repairs ($1,000, plus 13 percent interest) for misrepresenting the engine.

Repairs not done properly

Berta v. Gold Seal Engine Rebuilders, August 22, 1985, Ontario Small Claims Court (Toronto), No. C217/83, Justice Sigurdson. The plaintiff's engine was improperly repaired. Judge Sigurdson awarded $2,047.03 to the plaintiff after hearing the garage's employees testify in a "less than truthful" manner.

Canbec Auto v. De Levo, January 18, 1973, Quebec Provincial Court, No. 03-058009-72, Judge Page. The dealer sued the defendant for money owing on a bill for a general inspection and correction of defects. The car owner refused to pay the bill because the vehicle was still running poorly. Judgment was rendered in favour of the defendant. The Court held that the garage had an obligation of results, whereby the repairs would be expected to correct the problems complained of by the car's owner.

Collier v. McMaster's Auto Sales, April 26, 1991, New Brunswick Court of Queen's Bench, No. W/C 157/90. Judge McLellan ruled that the dealer's failure to repair the car properly under warranty justified the owner getting the engine repaired elsewhere at the dealer's expense. The failure to repair the plaintiff's car properly amounted to a breach of the manufacturer's expressed warranty.

Magloire v. Chomedy Toyota, December 1, 1982, Quebec Provincial Court, No. 500-02-014582-824, Judge Hodge. This Toyota dealer installed a defective oil pump that caused $1,494.28 in damages to the motor. Judge Hodge awarded the full amount to the plaintiff.

Mudge v. Corner Brooke Garage, 8 Nfld. & P.E.I.R., No. 374. This truck owner successfully sued the garage for negligent repairs to the rear frame assembly.

Pelleray v. Heritage Ford Sales Ltd., March 22, 1993, Ontario Small Claims Court (Scarborough), No. SC7688/91. This owner of a 1986 Ford Aerostar was awarded $1,691.29 as compensation for repairs to his automatic transmission, which had failed three times after having been repaired by the dealer.

Raiches Steel Works v. J. Clark & Son, 16 N.B.R. (2nd), No. 535. The brakes failed three weeks after being repaired. The judge found the mechanic negligent and awarded damages of $6,423.

Sigurdson v. Hillcrest Service & Acklands (1977) 1 W.W.R., No. 740. An accident was caused by a defective brake hose. The garage that installed it claimed that the parts distributor was responsible. The judge ruled that Saskatchewan's Sale of Goods Act made both garage and distributor responsible for damages.

Sylvain v. Carrosseries d'Automobiles Guy Inc. (1981), C.P., No. 333, Judge Page. The garage had an obligation of results that the paint job on the plaintiff's car would be satisfactory. It was not. The Court held the garage liable for the cost of repainting the car elsewhere.

Tremblay v. Au Grand Salon, September 19, 1973, Quebec Provincial Court, No. 02-054410-73, Judge Bousquet. The plaintiff asked that his brakes be checked and paid $30 for the inspection. After the inspection, the brakes failed and an accident ensued. The Court held the dealer responsible, although no repairs were done.

See also:
• *Acme v. Coziol* (1962), B.R.
• *Chomedy Ford v. Mash*, March 11, 1976, Quebec Provincial Court, No. 500-02-007671-767.
• *Gagnon v. Ford Motor Co.* (1974), C.S., No. 422.
• *Lazanick v. Ford Motor Co.*, June 15, 1965, Quebec Superior Court, No. 623504.

Repairs leading to vandalism or theft
Goulet v. Roberval Pontiac Buick, February 11, 1980, Quebec Small Claims Court, No. 155-32-000516-794, Judge Savard. The plaintiff's vehicle was vandalized while being repaired. The Court held the garage responsible because the car was under its care.

Water in fuel
Claridge v. Three Way Motors, July 20, 1987, Manitoba, No. 221/86, Judge Thompson. The owner of a 1980 Audi 5000 had starting problems and rusty fuel-injection nozzles caused by what he believed to be water-contaminated gasoline. He didn't have any direct proof that the gas station's pumps were contaminated, but the judge ruled that the balance of probabilities indicated this was likely, since the station owner had had problems with the storage pumps in the past.

Part Three
NEW VEHICLE RATINGS

What Makes a Good Car or Minivan?

Your new car or minivan must first live up to the promises made by the manufacturer and dealer. It should be crashworthy, reasonably durable (lasting at least ten years), cost no more than $800 a year to maintain, and provide you with a fair resale value a few years down the road. Parts should be reasonably priced and easily available, and servicing shouldn't be given with a shrug or a snarl.

This edition tries to publish up-to-date photographs of each new model rated, but some automakers disagree with our ratings and refuse to cooperate with us in any manner whatsoever, including sending us recent photos and current technical specifications. We regret any errors or omissions that may result. Our independence is more important than a squeaky-clean book with pretty pictures.

Under no circumstances are dealers or manufacturers solicited for free "test" vehicles, as is the case with most auto columnists and some consumer groups. When a test vehicle is needed, it's rented from a major rental agency or borrowed from its owner. I've adopted this practice from my early experiences as a consumer reporter 25 years ago. At that time, Nissan asked me to test-drive their new 1974 240Z—no strings attached. I took the car for a week, had it examined by an independent garage, spoke with satisfied and dissatisfied owners, and accessed internal service bulletins. I concluded that the car's faulty brakes made it unsafe to drive. Nissan sued me for $4 million, fixed the brakes in a "product improvement campaign," and dropped the lawsuit two years later. I never went back for another car.

Definitions of Terms

Ratings

This edition makes use of owner complaints, confidential dealer service bulletins, and test-drives to expose serious factory-related defects, design deficiencies, or servicing glitches. It should be noted that customer complaints alone do not make for a scientific sampling, and that's why they're used in conjunction with other sources of information. On the other hand, owner complaints combined with the inside information found in dealer service bulletins are a good starting point to cut through the automakers' hyperbole to a glimpse of reality.

Unlike most auto guides, *Lemon-Aid* isn't bedazzled by high-tech wizardry. Almost 30 years of consumer advocacy in the auto industry have taught me that complex components are usually quite troublesome during their first few years on the market (airbags and anti-lock brakes are particularly irritating). Complexity drives up ownership costs, reduces overall reliability, and puts extra stress on major and expensive parts like powertrain, fuel system, and emissions components. Computerized engine controls and sophisticated fuel-injection systems are also impossible to service without specialized training and diagnostic equipment. Although many garages are acquiring such equipment and retraining their personnel, few mechanics as yet have a sufficient background in the complex electronics found under the hood of most new cars. As a general rule, a car with fewer electronic accessories will be cheaper and easier to maintain.

Depreciation is the biggest—and most often ignored—expense you'll encounter when you trade in your vehicle, or when an accident forces you to buy another vehicle before the depreciated loss can be amortized. Most new cars depreciate a whopping 30 to 40 percent during the first two years of ownership. Fortunately, most minivans depreciate at a much slower rate.

Traditional Depreciation "Winners"

1. Honda Civic CX
2. Infiniti Q45
3. Mazda Miata
4. Honda Accord
5. VW Jetta GL
6. Toyota Camry
7. BMW 3 series
8. Ford Mustang GT
9. Acura Integra
10. Toyota Corolla
11. Toyota Supra
12. Chevrolet Camaro
13. Toyota Tercel
14. Eagle Talon TSI AWD
15. VW Golf GL

Traditional Depreciation "Losers"

1. Lincoln Continental Executive
2. Cadillac Concours
3. Lincoln Mark VIII
4. Cadillac Eldorado
5. Cadillac Seville SLS
6. Chrysler LHS
7. GM Park Avenue Ultra
8. Saab 900S
9. Ford Taurus SHO
10. Chrysler New Yorker
11. GM Park Avenue
12. Hyundai Elantra
13. Infiniti J30
14. Suzuki Swift
15. Ford Thunderbird

Leasing agents play this depreciation game to their advantage (while adding in the dealer's profit) when they establish your car's residual value upon the expiration of the lease. The only way to use depreciation rates to your advantage is to choose a vehicle listed as being economical to own and keep it for five to ten years.

During a vehicle's first year on the market it takes about six months to acquire enough information for a fair-minded evaluation, unless it's a hybrid that has been in service under another name or has only been re-badged. Most new cars hit the market before all of the bugs have been worked out, so it would be irresponsible to recommend them before they've been owner-driven, or before the quality of service from the dealer and manufacturer has been customer-tested. The Chrysler Caravan is a case in point. Hailed as Car of the Year by the motoring press upon its introduction in 1984, it's now noted mostly for its costly engine, transmission, AC, anti-lock brake, and paint problems and poor crashworthiness.

Warranty performance

I'm more impressed by performance than promise. A manufacturer's warranty is a legal commitment that the product it sells will perform in the normal and customary manner for which it is designed. It's an important factor in this edition's ratings, and is judged by how fairly it's applied—not by what's promised. Extended or supplementary warranties provide extended coverage and may be sold by the manufacturer, dealer, or an independent third party. If a part malfunctions or fails (not owing to owner negligence), the dealer will fix, repair, or replace the defective part or parts and bill the automaker for the cost.

Most new vehicle warranties fall into two categories: bumper-to-bumper for a period of three to five years, and powertrain for up to 6 years/130,000 km. (See the "1998 Warranties" table on page 91.) Automakers still sometimes charge an additional $50 to $100 fee for warranty repairs requested by owners of used cars with unexpired base warranties. For snowbirds, the federal and provincial governments can charge GST and sales tax on warranty and non-warranty repairs done south of the border. Beware.

After using longer, more comprehensive warranties to successfully sell its cars and minivans, Chrysler dropped its generous seven-year warranty in 1995 in favour of rebates and low interest rates even though its cars and minivans aren't sufficiently reliable to forego the extra protection. Now, much like Ford and GM, Chrysler uses secret warranties to pay for factory defects. Unlike other automakers, however, rarely do you see written confirmation of this fact in a service bulletin or dealer memo, leading to incredible variations (injustices?) in the treatment of warranty claims. Chrysler is also unique among automakers in having set up a special Review Committee last year to give out compensation to owners who were refused help through normal warranty channels. That Committee, available only to Canadians, is still operating today and is mostly preoccupied with automatic transmission, brake, and paint delamination claims. (See Appendix V).

General Motors is tougher to deal with than Chrysler. Once it rules upon a customer's complaint, the file is closed and won't be reopened unless there's a threat of court action or the media becomes interested in the case. Like Ford, GM informs its dealers and customers selectively of its goodwill policies through bulletins and memos. Nevertheless, the automaker likes to see its customers squirm, urging dealers to give them the third degree before warranty assistance is forthcoming.

Ford does much better, with an average warranty that's usually applied fairly and gives customers the benefit of the doubt. Where Ford fails its customers is in taking too long to come up with a consistent policy in dealing with what are obviously chronic, factory-related defects. For example, the automaker waited until June 1998 to extended the warranty on its 3.8L engine headgasket failures afflicting 1994–95 Taurus and Sables and 1995 Windstars, even though the problem had been evident since 1996. Furthermore, Ford still hasn't dealt with the myriad automatic transmission failures caused by a defective aluminum piston that affects over a decade's worth of its entire vehicle line.

Tires and batteries aren't covered by most car manufacturers' warranties (except for GM, which began covering tires on its 1996 models); they're warranted by their manufacturers on a pro-rated basis. Batteries, for example, are covered for at least a year against defects, and then generally for another 24 months on a pro-rated basis. This isn't really a good deal, because the manufacturer is making a profit by charging you the full list price. If you were to buy the same replacement battery from a discount store you'd likely pay less, even without the pro-rated rebate. The same caveat also applies to tires, because you're given a pro-rated rebate on the suggested list price, which almost nobody pays.

Safety restraints, such as airbags and seatbelts, usually mirror the basic warranty with coverage varying between 3 years/60,000 km and the lifetime of the vehicle/unlimited km. After-market products and services—such as gas-saving gadgets, rustproofing, paint protectors, AC, and van conversions—can render the manufacturer's warranty invalid, so be sure to check with your dealer before purchasing any optional equipment or services from an independent supplier.

This edition emphasizes important new features that add to a vehicle's safety, reliability, road performance, and comfort, and points out those changes that are merely gadgetry or styling revisions. Also noted are important improvements planned for the future, or the dropping of a model line. In addition to the "Recommended" or "Not Recommended" rating, each vehicle's strong and weak points are summarized.

Recommended
This rating indicates a best buy. This category includes new vehicles that combine a high level of crashworthiness with good road performance, decent reliability, and better-than-average resale value. Service must be readily available, and parts not expensive or difficult to find.

A vehicle may lose its "Recommended" rating from the previous edition whenever its price becomes unreasonable or its warranty inadequate, or when the competition offers comparable models at a lower price, or with more standard safety, mechanical, or convenience features.

Above Average
Vehicles in this class exhibit quality construction, durability, and safety features as standard equipment. They may have expensive parts and servicing, an unreasonably high price tag, or only satisfactory warranty performance, one or all of which may remove them from the "Recommended" category.

Average
Vehicles in this group have some deficiencies or flaws that make them a second choice. In many cases, certain components are prone to premature wear or breakdown, or some other positive aspect of long-term ownership is lacking. An "Average" rating can also be attributed to such factors as substandard assembly quality, lack of a solid long-term reliability record, or some flaw in the parts and service network.

Below Average
This is a rating category that I use less often. It denotes a vehicle that may have had a poor reliability record, but where improvements have been made with regard to durability and/or safety features. A "Below Average" vehicle may be a risky buy, but it's a cut above "Not Recommended." Ensure that you get an extended warranty with a vehicle in this category.

Not Recommended
Buy at your own risk. Substandard crashworthiness, poor overall reliability, inadequate road performance, poor dealer service, and other factors can make owning one of these vehicles a traumatic and expensive experience. It doesn't necessarily follow that every single vehicle produced in a "Not Recommended" model line will have exactly the same reliability shortcomings, but chances of having trouble are higher than normal.

Not Rated
Vehicles that haven't been on the road long enough to assess, or that are sold in such small numbers that owner feedback is insufficient, are left unrated.

Cost analysis/alternatives
Most 1999 model prices are unchanged due to stiff competition among American automakers, who are facing price rollbacks from Japanese manufacturers beset by a fallen yen. In most cases, where prices are higher this year, safety, performance, comfort, or convenience improvements don't usually add up to the extra money you'll have to pay. Selling prices are pretty straightforward, but beware of $99 and up add-on "administration fee" charges that have no place in either your leasing or purchase contract.

Each model's cost is analyzed in light of cheaper carry-over models, possible rebates, destination charges, insurance costs, servicing, parts costs, depreciation, and fuel consumption. According to the CAA, annual maintenance costs average about $800—vehicles are rated as to whether their estimated maintenance costs fall on the low or high side of this figure.

Quality/reliability/safety
Lemon-Aid bases its quality and reliability evaluations on owner comments, confidential manufacturer service bulletins, and government reports from the NHTSA safety complaint files, among other sources.

This 1999 edition also draws on the knowledge and expertise of professionals working in the automotive marketplace, including mechanics and fleet owners. The aim is to have a wide range of unbiased (and irrefutable) data on quality, reliability, and durability that you can use as proof that a safety-related or performance-related problem has been reported or investigated by others. Once you prove you're not alone, the dealer and manufacturer will treat your complaint more seriously. *Lemon-Aid* is unique in supplying this data.

Manufacturers' service bulletins listed in this section give the most probable cause of factory-related defects on 1999 models. These problems are often carried over several years, since manufacturers depend on dealer corrections outlined in their bulletins until a permanent, cost-effective engineering solution is found at the factory. In the meantime, owners can be charged for repairs, particularly if they can be convinced that the repair falls under normal maintenance.

Service bulletins cut down troubleshooting time considerably. In emergencies, independent mechanics can go right to the source of the trouble if dealer servicing is unavailable, incompetent, or just plain hostile. You can also get warranty repairs done more easily if you jog the dealer's memory with a service bulletin that shows a problem is factory-related and therefore not part of routine maintenance. Finally, bulletins are great tools for getting consequential compensation, including lost wages or money spent on towing, renting a car, or for an interrupted vacation.

Many of the bulletins listed in this edition come from American sources and may differ from Canadian bulletins where the parts numbers are concerned. Nevertheless, the problems and defects they treat are exactly the same on both sides of the border. Some cars have more DSBs than others, but this doesn't mean they're lemons—listed problems may affect only a small number of vehicles, or may be minor in nature and easily corrected. DSBs should also be used to verify that a problem was correctly diagnosed, the correct upgraded replacement part was used, and the billed labour time was fair.

Road performance

The main factors considered in this rating are acceleration and torque, transmission operation, routine handling, emergency handling, steering, and braking.

Every vehicle must be able to merge safely onto a highway and have adequate passing power for two-lane roads. Steering feel and handling should inspire confidence. The suspension ought to provide a reasonably well-controlled ride on most road surfaces. The passenger compartment, ideally, will be roomy enough to accommodate passengers comfortably on extended trips. The noise level inside the vehicle should not become tiresome and annoying. As a rule, handling and ride comfort are inversely proportional. Variations from this pattern are reflected in the ratings.

Comfort/convenience
Here we rate a vehicle based on the level of standard equipment, driving position, controls and displays, climate control, the ease of entry/exit, front and rear interior space/comfort, cargo space, trunk space and liftover, and interior quietness.

Driving pleasure is hard to define, but a cramped interior, controls that are hard to see or reach, poor climate control systems, and excessive engine, road, and wind noise can turn that pleasure into a distressing experience.

This edition points out possible deficiencies that you should check out in the showroom and during the test drive. Obvious deficiencies that aren't questioned at the time of sale are deemed to have been accepted by the customer, and cannot be used later to cancel that sale or to obtain a partial refund.

Cost
This edition lists the estimated manufacturer's suggested retail price (MSRP) applicable to the standard-equipped model, whether that price is firm or negotiable, the range of the dealer's markup, and the vehicle's estimated residual value over the next five years.

Manufacturers usually increase prices a few times during the year (although this year the major American automakers claim they won't raise prices), and these increases may boost prices 2 to 6 percent above those listed in this edition. If this happens, ask the dealer to show you the manufacturer's notice of the price increase. Space limitations do not allow the printing of every price for all of a particular model's levels of powertrain or trims, but there is a solid representation.

With all the attention given to the so-called "no haggle" sticker prices, keep in mind that there's a substantial gap between the cost of the vehicle to the dealer and the manufacturer's suggested retail price (the "sticker" price). This difference represents the dealer's markup or gross profit, and is usually augmented by other incentive programs and holdbacks that can add another 2 to 3 percent. To help you negotiate the best price, this edition indicates those prices that are firm and those that are negotiable, and gives the approximate price markup percentage in parentheses.

Keep in mind that the markup percentages can fluctuate considerably depending on the availability of dealer or customer rebates or the popularity of certain models. Some Volvo and Honda dealers will insist upon selling at full price, for example, because they know that their cars are so popular that they don't have to cut prices. Toyota dealers, on the other hand, have done the unthinkable and are selling their popular 1999 cars for thousands of dollars less than last year's models.

Residual values apply to the worth of the vehicle after a lease expires. These values can be a comparative guide to depreciation over the next five years if you plan to sell your car privately.

Destination charges and the PDI fee are outrageous $500–700 add-ons that you shouldn't pay. In fact, Infiniti dealers have been ordered by Nissan/Infiniti to forego both the delivery and preparation charges on 1999 models, and Land Rover has these costs built into the selling price (where they belong). If you get tired of haggling with the dealer, agree to pay no more than 1 percent of a vehicle's MSRP for these extra charges.

Technical data

Technical data and specifications are taken from the automakers' press kits. There's a huge amount of technical information to be presented in a limited amount of space. I welcome comments about the technical information that's most important to you and that you'd like to see in next year's edition. My mailing, fax, and email addresses are listed in Appendix VI.

Towing capacities differ depending on the kind of powertrain/suspension package or towing package you buy. Remember that there's a difference between how a vehicle is rated for cargo capacity or payload, and how heavy a boat or trailer it can pull. Do not purchase any new vehicle without receiving very clear information, in writing, about a vehicle's towing capacity and the kind of special equipment you'll need to meet your requirements. Have both the towing capacity and the necessary equipment written into your contract.

In the ratings, cargo capacity is expressed in cubic feet with the rear seat up. With the rear seat folded or removed, cargo capacity obviously becomes quite larger.

Safety features

Some of the main features weighed in the safety ratings are a model's crashworthiness and claims history (as assessed by the NHTSA and various insurers' groups, including the Highway Loss Data Institute and the Insurance Institute for Highway Safety), and the availability of such safety features as depowered airbags, airbag disablers, anti-lock brakes (rear-wheel-only systems aren't as effective as four-wheel ABS), integrated child safety seats, head restraints, traction control, and front and rearward visibility.

In addition to a listing for each model rated in Part Three, a two-year summary of U.S. government crash-test results can be found in Appendix IV. Crash protection figures are taken from the NHTSA's New Car Assessment Program. Vehicles are crashed into a fixed barrier, head-on, at 57 km/h (35 mph) to evaluate the effects of the consequent forces exerted on specially constructed dummies placed in the two front seats. Some 1997–99 models may have been tested for side impact protection as well. The latest results—even if several years old—have been included in the ratings.

The NHTSA shows a vehicle's level of crashworthiness by the likelihood, expressed as a percentage, of the belted occupants being seriously injured. The higher the number of stars, the greater the protection:

NHTSA Front Collision Ratings

★★★★★	— a 10% or less chance of serious injury
★★★★	— a 10% to 20% chance of serious injury
★★★	— a 20% to 35% chance of serious injury
★★	— a 35% to 45% chance of serious injury
★	— more than a 45% chance of serious injury

NHTSA tests don't necessarily provide an accurate picture of how a given model will perform in every accident; test figures are only valid if they're used to compare vehicles that are of the same size (i.e., small, midsize, or large). It's also unfortunate that vehicles aren't tested twice to confirm the validity of the first test.

Mercedes-Benz, proud of its reputation for building crashworthy cars, hasn't always fared well in the NHTSA head-on collisions, and questions the validity of the ratings. The company claims that its own crash data show that most frontal collisions occur at an angle (offset), and that that's the kind of test wherein its cars excel. The Insurance Institute for Highway Safety (IIHS) sides with Mercedes, and crash-tests its own vehicles at an angle and at 64 km/h (40 mph). The NHTSA doesn't do front offset testing, but it has tested some 1997–99 models for side-impact protection. Those test results can also be found in Appendix IV.

NHTSA Side Collision Ratings

★★★★★	— a 5% or less chance of serious injury
★★★★	— a 6% to 10% chance of serious injury
★★★	— an 11% to 20% chance of serious injury
★★	— a 21% to 25% chance of serious injury
★	— more than a 26% chance of serious injury

The laws of physics dictate that a larger and heavier vehicle will provide better crash protection than a smaller one, and that injuries vary substantially according to the angle of impact. For example, twice as many deaths occur in small cars as opposed to large cars. Furthermore, the frequency of damage claims for small, two-door cars is 35 percent higher than for large two-door cars. The same holds true for four-door cars. Midsize four-door cars generally have lower driver death rates and insurance claims history for injuries, compared with the average for all cars. This is not only the case when a small car hits a larger vehicle. In single-car crashes, the death rate for occupants of small cars is more than double the rate for large cars.

American Vehicles
CHRYSLER

Dammit, I like Chrysler. I know the company is capable of building top-quality vehicles and selling them at reasonable prices, as it once did with the Valiant, Dart, rear-drive New Yorker, and the whole slew of "muscle" machines we all longed for as we went through puberty.

Problem is, Chrysler has forgotten its roots.

Instead, it's making tons of money building stylish, roomy, poor-quality cars and minivans (but reasonably reliable trucks and full-sized vans). In fact, most of the recent higher-quality cars it once sold, like the Colt and Stealth, were merely re-badged Mitsubishis that have since been dropped. Presently, your best choices for Japanese quality in a so-called Chrysler product are the '98 Talon, Avenger, and Sebring.

The '99 Avenger: a winning combination of Japanese quality and Chrysler marketing.

Chrysler is hoping its merger with Daimler will return it as a force in the passenger-car side of the market, a niche where the automaker has had declining sales for more than a decade. Chrysler held a 20.9 percent share of car sales in 1983 and was ranked number two in Canada. Last year, it took fourth place, with sales representing only an 11.8 percent share. I have my doubts that the Daimler merger will improve the overall quality and reliability of Chrysler's cars and minivans (or boost Chrysler sales, for that matter). It didn't work with Saab when GM took them over, Ford's Jaguar acquisition hasn't been all that successful, and after Chrysler bought out American Motors, its approach to improving AMC quality was to dump most of the company's models (remember the Encore?).

Quality problems likely to continue

There are no signs whatsoever that Chrysler's poor quality control has been addressed in its '99 model cars and minivans, judging by the automaker's own service bulletins and press statements.

		DSB Summary: 1998 Chrysler Caravan
1.	SEP-97	BACKLIGHT WATER LEAKS
2.	DEC-97	BCM AUTO HEADLAMP SENSOR/SIGNAL CIRCUIT DTC
3.	OCT-97	CUSTOMER SATISFACTION NOTIFICATION #743-OWNERS MANUAL
4.	DEC-97	GASKET SURFACE PREPARATION ON ALUMINUM ENGINE COMPONENTS
5.	DEC-97	HONK NOISE DURING LOW SPEED MANEUVERS
6.	DEC-97	IMPROPER COOLING FAN RELAY ACTUATION
7.	OCT-97	INTERMITTENT MOMENTARY LOSS OF POWER ASSIST
8.	DEC-97	INTERMITTENT POPPING IN FRONT END
9.	SEP-97	NHTSA AUTHOSIZED AIRBAG DEACTIVATION/MEDICAL NECESSITY
10.	NOV-97	POOR DRIVEABILITY WITH HIGH D1 FUEL
11.	NOV-97	REMOTE KEYLESS TRANSMITTER BATTERY FAILURE
12.	FEB-98	SAFETY RECALL #762-INT. CHILD SEAT SHOULDER BELT ROUTING
13.	DEC-97	SEAT BACK CREAK NOISE DRIVERS SIDE
14.	NOV-97	SERVICE MANUAL REVISION
15.	OCT-97	THUMPING NOISE AT REAR OF VEHICLE DURING COLD OPERATIONS
16.	FEB-98	TRANSAXLE DESENSITIZATION TO INTERMITTENT FAULTS
17.	DEC-97	UNDERBODY CREAK OR KNOCK SOUND
18.	SEP-97	WATER LEAKS ONTO FLOOR FROM HVAC HOUSING

American vehicles

C'mon Chrysler, improve quality across the board and you won't need a special Warranty Review Committee to placate angry owners.

This is unfortunate—it means Chrysler bean-counters still reign supreme.

Five years ago, the automaker's cost-cutters came up with the not-so-bright idea that the company could save millions of dollars by cutting its base warranty down to 3 years/80,000 km, selling the previous seven-year protection for up to $1,000 extra (now sometimes as high as $1,400), and squeezing supplier prices, even if quality was compromised. Chrysler complied, and as a result has boasted both record-breaking profits during the past three years and a steady stream of complaints from disgruntled owners.

Since the warranty was shortened, most Chrysler products have finished at the bottom of most of the J. D. Power quality and customer satisfaction surveys, and, in light of the shorter warranty and member complaints, *Consumer Reports* says the company's midsize cars are no longer recommended. Other Chrysler vehicles have been similarly downgraded.

Now let's look at what Chrysler's failure-prone components mean from a dollar-and-cents standpoint. Automatic transmission failure—$3,000; paint delamination—$3,000; AC replacement—$1,500; and ABS failure—$1,500. That's a total potential cost during the first five years of $9,000. Now you understand why I don't recommend most Chrysler products unless they're covered by an optional, comprehensive warranty.

LHS, 300M

LHS

RATING: Not Recommended during the first model year. They really aren't new models; they're more a nicely packaged depository of generic components used on other Chrysler vehicles. This means they will have generic Chrysler-type problems in addition to traditional first-year model snafus. **Strong points:** Attractive styling, good acceleration and handling, plenty of passenger and cargo room, standard four-wheel ABS and traction control, and reasonable price. The LHS also has a large trunk with a wide opening. **Weak points:** Rough-running engine, excessive road and wind noise, five-passenger capacity, the 300M has limited rear legroom, narrow rear windshield reduces rear visibility and carries a smaller trunk with a smaller opening than the LHS, no side airbags, mediocre fit and finish, and questionable reliability.

NEW FOR '99: Entirely new models, costing $40,900 and $38,995, respectively.

GENERAL COMMENTS: These two models are, respectively, the near-luxury and the sport clones of the Chrysler Concorde and Dodge Intrepid. Although they use the same front-drive platform as the Concorde, their bodies are shorter and they're styled differently. In fact, the 300M is the shortest of Chrysler's midsize sedans.

Both cars are powered by a 253-hp 3.5L V6 and mated to Chrysler's AutoStick semi-automatic transmission. Braking is better than average. Opt for the handling package and you get crisper steering response, better brakes and tires, and stiffer springs that eliminate much of the body roll.

Only a few months after launching these cars this summer, Chrysler made engineering changes to reduce noise and vibration and smooth out what was thought to be an overly harsh ride. Automatic headlights were added as well. Owners have also complained of an annoying reflection on the inside of the windshield, particularly evident on vehicles with beige interiors. **Alternatives:** Acura RL, Audi A6, Lexus GS 300, and Toyota Avalon.

Prowler

Prowler

RATING: Recommended. Neither service bulletins nor owner comments show any problems. **Strong points:** Attractive styling, good acceleration and handling, reasonably priced, and slow to depreciate. **Weak points:** ABS is unavailable, limited visibility, difficult entry/exit, limited storage space, and the car shakes, rattles, and rolls like Elvis.

NEW FOR '99: There wasn't a 1998 model Prowler. However, it returns this year with a new 253-hp 3.5L V6 engine, an additional colour (yellow), an airbag cut-off switch, and side airbags.

GENERAL COMMENTS: This aluminum and plastic, rear-drive, two-seat, convertible isn't for introverts. With a $55,500 U.S. base price, the Prowler, much like the Viper (another head-turner), is one of Chrysler's most unusual cars. Despite its racy styling, the Prowler's no high-performance muscle car, even though it posts impressive 0–100 km/h acceleration times. The 4-speed automatic comes with AutoStick (also available on the Vision, Intrepid, and Stratus), which allows you to shift the transmission as you would with a manual gearbox. On climbs it prevents the transmission from changing gears back and forth, and on the downhill you can keep the car in a lower gear to prevent picking up excess speed.

On the downside, the Prowler has a kidney-pounding, stiff ride; no trunk (you have to buy an optional purple mini-trailer); no spare tire; and room only for two—as long as they're not too tall. **Alternatives:** Mercedes-Benz SLK230, Chevrolet Corvette convertible, and Porsche Boxster.

Viper

RATING: Recommended. **Strong points:** Good acceleration and handling. **Weak points:** No ABS, rapid depreciation, poor fuel economy, and passenger comfort is compromised by excessive wind noise. Only a hundred or so Vipers have been allocated to Canada.

NEW FOR '99: The Dodge Viper RT/10 and GTS coupe returns this year with 18-inch wheels, an additional colour (black) and minor interior refinements.

GENERAL COMMENTS: This red-hot $90,610, midsize, two-door, rear-drive roadster breaks all the marketing rules—and wins. Basically a limited production of less than 500 a year (only 303 were built in 1994), its awesome 450-hp 8.0L V10 engine, 6-speed manual gearbox and "in your face" styling aren't equalled by any other vehicle in its class. It also features depowered airbags and an airbag cut-off switch. Interestingly, service bulletins and owner comments paint a positive picture of the Viper's overall dependability. **Alternatives:** Acura NSX, Chevrolet Corvette, and Porsche Boxster.

Neon

RATING: Below Average. **Strong points:** Good acceleration and handling; optional ABS. **Weak points:** Imprecise manual shifter, clunky 3-speed automatic, mediocre braking, and excessive engine, road, and body noise.

NEW FOR '99: Depowered airbags are now offered on all Neons. The year 2000 Neon will go on sale early in 1999. Its main attribute will be a platform that is five inches shorter, potentially compromising both ride and handling.

GENERAL COMMENTS: Traditionally, Chrysler competed in the subcompact class by re-badging Mitsubishi-built cars and selling them under Chrysler nameplates. Now, with the Neon, it has a home-grown competitor that's roomy and reasonably powered. Interior room is where the Neon shines, though, with front and rear seating that easily accommodates six-footers.

Cost analysis/alternatives: Get the '99 version later in the model year. It should be deeply discounted, once the redesigned and costlier new model arrives. Other cars worth considering are the Ford Escort, Geo Metro, Honda Civic, Mazda Protegé and Toyota Corolla. If you're in the market for the sport coupe, make sure that you also check out the '98 Nissan 200SX, SE-R, and the VW Golf GTi. **Recommended options:** Built-in child safety seats (if available) and height adjustment for the steering wheel (for short drivers). Don't invest in the optional 150-hp 4-banger—you'll get just as much noise and not much more power. ABS is another option that hasn't got the bugs worked out yet. **Rebates:** $1,000–$1,500 rebates. **Destination charge:** $600. **Depreciation:** About average. **Insurance cost:** Average. **Parts supply/cost:** Average. **Annual maintenance cost:** Higher than average. **Warranty:** Bumper-to-bumper 3 years/60,000 km; rust perforation 5 years/160,000 km. **Supplementary warranty:** Don't buy a Neon without extra protection. **Highway/city fuel economy:** 6–9L/100 km with the base 2.0L engine, and 7–11L/100 km with the high-output powerplant. Owners say that real-world fuel economy is far less than what's hyped, so be wary of Chrysler's fuel economy claims, which are different than the figures listed above.

Quality/Reliability/Safety

Pro: Reinforced doors meet tough U.S. federal side-impact standards. Front adjustable shoulder belt anchors.

Con: Quality control: It may take longer than the base warranty's three-year limit to correct the Neon's many problems, notably its powertrain, electrical system, and body deficiencies. *Consumer Reports* says that its member survey found that first-year (1995 model) Neons had nearly twice the problems of the average 1995 model car. **Reliability:** When *Autoweek,* an American car enthusiast magazine, tested a '96 Neon Sport Coupe with only 16,566 miles (26,506 km) on the odometer for its March 4th edition, it concluded that "aliens" had invaded the test car. Some of the magazine's "close encounters": a raggedy shifter, premature front brake pad wear, excessive brake fade, a rumbling noise coming from under the car, distorted sound coming from the cassette player, frozen windshield wipers, and a defroster that won't clear the windshield or side windows and that produces a wheezing noise when operating. **Warranty performance:** Chrysler's shortened warranty is far from reassuring when one considers how tough Chrysler has been in interpreting its warranty obligations, and that most powertrain problems occur after the third year of ownership. Fortunately, you can always appeal any warranty repair refusal to the company's Review Committee (see Appendix V). **Owner-reported problems:** A perusal of owner comments confirms that these cars continue to have lots of serious factory-related defects, including an air-conditioning system that often requires expensive servicing, lots of interior noise and leaks, interior window film buildup, exposed screw heads, and uneven fit and finish, and poor-quality trim items that break or fall off easily. The finish isn't as good as most other subcompacts, either; the thickness of the coat varies considerably and will chip easily. **Service bulletin problems:** Steering wheel, column clunks and rattles; front brake squeaks and groans (see following page); front suspension and creaking; erratic tachometer; remote keyless transmitter battery failure; vehicle overheats and radiator fan inoperative, or runs continuously.

NO: 05-10-97
GROUP: Brakes
DATE: Dec. 19, 1997
SUBJECT:
Front Brake Squeal And/Or Creep/Groan
MODELS:
1995–1998 (PL) Neon
NOTE:
THIS BULLETIN APPLIES TO VEHICLES WITH 14" DISC/DRUM (SALES CODE BRA AND BRJ).
SYMPTOM/CONDITION:
Front brake squeal moderate brake pedal application, or creep/groan sound during zero speed creeping brake apply.
DIAGNOSIS:
1. Drive the vehicle at 10 to 20 MPH, with moderate pressure apply the brakes. If a squeal sound is heard perform the Repair Procedure.
2. With the brake pedal applied, place the transmission in "drive" and slowly release the brakes until the vehicle just begins to creep. If a loud grinding, crunching, or groaning noise is heard from the front brakes, perform the Repair Procedure.
PARTS REQUIRED:
1   05011069AA   Pad Set, Front Disc Brake
REPAIR PROCEDURE:
This bulletin involves the replacement of the front brake pads.
1. Remove and replace the front brake pads following the repair procedure provided in the appropriate Neon Service Manual, Group 5.
POLICY:
Reimbursable within the provisions of the warranty.
TIME ALLOWANCE:
Labor Operation No: 05-70-22-90   0.5 Hrs.
FAILURE CODE: P8 New Part

This is definitely a warranty repair. Don't let the dealer convince you it's a maintenance item.

NHTSA safety complaints/safety: Airbags fail to deploy or deploy inadvertently; Michelin tires fail prematurely; engine headgasket, intake manifold, front-end suspension, and drivetrain failure; front and rear head restraints are set too low; headlight switch is a "hide-and-go-seek" affair.

Road Performance

Pro: Better than average acceleration (0–100 km/h: 8.6 sec.) with plenty of low-end torque. The 2.0L engine's 132 horses and the Neon's low weight give it acceptable performance in lower gear ranges, but restricts it to mainly urban use. **Emergency handling:** Better than average. **Steering:** Precise and easy to control on smooth roads.

Con: Acceleration/torque: Base engine runs out of steam in high gear and is buzzy from 4,000 rpm on up. It runs particularly roughly after 5,000 rpm. This is especially irritating because horsepower and torque peak at 5,000 and 6,000 rpm. The optional 150-hp 4-cylinder engine isn't much better. Throttle "jerk" in traffic when you barely press the accelerator is probably caused by faulty fuel-injector calibration, because it can also be felt at cruising speed when the accelerator is depressed slightly. **Transmission:** The manual transmission is harsh and noisy—no comparison with Honda and Toyota vehicles. The manual gearbox also requires lots of downshifting when going over small hills. The 3-speed automatic transmission lacks sufficient torque in high gear, and shifts abruptly and often. The car cries out for the more economical and efficient 4-speed electronic transmission. **Routine handling:** The jittery ride becomes fairly rough when traversing anything but the smoothest roads. Ride deteriorates and the suspension bottoms with a vengeance with a full load. **Braking:** Worse than average (100–0 km/h: 143 ft.).

Comfort/Convenience

Pro: Driving position: Good driving position. **Controls and displays:** Easy-to-operate controls and clear gauges. Easy-to-use and effective heating-and-ventilation system (except for the defroster) that's illuminated at night. **Climate control:** Everything's within easy reach and easily read. **Entry/exit:** Good. Large door openings for long legs. **Interior space/comfort F/R:** The Neon seats five adults and has a spacious interior. Practical cloth bucket seats. Seats are firmer and more comfortable than one would expect. Plenty of leg room, head room, and elbow room. Rear seat is roomy enough for three adults. Rear seatbacks can be folded down to increase trunk space. **Cargo space:** Lots of little storage areas. **Trunk/liftover:** Versatile though narrow trunk with a low sill.

Con: Standard equipment: Low-quality interior appointments. Doormounted power window switches press uncomfortably against the driver's leg. Hard-to-access rear seat doesn't provide enough thigh support. Inadequate rear toe space. No locks for the inside trunk release or seatback sections that give access to the trunk. Hard-to-operate window cranks and only the front windows are power-assisted. Short, flimsy trunk lid restricts trunk access. **Quietness:** Noise, noise everywhere—engine boom, automatic transmission whine, air leaks through the frameless windows, tire thumping, road rumbling, and rattling front-seat shoulder harness mountings.

COST

List Price (negotiable)	Residual Values (months)			
	24	36	48	60
Base Neon 2d: $15,775 (12%)	$8500	$6500	$5000	$3500

TECHNICAL DATA

Powertrain (front-drive)
Engines: 2.0L 4-cyl. (132 hp)
• 2.0L 4-cyl. (150 hp)
Transmissions: 5-speed man. OD
• 3-speed auto.
Dimensions
Passengers: 5
Height/length/width:
53/171.8/67.5 in.

Head room F/R: 39.6/36.5 in.
Leg room F/R: 42.5/35.1 in.
Wheelbase: 104 in.
Cargo capacity: 42.6 cu. ft.
Towing capacity: 1,000 lbs.
Fuel tank: 47L/reg.
Weight: 2,400 lbs.

SAFETY FEATURES

	Std.	Opt.
Anti-lock brakes	❏	■
Seatbelt pretensioners	—	—
Integrated child safety seat	—	■
Airbag cut-off switch	—	—
Depowered airbags	■	❏
Side airbags	—	—
Traction control	—	—
Visibility (front/rear)	*****	*****
Crash protection D/P	***	****
Crash protection (side) D/P	**	***
HLDI injury claims	High	

Avenger/Sebring

Sebring

RATING: Above Average. **Strong points:** Comfortable ride, adequate interior room, and optional ABS. **Weak points:** No manual transmission with the V6, mediocre engine performance, lots of engine and road noise.

NEW FOR '99: Nothing much has changed this year on the Avenger, except for the 4-cylinder ES getting a sway bar, new 16-inch wheels and depowered airbags. Sebring gets depowered airbags, as well, plus an improved four-wheel ABS system offered with the traction control package.

GENERAL COMMENTS: The Avenger and its more luxuriously appointed Sebring twin are good buys mainly because they've had fewer new-model "teething" problems than other Chrysler-built compacts. Sebring is a reasonably priced luxury coupe equipped with standard amenities, including AC, bucket seats, and a tilt steering wheel, while the Avenger fills the sports coupe niche with standard tinted glass and an awesome sound system.

Except for the convertible version, these front-drive replacements for the failure-prone Dodge Daytona and LeBaron coupes are built in Normal, Illinois, in the same factory that produces the Talon. They share many safety features and mechanical components with the Talon, including standard dual airbags and a 140-hp 2.0L twin cam 4-cylinder engine. High-performance ES versions are powered by a 164-hp 2.5L V6 coupled to an electronically controlled 4-speed automatic transaxle.

The convertible, made in Mexico, is six inches longer than the Sebring coupe and is powered by a standard 2.0L twin cam, while the upscale JXi gets a performance injection with the 2.5L 6-cylinder powerplant coupled to an AutoStick transaxle, 4-wheel disc brakes, ABS, and traction control.

Cost analysis/alternatives: The 1999 Avenger and Sebring shouldn't cost more than last year's models. Avenger shoppers should take a look at other sporty coupes, including the Honda Accord and Toyota Celica. Convertibles worth a glance: Ford Mustang and Chevrolet Camaro. **Recommended options:** These cars come well-appointed. **Rebates:** $1,000 rebates on the '98s. **Destination charge:** $350. **Depreciation:** Much slower than average. **Insurance cost:** Average. **Parts supply/cost:** Even though these cars have only been on the market for a few years, reasonably priced parts are easily found. **Annual maintenance cost:** Average. **Warranty:** Bumper-to-bumper 3 years/60,000 km; rust perforation 5 years/160,000 km. **Supplementary warranty:** Not essential, due to Mitsubishi's high quality and above average body construction. **Highway/city fuel economy:** 6.8–10.7L/100 km with the base 4-cylinder; 8–12L/100 km with the V6.

Quality/Reliability/Safety

Pro: Quality control: Quality control is unusually good, thanks to Mitsubishi. Body construction and assembly are solid, with few gaps. **Service bulletin problems:** Nothing significant (see, I told you these were pretty reliable cars). **Owner-reported problems:** No major problems reported, yet. **Reliability:** Better than average. **Warranty performance:** Average. This may be because these cars haven't been on the market very long. Remember, you can always appeal any warranty repair refusal to the company's Review Committee (see Appendix V).

Con: NHTSA Safety complaints/safety: Space-saver spare tire is only good for a few miles and at slow speeds; electrical system fire; seatbelts too tight.

Road Performance

Pro: Acceleration/torque: Adequate, but far from sporty acceleration (0–100 km/h: 10 sec. with the V6). The base 4-cylinder is thrifty and adequate for most driving tasks. It works well with both the manual and automatic transmission. **Transmission:** Smooth and quiet operation in all gear ranges. **Routine handling:** Handling is exceptional with either engine, and there's little body lean when cornering under speed. The ride deteriorates only slightly on bad surfaces due to the car's compliant suspension. Jarring is reduced as the weight of passengers is added. **Emergency handling:** Better than average. **Steering:** Steering is responsive and light.

Con: The base 2.0L engine loses power when mated to the 4-speed automatic and, when pushed, it's noisy and less responsive than the V6. Unfortunately the V6 doesn't come with a manual gearbox, so its extra power doesn't translate into performance thrills. Some front-end plow in turns. The car's large turning circle makes parking a chore. **Braking:** Unimpressive (100–0 km/h: 141 ft.).

Comfort/Convenience

Pro: Standard equipment: Well-appointed with many standard features. **Interior space/comfort F/R:** The rear seat area is more adult-friendly than most sport coupes. Three tall passengers can sit in the rear for short trips, but the seating is really designed for two. **Controls and displays:** Controls and gauges are easily reached and seen. **Entry/exit:** Large doors facilitate entry and exit. **Cargo space:** Limited trunk cargo area can be extended by folding the split seatback. **Trunk/liftover:** Average trunk space with a low liftover. Rear seatback and remote trunk release can be locked.

Con: Driving position: Front seats need additional lateral support, and the seatback bulge is annoying to some drivers. The tilt steering wheel is set too low (almost in the driver's lap). Short drivers may have difficulty with forward vision, even with the seat raised to its maximum setting. **Climate control:** The climate control system is hampered by a noisy fan and uneven air distribution. The rear defroster leaves some of the glass untouched. With rear-quarter windows that won't open and the optional rear deck-lid spoiler cutting rear visibility, it's not hard to feel a bit claustrophobic. **Quietness:** Excessive tire/road noise intrudes into the passenger compartment.

COST				
List Price (negotiable)	**Residual Values** (months)			
	24	36	48	60
Base Avenger: $19,180 (15%)	$13,000	$11,000	$9500	$8000

TECHNICAL DATA	
Powertrain (front-drive)	Head room F/R: 37.6/36.5 in.
Engines: 2.0L 4-cyl. (140 hp)	Leg room F/R: 43.3/35 in.
• 2.5L V6 (163 hp)	Wheelbase: 103.7 in.
Transmissions: 5-speed man.	Cargo capacity: 13.1 cu. ft.
• 4-speed auto.	Towing capacity: 1,000 lbs.

Dimensions	Fuel tank: 60L/reg.
Passengers: 5	Weight: 3,000 lbs.
Height/length/width:	
53.3/187.2/69.1 in.	

SAFETY FEATURES

	Std.	Opt.
Anti-lock brakes	■	■
Seatbelt pretensioners	—	—
Integrated child safety seat	❑	■
Airbag cut-off switch	—	—
Depowered airbags	■	❑
Side airbags	—	—
Traction control	■	❑
Visibility (front/rear)	****	*****
Crash protection D/P	*****	*****
Crash protection (side) D/P	N/A	
HLDI injury claims	Average	

Talon ('98)

Talon

RATING: Recommended. **Strong points:** Impressive acceleration and handling, reasonably priced, durable, and a high resale value. **Weak points:** ABS is optional, limited rear visibility and rear interior room, Chrysler has a lousy warranty performance.

NEW FOR '99: 1998 was the Talon's last model year.

GENERAL COMMENTS: A twin of the Mitsubishi Eclipse, this front-drive, Japanese-American hybrid is a high-performance, sporty two-seater made in Illinois by Diamond Star Motors, a joint venture of Mitsubishi and Chrysler. The ESi comes with a 140-hp 2.0L engine (borrowed from the Neon Sport), and the TSi is powered by a 205-hp 2.0L Mitsubishi-bred engine. A turbocharged version of the same engine rated at 210 hp is also available. A manual 5-speed is standard, and an optional 4-speed automatic is available on all models except the Turbo RS.

All high-performance models cost thousands of dollars less than the Japanese competition, without compromising quality or performance. The 16-valve Talon 4X4 is at the top of the trim list and provides five horses more than the turbocharged TSi.

Cost analysis/alternatives: '98 versions may be hard to find now that word is out that this is the car's final model year. Other cars worth considering are the Ford Mustang, GM Camaro and Firebird, '98 Nissan 240SX, and Toyota Celica and '98 Supra. The Toyota Celica AWD Turbo is the best alternative to the Talon AWD. **Recommended options:** The turbo's extra horses aren't that significant and exact a 10 percent fuel penalty. **Rebates:** $2,000 rebates on the '98s. **Destination charge:** $375. **Depreciation:** Slower than average. **Insurance cost:** About average. **Parts supply/cost:** Parts aren't hard to find but the CAA says they're a bit more expensive than average. **Annual maintenance cost:** Less than average. **Warranty:** Bumper-to-bumper 3 years/60,000 km; rust perforation 5 years/160,000 km. **Supplementary warranty:** Not necessary. **Highway/city fuel economy:** 7–11L/100 km (non-turbo) and 9–12L/100 km on turbo-equipped AWD Talons.

Quality/Reliability/Safety

Pro: Quality control: Better than average. **Reliability:** Mitsubishi products have a reliability record that's above average. Fit and finish are beyond reproach. The AWD system provides sure-footed foul weather stability. **Owner-reported problems:** No serious problems reported. **NHTSA safety complaints/safety:** Nothing recorded.

Con: Warranty performance: Chrysler dealers may not be capable of adequately servicing these high-tech vehicles. Remember, you can always report any repair that was incompetently performed or appeal a warranty repair refusal to the company's Review Committee (see Appendix V). **Service bulletin problems:** Excessive brake noise.

Road Performance

Pro: Acceleration/torque: Impressively fast (0–100 km/h: 7.2 sec.). The base 16-valve 2.0L engine is quite powerful, but the optional 16-valve, turbocharged version gives more horsepower for the dollar than any other front-drive sports coupe, without any irritating turbo lag. **Transmission:** The 5-speed manual is the gearbox of choice, especially with its shorter shift stroke and comfortable feel. **Routine handling:** Very good. **Emergency handling:** Excellent. **Steering:** Very predictable and easy to control, as long as you aren't in a turbocharged version. **Braking:** Excellent (100–0 km/h: 117 ft.).

Con: Torque steer makes the car appear to try to twist out of your hands when all 210 turbocharged horses are unleashed.

Comfort/Convenience

Pro: Driving position: Excellent ergonomics, highlighted by a wraparound dash. **Controls and displays:** Good, old-fashioned analog gauges are easy to read and the controls are easy to adjust. Dashboard air vents provide excellent ventilation. Quiet riding, rattle-free construction. **Cargo space:** Lots of small storage spaces. **Quietness:** Fairly quiet. **Climate control:** Efficient, quiet, and easy to calibrate. **Standard equipment:** Loaded with standard features.

Con: Entry/exit: Difficult to get in or out of. Driving position is set too low and seats are a bit hard. **Interior space/comfort F/R:** Cramped interior has limited rear room. **Trunk/liftover:** Small, shallow trunk with a high sill.

COST

List Price (negotiable)	Residual Values (months)			
	24	**36**	**48**	**60**
'98 Talon DL: $19,885 (15%)	$8500	$7000	$6000	$5000

TECHNICAL DATA

Powertrain (front-drive)
Engines: 2.0L 4-cyl. (140 hp)
• 2.0L 4-cyl. turbo (205 hp)
• 2.0L 4-cyl. turbo (210 hp)
Transmissions: 5-speed man.
Dimensions
Passengers: 4
Height/length/width:
51.6/174.8/69.9 in.

Head room F/R: 37.9/34.1 in.
Leg room F/R: 43.3/28.4 in.
Wheelbase: 98.8 in.
Cargo capacity: 13.5 cu. ft.
Towing capacity: N/A.
Fuel tank: 64L/reg.
Weight: 2,729 lbs.

SAFETY FEATURES

	Std.	Opt.
Anti-lock brakes	❏	■
Seatbelt pretensioners	—	—
Integrated child safety seat	—	—
Airbag cut-off switch	—	—
Depowered airbags	■	❏
Side airbags	—	—
Traction control	❏	■
Visibility (front/rear)	*****	*****
Crash protection D/P	****	****
Crash protection (side) D/P	N/A	
HLDI injury claims	High	

Breeze/Cirrus/Stratus

Cirrus

RATING: Average. **Strong points:** Plenty of passenger room, well appointed, and excellent handling. **Weak points:** Cirrus airbags aren't depowered, insufficient 2.0L engine torque, and poor quality workmanship.

NEW FOR '99: Breeze: This year's model returns relatively unchanged. **Cirrus:** Standard four-wheel disc brakes for the LXI, easier-to-read instrument cluster graphics, and an upgraded suspension to reduce noise, vibration, and a harsh ride. **Stratus:** Revised instrument panel, new interior fabric, upgraded wheels, and a retuned suspension that improves handling and reduces noise, vibration, and harshness.

GENERAL COMMENTS: The Chrysler Cirrus and Dodge Stratus are identical midsize, front-drive sedans. The Cirrus LXi comes loaded with standard features that include AC, leather-trimmed interior with adjustable driver's seat, ABS, an upgraded sound system with cassette player, tilt steering, cruise control, and plenty of power-assisted accessories. Breeze, Plymouth's entry-level version, offers an optional 2.4L 4-cylinder engine, but won't carry the V6 in order to keep its base price low. Most of these cars' components have been used for some time on other Chrysler models, particularly the Neon subcompact and Avenger/Sebring sports coupes.

Power is supplied by three engines: a 2.0L 4-cylinder engine shared with the Neon powers the Stratus, while a base 2.4L 4-banger and optional 2.5L V6, used by the Avenger, propels the high-performance Cirrus and Stratus ES. Carrying Chrysler's "cab forward" design a step further up the evolutionary ladder, these cars have short rear decks, low noses, and massive sloping grilles. A wheelbase that's two inches longer than the Ford Taurus' makes both cars comfortable for five occupants, with wide door openings and plenty of trunk space.

Cost analysis/alternatives: Get the '99 Cirrus and Stratus for their upgrades; the '98 and '99 Breeze models are identical, so buy whichever one is cheapest. Other vehicles worth considering: Ford Taurus/Sable, Honda Accord, Toyota Camry, and Volvo S70 or V70. Recommended options: The 2.5L V6 and an integrated child safety seat for the rear centre seat. Rebates: $1,000 rebates on the '98s. Destination charge: $375. Depreciation: Slower than average. Insurance costs: A bit higher than average. Annual maintenance cost: Higher than average. Warranty: Bumper-to-bumper 3 years/60,000 km; rust perforation 5 years/160,000 km. Supplementary warranty: Essential. Invest the money you saved in buying a '98 model on an extended seven-year warranty. Highway/city fuel economy: 8–12L/100 km with the 2.5L engine.

Quality/Reliability/Safety

Pro: Reliability: Average. NHTSA safety complaints/safety: Nothing significant.

Con: Quality control: Spotty. Body construction and powertrain components leave much to be desired. Warranty performance: The three-year base warranty is clearly insufficient coverage in view of Chrysler's traditionally poor quality control and sub-par warranty performance. You'll likely wind up appealing for a warranty refund to the company's Review Committee (see Appendix V). Owner-reported problems: AC failures, frequent stalling, myriad body squeaks and rattles, and fragile body hardware. Service bulletin problems: Transaxle desensitization to intermittent faults causing all sorts of transmission failures (not again!); loose or broken antenna mount; steering column, wheel clunks and rattles; low frequency rumble, gear noise from front of vehicle; front door snapping on cladding; and seat adjuster rises when the seat is unoccupied.

Road Performance

Pro: Acceleration/torque: Although the base 2.4L 4-cylinder performs competently, the 2.5L V6 is a better choice from a noise and performance standpoint. It provides plenty of power in all gear ranges (0–100 km/h: 9.8 sec.) and this year's improvements have also reduced engine vibration and noise somewhat. Routine handling: Although high-performance handling isn't as sporty as the Contour's and the steering isn't quite as sensitive, overall handling is quite competent. Ride quality is generally smooth and pleasant and doesn't deteriorate as the load increases. Emergency handling: Fairly good, though not as precise as the Ford Contour/Mystique. Braking: Better than average (100–0 km/h: 122 ft.), although there is some brake fade after successive stops.

Con: Forget about the Neon-borrowed 2.0L 4-banger; it's overwhelmed by this car's size and accessories and is quite noisy. The V6 is also a bit noisy when pushed and lacks the aggressiveness of the Ford Contour and Mystique V6, particularly when passing. **Transmission:** When passing, the powertrain computer kicks the transmission down to second gear, pushing the tachometer to the redline without gaining much more speed. It's also sometimes slow to downshift. **Steering:** Steering response is vague and gives little feel of the road.

Comfort/Convenience

Pro: Standard equipment: Attractive, tasteful interior with lots of standard features. **Driving position:** Excellent, with a commanding view of the road. **Controls and displays:** Both tall and short drivers can see and access all controls and gauges. **Climate control:** Efficient and easy to adjust. Rear-seat comfort has been enhanced through floor ducts located under the front seats. The defroster also heats the side mirrors. **Interior space/comfort F/R:** Seats are generally comfortable, with nice side bolsters. They aren't quite as snug as the Contour and Mystique seats, but some drivers prefer the extra room. Plenty of front head and leg room. Rear seating is comfortable only for two adults. **Cargo space:** Rear seatback folds down, extending the trunk cargo space. **Trunk/liftover:** Fairly large with a low liftover.

Con: Front seat bottom cushion is a little short on thigh support for tall drivers. **Entry/exit:** Difficult access to the front seats due to the sharply slanted roof pillars. **Quietness:** In highway cruising between 100 and 120 km/h the powertrain emits an annoying high-pitched whine. Some suspension noise intrudes into the interior when going over rough surfaces. Noisy heater fan. Narrow rear-door armrests and the lack of a centre armrest leave you without much to lean on. The trunk's cargo net is poorly positioned.

COST				
List Price (negotiable)	**Residual Values** (months)			
	24	36	48	60
Cirrus LXi: $24,765 (23%)	$15,000	$12,500	$10,000	$8500

TECHNICAL DATA

Powertrain (front-drive)	Head room F/R: 38.1/36.8 in.
Engines: 2.0L 4-cyl. (132 hp)	Leg room F/R: 42.3/38.1 in.
• 2.4L 4-cyl. (150 hp)	Wheelbase: 108 in.
2.5L V6 (168 hp)	Cargo capacity: 15.7 cu. ft.
Transmissions: 5-speed man.	Towing capacity: 1,000 lbs.
• 4-speed auto.	Fuel tank: 60L/reg.
Dimensions	Weight: 3,100 lbs.
Passengers: 5	
Height/length/width:	
52.5/186/71.7 in.	

SAFETY FEATURES

	Std.	Opt.
Anti-lock brakes	■	■
Seatbelt pretensioners	—	—
Integrated child safety seat	❏	■
Airbag cut-off switch	—	—
Depowered airbags	■	❏
Side airbags	—	—
Traction control	—	—
Visibility (front/rear)	*****	*****
Crash protection D/P	***	****
Crash protection (side) D/P	***	**
HLDI injury claims	Low	
Breeze	N/A	

Concorde/Intrepid

Intrepid

RATING: Average. These cars give you more room than dependability. **Strong points:** Attractive styling, nice riding, easy entry/exit, and lots of passenger and cargo room. **Weak points:** Excessive road and wind noise, vague steering, optional ABS, limited rear visibility caused by the cars' high rear end, impractical trunk, poor reliability, and sub-par warranty performance on Chrysler's part.

NEW FOR '99: Redesigned last year, no significant changes will occur until midway through the model year when new sway bar links and tubular rear trailing arms will be added to smooth out the ride and reduce road noise.

GENERAL COMMENTS: These identical full-sized cars share the same chassis and offer most of the same standard and optional features. The

Intrepid, Vision, and Concorde were launched in early 1993, and the extended-wheelbase, upscale LHS hit dealer showrooms the following summer. This year's LHS, the sister to the 300M, is an entirely different car. The Vision has been discontinued.

Both cars have loads of passenger space and many standard features that usually sell as options, such as four-wheel disc brakes and independent rear suspension. The Concorde is marketed to the more conservative buyer. The Intrepid, the Dynasty's replacement and the most popular model, is the entry-level version. Base models are equipped with a 2.7L V6 aluminum engine that delivers 200 hp. Higher line variants get a more powerful 3.2L V6 220-hp powerplant.

Cost analysis/alternatives: Delay your purchase until the improved '99s arrive next spring, when rebates and dealer incentives will be more generous—particularly with the less popular Intrepid. If you want first-class quality, though, a Toyota Camry or Avalon, Honda Accord, or Nissan Maxima should be your first choice. **Recommended options:** The V6 upgrade. The harsh sports suspension, however, is a waste of money. Goodyear GA tires provide better handling, but they're noisy. The large rear windshield may need tinting to protect rear-seat passengers from the sun. **Rebates:** $1,500–$2,000 rebates on the '98s. **Destination charge:** $800. **Depreciation:** About average. The Intrepid suffers from a low level of owner loyalty—industry stats show that about nine out of ten Intrepid owners walk away from the model when considering their next vehicle purchase. **Insurance cost:** Higher than average. **Parts supply/cost:** Reasonably priced and easily found. **Annual maintenance cost:** Much higher than average. **Warranty:** Bumper-to-bumper 3 years/60,000 km; rust perforation 5 years/160,000 km. **Supplementary warranty:** Don't leave home without it. A wise investment, judging from the serious problems reported on previous models. **Highway/city fuel economy:** 8–13L/100 km with the base engine.

Quality/Reliability/Safety

Pro: Plastic front fenders are dent- and corrosion-resistant. Platinum-tipped spark plugs are expected to last 160,000 kilometres. Improved headlights introduced on the '98 models really illuminate the road, and the upgraded defroster now clears the entire windshield.

Con: Quality control: Way below average. **Reliability:** Poor overall. **Warranty performance:** Worse than average. Fortunately, you can always appeal any warranty repair refusal to the company's Review Committee (see Appendix V). **Owner-reported problems:** Glitches in the computerized transmission's shift timing, which cause driveability problems (stalling, hard starts, and surging). Amazingly, the 4-speed LE42 automatic transmission—a spinoff of Chrysler's failure-prone A604—appears to be just as problem-plagued as its predecessor, with reports of driveline shudder during 3–4 shifts and frequent transmission defaults into second gear (limp-in mode). Other owner-reported defects include premature brake wear and brake malfunctions, electrical problems, and sloppy body construction. For example, owners complain of water and air leaks into the interior, uneven fit and finish, poor-quality trim items that break or easily fall off, exposed screw heads, faulty door hinges that make the doors rattle and hard to open, windows that come off their tracks or are misaligned, and power-window motor failures. **Service bulletin problems:** Transaxle desensitization to intermittent faults causing all sorts of transmission failures; troubleshooting tips for eliminating body panel gaps; faulty wiper switch; exhaust drone (see below); tapping noise originating from the temperature door; and vehicle leads or pulls. **NHTSA safety complaints/safety:** Side seatbelts don't retract; front and rear windshields distort view; transmission won't shift to reverse, stalls; headlights sometimes shut off.

NO: 11-01-98
GROUP: Exhaust
DATE: Jan. 30, 1998
SUBJECT:
Exhaust Drone 1600-2000 RPM
MODELS:
1998 (LH) Concorde/Intrepid
NOTE:
THIS BULLETIN APPLIES TO VEHICLES BUILT PRIOR TO JANUARY 15, 1998 (MDH 0115XX).
SYMPTOM/CONDITION:
Exhaust drone and/or vibration felt at 1600-2000 engine RPM under load.
DIAGNOSIS:
If a drone can be felt at 1600-2000 engine RPM and/or vibration can be felt in the accelerator pedal or floor pan, check that the exhaust system is not grounded to the body or suspension. If exhaust system is free in the hangers perform the Repair Procedure.
PARTS REQUIRED:

1	04581705AF	Exhaust Pipe, 2.7L Engine, Left Side, Fed. Emissions (NAA)
1	04581707AF	Exhaust Pipe, 2.7L Engine, Left Side, Calf. Emissions (NAE)
1	04581701AF	Exhaust Pipe, 3.2L Engine, Left Side, Fed. Emissions (NAA)
1	04581703AF	Exhaust Pipe, 3.2L Engine, Left Side, Calf. Emissions (NAE)
1	04581013AC	Clamp, V-Band Exhaust Manifold

REPAIR PROCEDURE:
This bulletin involves replacing the left side front exhaust pipe with revised parts and removing the right side front exhaust pipe support bracket.
1. Replace the left front exhaust pipe/catalytic converter as described on page 11-7 of the 1998 Concorde/Intrepid Service Manual (Publication No. 81-270-8140).

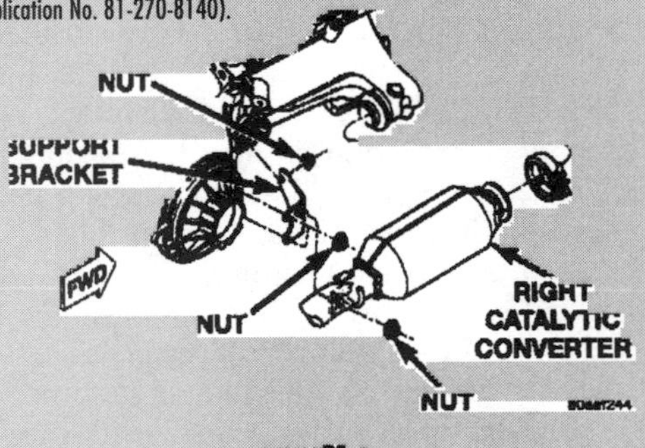

NUT

SUPPORT BRACKET

FWD

NUT

RIGHT CATALYTIC CONVERTER

NUT

FIGURE 1

Road Performance

Pro: Acceleration/torque: Both V6 engines provide plenty of low-end torque and acceleration (0–100 km/h: 9 sec.). **Transmission:** Smooth-shifting 4-speed automatic transaxle and user-friendly AutoStick semi-automatic transmission. **Routine handling:** Good or better handling and steering response than the Taurus, and the optional AutoStick clutchless manual transmission available with the Intrepid sports package improves overall performance even more. Independent suspension also maximizes control and provides lots of suspension travel so that you don't get bumped around on rough roads. The ride doesn't deteriorate as the load is increased. The best balance between performance and ride is found with the mid-level touring suspension. It's not as harsh as the optional sport suspension, and it's firmer than the standard settings. **Emergency handling:** Steering is a bit vague and ponderous with some tire squealing, but no worse than the competition. **Braking:** Good braking performance with standard brakes (100–0 km/h: 125 ft.).

Con: The smaller engine is inadequate to handle a fully loaded Concorde or Intrepid. The traction control system is noisy when activated. A considerable amount of body roll occurs in tight manoeuvring (a problem that may be corrected through the midyear suspension upgrade).

Comfort/Convenience

Pro: Standard equipment: Loaded with standard features. A sleeker, more aerodynamic body than the Taurus/Sable, the Honda Accord, and Chevrolet's Lumina. Excellent visibility due to the large windshield and low front end. **Controls and displays:** Very user-friendly. Analogue instruments are clearly laid out. **Climate control:** Automatic climate-control system is much improved. Efficient and easy to adjust. **Interior space/comfort F/R:** Extended front seat tracks for long-legged drivers or simply for people wanting to sit away from the airbag. Comfortable front bucket seats and rear seat sits three abreast. **Entry/exit:** Excellent front and rear access. The user-friendly interior features passenger grab handles for easy access. **Cargo space:** Lots of storage space, including map pockets in the door.

Con: Driving position: Front seat lacks lateral support and the adjustable lumbar support is uncomfortable. The trunk has a high deck lid, making for difficult loading and unloading, and there's no inside access by folding down the rear seat, as in the Camry. **Quietness:** Excessive engine, road, and wind noise comes mainly from the tires and poor sealing around the windows.

COST

List Price (very negotiable)	Residual Values (months)			
	24	36	48	60
Concorde LX: $26,815 (24%)	$16,000	$14,000	$12,000	$9500

TECHNICAL DATA

Powertrain (front-drive)
Engines: 2.7L V6 (200 hp)
• 3.2L V6 (225 hp)
Transmissions: 5-speed man.
• 4-speed auto.
Dimensions (Concorde)
Passengers: 5
Height/length/width:
55.9/209.1/74.4 in.

Head room F/R: 38.3/37.2 in.
Leg room F/R: 42.2/41.6 in.
Wheelbase: 113 in.
Cargo capacity: 18.7 cu. ft.
Towing capacity: 2,000 lbs.
Fuel tank: 68L/reg.
Weight: 3,550 lbs.

SAFETY FEATURES

	Std.	Opt.
Anti-lock brakes	■	■
Seatbelt pretensioners	—	—
Integrated child safety seat	❑	■
Airbag cut-off switch	—	—
Depowered airbags	■	❑
Side airbags	—	—
Traction control	❑	■
Visibility (front/rear)	*****	*****
Crash protection D/P	****	****
Crash protection (side) D/P	****	***
HLDI injury claims	Low	

Caravan/Voyager/Town & Country

Voyager

RATING: Above Average. Compromised by a history of poor quality control and worse than average reliability. Not to be bought without an extended warranty. **Strong points:** Comfortable ride, excellent braking, lots of innovative convenience features, user-friendly instruments and controls, driver-side sliding door, and plenty of interior room. **Weak points:** Poor acceleration with the base engine and mediocre handling with the extended versions. Both automatic transmissions perform poorly in different ways. A chintzy base warranty is inadequate to deal with serious powertrain, ABS, and body defects, and is exacerbated by the automaker's hard-nosed attitude in interpreting its warranty obligations. Crashworthiness has declined.

NEW FOR '99: Caravan: A carryover year with no substantive changes, except for slightly restyled front ends. AutoStick transmission is standard on the Grand Caravan ES. A second row integrated child safety seat can be ordered with the Quad bucket seats. **Town & Country:** Depowered airbags, a cargo net between the front seats, and the availability of an optional reclining integrated child safety seat.

GENERAL COMMENTS: These practical and stylish minivans return with a wide array of standard and optional features that include AWD, anti-lock brakes, child safety seats integrated into the seatbacks, flush design door handles, and front windshield wiper/washer controls located on the steering column lever for easier use. Extra care has been taken to reduce interior engine and road noise. Childproof locks are standard and the front bucket seats incorporate vertically adjustable head restraints. The Town & Country, a luxury version of the Caravan, comes equipped with a 3.8L V6 and standard luxury features that make the vehicle more fashionable for upscale buyers.

Cost analysis/alternatives: Chrysler says it will forego major price increases on this year's minivans. If this promise is kept, it would make this year's versions the better buy, even though they're practically identical to the '98s. Honda and Toyota have also promised to keep a lid on new minivan prices, so you may wish to consider the Honda Odyssey or Toyota Sienna as an alternative to the Caravan and its many variations. Two small minivans that may be better suited to your needs include the Ford Villager or Nissan Quest. On the other hand, some full-sized GM or Ford rear-drive cargo vans, ripe for conversion, might be a more affordable and practical buy if you intend to haul a full passenger load, do some regular heavy hauling, use lots of accessories, or take frequent motoring excursions. **Recommended options:** As you increase body length you lose manoeuvrability. Don't even consider the 4-cylinder engine—it has no place in a minivan, especially when hooked to the automatic transmission. If you buy a Grand version, stay away from the inadequate 3.0L V6 mated to the 3-speed automatic. That transmission lacks an Overdrive and will shift back and forth as speed varies, and it's slower and noisier than the other optional 6-cylinders when accelerating from a standing start. The 3.3L V6 is a better choice for most city-driving situations, but don't hesitate to get the 3.8L if you're planning lots of highway travel or carrying four or more passengers. The $600 sliding rear door on the driver's side makes it easy to load and unload children, install a child safety seat directly behind the driver, or remove the rear seat. Child safety seats integrated into the rear seatbacks are convenient and reasonably priced. Other important features to consider are the optional defroster, power mirrors, power door locks, and power driver's seat (if you're shorter than 5'9" or expect to have different drivers using the minivan). Town & Country buyers should pass on the optional all-wheel drive coupled with four-wheel disc brakes (instead of the standard rear drums). Although the disc brakes have been improved, Chrysler's large number of ABS failures are worrisome. **Rebates:** Now that the bloom has faded from the minivan rose, look for both '98 and '99 models getting rebates that top $2,000. **Destination charge:** $810. **Depreciation:** Slightly slower than average. There's currently a glut of used Chrysler minivans coming off leases with expired warranties, creating a buyer's market. Resale values have also fallen out of favour as buyers turn toward sport-utilities and pickups. **Insurance cost:** Higher than average, but about average for a minivan. **Parts supply/cost:** Average. Chrysler says that its 3.3L and 3.8L engines won't require tune-ups before 160,000 kilometres. Prepare to be disappointed; many owners have had to tune up their minivans way before then. **Annual maintenance cost:** Repair costs are average during the warranty period. Now that the base warranty has been cut back, owners won't have the luxury of time to get proper warranty servicing through repeat repair-bay visits. If your dealer or Chrysler starts to play the waiting game—waiting for the warranty to expire—don't hesitate to use an independent garage if that's where good service can be found. **Warranty:** Bumper-to-bumper 3 years/60,000 km; rust perforation

5 years/160,000 km. **Supplementary warranty:** A must-have—preferably a seven-year powertrain warranty. Paying over $1,000 for this protection is ridiculous; settle for a third or half as much. **Highway/city fuel economy:** Caravan/Voyager: 9–13L/100 km; Grand Caravan AWD: 10–14L/100 km; Town & Country: 9–14L/100 km; Town & Country AWD: 10–15L/100 km.

Quality/Reliability/Safety

Pro: ABS improvements on last year's models are promising in that consumer complaints have trailed off. Nevertheless, it will take several more years to be sure that these systems are functioning as they should. Dual airbags include knee bolsters to prevent front occupants from sliding under the seatbelts. Side-impact protection has been increased with steel beams in door panels. An improved engine compartment layout also makes for a larger "crumple zone" in the event of collision. Remote-control power door locks can be programmed to lock when the vehicle is put in gear. Chrysler has developed a mechanism that releases the power door locks and turns on the interior lights when the airbag is deployed. The rear wiper is extraordinarily efficient and the Grand Voyager's heated windshield wiper well keeps the blades from icing up in nasty weather.

Con: Quality control: There is nothing in the press releases I received from Chrysler or the service bulletins I accessed that reassures me that the '99 minivans won't continue to have chronic powertrain, brake, and body problems.

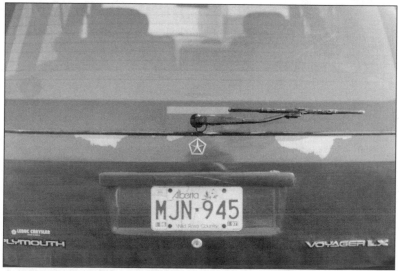

I estimate that fully 10–15 percent of Chrysler's minivans will have paint or transmission problems.

Although *Consumer Reports* rates only the extended versions as worse than average, Canadian *Lemon-Aid* readers report that the base versions are just as failure-prone. This isn't surprising—quality control has been below average since these vehicles were first launched 15 years ago. Quality has improved a bit over the years for some components like engines and brake durability, but it has also declined dramatically since the late '80s, as evidenced by an unending stream of automatic transmission, ABS, and paint delamination complaints. Once the warranty expires, these common problems (I estimate a one in five vehicle occurrence rate) can collectively produce repair bills that will easily reach $5,000. **Reliability:** Reliability is a major problem because Chrysler's deficiencies, notably transmission and ABS failures, make these minivans undriveable and require long periods of "shop time" to diagnose and repair. **Warranty performance:** Below average. As long as Chrysler makes money, it's unlikely to change its hard-nosed treatment of warranty claims. Nevertheless, you can always appeal any warranty repair refusal to the company's Review Committee (see Appendix V). Many owners have been compensated by the Committee, but it cannot replace better quality control and a more comprehensive base warranty.

NO: 21-03-98
GROUP: Transmission
DATE: Feb. 13, 1998
SUBJECT:
Transaxle Desensitization To Intermittent Faults/Driveability Improvements
MODELS:

1998 (FJ)	Avenger/Sebring/Talon
1998 (GS)	Chrysler Voyager (European Market)
1998 (JA)	Cirrus/Stratus/Breeze
1998 (JX)	Sebring Convertible
1998 (LH)	Concorde/Intrepid
1998 (NS)	Town & Country/Caravan/Voyager

NOTE:
THIS INFORMATION APPLIES TO VEHICLES BUILT PRIOR TO DEC. 13, 1997 (MDH 1213XX) WITH A 41TE/AE OR 42LE TRANSAXLE.
DISCUSSION:
New software has been released to address the following:
All models:
Be more tolerant of intermittent conditions that may cause MIL illumination, limp-in or DTC generation. Following is a list of symptom/conditions made more fault tolerant:
1. Corrects an error in extreme cold temperatures -27 C (-16 F) degrees or below. This allowed the transaxle to switch to the cold schedule too quickly. This may cause MIL Illumination and limp-in condition with associated DTC's due to slower than expected response from the fluid.
2. Reduce excessively long (more than 3 second) 3–2 shifts as the vehicle is coasting or braking to a stop with 4 C (40 F) degree or below fluid temperature. The driver may experience slight engine flare accelerating from a stop and/or sluggish acceleration due to the transaxle still being in 2nd gear instead of 1st.
On FJ/GS/JA/JX/NS models:
1. Improves the shift schedule while towing in hilly conditions. The driver may describe this condition as being in the wrong gear or delayed upshifts after cresting a hill.
On NS/GS models:
1. Reduces a shudder condition that may be experienced during a light to moderate throttle 1–2 upshift with -1 C (30 F) degree fluid temperature or higher. This condition can be experienced more frequently as the fluid becomes hotter.
2. Reduces a shudder condition that may be experienced during a 2–3 upshift just after a 3–2 or 4–2 kick-down. On FJ 2.0L (non turbo) models:
1. Reduces a closed or light throttle engine sag experienced between 9 and 27 mph with 7 C (45 F) degree or below fluid temperature.

Chrysler's transmission problems are déjà vu, all over again.

Service bulletin problems: Transaxle desensitization to intermittent faults causing all sorts of transmission failures (see previous page); faulty cooling fan, sudden loss of power assist, front end popping; thumping from rear end in cold temperatures; underbody creaking or knocking; driver's seatback creaking; honk noise during low-speed manoeuvres, as in this DSB.

NO: 19-11-97
GROUP: Steering
EFFECTIVE DATE: Dec. 5, 1997
SUBJECT:
"Honk" Noise During Parking Lot Maneuvers
FOR VEHICLES EQUIPPED WITH A 3.0L, 3.3L OR 3.8L ENGINE THIS BULLETIN SUPERSEDES TECHNICAL SERVICE BULLETIN 19-07-97, DATED MAY 9, 1997. FOR VEHICLES EQUIPPED WITH A 2.4L ENGINE CONTINUE TO USE TECHNICAL SERVICE BULLETIN 19-07-97.
MODELS:
1996 - 1998 (NS) Town & Country/Caravan/Voyager
1996 - 1998 (GS) Chrysler Voyager (International Market)
NOTE:
THIS BULLETIN APPLIES TO LEFT HAND DRIVE VEHICLES EQUIPPED WITH A 3.0L, 3.3L OR 3.8L ENGINE.
SYMPTOM/CONDITION:
'Honk' noise, which may also be described by vehicle operator as an intermittent groan or squawk noise, heard during stationary or low speed parking lot maneuvers, the duration is usually less than one second. The noise usually occurs near the ends of steering travel when reversing direction. This noise condition typically does not develop until the vehicle has accumulated at least a few hundred miles.
DIAGNOSIS:
The noise may or may not go away after the vehicle has been operated for 10–15 minutes, so it may be necessary to not operate the vehicle for approximately 60 minutes or more before the noise can be reproduced during the diagnostic procedure. The noise may decrease in severity or disappear when the ambient temperature is below 70C (45F). Any break, (loosening fittings, replacing pump or lines) made in the Power Steering (P/S) fluid system before the diagnostic procedure is performed, will temporarily eliminate the noise for approximately 200 miles.
Start the engine and turn the steering wheel to the right until it reaches the stop. Jerk (quickly move) the steering wheel back toward the left, repeat several times or if the noise is heard, perform the Repair Procedure. Turn the steering wheel to the left until it reaches the stop. Jerk the steering wheel back toward the right, repeat several times. If the noise is heard, perform the Repair Procedure.
PARTS REQUIRED:

1	05011872AA	Line, Power Steering Pressure
1	05011 873AA	Line, Power Steering Return
	AR 04883077	Fluid Power Steering
2	04546098	Clip, Line
1	04641780	Strap, Tie
1	06035824	Clamp, Hose

POLICY: Reimbursable within the provisions of the warranty.
TIME ALLOWANCE:
Labor Operation No: 19-50-17-90   0.4 Hrs.
FAILURE CODE: P8 - New Part

Honking is for horns, not power steering assemblies.

Remote keyless entry transmitter battery failure; water leaks onto floor from heater/AC housing; and backlight water leaks. **Owner-reported problems:** Some 2.4L engine headgasket leaks, constant stalling, fuel-injection glitches, and leaky oil pressure sending unit seals. Cruise control often malfunctions, causing excessive downshifting (although it's covered under warranty, dealers try to exclude it from the base warranty). The transmission has a hard time deciding which gear it wants, and when you approach a minor incline it shifts down one or two gears and then shifts up too late—a major cause for complaints of poor fuel economy. Premature wear-out occurs on these parts: cooling system, clutch, front suspension components, wheel bearings, front brake rotors, air-conditioning compressor, and body parts (trim becomes loose and falls off, plastic pieces rattle and break easily, and door handles pull away). In spite of improvements over the years, the front brakes need constant attention, if not to replace the pads, then to silence the excessive squeaks when braking. The plastic gas tank is mounted low and is vulnerable to damage from road hazards, and the fuel system develops leaks. Finally, owners report a persistent rotten egg smell caused by poor engine timing or a defective catalytic converter. **NHTSA safety complaints/safety:** *Caravan:* Exterior rear view mirror design distorts vision; transmission may slip out of Drive into Neutral during highway driving; when placing transmission into Park from Drive, it suddenly accelerated; ABS brake failure; excessive brake fade and long stopping distance; fuel leaking from the gas tank; right side sliding door opened while vehicle was in motion, slammed shut, but did not latch when brakes were applied. *Grand Caravan:* While driving, transmission fluid hose detached, causing fluid leakage and loss of engine power; steering failure; engine and engine camshaft failures; while driving at normal speed, vehicle jolts forward; engine noise caused by exhaust hitting engine; transmission failures; wheel bearing failed; faulty passenger door window and door locks; power door lock unlocked while driving, required replacement of sensors twice; when accelerating, fuel tank shifts against vehicle frame causing loud thumping noises; vehicle may catch fire when refilling fuel tank; side sliding door latch won't open from the outside; ABS fails or has a low pedal. *Town & Country:* Rear axle failure caused loss of control, accident, and injuries; broken steering control arm knuckle caused wheel to move sideways, causing an accident; vehicle suddenly accelerated when started; gas tank makes loud sounds when accelerating.

Road Performance

Pro: Acceleration/torque: The most versatile powertrain is the 3.3L V6 engine coupled with the 4-speed automatic transmission. Chrysler's top-of-the-line 3.8L engine is a good second choice: it's smooth and quiet with lots of much-needed low-end torque—0–100 km/h: 9.8 sec. for a base Voyager equipped with the 3.3L V6; a similarly equipped Grand Voyager posts an 11.2 sec. time. **Transmission:** The AWD transfers 90 percent of the engine power to the front wheels during normal driving conditions. It's easy to use and performs well. As the front wheels lose traction, the rear wheels get additional power until traction has been stabilized or the 55/45 percent front-to-rear limit is reached. **Routine handling:** These minivans are the closest thing to a passenger car when it comes to ride and handling. The redesigned chassis and improved steering provide a comfortable, no-surprise ride. Stiff springs greatly improve handling and comfort. Manoeuvrability around town is easy. Remember, the Grand version sacrifices handling for extra interior room. **Emergency handling:** Slow, but acceptable. **Steering:** Precise and predictable. **Braking:** Impressive ABS braking when it functions as it should (100–0 km/h: 118 ft. with the base Voyager and 132 ft. with the Grand Caravan).

Con: Sluggish highway acceleration until you move up to the 3.3L engine or better. And at that, you'll have to get used to excessive engine noise when passing. There is no transmission/brake interlock to prevent sudden acceleration. The 3-speed automatic transmission accelerates poorly and is noisy, while the optional 41TE 4-speed automatic transmission with Overdrive shifts slowly and imprecisely. Excessive transmission whine. Although it works well, the all-wheel drive option is overrated and not worth the fuel penalty for most driving situations. The stretched wheelbase version gives less-than-nimble handling. A large turning radius and long nose can make parking difficult. Power steering is vague and over-assisted as speed increases. Brake pedal feels mushy and the brakes tend to heat up after repeated applications, causing considerable loss of effectiveness (fade) and warping of the front discs. The 1997 upgraded ABS system has proved unreliable on older vans and repair costs are astronomical. Furthermore, the ABS control unit is located behind a front wheel, where it's susceptible to contamination by road salt and dirt.

Comfort/Convenience

Pro: Standard equipment: This is where Chrysler minivans shine. They offer plenty of standard comfort and versatility features. **Driving position:** Drivers are treated to a car-like driving position. Good overall view of the road. **Controls and displays:** The instrument panel features easy-to-read gauges and warning lights, and the large glove box and radio and heater controls are set close to the driver. The location of the turn signal indicators is particularly well thought out—they're in the lower portion of your field of vision. Lots of cupholders and interior reading lights. **Climate control:** Adequate. Dual-zone AC allows for different temperature settings for the driver and front-seat passenger. Overhead heating and ventilation ducts to the rear seat are well placed. **Entry/exit:** Easy. The step-up height isn't too high for most people. Another nice touch: grab handles on the rear hatch and sliding door. There's convenient "walk through" access to the rear seating area. **Interior space/comfort F/R:** Minivan doesn't mean "mini" in terms of passenger space. The aerodynamic exterior design, increased window area, and lower sills make for an attractive, roomier-feeling vehicle, and the interior is large and versatile with excellent outward visibility and plenty of storage space. Chrysler has copied the Windstar in providing theatre-type seating; each row is set a little higher than the row in front, giving most passengers a better view. A fairly high roofline—about four inches taller than the Ford Windstar—means that a six-foot-tall passenger will sit comfortably in the back seat, but would touch the roof in a Windstar. The rear seat will seat three adults. Chrysler's integrated child safety seat has a reclining back. An optional "Convert-a-Bed" package is available with the seven-passenger seating configuration. **Cargo space:** Plenty and practical. This is where the $600 driver-side sliding door comes in handy. No longer do you have to walk around to the passenger side to load or unload cargo. Rear seatbacks fold down, and removing the centre and rear seats is a "snap," thanks to the addition of little wheels on the base of the rear seat. Snap them down and you can roll the seat anywhere. **Trunk/liftover:** Easy to load and unload 4x8-foot sheets of plywood thanks to the wide doors and low floor. Courtesy lights in front and on the liftgate are an added convenience. Interestingly, with the rear seat removed, the regular-sized Caravan provides more cargo space than the Grand Caravan. **Quietness:** Better than average, thanks to better body soundproofing with polyurethane foam injected into body cavities (watch those allergies).

Con: Driver is faced with 44 switches, dials, and buttons on the dash/door panel/console. Console storage bin for small objects is sometimes hard to open and close, and the panel dimmer is hidden behind the steering wheel. Front seats lack sufficient lumbar support and the seatback comes up short against the shoulder blades. Tall drivers will find leg room a bit tight without an adequate left footrest. Wipers obstruct forward vision. AC and heater take a while to be felt. Three adults will find the third-row bench seat a bit cramped and the head restraints set too low. Both sliding side doors are unwieldy to slide and it takes lots of effort to push the buttons that unlatch them. 50- to 100-pound removable seats aren't as easy to remove as Chrysler would have you believe. Some road, engine, and transmission noise intruding into the interior.

COST				
List Price (very negotiable)	**Residual Values** (months)			
	24	36	48	60
Base Caravan: $20,405 (17%)	$15,000	$12,000	$9500	$7500

TECHNICAL DATA	
Powertrain (front-drive)	**Dimensions** (base)
Engines: 2.4L 4-cyl. (150 hp)	Height/length/width:
• 3.0L V6 (150 hp)	68.5/186.3/76.8 in.
• 3.3L V6 (158 hp)	Head room F: 39.8/R1: 40.1/R2: 38.1 in.
• 3.8L V6 (180 hp)	Leg room F: 41.2/R1: 36.6/R2: 35.8 in
Passengers: 7	Wheelbase: 113.3 in.
Transmissions: 3-speed auto.	Cargo capacity: 13.6 cu. ft.
• 4-speed auto.	Towing capacity: N/A
	Fuel tank: 76L/reg.
	Weight: 3,985 lbs.

SAFETY FEATURES

	Std.	Opt.
Anti-lock brakes	■	■
Seatbelt pretensioners	—	—
Integrated child safety seat	❏	■
Airbag cut-off switch	—	—
Depowered airbags	■	❏
Side airbags	—	—
Traction control	■	■
Visibility (front/rear)	*****	*****
Crash protection D/P	***	***
Crash protection D/P		
G. Caravan	***	***
Town & Country	***	***
Crash protection (side)	N/A	
HLDI injury claims	N/A	

FORD

Ford's vehicles appeal to four types of buyers: those wanting inexpensive and reliable front-drive econoboxes like the Escort; those opting for front- and rear-drive midsize sedans and coupes; muscle car enthusiasts who want a rear-drive machine; and those wanting the comfort and power of traditional rear-drive luxury cars. The small Escort and large-size Crown Victoria/Marquis have been particularly successful in fighting imports at both ends of the market while keeping Chrysler and GM on their toes. This is all the more ironic because the Escort is a knock-off of the Mazda 323/Protegé, and the rear-drive Crown Victoria/Marquis and Mustang are restyled 1970s products. The Taurus and Sable duo have also done well against Toyota's Camry and the Honda Accord, but this isn't likely to last, now that Ford has stopped heavily discounting the price, Taurus reliability problems keep surfacing, and the Camry and Accord redesigns attract more buyers.

Environmentalists are pleased that Ford has followed Daimler-Benz in showing an interest in Burnaby-based Ballard Power System's hydrogen fuel-cell engine in an effort to produce a zero-emission car. The automaker plans to have a vehicle prototype equipped with the new engine within a year. On the other hand, Ford lost much of the goodwill it garnered over the years with the NHTSA when the government agency learned earlier this year that the automaker intentionally hid many internal documents that showed that as many as 20 million 1983–95 cars and trucks have defective electronic ignition modules (TFI modules) that may cause sudden stalling. As a result of this disclosure, Ford will likely face more lawsuits over the TFI-induced injuries, have a harder time showing its goodwill, and likely come under increasing scrutiny from federal authorities.

Warranty performance

Ford's warranty performance is better than Chrysler's and General Motors' in that the company has been more forthcoming when extending its warranty to cover its own manufacturing errors. But it's been less than forthright when dealing with safety-related defects, emission warranty obligations, and secret warranties covering 3.8L engine headgasket failures (yes, the Mustang's new engine is a variation of the same ubiquitous powerplant), automatic transmission glitches, and paint defects.

Ford's quality control, although much improved, still lags behind that of Asian automakers. The quality of body components and their assembly and rust resistance are better than those of GM and Chrysler, but remain far below Japanese and European standards. Poor paint quality, a Ford problem for over a decade, was addressed in 1995 by a changeover in suppliers and the use of improved processes. It'll take a couple more years to notice any improvement (keep your fingers crossed).

Cougar

The new Cougar is a driver's car; styling and performance are its strengths.

RATING: Not Recommended during the first model year. **Strong points:** Attractive styling, good acceleration and handling, and a standard anti-theft system. **Weak points:** Narrow, claustrophobic interior, too many decontented standard features, an ugly and superfluous trunklid spoiler, and excessive interior squeaks and rattles.

NEW FOR '99: An entirely new model, priced at $19,995.

GENERAL COMMENTS: Part Contour and part Probe, the '99 Cougar, like the Contour and Mystique, is based on the European Mondeo sedan and is built at the Mazda-run Auto Alliance plant in Flat Rock, Michigan, home to the Probe, MX-6, and 626. The redesigned front-drive Cougar, restyled as a hatchback, went on sale last summer as an early '99 model. It's reasonably priced at $19,995 for the base version, equipped with a 16-valve, 125-hp 2.0L inline-four and $21,795 for a better equipped model carrying a 24-valve, 170-hp 2.5L V6. ABS and side airbags are optional.

The firm suspension and quick, responsive steering make the Cougar both nimble and stable when cornering under speed. Comfortable seatbacks and a split-fold rear seatback makes cargo hauling a breeze. Headlight illumination is impressive.

On the minus side, steering is a bit heavy in city traffic and the interior feels narrow and small—the Accord gives a much roomier impression. Short front seat cushions don't give enough thigh support, dashboard controls are cheap-looking, the small Clarion radio buttons aren't user-friendly, and the rear spoiler is both distracting and cuts rearward vision. There have also been a few reports of annoying body squeaks and groans. Cargo loading is made difficult by the high liftover.

Rather than raise prices, Ford has reduced content, making optional equipment that should be standard. This includes AC (standard in the States), ABS ($731 extra; standard with the Cavalier and Sunfire), and side airbags ($500 more). **Alternatives:** 4-cylinder version: Chevrolet Cavalier, Pontiac Sunfire, and Honda Civic; V6 version, '98 Eagle Talon.

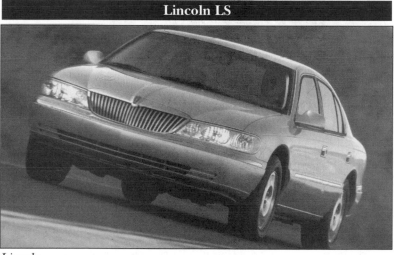

Lincoln LS

Lincoln

RATING: Not Recommended during its first year on the market.

GENERAL COMMENTS: Lincoln's new 2000 LS rear-drive sedan won't be launched until the spring of 1999. Ford needs the extra time to improve the fit and finish, fine-tune the suspension, and upgrade the powertrain performance. The entry-level LS6 will come with a high-performance 200-hp variant of the Taurus 3.0L V6 mated to an optional manual or a standard automatic gearbox. LS8 buyers get a 250-hp 3.9L V8 based on the Jaguar XK8 coupe coupled to a semi-automatic transmission Ford calls SelecShift. Although Lincoln has been outselling Cadillac for much of 1998, it desperately needs new and younger drivers to compete with BMW, Lexus, and Mercedes-Benz, and is counting on the LS series to do just that. Nevertheless, Lincoln has yet to divulge LS prices.

Escort/ZX2/Tracer ('98)

Escort

RATING: Above Average. Ideal for both city and highway use. **Strong points:** Comfortable ride, easy handling, good fuel economy. The ZX2 has a high-performance powertrain. **Weak points:** Slow throttle response, mediocre braking, and insufficient front leg room. The ZX2 has less cargo space and more difficult rear-seat access due to its sportier styling.

NEW FOR '99: Escorts return without any significant changes; the Tracer adds a sporty wagon, which won't be sold in Canada.

GENERAL COMMENTS: Ford's top-selling compacts, the Escort and Tracer, underwent significant changes two years ago, making them more attractive and smoother-riding, and giving them better handling. They've used the 323/Protegé platform for over seven years, but their latest redesign brings them closer to Ford than ever before. Ford is now responsible for interior and exterior features, the standard 2.0L engine, and the fuel-injection and ignition systems. Escorts come in three body styles: the similarly-equipped sedan and wagon, and a racier-styled, high-performance coupe called the ZX2.

Cost analysis/alternatives: Get the '99 model if it's discounted; only consider a '98 model if the price is cut 15 percent or more. You may also wish to consider the Honda Civic, Mazda Protegé, and Toyota Corolla. **Recommended options:** A rear wiper for wagons. Think twice about getting AC—the base engine may not be powerful enough to handle the extra load. Also, considering the limited head room, a sunroof isn't advisable. One optional keyless entry system only locks the driver's door; get a unit that activates both doors. **Rebates:** Look for $500–$1,000 rebates early in the new year. **Destination charge:** $250. **Depreciation:** Slower than average. **Insurance cost:** Average. **Parts supply/cost:** Parts are easily found, but the CAA says they may cost more than average. Price-shop independent suppliers. **Annual maintenance cost:** Below average. **Warranty:** Bumper-to-bumper 3 years/60,000 km; rust perforation 5 years/unlimited km. **Supplementary warranty:** Not needed. **Highway/city fuel economy:** 6–9L/100 km with the base 2.0L engine. Expect a bit less fuel economy with the ZX2's high-performance engine.

Quality/Reliability/Safety

Pro: Quality control: Escorts have been recommended since 1991 for their overall reliability, good road manners, and spaciousness. The 2.0L 130-hp ZX2's engine is borrowed from the Contour and has been quite dependable so far. Increased body rigidity means that doors, windows, trunks, hoods, and body panels fit together better, there's less body flexing, and most wind and road noise—a serious problem with previous models—is muted fairly successfully. **Reliability:** Above average. **Warranty performance:** Ford customer relations staffers are generally fair and efficient in handling warranty claims. **Service bulletin problems:** Nothing significant—just an inoperative dome lamp.

Con: Owner-reported problems: Premature front brake wear, paint delamination, and excessive interior noise. **NHTSA safety complaints/safety:** Faulty steering wheel assembly; brake failure; ABS failure; driver-side seatbelt buckle failure; defective child safety seat harness strap; engine stalling at high speed; inadvertent airbag deployment; airbags deployed during a minor "fender-bender" collision; sudden acceleration.

Road Performance

Pro: The ZX2's 0–100 km/h acceleration time of 7.9 seconds is impressive, and there's plenty of bottom-end torque for hill climbing. **Routine handling:** Very good. Overall handling and braking have been given a boost with a lighter, more responsive power steering unit, stronger front disc brakes, larger rear drums, and bigger, 14-inch wheels. **Emergency handling:** Better than average. The retuned suspension makes for a firmer, more controlled ride with less oversteer. **Steering:** Precise, with lots of road feel.

Con: Acceleration/torque: Mediocre acceleration with the manual transmission (0–100 km/h: 10.9 sec.) is much worse with the automatic. The engine stumbles and hesitates at idle with the AC system on and the throttle often takes several seconds to close when you take your foot off the pedal to downshift. **Transmission:** Hill climbing leads to annoying gear hunting. **Braking:** Unacceptably long stopping distances (100–0 km/h: 140 ft.) mandate the choice of optional ABS.

Comfort/Convenience

Pro: Sedan and wagon have rounded features similar to the Taurus design; the ZX2's styling resembles Hyundai's Tiburon. **Driving position:** Good, if you don't mind your leg rubbing against the centre console. **Climate control:** Quiet, efficient heating and ventilation system uses four large dash vents to control the temperature. **Entry/exit:** Not difficult. **Interior space/comfort F/R:** The interior isn't expansive, but it's adequate. The wagon borrows the most from Mazda and is the practical choice for interior room. Comfortable front seats with plenty of front leg room. **Cargo space:** Plenty of small storage areas. **Trunk/liftover:** Reasonably sized trunk.

Con: Standard equipment: Just the basics. GT styling is a yawner and the spoiler is out of place on this econobox. **Controls and displays:** Confusing climate control layout forces you to take your eyes off the road. Radio is hard to tune because of small buttons and a long reach. Rear leg room could be better, and three rear passengers will have a tight fit. The door stops often don't prevent the door from closing. The wagon's raised sill makes cargo loading difficult. The ZX2's trunk has 8 percent less space than the Escort sedan. **Quietness:** Excessive engine noise.

COST

List Price (negotiable)	Residual Values (months)			
	24	36	48	60
Escort LX: $14,895 (13%)	$11,500	$10,000	$8000	$6000

TECHNICAL DATA

Powertrain (front-drive)
Engines: 2.0L 4-cyl. (110 hp)
• 2.0L 4-cyl. (130 hp)
Transmissions: 5-speed man.
• 4-speed auto.
Dimensions (LX)
Passengers: 5
Height/length/width:
53.3/174.7/67 in.

Head room F/R: 39/36.7 in.
Leg room F/R: 42.5/34 in.
Wheelbase: 98 in.
Cargo capacity: 12.8 cu. ft.
Towing capacity: N/A.
Fuel tank: 48L/reg.
Weight: 2,450 lbs.

SAFETY FEATURES

	Std.	Opt.
Anti-lock brakes	❑	■
Seatbelt pretensioners	—	—
Integrated child safety seat	❑	■
Airbag cut-off switch	—	—
Depowered airbags	■	❑
Side airbags	—	—
Traction control	—	—
Visibility (front/rear)	*****	*****
Crash protection D/P	***	****
Crash protection (side) D/P	***	***
HLDI injury claims	N/A	

Contour/Mystique

Contour

RATING: Average. **Strong points:** The main advantages of the Contour and Mystique are exceptional handling, a smooth ride, and a powerful, limited-maintenance V6 engine. **Weak points:** An anemic 4-banger, erratic automatic gear shifting, cramped rear seating, and difficult entry/exit.

NEW FOR '99: The base model has been dropped. Front seat knee room is increased by a half-inch and rear seat legroom gets an additional 1.2 inches. Only the SE models get the 2.5L V6. Front suspension upgrades improve steering and handling. The SVT Contour gets five additional horses and larger, better performing tires.

GENERAL COMMENTS: These front-drive, midsize twin sedans are based on the European-designed Mondeo, which has met with respectable sales after many years on the market. The four-door, five-passenger Contour sells for a bit less than its practically identical Mercury counterpart.

Both vehicles are set on a wheelbase that's slightly larger than the Taurus' and come with two engines and transmissions: a base 16-valve 125-hp 2.0L 4-cylinder, and an optional 24-valve 170-hp 2.5L V6. Either engine can be hooked to a standard 5-speed transaxle or an optional 4-speed automatic. A smooth but firm ride and crisp handling are guaranteed by the standard MacPherson strut front suspension, an anti-roll bar, and fully independent rear suspension.

Other interesting standard features include dual airbags, adjustable head restraints, 60/40 split-fold rear seats, rear heater ducts, and a sophisticated air filtration system for the passenger compartment. Four-wheel disc brakes, a sport-tuned suspension, and high-performance tires are standard features on the V6.

Cost analysis/alternatives: Get the '99 model for the upgrades, if it's discounted; only consider a '98 model if the price is cut 15–20 percent. Marketed to fit between the compact Escort and Tracer and the larger midsize Taurus and Sable, their high manufacturer's suggested retail price (MSRP) have put both vehicles far beyond the budget of former Tempo/Topaz owners (whose cars they replaced). Even discounted 1997 models aren't much of a bargain, since they don't get the upgrades found with the '98s. Mazda's 626 is a worthwhile alternative to the Contour and Mystique. It's a more stylish, highway-proven sedan with better-than-average reliability, excellent parts supply, and also gets many improvements this year. Other vehicles worth considering: Nissan Altima, Honda Accord, Toyota Camry, and Oldsmobile Cutlass. Be wary of the Chrysler Cirrus: it's roomier and more stylish, but not very reliable. **Recommended options:** The V6 engine, but if you want better fuel economy stay with the standard 5-speed transmission. **Rebates:** $750 rebates on the '98s and $1,000 rebates on the '97s. There are plenty of unsold '97 models left on dealers' lots, so the longer you wait to buy, the greater your chances of snaring a car that's eligible for both a rebate and dealer incentive bonus. **Destination charge:** $350. **Depreciation:** Slower than average. **Insurance cost:** Higher than average. **Parts supply/cost:** Average cost, but sometimes hard to find. **Annual maintenance cost:** Average. **Warranty:** Bumper-to-bumper 3 years/60,000 km; rust perforation 5 years/unlimited km. **Supplementary warranty:** A good idea. **Highway/city fuel economy:** 7–11.5L/100 km.

Quality/Reliability/Safety

Pro: Quality control: Better than average. **Reliability:** Apart from computer glitches, few reliability problems reported. **Warranty performance:** Very good.

Con: Owner-reported problems: Owners report AC and computer module failures, long waiting periods for parts, and unsatisfactory repairs by mechanics who seem unfamiliar with the car. Other, more specific problems are listed on the Contour/Mystique web site (*http://www. contour. org/FAQ/probs.html*) along with possible corrections: upon startup, engine makes a clattering/rapping sound, like marbles in a tin can; coolant light comes on for first few minutes after startup; "throttle hang," where engine rpms hang during shifts or when backing off throttle; engine squeals then stalls in wet conditions or when accelerating/braking; V6 engine stalls, sputters when cold; loss of power, later followed by the sound of rushing air in the engine compartment (catalytic converter); '97 E61 manifold catalytic converter recall; rubbery manual transmission shift; emergency brake doesn't release completely or freezes; chronic rotor warping; vehicle pulls to one side; weak low-beam headlights; fuel door sticking; squeaking noise from rear passenger side upon startup; crunch noise during first acceleration; creaky rear suspension; clock illumination doesn't work; cupholders don't work well.

Service bulletin problems: Detonation, stalling, exhaust sulfur odour; fuel gauge won't read below ¼ full tank; broken PRNDL indicator; engine compartment hooting or moosing noise with AC on. (No, I don't know what a "moosing" noise sounds like. Ask your service manager, a zookeeper, or a moose.) **NHTSA safety complaints/safety:** Excessive brake wear and noise; airbag warning light goes on for no reason. Ford promises that its new Duratec V6 engine won't require a tune-up before 160,000 km. Would they kid us?

Road Performance

Pro: Acceleration/torque: The base 4-cylinder engine is quiet and smoother-running. Ford's 2.5L dual overhead cam 24-valve Duratec V6 is also reasonably quiet and smooth, and gives plenty of power without hesitation at low and moderate engine speeds (0–100 km/h: 8.8 sec.). **Transmission:** Very smooth and quiet over even terrain. Superb ride and handling qualities. Gear ratios in the 4-speed electronically controlled automatic transmission are well matched to the engine's output. **Routine handling:** Even with an automatic transmission, the Contour slices through corners with limited body roll and excellent control. **Emergency handling:** Although traction control is available, the car's front-drive configuration gives good traction on slippery roads without the option. **Steering:** Power steering is quick and precise. **Braking:** Braking is acceptable (100–0 km/h: 130 ft.).

Con: The base 4-cylinder engine is a yawner that isn't suited for passing or hilly terrain, particularly when hooked to the automatic transmission, as the following Contour owner discovered: "The trip was a white-knuckler all the way. Foot on the gas, pushing through the firewall, engine wheezing like crazy. Old VW Westphalias went by like we were standing still. The thing was so slow it was scary!" Poorly timed transmission upshifts when traversing hilly terrain.

Comfort/Convenience

Pro: Standard equipment: Well appointed with lots of standard features. **Driving position:** Very good. The Contour's front seats are first rate, even in the least expensive GL. Along with the more luxuriously upholstered seats in the Mystique, they're the best in their class. Plenty of front seat room for a six-footer. **Controls and displays:** The instrument panel is well laid out—a high-mounted coin bin is a thoughtful touch. **Climate control:** Efficient and easy to adjust. **Cargo space:** Better than average. **Trunk/liftover:** Surprisingly spacious trunk is easy to load.

Con: Interior space/comfort F/R: Door panels limit leg room. Sport seat bolsters are a bit too snug. The rear seat is inadequate—even with the extra inch added last year. The Mazda Protegé has more rear-seat leg room than the Contour. The heads of tall passengers will hit the headliner/roof where it meets the steeply sloped back window, and despite this year's redesign, rear leg room is still insufficient. Power-window switches are awkward to use and the radio controls are tiny push buttons requiring the driver's full attention, plus a steady hand, to operate when the car is moving. Slow-operating power door locks. **Entry/exit:** Difficult rear seat access. **Quietness:** Lots of road noise.

COST

List Price (negotiable)	Residual Values (months)			
	24	**36**	**48**	**60**
Contour LX: $17,595 (16%)	$15,000	$13,000	$11,000	$8500

TECHNICAL DATA

Powertrain (front-drive)
Engines: 2.0L 4-cyl. (125 hp)
• 2.5L V6 (170 hp)
Transmissions: 5-speed man.
• 4-speed auto.
Dimensions
Passengers: 5
Height/length/width:
54.5/183.9/69.1 in.

Head room F/R: 39/36.7 in.
Leg room F/R: 42.9/35.9 in.
Wheelbase: 106.5 in.
Cargo capacity: 13.9 cu. ft.
Towing capacity: 2,000 lbs.
Fuel tank: 55L/reg.
Weight: 2,750 lbs.

SAFETY FEATURES

	Std.	Opt.
Anti-lock brakes	❏	■
Seatbelt pretensioners	—	—
Integrated child safety seat	❏	■
Airbag cut-off switch	—	—
Depowered airbags	■	❏
Side airbags	—	—
Traction control	❏	■
Visibility (front/rear)	*****	*****
Crash protection D/P	*****	****
Crash protection (side) D/P	***	****
HLDI injury claims	Average	

Mustang

Mustang

RATING: Recommended. **Strong points:** Fast acceleration, impressive handling, braking, and resale value. **Weak points:** Insufficient rear seat room and limited cargo space.

NEW FOR '99: While GM seriously considers dropping its sporty Camaro and Firebird, Ford has renewed its commitment to the Mustang through a "retro" restyling, using sharp exterior creases that hearken back to the pony car's early years. Ford has also increased the Mustang's length and width by almost two inches and given the car a 40-hp boost to its "headgasket-challenged" 3.8L V6 (also used in the Taurus and Windstar) and 25 extra horses to its 4.6L V8 engine equipped '99s. Optional all-speed traction control is also available. Other changes: a stiffer chassis, plus improvements to steering, handling, and ride. A new Cobra with independent rear suspension will debut in mid-'99.

GENERAL COMMENTS: The Mustang carries a base 3.8L V6 and offers an optional 4.6L V8 along with a high performance, limited-edition Cobra variation that delivers 70 more horses than the stock 4.6L V8. The single and twin cam V8 options make the Mustang a powerful street machine. V6 models are an acceptable compromise, even though the engine fails to deliver the gobs of power expected of a Mustang by most performance enthusiasts. Base models come equipped with a host of luxury and convenience items. Furthermore, the price is hard to beat, and resale value stays relatively high.

This is definitely not a family car. But for those who want a sturdy and stylish second car, or who don't need room in the back or standard ABS, the Mustang is a pretty good sports car buy.

Cost analysis/alternatives: Get the '99 model for the upgrades. They are substantially improved and can be a real bargain if the dealer will sell you one at a discount and with a rebate. Other cars worth considering are the '98 Eagle Talon, GM Camaro/Firebird, and Toyota Celica and '98 Supra. **Recommended options:** Traction control, considering this rear-drive's tendency to "spin out" when pushed. **Rebates:** $500 rebates to clear out 1998 leftovers. **Destination charge:** $300. **Depreciation:** Slower than average. **Insurance cost:** Higher than average. **Parts supply/cost:** Inexpensive and easily found. **Annual maintenance cost:** Lower than average. Any mechanic is able to fix a Mustang. **Warranty:** Bumper-to-bumper 3 years/60,000 km; rust perforation 5 years/unlimited km. **Supplementary warranty:** Not necessary. **Highway/city fuel economy:** 7–12L/100 km with the 3.8L; 9–14.5L/100 km with the 4.6L.

Quality/Reliability/Safety

Pro: Quality control: Better than average. The Mustang's repair history has improved greatly and this is likely to continue with the '99 models, which use parts improved upon from previous years. **Reliability:** Very good. The engines and transmissions are durable, as are most other components. Body assembly has improved of late, with fewer rattles and a more solid feeling. **Warranty performance:** Better than GM or Chrysler. **Service bulletin problems:** Nothing significant.

Con: Owner-reported problems: The front suspension, brakes, and steering components remain the only consistent weak spots. The engine computer can be temperamental, and electrical problems are common. Keep an eye on the 3.8L engine: headgasket failures may be in the offing. Assembly quality not up to the level of Japanese vehicles. **NHTSA safety complaints/safety:** Sudden acceleration; left front wheel fell off when the lower control arm and ball joint became loose; a light rear end makes the car dangerously unstable on wet roads or when cornering at speed.

Road Performance

Pro: Acceleration/torque: The V8 provides very quick acceleration and smooth power delivery (0–100 km/h: 7.1 sec.), while the V6 performs fairly well with the automatic 4-speed transmission. **Transmission:** The clutch is reasonably smooth and the automatic shifts reasonably well most of the time. **Routine handling:** Models equipped with the sport suspension (which includes larger tires) provide sure and predictable handling on dry roads. The upgraded base suspension also makes the car more stable and controllable on most roads. **Emergency handling:** Slow but predictable. **Steering:** Quick and responsive. **Braking:** Excellent braking performance for a car this heavy (100–0 km/h: 123 ft.).

Con: The 3.8L V6 is rough and noisy when pushed. The V8s are a bit too powerful for the amount of traction available to the rear wheels, making for lots of wheelspin and instability on slippery surfaces. The manual transmission is notchy at times and the automatic sometimes hesitates between gears. The rear end tends to slip out under hard cornering. The GT rides harshly on rough roads. These cars are a bit clumsy around town because of a wide turning circle.

Comfort/Convenience

Pro: Standard equipment: Even the base Mustangs come well equipped with lots of standard features. **Driving position:** Excellent, with plenty of head and leg room for tall drivers. **Controls and displays:** First class. Complete and well laid-out dual-cowl dashboard and controls. **Climate control:** Efficient, easy to adjust, and quiet. **Interior space/comfort F/R:** Comfortable front seats on all models. **Cargo space:** The split folding rear seat frees up much-needed trunk storage space. Easy loading, thanks to the low liftover. **Quietness:** Improved body rigidity has reduced interior noise somewhat.

Con: Rear visibility is obstructed by the roof pillars and high parcel shelf. Front seats need at least an inch more travel, and the rear seat is best left to children, especially with the convertible version. **Entry/exit:** The wide doors make for clumsy entry and exit in tight spots. GT ride comfort is below average. **Trunk/liftover:** Very shallow trunk with a small opening.

COST				
List Price (negotiable)	\t**Residual Values** (months)			
	24	36	48	60
Base Mustang 3.8L: $22,595 (15%)	$18,000	$14,000	$11,000	$9000

TECHNICAL DATA	
Powertrain (front-drive)	Head room F/R: 38.2/35.9 in.
Engines: 3.8L V6 (190 hp)	Leg room F/R: 42.9/31.3 in.
• 4.6L V8 (250 hp)	Wheelbase: 101.3 in.
• 4.6L V8 (320 hp)	Cargo capacity: 10.3 cu. ft.
Transmissions: 5-speed man.	Towing capacity: 1,000 lbs.
• 4-speed auto.	Fuel tank: 58L/reg.
Dimensions	Weight: 3,300 lbs.
Passengers: 4	
Height/length/width: 53.4/181.5/71.8 in.	

SAFETY FEATURES		
	Std.	Opt.
Anti-lock brakes	❏	■
Seatbelt pretensioners	—	—
Integrated child safety seat	—	—
Airbag cut-off switch	—	—
Depowered airbags	■	❏
Side airbags	—	—
Traction control	—	■
Visibility (front/rear)	*****	**

Crash protection D/P	N/A	
Convertible	*****	*****
Crash protection (side) D/P	***	***
HLDI injury claims	Average	

Taurus/Sable

Taurus

RATING: Above Average, but only if bought with an extended warranty. **Strong points:** Quiet running, good handling, and comfortable ride. **Weak points:** Insufficient storage space, limited rear head room and access, and long-term reliability problems.

NEW FOR '99: A revised gauge cluster, five-passenger seating with a storage console replaces the flip-fold six-passenger seating console. The Sable gets a GS wagon.

GENERAL COMMENTS: Ford's most popular family car offers an attractive combination of safety, reliability, performance, handling, and comfort. The base 3.0L Vulcan V6 is adequate, though dated, and the high-performing 24-valve V6 provides plenty of power for most driving needs. Other nice standard features: heated outside mirrors, a 60/40 split-fold rear seatback for additional cargo space, a driver's foot rest, and reserve power to operate the power windows and moonroof after the engine is shut off.

The SHO high-performance version returns this year with a 3.4L, 32-valve V8 engine. It delivers sparkling performance and sports car handling—at a price. Acceleration rivals the Mustang GT with a top speed of over 140 mph, and it comes with an automatic transmission.

Cost analysis/alternatives: Get the '99 model for the upgrades, as minimal as they are; only consider a '98 model if the price is cut by at least 15 percent. Wagons are competent performers, but they're outclassed by some imports and most minivans as far as reliability and overall performance is concerned. The SHO has become a cult car for high-performance fans and its slow depreciation reflects this fact; bargains are hard to find. Other sedans worth considering are the Honda Accord, Mazda 626, Toyota Camry, and Volvo 850/S70. Wagons worth considering are the Honda Accord EX, Subaru Legacy, Toyota Camry LE V6, and Volvo 940/V90. **Recommended options:** Expect to spend about $300 more for the flexible-fuel Taurus (ethanol or methanol), currently sold only to fleets. The automatic climate control system, a rear integrated child safety seat, power seats, and a heavy-duty suspension are wise choices. Get the optional DOHC V6 variation, but tell the dealer to forget the wagon's uncomfortable rear-facing third seat. Don't buy the optional leather seats, either; they're slippery and not all that durable. The digital instrumentation is another useless option; it's gimmicky and distracting. On the other hand, Ford's optional InstaClear windshield is a boon in Canadian winters. **Rebates:** The redesigned Taurus and Sable have been heavily discounted during the past few years. As the Toyota Camry and Honda Accord eat into Ford's sales, generous dealer incentives and customer rebates will start kicking in before the year is up. Expect $1,000 rebates on the '99s and $2,000 on the '98s. **Destination charge:** $350. **Depreciation:** A bit slower than average. **Insurance cost:** Higher than average. **Parts supply/cost:** Parts are easily found, but they tend to be expensive. **Annual maintenance cost:** Average. The underhood area is crowded, making maintenance a little more complicated. **Warranty:** Bumper-to-bumper 3 years/60,000 km; rust perforation 5 years/unlimited km. **Supplementary warranty:** A wise investment, particularly if you have to replace the AC, automatic transmission, and fuel pump around the fifth year of use. **Highway/city fuel economy:** 7.5–12L/100 km with the 3.0L; 9–14L/100 km with the SHO V8.

Quality/Reliability/Safety

Pro: Quality control: Average for an American car, but not up to Japanese or European standards. The SHO engine has been particularly reliable. **Warranty performance:** Average. Ford has been remiss of late in handling both engine and automatic transmission warranty claims.

Con: Paint and body assembly are sub-par and body squeaks and rattles are omnipresent. Assembly quality depends a lot on where the car was put together: insiders tell me that Atlanta is tops, and Chicago is below average. **Reliability:** Mediocre long-term reliability. **Owner-reported problems:** Automatic transmission, AC, electrical system (lots of blown fuses), steering, fuel system, fuel pumps, front suspension, and ignition problems are frequently reported on these cars. There have been lots of complaints concerning paint delamination (fading, chalking, and peeling) and, surprisingly, premature rusting along the door edges, handles, taillight housings, deck lid, and inside hood area, as the photo of a three-year-old Taurus on the following page shows.

Service bulletin problems: No Forward/Reverse; torque converter clutch may not engage; intermittent neutral condition; rattling noise during acceleration with the 3.0L engine (last two bulletins are reprinted below and on the following page).

Article No.
98-3-7
02/16/98
TRANSAXLE - AX4N - INTERMITTENT NEUTRAL
CONDITION - NO FORWARD OR REVERSE
MOVEMENT - VEHICLES BUILT THROUGH 2/1/98
FORD:
1994–98 TAURUS
LINCOLN-MERCURY:
1994–98 SABLE
1995–98 CONTINENTAL
ISSUE:
Some vehicles may experience an intermittent Neutral condition after driving and coming to a stop. This may be caused by the bonded seals on the forward clutch piston intermittently not sealing during the 3–2 downshift.
ACTION:
Replace the forward clutch piston with a revised Forward Clutch Piston (F8DZ-7A262-AB). Refer to the following Service Procedure for details.
SERVICE PROCEDURE:
Clean and reseal the transaxle completely including replacement of the forward clutch piston with revised forward clutch piston and replace the forward clutch plates if darkened or discolored from heat. Refer to the appropriate Continental Service Manual, Section 07-01, or the appropriate Taurus/Sable Service Manual, Section 07-013, for details.
Be sure to check end clearance on all three (3) select fit thrust washers (# 16, # 8, 1.02-1.50 mm (0.040-0.059")). Be sure to clean and inspect the main control (pump and valve body) and servos. Prior to returning vehicle to customer recheck fluid level at operating temperature.

PART NUMBER	PART NAME
F5DZJ153-AA	Seal And Gasket kit
F8DZ-7A262-AB	Forward Clutch Piston
F8DZ-7B164-AC	Forward Clutch Plates - Friction (4)
F2DZ-7B442-A	Forward Clutch Plates - Steel (4)

OTHER APPLICABLE ARTICLES: NONE

The ubiquitous forward clutch piston fails again!

```
Article No.
97-26-11
12/22/97
NOISE - "RATTLING" NOISE DURING
ACCELERATION - ALL ENGINE TEMPERATURES -
3.0L VEHICLES BUILT THROUGH 10/30/97
FORD:
1996-98 TAURUS
LINCOLN-MERCURY:
1996-98 SABLE
ISSUE:
Some vehicles may experience a "baby rattle" noise during acceleration. This noise may be greatest at high engine rpms just
before the transaxle shifts into the next higher gear. This may be caused by exhaust flow within the flex coupling. This rat-
tle should not be confused with spark knock which occurs at low rpm, high engine load conditions.
ACTION:
Replace the exhaust pipe flex coupling. The new coupling has a revised interior to reduce the possibility of rattling. Refer to
the following text for details.
Verify the "rattling" noise occurs only on accelerations just before the transaxle shifts.
Replace the previous flex pine with a new Flex Pipe (F8DZ-5G203-AA). Refer to the Service Procedure outlined in the appro-
priate Taurus/Sable Service Manual.
PART NUMBER      PART NAME
F8DZ-5G203-AA    Flex Pipe
OTHER APPLICABLE ARTICLES:
NONE
WARRANTY STATUS:
Eligible Under The Provisions Of Bumper To Bumper Warranty Coverage
OPERATION        DESCRIPTION       TIME
972S11A          Replace Flex Pipe  0.8 Hr.
```

Remember, this exhaust pipe replacement is fully covered by the base warranty; it's not a maintenance item.

NHTSA safety complaints/safety: Excessive windshield glare; at highway speeds the Overdrive light flashes and the vehicle stalls; sudden stalling at all speeds; airbags deployed during a "fender-bender" accident; sudden acceleration; sudden loss of steering when bolt fell out of steering column. However, offset crash tests carried out by the Insurance Institute for Highway Safety concluded that both the driver and front passenger would be well protected.

Road Performance

Pro: Acceleration/torque: Better than average with the 3.0L engine (0–100 km/h: 8.7 sec.). The base 3.0L V6 is a decade-old engine that offers adequate power for most driving situations, while the twin cam Duratec version provides exhilarating, quiet acceleration equal to the European-influenced chassis dynamics. **Transmission:** The 4-speed automatic transmission shifts smoothly and responsively. **Routine handling:** The sedan's handling, both around town and on the highway, is better than average due primarily to its solid suspension and stiff body construction. **Emergency handling:** Better than average. **Steering:** The speed-sensitive variable-assist power steering makes the car easier to handle, but not as much as Ford claims.

Con: Ford's 3.0L Vulcan V6 is okay for rentals and city commuting, but it's unable to take full advantage of the car's excellent handling characteristics. Wagons handle poorly in turns and over uneven terrain. The high-performance SHO doesn't handle well in tight spaces, requiring four more feet to make a U-turn. **Braking:** Unimpressive braking (100–0 km/h: 134 ft.). ABS produces strong pedal pulsations.

Comfort/Convenience

Pro: Standard equipment: Lots of convenience features, but four-wheel disc anti-lock brakes are optional. The three-way front-seat console is a nice touch. It's a flip-fold affair that's a regular seat, an armrest, or a cup-and coin-carrying console. Armrest switches make it easy to activate the door locks and power windows. Efficient and quiet climate control system. **Interior space/comfort F/R:** Loads of room both in the front and in the rear. The standard seats are comfortable for most people, but the wagon's fabric-covered seats are more comfortable and supportive than the leather-covered sedan seats. The sedans will seat five in comfort, while the wagons offer an optional third seat. **Cargo space:** There's lots of cargo area in the wagon, and its innovative two-way tailgate allows the entire unit to swing out for large cargo or just the window glass to open for small packages. **Trunk/liftover:** The sedan's huge trunk has a low liftover and split rear seatbacks to facilitate easier loading.

Con: Ugly (in my opinion) elliptical styling makes the car look smaller, even though it's more than five inches longer and almost two inches wider than the original. The SHO sedan is loaded with exterior styling gimmicks that may not be to everyone's taste. The wagon's interior plastic trim is cheap. **Driving position:** Short drivers will have to strain to reach the accelerator and see over the dash and tall drivers will find thigh support lacking. Leather seats offer little lateral support. **Controls and displays:** The massive dash and digital treatment are gimmicky and take getting used to. The radio is set too low and too far forward, and the JBL Premium Sound System's push-button controls require a Ph.D. to understand. Radio reception quality is disappointing. **Climate control:** The rear window defroster is hard to find on the left side of the steering column. Air conditioning push buttons are difficult to understand and manipulate. The low-fuel warning light comes on with enough fuel to travel 160 km. The wagon's liftgate doesn't rise high enough to clear most people's heads. **Entry/exit:** Difficult third seat access and limited head room for the third seat passenger. **Quietness:** Both the sedan and wagon's noise levels are unusually high, with lots of wind noise and tire drumming from the rear.

COST				
List Price (negotiable)	**Residual Values** (months)			
	24	**36**	**48**	**60**
Taurus LX: $23,295 (20%)	$14,000	$12,000	$10,000	$7500

TECHNICAL DATA

Powertrain (front-drive)
Engines: 3.0L V6 (145 hp)
• 3.0L V6 (200 hp)
• 3.4L V8 (235 hp)
Transmissions: 5-speed man.
• 4-speed auto.
Dimensions (LX)
Passengers: 5

Height/length/width:
55.1/197.5/73.1 in.
Head room F/R: 39.2/36.2 in.
Leg room F/R: 42.2/38.9 in.
Wheelbase: 108.5 in.
Cargo capacity: 15.8 cu. ft.
Towing capacity: 1,750 lbs.
Fuel tank: 60L/reg.
Weight: 3,350 lbs.

SAFETY FEATURES

	Std.	Opt.
Anti-lock brakes	❑	■
Seatbelt pretensioners	—	—
Integrated child safety seat	—	—
Airbag cut-off switch	—	—
Depowered airbags	■	❑
Side airbags	—	—
Traction control	—	—
Visibility (front/rear)	*****	*****
Crash protection D/P	*****	*****
Crash protection (side) D/P	***	***
HLDI injury claims	N/A	

Crown Victoria/Grand Marquis/Town Car

Town Car

RATING: Recommended. Best suited for highway cruising and trailer towing. **Strong points:** Lots of interior room, quiet running, easy entry/exit, reliable, and excellent resale value. A natural gas V8 engine is available. **Weak points:** Difficult trunk access and terrible fuel economy.

NEW FOR '99: Completely revamped last year, this year's changes are more modest: front side airbags, ABS, an upgraded sound system, and an anti-theft system are standard, and sound insulation has been improved.

GENERAL COMMENTS: The industry's lowest-priced six-passenger V8 sedans, the Crown Victoria and Grand Marquis have always been a favourite with police, taxi drivers, farmers, and retirees. Now, with last year's addition of a 4.6L OHC V8, they're likely to stay around a relatively long time without many other changes.

Aside from the sheer wastefulness of the design and the high fuel cost of running one of these boats, they're fairly reliable and predictable highway cruisers. Handling isn't very responsive, but everyone is going to be comfortable inside. The mechanical design is straightforward and easy to troubleshoot (electronic gizmos excepted). The Crown Victoria and Grand Marquis have consistently come out on top in quality surveys of North American cars.

Speed-sensitive variable-assist power steering is a standard feature, as it is with most of Ford's luxury cars. The base model and LX are joined by the Touring Sedan, which offers a firmer ride, a more responsive handling package, and different exterior and interior styling touches. An electronically controlled automatic transmission has been around since early 1992.

The Lincoln Town Car still represents the epitome of large car luxury to many people, and it's a popular rear-drive base for Ford's luxury cars. A stretched version of the Crown Victoria/Marquis, its air-spring rear suspension provides a smooth ride and prevents tail-dragging, even when fully loaded.

Cost analysis/alternatives: Get the '99 model for the safety upgrades; only consider a '98 model if the price is cut considerably. The Marquis is a slightly more luxurious version of the Crown that costs more but gives little of consequence for the extra expense. Other cars worth considering: Nissan Maxima, Mazda Millenia, Toyota Avalon, and Volvo 900/S90 series. **Recommended options:** Invest in the "Handling and Performance" option to reduce body roll and increase traction, and in a power seat. **Rebates:** In the late fall expect $1,500 rebates on the '98 Crown Victoria and Grand Marquis and more generous rebates and dealer incentives applied to the '98 Town Car. **Destination charge:** $500. **Depreciation:** Slower than average. **Insurance cost:** Higher than average. **Parts supply/cost:** Parts aren't hard to find, but the CAA says that Crown Victoria parts are more expensive than most other cars in this class. **Annual maintenance cost:** Higher than average. Although repairs are relatively easy to carry out, these cars have complicated fuel and electronic systems that are a pain in the butt and wallet to troubleshoot. **Warranty:** *Crown Victoria and Grand Marquis*: Bumper-to-bumper 3 years/60,000 km; rust perforation 5 years/unlimited km. *Town Car*: Bumper-to-bumper 4 years/80,000 km; rust perforation 5 years/unlimited km. **Supplementary warranty:** A good idea as protection from costly diagnostic procedures. **Highway/city fuel economy:** 8.5–14L/100 km.

Quality/Reliability/Safety

Pro: Quality control: Body components and construction are first rate. **Reliability:** Overall reliability has been above average for the past several years. **Warranty performance:** Very good. **Service bulletin problems:** Nothing important.

Con: Owner-reported problems: Main problem areas are the engine computer module, the electrical system, air-conditioning compressor, prematurely worn brakes, faulty seat tracks and door mouldings, and the fuel system. **NHTSA safety complaints/safety:** Crown Victoria's front seats may suddenly come loose and tilt; sharp edges on the Crown Victoria's doors have injured several people; the Grand Marquis' poor gas/brake pedal design caused one minor accident.

Road Performance

Pro: Acceleration/torque: Respectable, though not impressive, acceleration with plenty of low-end torque (0–100 km/h: 10.2 sec.). The smooth, quiet-running 4.6L V8 provides more than enough power for a comfortable ride. Towing capacity is 2,250 kg (5,000 lbs.) with the Class III Towing or Handling and Performance packages offered with the Grand Marquis. **Transmission:** Flawless, most of the time. **Routine handling:** Fairly good for vehicles this large. Ride isn't overly soft. A '98 improvement smoothed out the ride and revised the steering to upgrade the handling. In effect, the rear end no longer sways when you turn the steering wheel. **Emergency handling:** A bit slow, but predictable and sure-footed. Less body lean in corners thanks to the upgraded suspension. **Steering:** Improved steering transmits more road feel than before. **Braking:** Better than average braking with the four-wheel disc brakes (100–0 km/h: 124 ft.).

Con: Transmission sometimes hesitates between gear changes. Handling still takes a backseat to ride quality. Despite improvements, steering is still rather vague.

Comfort/Convenience

Pro: Standard equipment: Lots of standard convenience features. **Driving position:** Very comfortable driving position. **Controls and displays:** Everything is within easy reach and well presented. **Climate control:** Powerful, quiet ventilation system. **Interior space/comfort F/R:** Spacious interior: three passengers are comfortable in the back, where there's lots of head, leg, and shoulder room. The individual front seats are large, comfortable, and supportive (the power seat option is recommended), particularly in the lumbar region. **Entry/exit:** Large doors make entry/exit a breeze. **Cargo space:** Plenty of storage areas. **Trunk/liftover:** Huge trunk. The Town Car's trunk, for example, is an impressive 22 cubic feet, with a low liftover. **Quietness:** Very quiet interior.

Con: Conservative styling. The driver's right knee frequently hits the dashboard/radio housing. Seatbelt anchor pokes into driver's right hip. Distracting continuous digital readout of your fuel economy. The Town Car's electronic dash is too gimmicky, and its moonroof cuts down on rear head room. Confusing power seat and controls. Climate control system is slow to warm up. Poor rear visibility. The split-bench front seat in the Crown Victoria isn't very comfortable due to its insufficient seatback padding and side support. Rear seats also lack sufficient seatback padding. Heater is a bit slow to warm up. Deep-dish trunk that's not very practical for everyday baggage. You have to do some acrobatics to get at the full-sized spare tire, which is placed far forward in the trunk.

COST

List Price (negotiable)	Residual Values (months)			
	24	36	48	60
Base Crown Victoria:				
$33,695 (22%)	$23,000	$18,000	$14,000	$12,000
Town Car Executive:				
$50,895 (31%)	$36,000	$27,000	$23,000	$19,000

TECHNICAL DATA

Powertrain (rear-drive)
Engines: 4.6 (175 hp) natural gas
• 4.6 (190 hp)
• 4.6 (200 hp)
• 4.6 (220 hp)
Transmission: 4-speed auto.
Dimensions (Crown Victoria)
Passengers: 6

Height/length/width:
56.8/212/77.9 in.
Head room F/R: 39.4/38 in.
Leg room F/R: 42.5/39.6 in.
Wheelbase: 114.4 in.
Cargo capacity: 20.6 cu. ft.
Towing capacity: 2,000 lbs.
Fuel tank: 75L/reg.
Weight: 3,800 lbs.

SAFETY FEATURES

	Std.	Opt.
Anti-lock brakes	■	■
Seatbelt pretensioners	—	—
Integrated child safety seat	—	—
Airbag cut-off switch	—	—
Depowered airbags	■	❑
Side airbags	■	—
Traction control	■	■
Visibility (front/rear)	*****	**
Crash protection D/P	*****	*****
Town Car	****	*****
Crash protection (side) D/P	****	****
HLDI injury claims	Low	

Lincoln Continental

Lincoln Continental

RATING: Average. Think of the Continental as a larger, fully loaded Ford Taurus. **Strong points:** Many standard features, comfortable ride, easy access, and lots of cargo room. **Weak points:** Limited rear seat room, delayed transmission engagement, and uncertain long-term reliability.

NEW FOR '99: Fifteen more horses, optional side airbags, and an upgraded sound system.

GENERAL COMMENTS: The Continental rests on a modified front-wheel drive Taurus chassis, which is one of the most up-to-date designs on the road. With the addition of a depowered 4.6L V8 used in the Mark VIII as the standard powerplant, performance has improved immeasurably, to the point that it's now comparable to other Lincolns. One of the Continental's strong selling points is its large array of standard features that would cost extra on many other luxury sedans.

Cost analysis/alternatives: Get the '99 model for the extra horses and airbags; only consider a '98 model if the price is cut 15–20 percent. Other cars you may wish to consider: the Ford Crown Victoria or Marquis, Lincoln Town Car, Infiniti, Lexus, Mercedes-Benz 300 series, or Toyota Avalon. The Continental is less expensive than imported luxury sedans, without sacrificing luxury features or innovative technology. On the other hand, German and Japanese models leave the Continental far behind in handling, braking, engine smoothness, and overall reliability. **Recommended options:** A one-touch panic button (RESCU) that alerts the police, ambulance, or tow truck to your whereabouts through a patch between the cellular phone network and global satellites; and run-flat Michelin ZP tires that can be driven up to 80 km (50 miles) without tire pressure. **Rebates:** Expect $3,000 dealer incentives on the '98s early in the new year. **Destination charge:** $500. **Depreciation:** Faster than average. **Insurance cost:** Higher than average. **Parts supply/cost:** Parts are easy to come by and reasonably priced, says CAA. **Annual maintenance cost:** Higher than average. The sequential fuel-injection system is difficult and costly to service when problems arise. **Warranty:** Bumper-to-bumper 4 years/80,000 km; rust perforation 5 years/unlimited km. **Supplementary warranty:** A good idea, not just because of the Continental's uncertain long-term reliability, but because the complicated mechanical and electrical components cost so much to troubleshoot and replace. **Highway/city fuel economy:** 9–13.5L/km.

Quality/Reliability/Safety

Pro: Quality control: Overall quality control is the best of domestic luxury cars, which is far from complimentary. **Reliability:** Average; the front brakes and suspension system aren't very durable. **Warranty performance:** Better than average.

Con: Owner-reported problems: AC, automatic transmission, and fuel pump failures and lots of body squeaks and rattles. The added complexity of ABS, an electronic air suspension, and all the other high-tech items found on these cars are likely to cause some headaches with age, which is reason enough to buy an extended warranty. **Service bulletin problems:** Intermittent neutral condition; no Forward/Reverse; noise from rear underbody/suspension; torque converter clutch failure; AM band static; troubleshooting tips for excessive wind and road noise; condensation buildup on inside of windows. **NHTSA safety complaints/safety:** Sudden failure of the tie rod.

Road Performance

Pro: Acceleration/torque: Brisk and smooth acceleration with lots of low-end torque (0–100 km/h: 8 sec.). **Routine handling:** Air suspension helps both ride and handling; the car is smooth on all but the worst roads, but cornering at highway speeds remains precise and predictable. **Emergency handling:** Better than average. **Steering:** The variable-ratio power steering gives the right amount of road feel and control. **Braking:** Acceptable braking, considering the Continental's size (100–0 km/h: 130 ft.).

Con: Transmission: The automatic transmission is sometimes slow to downshift and occasionally has trouble deciding if it wants to be in Overdrive or third gear. Despite its good handling, the Continental does feel clumsy around town. The computer-controlled air suspension emits an irritating hissing sound when it settles after parking. Some torque steer (steering twists a bit) when the accelerator pedal is floored.

Comfort/Convenience

Pro: Standard equipment: A sophisticated air cushion suspension allows the driver to dial in different suspension settings for all driving conditions. **Driving position:** Comfortable seating and good all-around visibility. **Entry/exit:** Easy front and rear access. **Interior space/comfort F/R:** Better than average. The interior is narrower than other domestic cars in this class, but it's plush and comfortable. **Trunk/liftover:** Large trunk and low liftover facilitate loading. **Quietness:** Very little engine, road, or wind noise.

Con: Ford's chintzy side is evident when you open the spacious trunk and find that it houses a temporary-service spare tire. Handset cradle is not user-friendly. The standard leather upholstery is slippery, and it's hot in summer and cold in winter. **Climate control:** Fresh air ventilation is adequate, but the automatic climate controls tend to overcompensate and perform erratically. The rear seats need more side and lower back support. **Controls and displays:** The digital dash is hard to read, and some operating controls are inconvenient and illogical. For example, you'll have to shut off the ignition and blindly grope inside the glove compartment for the trunk lid remote release and hope you don't hit the fuel-filler door release instead. Confusing power-window switches. Plus it takes far too many buttons to set the trip computer, suspension mode, and steering effort. Seats aren't as comfortable as the competition's and only two can sit up front. Loading the trunk is made difficult by the protruding rear bumper. **Cargo space:** The interior lacks storage bins for small objects.

COST

List Price (negotiable)	Residual Values (months)			
	24	36	48	60
Continental: $52,795 (31%)	$39,000	$27,000	$22,000	$19,000

TECHNICAL DATA

Powertrain (front-drive)
Engine: 4.6L V8 (275 hp)
Transmission: 4-speed auto.
Dimensions
Passengers: 5
Height/length/width:
56/206.3/73.6 in.

Head room F/R: 39/38 in.
Leg room F/R: 41.9/38.9 in.
Wheelbase: 109 in.
Cargo capacity: 18.1 cu. ft.
Towing capacity: 2,000 lbs.
Fuel tank: 67L/reg.
Weight: 3,900 lbs.

SAFETY FEATURES

	Std.	Opt.
Anti-lock brakes	■	❑
Seatbelt pretensioners	—	—
Integrated child safety seat	—	—
Airbag cut-off switch	—	—

Depowered airbags	■	❑
Side airbags	❑	■
Traction control	■	❑
Visibility (front/rear)	*****	*****
Crash protection D/P	****	*****
Crash protection (side) D/P	N/A	
HLDI injury claims	***	***

Lincoln Mark VIII ('98)

Lincoln Mark VIII

RATING: Above Average. **Strong points:** An exceptional ride, impressive handling, quiet interior, precise steering, and powerful engine make this behemoth a better highway cruiser than city-schlepper. **Weak points:** Limited rear seat room and difficult access.

NEW FOR '99: Nothing. It will be replaced by the Lincoln LS series late next year.

GENERAL COMMENTS: Lincoln's Mark VIII is the latest makeover of the series that began in 1955 with the Mark II. It's set on the Thunderbird platform (the Continental shares the Taurus platform) and uses a 4.6L aluminum V8 engine that puts out 280 hp—15 fewer horses than Cadillac's Northstar powerplant.

Cost analysis/alternatives: Mark VIII shoppers should also consider the Lincoln Town Car or Continental, a fully loaded Ford Crown Victoria/Mercury Grand Marquis, Nissan Maxima, or Toyota Avalon. **Recommended options:** Traction control. **Rebates:** $2,000 rebates by year's end to make room for the new LS models. **Destination charge:** $500. **Depreciation:** Faster than average. **Insurance cost:** Higher than average. **Parts supply/cost:** Parts are easy to find and reasonably priced. **Annual maintenance cost:** Average. **Warranty:** Bumper-to-bumper 4 years/80,000 km; rust perforation 5 years/unlimited km. **Supplementary**

warranty: A wise choice as protection from some of the more expensive repairs associated with the ABS, traction control, AC, and electronic glitches. **Highway/city fuel economy:** 9–13.5L/100 km.

Quality/Reliability/Safety

Pro: Quality control: Very good. **Reliability:** Overall reliability is above average. **Warranty performance:** Ford staffers generally handle warranty claims in a fair and efficient manner. **Service bulletin problems:** Nothing significant—just AM band static.

Con: Owner-reported problems: AC, fuel pump, electronic computer module, and front brakes may be troublesome. **NHTSA safety complaints/safety:** One incident of sudden brake failure.

Road Performance

Pro: Acceleration/torque: Unbelievably fast acceleration and lots of low-end torque. The smooth, quiet-running 4.6L V8 provides more than enough power for a comfortable ride and effortless passing ability—would you believe 0–100 km in 7.2 seconds? **Transmission:** Smooth and quiet-shifting automatic transmission. **Routine handling:** Superior ride quality on the highway. Air suspension provides a smooth ride, no matter what the load. **Emergency handling:** Better than average. The rear-drive Mark VIII handles much better than most of the front-drive luxury coupes. **Steering:** Sensitive steering is a plus around town. **Braking:** Excellent braking with relatively short stopping distances (100–0 km/h: 128 ft.).

Con: Power steering allows for little road feel on the highway and is a bit twitchy due to its too-quick response. Clumsy to manoeuvre and park around town. The ABS pulsing takes getting used to.

Comfort/Convenience

Pro: Driving position: First class. Lots of favourable comments highlighting the comfortable seating up front. **Standard equipment:** Well-appointed, with traction control the only important option available. **Controls and displays:** Controls and gauges are easy to see and reach. **Climate control:** Efficient and quiet climate control system. Plenty of front seat room for two. **Cargo space:** Pretty good. **Quietness:** Except for some wind noise, the interior is exceptionally quiet. **Trunk/liftover:** Large trunk has a wide, flat floor and low liftover to facilitate loading.

Con: Luxurious-looking leather seats don't *feel* luxurious (see "Dumb Options" in Part One). Rear visibility is obstructed by the large rear pillars and small rear window. **Entry/exit:** Rear access is difficult. **Interior space/comfort F/R:** Rear seating is surprisingly tight—two average-sized adults can barely squeeze in.

COST

List Price (negotiable)	Residual Values (months)			
	24	**36**	**48**	**60**
'98 Mark VIII: $53,695 (30%)	$38,000	$24,000	$21,000	$18,000

TECHNICAL DATA

Powertrain (rear-drive)
Engine: 4.6L V8 (280 hp)
Transmission: 4-speed auto.
Dimensions
Passengers: 5
Height/length/width:
53.6/207.3/74.8 in.

Head room F/R: 38.1/37.5 in.
Leg room F/R: 42.6/32.5 in.
Wheelbase: 113 in.
Cargo capacity: 14.4 cu. ft.
Towing capacity: 2,000 lbs.
Fuel tank: 68L/reg.
Weight: 3,800 lbs.

SAFETY FEATURES

	Std.	Opt.
Anti-lock brakes	■	❑
Seatbelt pretensioners	—	—
Integrated child safety seat	—	—
Airbag cut-off switch	—	—
Depowered airbags	■	❑
Side airbags	—	—
Traction control	■	❑
Visibility (front/rear)	*****	**
Crash protection D/P	N/A	
Crash protection (side) D/P	N/A	
HLDI injury claims	Low	

Villager ('98), Quest

Villager

RATING: Recommended. Maxima reliability and Ford styling. **Strong points:** Plenty of passenger and cargo room, comfortable ride with lots of seating choices. Strong Nissan warranty. **Weak points:** Mediocre reliability, difficult rear seat access, limited rear visibility, horrendous gas consumption.

NEW FOR '99: The '99 model Villager is not available in Canada. The Pathfinder's 3.3L V6 replaces the 3.0L V6, giving the Quest an additional 19 horses. Other changes: a fourth door, more interior room, a revised instrument panel that's easier to reach, restyled front and rear ends, improved shifting, acceleration, and braking (ABS takes less effort and is supposedly more durable), the suspension has been retuned to give a more car-like ride and handling, the old climate control system has been ditched for a more sophisticated version with air filtration, and optional ABS is available with all models. Mercury's top-of-the-line model, the Nautica, has been dropped.

GENERAL COMMENTS: Smaller and more car-like than most minivans, these two minivans are built by Ford at its truck factory in Avon Lake, Ohio, and sized comfortably between the regular and extended Chrysler minivans. These front-drive, five- or seven-passenger minivans come without aero-styling gimmicks, having adopted a bit of Chrysler's boxy look and interior dimensions.

Of all the small minivans, the Mercury Villager/Nissan Quest are the most economical to maintain, the least expensive to purchase, and the most fun to whip around the city in. Their strongest assets are car-like handling, modular seating, and reliable mechanical components that have been tested for years on the Maxima.

Mercury, unlike Nissan, offers a cargo version in addition to its five- and seven-passenger models. It's also quite different from the lighter weight, truck-like Ford Aerostar because its front-drive setup and 151-hp 3.0L V6 engine give the Villager car-like handling, ride, and cornering. Nissan borrowed the powertrain, suspension, and steering assembly from its Maxima, mixed in some creative sheet metal, and left the job of outfitting the sound system, climate control, dashboard, steering column, and wheels to Ford. This has resulted in an attractive and not overly aero-styled minivan.

Cost analysis/alternatives: Get the '99 Quest model for the upgrades; don't even consider a '98 model. Expect heavy discounting: Villager sales have suffered a 16 percent decline over the last year. Other minivans worth considering are the Honda Odyssey, or Toyota Sienna. **Recommended options:** The integrated child safety seat is a must-have and the seat height adjuster will benefit short drivers. A separate rear air conditioner/heater and power side windows are also worth considering. The optional performance handling equipment makes little improvement to the standard suspension, and the '98 model Nautica option is simply a high-priced cosmetic makeover. **Rebates:** '98s get $2,000 rebates; the '99 Quest gets $400. **Destination charge:** $875. **Depreciation:** Average. **Insurance cost:** Above average. **Annual**

maintenance cost: Average. **Parts supply/cost:** Good supply and reasonable costs. **Warranty:** *Mercury:* Bumper-to-bumper 3 years/60,000 km; rust perforation 5 years/unlimited km. *Nissan:* Bumper-to-bumper 3 years/80,000 km; powertrain 5 years/100,000 km; rust perforation 5 years/unlimited km. **Supplementary warranty:** An extended warranty isn't needed. **Highway/city fuel economy:** 9.5–13.5L/100 km.

Quality/Reliability/Safety

Pro: Quality control: Much-better-than-average quality control—Nissan designs and develops the minivans while Ford manufactures them. **Reliability:** The engine and drivetrain are borrowed from the Nissan Maxima, a very reliable vehicle. Excellent fit and finish. A large dealer network means that servicing and parts are easily available. According to CAA, parts are less expensive than most other cars in this class. Plenty of glass provides excellent front and rear visibility. **Warranty performance:** Average with Ford and Nissan.

Con: Owner-reported problems: Most owner-reported problems involve interior and exterior noise and driveline vibrations. **Service bulletin problems:** Fuel odour in the passenger compartment; intermittent self-activation of the power door lock; rattling, creaking noise at rear of floor or sliding door (see below).

Article No.
98-3-19
02/16/98
NOISE - "RATTLING/CREAKING NOISE FROM REAR
OF VEHICLE AT FLOOR NEXT TO SLIDING DOOR -
VEHICLES BUILT THROUGH 2/1/98
LIGHT TRUCK:
1997-98 VILLAGER
ISSUE:
A "rattling/creaking" noise may come from the rear of some vehicles. The noise may be present in the floor area or the sliding door. On some vehicles, it may be heard on the left side This may be caused by excessive clearance between the spring shackle plate mounting bolt shoulders and the shackle plate.
ACTION:
Replace both shackle plates and upper bolts. Refer to the following Service Procedure for details.

PART NUMBER	PART NAME
F3XY-5780-A	Bolt
08911-6421A	Nut
08915-3421A	Lockwasher
F3XY-5A765-B	Bracket - Inner
F3XY-5A765-A	Bracket - Outer

OTHER APPLICABLE ARTICLES: NONE
WARRANTY STATUS: Eligible Under The Provisions Of Bumper To Bumper Warranty Coverage

OPERATION	DESCRIPTION	TIME
980319A	Replace Mounting Plates As Outlined	0.8 Hr.

NHTSA safety complaints/safety: ABS failures; brake and accelerator pedals are the same height, so driver's foot can easily slip and step on both at the same time; 22-month-old child was able to pull the clasp apart on integrated child safety seat; rear window on liftgate door shattered for unknown reason. Dealer was aware of problem and replaced window under warranty; door hinge allows the door to damage the fender during average wind storms. Safety investigators are also looking into reports of electric door lock and power window failures that have trapped occupants in their vehicles. Unlike the Windstar, you won't find side airbags on this year's Quest.

Road Performance

Pro: Acceleration/torque: Upgraded V6 engine delivers plenty of power for city and highway driving needs (0–100 km/h: 11.5 sec.). **Transmission:** The 4-speed automatic transmission is much quieter and smoother this year—you can switch from Economy to Power shift mode by pressing a dashboard button. Fourth gear can be locked out to prevent constant gear hunting when going over hilly terrain. **Routine handling:** Handles and manoeuvres like a large station wagon. Agile (the short wheelbase and revised suspension help in this area) and easy to drive, the Villager delivers a no-surprise, smooth, quiet ride on the highway that isn't compromised by a full load. **Emergency handling:** Impressive highway stability. **Steering:** Precise steering makes the Villager quite responsive at highway speeds and in emergency manoeuvres. **Braking:** Braking performance is excellent, because four-wheel ABS improves directional control by eliminating wheel lockup (100–0 km/h: 138 ft.).

Con: Long-legged drivers may find the leg room a bit short. Not the minivan for high-speed cruising or carrying lots of cargo or passengers. Rough terrain or uneven pavement makes for a busy to rough ride. Don't make too much of the Villager's car-like handling. Sure, it handles much better than truck-based minivans like the GM Astro and Ford Aerostar, but it isn't superior to other front-drive minivans. It requires a rather wide turning circle. Towing capacity of 3,500 pounds is possible only with an optional towing package.

Comfort/Convenience

Pro: Standard equipment: Comfortable and well-appointed interior. The standard radio gives great sound. The Villager and Quest offer a large array of standard safety features that include airbags, side-impact beams, reinforced centre pillars, front and rear impact absorbing zones, rear outboard three-point safety belts, ABS, and a childproof door lock in the sliding door. An integrated child seat is optional. **Driving position:** Car-like driving position and comfortable seats, which include a power lumbar support in the driver's seat. **Climate control:** Efficient, powerful climate control system; you can turn on the AC and control the air outlet location separately. All side windows can be opened for maximum ventilation. **Controls and displays:** Most controls and instruments are generally easy to use and read. **Entry/exit:** Easy. Helpful assist grab handles over the front and sliding doors. The front captain's chairs are easily removed, and the modular interior allows 14 possible seating and cargo configurations, making for better seating for three adults in the rear than with most other small vans or wagons. An additional 4.8 inches in length gives second row passengers an extra inch of leg room and two more inches of cargo space. **Cargo space:** Expanded this year. Flexibility and the easy-to-use sliding rear seat make up for the Villager's modest cargo-carrying capacity. Middle seatback folds flat, and the rear seats have tracks that allow them to slide forward all the way to the front. Low liftover height makes for convenient loading from the rear.

Con: Front seats could use more lateral support. **Quietness:** Some wind and road noise.

COST

List Price (negotiable)   **Residual Values** (months)

	24	36	48	60
'98 Villager GS: $23,995 (19%)	$15,000	$12,000	$10,000	$8500

TECHNICAL DATA

Head room F: 39.4/R1: 39.7/
Leg room F:39.9/R1: 34.8/
R2: 36.7 in.
Powertrain (front-drive)
Engine: 3.3L V6 (170 hp)
Transmission: 4-speed auto.
Dimensions ('98 Villager)
Height/length/width:
65.9/190.2/73.8 in.
Wheelbase: 112.2 in.
Passengers: 7
Cargo capacity: 11.8 cu. ft.

Head room F: 39.4/R1: 39.7/R2: 37.3 in.
R2: 37.3 in.
Leg room F:39.9/R1: 36.3/R2: 36.7 in.
Towing capacity: 2,000–3,500 lbs.
Fuel tank: 75L/reg.
Weight: 3,850 lbs.
Dimensions ('98 Quest)
Height/length/width:
65.6/189.9/73.7 in.
Cargo capacity: 14.1 cu. ft.
Weight: 3,850 lbs.

SAFETY FEATURES

	Std.	Opt.
Anti-lock brakes	❑	■
Seatbelt pretensioners	—	—
Integrated child safety seat	❑	■
Airbag cut-off switch	—	—
Depowered airbags	■	❑
Side airbags	—	—
Traction control	—	—
Visibility (front/rear)	*****	*****
Crash protection D/P	****	***
Crash protection (side) D/P	N/A	
HLDI injury claims	Low	

Windstar

Windstar

RATING: Windstar has been downgraded this year from Recommended to Above Average, and an extended warranty is strongly recommended.

I was tempted not to recommend the Windstar, but instead, I've asked for a meeting with Ford's Canadian president to extend the base warranty and compensate owners who I believe were unfairly denied warranty repairs. In the meantime, I'll give her and the '99 Windstar the benefit of the doubt. **Strong points:** Five-star crashworthiness rating (see caveat below); 3.8L engine and automatic 4-speed transmission beat out the Chrysler and GM competition; well-controlled, comfortable ride; good instrument/controls layout; plenty of passenger space. **Weak points:** Powertrain mechanical components don't hold up well from day one. Mediocre city handling and restricted side and rear visibility; poor warranty performance.

NEW FOR '99: A standard fourth door, body stiffness has been increased by 30 percent, optional seat-mounted side airbags, optional rear-bumper sonar sensors, improved steering and brakes, standard ABS, an anti-theft system, new side panels, a new liftgate, larger headlights, and taillights, and a revised instrument panel. The second-row bench seat can now be moved to the right or left to make it easier to access the third row seats.

Exterior dimensions have all decreased slightly; height has been cut by an unusual 2.4 inches. The reworking of the hood makes it easier for drivers to see where the nose of the van is, particularly when parking.

GENERAL COMMENTS: Windstar is a front-drive minivan that looks a bit like a stretched Mercury Villager. It's longer, larger, and lower than most other minivans. It's also one of the few minivans not built on a truck platform (it uses the Taurus platform instead), and so it has some of the car-like handling characteristics of Chrysler's minivans and some of the engine and automatic transmission problems experienced by Taurus and Sable owners. It's offered in two body styles—a seven-passenger people-hauler and the less expensive basic cargo van. Buyers have the choice of two 6-cylinder engines: a standard 147-hp 3.0L V6 or a 200-hp 3.8L V6. Both motors are hooked to a 4-speed electronic automatic transmission.

Cost analysis/alternatives: Get the '99 model for the upgrades; don't even think about getting a '98 model. Chrysler Caravan/Voyager, Honda Odyssey, Mercury Villager ('98)/Nissan Quest, and the Toyota Sienna are recommended alternatives. **Recommended options:** Automatic levelling suspension ($385); dual integrated child safety seats for the middle bench seat; power side windows; and rear air conditioner, defroster, and heater. Don't spring for the centre console option unless you're prepared to sacrifice rear seat access. **Rebates:** $1,500 on the '98s. With minivan sales slowing down, heftier rebates won't be far behind. By the end of the year, look for more generous rebates and dealer incentives. **Destination charge:** $875. **Depreciation:** Much slower than average. **Insurance cost:** Above average. **Annual maintenance cost:** Average. **Parts supply/cost:** Parts are widely available and reasonably priced. **Warranty:** Bumper-to-bumper 3 years/60,000 km; rust perforation 5 years/unlimited km. **Supplementary warranty:** An extended warranty is a good idea. **Highway/city fuel economy:** With the 3.8L V6: 9.5–14L/100 km.

Quality/Reliability/Safety

Pro: Quality control: Good assembly quality. Unlike Chrysler and GM minivans, Windstars don't depend on shims, slots, and toy-tabs on sheet metal to permit inexact parts to be manoeuvred into a fit (akin to putting a round peg into a square hole). This ensures a quiet interior with little engine or road noise.

Con: The last four years have been a disaster from a quality control standpoint. Mechanical components are based on the old Ford Taurus, which had a below-average reliability rating after the third year. **Reliability:** Serious problems affecting 3.8L engine and automatic transmission reliability. Electrical system, fuel pump, and brake defects also frequently sideline the Windstar. **Warranty performance:** Much worse than average. Ford staffers have lost or ignored letters and treated customers with an arrogance that surpasses Chrysler, a company that improved its own attitude after the formation of Canadian CLOG (Chrysler Lemon Owners Group) chapters. Will Ford's poor warranty performance and insensitive attitude lead to the creation of Canadian FLOG groups this year? Stay tuned. **Owner-reported problems:** As stated above, engine and transmission defects lead the list, but there have also been a worrisome number of complaints concerning the electrical components, AC failures, and premature brake wear. Other problems include: coolant leaks; premature tie rod wear; noisy power steering pumps; a rear heating duct behind the driver's seat that gets so hot it can burn an unsuspecting driver's fingers; rear windows that break suddenly because of auxiliary rear heater overheating; and a front windshield that cracks from the base upwards due to faulty mounting or sudden temperature changes. Ford—not your insurance company—should pay the damage claims arising from these windshield problems.

Service bulletin problems: Upper radiator hose leaks; accelerator pedal buzz and exhaust system drone; excessive AC odours; diagnostic tips for finding and fixing suspension noise; rattling, clunking noise from front of vehicle and when moving gearshift lever out of Park (see below); whistling noise from front AC-heater plenum; intermittent neutral condition after coming to a stop (a complaint often reported to NHTSA officials); stalling when decelerating, parking, or coasting (see following page).

Article No.

12/22/97
NOISE - "RATTLING" AND/OR "CLUNKING" NOISE
FROM FRONT OF VEHICLE
LIGHT TRUCK:
1997-98 WINDSTAR
ISSUE:
A "rattling" and/or "clunking" noise may be heard from the front of the vehicle. This may be caused by a loose front tension strut bushing retainer in the subframe front crossmember.
ACTION:
Weld the front tension strut bushing retainer back into place. Refer to the following Service Procedure for details.

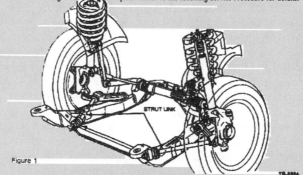

Figure 1

SERVICE PROCEDURE
1. Check to see if the front tension strut retainer is loose by pushing/pulling the strut link side-to-side while watching the retainer for movement. Refer to Figure 1. If no movement is found, stop here. It movement is found, proceed to Step 2.
2. Remove the front strut and bushings from the front crossmember. Refer to Page 04-00-11 in the 1998 Windstar Service Manual for details.
3. Clear the area around the bushing.

Lemon-Aid

Article No.
97-26-15
STALL-DURING DECELERATION TO A STOP, PARKING AND/OR COASTING DURING SLOW SPEED TURNS-VEHICLES BUILT
THROUGH 12/97 EQUIPPED WITH 3.8L ENGINE
LIGHT TRUCK:
1998 WINDSTAR
CALIBRATION:
8-62J-R11, 8-62J-R12, 8-62J-R17, 8-62K-R11, 8-62K-R12, 8-62K-R17, 8-62P-R05, 8-62P-R17, 8-62Q-R05, 8-62Q-R17,
8-62S-R11, 8-62T-R11
ISSUE:
Some vehicles my stall during deceleration when coming to a stop, during slow speed parking maneuvers and/or coasting
through slow sweeping turns. This may be caused by the Powertrain Control Module (PCM) calibration dropping the rpms
too quickly during deceleration.
ACTION:
Reprogram the PCM. The revised calibration will allow the engine rpms to drop slowly during low speed maneuvers to reduce
the possibility of stall. Refer to the following Service Procedure and the Recalibration Cross Reference Chart for the correct
PCM calibration.

NHTSA safety complaints/safety: Fire caused by snow short-circuiting the cooling fan; sudden acceleration; chronic stalling, particularly when decelerating or turning; fuel pump sensor failure causes the fuel pump to shut down; stalling when brakes are applied; automatic transmission failures; transmission jolts continuously; while parked in Park, vehicle jumped into reverse and rolled away; when driving or parked on an incline, transmission jumps from Drive to Neutral; driver made a 90-degree right turn and then the axle disconnected from the transmission; when stopping, brake pedal goes all the way to the floor and causes extended stopping distances; left front brake caliper (ABS) locks up and won't retract; driver's side lower brake caliper fell off; sudden brake loss and brake pedal fell off; power steering hose came loose, spewing fluid; vehicle's rear end sways when reaching cruising speeds; driver's seat shifts on its tracks, won't lock when coming to a stop, seat moves forward; electric windows work only with key off and out of the ignition; trunk lid crashed down upon driver's head while unloading vehicle; Ford says its integrated child safety seat will hold a child up to a maximum weight of 60 lbs., however children up to 43 lbs. may not fit; seatbelts in second row middle seat are too tight, and a passenger can't lean forward; speedometer doesn't reset to zero; ran out of fuel, but fuel gauge indicated plenty of fuel left.

Windstar's five-star crash rating may decline after the revised van is tested. Chrysler's additional door compromised its crash rating. The '98 Windstar has been recalled for two problems: a defective rack-and-pinion input shaft bearing that could affect steering, and a faulty transmission low/intermediate servo cover may leak fluid creating the possibility of a fire.

Road Performance

Pro: Acceleration/torque: The 3.8L V6 is usually competent and smooth, with lots of low-end torque (0–100 km/h: 10.7 sec.). In fact, when mated with the 4-speed transmission its overall performance is superior to what GM and Chrysler offer. **Transmission:** The electronic

4-speed automatic responds well and shifts smoothly, most of the time (see "Con"). Fourth gear can be locked out for towing. **Routine handling:** Easy to drive. Smooth and supple ride under most driving conditions improves as the load increases. **Emergency handling:** High-speed handling is acceptably stable and predictable, and the steering is particularly precise and light. **Steering:** Light and responsive, though not as effortless as the competition.

Con: Engine frequently stalls due to fuel pump, computer module, and electrical system glitches. Erratically performing automatic gearbox often slips out of gear, lurches into gear, or simply refuses to engage whichever gear you choose. The Windstar's city manners aren't impressive: excessive body lean makes highway driving less car-like than the shorter base Chrysler minivans. It also has a large turning radius. Lots of wind noise on the highway. **Braking:** Average braking that's a bit difficult to modulate.

Comfort/Convenience

Pro: Standard equipment: Comfortable and well-appointed interior. Superior sound system. One innovative touch that many families will appreciate: a wide-angle mirror housed in the ceiling console lets the driver watch the little darlings in the rear without turning around. **Driving position:** Excellent driving position gives most drivers a commanding view of the road. **Controls and displays:** Well laid-out instrument panel with easy-to-read gauges. **Climate control:** Adequate and easily adjusted. **Entry/exit:** Acceptable. **Cargo space:** Lots of small storage spaces in addition to the large amount of space for larger items. Another nice touch is the optional power lock switch just inside the rear hatch, which saves you from having to walk to the front of the van to lock up. **Trunk/liftover:** Rear hatch is easy to open and shut, and the low floor improves cargo handling. **Quietness:** Generally quiet interior.

Con: The Windstar's driver's seat isn't comfortable for big, tall drivers, who complain of the lack of leg room, seat contouring, and lower back support. Uncomfortable driver's shoulder belt can ride on a tall driver's collarbone because it's anchored too far back. It's also a long reach to put on. Headlight switch is partly obscured by the steering wheel. Tiny, flat buttons on the Windstar's radio make it hard to calibrate. Weak AC and heater airflow to the floor makes an auxiliary heater a good idea. **Interior space/comfort F/R:** Although the seats are easily removed, getting them in and out of the vehicle is more of a chore than it is for the Chrysler minivans (the rear bench seat alone weighs 110 lbs., or almost 50 kg). Restricted side/rear visibility. **Cargo space:** Unlike Chrysler, Ford still hasn't figured out a way to reconfigure the Windstar's storage space so that it will hold bulky items like 4x8 sheets of building material. The right sliding door takes a lot of effort to open and close. Some wind and road noise.

COST

List Price (firm)   **Residual Values** (months)

	24	36	48	60
Windstar 3.0L: $24,295 (20%)	$18,000	$15,000	$11,000	$8000

TECHNICAL DATA

Powertrain (front-drive)
Engines: 3.0L V6 (147 hp)
• 3.8L (200 hp)
Transmission: 4-speed auto.
Dimensions ('98 LX)
Height/length/width:
68/201.2/74.3 in.

Head room F: 39.3/R1: 38.9 /R2: 38.1 in.
Leg room F:41.8/R1: 39.2/R2: 35.3 in.
Wheelbase: 120.7 in.
Passengers: 7
Cargo capacity: 21.7 cu. ft.
Towing capacity: 3,500 lbs.
Fuel tank: 75/94L
Weight: 3,850 lbs.

SAFETY FEATURES

	Std.	Opt.
Anti-lock brakes	■	❏
Seatbelt pretensioners	—	—
Integrated child safety seat	❏	■
Airbag cut-off switch	—	—
Depowered airbags	■	❏
Side airbags	—	❏
Traction control	—	—
Visibility (front/rear)	*****	*****
Crash protection D/P	*****	*****
Crash protection (side) D/P	N/A	
HLDI injury claims	Low	

JAGUAR

XJ8, XJ8L, XJR, Vanden Plas, XK8

XJ8

RATING: Not Recommended. As far as interior space, reliability, and overall quality are concerned, other automakers offer better products for less. **Strong points:** Impressive engine performance, superb handling, and a well-appointed interior. **Weak points:** Not much room for cargo, a cramped interior, uncertain reliability and dealer servicing, and accelerated depreciation.

NEW FOR '99: Few significant changes for the XJ- or the XK-series. Sharing its rear-drive platform with Ford's new Lincoln LS sedan, the S-Type will be Jaguar's smallest luxury car, and is scheduled to debut in mid 1999. The XJ8 will be replaced next year by a new 2000 model.

GENERAL COMMENTS: Jaguar's name conjures up images of posh sedans and fast sports cars rolling through the English countryside. Jaguars reek of elegance, taste, and money. The car's styling, ride, handling, and comfort still entice motorists full of nostalgia for British cars of the 1960s, but mechanical, electronic, and body problems persist, though there aren't as many as a decade ago. Interestingly, that may explain why Jaguars have such a high rate of depreciation, and why 70 percent of buyers prefer to lease rather than purchase their "Jag."

There are two models to choose from: the XJ8 and the XK8. XJ8s have four variations to choose from: the entry-level XJ8 ($76,900), the long-wheelbase XJ8L, the luxurious long-wheelbase Vanden Plas ($89,900), and the standard-length, supercharged XJR ($92,900). XK8 models are available as coupes or convertibles ($91,900 and $99,900).

Caught in a dilemma similar to that of the Corvette, the Jaguar's excess weight makes it necessary to install lots of complicated and difficult-to-troubleshoot devices, as well as larger engines, in order to make these cars decent highway performers.

Now that Ford has taken over the company, long-term reliability is still a rather large question mark. Nevertheless, the company does offer a 30-day, money-back guarantee (about 2 percent of the cars have been taken back) and a comprehensive 4-year/80,000-km base mechanical warranty. The automaker also provides a 6-year/unlimited-km rust perforation warranty, and Jaguar Club benefits that include no-cost maintenance, roadside assistance, and trip interruption services.

Poor servicing has compounded the quality-control problem. Owners report long delays for service appointments and then even longer waits for the right parts to arrive. Unfortunately, there aren't many Jaguar dealers to choose from, so if you don't find a competent and conscientious one it's doubtful that you'll be able to go elsewhere for a second opinion.

XJ8

XJ8s continue to use the 1994 XJ body design with just minor trim changes, upgraded headlights and taillights, more rounded bumpers, and a slightly larger grille. As with the XK8, the only available engine is a 4.0L 290-hp V8, but the XJR adds a supercharger that raises output to 370 hp. Mechanical components have been enhanced with a suspension upgrade borrowed from the XK8, larger front disc brakes, a 5-speed automatic transmission, and standard traction control.

Interior features include upgraded front seats incorporating standard side airbags and seatbelt pretensioners. The cramped interior was restyled last year rather than enlarged (the longer-wheelbase Vanden Plas used its extra room mostly for rear seat passengers).

The XK8's race car styling is a sure-fire head-turner.

XK8

Jaguar's replacement for the XJS, the rear-drive XK8 is a beautifully styled coupe and convertible that has lines similar to its XK 120 and E Type predecessors. It comes with an extensive list of bells and whistles and a 4.0L V8 engine that's identical to the one used by the XJ8. Automatic stability control is standard, and traction control is optional. Billed as a four-seater, the XK8 is actually a two-seater with practically no rear-seat leg room. Fortunately, it does have a fairly spacious trunk when compared with other roadsters and coupes in its class.

Cost analysis/alternatives: Although sales through August '98 have been much better than last year, Jaguar still is a low volume seller (856 vs. 692 units through August) and deep discounting is quite common. There isn't any compelling reason to buy or lease a '98 or '99 Jaguar when the car is compared with less expensive convertible/roadsters like the BMW Z3, Mercedes SLK, and Porsche Boxster. Other more reliable luxury cars you may wish to consider are the BMW 7 series, Lexus models, the Lincoln Town Car and '98 Mark VIII, Infiniti models, Mercedes' S-class, Nissan's Maxima, and the Toyota Camry or Avalon. **Recommended options:** Traction control. **Rebates:** Expect $2,000–$3,000 rebates on unsold '98s by year's end. **Destination charge:** $600. **Depreciation:** Resale price plummets about as quickly as Bre-X stock. **Insurance cost:** Higher than average. **Parts supply/cost:** Parts are often back-ordered because not a lot of Ford dealer inventory goes into stocking Jaguar parts. Parts are moderately expensive as well, and there aren't any independent suppliers that could inject price competition into the equation. **Annual maintenance cost:** Higher than average. **Warranty:** Bumper-to-bumper 4 years/80,000 km; rust perforation 6 years/unlimited km. **Supplementary warranty:** Don't leave home without it. **Highway/city fuel economy:** 9.5–14L/100 km (Vanden Plas); 10.5–16L/100 km (XJR); 13–20L/100 km (XJS); 13.5–20.3L/100 km (XJ12).

GENERAL MOTORS

Redundant models, little focus

Ever since GM began switching over to front-drives, almost two decades ago, it has earned a reputation for making look-alike low-quality vehicles. This is one of the main reasons why GM's U.S. market share has plummeted from nearly 50 percent in the late 1970s to its current 30 percent.

Although it may be hard to believe, America's largest automaker has still managed to make record profits selling fewer cars and trucks. That's because they've cut production costs by closing plants, slashing jobs, reducing the number of parts, and using common parts across several product lines. But GM's labour costs to build a single car are still the highest of the Big Three. GM spends almost 30 hours per vehicle— 20 percent longer than Ford's average time.

Pressure is mounting for GM to reinvent itself. Although the automaker's profits have been substantial, its market share over the past decade has plummeted to less than 30 percent (25 percent during last fall's two-month strike), thinly spread over six vehicle divisions.

GM knows it has become the marginal car champ, with too many nameplates for models that are both identical and bland. Its various divisions are in serious need of pruning and restructuring. While axing the Olds 88 and Riviera are smart moves, GM's entire Olds division should be dropped—it makes no sense at all to have seven Olds nameplates on seven different model platforms. In fact, Olds sales have declined over the past ten years almost as much as Saturn sales have increased.

Saturn

Having had only one facelift in eight model years, Saturn is starved for new product, and is presently being forced to act like GM's other divisions—despite GM's promises that Saturn would be treated differently. Saturn Corp. will be marketing its cars differently this year, as well. Instead of using actual owners and plant workers in its TV ads, the company will use actors to tell customer stories. Critics say this is another indication that Saturn is "morphing" into a car division no different than GM's other car divisions. In fact, GM has announced that it intends to fold Saturn into its year 2002 Delta platform where it will join the Cavalier and Sunfire.

Post-strike pricing, quality control

GM was hurt by the recent two-month strike and can't afford to lose any more market share. Consequently, the automaker intends to cut '98 and '99 model prices way below what the competition can afford. This should mean substantial rebates, dealer incentives, and cut-rate financing applicable to the entire model lineup, including minivans.

Make sure, though, that what you save through a lower price isn't taken away by other charges. Your best bet is to consider how the bottom-line price, essential options, dealer incentives, rebates, and included taxes measure up against comparable domestic and Japanese makes. Remember, the bottom-line price should exclude all the little "extras" that dealers like to tack on just before getting your signature (administration fee, acquisition fee, and destination and pre-delivery charges).

As for the no-price-haggling stipulation, haggle away. *Lemon-Aid* readers report that salespeople often ignore the no-haggle edict if they feel that the customer is a serious prospect.

The downside to GM's recent strike settlement is that most of its first-series '99 models will have serious factory-related defects, caused by a rush to production in order to meet dealer backorders, employees working at new assembly line stations, and an influx of insufficiently field-tested supplier components.

Smart shoppers will wait until early next spring and pick out a GM "second-series" vehicle that was made in March or later (check the driver-side doorplate) and also take advantage of the flurry of new rebates that are announced at that time.

Metro/Firefly, Swift

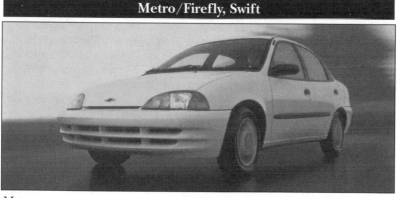

Metro

RATING: Average. Acceptable only for bare-bones city commuting, where fuel savings and agility are paramount. **Strong points:** Cheap to buy and cheap to run, better than average quality control, fun to drive with a manual shifter. **Weak points:** Anemic, noisy engine makes these cars the antithesis of "swift"; harsh, choppy ride; lots of interior noise; a spartan interior; poorly performing original equipment tires; and terrible braking.

NEW FOR '99: Several new exterior colours. Swift is a carried-over model, only available in limited quantities while Suzuki gears up its Vitara production.

GENERAL COMMENTS: Good city and commuter cars that are capable of fitting into the tiniest of parking spaces and nipping through narrow city streets, but still provide sufficient room inside for two adults and their cargo. Interestingly, only GM offers optional power steering. These cars deliver outstanding fuel economy because of an unusual aluminum 1.0L 3-cylinder engine, which is a little rough around the edges but gets the job done efficiently. People who'd like a little more zest from their city scooter can order the fuel-injected 1.3L 4-banger.

Cost analysis/alternatives: Get the '99 model if it's discounted; only consider a '98 model if the price is cut at least 10 percent. The XFi bare-bones Metro is the fuel economy champion, but it sacrifices an automatic transmission and a host of other amenities. Actually, a better-equipped model would be almost as economical. Convertibles are the best choice for ragtop thrills that won't break your budget. Compare prices with the Suzuki Swift, the Metro's twin; it offers a longer warranty and more standard features for less. Other cars to consider are the Honda Civic, Hyundai Accent, and Toyota Tercel. **Recommended options:** The larger engine with fuel injection, a remote trunk release, and split folding rear seats (sedans). Premium tires. **Rebates:** $500 on '99 Metros and Fireflys and $750 on the '98s; '97 and '98 Swifts get a $500 dealer incentive. **Destination charge:** $525. **Depreciation:** Faster than average. **Insurance cost:** Lower than average. **Parts supply/cost:** Average availability and reasonably priced (powertrain components tend to be pricey). Shop around for the best price among GM and Suzuki dealers. **Annual maintenance cost:** Below average. Maintenance is made simple by an uncluttered underhood layout and the availability of two dealer networks for servicing. **Warranty:** Bumper-to-bumper 3 years/60,000 km; rust perforation 6 years/160,000 km. *Suzuki:* Bumper-to-bumper 3 years/80,000 km; rust perforation 5 years/unlimited km. **Supplementary warranty:** Not needed. **Highway/city fuel economy:** 4.5–5.4L/100 km with the 1.0L and 5-speed manual; 5–6.5L/100 km with the 1.3L and 5-speed manual; 6.2–8L/100 km with the 1.3L and 3-speed automatic.

Quality/Reliability/Safety

Pro: Quality control: Better than average. This is a low-cost and low-maintenance econobox with a better than average repair record that goes back many years. The trend seems to be continuing, judging by the absence of significant problems reported by owners. **Reliability:** Fairly good, except for some fuel-injection glitches and engine headgasket failures. If not checked often for corrosion and leaks the cooling system will eventually fail, causing serious damage to the aluminum engine. **Warranty performance:** Very good with Suzuki; average at GM. **Service bulletin problems:** Nothing significant. **NHTSA safety complaints/safety:** *Metro:* Sudden acceleration; taillight failure when daylight running lights are on; strut failures; transmission failures; clutch failures; brakes are noisy and make for extended stopping distances; emergency brake applied, but vehicle still rolled backwards. Chassis rigidity and crash safety have been enhanced with the placement of a steel beam behind the instrument panel.

Con: Owner-reported problems: Premature brake wear (the front discs warp easily), and the front metallic brake pads are noisy. Some owners complain about fragile body hardware. Stopping distances are greater than average and the car is very sensitive to crosswinds and passing trucks on the highway.

Road Performance

Pro: The tiny 1.0L 3-cylinder powerplant has no trouble keeping up with city traffic, but the optional 1.3L 4-cylinder handles the automatic gearbox and highways much better. **Transmission:** The 5-speed manual with Overdrive shifts easily. **Routine handling:** Handling is nimble and stable most of the time, thanks in part to the independent suspension. **Steering:** The non-power steering is fairly precise and always predictable.

Con: Acceleration/torque: Very slow and without much torque (0–100 km/h: 12.3 sec.), which means that you'll quickly become expert at using the manual shifter—and get just as quickly fed up with the constant shifting of the 3-speed automatic. Even with the optional 4-cylinder engine, these cars are not great highway or long-distance cruisers. Some stalling and hesitation under full throttle. If you hear a constant knocking when accelerating or decelerating, blame it on the unusually pliable engine mounts that allow the engine and exhaust system to knock against the floor pan. The clutch is abrupt, and the automatic transmission robs the engine of what little power it produces. The absence of an Overdrive gear on the automatic makes for excessive engine noise at highway speeds. The suspension thumps and bounces in hard turns. Cheap original equipment tires compromise handling, ride, and braking. **Emergency handling:** Cornering becomes sloppier and less predictable as speed increases. The added weight of the 4-cylinder engine makes for hard steering while parking. **Braking:** Incredibly bad without ABS (100–0 km/h: varies between 139 and 152 ft.).

Comfort/Convenience

Pro: Standard equipment: Well-appointed interior with complete instrumentation. **Driving position:** Good. The plunging hood, sweeping window glass, and thin side pillars give the interior an airy look that heightens visibility in all directions. **Controls and displays:** Convenient, easy-to-read controls. **Interior space/comfort F/R:** Despite their diminutive proportions, these cars will easily accommodate tall occupants in front. Standard seats are reasonably comfortable for short rides. **Cargo space:** The area behind the front seats is a compromise; either you get limited space for two people and no room for cargo, or a spacious cargo area with the rear seat folded down. **Trunk/liftover:** Fairly large trunk with a low liftover to facilitate loading.

Con: Coupes don't offer power steering. Some radios furnished by GM dealers are poorly calibrated, producing an irritating, tinny sound. **Entry/exit:** Very difficult rear access. Not much room for your feet in the rear. **Climate control:** Mediocre heating and ventilation. Seats become cramped and generally uncomfortable during long trips. **Quietness:** The interior is quite noisy, due mainly to poor soundproofing and the car's small size.

COST

List Price (firm)	Residual Values (months)			
	24	36	48	60
Base Metro: $10,690 (10%)	$8500	$6000	$4000	$3000

TECHNICAL DATA

Powertrain (front-drive)
Engines: 1.0L 3-cyl. (55 hp)
• 1.3L 4-cyl. (79 hp)
Transmissions: 5-speed man.
• 3-speed auto.
Dimensions (Metro LSi)
Passengers: 4
Height/length/width:
55.4/164/62.6 in.

Head room F/R: 39.3/37.3 in.
Leg room F/R: 42.5/32.2 in.
Wheelbase: 93.1 in.
Cargo capacity: 10.3 cu. ft.
Towing capacity: N/A
Fuel tank: 40L/reg.
Weight: 2,000 lbs.

SAFETY FEATURES

	Std.	Opt.
Anti-lock brakes	❏	■
Seatbelt pretensioners	—	—
Integrated child safety seat	—	—
Airbag cut-off switch	—	—
Depowered airbags	■	❏
Side airbags	—	—
Traction control	—	—
Visibility (front/rear)	*****	*****
Crash protection D/P	****	****
Crash protection (side) D/P	N/A	
HLDI injury claims	High	

Saturn

Saturn

RATING: Above Average. **Strong points:** Excellent braking, good driving position, unobstructed visibility, standard traction control, dent-resistant body panels, and good warranty performance supported by unusually competent servicing. **Weak points:** Some annoying engine noise persists, limited rear seat room, optional ABS, and mediocre quality control (regardless of what the advertising hype says).

NEW FOR '99: Engine modifications to reduce noise, vibration, and harshness and user-friendly front seatbelt inboard latches.

GENERAL COMMENTS: Promises of strict quality control at the factory level, posted sticker prices, no haggling over prices, and a 30-day money-back guarantee have all contributed to Saturn's sales success. Nevertheless, GM has announced that it will consider merging Saturn's operations into one of its other operations. This means that General Motors is cutting Saturn's umbilical cord and will force the company to sink or swim depending on its own balance sheet. In other words, Saturn will henceforth be like all of GM's other car divisions.

Launched in 1992 as an all-American effort to beat the Japanese in the small-car market, the Saturn compact was GM's first totally new car touted as being practically as reliable as the Japanese competition. Is almost as good as Toyota good enough? No, not when GM has its own Prizm (sold only in the States), Suzuki, and other captive imports and hybrids to market at less cost and risk.

Nevertheless, the Saturn is a better car than GM's other home-grown compacts (which we've learned to be wary of over the past 20 years). Rust protection is maximized with the stainless-steel exhaust system and plastic body panels. Another positive step that should be extended to other models is GM's offer of a complete refund or exchange if the buyer brings the car back within 30 days or 2,400 km (a pro-rata deduction is made in the U.S. but not in Canada).

Cost analysis/alternatives: Get the quieter '99 model; only consider a '98 model if the price is cut 15 percent or more and you can tolerate the engine noise. The Honda Civic and Toyota Corolla perform well and offer better quality. The Hyundai Tiburon, '98 Nissan 200SX and '98 Toyota Paseo compare well with the Saturn SC. **Recommended options:** Four-wheel anti-lock brakes. **Rebates:** Nothing reported yet, but the new year should see some price cutting. **Destination charge:** $455. **Depreciation:** Slower than average. **Insurance cost:** Average. **Parts supply/cost:** Average parts availability. According to CAA, parts are reasonably priced, with heavy discounting by dealers. **Annual maintenance cost:** Average. **Warranty:** Bumper-to-bumper 3 years/60,000 km; rust perforation 6 years/160,000 km. **Supplementary warranty:** A good idea in view of Saturn's uncertain future at the hands of GM. **Highway/city fuel economy:** 6–9L/100 km with the manual 5-speed and automatic transmission; the High Output engine adds another litre to the figure.

Quality/Reliability/Safety

Pro: Reliability: Reliability and dealer servicing have been overhyped, but why not? They're still much better than what you'll find among GM's other car divisions. You may be surprised to learn that Saturns aren't built that much better than other vehicles. It's just that when problems occur they're dealt with quickly, and repair costs are frequently covered by GM. **Warranty performance:** Much better than average, because GM wants to nurture owner loyalty. Nevertheless, Saturn dealers say that GM is no longer as generous in paying warranty goodwill claims. They're worried that this may be a harbinger of a new "tough love" approach advocated by GM dealers in other divisions who are frustrated by the special treatment given Saturn customers. Another cloud on the horizon: if GM carries out its plan to merge Saturn with its other car divisions and add larger Saturn models to the lineup, it's unlikely that Saturn dealers and customers will get the same high level of service that Saturn ads promise.

Con: Owner-reported problems: Engine, powertrain, and body defects. Defrosting system doesn't work properly, causing moisture damage and poor visibility. **Quality control:** Paint quality and body assembly are much better than other Big Three competitors, but not up to Japanese car standards. Some engine coolant and power steering leaks, premature brake wear, and excessive brake noise. **Service bulletin problems:** Fluid leaks from automatic transmission case; loss of airflow from AC outlets (see bulletin on following page); clunk, rattle, buzz, squeak, creak, and pop noise from front of vehicle; rattle, buzz, clunk from front doors when passing over rough roads; rattle, click from rear when turning or passing on uneven roads; license plate rattles when closing rear lid; sunroof sunshade binds or rattles. **NHTSA safety complaints/ safety:** *SC1:* When applying brakes there's excessive noise coming from the rear end; fuel sloshing sound when fuel tank is half full. *SC2:* Seatbelt tightens on any sudden movement, however slight; the small, recessed horn buttons make it hard to find and activate the horn without looking down. *SL:* Steering wheel came apart while driving; total loss of steering when the retaining clip was omitted during assembly. *SL1:* Windshield wipers fail to adequately clean the windshield; defrosting system doesn't work properly, causing moisture damage and poor visibility. *SL2:* Sudden acceleration; turn signal indicator sticks in the resume position; seatbelts are hard to engage; when driving at night, one sees multiple lights when looking through the rear view mirror at the vehicle in back, as well as the reflection of the defroster lights; during rainy weather, rear windshield view is distorted or wavy; sudden brake failure. *SW2:* automatic transmission slippage caused collision.

BULLETIN NO.: 98-T-10
ISSUE DATE: February, 1998
GROUP/SEQ. NO.: HVAC-03
CORPORATION NO.: 781204
SUBJECT:
Loss of Airflow from A/C Outlets after Extended Periods of Highway Driving (Adjust A/C Compressor Set Point)
MODELS AFFECTED:
1994-1998 Saturns equipped with R-134a air conditioning
CONDITION:
After extended periods of highway driving, some customers may notice a loss of airflow from the A/C outlets.
CAUSE:
A/C compressor suction set point may be low for some customers usage and driving patterns, resulting in evaporator freeze after extended periods of highway driving.
CORRECTION:
Adjust A/C compressor set point using the following procedure.
NOTICE:
This procedure should never be repeated on the same A/C compressor. If condition is not corrected by this bulletin, refer to the diagnostic flow chart in the appropriate year "VAC Service Manual."
PARTS REQUIREMENTS:
21031284   Label-A/C Refrig Caution
CLAIM INFORMATION:

Case Type	Description	Labor Operation Code	Time
VW	Adjust A/C Compressor Set-Point	T9769	0.3 hrs

To receive credit for this repair during the warranty coverage period, submit a claim through the Saturn Dealer System as shown.

GM will pay for this air conditioning fix under the base warranty.

Road Performance

Pro: Acceleration/torque: Brisk acceleration with the DOHC 124-hp 4-banger (0–100 km/h: 8.5 sec.). It delivers excellent fuel economy and performance. **Transmission:** The manual transmission lever is precise and easily shifted. The automatic has a useful performance setting. **Routine handling:** Better than average. The firm suspension gives a comfortable ride. Nimble handling with only a slight tendency to understeer. **Emergency handling:** First class. **Steering:** Fairly precise and predictable, with plenty of assist and road feedback. There's no torque steer, owing to the use of equal-length driveshafts. **Braking:** Excellent braking with the four-wheel ABS (100–0 km/h: 124 ft.).

Con: The 1.9L 100-hp 4-cylinder engine found on the sporty SC coupe gives barely adequate acceleration times (11.5 seconds to reach 100 km/h) with the manual transmission. This time is increased to a near-glacial 13.7 seconds with the 4-speed automatic gearbox, which robs the engine of what little power it produces. Excessive automatic gearbox shudder when the kickdown is engaged while passing. Some wallowing in tight turns, and ride quality deteriorates if the car is loaded.

Comfort/Convenience

Pro: Standard equipment: Base Saturns come with a wide range of standard equipment. Interior trim is first class. Large glove box and convenient door pockets. **Driving position:** Very good. Excellent visibility in all directions. **Controls and displays:** Most everything's within easy reach and well presented. **Climate control:** Efficient, quiet, and easy to adjust. **Interior space/comfort F/R:** Comfortable front seats, with a fair amount of head and leg room. **Cargo space:** The rear seatbacks fold down 60/40 for cargo flexibility. **Trunk/liftover:** Huge trunk has a large opening and low liftover height.

Con: Steering wheel is too close for comfort and tiny horn buttons would be hard to find in an emergency. People with small hands can't reach the turn signal lever without taking their hand off the steering wheel. Traction control light stays lit when the traction control is on. **Entry/exit:** Difficult rear access. The rear is not the place to be—door sills are high, seat cushions are short and hard, and the seatbacks are too upright. **Quietness:** Lots of rattles and road and wind noise. Some engine noise at cruising speed.

COST				
List Price (negotiable)	**Residual Values** (months)			
	24	**36**	**48**	**60**
SL1: $14,398 (11%)	$11,000	$9500	$7500	$6000

TECHNICAL DATA	
Powertrain (front-drive)	Head room F/R: 39.3/38 in.
Engines: 1.9L 4-cyl. (100 hp)	Leg room F/R: 42.5/32.8 in.
• 1.9L 4-cyl. (124 hp)	Wheelbase: 102.4 in.
Transmissions: 5-speed man.	Cargo capacity: 12.1 cu. ft.
• 4-speed auto.	Towing capacity: 1,000 lbs.
Dimensions (SL/SC)	Fuel tank: 46–49L/reg.
Passengers: 5	Weight: 2,400 lbs.

Height/length/width:
53.8/176.9/66.7 in.

SAFETY FEATURES

	Std.	Opt.
Anti-lock brakes	❑	■
Seatbelt pretensioners	—	—
Integrated child safety seat	—	—
Airbag cut-off switch	—	—
Depowered airbags	■	❑
Side airbags	—	—
Traction control	—	■
Visibility (front/rear)	*****	*****
Crash protection D/P	****	****
Crash protection (side) D/P	***	***
HLDI injury claims	N/A	

Cavalier/Sunfire

Cavalier

RATING: Above Average if you also get an extended warranty. **Strong points:** Plenty of passenger and cargo room, comfortable riding, standard ABS, and good fuel economy. **Weak points:** Noisy engine and mediocre steering and handling. Crash safety and quality control still need some improvement.

NEW FOR '99: A new bi-fuel sedan that uses compressed natural gas.

GENERAL COMMENTS: These twins are two of the lowest-priced cars to come equipped with standard ABS and dual airbags. They have exceptional styling (especially the coupe) and lots of interior room, with a nicely tuned suspension (making for an improved ride). The ride and handling have also improved markedly over the past two years, with power rack-and-pinion steering, a longer wheelbase, and a wider track. The Sunfire is identical to the Cavalier, except for its more rakish look.

The Cavalier Z24/Sunfire GT are performance versions of the compacts introduced two years ago. They use a reworked version of the failure-prone Quad 4 2.4L DOHC 16-valve 4-cylinder powerplant. GM promises that its past problems have been cured through the addition of a balance shaft for smoother engine performance and a longer operating life. I have my doubts.

Cost analysis/alternatives: Get the '99 model if it's sufficiently discounted; consider a '98 model if the price is cut by at least ten percent. Also look at the Honda Civic, Hyundai Tiburon, Mazda Protegé, or Nissan Sentra. **Recommended options:** The 4-speed automatic transmission will reduce engine noise and make for more responsive performance, a suspension upgrade, traction control, and air conditioning. If you want more performance, the best combination is the 2.4L engine hooked to a 5-speed manual transmission. Of course, you'll have to deal with the engine's uncertain reliability. **Rebates:** $2,000 rebates on the '98 and '99 convertibles and $750–$1,000 rebates on the '98 sedans and coupes. **Destination charge:** $620. **Depreciation:** Slower than average. **Insurance cost:** Average. **Parts supply/cost:** Parts are easy to find and CAA says they're reasonably priced, with heavy discounting by dealers. **Annual maintenance cost:** Average. Maintenance on 4-cylinder models is reasonably straightforward. **Warranty:** Bumper-to-bumper 3 years/60,000 km; rust perforation 6 years/160,000 km. **Supplementary warranty:** A wise investment. **Highway/city fuel economy:** 6–10L/100 km with the 2.2L and manual 5-speed; 7–10L/100 km with the 2.2L and automatic 3-speed; 7.5–12L/100 km with the 2.4L and manual 5-speed; 7.5–11.5L/100 km with the 2.4L and automatic 4-speed.

Quality/Reliability/Safety

Pro: Reliability: Overall reliability has been average. **Warranty performance:** Better than Chrysler; on par with Ford.

Con: Quality control: Quality control is variable, often leading to poor paint application, inside and outside body panel gaps, and lots of exposed screw heads. Most body hardware is fragile. **Owner-reported problems:** The Quad 4 engine, despite its new refinements, has had a poor reliability history; headgasket failures have been a frequent problem. Computer modules have also been one of the most common sources of complaints; symptoms include stalling and a shaky idle. Fuel-injection and cooling systems are temperamental as well. The power steering may lead or pull, and the steering rack tends to deteriorate quickly, usually requiring replacement some time shortly after 80,000 km. The front MacPherson struts also wear out rapidly, as do the rear shock absorbers. Many owners complain of rapid front brake wear and warped brake discs after a year or so. **Service bulletin problems:** Seatbelt latch slides to seatbelt anchor sleeve. **NHTSA safety complaints/safety:** *Cavalier:* Engine fires; chronic hesitation or stalling; brake failure due to leaking master cylinder fluid; transmission failed to engage upon start-up; passenger-side airbag failed to deploy; when driving with door locked, it came ajar; when vehicle is in Drive with foot on the brake it lurches forward, stalls, and produces a crashing sound; during highway driving the vehicle suddenly accelerated without steering control; sudden brake cable breakage while driving. *Sunfire:* Brake master cylinder leaks; dash warning light indicating time to upshift comes on at the wrong time; fuel tank leakage; airbags failed to fully inflate. On both cars the trunk lid remains open at such a low angle that it's easy to hit your head.

Road Performance

Pro: Acceleration/torque: Acceptable acceleration with the 2.2L (0–100 km/h: 9.6 sec.), but the 2.4L is a much better performer. The fuel-injected 2.2L 4-cylinder engine provides adequate power when used with the manual transmission or with the smoother, more responsive 4-speed automatic. The 150-hp 2.4L Quad 4 produces lots more torque, shaving 0–100 km/h times by over a second (to 8 seconds). Models equipped with an optional suspension package offer the best handling at highway speeds and the best ride control on bad roads. **Braking:** Acceptable (100–0 km/h: 131 ft.).

Con: Even with the torque upgrade this year, when hooked to the 3-speed transaxle the 2.2L 4-cylinder lacks sufficient power to distinguish these J-cars from the competition. **Transmission:** The 5-speed manual transaxle has an abrupt clutch. The 3-speed automatic strains to get into the proper gear range. **Routine handling:** Base models don't handle as well as do most other vehicles in this class. **Steering:** Power steering feels over-assisted, resulting in insufficient road feel. **Emergency handling:** Excessive lean when cornering under power and standard tires corner poorly.

Comfort/Convenience

Pro: Driving position: Generous up-front head room, although tall drivers may find the driving position a bit confining. **Controls and displays:** Well laid-out dashboard and controls. **Entry/exit:** Lots of foot space and large door openings make for easy access into the front or rear areas. **Interior space/comfort F/R:** Plenty of interior room to seat four adults comfortably. **Quietness:** Quiet interior with minimal road/wind noise intrusion. **Cargo space:** Fairly generous for a compact. **Trunk/liftover:** Good-sized trunk with a low liftover.

Con: Poor visibility on the Z24. **Climate control:** Interior ventilation is feeble without the air conditioning option. Lots of engine resonance invades the car's interior. Watch out for the low-hanging trunk lid.

COST

List Price (firm)	Residual Values (months)			
	24	**36**	**48**	**60**
Cavalier Sedan: $15,365 (12%) $11,000	$8000	$6000	$4500

TECHNICAL DATA

Powertrain (front-drive)
Engines: 2.2L 4-cyl. (120 hp)
• 2.4L 4-cyl. (150 hp)
Transmissions: 5-speed man. OD
• 3-speed auto.
• 4-speed auto.
Dimensions
Passengers: 5

Height/length/width:
54.8/180.3/67.4 in.
Head room F/R: 38.9/37.2 in.
Leg room F/R: 42.3/34.6 in.
Wheelbase: 104.1 in.
Cargo capacity: 13.6 cu. ft.
Towing capacity: 1,000 lbs.
Fuel tank: 58L/reg.
Weight: 2,700 lbs.

SAFETY FEATURES

	Std.	Opt.
Anti-lock brakes	■	❑
Seatbelt pretensioners	—	—
Integrated child safety seat	—	—
Airbag cut-off switch	—	—
Depowered airbags	■	❑
Side airbags	—	—
Traction control	❑	■
Visibility (front/rear)	*****	*****
Crash protection D/P	***	****
Crash protection (side) D/P	*	**
Crash protection 4d (side) D/P	*	***
HLDI injury claims	High	

Grand Am

Grand Am

RATING: Average. **Strong points:** Competent V6, good steering and handling, roomy interior, standard ABS and traction control, and average quality control. **Weak points:** Mediocre ride over rough terrain, excessive 4-cylinder noise, noisy interior, difficult rear seat access (coupe), awkward radio controls, and long-term powertrain reliability is still a question mark.

NEW FOR '99: An entirely new car offers a stiffer chassis that's shorter by about a half-inch, wider by three-and-a-half inches, and set on a 3.6-inch longer wheelbase. A 170-hp 3.4L V6 engine replaces last year's 155-hp 3.1L V6. ABS, traction control, an independent, softer suspension, and new cornering lights are standard. The interior has also been upgraded. A sportier GT version with five extra horses is due later in the year.

There's been a lot of hype about the Quad 4 engine, but little of this translates into benefits for the average driver. Multi-valve motors produce more power than a standard engine, but always at higher rpms and with a fuel penalty. The Quad 4 is rougher than most multi-valve engines when revved to cruising speed, and so does little to encourage drivers to get the maximum power from it.

GENERAL COMMENTS: Taking its styling cues from GM's redesigned Grand Prix, this year's Grand Am offers a roomy, comfortable interior in two- and four-door body styles. Sharing its platform and mechanical components with the new 1999 Oldsmobile Alero, the base Grand Am uses a 150-hp Quad DOHC engine; a 170-hp 3.4L V6 engine is optional on the SE1 and standard on the SE2.

Cost analysis/alternatives: Get the '99 model Grand Am for the upgrades; don't even think of getting any one of last year's Achieva or Skylark models, even if they are heavily discounted. Other cars worth considering are the '98 Eagle Talon, Ford Taurus and Sable, Honda Accord, Nissan Altima, Toyota Camry and Avalon, or the VW Passat. **Recommended options:** The best engine choice for power, smoothness, and value retention is the 170-hp 3.4L V6. Stay away from the Computer Command Ride option: true, it allows you to choose your own suspension setting, but the settings aren't quite what they pretend to be. **Rebates:** $2,000 on the '98 Grand Am coupe and sedan. The '99s will get rebates in the new year. **Destination charge:** $650. **Depreciation:** Faster than average. **Insurance cost:** Higher than average. **Parts supply/cost:** Predicted to be average. **Annual maintenance cost:** Should be about average. **Warranty:** Bumper-to-bumper 3 years/60,000 km; rust perforation 6 years/160,000 km. **Supplementary warranty:** A good idea. **Highway/city fuel economy:** 7.5–12L/100 km with the 2.4L and manual 5-speed, 7.5–11.5L/100 km with the 2.4L and automatic 4-speed.

Quality/Reliability/Safety

Pro: Quality control: The 4-speed automatic and 5-speed manual have had few major mechanical problems. The stainless-steel exhaust system is impervious to rust. New rear cornering lights shine at a 45 degree angle and make backing up both easier and safer.

Con: Body assembly and paint application are substandard. **Reliability:** The Quad 4 has proven to be unreliable in the past, and parts are often in short supply. **Warranty performance:** Not very good. **Owner-reported problems:** Powertrain malfunctions, electrical problems, and substandard body assembly. **Service bulletin problems:** Squawk coming from front suspension or engine area; seatbelt latch slides to anchor sleeve; fuel injector deposits causing chronic stalling, poor idling, or hard starts. **NHTSA safety complaints/safety:** Optional rear spoiler blocks rear vision.

Road Performance

Pro: Acceleration/torque: Fair acceleration (0–100 km/h: 9.9 sec.) with the four-cylinder engine. V6 acceleration is impressive with powered delivered smoothly and quietly. **Transmission:** Well-suited to the V6. **Routine handling:** Better than average on the highway. Suspension improvements have made for better handling and have smoothed out the ride considerably. **Emergency handling:** Better than average. **Steering:** Steering is predictably responsive. **Braking:** Reasonably good (100–0 km/h: 121 ft.) with some brake fade after repeated stops.

Con: Transmission: The Quad 4 powerplant accentuates the harsh shifting of the 4-speed automatic; it's over-eager to enter lockup mode in high gear, causing sluggish response in city driving.

Comfort/Convenience

Pro: Standard equipment: Well-appointed. **Driving position:** Comfortable cockpit with an easily adjusted, supportive driver's seat and plenty of head and leg room. **Controls and displays:** Good interior and exterior styling. Well laid-out, user-friendly dash. **Climate control:** Efficient heating/defrosting and ventilation system. Rear windows roll all the way down. **Interior space/comfort F/R:** *Sedan:* has better than average room in front and back. Standard split-folding rear seats are quite useful. **Trunk/liftover:** Spacious trunk; high sill and small opening makes loading difficult.

Con: Interior space/comfort F/R: *Coupe:* back seat will only hold two adults comfortably due to its narrower seats and reduced head room. **Entry/exit:** The doors on two-door models are heavy and awkward to open in tight spaces. The front seatbelts interfere with getting in and out. **Cargo space:** Limited storage space. **Trunk/liftover:** High sill and small opening makes loading difficult. **Quietness:** Excessive road noise and annoying exhaust drone.

COST

List Price (firm)	Residual Values (months)			
	24	36	48	60
Grand Am SE:				
$21,795 (16%)	$15,000	$12,000	$9500	$7500

TECHNICAL DATA

Powertrain (front-drive)
Engines: 2.4L 4-cyl. (150 hp)
• 3.4L V6 (170 hp)
Transmissions: 5-speed man. OD
• 4-speed auto.
Dimensions ('98 Grand Am)
Passengers: 5
Height/length/width:
53.5/186.9/68.3 in.

Head room F/R: 37.8/36.5 in.
Leg room F/R: 43.1/33.9 in.
Wheelbase: 103.4 in.
Cargo capacity: 13.4 cu. ft.
Towing capacity: 1,000 lbs.
Fuel tank: 47L/reg.
Weight: 3,066 lbs.

SAFETY FEATURES

	Std.	Opt.
Anti-lock brakes	■	❏
Seatbelt pretensioners	—	—
Integrated child safety seat	—	—
Airbag cut-off switch	—	—
Depowered airbags	■	❏
Side airbags	—	—
Traction control	■	❏
Visibility (front/rear)	*****	*
Crash protection D/P	N/A	N/A
Crash protection (side) D/P	N/A	N/A
HLDI injury claims	Average	

Olds Cutlass/Chevrolet Malibu

Malibu

RATING: Above Average, but only if an extended warranty is purchased to protect you from the early production bugs. **Strong points:** Good V6 powertrain setup. Comfortable ride, easy handling, and precise steering. **Weak points:** Noisy base engine lacks guts, mediocre seats, uneven quality control, and an uncertain future.

NEW FOR '99: *Cutlass:* Returns relatively unchanged, except for a new gold trim package; this is the car's last model year. *Malibu:* No changes.

GENERAL COMMENTS: The Cutlass and Malibu are identical front-drive, five-passenger, midsize sedans that replaced the long-discontinued Celebrity and Ciera. They're conventionally styled cars that use a more rigid body structure to cut down on noise and improve handling. Standard mechanical components include a 2.4L, twin-cam 4-cylinder engine for the Malibu and a 3.1L V6 for the Cutlass (optional on the Malibu). The ignition switch is mounted on the dash (a throwback to your dad's Oldsmobile). There's plenty of passenger and luggage space. Other points to consider: outside mirrors are too small, the stiffer suspension may be too firm for some, and there's no traction control.

Cost analysis/alternatives: It's a toss-up; buy whichever model year is the cheapest. Remember, the base Cutlass has more standard features than the base Malibu. Other cars worth considering: Ford Contour and Mystique, the Plymouth Breeze, Toyota Camry, Honda Accord, or Mazda 626. **Recommended options:** The quieter, "torquier" 3.1L V6 and LS package. Premium tires. **Rebates:** '98s get $1,000 rebates and '99s get $500. **Destination charge:** $750. **Depreciation:** Average. **Insurance cost:** Higher than average. **Parts supply/cost:** These new models use GM generic parts that are found everywhere and are reasonably priced. **Annual maintenance cost:** Estimated to be a bit higher than average. **Warranty:** Bumper-to-bumper 3 years/60,000 km; rust perforation

6 years/160,000 km. **Supplementary warranty:** A wise investment. **Highway/city fuel economy:** 7.8–12.3L/100 km with the 2.4L.

Quality/Reliability/Safety

Pro: Reliability: Nothing of a serious nature. **Warranty performance:** Nothing negative, yet. **Safety:** The automatic headlight control that turns on automatically at dusk is a useful feature.

Con: Quality control: Below average quality control. **Owner-reported problems:** Some hard starting and stalling; malfunctioning theft lock prevents the car from starting; leaking steering rack; glove box door won't close; faulty window control pod; and sticking power windows. **Service bulletin problems:** Seatbelt latch slides to anchor sleeve; fuel injector deposits causing chronic stalling, poor idling, or hard starts. **NHTSA safety complaints/safety:** *Cutlass:* ABS malfunctioned, causing extended stopping distance and producing a grinding noise; in a "fender-bender" rear-end collision the driver and passenger seatbacks collapsed rearward. *Malibu:* Excessive vibration at any speed; transmission doesn't lock when the key is in the accessory position; very loose steering; faulty high-beam light switch; needs tires with better gripping power.

Road Performance

Pro: Acceleration/torque: Brisk acceleration with plenty of low-end torque with the V6 engine (0–100 km/h: 8.8 sec.). **Transmission:** Smooth and predictable shifting. **Routine handling:** Better than average, thanks to an independent suspension that doesn't sacrifice solid handling for passenger comfort. **Emergency handling:** Very good. Cornering under speed is well controlled, with little front-end plowing or excessive body roll. **Steering:** Quite precise, with lots of road feedback.

Con: Malibu's base 2.4L engine is noisy and lacks sufficient torque in the higher gear ranges. Push-rod V6 is rougher than the overhead-cam V6s used by the competition. **Braking:** Antiquated rear drum brakes provide mediocre braking with standard ABS (100–0 km/h: 128 ft.). Some brake fade after repeated stops.

Comfort/Convenience

Pro: Standard equipment: Well-appointed for the price, but the better-equipped LS version has more of what you need. **Driving position:** Seating is adequate, though a bit low. Large side mirrors help provide good all-around visibility. **Controls and displays:** Very well thought-out instrumentation, and gauges that are easy to access and read. For example, the ignition switch is located on the instrument panel, a radical departure for GM. **Climate control:** Excellent ventilation system and first-class controls that are easy to use. AC vents are mounted high enough to direct cool air at your face. **Interior space/comfort F/R:** More head and leg room than the Ford Contour/Mystique or the Chrysler Cirrus/Stratus. Unusually spacious rear seat area can accommodate three adults in comfort. **Cargo space:** Lots of interior storage space. **Entry/exit:** Easy access to both front and rear interiors. **Trunk/liftover:** Plenty of trunk space that can be expanded through the split-folding rear seatbacks. Low liftover and practical cargo net facilitate loading.

Con: Bland styling. Seats could use better lumbar support and side bolstering. Some gauges are hard to read in direct sunlight. Heating to the floor area is a bit slow. Door checks may not hold the doors open when parked facing uphill. Rear seatbacks don't lie flat when folded. Trunk hinges intrude into the trunk area, possibly damaging contents in a stuffed trunk. The 2.4L engine's noise intrudes into the passenger compartment. **Quietness:** Excessive engine noise. Interior not as quiet as GM claims; lots of front suspension squeaks and rattles.

COST

List Price (firm)	Residual Values (months)			
	24	**36**	**48**	**60**
Malibu Sedan: $20,895 (18%)	$16,000	$12,000	$10,000	$8000

TECHNICAL DATA

Powertrain (front-drive)
Engines: 2.4L 4-cyl. (150 hp)
• 3.1L V6 (155 hp)
Transmission: 4-speed auto.
Dimensions (Malibu)
Passengers: 5
Height/length/width:
56.4/190.4/69.4 in.

Head room F/R: 39.4/37.6 in.
Leg room F/R: 41.9/38 in.
Wheelbase: 107 in.
Cargo capacity: 16 cu. ft.
Towing capacity: 1,000 lbs.
Fuel tank: N/A
Weight: 3,100 lbs.

SAFETY FEATURES

	Std.	Opt.
Anti-lock brakes	■	❑
Seatbelt pretensioners	—	—
Integrated child safety seat	—	—
Airbag cut-off switch	—	—
Depowered airbags	■	❑
Side airbags	—	—
Traction control		
Visibility (front/rear)	*****	*****
Crash protection D/P	****	****
Crash protection (side) D/P	*	***
HLDI injury claims	N/A	

Century/Intrigue/Grand Prix/Regal

Grand Prix

RATING: Average. The Intrigue is Above Average. **Strong points:** Standard ABS and traction control, good choice of powertrains, comfortable ride, easily accessed and roomy interior. **Weak points:** Rear seating for two (Grand Prix) and obstructed rear visibility.

NEW FOR '99: *Intrigue:* Traction control is now available with the new DOHC V6, as well as an optional high-performance AutoBahn package. *Regal:* LS gets five additional horses, larger front and rear stabilizer bars (reducing body roll and making for a stiffer ride). Both the LS and GS will have enhanced traction control, more efficient anti-lock brakes, and a new array of optional features, ranging from an outside rear-view mirror that automatically dims when a car approaches from the rear to an awesome, 200-watt sound system with eight speakers. *Century:* Enhanced traction control, more efficient anti-lock brakes, an upgraded suspension, and a new array of optional features, including a tire inflation monitor and more powerful and versatile sound system.

GENERAL COMMENTS: *Grand Prix:* the new sport sedan, cousin to the Buick Century and Olds Intrigue, comes as a two- or four-door model and is powered by the Chevy Lumina's 3.1L V6 and an optional 3.8L V6—or supercharged variation—borrowed from the Pontiac Bonneville. Larger brakes, upgraded power steering, and a two-inch longer body, a three-inch longer wheelbase, and a two-inch wider track are also featured.

The A-body line, long a mainstay in GM's family sedan market, is quickly disappearing. This is good news, because these cars are outclassed by the competition and are in desperate need of high-quality components and fresher styling. Overall quality has improved somewhat, but with the arrival of the better-quality Japanese imports, only the Intrigue is really in the running.

Intrigue
Although it shares its platform with the Century, Grand Prix, and Regal, the near-luxury-class Oldsmobile Intrigue is a much better performer than any of the three. It's got plenty of interior room, a competent base 3.8L V6 and a more powerful optional 3.5L 220-hp 24-valve V6, four-wheel disc ABS, traction control, and knockout styling. Initial reports give it high marks for handling *and* ride comfort, exceptional braking with the AutoBahn package, and a superb suspension that provides a firm, though not unpleasant, ride.

Cost analysis/alternatives: Get the '99 models for the upgrades, consider a '98 model only if the price is cut 15–20 percent. Don't buy a first-year '98 model Intrigue; instead, check out the Olds Cutlass: it's only a bit smaller than the Intrigue, but it's much cheaper. Look at the Acura Integra, Ford Taurus and Sable, Honda Accord, Nissan Altima and Maxima, and Toyota Camry and Avalon. Intrigue shoppers should also look at the BMW 328. **Recommended options:** The rear-mounted child safety seat and traction control. The Intrigue's AutoBahn package with larger brake rotors and better-performing tires, or the GL version, both of which offer lots of useful features for only $1,700 more. **Rebates:** $750 on all '98s. Expect $1,500 customer rebates in the new year. **Destination charge:** $785. **Depreciation:** A bit slower than average. **Insurance cost:** Higher than average. **Parts supply/cost:** Moderately priced parts aren't hard to find. **Annual maintenance cost:** Higher than average. Servicing can be performed by most neighbourhood mechanics. **Warranty:** Bumper-to-bumper 3 years/60,000 km; rust perforation 6 years/160,000 km. **Supplementary warranty:** Essential, especially after the third year of ownership. **Highway/city fuel economy**: 8–13L/100 km with the 3.1L for the base sedan. *Regal:* 9–14.5L/100 km with the High Output engine.

Quality/Reliability/Safety

Pro: The Intrigue's quality control and overall reliability is predicted to be better than average due to the care GM has taken in its production. **Warranty performance:** Average.

Con: Quality control: Below average for powertrain and body construction. **Reliability:** The 3.1L V6 engine has had more than its share of fuel system and engine computer problems. The 4-speed automatic is easily damaged if left in Overdrive during prolonged city driving or when pulling heavy loads. **Owner-reported problems:** Electrical system problems are common on cars loaded with power accessories. The front brakes wear out early and the discs warp far too easily. Shock absorbers and MacPherson struts wear out or leak prematurely. The power rack-and-pinion steering system degenerates quickly after three years and is characterized by chronic leaking. Poor body fit, particularly around the doors, leads to excessive wind noise and water leaks into

the interior. Door locks freeze up easily. **Service bulletin problems:**
Century: Fuel injector deposits causing chronic stalling, poor idling, or
hard starts. *Grand Prix*: Erratic automatic transmission shifting (see
DSB and illustration below); high deck lid opening or closing efforts or
low "pop up" lift height (see following page).

File In Section: 7 - Transmission
Bulletin No.: 73-71-06
Date: December, 1997
Subject:
Transaxle Erratic and/or No Shifts, Stuck in 3rd Gear, MIL On
(Repair Wire(s) Under Air Cleaner)
Model:
1998 Pontiac Grand Prix - Built Prior to VIN Breakpoint WF249884 with HYDRA-MATIC 4T65E Transaxle (RPOs MN7, M15)
and 3.8L Engine (VINS K, 1 - RPOs L36, L67)
Condition
Some owners may comment on one or more of the following conditions:
- Transaxle erratic and/or no shifts
- No power when accelerating
- Stuck in 3rd gear and/or Torque Convertor Clutch (TCC) fuse blows
- Intermittent MIL/Service Engine Soon indicator illuminated
Cause
Wires to the Torque Converter Clutch (TCC) switch may chafe against a reinforcement rig on the transaxle's side cover and the
bottom of the air cleaner assembly. Damage to the harness may result in stored diagnostic trouble codes of P0711, P0753,
P1860 and/or open fuse in the TCC circuit. This condition may cause one or more shifting concerns, or stuck in 3rd gear.
Correction
Inspect and repair any damaged wires and install P-clip to re-route wiring harness.

Figure 1

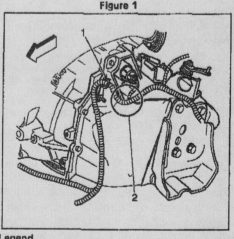

Legend
1. P-clip Installed
2. Possible wire damage area

File In Section: 10 Body
Bulletin No.: 73-15-13
Date: January, 1998
Subject:
High Deck Lid Opening and Closing Efforts or Low "Pop Up" Lift Height
(Install New Supports or Hinges and Supports)
Model:
1997–98 Pontiac Grand Prix
Built with the Following VIN Breakpoints:

Year	VIN Breakpoints
1997 (with or without rear spoiler - D81)	Prior to VF349965
1997–98 (without rear spoiler - D81; vehicles with rear spoiler not included)	After VF349964

Condition
Some owners may comment that significant effort is required to open and/or close the deck (trunk) lid. Also, some may comment that the deck lid doesn't "pop up" or lift very high when the Remote Keyless Entry (RKE) button is depressed on the key ring transmitter.
Correction
Important:
The new hinges and supports listed below will only allow the deck lid to "pop up" or lift approximately one inch when the RKE transmitter button is depressed. The amount of "pop up" may vary with temperature.

P/N	Description	Quantity
10410705	Hinge - Rear Compartment, Left	1
10410706	Hinge - Rear Compartment, Right	1
10405723	Support Assembly - Rear Compartment with Spoiler (D81)	2
10409072	Support Assembly - Rear Compartment without Spoiler (D81)	2

Important:
The new hinges listed have revised pivot points and support attaching locations. The new supports listed are of a different length and internal pressure than the original supports. As a result, the new supports listed can only be used with the new hinges listed. See the Service Parts Catalog for additional information on parts identification and usage.
For 1997–98 Vehicles Without Rear Spoiler (D81) Built After VIN Breakpoint VF349964 -
Important:
Vehicles with rear spoiler (D-81) built after VIN Breakpoint VF349964 are not included in this bulletin. Those vehicles were manufactured with the new design supports.

NHTSA safety complaints/safety: *Century:* Sudden brake failure; constant reflection of curved dashboard in windshield with or without sunlight. *Grand Prix:* Chronic stalling; false airbag deployment; airbag failed to deploy; seatbacks designed with an inertia lock that only locks when braking aggressively, allowing unoccupied seatback to flop around and distract driver; ABS failure; windshield wipers malfunction; windshield wiper system freezes up in cold weather; lap/shoulder seatbelts become twisted when reaching up and pulling down from the guide loop; cruise control suddenly engaged on its own and wouldn't release; sometimes cruise control causes the vehicle to suddenly accelerate and then slow down. *Regal:* Vehicle was on a medium incline, with the ignition on and the shift indicator in the Drive position, when driver took foot off the brake pedal and the vehicle rolled backward; passenger-side airbag cover came loose.

Road Performance

Pro: Acceleration/torque: The 3.1L V6 engine produces sufficient power for smooth acceleration and works well with the 4-speed automatic transmission (0–100 km/h: 10.5 sec.). However, for extended highway use you'll find the 3.8L powerplant better suited to your needs. Intrigue buyers will want to get the 220-hp 3.5L engine. **Transmission:** The automatic transmission is quiet and smooth under most conditions. **Routine handling:** Handling and ride are better than average due to recent suspension and steering refinements. **Emergency handling:** Better than average, thanks to standard traction control. **Steering:** Precise and predictable. **Braking:** Better than average, thanks to GM's '99 model refinements. Last year's models had sub-par ABS.

Con: Fully-loaded, the base V6 engine lacks guts; when pushed, there's excessive engine noise intrusion into the interior. The automatic 4-speed transmission is sometimes slow to downshift.

Comfort/Convenience

Pro: Standard equipment: Reasonably well-appointed, with such innovative features as automatic headlights that turn on at dusk and a system that prevents the doors from locking automatically if the key is in the ignition. Large side mirrors help overcome the obstructed rear view. **Driving position:** The cockpit area is much more user-friendly this year; lots of room; good all-around visibility; optional power driver's seat is a boon for short drivers. A tilt steering wheel is standard. **Controls and displays:** Improved instrumentation and easy-to-read gauges and controls. **Climate control:** Excellent heating-defrosting-ventilation system that even includes a pollen filter. **Entry/exit:** Not difficult. **Interior space/comfort F/R:** Front bench seats accommodate two with plenty of head and leg room. Rear seats have enough space for three adults. Grand Prix seating is quite firm, but not uncomfortable. **Trunk/liftover:** Large trunk and a low liftover. **Quietness:** Fairly quiet, except for some engine noise.

Con: Luxury models use tacky imitation wood and cheap cloth covers. Flimsy cupholders. Confusing climate-control panel, and low dash vents can chill a driver's hands. The Grand Prix sport sedan's head room has been sacrificed to give the car a sleeker appearance. Seats are too soft and lack support. Insufficient rear leg room. **Cargo space:** Absence of truly functional interior storage areas. There are lots of little storage spaces, but they're generally small and narrow. **Trunk/liftover:** *Grand Prix:* High trunk sill and narrow opening make for difficult loading and unloading, and large decklid hinges reduce usable trunk space. Rear seatbacks don't fold down to increase trunk space.

COST

List Price (negotiable)	Residual Values (months)			
	24	**36**	**48**	**60**
Grand Prix SE Sedan:				
$25,399 (22%)	$16,000	$13,000	$11,000	$8000

TECHNICAL DATA

Powertrain (front-drive)
Engines: 3.1L V6 (160 hp)
3.8L V6 (195 hp)
3.8L V6 SC (240 hp)
3.5L V6 (220 hp)
Transmissions: 5-speed man.
• 4-speed auto.
Dimensions (Grand Prix)
Passengers: 5
Height/length/width:
54.7/196.5/72.7 in.
Head room F/R: 38.3/36.7 in.
Leg room F/R: 42.4/35.8 in.
Dimensions (Century)
Passengers: 6
Height/length/width:
56.6/194.6/72.7 in.
Head room F/R: 39.3/37.4 in.
Leg room F/R: 42.4/36.9 in.

Dimensions (Regal)
Passengers: 5
Height/length/width:
56.6/196.2/72.7 in.
Head room F/R: 39.3/37.4 in.
Leg room F/R: 42.4/36.9 in.
Dimensions (Intrigue)
Passengers: 5
Height/length/width:
56.6/195.9/73.6 in.
Head room F/R: 39.3/37.4 in.
Leg room F/R: 42.4/36.9 in.
Wheelbase: Grand Prix: 110.5 in.;
Century, Intrigue, and Regal: 109 in.
Cargo capacity: 16 cu. ft.
Towing capacity: 1,000 lbs.
Fuel tank: 62L/reg.
Weight: 3,400 lbs.

SAFETY FEATURES

	Std.	Opt.
Anti-lock brakes	■	❑
Seatbelt pretensioners	—	—
Integrated child safety seat	❑	■
Airbag cut-off switch	—	—
Depowered airbags	■	❑
Side airbags	—	—
Traction control	❑	■
Visibility (front/rear)	*****	***
Crash protection D/P		
Century	N/A	
Grand Prix	****	****
Intrigue	****	***
Regal	N/A	
Crash protection (side) D/P		
Century	***	***
Grand Prix	N/A	
Intrigue	***	*
Regal	***	***
HLDI injury claims	Average	
Grand Prix	Poor	

Lumina/Monte Carlo

Lumina

RATING: Average, but only with an extended warranty. Different bodies, but the same poor-quality components. **Strong points:** Well-matched base engine and transmission and plenty of front seat and cargo room. **Weak points:** Light steering transmits little road feel, limited instrumentation, seats aren't comfortable on long drives, and serious past reliability problems.

NEW FOR '99: No significant changes.

GENERAL COMMENTS: The Lumina and Monte Carlo are popular two- and four-door versions of Chevy's midsize cars, featuring standard dual airbags, ABS, and 160-hp V6 power. The Monte Carlo was formerly sold as the Lumina Z34. Powertrain enhancements have increased horsepower and fuel efficiency. Each car has been given a slightly different exterior appearance and a distinct "personality." A 3.1L V6 is the standard engine, while a 3.8L V6 equips the more upscale versions.

Cost analysis/alternatives: Buy whichever model year is the cheapest. Other good choices: the Ford Taurus/Sable, Honda Accord, Mazda 626, and Toyota Camry and Avalon. **Recommended options:** Braking is the pits on these cars without ABS, so spring for the $500 or so extra cost. The sunroof option isn't a good idea if you're taller than 5'11". The Lumina's LTZ and the Monte Carlo's Z34 version gives you significant performance and comfort upgrades. **Rebates:** $1,250 rebates are currently being offered on the '98 Lumina LTZ and $750 for other '98 Luminas. Expect sizeable customer rebates and dealer incentives on the '99s early in the new year. **Destination charge:** $785. **Depreciation:** About average. **Insurance cost:** Higher than average. **Parts supply/cost:** No problem finding moderately priced parts, especially from independent suppliers. **Annual maintenance cost:** Higher than average. The 3.8L V6 (3800 TPI) engine is difficult to service due to its highly sophisticated fuel system and difficult-to-diagnose electronic controls. **Warranty:** Bumper-to-bumper 3 years/60,000 km; rust perforation 6 years/160,000 km. **Supplementary warranty:** A good idea, particularly in view of the fact that these cars often develop serious powertrain problems after their third year of use. **Highway/city fuel economy:** *Lumina* and *Monte Carlo:* 8–13L/100 km.

Quality/Reliability/Safety

Pro: Reliability: Overall reliability is better than Chrysler front-drives, but below the Ford and Japanese equivalent. **Service bulletin problems:** Nothing significant.

Con: Quality control: Below average. **Warranty performance:** Mediocre. **Owner-reported problems:** In spite of some noise reduction progress, body construction is still below par—loose door panel mouldings, poorly fitted door fabric, and misaligned panels. Other common problems: fuel pump whistling, frequent stalling, vague steering, premature paint peeling on the hood and trunk, heavy accumulation of hard-to-remove brake dust inside the honeycomb design wheels, and front tires that scrape the fenders when the wheel is turned. Despite its own recent redesign, the 3.1L engine isn't entirely problem-free. Electronic fuel-injection systems and engine controls have created many problems for GM owners. The 4-speed automatic transmission still has bugs. The front brakes wear quickly, as do the MacPherson struts and shock absorbers. Steering assemblies tend to fail prematurely. The electrical system is temperamental. The sunroof motor is failure-prone. Owners report water leaks from the front windshield. Front-end squeaks may require the replacement of the exhaust manifold pipe springs with dampers. **NHTSA safety complaints/safety:** *Lumina:* Horn button not easily accessible; brake booster diaphragm failure; driver has to keep foot on brake when stopped on a hill; cruise control suddenly cuts out and can't be reset until brake pedal is applied. *Monte Carlo:* During a collision the passenger-side airbag deployed and exploded, burning the driver's face and neck.

Road Performance

Pro: Acceleration/torque: Acceptable acceleration with the 3.1L V6 (0–100 km/h: 9.4 sec.). It's the engine of choice for reliability, but it doesn't have enough grunt (particularly in passing power) to handle all highway situations. The 3.8L powerplant is smoother and more powerful, and dealer service bulletins don't show any serious problems. **Routine handling:** Above average. The upgraded rear suspension has improved both ride and handling under either a light or full load. **Emergency handling:** Average for the Cutlass; better than average with the Lumina and Monte Carlo. **Braking:** Acceptable (100–0 km/h: 135 ft.). Anti-lock brakes control directional stability by preventing wheel lockup, but take an unacceptably long time to work under normal conditions.

Con: Transmission: The 4-speed automatic occasionally has trouble choosing the right gear. **Steering:** Too light and vague. A fully loaded car causes the back end to sag and makes for a poor ride.

Comfort/Convenience

Pro: Standard equipment: User-friendly cockpit area. Good visibility. Spacious interior has more room than the Taurus/Sable. The comfortable front bench seats will accommodate just about anyone. **Cargo space:** Plenty of cargo space. **Trunk/liftover:** Large trunk and low liftover. **Quietness:** Although styling is rather plain, a more rigid body structure, thicker side windows, and additional soundproofing material have practically eliminated interior rattles as well as wind and road noise.

Con: Driving position: Uncomfortable driving position without the optional power seat, and the bucket seats are best suited for bucket bottoms. The low-cut side bolstering leaves much of the back unsupported. The seat can't be lowered sufficiently to prevent your head from touching the roof. **Controls and displays:** The interior is too "space age," with omnipresent small buttons and paddle switches that are distracting and difficult to fiddle with, particularly when adjusting the AC system. **Climate control:** Mediocre heating/defrosting. **Entry/exit:** Getting in and out of this car takes real effort and determination, particularly as a result of the heavy, stiff front doors. **Interior space/comfort F/R:** The rear seat isn't very comfortable and there's only marginal room for three adults.

COST				
List Price (negotiable)		**Residual Values** (months)		
	24	36	48	60
Lumina Sedan: $22,329 (20%) $15,000		$11,500	$9500	$8000

TECHNICAL DATA	
Powertrain (front-drive)	Head room F/R: 38.4/37.4 in.
Engines: 3.1L V6 (160 hp)	Leg room F/R: 42.4/36.6 in.
• 3.8L V6 (200 hp)	Wheelbase: 107.5 in.
Transmissions: 5-speed man.	Cargo capacity: 15.5 cu. ft.
• 4-speed auto.	Towing capacity: 1,000 lbs.
Dimensions	Fuel tank: 65L/reg.
Passengers: 6	Weight: 3,650 lbs.
Height/length/width:	
55.2/200.9/72.5 in.	

SAFETY FEATURES

	Std.	Opt.
Anti-lock brakes	■	❏
Seatbelt pretensioners	—	—
Integrated child safety seat	■	❏
Airbag cut-off switch	—	—
Depowered airbags	■	❏
Side airbags	—	—
Traction control	—	—
Visibility (front/rear)	*****	*****
Crash protection D/P		
Lumina	****	***
Crash protection (side) D/P		
Lumina	****	***
HLDI injury claims		
Lumina	Low	

88/LSS/Regency/Bonneville/LeSabre

88

RATING: Average, but only with an extended warranty. These luxurious family sedans are outclassed by more reliable and better-performing Japanese competitors. **Strong points:** Well-matched engine and transmission, good braking, easy access, and roomy interior. **Weak points:** Limited rear visibility, uncomfortable seats, poor fuel economy, and a history of expensive powertrain defects.

NEW FOR '99: Olds 88 will be dropped in December. It will be replaced next summer by a redesigned 6- and 8-cylinder equipped full-sized sedan that will adopt the Aurora name. The other models are carried over virtually unchanged, except for the addition of new exterior colours.

GENERAL COMMENTS: Set on a modified Seville/Eldorado platform, these large, front-wheel drive sedans represent the state of the art in GM's concept of family motoring, which in turn exemplifies the malaise afflicting the company these days. The LeSabre is the bargain of the group. It offers all the technical features of the more expensive Park Avenue but in a smaller package.

Don't be conned by GM's name game: the LSS was once just a higher trim level for the 88, but it's now marketed as a separate model. The Regency, the '98's replacement, is really just an 88 with chrome grille and whitewalls.

Pontiac continues this year to break away from the pack by offering its stylish Bonneville SSE to those buyers who want more bark and bite. The SSEi uses the same supercharged 240-hp 3.8L engine that powers the Buick Ultra.

Although the interiors will seat six in a pinch, and the decor is suitably "upscale," these large cars still feel as though they got stuck in the 1970s, when conservative styling, uninspiring handling, and a floating, cushiony, extra-quiet ride were the norm. A retuned 3800 TPI 3.8L V6 engine and electronically controlled 4-speed transmission form the base drivetrain for all models.

Cost analysis/alternatives: If you can get a 15–20 percent discount on a '98 model, buy it; there's no reason to pay more for an identical '99 version. The Olds 88 Royale LS and Bonneville SE with a V6 and optional sport suspension are cheaper alternatives to the Bonneville SSEi. Other cars worth considering include the Ford Taurus/Sable, Crown Victoria, and Lincoln Town Car. **Recommended options:** Traction control, automatic levelling suspension, and power mirrors to compensate for the poor rear visibility. You may wish to buy the optional firmer suspension to counteract the base suspension's unsettling jiggle. It includes quicker-ratio steering, firmer shocks, thicker sway bars, and high-performance Goodyear tires. Stay away from the optional digital cluster—all you get are large digital read-outs and bar graphs. The sports suspension and Grand Touring package also promise much more than they deliver. **Rebates:** Expect $2,000 rebates on '98 88, LSS, and Regency models; the limited-run '99s get a $1,500 rebate. The '98 Bonneville gets a $2,000 rebate; the '99 version: $1,250. Only the '98 LeSabre gets a $2,000 rebate. When dealer incentives are added next fall you could get more. **Destination charge:** $895. **Depreciation:** Slightly slower than average. **Insurance cost:** Expensive. **Parts supply/cost:** Parts are easily found, but they tend to be fairly expensive. **Annual maintenance cost:** Higher than average. **Warranty:** Bumper-to-bumper 3 years/60,000 km; rust perforation 6 years/160,000 km. **Supplementary warranty:** Should be seriously considered, since these cars tend to incur serious repair expenses after their third year on the road. **Highway/city fuel economy:** *88:* 8.5–14L/100 km and 9–14.5L/100 km with the High Output engine; *Bonneville:* 8.5–14L/100 km and 9–14.5L/100 km with the High Output engine; *LeSabre:* 8–13L/100 km.

Quality/Reliability/Safety

Pro: Reliability: The 3.8 V6 engine has proven to be much more reliable than its Quad 4 predecessor.

Con: Warranty performance: Below average. GM doesn't stand for "generous" motors. **Quality control:** Not very good. Powertrain failures, computer glitches, and body defects indicate poor overall quality. **Owner-reported problems:** The electronic controls and sequential fuel-injection system are particularly failure-prone. The electrical system in general is plagued by an alarming frequency of short circuits and other failures, and it's difficult to troubleshoot. Front shock absorbers and steering assembly are likely to wear out quickly. Body hardware is fragile. Many mechanics, including GM's own, find the under-hood systems a mystery—even when there's no problem. Paint application is substandard. **Service bulletin problems:** Engine runs rough, lack of power, or knock noise (see DSB below).

File In Section: 6E - Engine Fuel & Emission
Bulletin No.: 77-65-30
Date: December, 1997
Subject:
Engine Runs Rough, Lack of Power, Knock Noise, MIL illuminated
(Replace Spark Plugs and Reflash PCM)
Models:
1998 Buick LeSabre, Park Avenue
1998 Oldsmobile Eighty Eight, LS, LSS, Regency
1998 Pontiac Bonneville
with 3.8L Engine (VIN K - RPO L36)
Condition
Some owners may comment that the engine runs rough, has lack of power, has a knock noise, and/or the MIL (Malfunction Indicator Light) is illuminated. The service technician may determine that DTC Diagnostic Trouble Code) P0300 is stored in the PCM (Powertrain Control Module). The service technician further determines that the affected cylinders have eroded spark plug electrodes.
Cause
The ESC (Electronic Spark Control) calibration within the PCM may not control the spark timing properly resulting in pre-ignition. The pre-ignition may cause the spark plug electrodes to erode and produce the customer concern.
Correction
1.　Install a scan tool and verify DTC P0300 (engine misfire detected) is set.
2.　Note the calibration ID currently in the PCM.
3.　Remove all six spark plugs and inspect for eroded electrodes.

Make/Model	Engine Code	Axle Ratio	Emission Standards	Calibration ID
Buick				
LeSabre	K	2.86	USA-Fed Canada	09357164
LeSabre	K	2.86	California TLEV	09357174
LeSabre	K	2.86	Unleaded Export	09357184
LeSabre	K	3.05	USA-Fed Canada	09357194

NHTSA safety complaints/safety: *Olds 88:* Steering wheel suddenly locked up, causing the vehicle to pull sharply to the left; design of the passenger-side seatbelt causes it to stab the passenger in the back. *Bonneville:* Sudden acceleration; airbag failed to deploy; dash fire ignited behind the radio. *LeSabre:* Throttle sticks, causing high rpms; chronic stalling; inoperative rear seatbelt buckles; turn signal arm doesn't return to Neutral position; plastic part of seatbelt buckle came off when buckling up; location of rear seatbelts makes it difficult to buckle up; parking brake is hard to engage or release and sometimes won't stay locked; broken short steering gear; ABS brake failure; sudden steering failure; when lowering both rear windows while driving the vehicle begins to vibrate excessively; when decelerating or stopping the headlights dim or flicker; rear seatbelts are too short for a child safety seat or for some adults.

Road Performance

Pro: Acceleration/torque: The base 3.8L V6 engine is quiet, smooth, and relatively more economical than some competitive V6 powerplants. It provides lots of power through the lower gear ranges, but runs out of steam as it gets to the top end of its power curve (0–100 km/h: 8.2 sec.). **Transmission:** Smooth and quiet shifting with the 4-speed automatic. One major improvement: you can leave the car in Overdrive and drive around town without the transmission constantly shifting up and down. The Olds' suspension is calibrated more on the firm side than most cars in this class. **Braking:** Very good for cars of this heft (100–0 km/h: 127 ft.).

Con: Steering: The power steering transmits very little road feel. **Routine handling:** Highway handling is clumsy, with too much body lean when cornering. The Bonneville SSE handles better than the others, but it still rides harshly for such a large car. **Emergency handling:** The ride deteriorates rapidly as the suspension bottoms out on rough roads. This effect worsens as the passenger and cargo loads increase. **Braking:** The Oldsmobile versions require more pedal effort.

Comfort/Convenience

Pro: Standard equipment: All these cars are loaded with standard features and plush interiors, but their styling is fairly bland, except for the 88 and Bonneville. The Bonneville SSE interior is stylish, without a lot of steering wheel mounted controls, and its dash layout makes for easy reading of the gauges and controls. The SSEi's trunk contains a road emergency kit and a trunk-mounted air compressor. **Driving position:** Good driving position if your buttocks fit the predefined indents. The optional power seat is essential for a comfortable driving position. **Controls and displays:** A more pleasing and practical half-eyebrow dash copies that of the Japanese and European automakers. User-friendly instruments, climate-control system, and radio. **Climate control:** Improved climate controls and a higher-efficiency AC compressor provide excellent ventilation with little noise. You may also choose different temperature settings for either side of the car. **Entry/exit:** Very good. **Interior space/comfort F/R:** The interior feels spacious and airy and will comfortably seat five adults. There's plenty of rear seat leg room, thanks to the limited rearward travel of the front seats. **Cargo space:** Lots of small storage areas, and long objects can be passed from the trunk through the rear-seat armrest port. **Trunk/liftover:** Large trunk with a low liftover. **Quietness:** Quiet ride.

Con: Rear visibility is hampered by the thick rear roof pillars. Front quarter windows don't open. Limited rear travel on the front seats can put the driver too close to the steering wheel. Rear-seat access a problem. Be wary of GM's claims of a six-passenger carrying capacity; only five passengers will ride in comfort. Front seats require a bit more back support, and the rear seats offer little thigh support and aren't sufficiently padded.

COST

List Price (negotiable)

	Residual Values (months)			
	24	36	48	60
LeSabre Custom: $28,845	$23,000	$15,000	$13,000	$11,000

TECHNICAL DATA

Powertrain (front-drive)
Engines: 3.8L V6 (205 hp)
• 3.8L V6 (240 hp)
Transmissions: 5-speed man.
• 4-speed auto.
Dimensions (LeSabre)
Passengers: 6
Height/length/width:
55.6/200.8/74.4 in.

Head room F/R: 38.8/37.8 in.
Leg room F/R: 42.6/40.4 in.
Wheelbase: 110.8 in.
Cargo capacity: 17 cu. ft.
Towing capacity: 2,000 lbs.
Fuel tank: 68L/reg.
Weight: 3,450 lbs.

SAFETY FEATURES

	Std.	Opt.
Anti-lock brakes	■	❏
Seatbelt pretensioners	—	—
Integrated child safety seat	—	—
Airbag cut-off switch	—	—
Depowered airbags	■	❏
Side airbags	—	—
Traction control	❏	■
Visibility (front/rear)	*****	**
Crash protection D/P		
Bonneville	*****	***
LeSabre	****	****
Crash protection (side) D/P		
LeSabre	***	***
HLDI injury claims		
Bonneville	Low	

Aurora/Riviera ('98)

Aurora

RATING: Average. **Strong points:** Standard ABS and traction control, comfortable ride, good steering and handling, roomy interior, and well-appointed. **Weak points:** Underpowered base engine, requires premium fuel, no side airbags, excessive wind noise, and rear seats aren't easy to get into.

NEW FOR '99: Minor steering and suspension adjustments, two additional engine mounts to dampen noise and vibration, and four new exterior colours. The Aurora nameplate will be affixed to an entirely new sedan set to debut early next year. The Riviera will be dropped in 1999. No changes will be made to the 2000 carried-over units to be built before the model is discontinued.

GENERAL COMMENTS: Essentially a two-door Aurora, the Riviera is a luxury coupe that shares its G-platform with the Oldsmobile Aurora, also introduced in 1995. Its main claim to fame is the availability of a 225-hp 3.8L V6 supercharged engine that provides 0–100 km/h acceleration in 8.2 seconds. Optional in the U.S., GM Canada has made the supercharged version its standard powerplant in Canada.

The Aurora is the epitome of ugly styling. Built on the Riviera and Park Avenue platform and similar in size to the Lexus LS 400, the Aurora is a five-passenger sports sedan that targets Lexus, Infiniti, Mazda's Millenia, and Toyota's Avalon. GM is shooting at moving targets, however, and has missed the mark with the Aurora. For example, its five-passenger seating can't compete with Avalon's six-passenger capacity; its failure-prone front-drive (based on past complaints when used with other vehicles) competes poorly in a market that has more reliable powertrains and that includes rear-drives; and exterior fit and finish just don't compare.

The Aurora is powered by a 250-hp 4.0L V8 Northstar engine—a smaller version of the Cadillac powerplant—coupled to a standard 4-speed automatic transmission. Standard features include dual airbags, four-wheel ABS, traction control, adjustable shoulder height manual seatbelts, cruise control, keyless remote entry and security system, and power-assisted everything.

Cost analysis/alternatives: The 1999 Aurora is the better choice for the upgrades; the '98 Riviera is an also-ran that will have little value as a collector's car. Other cars worth considering are the Acura TL, Ford Crown Victoria and Mercury Marquis, Infiniti I30, Lexus ES 300, Lincoln Mark VIII and Town Car, Mazda Millenia, Nissan Maxima, and Toyota Avalon. The Olds 88 LSS matches the Aurora's supercharged performance for less money. **Recommended options:** The AutoBahn Package is not for everyone; it makes for a harsher ride than the more forgiving base suspension. Bucket seats provide more comfortable support. **Rebates:** $3,000 on the '98 Aurora and Riviera; $2,000 on the '99 Aurora. **Destination charge:** $895. **Depreciation:** Faster than average. **Insurance cost:** Higher than average. **Parts supply/cost:** Moderately priced parts aren't hard to find. **Annual maintenance cost:** Above average. **Warranty:** Bumper-to-bumper 3 years/60,000 km; rust perforation 5 years/160,000 km. **Supplementary warranty:** A good buy. **Highway/city fuel economy:** 9–14.5L/100 km.

Quality/Reliability/Safety

Pro: Quality control: It's been spotty so far, but no worse than GM's other models. Improved structural integrity cuts flexing and reduces squeaks and rattles. **Reliability:** Few major reliability problems reported, due to the short time this reworked version has been on the market. The supercharged engine can't be repaired at your corner garage.

Con: Warranty performance: Below average. **Owner-reported problems:** Transmission malfunctions, electrical glitches, and sloppy body construction. **Service bulletin problems:** Front brake noise (see following DSB); headliner sags; parallel park assist mode/both mirrors inoperative. **NHTSA safety complaints/safety:** ABS failure.

File In Section: 5 - Brakes
Bulletin No.: 73-50-23A
Date: January, 1998
Subject:
Brake Noise (Grunt/Groan/Grind/Crunch/Squeal) Coming from Front Brakes (Replace Front Brake Pads/Rotors)
Models:
1997–98 Buick Riviera, Park Avenue
1997–98 Cadillac Concours, DeVille, Eldorado, Seville
1997–98 Oldsmobile Aurora
1998 Models Affected Were Built Prior to November 1, 1997
This bulletin is being revised to update the model years affected and to include replacement of the brake rotors. Please discard Corporate Bulletin Number 73-50-23 (Section 5 - Brakes).
Condition
Same owners may comment on a grunt, groan, grind, crunch or squeal noise coming from the front brakes when applying the brakes at low speeds (35 mph–0 mph).
Important:
The previous bulletin number (73-50-30) instructed to replace the front brake pads. Owners of vehicles that were serviced under the original bulletin guidelines may now comment on a squeal noise after the brake pads were replaced.
Correction
For 1997 vehicles that have not been previously serviced for the grunt, groan, grind or crunch condition, replace the front brake pads and rotors with new brake pads, P/N 18024961, and brake rotors, P/N 18026591.
For vehicles that have been previously serviced for these various noise conditions and now exhibit a squeal condition, replace the brake rotors only with the larger 8 mm (0.32 in.) cheek rotors, P/N 18026591.
For 1998 vehicles built prior to November 1, 1997, measure the rotor cheek to verify the size of the rotors on that vehicle. Vehicles produced after approximately November 1, 1997, will be built with the larger 8 mm (0.32 in.) cheek rotors and the updated brake pads and should not exhibit the above conditions. To achieve the proper rotor measurement, measure only one side of the rotor from the cooling fin area to the outer braking surface (measure only 1 rotor cheek). The old design rotors have 6 mm (0.24 in.) cheeks. The new design rotors have 8 mm (0.32 in.) cheeks.
Parts Information
Parts are currently available from GMSPO.
Warranty Information

Labor Operation	Description	Labor Time
H0042	Pad and Rotor Replacement	Use published
H0127	Rotor Replacement Only	labor operation
		time

Road Performance

Pro: Acceleration/torque: Acceptable acceleration with the base engine; lots of power and torque produced by the supercharged powerplant (0–100 km/h: 8.6 sec.). **Transmission:** Smooth and quiet shifting. **Routine handling:** Better than average handling and ride quality. **Emergency handling:** Average. **Steering:** Excellent, with better road feel at high speeds. **Braking:** Excellent braking (100–0 km/h: 123 ft.), although pedal effort is a bit high.

Con: Emergency handling: Some excessive body lean; not as nimble as the competition.

Comfort/Convenience

Pro: Standard equipment: Fairly well-appointed despite some lapses. **Driving position:** Excellent driving position. Impressive styling combined with a roomy interior. Well thought-out interior ergonomics. Plush interior includes comfortable front seats and generous amounts of head and leg room. **Controls and displays:** State of the art, particularly the highly functional analogue instrument cluster. **Climate control:** Efficient, quiet, and easily calibrated. **Interior space/comfort F/R:** Roomy interior provides generous room for five adults. Seating is exceptionally comfortable, with just the right amount of thigh and lumbar support. **Cargo space:** Lots of storage areas that are easily accessed. **Trunk/liftover:** Huge trunk. **Quietness:** Excellent soundproofing and few vibrations.

Con: Lacks some features that are standard with the competition, like side airbags, height-adjustable shoulder belts, fold-away side mirrors, and a passenger-side heated seat. Rear visibility is obstructed by the wide rear pillars and the undersized door mirrors don't help. **Entry/exit:** The low roof complicates access and creates a claustrophobic interior. This is not a five-passenger car: the middle occupant, front or rear, won't be comfortable for long. **Trunk/liftover:** The small opening and high liftover make for difficult loading and it's hard to lift the handle-less trunk lid except when it's opened by remote control. Rear seatbacks don't fold flat to expand storage capability. **Quietness:** Some wind noise still intrudes into the passenger compartment.

COST

List Price (negotiable)		**Residual Values** (months)		
	24	**36**	**48**	**60**
Aurora Sedan: $46,190 (30%)	$27,000	$21,000	$17,000	$14,000

TECHNICAL DATA

Powertrain (front-drive)
Engines: 3.8L V6 (240 hp)
• 4.0L V8 (250 hp)
Transmission: 4-speed auto.
Dimensions (Riviera)
Passengers: 4
Height/length/width:
54.6/207.2/75 in.

Head room F/R: 38.2/36.2 in.
Leg room F/R: 42.6/37.1 in.
Wheelbase: 113.8 in.
Cargo capacity: 17.4 cu. ft.
Towing capacity: 3,000 lbs.
Fuel tank: 76L/premium
Weight: 3,750 lbs.

SAFETY FEATURES

	Std.	Opt.
Anti-lock brakes	■	❏
Seatbelt pretensioners	—	—
Integrated child safety seat	—	—
Airbag cut-off switch	—	—
Depowered airbags	■	❏
Side airbags	—	—
Traction control	■	■
Visibility (front/rear)	*****	*****
Riviera	*****	**
Crash protection D/P	***	***
Crash protection (side) D/P	N/A	
HLDI injury claims	Low	

Park Avenue, Ultra

Park Avenue

RATING: *Park Avenue:* Average; *Ultra:* Above Average. **Strong points:** Great powertrain performance, standard ABS, well-appointed, and quiet-running. Ultra provides excellent steering and handling. **Weak points:** Ponderous handling caused partly by a mediocre suspension and over-assisted steering with the base model, excessive fuel consumption (premium fuel) with the supercharged engine, and no side airbags.

NEW FOR '99: Restyled taillights, standard Michelin tires, a walnut-trimmed interior, an upgraded stereo system, and the addition of four new exterior colours.

GENERAL COMMENTS: Full-size luxury sedan aficionados love the flush glass, wrap-around windshield and bumpers, and clean body lines that make for an aerodynamic, pleasing appearance. But these cars are more than a pretty package; they provide lots of room, luxury, style, and, dare I say, performance. Plenty of power is available with the Park Avenue's 205-hp 3.8L V6 engine and the Ultra's 240-hp supercharged version of the same powerplant. It does a 0–100 km/h time in under 9 seconds (impressive, considering the heft of these vehicles), and improves low- and mid-range throttle response. Power is transmitted to the front wheels through an electronically controlled transmission that features "free-wheeling" clutches designed to eliminate abrupt gear changes. Both the Park Avenue and Ultra use a stretched version of the more rigid Buick Riviera and Olds Aurora platform.

Cost analysis/alternatives: Get the '99 version for the upgrades. Other cars worth considering: an Olds Aurora, Ford Crown Victoria/Mercury Grand Marquis, Infiniti I30, Lexus ES 300, or Nissan Maxima. **Recommended options:** The Grand Touring suspension is a good middle ground between sporty firmness and luxurious cruising comfort. On the other hand, the Head Up display is more of a gimmick than anything else. **Rebates:** $3,000 applicable to the base Park Avenue. **Destination charge:** $895. **Depreciation:** Faster than average. **Insurance cost:** Higher than average. **Parts supply/cost:** Parts aren't hard to find, but they can be pricey (particularly the supercharged engine components). **Annual maintenance cost:** Higher than average. **Warranty:** Bumper-to-bumper 3 years/60,000 km; rust perforation 5 years/160,000 km. **Supplementary warranty:** It'll come in handy after the third year of use. **Highway/city fuel economy:** 8–13L/100 km; 9–14.5L/100 km with the High Output engine. Supercharged V6 sips fuel, unlike the V8-equipped competition.

Quality/Reliability/Safety

Pro: Quality control: Average. Quality control has improved a lot during the past few years. **Warranty performance:** Better than average. **Safety:** A personalized vehicle security system disables the starting and fuel systems if a non-matching key is used. Rear shoulder belts have a strap to pull the belt away from the neck of small passengers and children. Right-side mirror tilts down when Reverse is engaged (standard on the Ultra).

Con: Reliability: Mediocre. **Owner-reported problems:** Some engine, transmission, and electronic module malfunctions. **Service bulletin problems:** Front brake noise; engine runs rough, lack of power, or knock noise. **NHTSA safety complaints/safety:** Hard-to-read speedometer; difficulty seeing dashboard controls due to dash-top design; a reflection in the windshield coming from the dashboard obstructs view; ABS and service light come on for no reason; horn is hard to operate.

Road Performance

Pro: Acceleration/torque: The 3.8L V6 engine is competent, quiet, and smooth running, with lots of low-end torque. Impressively fast with the supercharged engine (0–100 km/h: 8 sec.). **Transmission:** The F31 electronic 4-speed transmission works imperceptibly. Cruise control is much smoother without all those annoying downshifts we've learned to hate in GM cars. **Routine handling:** Acceptably predictable, though quite slow with variable-assist power steering and shocks that are a bit firmer than usual. Body roll has been reduced thanks to the retuned suspension. With its stiffer suspension the Ultra performs well on winding roads, while the softly sprung Park Avenue is best for city use. **Emergency handling:** Fairly quick and sure-footed. **Braking:** Good braking with or without ABS (100–0 km/h: 135 ft.).

Con: Acceleration/torque: Acceleration isn't breathtaking with the base 3.8L engine; at higher revs torque falls off quickly. **Steering:** Power steering is a bit vague at highway speeds. Panic braking causes considerable nose-diving that compromises handling.

Comfort/Convenience

Pro: Standard equipment: Very well equipped, with many performance and convenience features included as standard equipment. **Driving position:** Excellent. Modern, aerodynamic styling maximizes front and rear visibility. **Controls and displays:** Complete and easy-to-read instruments and gauges. **Climate control:** Much improved interior ventilation and AC performance. Easy-to-adjust controls allow the driver and passenger to choose different temperature settings for their own comfort. **Entry/exit:** No problem. **Interior space/comfort F/R:** Exceptionally spacious interior will seat four in total comfort. **Cargo space:** Plenty of storage areas that are easily accessible. **Trunk/liftover:** Huge trunk has a low liftover. **Quietness:** Excellent soundproofing. The entire body has a more solid feel than what one normally finds with GM.

Con: Driving positon: Driver seat lacks lateral support. Wide rear pillars block visibility, but large side mirrors compensate. **Quietness:** Some wind noise and tire vibration.

COST

List Price (negotiable)	Residual Values (months)			
	24	36	48	60
Park Avenue: $41,060 (30%)	$26,000	$22,000	$18,000	$15,000

TECHNICAL DATA

Powertrain (front-drive)
Engines: 3.8L V6 (205 hp)
• 3.8L V6 (240 hp)
Transmission: 4-speed auto.
Dimensions
Passengers: 4 in comfort
Height/length/width:
57/206.8/74.7 in.

Head room F/R: 39.8/38 in.
Leg room F/R: 42.4/41.4 in.
Wheelbase: 113.8 in.
Cargo capacity: 19.1 cu. ft.
Towing capacity: 3,000 lbs.
Fuel tank: 68L/premium
Weight: 3,950 lbs.

SAFETY FEATURES

	Std.	Opt.
Anti-lock brakes	■	❏
Seatbelt pretensioners	—	—
Integrated child safety seat	—	—
Airbag cut-off switch	—	—
Depowered airbags	■	❏
Side airbags	—	—
Traction control	■	■
Visibility (front/rear)	*****	***
Crash protection D/P	N/A	
Crash protection (side) D/P	N/A	
HLDI injury claims	N/A	

Cadillac Catera

Catera

RATING: Below Average. If Cadillac is to once again lure luxury buyers into the GM fold, the automaker has to copy European automakers with something more substantial than a warmed-over Opel. **Strong points:** Well-appointed, comfortable ride, standard ABS and traction control. **Weak points:** Merely adequate acceleration, mediocre handling, limited rear visibility, potentially problematic emissions system, styling isn't for everyone, and an uncertain future if sales don't pick up.

NEW FOR '99: Not much new. The gas cap has been redesigned, the chrome grill will be blacker, and GM has retired that crazy duck used in its "the car that zigs" commercials. Cadillac has also reworked its emissions control system by adding new powertrain control computers, an electronic throttle control, and an upgraded fuel tank and evaporative system. This changeover in the emissions hardware came during the GM strike, and therefore hasn't been fully validated as being glitch-free. I expect driveability problems to arise (hard starting, poor idling, stalling, and high fuel consumption).

GENERAL COMMENTS: Assembled in Germany and based on the Opel Omega, the rear-drive, midsize Catera comes with a 200-hp V6 engine, 4-speed automatic transmission, 16-inch alloy wheels, four-wheel disc brakes, a limited-slip differential, traction control, and standard dual side airbags.

The last time Cadillac introduced an entry level model was in 1981 when the automaker launched the Cimarron, a fully loaded, Chevrolet Cavalier-derived Cadillac that carried a $4,000 premium over a comparably equipped Cavalier. Back then, most auto critics and consumer advocates considered the Cavalier to be at the back of the pack as far as performance and quality control were concerned. The Catera, on the other hand, has gotten good reviews from the European press for its quiet, spacious, and comfortable interior, responsive handling, precise steering, fine-tuned suspension, and almost nonexistent lean or body roll when cornering. Without a doubt this is one Cadillac that's meant to be driven. The only question that remains is whether it's worth $43,000. I think not.

Cost analysis/alternatives: If it's discounted at least 20 percent, you can get away with buying a '98 Catera and miss nothing. Other "driver's" cars worth considering: the Audi A6, BMW 328i, Infiniti I30, Lexus ES 300, and Mercedes Benz C280 or CLK. **Recommended options:** None. This car comes fully loaded. **Rebates:** $1,000 on all '98 models. **Destination charge:** $895. **Depreciation:** Predicted to be higher than average. **Insurance cost:** Also higher than average. **Parts supply/cost:** Parts are expensive and not easily found. **Annual maintenance cost:** Predicted to be higher than average after the fourth year when the warranty expires. **Warranty:** Bumper-to-bumper 4 years/80,000 km; rust perforation 6 years/160,000 km. **Supplementary warranty:** Essential, until the Catera has proven its long-term reliability, to ensure that you won't be stuck with huge fifth-year repair bills. **Highway/city fuel economy:** 8.7–12.9L/100 km.

Quality/Reliability/Safety

Pro: Quality control: Above average. Just a few computer module and body problems have been reported. **Reliability:** Reliability hasn't been a concern, partly because the Catera has been out for only a short time and partly because it's still under warranty. **Warranty performance:** Unblemished. Now if only all of GM's customers were treated so well. **Service bulletin problems:** Nothing significant.

Con: GM dealers are notoriously bad when it comes to understanding and repairing European-transplanted cars (just ask any Saab owner). **Owner-reported problems:** Premature front brake wear, electrical glitches, and some body imperfections. **NHTSA safety complaints/safety:** Front seatbelts malfunction; airbag failed to deploy; brakes squeal and pull vehicle sharply to the right when applied; rear visibility is obstructed by a narrow window and large rear head restraints.

Road Performance

Pro: Acceleration/torque: German-built V6 engine has plenty of low-end torque and accelerates smoothly (0–100 km/h: 8.9 sec.). **Transmission:** Smooth and quiet, and the automatic transmission allows for third-gear starts for maximum traction on snow or ice. **Routine handling:** "European" ride is firm but comfortable. **Braking:** Respectable for a vehicle this heavy (100–0 km/h: 129 ft.).

Con: Engine runs out of steam in higher gear ranges. **Transmission:** The transmission has to kick down two gears to achieve adequate highway passing power. **Routine handling:** When you pass over a large expansion joint the floorpan vibrates annoyingly; drive over a bump when turning and the steering wheel kicks back in your hands.

Emergency handling: Surprisingly slow for a European-bred luxury car.
Steering: Vague, with little road feel.

Comfort/Convenience

Pro: Standard equipment: Loaded with convenience and performance
features that would be optional on other cars. **Driving position:**
Excellent, with good front and rear visibility. **Controls and displays:**
Complete, logically presented, and easy to read. **Climate control:** Quite
efficient and quiet. **Entry/exit:** Wide door openings make for easy
front and rear access. **Interior space/comfort F/R:** Plush interior will
seat four adults comfortably. **Cargo space:** Split folding rear seatbacks
increase storage capability. **Trunk/liftover:** The large trunk has a low
liftover. **Quietness:** Fairly quiet interior.

Con: The uninspired styling has Lumina written all over it. Unmarked
power window switches are mounted on the centre console where they
are less convenient. **Quietness:** Some wind noise at highway speeds.

COST

List Price (very negotiable)	Residual Values (months)			
	24	**36**	**48**	**60**
Catera Sedan: $42,310 (30%)	$25,000	$21,000	$17,000	$13,000

TECHNICAL DATA

Powertrain (front-drive)
Engine: 3.0L V6 (200 hp)
Transmissions: 4-speed auto.
Dimensions
Passengers: 4 in comfort
Height/length/width:
57.4/193.8/70.3 in.

Head room F/R: 38.6/37.8 in.
Leg room F/R: 42/36.2 in.
Wheelbase: 107.4 in.
Cargo capacity: 16.6 cu. ft.
Towing capacity: 2,000 lbs.
Fuel tank: 68L/reg.
Weight: 3,800 lbs.

SAFETY FEATURES

	Std.	Opt.
Anti-lock brakes	■	❑
Seatbelt pretensioners	■	❑
Integrated child safety seat	—	—
Airbag cut-off switch	—	—
Depowered airbags	■	❑
Side airbags	■	❑
Traction control	■	❑
Visibility (front/rear)	*****	*****
Crash protection D/P	N/A	
Crash protection (side) D/P	N/A	
HLDI Injury claims	N/A	

Cadillac DeVille/d'Elegance/Concours

DeVille

RATING: Average. **Strong points:** Well-matched engine and transmission, comfortable riding and easy handling, standard side airbags and traction control, and lots of passenger and cargo room. **Weak points:** Limited rear and side visibility, base DeVille and d'Elegance climate controls aren't user-friendly, poor fuel economy (premium fuel), and mediocre body assembly quality.

NEW FOR '99: The anti-theft alarm and inside compass mirror become standard features, the OnStar communication system will now alert the customer service centre of a front or side airbag deployment, and a massaging lumbar front seat is optional on the Concours and d'Elegance.

GENERAL COMMENTS: Now that the rear-drive Fleetwood is gone, these two Cadillacs step in to fill the void. There are really two DeVilles: the Sedan DeVille (GM's most popular Cadillac) aimed at traditional Cadillac buyers, and the Concours, which offers sportier performance. Essentially a front-drive clone of the rear-drive Fleetwood, the sedan is a chrome-ridden, overly large luxury car whose new Northstar powerplant blurs the distinction between it and the Concours. It uses a "brake only" traction-control system, which counters wheelspin at low speeds by applying the front brakes, and a softer suspension. Michelin whitewalls are standard.

The Concours version carries the powerful 4.6L 300-hp Northstar engine and 4-speed automatic transmission, improved traction control, electronic variable-dampening suspension (programmed for a firmer ride), four-wheel anti-lock disc brakes, and 225/6016 Eagle GA touring tires. Both Cadillacs have moved from GM's C platform—which they used to share with the Buick Park Avenue and Olds Ninety Eight—to a K-Special chassis, a stretched version of the Seville/Eldorado platform.

Cost analysis/alternatives: Get the '99 model if you feel the upgrades are worth the extra cost; consider a '98 model if the price is cut 15–20 percent. Other cars worth considering: the Buick Park Avenue, the Ford Crown Victoria and Lincoln Town Car. **Recommended options:** Stay away from the optional digital cluster; all you get are large digital read-outs and bar graphs. Buy the optional firmer suspension to counteract the base suspension's unsettling jiggle. It includes quicker-ratio steering, firmer shocks, thicker sway bars, and high-performance Goodyear tires. **Rebates:** Up to $5,000 on the '98s; $1,000 on the '99s. **Destination charge:** $895. **Depreciation:** Faster than average. **Insurance cost:** Higher than average. **Parts supply/cost:** Except for engine components, most parts are easily found, though a bit expensive. **Annual maintenance cost:** Average during the first four years of ownership. Engine control and electrical systems are too complicated for most garages to service. **Warranty:** Bumper-to-bumper 4 years/80,000 km; rust perforation 6 years/160,000 km. **Supplementary warranty:** If you plan to keep the car after the fourth year, an extended warranty is essential. **Highway/city fuel economy:** 9–16L/100 km; *DeVille Concours:* 9–14.5L/100 km.

Quality/Reliability/Safety

Pro: Warranty performance: Better than average.

Con: Quality control: Assembly quality isn't anywhere near luxury car standards, and paint is often poorly applied. Fragile body hardware. Large gaps between sheet metal panels and doors. **Reliability:** Long-term ownership of any of these models doesn't look promising. Reliability histories are replete with major faults, constant malfunctions, and mind-spinning depreciation. **Owner-reported problems:** The front brakes and shock absorbers wear out quickly. Serious fit and finish deficiencies. Intermittent stalling, rough idling, hesitation, and no-starts. **Service bulletin problems:** Front brake noise. **NHTSA safety complaints/safety:** *DeVille:* Traction control light comes on for no reason; premature brake wear; seats protrude out too far in the back area, preventing passengers from sitting back and making head restraints set too far back; sudden headlight failure; suddenly stalled while driving uphill and then started rolling backwards. *Concours:* Premature brake pad wear.

Road Performance

Pro: Acceleration/torque: Plenty of power and torque with the base 275-hp 4.6L V8 engine, delivered with minimal harshness, vibration, and noise (0–100 km/h: 7.6 sec.). The 300-hp variant is even more impressive. **Transmission:** The 4-speed automatic with Overdrive is responsive, smooth, and quiet. **Routine handling:** Very good. Little body roll and crisp handling. **Steering:** Speed-sensitive power steering is precise, with lots of road feel. **Emergency handling:** Very good. Road Sensing suspension prevents excessive body lean when cornering at high speed. **Braking:** Best in its class (100–0 km/h: 120 ft.).

Con: The 4.6L V8 overpowers the front-drive chassis. Some torque steer is evident. 41-foot turning radius can make parking a chore.

Comfort/Convenience

Pro: Standard equipment: These cars come equipped with just about every imaginable electrical and power-assisted gadget, in addition to an ultra-plush interior. **Driving position:** Excellent. **Climate control:** Efficient and quiet, though the controls may be hard to reach (Concours). **Entry/exit:** Easy front and rear access. **Interior space/ comfort F/R:** This is one huge front-drive Cadillac. Impressively large interior easily accommodates six adults in comfort. **Cargo space:** Lots of storage areas. **Trunk/liftover:** Fairly large trunk has a low liftover. **Quietness:** Very little engine or road noise seeps into the interior.

Con: Tacky imitation wood dash. All seats lack sufficient lumbar support and the front seats lack adequate thigh support. Rear visibility is blocked by wide rear roof pillars, and rear view mirrors are too small to be of much help. **Controls and displays:** Dashboard controls are too fussy for safe operation; the driver must often look away from the road to do such simple things as tune the radio or adjust the climate controls.

COST

List Price (negotiable)	Residual Values (months)			
	24	**36**	**48**	**60**
DeVille: $49,910 (30%)	$35,000	$24,000	$21,000	$18,000

TECHNICAL DATA

Powertrain (front-drive)	Head room F/R: 38.5/38.4 in.
Engines: 4.6L (275 hp)	Leg room F/R: 42.6/43.3 in.
• 4.6L (300 hp)	Wheelbase: 113.8 in.
Transmission: 4-speed auto.	Cargo capacity: 20 cu. ft.
Dimensions	Towing capacity: 3,000 lbs.
Passengers: 6	Fuel tank: 76L/premium
Height/length/width:	Weight: 4,000 lbs.
56.4/209.7/76.5 in.	

SAFETY FEATURES

	Std.	Opt.
Anti-lock brakes	■	❑
Seatbelt pretensioners	—	—
Integrated child safety seat	—	—
Airbag cut-off switch	—	—
Depowered airbags	■	❑
Side airbags	■	❑
Traction control	■	■
Visibility (front/rear)	*****	**
Crash protection D/P	****	****
Crash protection (side) D/P	****	****
HLDI injury claims	Low	

Eldorado, Seville

Eldorado

RATING: Average. **Strong points:** Standard ABS and traction control, impressive engine performance, good handling, and a comfortable ride. **Weak points:** Limited rear visibility, rear seating for two (Eldorado), climate controls hard to find on the base model, poor fuel economy, sloppy body assembly.

NEW FOR '99: *Eldorado:* A standard anti-theft alarm and inside compass mirror. ETC version gets optional massaging lumbar front seat and a standard Bose sound system. *Seville:* A massaging lumbar front seat is optional on the STS, an adaptive seat used by the '98 STS will come with the SLS. A heated seat will also be available for the adaptive seat. The OnStar communication system will now alert the customer service centre of a front or side airbag deployment.

GENERAL COMMENTS: The Eldorado is Cadillac's front-drive sports luxury coupe. It shares its chassis and engine with the Seville. Eldorado and its sporty Sports Coupe twin are both equipped with the Northstar V8 and built on identical platforms with the same components. This provides a quiet, comfortable ride along with impressive acceleration.

Last year, the Seville was dramatically restyled and adopted GM's G-body, the stiffened chassis created for the Oldsmobile Aurora, Buick Riviera, and Park Avenue. This gives it a wider stance, longer wheelbase, and shorter length.

On the safety front, seatbelts are attached to the seat itself rather than the B-pillar, the tires and rear brakes have been enlarged and seat-mounted side airbags are standard. Other standard safety features include: traction control, anti-lock brakes, and anti-spin technology from GM's Delphi division.

Most Cadillacs are offered with some sort of performance package, usually in a special model, and the Eldorado and Seville are no different. Granted, this makes them more pleasant to drive, but these are usually only half-hearted efforts when compared to the sterling performance offered by the Japanese and German imports.

Although there doesn't seem to be much hope for this model line when one takes a hard look at the Catera, the engineering improvements invested in last year's Seville send an altogether different message. But a message isn't a mindset. Nevertheless, the Seville is a step in the right direction.

Cost analysis/alternatives: *Eldorado:* Get the '99 model if you feel the upgrades are worth it; consider a '98 model only if the price is cut by at least 20 percent. *Seville:* The '99 Seville, the second year of its redesign, is the better choice. Other cars worth considering: a BMW 5-series, Infiniti Q45, Lexus LS 400, or Mercedes-Benz E-class. **Recommended options:** Be wary of the hard-riding ETC package; the base model's standard suspension gives a more comfortable ride and better low-speed performance. **Rebates:** *Eldorado:* $4,000 on the '98 Touring Coupe; $1,000 on the '99 Seville. **Destination charge:** $895. **Depreciation:** Faster than average. **Insurance cost:** Higher than average. **Parts supply/cost:** Parts aren't hard to find, and CAA says they're reasonably priced. **Annual maintenance cost:** Average. **Warranty:** Bumper-to-bumper 4 years/80,000 km; rust perforation 6 years/160,000 km. **Supplementary warranty:** Not necessary. **Highway/city fuel economy:** 9–14.5L/100 km for both vehicles.

Quality/Reliability/Safety

Pro: Warranty performance: Better than average. All Cadillacs come with GM's PASS KEY theft-deterrent system that shuts down the starter and fuel system if the right key isn't used.

Con: Quality control: Little has escaped the gremlins' hands on these cars. Assembly quality isn't anywhere near luxury car standards, and paint is often poorly applied. Fragile body hardware. Large gaps between sheet metal panels and doors that are poorly hung and not entirely square. **Reliability:** If you're planning to spend big bucks on either the Eldorado or the Seville, the likelihood of multiple reliability and body problems should make you think twice. Like most of GM's front-drives, these models have amassed a terrible reputation for being unreliable and expensive to maintain. In all, there is little to recommend them; there are cheaper vehicles that offer better performance and interior comfort. **Owner-reported problems:** The front brakes and shock absorbers wear out quickly. The Seville and Eldorado have serious fit and finish deficiencies. Some sample problems: cracking of front outside door handles; door rattles (Eldorado); poor bumper fit; loose sun visor mounting; rear taillight condensation (Seville); interior window fogging; "creaking" body mounts; water leaks into trunk from licence plate holder (Eldorado); noisy roof panels and seatback lumbar motors; and excessive brake pedal travel to disengage the cruise control or activate the brake lights. Intermittent stalling, rough idling, hesitation, and no-starts. **Service bulletin problems:** Front brake noise. **NHTSA safety complaints/safety:** No incidents reported. Plastic fuel tanks improve Seville and Eldorado crashworthiness. Drivers complain that the shoulder belt chafes the neck and that the traction control lacks an override feature. The 1998 Sevilles have been recalled to correct premature windshield wiper failures.

Road Performance

Pro: Acceleration/torque: Tire-burning acceleration (0–100 km/h: 7.1 sec.) with gobs of torque and minimal harshness, vibration, and noise. **Transmission:** The 4-speed automatic with Overdrive is responsive, despite occasional confusion about which gear it should be in. **Routine handling:** Better than average, although it floats a bit. Road Sensing suspension prevents excessive body lean in turns. **Emergency handling:** Average. Suspension improvements make for much less body roll, more responsive handling, and a softer ride. **Steering:** Steering is crisp and predictable. **Braking:** Acceptable, though not impressive (100–0 km/h: 134 ft.).

Con: The 4.6L V8 engine overpowers the Eldorado's front-drive chassis. Some torque steer is evident.

Comfort/Convenience

Pro: Standard equipment: These cars come equipped with just about every imaginable electrical and power-assisted gadget. **Driving position:** First class on the Seville. **Controls and displays:** Most controls are within easy reach, and instruments aren't hard to decipher. **Climate control:** Efficient and quiet. **Interior space/comfort F/R:** Spacious seating due to the Seville's extra length and width, which gives rear passengers considerable room and easy access. The Eldorado also has a surprisingly spacious interior for a coupe, and it actually offers more head room in the rear than up front. **Cargo space:** Plenty of small storage areas that are easily accessed. **Trunk/liftover:** Large trunk with a low liftover. **Quietness:** Better than average. Almost no engine, road, or wind noise finds its way into the passenger compartment.

Con: Driving position: The Eldorado's wide rear pillars obstruct the driver's view to the right rear; front seats lack adequate thigh and lumbar support. **Climate control:** The climate control system has limited manual override and the steering wheel blocks the view of the controls. **Entry/exit:** *Eldorado:* Getting to the back seat requires very inelegant contortions. **Interior space/comfort F/R:** *Eldorado:* Limited interior space. Rear seat won't accommodate three adults comfortably.

COST

List Price (very negotiable)

Eldorado: $52,120 (30%)

	Residual Values (months)			
	24	**36**	**48**	**60**
	$33,000	$24,000	$21,000	$18,000

Technical Data

Powertrain (front-drive)
Engines: 4.6L (275 hp)
• 4.6L (300 hp)
Transmission: 4-speed auto.
Dimensions (Eldorado)
Passengers: 4 in comfort
Height/length/width:
53.6/202.2/75.5 in.

Head room F/R: 37.8/38.3 in.
Leg room F/R: 42.6/36.1 in.
Wheelbase: 108 in.
Cargo capacity: 15.3 cu. ft.
Towing capacity: 3,000 lbs.
Fuel tank: 76L/premium
Weight: 3,800 lbs.

SAFETY FEATURES

	Std.	Opt.
Anti-lock brakes	■	❑
Seatbelt pretensioners	—	—
Integrated child safety seat	—	—
Airbag cut-off switch	—	—
Depowered airbags	■	❑
Side airbags	■	❑
Traction control	■	❑
Visibility (front/rear)	*****	**
Crash protection D/P	N/A	
Crash protection (side) D/P	N/A	
HLDI injury claims	Low	

Camaro/Firebird

Camaro

RATING: Recommended. **Strong points:** Safer, better-performing muscle cars with above-average crash protection and high resale value. Standard ABS and a reasonably good reliability record. Good engine performance (Z28) and crisp handling. **Weak points:** Poor wet-weather traction without traction control, limited rear seat room, hard-riding, difficult access, wide rear pillars impede rear visibility, and limited cargo space.

NEW FOR '99: Optional traction control, a larger fuel tank, electronic throttle control for the standard V6, an oil-life monitor that tracks how well the engine functions.

GENERAL COMMENTS: These sporty convertibles and coupes are almost identical in the features they offer and in their pricing. Both cars have been extensively upgraded (for the second time in five years), making them more powerful and aerodynamic with less spine-jarring performance.

As one moves up the scale overall performance improves considerably. The aluminum-block LS1 V8 engine gives these cars lots of sparkle and tire-spinning torque, but there's a fuel penalty to pay. A 4-speed automatic transmission is standard on the 5.7L-equipped Z28; other versions come with a standard 5-speed manual gearbox or an optional 6-speed. All cars can be ordered with lots of extra performance and luxury options, including a T-roof package guaranteed to include a full assortment of creaks and groans.

Both cars are equipped with an impressively effective PASS KEY theft-deterrent system similar to the one used successfully in the Corvette. A resistor pellet in the ignition disables the starter and fuel system when the key code doesn't match the ignition lock.

Cost analysis/alternatives: Even though last year's leftovers may be less expensive, the '99's refinements make it by far the better buy. Get a firm delivery date; long delivery delays have been caused by GM's recently settled two-month strike. A V8-equipped Camaro or convertible is the best choice for retained value a few years hence. But you can do quite well with the base coupe equipped with the performance handling package (about $800) and 235 tires. Other cars worth considering are the Eagle Talon, Ford Mustang, and the Toyota Celica and '98 Supra. Base Camaros usually outperform V6-equipped Mustangs and they get better gas mileage, as well. **Recommended options:** GM's Performance Handling Package and 235/55 tires on 16-inch aluminum wheels. Most drivers will find the optional traction control system more useful than the limited-slip differential. **Rebates:** $2,000 rebate for '98 V6 models; $750 on '98 V6 versions. **Destination charge:** $680. **Depreciation:** Much slower than average. Interestingly, the Camaro holds its value a wee bit better than do the Firebird variants. **Insurance cost:** Much higher than average. Expect to pay about $2,500, or three times the cost of a Japanese econobox. **Parts supply/cost:** No problem finding reasonably priced parts. **Annual maintenance cost:** Average. Servicing the fuel-injection system is an exercise in frustration and drives up maintenance costs. **Warranty:** Bumper-to-bumper 3 years/60,000 km; rust perforation 6 years/160,000 km. **Supplementary warranty:** Not needed. **Highway/city fuel economy:** 7.1–12.2L/100 km with the base 3.8L and manual 5-speed; 9–15L/100 km with the 5.7L and manual 6-speed; 9–14L/100 km with the 5.7L and 4-speed automatic.

Quality/Reliability/Safety

Pro: Quality control: Average. The new plastic body panels are dent- and rust-resistant. **Warranty performance:** Average. Most repairs are simple to perform and relatively inexpensive. **Service bulletin problems:** Nothing significant.

Con: Reliability: Powertrain components frequently fail, causing extended periods of downtime while they're repaired. **Owner-reported problems:** The 5.7L V8 fuel and electrical systems have been troublesome in the past. Engine cooling and ignition systems are also bug-plagued. Poor air-conditioner performance is a common complaint. The front brakes and MacPherson struts wear out quickly. Body problems include door rattles, poor fit and finish, misaligned doors and hatch, and a sticking hatch power release. **NHTSA safety complaints/ safety:** *Camaro:* Airbags failed to deploy; driving down the highway, locked T-top flew off. *Firebird:* Airbags failed to deploy.

Road Performance

Pro: Acceleration/torque: Better-than-average acceleration with the base V6. Thrilling performance with either the base 305-hp V8 or the optional 320-hp 5.7L V8. Engines start well in cold weather and give ample pulling power. In fact, these cars have so much power in reserve that the automatic transmission doesn't compromise fuel economy or performance. **Routine handling:** Handling is best on the sports models, but even the base coupes perform respectably on the road, and the stiffer suspension makes for much tighter cornering. **Steering:** The rack-and-pinion steering is responsive and precise with lots of road feedback. **Braking:** Much better than average, due primarily to the standard four-wheel anti-lock brakes (100–0 km/h: 117 ft.).

Con: Transmission: The 6-speed manual transmission's clutch is heavy and gets tiring in city driving—the shifter takes getting used to due to the pattern of the gear throws. Furthermore, it has a fuel-saving feature that automatically shifts to fourth from first gear if you're not driving aggressively enough. The upgraded 4-speed automatic with Overdrive tends to shift late, putting extra strain on the engine. **Emergency handling:** Without traction control the tires lose traction, and directional stability is compromised on wet pavement. Due to the rear axle suspension, the ride is constantly busy and particularly bouncy on poor roads. A stiffer suspension adds to this effect. These cars cry out for independent rear suspension.

Comfort/Convenience

Pro: Standard equipment: Even the base models come loaded with such useful features as anti-lock brakes. Most people find the Firebird's front seats more comfortable, but they're comfortable and supportive on both cars. **Controls and displays:** Dash is well laid-out with easy-to-read gauges and complete instrumentation. **Climate control:** Good fresh air ventilation system. Large doors make access into the interior a breeze, but they're a bit unwieldy, especially in tight parking spaces. **Cargo space:** Quite limited, but folding back seat expands cargo storage capability. **Quietness:** A tighter chassis has eliminated most of the creaks and groans that have accompanied these cars for decades.

Con: Driving position: Driving position is too low for short drivers and rear visibility is compromised by wide roof pillars and the high rear end. The obtrusive centre console gets in the way when shifting. The front windshield has only a single de-mister vent. **Interior space/comfort F/R:** Limited leg room for the front seat passenger. The rear buckets are just that—buckets. Consider this car a two-seater: the split rear seat is a joke (or a place to put people you don't like). **Entry/exit:** Very difficult rear seat access. Door detents are too weak to keep the heavy doors open. **Cargo space:** The cargo area is small and awkwardly shaped. Large objects won't fit under the hatch. **Trunk/liftover:** Small trunk with a high liftover; the convertible has 40 percent less trunk space. Excessive tire, road, and engine noise.

COST

List Price (negotiable)

Camaro (base):
  $23,100 (17%)

	Residual Values (months)			
	24	**36**	**48**	**60**
	$17,000	$15,000	$12,000	$9500

TECHNICAL DATA

Powertrain (front-drive)
Engines: 3.8L V6 (200 hp)
• 5.7L V8(305 hp)
• 5.7L V8(320 hp)
Transmissions: 6-speed man.
• 4-speed auto.
Dimensions (Z28)
Passengers: 4
Height/length/width:
52/193.2/74.1 in.

Head room F/R: 37.2/35.3 in.
Leg room F/R: 42.9/26.8 in.
Wheelbase: 101.1 in.
Cargo capacity: 7.6 cu. ft.
Towing capacity: 1,000 lbs.
Fuel tank: 59L/premium
Weight: 3,600 lbs.

SAFETY FEATURES

	Std.	Opt.
Anti-lock brakes	■	❏
Seatbelt pretensioners	—	—
Integrated child safety seat		—
Airbag cut-off switch	—	—
Depowered airbags	■	❏
Side airbags	—	—
Traction control	❏	■
Visibility (front/rear)	**	**
Crash protection D/P	****	*****
Crash protection (side) D/P	***	****
HLDI injury claims	Average	

Corvette

Corvette

RATING: Average. A brawny sports coupe that's slowly evolving into a more refined machine. **Strong points:** Standard ABS and traction control. Powerful powertrain, easy handling, supple ride, attractively styled, and lots of standard convenience features. **Weak points:** Poorly performing "skip shift" manual gearbox, ride (Z51 suspension), rear visibility, limited storage space, and poor-quality fit and finish.

NEW FOR '99: The debut of a high-performance hardtop version and additional options for the coupe and convertible that include: a head-up display that projects instrumentation readouts onto the windshield, a power telescoping steering column, and an active handling system.

GENERAL COMMENTS: Introduced in 1953 as a futuristic show car, and the first American car to use fuel injection (in 1957), Chevrolet has sold more than a million Corvettes over the past 40 years, with an estimated 500,000 still on the roads. Its peak year was 1984, when over 84,000 coupes and convertibles were sold in North America, for about half of today's price.

This year's Corvette returns with its 345-hp 5.7L LS1 powerplant, harnessed to either a 4-speed automatic or a 6-speed manual transmission. The engine is made from aluminum and most transmission components have been shifted to the rear for better handling and increased passenger room.

Cost analysis/alternatives: Get the '99 Corvette for the upgrades; only consider a '98 model if the price is cut 10 percent or more. Keep in mind that premium fuel and astronomical insurance rates will further drive up your operating costs. Other sporty models worth considering are the Dodge Viper, '98 Eagle Talon, Ford Taurus SHO, Porsche Boxster, and '98 Toyota Supra. **Recommended options:** The 6-speed manual transmission and Z51 suspension, if you want the extra performance thrills, but you may find the suspension a bit harsh. Run-flat tires from Goodyear are an excellent investment. A dash indicator tells you when the tire is flat, even though you can continue to drive at a steady 90 km/h for 85 kilometres and the only noticeable change you'll feel will be a stiffer ride. **Rebates:** The Corvette is so popular GM doesn't have to offer rebates to boost sales. **Destination charge:** $820. **Depreciation:** Much slower than average. **Insurance cost:** Astronomical. **Parts supply/cost:** Good availability, but parts are pricey. **Annual maintenance cost:** Higher than average. **Warranty:** Bumper-to-bumper 3 years/60,000 km; rust perforation 6 years/160,000 km. **Supplementary warranty:** A smart idea. **Highway/city fuel economy:** 9–15L/100 km with the 6-speed manual, 9–14L/100 km with the 6-speed manual hooked to the High Output engine, and 9–14L/100 km with the automatic.

Quality/Reliability/Safety

Pro: Warranty performance: Average. GM has beefed up its warranty and given more authority to its dealers to resolve warranty disputes. Key-controlled lockout feature discourages joy riding by cutting engine power in half. Both Corvette versions are equipped with an impressively effective PASS KEY theft-deterrent system that uses a resistor pellet in the ignition to disable the starter and fuel system when the key code doesn't match the ignition lock. **Safety:** The tires have built-in low-pressure sensors that warn the driver through a light on the centre console. Run-flat tires eliminate the need for a spare tire.

Con: Quality control: Below average, especially body construction. **Reliability:** Spotty. The Corvette's sophisticated electronic and powertrain components have low tolerance for real-world conditions. Expect lots of visits to the dealer's repair bays and extended periods when the car will be out of action. **Owner-reported problems:** Electronically controlled suspension systems have been glitch-plagued over the past several years. Squeaks and rattles due to the car's structural deficiencies. The car was built as a convertible, and therefore has too much body flex. Servicing the different sophisticated fuel-injection systems isn't easy, even (especially) for GM mechanics. **Service bulletin problems:** Loose lower front fascia valance panel. **NHTSA safety complaints/safety:** Faulty fuel line clip may cause chronic stalling; seatbelts twist easily and tend to pull down uncomfortably against the shoulder; the glass rearview window limits rear vision; there is no factory installed airbag cut-off switch, as found in the Miata and BMW Z3.

Road Performance

Pro: Acceleration/torque: Gobs of torque and horsepower with a top speed of 172 mph (0–100 km/h: 5 sec.). **Transmission:** The 6-speed gearbox performs well in all gear ranges and makes shifting smooth with short throws and easy entry into all gears. **Routine handling:** Above average. The car's so low that its front air dam scrapes over the smallest rise in the road, but still gives no-surprise handling and responds quickly to the throttle. The Bilstein FX-3 Selective Ride Control suspension can be preset to Touring, Sport, or Performance. Under acceleration, an electronic module automatically varies the suspension as the speed increases. **Emergency handling:** Very good. No oversteer, wheel spinning, breakaway rear ends, or nasty surprises. **Steering:** Predictable, with good road feel. **Braking:** Better than average. The ABS-vented disc brakes are easy to modulate, fade-free, and incorporate a Bosch system that GM engineers claim will pull over 1.0 G deceleration rates.

Con: Optional Z51 suspension's ride is too firm for some. This is one large and heavy sports car, whose weight compromises its fuel economy. True, the 6-speed manual does provides quicker acceleration and better fuel economy, but it's not particularly user-friendly.

Comfort/Convenience

Pro: Standard equipment: Attractively styled and full of power-assisted accessories. Rust-resistant fiberglass body. Simple-to-operate convertible top. Innovative Passive Keyless Entry System. **Driving position:** Excellent, with everything within easy reach, good front and rear visibility, and a roomy cockpit. **Controls and displays:** Complete instrumentation that's easy to decipher, and user-friendly controls. **Climate control:** Easy to adjust and quiet. **Entry/exit:** Acceptable. Tall drivers will find the interior confining. **Interior space/comfort F/R:** Snug, but not uncomfortable for two adults.

Con: The electronic dash never quite works right (speedometer lag, for example). Steering wheel hides some controls. No room in the engine compartment for a sophisticated climate-control system. Dual-zone climate control system takes time to warm up. Lowering the top takes patience: you release two latches, lift the plastic panel, and manually fold the top into its storage compartment. **Cargo space:** Insufficient storage space, which is no surprise to sports car enthusiasts. The lowered top cuts trunk space in half. **Trunk/liftover:** Skimpy storage space; high sill makes loading baggage difficult. **Quietness:** In addition to an irritating engine boom, there's excessive tire noise, wind whistling through the car's A- and C-pillars, and the all-too-familiar fiberglass body squeaks caused by excessive body flexing on rough surfaces.

COST				
List Price (firm)	**Residual Values** (months)			
	24	36	48	60
Corvette: $50,165 (30%)	$37,000	$30,000	$26,000	$22,000

TECHNICAL DATA

Powertrain (rear-drive)
Engine: 5.7L V8 (345 hp)
Transmissions: 6-speed man.
• 4-speed auto.
Dimensions (Coupe/Convertible)
Passengers: 2
Height/length/width:
47.7/179.7/73.6 in.

Head room: 37.8 in.
Leg room: 42.7 in.
Wheelbase: 104.5 in.
Cargo capacity: 24.8 cu. ft.
Towing capacity: N/A
Fuel tank: 72L/premium
Weight: 3,245 lbs.

SAFETY FEATURES

	Std.	Opt.
Anti-lock brakes	■	❏
Seatbelt pretensioners	—	—
Integrated child safety seat	—	—
Airbag cut-off switch	—	—
Depowered airbags	■	❏
Side airbags	—	—
Traction control	■	❏
Visibility (front/rear)	*****	*****
Crash protection D/P	N/A	
Crash protection (side) D/P	N/A	
HLDI injury claims	N/A	

Silhouette/Trans Sport/Venture

Venture

RATING: Above Average if you don't overwhelm the engine. **Strong points:** Standard ABS, side airbags, a comfortable ride, easy handling, dual sliding doors, plenty of comfort and convenience features, flexible seating arrangements. **Weak points:** Average acceleration with a light load, optional traction control, uncomfortable, low rear seats, excessive brake fading, and disappointing fuel economy.

NEW FOR '99: *Silhouette:* A five horsepower boost to the base V6 engine (185-hp), heated rear-view mirrors, and the debut of a Premiere model offering a mobile entertainment centre that includes a videocassette player and colour monitor. *Venture:* Depowered airbags, upgraded electronically-controlled automatic transmission, and a standard rear-window defogger.

GENERAL COMMENTS: This practically identical trio of minivans comes in regular and extended wheelbase versions. The extended wheelbase models get more bells and whistles, including optional power slide-open passenger- and driver-side doors. The Venture and Silhouette seat seven, while the Trans Sport manages to squeeze in one more passenger. Longer versions have dual sliding doors with optional power assist.

Cost analysis/alternatives: Get the '99 minivans for their upgrades; only consider a '98 model if the price is cut 15–20 percent. This year's minivans are a definite step up from the GM minivans they replaced several years ago. Keep in mind that if you opt for a cheaper, identical '98 leftover, you should get a second-series version made after March '98, otherwise, you're likely to have many first-year quality and reliability problems. Other vehicles worth considering: Ford Windstar, Nissan Quest, and Toyota Sienna. **Recommended options:** Consider the $235 load-levelling feature—a must-have for front-drive minivans. It keeps the weight on the front wheels, giving you better steering, traction, and braking. Other options that are worth buying: General XP2000 tires (about $100 for all four), traction control, integrated child safety seats, power side windows, and rear air conditioner, defroster, and heater. The Montana Package offers a firmer suspension and self-sealing tires. **Rebates:** $1,500 on the '98 models. **Destination charge:** $840. **Depreciation:** A bit slower than average. **Insurance cost:** High, but about average for a minivan. **Annual maintenance cost:** Average during the warranty period. Transmission, ABS, and electrical malfunction will likely cause maintenance costs to rise after the third year of ownership. **Parts supply/cost:** Parts are generic to GM's other models, so they should be reasonably priced and not hard to find. Body parts are likely to be more problematic and costly. **Warranty:** Bumper-to-bumper 3 years/60,000 km; rust perforation 6 years/160,000 km. **Supplementary warranty:** An extended warranty is a good idea until long-term reliability has been assessed. **Highway/city fuel economy:** 10–15.7L/100 km.

Quality/Reliability/Safety

Pro: Quality control: Above Average. Less rattle-prone due to a more rigid body structure than their predecessors. **Reliability:** No serious reliability problems. **Warranty performance:** Below average. **Owner-reported problems:** Electrical glitches, windshield wiper motor failures, excessive front brake noise, and assorted body deficiencies. **Service**

bulletin problems: Fuel injector deposits causing chronic stalling, poor idling, or hard starts; loose lumber noise from rear of vehicle when passing over small bumps (see bulletin below). **NHTSA safety complaints/safety:** *Venture:* Excess padding around horn makes it difficult to depress horn button in an emergency; weak-sounding horn; loose fuel tank due to loose bolts/bracket; steering idler arm fell off due to missing bolt; frequent windshield wiper motor failures. Some '98 models have been recalled to prevent the vehicle from rolling away while in Park and to install safety guards on seat latches.

File In Section: 3 - Steering/Suspension
Bulletin No.: 73-34-06
Date: November, 1997
Subject:
Loose Lumber Noise from Rear of Vehicle when Driving Over Small Bumps (Replace Rear Shock Absorbers)
Models:
1997–98 Chevrolet Venture
1997–98 Oldsmobile Silhouette
1997–98 Pontiac Trans Sport
Long Wheel Base Models Only with Electronic Level Control (G67) and Built Prior to the Following VIN Breakpoints:

Model	VIN Breakpoints
Chevrolet	WD131456
Oldsmobile	WD131384
Pontiac	WD131452

Important:
This condition does not apply to the Opel Sintra.
Condition
Some owners may comment on a "loose lumber" type noise coming from the rear of the vehicle and audible in the vehicle's passenger compartment. This condition is most apparent when driving over a series of small to moderate bumps (washboard gravel or roughly patched asphalt road surface), which cause high frequency, low displacement, wheel motions.
Cause
The noise condition may be generated by the internal valving mechanism of the rear shock absorbers and is transmitted into the body by the upper shock absorber mount. Variation in shock absorbers can make some vehicles worse than others.
Correction
Replace both rear shock absorbers with new assemblies, P/N 22064847, following the procedure in Section 3D, Rear Suspension, of the applicable Service Manual.

Road Performance

Pro: Acceleration/torque: Nice powertrain setup with smooth acceleration for most light-duty work. The 3.4L engine is smooth and responsive (0–100 km/h: 10.7 sec.). These minivans use the same quiet-running V6 powerplant that harnesses a few more horses than the Chrysler minivans' top-line 3.8L 6-cylinder, providing good mid-range and top-end power. Chrysler's engines do have a bit more torque, however. **Transmission:** The electronically controlled 4-speed automatic transmission shifts smoothly and quietly, another advantage over Chrysler. **Routine handling:** Pretty good. Sedan-like handling is better than most of the competition, particularly when equipped with the load-levelling option. **Steering:** The steering takes some effort, but it's responsive and fairly predictable. Longer, loaded versions have a smoother ride than the base versions, which tend to be more choppy.

Emergency handling: Better than average, due to the responsive powertrain, steering, and ABS. **Braking:** Unimpressive for the Venture (100–0 km/h: 147 ft.); much better with the Trans Sport (100–0 km/h: 134 ft.) and Silhouette (100–0 km/h: 135 ft.).

Con: Some body roll in hard turns. Powertrain isn't suitable for heavy towing or carrying a full passenger load. The GM engine is hampered by less torque, making for less grunt when accelerating and frequently downshifting out of Overdrive when climbing moderate grades (there's no Overdrive on/off switch). This is the main reason why owners feel that the GM minivans are underpowered when compared with Chrysler's. Watch out for excessive brake fading; the brakes lose their effectiveness progressively after repeated application.

Comfort/Convenience

Pro: Standard equipment: Fairly well-equipped. **Driving position:** Drivers are treated to a car-like driving position. Comfortable left footrest. Concealed windshield wipers, a large windshield, and larger side mirrors enhance visibility fore and aft. **Controls and displays:** Everything is easy to read and within reach. **Climate control:** Efficient and easy to use. AC has a pollen control feature. **Entry/exit:** Easy, especially with the low interior step-in, side interior door handles, power remote sliding door on the curb-side and a manual sliding door on the street-side of extended-wheelbase models (short-wheelbase models will have it phased in later this year). **Interior space/comfort F/R:** Plenty of room in the first two rows, while the third row is more problematic. Comfortable seats, particularly on the Venture. There are two reclining bucket seats in the front row and the second and third rows can accommodate modular or bench seats. Easy-to-fold seats drop down to increase storage space; the second seat flips forward for access to the third seat. **Cargo space:** Lots of storage bins and compartments. **Trunk/liftover:** A breeze. Dual sliding doors mean that you no longer have to walk around to the passenger side to load or unload cargo. Rear seats can be flipped down to carry a 4x8 sheet of plywood. **Quietness:** One of the quietest minivans in its class.

Con: Tall drivers will find insufficient head room and short drivers may find it hard to see where the front ends. Uncomfortable centre and rear bench seats; cushions are hard, flat, and too short; and the seatbacks lack sufficient lower-back support. Low rear seats force passengers into an uncomfortable knees-up position. These minivans take a while to warm up the interior. One convenience item that can easily become an inconvenience: the two cargo nets found between the front seats and behind the rear seat are easily entangled and complicate the removal of the rear seats. Also, eight of the Venture's 12 cupholders— 14 on the Trans Sport—are only usable if the seats are folded down. Cargo may not slide out easily due to the rear sill sticking up a few inches. Some wind noise.

COST

List Price (negotiable)	**Residual Values** (months)			
	24	**36**	**48**	**60**
Venture SW: $24,625 (22%)	$17,000	$14,000	$12,000	$9500

TECHNICAL DATA

Powertrain (front-drive)
Engine: 3.4L V6 (185 hp)
Transmission: 4-speed auto.
Dimensions (Venture/Trans Sport)
Height/length/width:
67.4/186.9/72 in.;
68.1/201.3/72.7 in.

Leg room F: 39.9/R1: 39/R2: 36.7 in.
Head room F: 39.9/R1: 39.3 /R2: 38.9 in.
Wheelbase: 112/120 in.
Passengers: 7/8
Cargo capacity: 16.3 cu. ft./24.2 cu. ft.
Towing capacity: 3,500 lbs.
Fuel tank: 76/95L
Weight: 3,650 lbs./3,900 lbs.

SAFETY FEATURES

	Std.	**Opt.**
Anti-lock brakes	■	❑
Seatbelt pretensioners	—	—
Integrated child safety seat	❑	■
Airbag cut-off switch	—	—
Depowered airbags	■	❑
Side airbags	■	❑
Traction control	❑	■
Visibility (front/rear)	*****	*****
Crash protection D/P	****	❣❣❣
Crash protection (side) D/P	N/A	
HLDI injury claims	N/A	

Astro/Safari

Safari

RATING: Average. More a utility truck than a comfortable minivan. **Strong points:** Standard ABS, brisk acceleration, trailer towing capability, and lots of passenger room and cargo space. **Weak points:** Harsh riding, limited front seat room, poor quality control and reliability, excessive fuel consumption made worse by the AWD option, and terrible fuel economy.

NEW FOR '99: Depowered airbags, a new standard anti-theft system, and an upgraded AWD active transfer case.

GENERAL COMMENTS: These boxy, rear-drive minivans are built on a reworked S-10 pickup chassis. As such, they offer uninspiring handling, trouble-prone mechanical and body components, and relatively high fuel consumption. Both Astro and Safari come in a choice of either cargo or passenger van. The cargo van is used either commercially or as an inexpensive starting point for a fully customized vehicle. The Safari is identical to the Astro, except for a slightly higher base price.

The engine is a 4.3L 190-hp V6. Dual airbags are standard. Also offered are an optional rear door and rear bench seats that can be adjusted fore and aft. Carried-over standard features are a 4-speed automatic transmission with Overdrive, power steering, a front stabilizer bar, a 102 L fuel tank (a Lumina offers 76 L), and anti-lock brakes. All-wheel-drive with a single-speed transfer case with viscous-controlled differential (no switches to throw) is available on the regular length and extended models. The sport package includes louvred rear-quarter body panels, two-tone paint, fog lights, and a front air dam. With the right options, the Astro and Safari have the advantage of being versatile cargo haulers when equipped with a heavy-duty suspension. In fact, Astro's 5,500-pound trailer-towing capability is 2,000 more than that of the front-drive Venture.

Cost analysis/alternatives: Get the '99 minivans for their upgrades; only consider a '98 model if the price is cut 20 percent or more. Front-drive minivans made by Ford, Mercury, Nissan, and Toyota have better handling and are more reliable and economical people carriers; unfortunately they lack the grunt needed for cargo hauling and trailer towing. **Recommended options:** Integrated child safety seats, rear AC, and rear Dutch doors. Be wary of the AWD option; it exacts a high fuel penalty. **Rebates:** '99 Astro conversion minivan: $500; '98 Astro passenger minivan: $2,000. **Destination charge:** $845. **Depreciation:** Much faster than the average minivan. **Insurance cost:** Slightly higher than average. **Annual maintenance cost:** Average. **Parts supply/cost:** Good supply of cheap parts. A large contingent of independent parts suppliers keeps repair costs down. Parts are less expensive than they are for other vehicles in this class, according to CAA. **Warranty:** Bumper-to-bumper 3 years/60,000 km; rust perforation 6 years/160,000 km. **Supplementary warranty:** A wise investment. Individual repairs won't cost a lot, but there'll be many of them. **Highway/city fuel economy:** 10.4–14.6L/100 km for two-wheel drive and 11.5–16L/100 km with AWD.

Quality/Reliability/Safety

Pro: Most of the Astro/Safari's defects are easy to diagnose, leading to a minimum of downtime in the repair bay. **Service bulletin problems:** Nothing significant.

Con: Quality control: Below average. **Reliability:** Below average, primarily because of this minivan's powertrain and electrical system malfunctions. Engine and transmission located under the dashboard make maintenance and repairs a chore. **Owner-reported problems:** Frequent problems with engine headgaskets, automatic transmission, steering, electrical system, heating and defrosting system, and suspension components. Poor body construction and sloppy paint application also figure prominently among owner beefs. **Warranty performance:** Very disappointing. **NHTSA safety complaints/safety:** Power steering pump failures; loss of power steering; sudden brake failure; extended stopping distance with ABS; differential in transfer case locked up while driving.

Road Performance

Pro: Acceleration/torque: The V6 engine is more than adequate for most driving chores and has plenty of reserve power for trailer towing and heavy hauling (0–100 km/h: 11.8 sec.). **Braking:** Excellent braking for a minivan (100–0 km/h: 137 ft.). AWD works well.

Con: The V6 is thirsty in city driving. **Transmission:** Clunky automatic transmission. **Routine handling:** Handling isn't very precise; overall behaviour is competent, but sloppy. A heavy-duty suspension will improve both ride and handling. Busy, harsh ride caused by stiff springs. **Emergency handling:** Ponderous, but still fairly predictable. **Steering:** Very light power steering, but still handles and manoeuvres like a large truck.

Comfort/Convenience

Pro: Standard equipment: Adequate. **Controls and displays:** Well laid-out instrument panel with easy-to-read gauges. **Climate control:** Very good climate control system. **Interior space/comfort F/R:** Spacious interior provides plenty of room for passengers. All seats are comfortable, although the front two are the best. The rear seat can be removed by a single person, but not as easily as the automaker's front-drive minivan seats. **Cargo space:** An incredible amount of cargo space can handle all kinds of bulky items, including 4x8 sheets of plywood. **Trunk/liftover:** No problem. In fact, the optional Dutch doors provide better rear-view visibility and include a convenient lift-open glass and defroster.

Con: Driving position: The driving position is awkward for most drivers—more like a truck than a passenger car. Tall drivers will find the pedals too close. Obtrusive engine makes for very narrow front footwells that give little room for the driver's left foot to rest. Some dashboard controls are hard to reach. **Entry/exit:** Difficult due to the high step-up and the intruding wheel well. **Quietness:** Interior noise levels rise sharply at highway speeds.

COST

List Price (very negotiable)	Residual Values (months)			
	24	36	48	60
Base Astro: $22,660 (22%)	$17,000	$13,000	$11,000	$9000

TECHNICAL DATA

Powertrain (rear drive)
Engine: 4.3L V6 (190 hp)
Transmission: 4-speed auto.
Dimensions
Height/length/width:
76/189.8/77.5 in.
Leg room F:41.6/R1: 36.5/
R2: 38.5 in.

Head room F: 39.2/R1: 37.9 /R2: 38.7 in.
Wheelbase: 111 in.
Passengers: 8
Cargo capacity: 41.3 cu. ft.
Towing capacity: 5,500 lbs.
Fuel tank: 95L
Weight: 4,200 lbs.

SAFETY FEATURES

	Std.	Opt.
Anti-lock brakes	■	❑
Seatbelt pretensioners	—	—
Integrated child safety seat	❑	■
Airbag cut-off switch	—	—
Depowered airbags	■	❑
Side airbags	—	—
Traction control	—	—
Visibility (front/rear)	*****	*****
Crash protection D/P	***	***
Crash protection (side) D/P	N/A	
HLDI Injury claims	Low	

SAAB

What's so special about Saabs? Their unusual, aerodynamic styling is (to put it mildly) distinctive; passenger comfort is unbeatable; and they handle very well, with precise steering and lots of road feel. Unfortunately, a lot of less expensive cars offer just as much road performance and are more reliable and easier to repair.

No one can accuse GM of opportunism in buying Saab for $600 million in late 1989—just before the Swedish automaker announced a $380-million operating loss for that year, followed by stunning 1990–91 losses exceeding a billion dollars. North American sales fell 30.7 percent during the first half of 1993, despite the huge effort put into attractive leasing and low financing deals. In 1994 Saab made a small profit for the first time since GM bought the company, and in 1995 it earned a profit of $22.3 million. Unfortunately, these profits were wiped out when sales plunged for the first quarter of 1996, causing a pre-tax loss of $50.15 million—more than double what it had earned for the entire previous year.

After three straight years of losses, Saab says it will be profitable in '99 due to its new products and improved European sales. The company blames its losses on a lack of new product, a Danish national strike, and unexpected costs in launching its new 9-3 and 9-5 models.

Saab's growth has been undeniably slowed by increased competition from European and Japanese luxury sedans that are more smartly styled, have greater market penetration than the rather dated 900 and 9000, and are marketed through attractive and innovative leasing plans that Saab is only beginning to adopt. Furthermore, Saab's reliability and servicing problems haven't been tackled by General Motors, a company with similar quality deficiencies.

9-3

RATING: Not Recommended during the first year on the market.
Strong points: Standard ABS, side airbags, and "smart" head restraint,
good highway performer with excellent handling, steering, and braking, comfortable seating, lots of storage capability, and good fuel economy. **Weak points:** Turbo lag, poor ride with premium tires, convertible
has minimal rear seat room, less comfortable seating, and shakes and
rattles, obstructed rear visibility in both the sedan and convertible, and
the servicing network is rather limited.

NEW FOR '99: Introduced last year as a '99 model, only small running
changes will be phased in during 1999.

GENERAL COMMENTS: Selling for about $33,200, the 9-3 is essen-
tially the old 900 loaded with what Saab claims are 1,000 engineering
upgrades that include a strengthened platform, restyled exterior, standard side airbags, "smart" head restraints, optional dual integrated
child safety seats, a hydraulically controlled soft top, and a larger glass
window. The upgraded 2.0L engine got a slight power boost to 200-hp
and the 2.3L version is now turbocharged.
      Don't expect fast starts uphill. The turbo kicks in at about 3,000 rpm
(which means lots of time spent in second gear waiting for a much-
needed turbo boost), in addition to a lurching transmission, uncomfortably long passing times, and sudden torque steer that may tug at the
steering wheel.
      Notwithstanding the turbo's deficiencies, the 9-3 is a driver's car,
with excellent braking performance, sporty handling, and sure-footed
cornering. Nevertheless, the SE's high-performance, premium tires
accentuate the smallest bumps, and make for a harsh, jiggly ride. The
standard V-rated tires give a much smoother ride.
      There's plenty of cargo space and room for five adults, except in the
convertible version, and the soft top is easily raised or lowered electri-

cally. Climate settings on the SE, though, have to be re-adjusted between startups, the ignition is still floor-mounted, rear visibility is not very good in the sedans and even worse in the convertible with the top raised, and the convertible's less-rigid chassis tends to shake and rattle.

9-5

RATING: Not Recommended during the first year on the market. **Strong points:** Standard ABS, side airbags, traction control (V6 only), "smart" head restraints. A superb highway performer, except for some "turbo lag." Excellent handling and braking, comfortable seating, lots of storage capability, better than average build quality and fit and finish, and good fuel economy. **Weak points:** Turbo lag, excessive tire noise, the steering feels a bit over-assisted, climate controls aren't very user-friendly, and the servicing network is rather limited.

NEW FOR '99: Introduced last year as a '99 model, only small running changes will be phased in during 1999. A high-performance sedan and station wagon will be added next summer.

GENERAL COMMENTS: Launched last March, the $39,800 9-5 SE is Saab's replacement for the 9000. It uses suspension and brake parts taken from GM's Opel Vectra, with a stiffened chassis and added four-wheel independent suspension. It floats less, though there's still too much body lean, and cornering has been improved. Saab has also turbocharged its V6 engine, while not boosting horsepower, so that it provides lots of low-end torque. It doesn't kick in under 3,000 rpm, however. Unfortunately, the V6 comes only with an automatic transmission.

There's plenty of cargo space and room for five adults. In addition to providing a spacious trunk, Saab pays lots of attention to detail. For example, work gloves and a plastic bag are provided so you don't soil your hands when changing the tire, the "smart" head restraint is specially

designed to prevent neck injuries, the glove box has an air conditioning
duct that keeps drinks cold, there are air vents in the back of the centre
console for added comfort, rear seats fold flat for added cargo room, and,
for added safety, a passenger-side rear-view mirror automatically tilts down
so you can get a better view when you engage Reverse .

Some things you won't like about the 9-5: power steering is over-
assisted and doesn't transmit sufficient road feel, only two adults can sit
comfortably in the rear, the remote lock/unlock key fob won't fit into
the average-sized pocket and is hard to decipher, the outside mirrors
are unacceptably small, the in-dash cupholder won't support a tall cof-
fee cup, the fan-cooled seats are more gimmicky than practical, climate
controls are set too low to be easily adjusted and have to be recalibrat-
ed after each startup, the ignition is still floor-mounted, front-seat head
restraints dig into your shoulder and neck, rear visibility is obstructed,
and servicing isn't widely available.

Cost analysis/alternatives: Choose a second-series '99 model made
after March to benefit from the numerous assembly line fixes carried
out during the first six months of the model run. Other cars 9-3 shoppers should consider are the Audi A6, BMW 3-series, Lexus ES 300,
Mazda Millenia, Toyota Avalon, Volvo S70 sedan or V70 wagon. 9-5
shoppers should also look at the BMW 5-series, Lexus GS 300 or 400,
or the Mercedes E-class. **Recommended options:** Integrated child safety seats. **Rebates:** Expect sizeable rebates and dealer incentives early in
the new year. **Destination charge:** $770. **Depreciation:** Faster than aver-
age. Saabs depreciate much more quickly now that GM has bought the
company, so if you plan to keep it for only a few years and don't want
to lose much money through depreciation, choose the popular 900
drop-top—the 9-3; it keeps its value longer. **Insurance cost:** Higher
than average. **Parts supply/cost:** Parts are moderately expensive and
servicing is a major liability (the dealership network is spotty and relatively inexperienced) due to GM's inept administration of its Saab
franchises. GM threw out many Saab dealers when it bought the company, and gave the Saab franchise to inexperienced Passport dealers
who primarily serviced Isuzus. After fielding a deluge of customer
complaints, GM realized this was a mistake and closed a third of its 60
dealerships. **Annual maintenance cost:** Higher than average. **Warranty:**
Bumper-to-bumper 4 years/80,000 km; rust perforation 6
years/unlimited km. **Supplementary warranty:** A very good idea, considering that these cars are complicated to diagnose and expensive to
repair. **Highway/city fuel economy:** 8–12L/100 km. The turbo models
add about two litres to city driving.

SAFETY FEATURES

	Std.	Opt.
Anti-lock brakes	■	❏
Seatbelt pretensioners	■	❏
Integrated child safety seat	—	—
Airbag cut-off switch	—	—
Depowered airbags	■	❏
Side airbags	—	—
Traction control	■	■
Visibility (front/rear)	*****	*
Crash protection D/P	N/A	
Crash protection (side) D/P	N/A	
HLDI injury claims	N/A	

Asian Vehicles

What a year! A devalued yen and cutthroat competition following GM's two-month strike have forced down Asian car prices, and for the first time in many years, Canadian car buyers can finally get top quality cars and minivans at reasonable prices. In fact, Auto Advisory, an Ontario new and used car broker I've recommended for years, tells me he is getting 10–15 percent discounts on new Toyota cars and minivans— vehicles that sold for full-list or at a premium last year.

Nevertheless, you're still going to pay too much for your Asian import—and those with the most generous rebates aren't likely to be the ones you'd want to buy in the first place. Still, look for some hefty price reductions from Asian automakers as they attempt to clear out '98 inventory and counter price rollbacks announced by the Big Three American automakers.

ACURA

When Acura first came to Canada in 1986 it did very well in selling reasonably priced compact cars that many considered to be no more than all-dressed Honda clones. Then the company got cocky and, rather than counting on lower profits and more sales, they raised prices (over dealers' objections) to what the market would bear. Fortunately, competitive pressures—not the least from Lexus and Nissan—forced the automaker to cut Acura prices with cash rebates and low-interest financing programs. Nevertheless, this move was too little, too late. Acura sales have been way off since 1991, when they peaked at almost 16,000 units. In fact, although Honda sales have been phenomenal, its Acura division continues to post disappointing sales, off 30 percent for the month of September.

Although they've been somewhat pacified through higher dealer profit margins and an improved product lineup, Canadian Acura dealers are still ticked off by what they consider to be the company's "take it or leave it" attitude toward them. One Canadian Federation of Automobile Dealer Association (FADA) dealer survey blasted Acura management for being insensitive to dealers' concerns and for dragging their feet in launching the 1.6 EL, a Canada-exclusive entry-level model.

Six models are sold under the Acura nameplate: the Integra, CL coupe, TL, RL, SLX sport-utility, and NSX sports car. Except for the SLX sport-utility, which is based on the Isuzu Trooper, Acura's lineup comprises overpriced, upscale Honda variants that have been sold and serviced by a separate Acura network since 1986. The NSX and SLX return this year unchanged; the SLX may be dropped in the spring of 2000 when the Alliston, Ontario, Odyssey-based MAV sport-utility debuts.

Acura products are generally good buys because maintenance costs are low, reliability is way above average, and Acura's warranty performance has been more generous than that of most automakers.

1.6 EL

EL

RATING: Above Average. **Strong points:** High level of performance and comfort, slow depreciation, and high-quality construction. **Weak points:** Optional anti lock brakes (inexcusable, when you consider that GM's $14,915 entry-level Cavalier coupe has standard ABS), no crashworthiness data, limited rear seat room, and difficult rear access.

NEW FOR '99: Nothing significant.

GENERAL COMMENTS: With an $18,800 base price, the recently launched 1.6 EL has sold quite well for what is essentially a restyled, luxury version of the Honda Civic Si with the following features: conservative styling, different bumpers and front headlights, upgraded wipers, heated power door mirrors, restyled dash, different seat covers, upgraded soundproofing, 15-inch wheels, and a rear sway bar.

Taken from the Civic Coupe Si, the VTEC 4-cylinder puts out 127 hp, which is 21 more than the base Civics and only three less than the '97 Accord. This gives it good all-around acceleration, but not a sports car personality like that offered by the Integra 1.8, which gives you a sportier 142-hp engine in a two-door body style. (Of course, you're looking at about $6,200 more for the Integra and $500 less for the Civic Si.)

Expect similar performance as that described for the Civic Si. Consumer feedback notes that the 4-speed gearbox is well-designed in that it doesn't "hunt" for the right gear when traversing hilly terrain. On the safety front, anti-lock brakes are optional, childproof rear door locks are standard, and no crash tests have yet been carried out.

Some of the 1.6 EL's weak points: relatively expensive for what is essentially a four-door Civic with a bit more horsepower (still, a low depreciation rate may give you back a greater portion of your initial investment); a narrow interior, with seats and seatbacks not to everyone's liking; emergency braking that's only average; and despite upgraded soundproofing, owners have complained of excessive engine noise intruding into the passenger compartment.

Cost analysis/alternatives: Get either the '98 or '99 model; they're practically identical. Other vehicles worth a look: Acura Integra and Honda Civic Si. **Recommended options:** A block heater. **Rebates:** Not likely, but look for 10–15 percent discounts. **Destination charge:** $400. **Depreciation:** Much slower than average. **Insurance cost:** Higher than average. **Parts supply/cost:** Moderately priced parts can be found at Acura or Honda dealers. **Annual maintenance cost:** Lower than average. **Warranty:** Bumper-to-bumper 3 years/60,000 km; powertrain 5 years/100,000 km; rust perforation 6 years/unlimited km. **Supplementary warranty:** Not needed. **Highway/city fuel economy:** 6.3–8.1L/100 km. VTEC 4-banger requires premium fuel.

CL Series

CL

RATING: Average. An attractive, loaded luxury coupe, but you can get the latest redesigned Accord for less. **Strong points:** Styling, plenty of standard features, and comfortable riding. **Weak points:** Engine isn't exactly high-performance, limited rear seat room, and a harsh-shifting automatic transmission (get the manual shifter).

NEW FOR '99: Standard leather interior trim; the coupe adopts the Accord's platform for the year 2000.

GENERAL COMMENTS: Priced from $30,000 to $34,000, these cars are stylish, front-drive, five-passenger, American built and designed luxury coupes. They have a flowing, slanted back end, and no apparent trunk lock (a standard remote keyless entry system opens the trunk from the outside and a lever opens it from the inside). And while other Japanese automakers are taking content out of their vehicles, Acura has put content into the CL, making it one of the most feature-laden cars in its class. Sure, we all know that the coupe's mechanical components and platform aren't that different from the Accord's, but when you add up all of its standard bells and whistles, you get a fully loaded small car that costs thousands of dollars less than such competing luxury coupes as the BMW 318is and the Lexus SC300. Consider this array of standard features: power windows, power mirrors, power moonroof, six-way power driver seat, a remote keyless entry system, ABS, leather-wrapped steering wheel, simulated wood trim, automatic climate control, dual airbags, tilt steering wheel, cruise control, CD player, and an AM/FM stereo with six speakers.

Although no one would consider the CL a high-performance car, it gets plenty of power from an optional 3.0L 24-valve SOHC Variable Valve Timing and Lift Electronic Control (VTEC) V6, in addition to its base 2.3L, single overhead cam 4-cylinder VTEC engine. Handling is better than average, thanks to upgraded suspension, variable-assisted steering, and 16-inch wheels. Excellent braking (100–0 km/h: 115 ft.).

On the minus side, the automatic transmission shifts are harsh and ill-timed (a good argument for getting a manual gearbox). This is not a car for passengers in the rear, either. Rear windows don't roll down and back seat room is insufficient, unless the front seats are pushed all the way forward. Front shoulder belts have no height adjustment, rear entry/exit is a bit difficult, and storage space is skimpy.

Cost analysis/alternatives: Let the bottom line be your guide, since the '98 and '99 models are practically identical. Look for a price cut of at least 20 percent on last year's models. The only difference between these two coupes is the 3.0/CL's larger engine, different wheels, and larger exhaust tip. Other vehicles worth considering, but with fewer standard features: the BMW 318i, Honda Accord, Lexus SC300, Nissan Maxima, and Toyota Camry. **Recommended options:** The manual transmission. **Rebates:** Likely by the end of the year. **Destination charge:** $350. **Depreciation:** Much slower than average. **Insurance cost:** Higher than average. **Parts supply/cost:** It's not hard to find moderately priced parts at Acura or Honda dealers. Body parts, though, may be back-ordered and rather pricey. **Annual maintenance cost:** Expected to be about average. **Warranty:** Bumper-to-bumper 3 years/60,000 km; powertrain 5 years/100,000 km; rust perforation 6 years/unlimited km. **Supplementary warranty:** Not needed. **Highway/city fuel economy:** 8.5–12L/100 km.

TL Series

TL

RATING: Average. **Strong points:** Handles well, rides comfortably, and is well put together with quality mechanical and body components. **Weak points:** Excessive engine noise with the 4-cylinder, harsh shifting, the standard auto-manual gearbox shift lever is awkward to use and too close, forcing elbow-close-to-the-ribs shifting. No manual transmission or side airbags.

NEW FOR '99: Wider and longer overall; sportier styling. Set on the Accord's platform, the 5-cylinder engine has been replaced by the Accord's 3.2L VTEC powerplant. Acura has pledged to keep a lid on prices, possibly making the TL a cheaper alternative to the Lexus ES 300 and the Infiniti I30.

GENERAL COMMENTS: Retailing for about $37,000 ($5,000 less than the 3.2L), this isn't a particularly impressive car, with its conservative, Legend-like styling and unusual 2.5L 176-hp 5-cylinder powerplant carried over from previous years. Last year it was joined by a 3.2L 200-hp V6 variant.

The base engine provides smooth but less than dazzling acceleration. It feels sportier, though, because the 2.5TL isn't loaded down with the extra weight that hampers its big brother. Despite its extra horses, the optional V6 can't compare with most sports sedans and performs decently only on the open road.

Although the TL is roomier than the Vigor it replaced in 1995, its rear seat still feels cramped. The Vigor had a better than average repair record, so the TL variants should be just as reliable. The only areas that have proven troublesome in the past have been poor body fits and premature brake wear.

Be wary of Acura's claim that the TL is "a personal performance sports sedan...with a higher level of performance than that available in the Integra." For despite its five cylinders, the TL lacks vigour (no pun intended) and smoothness and is seriously outclassed by the competition.

Standard safety features include ABS, dual airbags, childproof door locks, three-point seatbelts, and a transmission/brake interlock. Traction control is offered as an option on the 3.2L version. Crash tests give four stars for driver and passenger crash protection in a frontal collision.

Cost analysis/alternatives: Get the '99 model for the upgrades; it's likely to cost much less this year due to its American production (last year it was imported). Also consider a CL coupe: it's not as expensive, and is as close as you can get to the Accord with lots of standard bells and whistles thrown in. Other cars worth considering are the Infiniti I30, Lexus ES 300, Mazda Millenia, and Toyota Camry V6. **Recommended options:** None. **Rebates:** No incentives or rebates are likely, but some discounting can be expected early in the new year. **Destination charge:** $350. **Depreciation:** Much slower than average. **Insurance cost:** Higher than average. **Parts supply/cost:** Except for some body parts, most mechanical and electronic components are easily found and moderately priced. **Annual maintenance cost:** Less than average. **Warranty:** Bumper-to-bumper 3 years/60,000 km; powertrain 5 years/100,000 km; rust perforation 6 years/unlimited km. **Supplementary warranty:** Not needed. **Highway/city fuel economy:** 8.5–11.9L/100 km.

RL Series

RL

RATING: Average. **Strong points:** Styling, plenty of standard features, comfortable ride, and excellent braking. **Weak points:** Excessive engine vibrations, limited rear seat room, and pricey.

NEW FOR '99: New front airbags vary the speed of deployment depending upon the speed of impact, and "smart" side airbags, and pedestrian-friendly hood and front body components that absorb impact energy.

GENERAL COMMENTS: Although Acura's $55,000 top-of-the-line RL sedan replaced the Legend, it has far more standard features and is better-performing than its predecessor. Equipped with a powerful 210-hp 3.5L V6, the RL posts a 0–100 km/h time of 8.1 seconds— remarkable for a car hauling 3,600 lbs. Even more remarkable are the excessive engine vibrations felt through the steering wheel. Excellent braking (100–0 km/h: 115 ft.).

This luxury sedan comes fully loaded with every convenience feature imaginable, but it lacks the safety features found in other cars in its class, like dual side airbags, automatic stability control, traction control, and an occupancy detector for the front airbag.

Overall highway performance combines a soft, comfortable ride with superb routine and emergency handling, thanks to the efficient anti-lock brakes (100–0 km/h: 125 ft.).

Some minuses: the 4-speed automatic transmission is occasionally harsh-shifting and hesitates before downshifts, moderate body roll when cornering, and the centre console limits the driver's right leg room.

Cost analysis/alternatives: Get the '99 model for the upgrades; it should be discounted by about 20 percent early next year. Other vehicles worth considering: the Lexus GS 300 and 400, Lincoln Mark VIII or Town Car, and Mazda Millenia. **Recommended options:** None. **Rebates:** No incentives or rebates are likely. **Destination charge:** $350. **Depreciation:** Slower than average. **Insurance cost:** Higher than average. **Parts supply/cost:** Mostly generic Honda parts are easily found and moderately priced. Body parts, however, may be back-ordered. **Annual maintenance cost:** Average. **Warranty:** Bumper-to-bumper 3 years/60,000 km; powertrain 5 years/100,000 km; rust perforation 6 years/unlimited km. **Supplementary warranty:** Not necessary. **Highway/city fuel economy:** 8.8–12.6L/100 km.

Integra

Integra

RATING: Average. The performance and reliability aren't worth $25,500. **Strong points:** Better than average powertrain performance, low depreciation, and high-quality construction. **Weak points:** Way overpriced; more Honda than Acura. Skimpy rear seat room, difficult rear access, and too much low-speed steering effort.

NEW FOR '99: No significant changes. Acura has dropped its base RS sedan and expects to build over 1,000 high-performance Type R coupes.

GENERAL COMMENTS: The Integra doesn't quite fit into any category; it's a comfortable and practical small sedan with a high price. Its sporty pretensions lack the sizzle you'll find with the '98 Eagle Talon or Mazda Miata. On the whole, there's little to be said against the Integra and little to be said for it. One can get the same size four-door compact with a bit less performance for a lot less money—or a similar car with a lot more performance for just a little more money.

Cost analysis/alternatives: Either a '98 or '99 model will do; since they're practically identical, choose whichever one offers the best discount. Other cars worth considering are the Ford Escort ZX2, Honda Civic, or VW Golf or Jetta. **Rebates:** Expect sizeable discounts early next year. **Recommended options:** Don't get the GS-R. You'll quickly tire of its fussy VTEC engine. **Destination charge:** $400. **Depreciation:** Slower than average. **Insurance cost:** Higher than average. **Parts supply/cost:** No problem getting moderately priced parts from Acura or Honda dealers. **Warranty:** Bumper-to-bumper 3 years/60,000 km; powertrain 5 years/100,000 km; rust perforation 6 years/unlimited km. **Supplementary warranty:** Not needed. **Highway/city fuel economy:** 7–10L/100 km. VTEC 4-banger requires premium fuel.

Quality/Reliability/Safety

Pro: Quality control: Typical Honda (oops—I mean Acura): first class. **Reliability:** Few complaints that affect the Integra's overall reliability. The Integra has earned a good reliability record because it shares half of its components with the indestructible Civic. **Warranty performance:** Better than average. Acura has a comprehensive standard warranty, and there have been few occasions where warranty disputes have had to be settled by third parties. **Service bulletin problems:** Nothing important.

Con: Owner-reported problems: Owners complain of clutch failures, premature front brake wear, poorly performing tires for winter conditions, and the antenna sticks when the temperature falls. Squeaks and rattles frequently crop up on both the coupes and sedans. The sedan's frameless windows occasionally have sealing problems. **NHTSA safety complaints/safety:** Windshield wipers suddenly stop working until you shut off the ignition and wait a few minutes; steering wheel locked up while driving; the sunroof shattered; key can be removed from the ignition without the transmission lever in Park.

Road Performance

Pro: Acceleration/torque: Acceptable acceleration from the base engine; more impressive with the high-performance, 170-hp GS-R powerplant (0–100 km/h: 7.2 sec.). **Transmission:** The standard 5-speed manual transmission shifter and clutch mechanism were substantially beefed up last year, giving slightly higher ratios in third and fourth and a taller fifth gear. An optional electronic 4-speed automatic uses "fuzzy logic" to reduce the annoying shifting back and forth over hilly terrain. **Routine handling:** Good handling under almost all circumstances. Gas shocks and improved body rigidity create a smooth and firm ride. Ride doesn't deteriorate as load is increased. **Emergency handling:** Better than average, with little body lean or front end plow. **Steering:** Variable-assisted power steering is quick and precise at high speeds. **Braking:** Quite respectable (100–0 km/h: 118 ft.).

Con: Base engine whines at high speed. The GS-R's VTEC engine requires expert throttle control, frequent gear shifts, and constant attention in order to work properly. Some torque steer when accelerating. GS-R is hard riding. Steering exhibits a bit of understeer and isn't sufficiently assisted for parking. Base tires just don't have sufficient grip.

Comfort/Convenience

Pro: Driving position: Very good. Comfortable, manually adjusted front bucket seats. **Controls and displays:** The attractive interior includes an easy-to-read dashboard layout with large analogue gauges that are complete and clear, and climate controls that are easy to operate. **Climate control:** The climate control system works flawlessly. **Interior space/comfort F/R:** Plenty of front head and leg room. The coupe's seat cushions provide good thigh support, its windows have frames for better sealing, and a reinforced body makes for a stiffer body shell. The four-door sedan carries four passengers in comfort. The cloth-covered seats are fairly comfortable and supportive for short drives. The sedan has comfortable rear seating for two adults, and the rear seats fold down completely. **Cargo space:** Average.

Con: Standard equipment: Not impressive. A $25,000 base price and anti-lock brakes are optional, and traction control is unavailable. The coupe's four small headlights are a throwback to the Isuzu Impulse, and the side-view mirrors resemble those of both the Prelude and Civic. The sunroof switch is too far from the sunroof, the radio controls aren't easily reached, and the sun visors are cheap-looking. The steering column, even when tilted to the max, practically rests on your kneecaps. Spoiler restricts rear visibility. **Entry/exit:** Entry/exit is made difficult by the curved windows and the doors' awkward design. The three-door model's rear seat is cramped and suitable only for luggage on trips longer than to the corner grocery store. Seats are lower than usual and tend to be uncomfortable on long trips. **Trunk/liftover:** The trunk on the coupe and sedan is awkward to load because of its narrow opening and high liftover. **Quietness:** Poor sealing around the sedan's side windows. Lots of road and engine noise, especially at full throttle.

COST

List Price (negotiable)	Residual Values (months)			
	24	**36**	**48**	**60**
Integra GS: $25,500 (20%)	$18,000	$15,000	$12,000	$9000

TECHNICAL DATA

Powertrain (front-drive)
Engines: 1.8L 4-cyl. (139 hp)
• 1.8L VTEC (170 hp)
Transmissions: 5-speed man.
• 4-speed auto.
Dimensions
Passengers: 4
Height/length/width:
52.6/172.4/67.3 in.

Head room F/R: 38.6/35 in.
Leg room F/R: 42.7/28.1 in.
Wheelbase: 101.2 in.
Cargo capacity: 13.3 cu. ft.
Towing capacity: N/A
Fuel tank: 50L/reg.
Weight: 2,650 lbs.

SAFETY FEATURES

	Std.	**Opt.**
Anti-lock brakes	❏	■
Seatbelt pretensioners	—	—
Integrated child safety seat	—	—
Airbag cut-off switch	—	—

Depowered airbags	—	—
Side airbags	—	—
Traction control	—	—
Visibility (front/rear)	*****	**
Crash protection D/P	****	***
Crash protection (side) D/P	N/A	
HLDI injury claims	Average	

NSX

NSX

RATING: Above Average. Acura has allocated only a few hundred NSXs to this country, and will likely drop the model if sales don't pick up.

NEW FOR '99: A carried-over model that may be dropped next year.

GENERAL COMMENTS: Selling for about $138,000 and touted by the automotive press as the world's best-handling car, this 3.2L 300-hp V6, rear-drive, mid-engine, aluminum-bodied sports car goes from 0 to 100 km/h in less than 6 seconds and covers the quarter-mile in just under 14 seconds. These are impressive figures, but they're matched by lots of other sports cars that cost much less. Without its roof, the NSX-T's cramped interior is invaded by wind turbulence and road noise. And forget about carrying luggage.

Standard safety features include ABS, dual airbags, traction control, three-point seatbelts, and a transmission/brake interlock. The car hasn't been tested by the NHTSA for crashworthiness.

Acura's high-priced exotic sports car, the NSX, returns this year with its VTEC engine, recently upgraded from a 3.0 to a 3.2L, boosting its horsepower and torque.

Cost analysis/alternatives: Get the '99 model for the upgrades, if it's discounted; only consider a '98 model if the price is cut 15–20 percent. Other two-seaters worth considering are the Corvette and the Porsche 911 Carrera. **Recommended options:** None. **Rebates:** Not likely before mid-summer. **Destination charge:** $350. **Depreciation:** Much slower than average. **Insurance cost:** Much higher than average. **Parts supply/cost:** Tough-to-find body parts can sometimes be costly. **Annual maintenance cost:** Average. **Warranty:** Bumper-to-bumper 3 years/60,000 km; power-train 5 years/100,000 km; rust perforation 3 years/unlimited km. **Supplementary warranty:** A good idea, considering the cost of parts. **Highway/city fuel economy:** 9.0–12.9L/100 km.

HONDA

Look to Honda for some price reductions this year, but nothing like the cuts planned by Hyundai and Mazda. Although Honda's '99 product lineup has changed very little, its cars and sport-utilities are so popular it can sell most of them with minimal discounting.

This year, only the Odyssey will be redesigned, but the CRV will get a small horsepower boost, and the Civic gets a restyled front and rear end.

Civic, del Sol ('98)

Civic

RATING: Recommended. The overweight del Sol is Not Recommended, because of its poor handling and an exorbitant price for what is essentially a two-seater commuter car with sporty pretensions. **Strong points:** Great handling, comfortable, high-quality construction, and bulletproof reliability. **Weak points:** Seats lack support, difficult rear access, rear seat room limited to two adults.

NEW FOR '99: The del Sol has been dropped. Civics gets restyled front and rear ends, instrument panel, and manual seat-height adjusters.

GENERAL COMMENTS: Barely two years ago the Civic underwent its sixth design change since 1973, and is now one of the most refined and competent subcompacts on the market today. Few larger and more expensive cars can match its quality, performance, and roominess. The hatchback line is available in a wide range of models: a base CX, a mid-level DX, a VX econobox, and the high-performance Si. Sedans are designated in a fashion similar to that of the Accord's, with a base DX, a mid-level LX, and a high-performance EX that carries the most powerful Civic powerplant.

The Civic DX hatchback lacks many of the luxury items that are standard on the LX, but it also lacks the 200 to 300 pounds in extra curb weight, giving it the performance and handling edge. Civics are easy to resell as used cars and command premium prices. Unfortunately, Civics in any form are now very expensive, especially when compared with domestic offerings. On the other hand, they're stylish, have lots of interior room, and are tops in fuel efficiency, thanks to Honda's new VTEC system.

Imported from Japan, the '98 del Sol is a semi-convertible sporty coupe that's less fuel efficient and less responsive than the CRX it replaced five years ago. It comes with a sporty twin-cam VTEC 160-hp variant of the 1.6L powerplant, standard ABS, power door locks, an interior trunk release, low fuel warning light, and driver-side vent control.

Cost analysis/alternatives: Get the '99 model for the upgrades, if it's discounted; only consider a '98 model if the price is cut 15–20 percent. Choose the reasonably priced Civic CX or DX for the best combination of comfort, performance, and fuel economy. Other cars worth considering are the Ford Escort, Mazda Protegé, Nissan Sentra, Hyundai Accent, and Toyota Tercel. Mazda's Miata is a good del Sol alternative. Don't even think of getting the year-old del Sol, no matter what the price; its performance shortcomings make it a poor buy. **Recommended options:** Four-wheel anti-lock brakes and the "fuzzy logic" automatic transmission are wise buys. Since these cars are popular with thieves, buy an anti-theft system device from an independent retailer. Remember, Honda dealers have higher-than-average markups on options, so this is the best area to bring the retail price down. Steer clear of the standard-issue radio. **Rebates:** Not likely. **Destination charge:** $300. **Depreciation:** Much slower than average for the Civic. Average depreciation for the discontinued del Sol. **Insurance cost:** Average. **Parts supply/cost:** Parts are easily found at dealers and independent suppliers. According to CAA, parts are a bit more expensive than for most other cars in this class. **Annual maintenance cost:** Less than average. **Warranty:** *Civic:* Bumper-to-bumper 3 years/60,000 km; powertrain 5 years/100,000 km; rust perforation 6 years/unlimited km. *del Sol:* Bumper-to-bumper 3 years/60,000 km; powertrain 5 years/100,000 km; rust perforation 3 years/unlimited km.

Supplementary warranty: Not necessary. **Highway/city fuel economy:** 5.7–7.5L/100 km.

Quality/Reliability/Safety

Pro: Quality control: Assembly, as well as the quality of materials used in these cars, is first class. **Reliability:** Outstanding. Civics have proven to be mostly trouble-free. **Warranty performance:** Not generous, but acceptable. **Service bulletin problems:** Nothing published, yet. This should reinforce owners' impressions that the Civic is a top-quality car.

Con: Owner-reported problems: Main problem areas have been engine timing belts, constant velocity joints, steering components, premature front brake wear, and excessive brake noise. The 16-valve engine's extra mechanical and electronic complexity means that the corner mechanic won't have a good idea what to do if a problem occurs. Air-conditioner condensers frequently fail after a few years. The two-piece tailgate is a paradise for rattles, and is complicated without any reason to be. Metallic paint has a few problems. **NHTSA safety complaints/ safety:** Airbags failed to deploy; accelerator pedal sticks to cables mounted too tight; accelerator cable got hung up in the cruise control, causing the vehicle to suddenly accelerate; while driving vehicle suddenly accelerated due to the throttle sticking open, and brakes couldn't stop the car; sudden steering loss while driving; gas pedal keeps sticking; brakes locked up and vehicle pulled to the left when coming to an emergency stop; excessive vibration due to engine main bearing failure; transmission sometimes fails to change gear; dome light won't work when doors are open; sheet metal fatigue on both front fenders; faulty hood support rod causes the hood to come crashing down; exterior rear view mirror becomes loose, despite dealer efforts to tighten it.

Road Performance

Pro: Acceleration/torque: The 1.6L engine is smooth and responsive once it attains cruising speed (0–100 km/h: 9.1 sec.). The only disadvantage with these multi-valve engines is that peak power is developed at high engine rpm. The lack of low-end grunt (torque) means lots of gear shifting. The del Sol's VTEC engine gives the car a much-needed acceleration boost, particularly when shifting through the higher gear ranges. **Routine handling:** Handling is excellent, and the ride, though stiff, is among the best in the subcompact class. All Civics give a smooth ride over uneven terrain, thanks to a re-tuning of the double-wishbone suspension last year. **Braking:** Very good (100–0 km/h: 125 ft.).

Con: It's hard to modulate the throttle without having the car surge or lurch. The base engine loses its pep when the Overdrive gear on the automatic transmission engages in city driving, and the VTEC variant is noisy. Furthermore, get the VTEC option only if you enjoy constant gear shifting and intend to do a lot of highway driving, where it's most useful and less interactive. The VX gets its impressive fuel economy by sacrificing acceleration power through its extremely tall gearing. Get used to using second gear for cornering under speed or passing other cars unless you want to stall out. **Transmission:** The 4-speed automatic transmission jerks into gear during hard acceleration, and the 5-speed manual is hard to shift when it's cold. **Steering:** Optional power steering is imprecise and doesn't communicate much road feel. **Emergency handling:** Moderate body roll when cornering at highway speeds. Skinny tires add to overall noise and harshness.

Comfort/Convenience

Pro: Standard equipment: Reasonably well-appointed. **Driving position:** Very good. A large cockpit area, along with interior refinements and the large window area, make for excellent visibility and a feeling of spaciousness. **Controls and displays:** Excellent dashboard design, with easy-to-read gauges and accessible controls. **Climate control:** Heating and ventilation are first class. **Interior space/comfort F/R:** Spacious front seating, less roomy in the rear. **Cargo space:** Versatile and spacious cargo areas. **Quietness:** Engine/road noise has been cut considerably.

Con: Standard features: Base Honda has few standard features in order to keep the base price down. The basic Civic is very plasticky inside. Dual cup holders aren't very accessible. The tiny sun visors are practically useless, tiny horn buttons may be hard to find in an emergency, and the ignition switch is hidden away under the steering wheel. The Targa-style top is tough to remove. Doors give a "tinny" sound when closed. **Interior space/comfort F/R:** Both front and rear seats are uncomfortable on long trips. The del Sol's front seats are a bit too firm and are set too low to permit short drivers to see over the hood, and the back seat will hold only two adults. **Entry/exit:** The small door openings and low seating make for difficult entry and exit, and restrict overall visibility. **Trunk/liftover:** The trunk has limited cargo space and a high sill. **Quietness:** The del Sol's body produces more squeaks and rattles than you'll find in other, more structurally rigid Civics.

COST				
List Price (firm)	**Residual Values** (months)			
	24	36	48	60
Civic LX: $15,700 (11%)	$12,000	$10,000	$8000	$6500

TECHNICAL DATA	
Powertrain (front-drive)	Head room F/R: 38.2/36.2 in.
Engines: 1.6L 4-cyl. (106 hp)	Leg room F/R: 42.7/34.1 in.
• 1.6L 4-cyl. (127 hp)	Wheelbase: 103.2 in.
Transmissions: 5-speed man.	Cargo capacity: 11.9 cu. ft.
• 4-speed auto.	Towing capacity: N/A

Dimensions	Fuel tank: 45L/reg.
Passengers: 5	Weight: 2,500 lbs.
Height/length/width:	
54.7/175.1/67.1 in.	

SAFETY FEATURES

	Std.	Opt.
Anti-lock brakes	❏	■
Seatbelt pretensioners	—	—
Integrated child safety seat	—	—
Airbag cut-off switch	—	—
Depowered airbags	—	—
Side airbags	—	—
Traction control	—	—
Visibility (front/rear)	***	***
Crash protection D/P		
2d	****	****
4d	N/A	
Crash protection (side) D/P		
2d	**	***
4d	***	***
HLDI Injury claims	N/A	

Accord

Accord

RATING: Recommended. Having competed toe-to-toe for over a decade with the Camry and Ford Taurus/Sable, the '99 Accord's latest redesign puts it in the forefront of midsize family sedans. **Strong points:** Bigger, better equipped, better handling, comfortable ride, first-class craftsmanship, legendary reliability, and high resale value. **Weak points:** Low torque base engine makes for constant highway downshifting; average braking; and better-equipped models break the $30,000 barrier.

NEW FOR '99: Nothing significant.

GENERAL COMMENTS: Having undergone its sixth-generation redesign last year, the '99 Accord is better than ever. You want performance? Well, you can choose among three engines that include two competent 4-bangers and a powerful V6. You want ride comfort and responsive handling? Accord gives you that too, through a more refined suspension and steering setup. What about space? Look out, Taurus/Sable—the Accord sedans are roomier than ever before, with interior dimensions that provide more interior space than Ford's mid-size duo. That could be why Honda has regained its lead over Ford in midsize sedan sales.

Overall, the Honda Accord is smooth, quiet, mannerly, and predictable. Every time Honda has redesigned this line it not only caught up with the latest advances, but went slightly ahead. Other strong points are ergonomics that prioritize comfort, easy driveability, high-quality fit and finish inside and out, impressive assembly quality, and outstanding reliability.

Fast and nimble without a V6, this is the midsize sedan of choice for drivers who want maximum fuel economy and comfort along with lots of space for grocery hauling and occasional highway cruising. With the optional 16-valve 4-cylinder engine or V6, the Accord is one of the most versatile midsize cars you can find. It offers something for everyone, and its top-drawer quality and high resale value means there's no way you can lose money buying one.

Cost analysis/alternatives: Only consider a '98 model if the price is cut by at least 10 percent. Some other vehicles worth considering: Ford Taurus and Sable, BMW 325i, Mazda Protegé and 626, Nissan Altima, Toyota Camry, and VW Golf and Jetta. **Recommended options:** V6 for a smoother ride. If you're likely to do a lot of driving in the snow or over wet pavement, don't let the dealer sell you Michelin MXV4 tires— they're terrible snow performers. Choose instead one of the brands recommended in Part One. **Rebates:** Not likely. **Destination charge:** $500. **Depreciation:** Slower than average. **Insurance cost:** Higher than average. **Parts supply/cost:** Latest redesign means that most parts will be back-ordered and pricey. **Annual maintenance cost:** Less than average. **Warranty:** Bumper-to-bumper 3 years/60,000 km; powertrain 5 years/100,000 km; rust perforation 5 years/unlimited km. **Supplementary warranty:** Not needed. Even though this is a redesign, Hondas don't have as many "teething" problems with newly launched models as do other automakers. **Highway/city fuel economy:** 7.5–10L/100 km with the 16-valve 2.3L; 9–13L/100 km with the V6 engine.

Quality/Reliability/Safety

Pro: Quality control: Traditionally first class. These cars are built with care; rarely is a misaligned piece of trim or a crooked seam to be found.

Corrosion-prone overlapping metal panels have been eliminated and galvanized steel used instead. **Reliability:** Excellent for the first five years. **Warranty performance:** Predicted to be average. CAA surveys show that customer satisfaction is an impressive 88 percent, compared to 85 percent for both the Toyota Camry and Mazda 626. **Service bulletin problems:** Nothing significant.

Con: Owner-reported problems: Excessive wind noise. **NHTSA safety complaints/safety:** Airbags failed to deploy; vehicle hit from behind at stoplight and then suddenly accelerated; fuel tank never shows more than 2/3 when tank is full; brake pedal has to be pushed down with both feet to stop vehicle; sudden loss of power steering fluid while driving; loss of power steering fluid when making a U-turn; ABS light continually stays lit; check engine light stays lit; vehicle suddenly stalls while driving, which dealer says is caused by a faulty computer module; engine hesitates when accelerating to merge with traffic; when cruise control is engaged, the transmission suddenly downshifts; while parked on an incline, vehicle rolled forward, despite having gear lever in the Park position; premature brake wear; due to the design of the dash lighting, it's hard to read the odometer, clock, and radio indicator; driver's side seatback rocks; automatic transmission's gears disengage and make a loud noise when engaging.

Road Performance

Pro: Acceleration/torque: Excellent with both the 4- and 6-cylinder engines (0–100 km/h: 7.6 sec. with the V6). The 16-valve 2.3L engine delivers a sportier performance than the more sedate V6. Both engines give sparkling performance with plenty of low-end torque and minimal noise. The new 200-hp V6 doesn't offer a stick shift, but the automatic transmission doesn't sacrifice performance. **Transmission:** The 5-speed manual transmission works very well with smooth and light clutch action. The 4-speed automatic has Overdrive to help save fuel. It also has a Grade Logic feature that reduces gear hunting when climbing hills and automatically downshifts when descending, using engine compression to brake. **Routine handling:** Excellent handling in town or on the highway. It's also amazingly smooth and quiet. There isn't a trace of vibration throughout the operating range, including at idle. Excels in smoothness when passing over freeway expansion joints and potholes, where it damps out the jolts better than most cars in its class. The emphasis on comfort also dominates the Accord's ride and handling. Although its chassis is as good as any, Honda's suspension settings aren't as firm as those of the other cars in this class. **Emergency handling:** Very good. A firm but well-controlled ride is achieved through increased body rigidity and a reworked suspension. **Steering:** Improved variable-assist power steering provides excellent road feel. **Braking:** Average (100–0 km/h: 133 ft.).

Con: VTEC 150-hp 2.3L engine lacks guts and is a bit buzzy in the higher ranges. Could use a bit more high-end torque. No all-wheel drive option, available on many cars in the Accord class. Sometimes, the tall centre console gets in the way of shifting. The four-doors have a less rigid suspension and softer ride than does the coupe. Standard Bridgestone tires don't grip enough in corners.

Comfort/Convenience

Pro: Standard equipment: A nice array of standard features on the base model. Wood and leather on upper-end models. **Driving position:** Excellent driving position and visibility. Very comfortable sporty front seats are well-padded and supportive. Everything is right where it should be, easily seen and easily reached. **Controls and displays:** The well-designed dashboard looks like it's one big moulding rather than a lot of pieces thrown together. Clear gauges and instruments. User-friendly controls and instrumentation. The radio and AC controls have been moved closer to eye level. **Climate control:** Much improved this year. Quiet, efficient, and easily calibrated. **Entry/exit:** Easy entry and exit. **Interior space/comfort F/R:** Seven more cubic feet of passenger space gives this year's Accord more interior space than the BMW 740i, Ford Taurus, or Toyota Camry. Redesigned front seat bases provide more rear foot room. **Cargo space:** The LX and DX sedans' pass-through rear seats allow for more convenient cargo handling. **Trunk/liftover:** Large trunk on sedans, and versatile hatchback design; high liftover, however. **Quietness:** Excessive engine and road noise, particularly at full throttle, has been reduced considerably in this year's redesign.

Con: Rear seating is too low. Rear room for three is a bit tight and the middle passenger will be squeezed from both sides. The remote lock key fob is quirky: sometimes it refuses to unlock the doors.

COST				
List Price (firm)	**Residual Values** (months)			
	24	36	48	60
Accord DX Sedan:				
$22,000 (12%)	$17,000	$14,000	$12,000	$9000

TECHNICAL DATA	
Powertrain (front-drive)	Height/length/width:
Engines: 2.3L 4-cyl. (135 hp)	57.2/188.8/70.3 in
• 2.3L 4-cyl. (150 hp)	Head room F/R: 40/37.6 in.
• 3.0L V6 (200 hp)	Leg room F/R: 42.1/37.9 in.
Transmissions: 5-speed man.	Wheelbase: 106.9 in.
• 4-speed auto.	Cargo capacity: 14.1 cu. ft.
Dimensions (sedan)	Towing capacity: 1,000 lbs.
Passengers: 5	Fuel tank: 65L/reg.
	Weight: 3,230 lbs.

SAFETY FEATURES

	Std.	Opt.
Anti-lock brakes	❏	■
Seatbelt pretensioners	—	—
Integrated child safety seat	—	—
Airbag cut-off switch	—	—
Depowered airbags	—	—
Side airbags	—	—
Traction control	—	—
Visibility (front/rear)	*****	*****
Crash protection D/P	****	****
Crash protection (side) D/P	****	****
HLDI injury claims	Average	

Prelude

Prelude

RATING: Above Average. **Strong points:** Powerful engine, easy handling, lots of standard features, and impressive reliability and quality control. **Weak points:** A bit hard-riding, no VTEC-coupled 6-speed manual transmission, difficult rear seat access, limited rear seat room, and insufficient trunk space.

NEW FOR '99: An additional five horses, a new grille, and an upgraded air filter for the climate control system.

GENERAL COMMENTS: This fifth-generation Prelude sports coupe is complete, functional, and rational without any hint of aggression in its styling or performance components. In fact, most of its performance upgrades won't be noticed by the average driver. It comes with a standard 2.2L 195-hp VTEC engine. There are two trim levels available: the base Prelude and the Prelude Type SH.

Cost analysis/alternatives: If you don't know it already, the 1998 Prelude is practically identical to this year's version, and is a real bargain if you can find a reasonably priced leftover. Other worthwhile cars to consider are the Acura Integra, '98 Eagle Talon, Ford Mustang, GM Camaro and Firebird, and the Toyota Celica. **Recommended options:** None. **Rebates:** Not likely. **Destination charge:** $300. **Depreciation:** Slower than average. **Insurance cost:** Higher than average. **Parts supply/cost:** Parts are easily found, but CAA says they're a bit more expensive than for other cars in this class. Most corner mechanics are ill-equipped to service these cars, and the new Automatic Torque Transfer System (ATTS) won't make their job any easier. **Annual maintenance cost:** Less than average. **Warranty:** Bumper-to-bumper 3 years/60,000 km; powertrain 5 years/100,000 km; rust perforation 5 years/unlimited km. **Supplementary warranty:** Not needed. **Highway/city fuel economy:** 8.5–11L/100 km.

Quality/Reliability/Safety

Pro: Quality control: Exceptional quality control. **Reliability:** No problems have been reported that would make the Prelude unreliable. **Warranty performance:** Better than average. **Owner-reported problems:** Preludes usually give their owners excellent service for the first five years. Even later on, the few problems that surface aren't difficult to diagnose or expensive to repair. **Service bulletin problems:** Nothing published, yet.

Con: Owner-reported problems: Air-conditioner condensers frequently fail after a few years and often need cleaning to eliminate disagreeable odours. Owners have complained about minor electrical problems, brake squealing, and prematurely warped front brake rotors. **NHTSA safety complaints/safety:** Door locks frequently malfunction, causing the driver's door to lock unexpectedly and not unlock. Without ABS, wheels tend to lock up easily during emergency braking.

Road Performance

Pro: Acceleration/torque: Plenty of power (0–100 km/h: 7 sec.), but insufficient torque means you'll do a lot of shifting to keep pace in traffic or on the highway. The Automatic Torque Transfer System (ATTS) is an interesting gizmo that transfers torque to the outside wheel in a turn, making for quicker high-speed cornering. **Transmission:** The manual and automatic transmissions are precise, smooth shifting, and require little effort. **Routine handling:** Very responsive. The ride is quite comfortable, due mainly to suspension refinements and four-wheel disc brakes. **Emergency handling:** Handling is excellent in all conditions. Suspension travel is long enough to reduce bottoming out when fully loaded or when encountering irregular terrain. Last year's suspension upgrade gives a better feel of the road while reducing throttle-lift over-steer, bump, and torque steer (high-performance enthusiasts, rejoice!). **Steering:** Direct and predictable. **Braking:** Better than average.

Con: Even though the 195-hp engine is ideal for sporty performance, this car cries out for a V6 powerplant that provides more torque in all gears. It could also use a 6-speed transmission to more efficiently harness the VTEC's high-revving engine.

Comfort/Convenience

Pro: Standard equipment: Lots of standard features. Height-adjustable bucket seat. Excellent visibility. **Controls and displays:** Greatly improved, user-friendly dash. **Climate control:** Competent climate control system is quiet and easy to adjust. **Interior space/comfort F/R:** Last year's extended wheelbase increased rear head room by 1.5 inches, knee room by 2.5 inches, and foot room by almost 3 inches. Comfortable front seats are well padded and supportive. **Quietness:** More rigid body cuts down on wind and road noise.

Con: Driving position: All drivers may find head room lacking, especially with a sunroof. Insufficient rear passenger room. **Entry/exit:** Very difficult for both the driver and passengers. **Cargo space:** Rather limited. **Trunk/liftover:** Small trunk has a low liftover.

COST

List Price (negotiable)	Residual Values (months)			
	24	36	48	60
Base Prelude: $27,600 (20%)	$19,000	$16,000	$13,000	$10,000

TECHNICAL DATA

Powertrain (front-drive)
Engine: 2.2L 4-cyl. (195 hp)
Transmissions: 5-speed man.
• 4-speed auto.
Dimensions
Passengers: 4
Height/length/width:
51.8/178/69 in.

Head room F/R: 37.9/35.3 in.
Leg room F/R: 43/28.1 in.
Wheelbase: 101.8 in.
Cargo capacity: 8.7 cu. ft.
Towing capacity: 1,000 lbs.
Fuel tank: 60L/reg.
Weight: 2,950 lbs.

SAFETY FEATURES

	Std.	Opt.
Anti-lock brakes	❑	■
Seatbelt pretensioners	■	❑
Integrated child safety seat	—	—
Airbag cut-off switch	—	—
Depowered airbags	—	—
Side airbags	—	—

Traction control	■	❑
Visibility (front/rear)	*****	*****
Crash protection D/P	N/A	
Crash protection (side) D/P	N/A	
HLDI injury claims	N/A	

Odyssey, Isuzu Oasis

Odyssey

RATING: *Odyssey*: Recommended. Watch out, Chrysler and Ford! Here comes Honda's Caravan-and-Windstar-basher. *Oasis*: Not Recommended; a totally different, utterly inferior minivan. **Strong points:** Standard ABS and traction control (EX model only), car-like ride and handling, easy entry/exit, second driver-side door, quiet interior, lots of passenger and cargo room, impressive reliability, and an extensive list of standard equipment. **Weak points:** A high base price, premium fuel required, and rear seat head restraints impede side and rear visibility.

NEW FOR '99: Bigger engine and dimensions that rival the Dodge Caravan.

GENERAL COMMENTS: No longer simply an Accord masquerading as a minivan, the redesigned front-drive, Alliston, Ontario-built Odyssey is longer, wider, taller and more powerful than last year's model. In fact, it matches the Ford Windstar as the longest front-drive minivan on the market. Two sliding doors are offered as standard equipment and, if you buy the EX version, they will both be power-assisted.

You can only get one engine; the largest one among minivans, a powerful 210-hp V6 easily handles most driving chores. Odyssey also offers an upgraded suspension, front and rear AC, and second row captain's chairs that can be shoved side by side to create a bench seat, and a convenient third-row bench seat that folds into the floor when not in use.

Despite its high price, the Odyssey is more reliable and handles more easily than its American competition.

Cost analysis/alternatives: Get the '99 model for the upgrades, don't even consider a '98 model. Be wary of the '99 Isuzu Oasis; it's simply a carried-over '98 Honda Odyssey with none of the important performance upgrades that Honda's '99 Odyssey offers. Ford's Windstar, '98 Mercury Villager, and Nissan Quest are also worth considering if you plan mostly light-duty urban commuting. However, if you want better handling and reliability, the closest competitor to the Odyssey is Toyota's Sienna minivan. **Recommended options:** Traction control. **Rebates:** Look for $1,500 mid-year dealer incentives or rebates. **Destination charge:** $400. **Depreciation:** Slower than average. **Insurance cost:** Higher than average. **Annual maintenance cost:** Higher than average. **Parts supply/cost:** Supply is better than average because the Odyssey uses mostly generic Accord parts. Parts can be expensive, though. **Warranty:** Bumper-to-bumper 3 years/60,000 km; powertrain 5 years/100,000 km; rust perforation 5 years/unlimited mileage. **Supplementary warranty:** Not needed. **Highway/city fuel economy:** N/A.

Quality/Reliability/Safety

Pro: Quality control: Component quality and assembly are similar to the Accord: first class. A minimum of buzzes and rattles. First-year defects, although historically few, won't be ironed out until the middle of next year. Prices are at their highest during the fall, and most of the initial supply will be snapped up by leasing agencies and rental car firms, creating delays of 90 days or more for everyday buyers (make sure you have a *specific* delivery date spelled out in the contract along with a *protected* price, in case there's a price increase while you're waiting for delivery). **Reliability:** Hinged doors are a good idea from a reliability standpoint, since sliding doors often malfunction or wear out prematurely. **Warranty performance:** Comprehensive base warranty that's applied fairly. **Safety:** Each seat has its own head restraint. **Service bulletin problems:** Nothing reported.

Con: Owner-reported problems: Predicted premature front brake wear, excessive front brake noise, and rim and accessory items that will come loose, break away, or won't work. **NHTSA safety complaints/safety:** *Odyssey:* Low-speed airbag deployment; too much play in rear lapbelts, which won't tighten adequately, making it difficult to install a child safety seat securely.

Road Performance

Pro: Acceleration/torque: Impressive V6 engine performance with plenty of torque throughout the power band. **Transmission:** Smooth and quiet shifting. **Routine handling:** Best in its class, thanks to this year's improvements. Road manners are very car-like; steering is light to the touch and responsive. It performs flawlessly in terms of all-around handling and ride quality. **Emergency handling:** Predictable and well controlled. **Braking:** Better than average braking, with little fading after repeated stops.

Con: Steering: A bit heavy at low speeds.

Comfort/Convenience

Pro: Standard equipment: Well-appointed. **Driving position:** Comfortable, commanding driving position. **Controls and displays:** Controls and displays are easy to reach and read. **Climate control:** Much improved. Quiet and efficient. Each seat has its own AC and heating vent. **Entry/exit:** Low step-up. The Odyssey provides car-like room in the front two rows of seats; getting in is no more difficult than climbing into an Accord. Having two hinged rear doors makes it easier to climb in and out of the second row, and having those seats extend right out to the doors, as in a station wagon or sedan, also has its advantages. **Interior space/comfort F/R:** It's easy to strap a child seat into the Odyssey because there's far less lifting and reaching. The bench seat in the centre row is more practical than the captain's chairs, which can't be removed. It's more like a seven-seater station wagon than a minivan. Lots of little storage areas. **Trunk/liftover:** There's space enough for groceries, and the edging around the storage area will help keep your apples from rolling around. **Cargo space:** If you need to expand the cargo area, the third seat folds flat into the floor. **Quietness:** The interior is quiet in most situations.

Con: Power outlet, located at the base of the centre console, is awkward to access.

COST				
List Price (firm)	**Residual Values** (months)			
	24	36	48	60
Base: Odyssey: $29,800 (21%)	$15,000	$13,000	$11,000	$8500

TECHNICAL DATA	
Powertrain (front-drive)	Leg room F: 40.7/R1: 40.2/R2: 34 in.
Engine: 3.5L V6 (210 hp)	Head room F: 40.1/R1: 39.3/R2: 37.5 in.
Transmission: 4-speed auto.	Wheelbase: 111.4 in.
Dimensions ('98 LX)	Cargo capacity: N/A
Passengers: 7	Towing capacity: 1,000 lbs.
Height/length/width:	Fuel tank: 65L
64.6/187.2/70.6 in.	Weight: 3,450 lbs.

SAFETY FEATURES

	Std.	Opt.
Anti-lock brakes	■	❏
Seatbelt pretensioners	—	—
Integrated child safety seat	—	—
Airbag cut-off switch	—	—
Depowered airbags	—	—
Side airbags	—	—
Traction control	❏	■
Visibility (front/rear)	***	***
Crash protection D/P	N/A	
Crash protection (side) D/P	N/A	
HLDI injury claims	N/A	

HYUNDAI

Hyundai doesn't make top-quality cars—a fact repeated time and again by consumer groups on both sides of the border. But Hyundai quality is improving, backed by a more comprehensive warranty, and its cars are relatively inexpensive—three reasons to give their cars more consideration this year.

Over the past several years, Hyundai has been beset by tons of bad luck. Just when it was getting on its feet with such promising new models as the sporty Tiburon and re-engineered Sonata, strikes, product shortages, and a falling currency have combined to keep the company awash in red ink. North American sales have been in steady decline, dropping below 100,000 units—far short of the 240,000 units the company has set as its target for the year 2000. Although sales seem to have bottomed out, dealers complain that they are kept in the dark about the company's future plans and say Hyundai is presently drifting about in limbo following a management shakeup last year.

Naturally, the company is desperate to sell its products even if this means angering its dealers through direct sales, or risking its own financial stability by collecting a lot of bad debt. Earlier this year, *Automotive News* reported that smart shoppers were getting lower prices by "cyber-shopping" at Hyundai's head office (fax-shoppers may be able to get in on similar discounts) than those quoted in national ads featuring the higher MSRP used widely by dealers. Hyundai denied it was competing unfairly with its own dealers and blamed the whole affair on a communications foul-up. Unfortunately, the company's dealers got the message that Hyundai was prepared to undermine their interests through backdoor sales.

Presently, Hyundai is swimming in bad debt, from loans from the 10–12.5 percent of its clients who stiff the company by defaulting on their car loans (a 5 percent default rate is considered frightfully high by most lenders). Hyundai blames the defaults on the low-end nature of its vehicles, which it says attracts higher credit risks. The company says it is trying to fill out its product lineup with more upscale, more profitable vehicles that would attract a more credit-worthy buyers, but until then, it has to deal with customers who have what is delicately called in the industry "non-prime" credit ratings.

For the 1999 model year Hyundai launches its extensively reworked Sonata along with a re-powered Elantra. Both the Accent and Tiburon are carried over without any significant changes.

Accent

Accent

RATING: Above Average. Think of it as a better-quality Chevy Metro from South Korea. **Strong points:** Reasonable engine and automatic transmission performance, good fuel economy, and low base price. **Weak points:** Primitive manual transmission, mediocre braking, excessive engine, road, and wind noise, smelly vinyl coverings, and uncertain long-term reliability.

NEW FOR '99: No changes; may be axed next year.

GENERAL COMMENTS: An upgraded Excel masquerading as an Accent, this front-drive 4-cylinder sedan retains most of the Excel's underpinnings while dropping the Mitsubishi powerplant in favour of its own home-grown 1.5L 4-cylinder, which nevertheless borrows heavily from Mitsubishi. It's better than the old Excel, though, with its upgraded, smoother-shifting automatic transmission stiffer, better-performing suspension, stronger and quieter-running engine, dual airbags, and optional ABS. The three-door matches the Excel in length; the four-door is six inches shorter. Interior space has been increased by an inch.

Cost analysis/alternatives: Get the '99 model for the upgrades, if it's discounted; only consider a '98 model if the price is cut 15–20 percent. Other vehicles worth considering: the Chevrolet Metro, Honda Civic, Nissan Sentra, Suzuki Swift, Toyota Corolla, and VW Golf. Recommended options: An automatic transmission and power steering are essential. Get the GT package for a bit more powerful engine and better tires. Rebates: Expect $1,500 rebates to clear out the '97 and '98 models. Destination charge: $350. Depreciation: Slower than average. Insurance cost: Average. Parts supply/cost: Parts aren't hard to find and they're reasonably priced. Annual maintenance cost: Average. Hyundai says the timing chain should be replaced every 100,000 km. Warranty: Bumper-to-bumper 3 years/60,000 km; powertrain 5 years/100,000 km; rust perforation 5 years/unlimited km. Supplementary warranty: Not needed. Highway/city fuel economy: 6–8.5L/100 km.

Quality/Reliability/Safety

Pro: Quality control: Average. Repairs are straightforward because of a fairly simple design, and parts are less expensive than average. Warranty performance: Average. Service bulletin problems: Nothing published, yet.

Con: Reliability: Excels have always had a checkered reliability and servicing history, so the Accent has a lot of bad karma to overcome. Owner-reported problems: Past problem areas include the engine cooling system and cylinder headgaskets, automatic transmission, premature front brake wear and excessive noise when braking, wheel bearings, and fuel system and electrical components. Body assembly is mediocre and paint is poorly applied. NHTSA safety complaints/safety: Fire caused by alternator failure; sudden transmission and brake failure; chronic stalling; premature suspension strut failure; electrical system failure caused by loose solenoid wire; horn controls may be hard to find in an emergency; the rear seatbelt configuration complicates the installation of a child safety seat.

Road Performance

Pro: Although the 1.5L engine is no pocket rocket, it performs very well in city traffic. Transmission: Surprisingly, this is one car where the automatic transmission performs better than the manual gearbox. Routine handling: Above average. The Accent rides comfortably and handles responsively. Emergency handling: Slow, but predictable. Steering: The non-power steering is precise and transmits plenty of road feedback at higher speeds.

Con: Acceleration/torque: The 1.5L engine provides glacial acceleration (0–100 km/h: 11.2 sec.). The manual transmission is hard to shift correctly due to its balky linkage and long lever movements. Uneven pavement makes for a busy, jittery ride that's accentuated as passengers are added. Steering takes a lot of effort without the power-assist option. **Braking:** Unacceptably long stopping distances (100–0 km/h: 139 ft.).

Comfort/Convenience

Pro: Driving position: Very good. Multiple front seat adjustments and a well-appointed interior make for a pleasant driving environment with a good view of the road. **Controls and displays:** Well laid-out dashboard and controls. **Climate control:** Efficient, easy-to-understand climate control system. **Interior space/comfort F/R:** Room for two adults in the rear. Plenty of front head room. Fairly comfortable but very firm and narrow front seats. **Entry/exit:** Front and rear access is impressively easy. **Cargo space:** Reasonable amount of luggage space, but the hatchback is more versatile with its folding rear seatbacks. **Trunk/liftover:** Average-sized trunk with a low liftover.

Con: Standard equipment: Few standard features, and there aren't a lot of options to choose from. Limited front leg room for tall passengers. Temperature controls aren't within easy reach. **Quietness:** Excessive engine, road, and wind noise.

COST

List Price (negotiable)	Residual Values (months)			
	24	**36**	**48**	**60**
Accent L: $11,565 (11%)	$7000	$5500	$4500	$3500

TECHNICAL DATA

Powertrain (front-drive)	Head room F/R: 38.7/38 in.
Engines: 1.5L 4-cyl. (92 hp)	Leg room F/R: 42.6/32.7 in.
Transmissions: 5-speed man.	Wheelbase: 94.5 in.
• 4-speed auto.	Cargo capacity: 10.7 cu. ft.
Dimensions	Towing capacity: N/A
Passengers: 4	Fuel tank: 46L/reg.
Height/length/width:	Weight: 2,100 lbs.
54.9/162.1/63.8 in.	

SAFETY FEATURES

	Std.	Opt.
Anti-lock brakes	❑	■
Seatbelt pretensioners	—	—
Integrated child safety seat	—	—
Airbag cut-off switch	—	—
Depowered airbags	—	—
Side airbags	—	—
Traction control	—	—
Visibility (front/rear)	*****	*****
Crash protection D/P	***	****
Crash protection (side) D/P	N/A	
HLDI injury claims	High	

Elantra

RATING: Average. **Strong points:** Reasonably priced, pleasant riding, and handles easily. **Weak points:** Noisy, weak engine, mediocre braking, lots of wind noise, and uncertain reliability.

NEW FOR '99: The Tiburon's 2.0L 140-hp 4-cylinder powerplant becomes the base engine, standard AC and seatbelt pretensioners, restyled front and rear ends, and interior trim, and the addition of upgraded components to smooth out the ride and reduce interior noise and vibration.

GENERAL COMMENTS: This Italian-designed, front-drive, conservatively styled subcompact comes either as a sedan or wagon. It's only marginally larger than the discontinued Excel. Nevertheless, its powerful 1.8L engine supplies the much-needed power that you won't find with the Excel. The ride and handling are also improved, due mainly to the Elantra's longer wheelbase and more sophisticated suspension.

Elantra comes in two body styles: the base model and the GLS. As with most Asian cars, the base Elantra is loaded with standard equipment, including intermittent wipers, full centre console, dual remote-control outside mirrors, remote fuel-filler door and trunk release, reclining bucket seats, and tinted glass. Upgrading to the GLS will get you more instruments, power accessories, better tires, a tilt steering wheel, and a premium sound system.

Cost analysis/alternatives: Get the '99 model for the upgrades, if it's discounted; only consider a '98 model if the price is cut 15–20 percent. Other cars worth considering are the GM Saturn SL, Honda Civic, Nissan Sentra, and Toyota Corolla. **Recommended options:** None. **Rebates:** Expect $1,500–$2,000 rebates to clear out the '97 and '98 models. **Destination charge:** $300. **Depreciation:** Faster than average.

Insurance cost: A bit higher than average. **Parts supply/cost:** Easy to find and CAA says that parts are reasonably priced, with heavy discounting by dealers. **Annual maintenance cost:** Average. **Warranty:** Bumper-to-bumper 3 years/60,000 km; powertrain 5 years/100,000 km; rust perforation 5 years/unlimited km. **Supplementary warranty:** A wise investment. **Highway/city fuel economy:** 6–10L/100 km.

Quality/Reliability/Safety

Pro: Quality control: Few quality control problems, so far. **Reliability:** Average. **Warranty performance:** Average. Hyundai customer relations staff usually deal with customer claims in a fair and efficient manner. **Service bulletin problems:** Nothing published, yet.

Con: Reliability: Overall reliability has been slightly below average after the fifth year of ownership. The Elantra's brethren have racked up a sorry history of factory-related defects. If it follows in the Excel/Sonata's footsteps, overall reliability is likely to be considerably below average. **Owner-reported problems:** Powertrain and electrical system failures. **NHTSA safety complaints/safety:** Airbag failed to deploy; accelerator pedal floored, but vehicle failed to pick up speed; chronic transmission failures; automatic transmission slips; transmission goes into low gear periodically and gets stuck there; vehicle rolled forward even though emergency brake was applied; clutch slave cylinder failure; brakes not very efficient; brake master cylinder failure; sudden steering failure; loose steering; defective side moulding.

Road Performance

Pro: Routine handling: Independent suspension helps make for a pleasant ride with exceptional handling and control. **Emergency handling:** Better than average. **Steering:** Accurate and responsive.

Con: Acceleration/torque: Leisurely acceleration (0–100 km/h: 10.5 sec.). Around town this is no problem, but highway cruising and hilly terrain bring out the worst in this low-torque engine. **Transmission:** The optional 4-speed automatic transmission robs the base engine of at least ten horses, and it isn't as smooth as it should be. It shifts frequently trying to keep up with the overburdened engine. **Braking:** Worse than average without anti-lock brakes (100–0 km/h: 146 ft.). Brakes are difficult to modulate.

Comfort/Convenience

Pro: Driving position: Good driving environment with excellent all-around visibility. **Controls and displays:** The attractive interior includes an easy-to-read dashboard with large analogue gauges that are complete and clear, and climate and radio controls that are effective and easy to operate. **Climate control:** The climate control system works without a hitch. Comfortable rear seating for two adults. **Entry/exit:** Good up front; difficult access to the rear. **Cargo space:** Average. **Trunk/liftover:** Average, with a low liftover.

Con: Firm seats are uncomfortable for long trips. Small radio controls. **Interior space/comfort F/R:** Interior room is limited, and head room is particularly tight for tall drivers. **Quietness:** Excessive high-speed engine and road noise.

COST

List Price (negotiable)	Residual Values (months)			
	24	**36**	**48**	**60**
Elantra GL: $14,595 (13%)	$9000	$7000	$5500	$4500

TECHNICAL DATA

Powertrain (front-drive)
Engine: 1.8L 4-cyl. (130 hp)
Transmissions: 5-speed man.
• 4-speed auto.
Dimensions
Passengers: 5
Height/length/width:
54.9/174/66.9 in.

Head room F/R: 38.6/37.6 in.
Leg room F/R: 43.2/34.6 in.
Wheelbase: 100.4 in.
Cargo capacity: 11.9 cu. ft.
Towing capacity: N/A
Fuel tank: 55L/reg.
Weight: 2,500 lbs.

SAFETY FEATURES

	Std.	Opt.
Anti-lock brakes	❑	■
Seatbelt pretensioners	■	❑
Integrated child safety seat	—	—
Airbag cut-off switch	—	—
Depowered airbags	—	—
Side airbags	—	—
Traction control	—	—
Visibility (front/rear)	*****	*****
Crash protection D/P	***	***
Crash protection (side) D/P	***	*
HLDI injury claims	N/A	

Sonata

RATING: Average, but only with an extended warranty. **Strong points:** Nice riding, well-appointed, stylish, and reasonably priced. **Weak points:** Base engine lacks sufficient torque for highway cruising, clunky automatic transmission (a chronic problem with Chrysler and GM as well), and possible long-term reliability/servicing problems.

NEW FOR '99: Hyundai has put the accent on safety this year, giving buyers a lot more safety features for their money than competing models. Standard features include: side airbags, seatbelt pretensioners, an integrated rear child safety seat, and a "smart" passenger-side airbag that won't deploy if the passenger weighs less than 66 lbs. An optional ABS/traction control is also offered. Important powertrain revisions have also been made. The base 2.4L 149-hp 4-cylinder engine has been reworked and a new 165-hp 2.5L V6 has been added. Both the manual and automatic transmissions are upgraded this year for smoother shifting (the new automatic is excluded from the base models). Additionally, the body is wider, with almost an inch more head room, and the instrument panel and centre console have been made more user-friendly.

GENERAL COMMENTS: The Sonata, Hyundai's compact sedan, is loaded with standard features that are optional on competitive makes like the Ford Taurus and Sable, Honda Accord, and Toyota Camry. Some of those standard features include air conditioning, power steering, and a 2.0L 16-valve 4-cylinder engine. It also features an optional 3.0L V6 Mitsubishi engine and ABS.

　　If you don't want to risk a "Stellar" experience, plan on selling your Sonata before its warranty ends and depreciation takes its toll. Even during the warranty period owners report horrendous experiences in getting service from the generally weak dealer network. One Regina,

Saskatchewan, owner of a 1990 Sonata with only 35,000 km wrote me the following litany of disappointments:

...Now that the dealer has closed, I have to travel more than 500 km to change the oil to keep the warranty valid. And there is no 1-800 number, so I have to pay the long-distance telephone calls myself. After several months they opened a dealership in Regina, but the service coupons given by the previous dealer were not honoured.

I still keep asking myself how the 1990 Sonata was selected as "Car of the Year"...The only thing I can say to you, Mr. Lemon-Aid, and to the many thousands of potential buyers of Hyundai cars today and in the years to come, is NEVER BUY A HYUNDAI PRODUCT because you will really get a LEMON. If you are willing to expend your money, your own time, and have your health deteriorate due to stress, then go ahead. . . . The car may be gone in a few more years (if not before), but the memories of this nightmare will remain in our minds for the rest of our lives, and every time and anywhere that somebody starts talking about cars, I will relate my Hyundai experience. I think I got screwed and there is nothing I can do, but I don't want other innocent people to have the same misfortune as I did, and to finish the letter, the only thing I can say is, look before you even think of buying a HYUNDAI.

Cost analysis/alternatives: Get the '99 model for the upgrades, if it's discounted; only consider a '98 model if the price is cut 15–20 percent. My suggestion is to buy a deeply discounted '98 model, plan to keep it at least five years to shake off the additional year's depreciation, and put some of the savings on the purchase price of a comprehensive supplementary warranty to protect you during that period. Other cars worth considering are the Ford Taurus, Honda Accord, Mazda 626, Nissan Altima, and Toyota Camry. **Recommended options:** The V6 engine; if you get the 4-banger version, keep in mind that good fuel economy means putting up with an engine that's rougher and noisier than the V6. Be wary of the sunroof; it eats up a lot of head room. **Rebates:** Expect $2,000 rebates to clear out the '97 and '98 models. **Destination charge:** $300. **Depreciation:** Average. **Insurance cost:** Average. **Parts supply/cost:** Easy to find and relatively inexpensive, says CAA. Large engine compartment for easy servicing. **Annual maintenance cost:** Higher than average. **Warranty:** Bumper-to-bumper 3 years/60,000 km; powertrain 5 years/100,000 km; rust perforation 5 years/unlimited km. **Supplementary warranty:** A good idea to get you through the critical fifth year of ownership, when major components start to self-destruct. **Highway/city fuel economy:** 7.5–11L/100 km with the 2.0L; 9–13L/100 km with the 3.0L engine.

Quality/Reliability/Safety

Pro: No serious problems reported with the 3.0L Mitsubishi power-plant. Repair is straightforward because of the Sonata's simple design. **Service bulletin problems:** Nothing important. **Warranty performance:** Average.

Con: Quality control: *Consumer Reports* magazine says that 1990–92 Sonata owners found their cars to be 120 percent worse than average in terms of complaints. Sonatas have had body assembly and preparation deficiencies that show that Hyundai doesn't yet have a firm grip on quality control. **Reliability:** If the Stellar, Pony, and early Sonata's experience hold true, the third and fourth year of ownership will show serious reliability problems. **Owner-reported problems:** Poor engine performance (hard starting, poor idling, stalling). The engine runs hot, and when you're stopped at a traffic light, it shakes like a boiling kettle. The #3 spark plug often needs replacement or cleaning. Rough engine rattle. Oil consumption is quite high (one litre every two to three months). Excessive front brake pulsation and premature wear. Steering defects (when the steering wheel is turned to either extreme, it makes a sound like metal cracking). Cruise control malfunctions and electrical short circuits, battery life of only 18 months, malfunctioning lights, radio failures, falling interior roof liner, faulty hood locks, a rotten-egg smell coming from the catalytic converter, broken muffler, faulty resonator, defective exhaust pipe, poor door and window sealing (water leaking into the interior when the car is washed), and premature paint peeling and rusting. **NHTSA safety complaints/safety:** Airbags failed to deploy; transmission shifter will not lock into place and slips into Neutral if bumped.

Road Performance

Pro: Acceleration/torque: Reasonably good acceleration, but the base engine's insufficient torque makes the optional V6 a prerequisite for highway cruising, especially over hilly terrain (0–100 km/h: 9.8 sec.). Don't expect more power, though. The V6 has only five more horses, but it's torquier and that's what counts most. **Transmission:** The 4-speed automatic transmission with Overdrive (a fuel-saving feature) works smoothly and is well adapted to the engine's power range. An improved electronic automatic transmission uses "fuzzy logic" to make shifting smooth and predictable. **Routine handling:** Better than average. Hyundai has changed the suspension setting to provide a less bouncy ride. **Emergency handling:** Average. **Steering:** Very good. Predictable, with lots of road feedback.

Con: The V6 engine is still a bit rough-running and noisy despite last year's improvements. Harsh slow-speed or Forward to Reverse shifting. Ride quality deteriorates as load increases. **Braking:** Worse than average braking produces unacceptable stopping distances (100–0 km/h: 145 ft.).

Comfort/Convenience

Pro: Standard equipment: Well equipped for the price. **Driving position:** Very good. Great visibility and fairly supportive seats are set high off the floor. **Controls and displays:** Well laid-out dashboard and controls. Easy-to-read gauges. **Climate control:** Good heating-defrosting-ventilation system. **Entry/exit:** Easy front and rear access. **Interior space/comfort F/R:** One of the roomiest midsize vehicles around—almost as wide as the Accord and as tall as the Altima. Ample front knee room. **Cargo space:** Many storage bins. **Quietness:** Much quieter than previous models.

Con: Trunk/liftover: Surprisingly shallow trunk has a low liftover.

COST				
List Price (very negotiable)	**Residual Values** (months)			
	24	**36**	**48**	**60**
Base Sonata: $19,495 (15%)	$13,000	$12,000	$9500	$7500

TECHNICAL DATA	
Powertrain (front-drive)	Head room F/R: 38.5/37.7 in.
Engines: 2.0L 4-cyl. (137 hp)	Leg room F/R: 43.3/36.6 in.
• 3.0L V6 (142 hp)	Wheelbase: 106.3 in.
Transmissions: 5-speed man.	Cargo capacity: 13.2 cu. ft.
• 4-speed auto.	Towing capacity: N/A
Dimensions	Fuel tank: 47L/reg.
Passengers: 5	Weight: 3,100 lbs.
Height/length/width:	
55.3/185/69.7 in.	

SAFETY FEATURES		
	Std.	**Opt.**
Anti-lock brakes	❏	■
Seatbelt pretensioners	■	❏
Integrated child safety seat	■	❏
Airbag cut-off switch	—	—
Depowered airbags	—	—
Side airbags	■	❏
Traction control	❏	■
Visibility (front/rear)	*****	*****
Crash protection D/P	***	****
Crash protection (side) D/P	*	**
HLDI injury claims	High	

Tiburon

RATING: Average. **Strong points:** Good overall performance, exceptional handling, good fit and finish, and stylish. **Weak points:** Mediocre base engine, restricted rear visibility, and uncertain long-term reliability.

NEW FOR '99: No significant changes.

GENERAL COMMENTS: Although the Tiburon (it means shark in Spanish) is a two-door spinoff of the Elantra sedan, its stylish exterior promises sports car thrills in a compact coupe. Powered by a base 130-hp 1.8L or an optional 140-hp 2.0L, and mated to a 4-speed electronically controlled automatic or a 5-speed manual transmission, the Tiburon is a competent, but not impressive, performer. It handles well, with gas-charged shocks inside coil springs at all four corners, and front MacPherson struts. Steering is light and responsive with a minimum of body flex. Standard brakes consist of discs up front and drums in the rear; the FX package includes four-wheel discs and ABS.

Cost analysis/alternatives: Get the '99 model for the upgrades, if it's discounted; only consider a '98 model if the price is cut 15–20 percent. Other vehicles worth considering: the GM Cavalier, Sunfire, Ford Escort ZX2, and Mercury Cougar. **Recommended options:** The FX package with better-gripping tires, four-wheel disc brakes, and ABS. **Rebates:** Nothing yet on the '99s, but Hyundai is expected to offer attractive rebates on the '99s early in the new year. $1,500 on the '98s; $2,500 on unsold '97s. **Destination charge:** $350. **Depreciation:** Average. **Insurance cost:** Higher than average. **Parts supply/cost:** Parts aren't hard to find and they're less expensive than average. Repair is straightforward because of a fairly simple design. **Annual maintenance cost:** Predicted to be average during the first three years of ownership. **Warranty:** Bumper-to-bumper 3 years/60,000 km; powertrain 5 years/100,000 km; rust perforation 5 years/unlimited km.

Supplementary warranty: A smart buy. **Highway/city fuel economy:** 7–10.6L/100 km.

Quality/Reliability/Safety

Pro: Quality control: Average, but much improved. **Reliability:** Better than average. **Service bulletin problems:** Nothing published, yet. **Warranty performance:** Average. **Safety:** Impressive headlight illumination (take heed, Chrysler).

Con: Owner-reported problems: Premature front brake wear and excessive brake noise. Some electrical glitches. **NHTSA safety complaints/ safety:** Airbag deployed when it shouldn't have; airbag didn't deploy when it should have; reflection of the sun on the dash distracts vision; horn controls may be hard to find in an emergency; rear head restraints appear to be too low to protect occupants; the rear seatbelt configuration complicates the installation of a child safety seat. The rear spoiler is distracting and cuts rearward vision.

Road Performance

Pro: Acceleration/torque: Mediocre performance with the base 1.8L engine. The 2.0L gives respectable power (0–100 km/h: 9.1 sec.), but both engines lack sufficient torque. **Transmission:** The 5-speed manual transmission shifts smoothly and is well adapted to the engine's power range. The ride is reasonably soft on good roads. **Emergency handling:** Very good. Well-controlled, with minimal body roll. **Steering:** The light responsive steering is precise and predictable. **Braking:** Acceptable, though not impressive (100–0 km/h: 132 ft.).

Con: The 4-speed automatic transmission shifts roughly under full throttle and is noisy at high revs. **Routine handling:** Uneven pavement makes for a busy, jittery ride that's accentuated as passengers are added. Poor braking on wet pavement.

Comfort/Convenience

Pro: Attractive styling and a well-appointed interior. **Interior space/comfort F/R:** Comfortable seatbacks. Multiple front seat adjustments. Plenty of front head room. **Controls and displays:** Well laid-out dashboard and controls (except for the radio). **Climate control:** Efficient, easy-to-understand climate control system. **Cargo space:** Average. **Trunk/liftover:** Reasonable amount of luggage space, but the hatchback is more versatile with its folding rear seatbacks.

Con: Rear view is obstructed by the Tiburon's high tail and wide pillars. Tiny radio controls and temperature controls aren't within easy reach. **Entry/exit:** Front and rear access isn't easy. **Interior space/comfort F/R:** Short front seat cushions come up short for thigh support.

Limited front leg room for tall passengers, and rear head room is tight. Very firm and narrow front seats. Barely enough back seat room for two adults. High liftover to the cargo area. **Quietness:** Plenty of engine, road, and wind noise.

COST

List Price (very negotiable)	Residual Values (months)			
	24	**36**	**48**	**60**
Base: $17,595 (15%)	$ 9500	$7500	$6000	$4500
FX: $19,495 (17%)	$11,000	$9500	$8000	$6000

TECHNICAL DATA

Powertrain (front-drive)
Engines: 1.8L 4-cyl. (130 hp)
• 2.0L 4-cyl. (140 hp)
Transmissions: 5-speed man.
• 4-speed auto.
Dimensions
Passengers: 4
Height/length/width:
51.3/170.9/68.1 in.

Head room F/R: 38/34.4 in.
Leg room F/R: 43.1/29.9 in.
Wheelbase: 97.4 in.
Cargo capacity: 12.8 cu. ft.
Towing capacity: N/A
Fuel tank: 55L/reg.
Weight: 2,600 lbs.

SAFETY FEATURES

	Std.	Opt.
Anti-lock brakes	❏	■
Seatbelt pretensioners	—	—
Integrated child safety seat	—	—
Airbag cut-off switch	—	—
Depowered airbags	—	—
Side airbags	—	—
Traction control	—	—
Visibility (front/rear)	*****	**
Crash protection D/P	N/A	
Crash protection (side) D/P	N/A	
HLDI injury claims	N/A	

INFINITI

Infiniti has historically stressed performance over comfort and opulence. Lately, though, it's become a more mainstream luxury automaker and has lost its performance edge, particularly after dropping the J30 and J30t. When Nissan launched its Infiniti line it promised that Infinitis wouldn't be merely restyled Nissans selling at a premium. It lied.

Infiniti makes three vehicles: the I30, an entry-level luxury sedan; the top-of-the-line Q45 four-door sedan; and the QX4 sport-utility. All Infinitis come fully equipped and offer owners the prestige of driving a reliable and nicely styled luxury car.

Infinitis are sold and serviced by dozens of dealers across Canada. This small number doesn't affect either the availability or quality of servicing, since any Nissan dealer can carry out most non-warranty maintenance work.

Except for the G20's debut and some cosmetic revamping of the Q45, the Infinti lineup is carried over this year relatively unchanged.

G20

RATING: Not Recommended. **Strong points:** Standard side airbags and ABS, competent steering and handling, well laid out controls and instruments, good overall visibility. **Weak points:** Mediocre automatic transmission performance, inadequate passenger room, not very well appointed.

NEW FOR '99: New model.

GENERAL COMMENTS: After pulling its original G20 off the market in 1996 after a five-year run, Nissan has been lusting after the entry-level luxury car niche it abandoned. It hopes the $32,950 G20 will fill the bill.

It won't.

Nissan's "spirited performance" claim is pure hype. Looking a lot like its poor-selling predecessor, this year's front-drive G20 is merely an entry-level Sentra disguised as a luxury car. Nissan should be ashamed of itself for attempting this automotive charade. The 140-hp 2.0L engine and live-axle rear suspension are borrowed from the Sentra and the rest of its underpinnings are derived from the European Nissan Primera.

Slightly larger than its 1996 iteration, the G20 comes with additional features like four-wheel ABS, side-impact airbags, seatbelt pretensioners, and a Bose 100-watt sound system. Interestingly, Infiniti doesn't charge for shipping or the pre-delivery inspection, and throws in a free tank of gas along with a comprehensive 4-year/100,000 km warranty. A G20t "touring" model adds a viscous limited-slip differential, fog lamps, and a spoiler starts—all for $29,950. Competitive models you may wish to look at are the Audi A4 1.8T and the Lexus ES 300.

I30

RATING: Above Average. **Strong points:** Competent powertrain, standard traction control and side airbags, comfortable ride, and first-class quality control. **Weak points:** A warmed over, restyled Maxima, obstructed rear visibility, and poor fuel economy (premium fuel suggested).

NEW FOR '99: Carried over this year relatively unchanged, except for standard traction control, front side airbags, an anti-theft system that includes an ignition immobilizer, and an upgraded audio unit.

GENERAL COMMENTS: The I30's $41,350 base price makes it the world's most expensive Maxima, incorporating many of that car's chassis and drivetrain components, including the 190-hp 24-valve 3.0L V6 engine and rear multi-link suspension.

Apart from the Maxima, there are two classes of alternative vehicles that compete with the I30: those costing $40,000 to $50,000, like the BMW 328, Lexus ES 300, Mazda Millenia, Mercedes-Benz C230, and Volvo 960 or S90; and those costing $50,000 or more, such as the BMW 5-series. For my money, the Maxima looks to be the better buy.

Cost analysis/alternatives: Get the '99 model for the upgrades, if it's discounted; only consider a '98 model if the price is cut 15–20 percent. The Maxima SE is a worthy competitor from a price/performance standpoint. **Recommended options:** Limited-slip differential. **Rebates:** Not likely. **Destination charge:** $350. **Depreciation:** Average. **Insurance cost:** Higher than average. **Parts supply/cost:** Moderately priced parts are available only from Nissan or Infiniti dealers. **Annual maintenance cost:** Much less than average. **Warranty:** Bumper-to-bumper 4 years/100,000 km; powertrain 6 years/100,000 km; rust perforation 7 years/unlimited km. **Supplementary warranty:** Not necessary. **Highway/city fuel economy:** 7.8–11.4L/100 km.

Quality/Reliability/Safety

Pro: Quality control: Excellent. **Reliability:** Much better than average. **Warranty performance:** Very good. **Owner-reported problems:** Nothing significant. **Service bulletin problems:** Nothing reported, yet.

Con: NHTSA safety complaints/safety: *I30:* ABS failure; sudden acceleration. *J30:* Sudden acceleration; steering suddenly jerked from left to right, causing driver to lose control.

Road Performance

Pro: Acceleration/torque: Better than average. The engine performs well throughout the power band (0–100 km/h: 8.9 sec.). **Transmission:** The automatic transmission is imperceptible, and the viscous limited-slip differential assists traction over slippery roads. **Routine handling:** Handles acceptably and provides a quiet, comfortable ride when cruising. **Emergency handling:** Average. Little body lean or front-end plow during high-speed cornering. **Braking:** Braking is acceptable, with little fading or loss of directional stability (100–0 km/h: 131 ft.).

Con: Don't take Infiniti's 130 mph (208 km/h) pretensions seriously—the car's weight works against the hp. Rear headrests obstruct visibility.

Comfort/Convenience

Pro: Standard equipment: The I30 has many standard features that are optional on other cars in its class. **Driving position:** Excellent driving position with good front and rear visibility. **Controls and displays:** Very well laid-out, accessible, and easy to understand. **Climate control:** Efficient and quiet. **Entry/exit:** Large door openings make access a breeze. **Trunk/liftover:** The spacious trunk has a pass-through for carrying long items. **Cargo space:** Lots of small storage areas. **Quietness:** Extra damping makes for an exceptionally quiet interior.

Con: Tacky faux wood-grain console. **Interior space/comfort F/R:** Only enough room to sit four passengers comfortably. Rear seat backrest is too inclined for comfort.

COST				
List Price (firm)	**Residual Values** (months)			
	24	**36**	**48**	**60**
I30: $41,350 (30%)	$30,000	$20,000	$17,000	$14,000

TECHNICAL DATA

Powertrain (front-drive)
Engine: 3.0L V6 (190 hp)
Transmission: 4-speed auto.
Dimensions (I30)
Passengers: 5
Height/length/width:
55.7/189.6/69.7 in.

Head room F/R: 40.1/37.4 in.
Leg room F/R: 43.9/34.3 in.
Wheelbase: 106.3 in.
Cargo capacity: 14.1 cu. ft.
Towing capacity: N/A
Fuel tank: 70L/premium
Weight: 3,150 lbs.

SAFETY FEATURES

	Std.	Opt.
Anti-lock brakes	■	❑
Seatbelt pretensioners	■	❑
Integrated child safety seat	—	—
Airbag cut-off switch	—	—
Depowered airbags	■	❑
Side airbags	■	❑
Traction control	■	❑
Visibility (front/rear)	*****	*****
Crash protection D/P	****	****
Crash protection (side) D/P	****	***

Q45

Q45

RATING: Recommended. A nice compromise between luxury and performance; a Japanese BMW with good rear seating. **Strong points:** Well-appointed, standard side airbags, pleasant riding, stylish, plenty of rear leg room, excellent braking, and excellent workmanship. **Weak points:** Limited trunk space, and requires premium fuel.

NEW FOR '99: Front seat side airbags, electronically modulated shocks, revised grille, restyled and upgraded headlights, an upgraded moonroof switch, a power-assisted rear-window sunshade and remote-closing trunk lid.

GENERAL COMMENTS: Infiniti has shifted the Q45's emphasis from performance to luxury and comfort. This is unfortunate, because it reduces the distinction between the Q45 and Lexus LS 400. In fact, now that the engine has been downsized from a 4.5 to a 4.1L one wonders if the Q45 moniker isn't misleading advertising. Nevertheless, in spite of its downsized engine this luxury sedan is faster and more glitzy than many cars in its category.

The Q45 uses a 32-valve 266-hp 4.5L V8 not frequently found on Japanese luxury compacts. It's a refined powerplant that has been both reliable and durable over the years.

Redesigned for the 1997 model year, the Infiniti Q45 has front and side airbags (side airbags added mid-year) for both driver and right front passenger plus dual-locking shoulder belts. Belts in the front seat have tensioners that activate in a crash to reduce belt slack.

Cost analysis/alternatives: Get the '99 model for the upgrades, if it's discounted; only consider a '98 model if the price is cut 15–20 percent. **Recommended options:** Forget about the active suspension option; it doesn't improve the handling or ride very much. **Rebates:** Not likely. **Destination charge:** $350. **Depreciation:** Much slower than average.

Insurance cost: Much higher than average. **Parts supply/cost:** Parts are more expensive than other cars in this class, according to CAA and they're available only from Nissan or Infiniti dealers. **Annual maintenance cost:** Much less than average. **Warranty:** Bumper-to-bumper 4 years/100,000 km; powertrain 6 years/100,000 km; rust perforation 7 years/unlimited km. **Supplementary warranty:** Not necessary. **Highway/city fuel economy:** 10–14.5L/100 km with the 4.5L engine.

Quality/Reliability/Safety

Pro: Quality control: High-quality components and superior workmanship. **Reliability:** No reliability problems reported. **Warranty performance:** Better than average. **Service bulletin problems:** Nothing significant.

Con: Owner-reported problems: Tire thumping, some interior rattles, and excessive wind noise around the A-pillars. **NHTSA safety complaints/safety:** N/A.

Road Performance

Pro: Acceleration/torque: Impressive acceleration and plenty of torque (0–100 km/h: 8.6 sec.). The car accelerates without a hint of noise or abrupt shifting. The engine supplies plenty of upper-range torque as well. **Transmission:** Smooth-shifting and quiet automatic transmission. **Routine handling:** Quite nimble handling for such a heavy car. **Emergency handling:** Very good. Standard traction control works well in preventing the car's rear end from sliding out on slippery roads. **Steering:** Precise, with plenty of road feedback. **Braking:** Incredibly short stopping distances, thanks to four-wheel ABS (100–0 km/h: 121 ft.).

Comfort/Convenience

Pro: Standard equipment: Incredibly well-appointed, with lots of standard safety and convenience features. **Driving position:** Excellent. Unobstructed front and rear visibility. **Controls and displays:** Well-positioned and easy to decipher. Complete instrumentation. **Climate control:** Efficient, quiet, and very easy to adjust. **Entry/exit:** Both the front and rear seats can be easily accessed without undue acrobatics. **Interior space/comfort F/R:** Luxury seating both fore and aft. Rear seating is particularly comfortable. **Quietness:** Cocoon-like quiet.

Con: Cargo space: Limited room for storage of bulky items. **Trunk/liftover:** Small trunk has a low liftover.

COST				
List Price (negotiable)	**Residual Values** (months)			
	24	36	48	60
Q45t: $69,000 (30%)	$55,000	$45,000	$38,000	$29,000

TECHNICAL DATA

Powertrain (front-drive)
Engine: 4.1L V8 (266 hp)
Transmission: 4-speed auto.
Dimensions
Passengers: 5
Height/length/width:
56.9/199.2/71.7 in.

Head room F/R: 37.6/36.9 in.
Leg room F/R: 43.6/35.9 in.
Wheelbase: 111.4 in.
Cargo capacity: 12.6 cu. ft.
Towing capacity: N/A
Fuel tank: 81L/premium
Weight: 3,900 lbs.

SAFETY FEATURES

	Std.	Opt.
Anti-lock brakes	■	❏
Seatbelt pretensioners	■	❏
Integrated child safety seat	—	—
Airbag cut-off switch	—	—
Depowered airbags	■	❏
Side airbags	■	❏
Traction control	■	❏
Visibility (front/rear)	*****	*****
Crash protection D/P	N/A	
Crash protection (side) D/P	N/A	
HLDI injury claims	Low	

LEXUS

This has been another year of record sales for Toyota and Lexus. Lexus has become a luxury automaker on its own merits, even though it started out selling dressed-up Camrys as upscale models (only the ES 300 fits that description now). But so did Acura and Infiniti, right? Unlike Infiniti, though, Lexus isn't morphing into anything other than what it's always been: the epitome of luxury and comfort, with a small dab of performance thrown in. While Infiniti engineers see the highway as a challenge, Lexus sees it as an irritant, successfully isolating the driver from the driving experience. And guess what? It's a winning formula. No matter how often car enthusiast magazines say that drivers want "road feel," "responsive handling," and "high-performance" thrills, the truth of the matter is that most drivers simply want to travel from point A to point B in safety and comfort, without interruption. Infiniti bucked that concept, and lost.

Don't get the impression that Lexus does everything right. For example, the automaker knew its new GS 300 and RX 300 would take some sales from the popular ES 300, but additional competition from the Audi A6, Volvo S70, Acura 3.2TL, and BMW 3-series has caused ES 300 sales to nosedive by 20 percent through last September. And apparently nobody wants Lexus' luxury coupes, either, so models like the SC

300 and SC 400, with their decade-old design, are languishing on dealers' lots. Finally, there's the question of service. Lexus has half as many dealers as Mercedes and BMW, yet its models and units sold have proliferated over the years to the point where servicing is strained. The automaker wants to add dealers, but the dealer body—mesmerized by high profits per dealer—is resisting. This has created a customer service crisis that will only worsen as sales continue to soar.

Lexus hasn't scheduled any major changes for this year. The few improvements that have been announced include a 10-hp boost for the 3.0L V6, standard side-mounted airbags, standard traction control on some models, an anti-theft device that immobilizes the car, and an auto-tilt-down left-side mirror for backing up.

Although these luxury imports do set advanced benchmarks for quality control, they're not engineering perfection (they do average about half a defect per car during the first 90 days of ownership). Cheaper luxury cars like the Acura 3.0L CL, Mazda Millenia, Nissan Maxima, and Toyota Avalon give you almost as much comfort and reliability, but without the Lexus cachet.

Dealer service bulletins show that these cars are affected by some minor body fit and trim glitches. Most owners haven't heard of these problems, because Lexus dealers have been particularly adept at fixing many of them before they become chronic. One problem that's recently cropped up may not be fixed as easily, however. The California Air Resources Board has determined that the entire lineup of 1996–98 Toyota and Lexus models have defective emissions control hardware that requires the replacement of the OBD-II computer (at $250 U.S. each). This problem impacts Canadians because the faulty equipment can cause driveability problems and create emissions that exceed the provincial norm. Toyota has until January 1, 1999, to initiate a voluntary fix or face a mandatory recall.

In summary, the Lexus lineup is geared more to the luxury cruiser crowd, which prefers comfort over performance thrills. All models come with such important standard safety features as ABS and side airbags, automatically adjusted head restraints, an automatic transmission shifter interlocked with the ignition and brakes, childproof door locks, and easily adjusted three-point seatbelts.

ES 300

ES 300

RATING: Recommended. **Strong points:** Standard side airbags and ABS, good acceleration, pleasant, quiet ride, and excellent quality control and warranty performance. **Weak points:** Primarily a four-seater; three adults won't sit comfortably in the rear. Muted steering feel, some nosedive in panic stops, and overall handling isn't as nimble as its BMW or Mercedes rivals. Trunk space is limited (low liftover, though) and rear corner visibility is hampered by the high rear end.

NEW FOR '99: A 10-hp boost for the 3.0L V6, active-control engine mounts to reduce engine vibration, a new transmission borrowed from the RX300 sport-utility, standard side-mounted airbags, an anti-theft device that immobilizes the car, up/down power windows, and headlights that stay illuminated for 15 seconds after engine shut-off.

GENERAL COMMENTS: A Camry clone with some additional features, this $44,236 entry-level Lexus front-drive returns relatively unchanged. The sole engine is a 210-hp V6 mated to an electronically controlled 4-speed automatic transmission that handles the 3.0L engine's horses effortlessly—making for 0 to 100 km/h times in the low eights—without sacrificing fuel economy. All ES 300s feature dual front and side airbags, anti-lock brakes, improved double-piston front brake calipers, 60/40 split folding rear seats, and one of the rarest features of all, a conventional spare tire.

Cost analysis/alternatives: Get the '99 model for the extra horsepower, improved transmission, and safety upgrades. Forget about a leftover '98; it's unlikely any will be left and what you will find won't cost that much less than a '99 version. Other cars worth considering are the Acura TL, Audi A4, Infiniti I30, Mercedes-Benz E420, Mazda Millenia, Toyota Avalon, and Volvo's S70 and S90 series. **Recommended options:** Traction control. I don't recommend the Adaptive Variable Suspension option; it's mostly a gimmick with little functional improvement. **Rebates:** None.

Look for discounting on the MSRP by at least 5 percent. **Destination charge:** $350. **Depreciation:** Depreciation is much lower than average. **Insurance cost:** Much higher than average. **Parts supply/cost:** Average availability, and CAA says that parts cost a bit less than for other cars in this class. **Annual maintenance cost:** Below average. **Warranty:** Bumper-to-bumper 4 years/80,000 km; powertrain 6 years/110,000 km; rust perforation 6 years/unlimited km. **Supplementary warranty:** Not necessary. **Highway/city fuel economy:** 8–12L/100 km.

Road Performance

Pro: Acceleration/torque: Incredibly fast acceleration and lots of torque (0–100 km/h: 7.2 sec.); beats out the Infiniti Q45. **Braking:** Better than average braking that's almost as effective as the Q45's (100–0 km/h: 121 ft.).

Quality/Reliability/Safety

NHTSA safety complaints/safety: Instrument panel lights aren't bright enough at night; middle rear shoulder belt locks up, making it difficult to get the occupant out from the middle seat.

COST

List Price (negotiable)	Residual Values (months)			
	24	36	48	60
ES 300: $44,236 (30%)	$34,000	$27,000	$23,000	$18,000

TECHNICAL DATA

Powertrain (front-drive)
Engine: 3.0L V6 (210 hp)
Transmission: 4-speed auto.
Dimensions
Passengers: 4
Height/length/width:
54.9/190.2/70.5 in.

Head room F/R: 36.8/36.2 in.
Leg room F/R: 43.5/34.4 in.
Wheelbase: 105.1 in.
Cargo capacity: 13 cu. ft.
Towing capacity: N/A
Fuel tank: 70L/premium
Weight: 3,300 lbs.

SAFETY FEATURES

	Std.	Opt.
Anti-lock brakes	■	❑
Seatbelt pretensioners	■	❑
Integrated child safety seat	—	—
Airbag cut-off switch	—	—
Depowered airbags	■	❑
Side airbags	■	❑
Traction control	❑	■
Visibility (front/rear)	*****	*****
Crash protection D/P	****	****
Crash protection (side) D/P	*****	****
HLDI injury claims	N/A	

GS 300, 400

GS 300

RATING: Recommended. **Strong points:** Standard side airbags, ABS, and Vehicle Stability Control anti-skid system. Excellent high-performance powertrain setup, pleasantly quiet ride, superb handling and braking, and exceptional quality control and warranty performance. **Weak points:** Primarily a four-seater with limited head room for six-footers. High window line impedes rear visibility, poor fuel economy (premium fuel), some instruments hidden by the steering wheel, trunk and fuel-door releases hidden at the base of the dash, and the fuel gauge may give inaccurate readings (there's a service bulletin on this problem).

NEW FOR '99: Carried over unchanged.

GENERAL COMMENTS: Redesigned last year, these rear-drives are shorter, the wheelbase is longer, the trunk is larger, and there's a lot more interior room. Two models are available: one carries the in-line 6 engine and the other is V8-powered. Both engines have VVT-i (variable valve timing with intelligence), a feature that continually changes the engine timing to achieve peak horsepower with low emissions and high fuel economy. Other innovative features include vehicle skid control (VSC), dual side airbags, and dual-zone climate controls.

Cost analysis/alternatives: It's a toss-up whether to buy a '98 or '99 version, since they're identical. Choose whichever has been discounted the most. Other cars worth considering are the Acura RL, BMW 5-series, and Mercedes-Benz E-class. **Recommended options:** 17-inch tires. **Rebates:** Not likely. Look for discounting on the MSRP by at least five percent. **Destination charge:** $350. **Depreciation:** Much slower than average. **Insurance cost:** Much higher than average. **Parts supply/cost:** Engine and body parts will be relatively rare and costly. **Annual maintenance cost:** Less than average. **Warranty:** Bumper-to-bumper 4 years/80,000 km; powertrain 6 years/110,000 km; rust perforation 6 years/unlimited km. **Supplementary warranty:** Not necessary. **Highway/city fuel economy:** 8.9–12.1L/100 km.

Road Performance

Acceleration/torque: Hot rod acceleration with lots of torque (0–100 km/h: 6.1 sec. with the V8). **Braking:** Exceptional braking for a car this heavy (100–0 km/h: 122 ft.).

COST				
List Price (firm)	**Residual Values** (months)			
	24	**36**	**48**	**60**
GS 300: $59,220 (30%)	$40,000	$34,000	$28,000	$23,000
GS 400: $67,360 (30%)	$45,000	$39,000	$33,000	$28,000

TECHNICAL DATA

Powertrain (rear-drive)
Engines: 3.0L V6 (225 hp)
• 4.0L V8 (300 hp)
Transmissions: 4-speed auto.
• 5-speed auto.
Dimensions
Passengers: 4
Height/length/width: 56.7/189/70.9 in.

Head room F/R: 39.2/37 in.
Leg room F/R: 44.5/34.3 in.
Wheelbase: 110.2 in.
Cargo capacity: 13 cu. ft.
Towing capacity: N/A
Fuel tank: 70L/premium
Weight: 3,300 lbs.

SAFETY FEATURES

	Std.	Opt.
Anti-lock brakes	■	❏
Seatbelt pretensioners	■	❏
Integrated child safety seat	—	—
Airbag cut-off switch	—	—
Depowered airbags	■	❏
Side airbags	■	❏
Traction control	■	❏
Visibility (front/rear)	*****	*****
Crash protection D/P	***	***
Crash protection (side) D/P	N/A	
HLDI injury claims	Average	

LS 400

LS 400

RATING: Recommended. **Strong points:** Comfortable ride, quiet interior, and well-appointed, with lots of standard safety features. **Weak points:** Ponderous handling and limited trunk space.

NEW FOR '99: Standard wood and leather steering wheel, shift knob, and floor mats.

GENERAL COMMENTS: This attractive, rear-drive luxury sedan returns considerably improved. Designed using a traditional European approach, Lexus outclasses Cadillac and Lincoln both in styling and function. The long wheelbase makes for a comfortable ride, lots of interior room (exceeding that of the Mercedes S-class and BMW 7-series), and easy entry/exit.

The base engine is a 290-hp 4.0L V8 that provides impressive acceleration and superior highway passing ability at all speeds. Its transmission is smooth and efficient. The suspension provides an easy ride without body roll or front-end plow during emergency stops, thereby delivering a major comfort advantage over other luxury compacts. There's an absence of engine or wind noise. The $1,000 optional memory feature resets the driver's seat, steering wheel, headrest, mirrors, and seatbelt. It's particularly useful if several people will be driving the car.

Lexus has issued service bulletins to correct serpentine belt squeal and incorrect fuel gauge readings on its '98 versions.

Cost analysis/alternatives: Again, it's a toss-up whether to buy a '98 or '99 version since they're nearly identical (c'mon, who really cares about new floor mats or a leather steering wheel?). Other cars worth considering are the BMW 540i and 740i, Infiniti Q45, Mercedes-Benz E- and S-class, and BMW 5- and 7-series. **Recommended options:** None. **Rebates:** Not likely. Look for discounting on the MSRP by at least

10 percent. **Destination charge:** $350. **Depreciation:** Slower than average. **Insurance cost:** Higher than average. **Parts supply/cost:** Moderately priced parts aren't hard to find, except for engine components and body panels, which are likely to be back-ordered. **Annual maintenance cost:** Much less than average. **Warranty:** Bumper-to-bumper 4 years/80,000 km; powertrain 6 years/110,000 km; rust perforation 6 years/unlimited km. **Supplementary warranty:** Not needed. **Highway/city fuel economy:** 8.8–12.4L/100 km with premium fuel.

Road Performance

NHTSA safety complaints/safety: N/A. LS 400 models were rated better than average overall for injury claims by the Highway Loss Data Institute, an insurance industry-sponsored safety group. No NHTSA crash data are available.

Quality/Reliability/Safety

Acceleration/torque: Excellent acceleration times with lots of torque (0–100 km/h: 7.9 sec.). **Braking:** Respectable braking performance (100–0 km/h: 126 ft.).

COST				
List Price (negotiable)	**Residual Values** (months)			
	24	**36**	**48**	**60**
LS 400: $78,300 (30%)	$55,000	$42,000	$35,000	$28,000

TECHNICAL DATA	
Powertrain (rear-drive)	Head room F/R: 38.9/36.9 in.
Engine: 4.0L V8 (290 hp)	Leg room F/R: 43.7/36.9 in.
Transmissions: 5-speed auto.	Wheelbase: 112.2 in.
Dimensions	Cargo capacity: 13.9 cu. ft.
Passengers: 5	Towing capacity: N/A
Height/length/width:	Fuel tank: 85L/premium
56.5/196.7/72 in.	Weight: 3,890 lbs.

SAFETY FEATURES		
	Std.	**Opt.**
Anti-lock brakes	■	❏
Seatbelt pretensioners	■	❏
Integrated child safety seat	—	—
Airbag cut-off switch	—	—
Depowered airbags	■	❏
Side airbags	■	❏
Traction control	■	❏
Visibility (front/rear)	*****	*****
Crash protection D/P	N/A	
Crash protection (side) D/P	N/A	
HLDI injury claims	N/A	

MAZDA

Mazda's Canadian sales were slightly off last year. In the U.S., Mazda sales appear to be making a comeback—improving to the '95 levels. Mazda is more vulnerable to downturns than other Japanese automakers because it doesn't have the huge cash reserves of Toyota (almost $30 billion), and has only one overseas plant (a Michigan plant co-owned by Ford) to which it can shift production. The company has been hit hard by a devalued yen and a softening in the entry-level market that has sent sales spinning downward. In an effort to improve its sales, Mazda revamped the aging 626 compact sedan last year.

Mazda's misery represents a buying opportunity for smart shoppers, who can take advantage of the company's many rebates and dealer incentives to pick up some good-quality cars and trucks. The only caveat is the spotty servicing and high parts cost, both of which can be overcome partly through the purchase of a supplementary warranty or servicing by an independent repair facility.

Protegé

Protegé

RATING: Recommended. **Strong points:** Much improved powertrain, comfortable ride, plenty of interior room, good fuel economy, and quality workmanship. **Weak points:** Difficult rear entry/exit and rear seating for two adults only.

NEW FOR '99: Two new engines and a transmission that uses 26 percent fewer parts. The new base engine is a 1.6L, 106-hp (up from 92-hp DOHC in-line four); last year's Miata-based 1.8L powerplant has been replaced by a smaller, torquier variant that provides identical horsepower. Rear disc brakes have been dropped on the top-line model in favour of revised pads and calipers that Mazda says brake more efficiently. The suspension has also been upgraded to smooth out the ride. Restyled, unibody construction makes for a more rigid body and less squeaks and rattles. The '99s come with a slightly longer wheelbase and are narrower and lower, with improved interior ergonomics.

GENERAL COMMENTS: Now that the 323 has been dropped, the Protegé is Mazda's least costly model. It shares platforms with the Escort and Tracer, but keeps its own sheet metal, engine, and interior styling. Powered by a standard, fuel-efficient 1.6L engine mated to a manual 5-speed transmission, the Protegé is one of the most responsive and roomiest small cars around.

Cost analysis/alternatives: Get the '99 model for the upgrades; don't even consider the '98 version even though it comes with hefty rebates. Other cars worth considering are the Ford Escort and '98 Tracer (Protegé clones), Honda Civic, Hyundai Accent, Suzuki Swift, Toyota '98 Tercel and Corolla, and VW Golf and Jetta. **Recommended options:** The 1.8L engine and anti-lock brakes. **Rebates:** $750–$2,250 on the '98s. **Destination charge:** $400. **Depreciation:** Faster than average. **Insurance cost:** Average. **Parts supply/cost:** According to CAA, Mazda parts cost far more than average, but they aren't difficult to find. Plus, these cars are easily serviced by dealers or independents. In fact, most Ford dealers have parts that can be used on Mazda products because the Ford Escort uses lots of Mazda mechanical components. This knowledge may be useful if you find your Mazda dealer jacking up parts prices to an unreasonable level. **Annual maintenance cost:** Below average. **Warranty:** Bumper-to-bumper 3 years/80,000 km; powertrain 5 years/100,000 km; rust perforation 5 years/unlimited km. **Supplementary warranty:** A good idea while waiting for improved service. **Highway/city fuel economy:** 5.7–7.7L/100 km with the base 1.5L engine and a manual transmission; 6.5–9.0L/100 km with the 1.8L engine and manual transmission; 7–9.5L/100 km with the 1.8L and an automatic transmission.

Quality/Reliability/Safety

Pro: Quality control: Very good. Few quality-control complaints. **Reliability:** Better than average reliability. **Warranty performance:** Acceptable, though a lot depends on the dealer going to bat for you. There's a valet lock that locks the folding rear seatbacks to prevent access to the trunk's contents. ABS is standard on the ES and optional on the LX.

Con: Owner-reported problems: The front brakes tend to wear out quickly, and MacPherson struts and rear shock absorbers don't last as long as they should. Some complaints of poor fit and paint defects. **Service bulletin problems:** Nothing published yet, but you may find some helpful hints in the Ford Escort section. **NHTSA safety complaints/safety:** Brake pedal pushed almost to the floor before brakes work, and they produce excessive noise.

Road Performance

Pro: Acceleration/torque: Excellent overall performance with either engine. The 1.6L twin-cam 4-cylinder engine is surprisingly responsive and quiet. Impressive acceleration with the 1.8L optional powerplant. **Transmission:** Both transmissions shift smoothly. The 5-speed manual has a handy "Hold" feature that allows the driver to select and hold any of three lower gears through the shift lever. Two other advantages: the automatic transaxle can be driven away in second gear, an asset on snow and ice; and you can lock out Overdrive with the push of a button, allowing you to traverse hilly terrain or urban traffic without constant shifting. **Routine handling:** Although the suspension is less firm this year, handling is quite nimble. **Emergency handling:** Comfortable, firm, no-surprise ride doesn't deteriorate as passenger load increases or when cornering at high speed. **Steering:** Predictable, well-controlled, and transmits good road feedback.

Con: The automatic transmission robs the base engine of much-needed power. Some body roll in turns. **Braking:** Average braking without ABS.

Comfort/Convenience

Pro: Driving position: Better than average. The driver and front passenger are pampered with firm, comfortable front bucket seats and multiple-seat steering wheel adjustments. Great all-around visibility. **Controls and displays:** Clear and well laid-out controls. **Climate control:** Efficient, quiet heating and defrosting. **Entry/exit:** Large doors make for easy access to the front. **Interior space/comfort F/R:** A comfortable four-seater. **Cargo space:** Lots of interior space to store large and small items. **Trunk/liftover:** Trunk space is expanded with locking, folding rear seatbacks. A low liftover facilitates loading.

Con: Standard equipment: Cheap-looking, sober interior. The sunroof drastically reduces head room. Even with a tilt steering column, the steering wheel may be too low for some tall drivers. Others may find the gear shift lever a bit too far away when shifting into fifth gear. **Climate control:** Climate controls aren't user-friendly. **Entry/exit:** Difficult rear access due to the narrow rear doors. **Interior space/comfort F/R:** The rear seating is better suited for two average-sized adults and the rear seatbacks are hard, offer little side support, and are too vertical. **Quietness:** Some engine and tire noise intrusion into the interior.

COST

List Price (negotiable)	Residual Values (months)			
	24	**36**	**48**	**60**
Protegé DX: $14,870 (12%)	$11,000	$9000	$7500	$6000

TECHNICAL DATA

Powertrain (front-drive)
Engines: 1.6L 4-cyl. (106 hp)
• 1.8L 4-cyl. (122 hp)
Transmissions: 5-speed man.
• 4-speed auto.
Dimensions
Passengers: 5
Height/length/width:
55.5/174/67.1 in.

Head room F/R: 37.9/36.7 in.
Leg room F/R: 42.2/35.6 in.
Wheelbase: 102.8 in.
Cargo capacity: 13.1 cu. ft.
Towing capacity: N/A
Fuel tank: 50L/reg
Weight: 2,350 lbs.

SAFETY FEATURES

	Std.	Opt.
Anti-lock brakes	❏	■
Seatbelt pretensioners	—	—
Integrated child safety seat	—	—
Airbag cut-off switch	—	—
Depowered airbags	■	❏
Side airbags	—	—
Traction control	—	—
Visibility (front/rear)	*****	*****
Crash protection D/P	***	N/A
Crash protection (side) D/P	N/A	
HLDI injury claims	N/A	

626

RATING: Above Average. **Strong points:** Strong V6 acceleration, standard traction control (V6 only) pleasant handling, comfortable front seating, easy entry/exit, and good overall reliability. **Weak points:** Sluggish 4-cylinder performance, jerky automatic transmission, and excessive road noise.

NEW FOR '99: No significant changes.

GENERAL COMMENTS: Restyled last year to resemble the more luxurious Mazda Millenia, the 626 is a stylish front-drive compact sedan that does everything well. It comes in three trim levels with a choice of two engines, coupled to either a 5-speed manual or a 4-speed automatic transmission. The base DX is touted as the price leader, but with the low price you have to take the 4-cylinder engine and few standard features. The top-of-the-line ES has more bells and whistles in addition to a V6 engine. A good compromise model is the LX: it's cheaper than the ES, yet offers many of its amenities.

These sedans provide room for five, along with either a high level of luxury and comfort. In spite of all the gimmicks, the 626 rates among the best midsize cars currently available on the market. Mazda's poor sales over the past few years will presumably generate substantial price discounting by mid-'99.

Cost analysis/alternatives: Get the cheapest '98 or '99 model; they're practically identical. When buying the '98, however, try to get a better-quality second-series version made in March 1998 or later. The standard 2.0L 4-banger competes with the Nissan Altima and Toyota Camry. Now that there's so little difference between the 626 and the upscale Millenia, consider the 626 as a cheaper alternative. **Recommended options:** Consider the LX for its V6 engine, traction control, and various power accessories. **Rebates:** Expect $1,500 rebates to clear out the '98s. **Destination charge:** $400. **Depreciation:** Faster than average. **Insurance cost:** Slightly higher than average. **Parts supply/cost:** Parts aren't difficult to find, and the cars are easily serviced by dealers or independents. CAA says that parts may cost twice as much as other cars in the 626 class. Keep in mind, though, that most Ford dealers have parts that can be used on Mazda products. This knowledge may be useful if your Mazda dealer is too greedy when it comes to parts prices (more than cost plus 50 percent). **Annual maintenance cost:** Less than average. **Warranty:** Bumper-to-bumper 3 years/80,000 km; powertrain 5 years/100,000 km; rust perforation 5 years/unlimited km. **Supplementary warranty:** Not necessary. **Highway/city fuel economy:** 6.6–9L/100 km. with the base 4-banger.

Quality/Reliability/Safety

Pro: Quality control: Few quality control complaints. Assembly and component quality are high. **Reliability:** Better than average. **Warranty performance:** Not generous, but fair. **Service bulletin problems:** Nothing published yet.

Con: NHTSA safety complaints/safety: Crash ratings may not apply to the redesigned '98 626. **Owner-reported problems:** Complex electronics cause trouble with age, air-conditioning defects, headgasket leaks, automatic transmission malfunctions, excessive hydraulic lifter noise, sunroof rattles, and premature wear-out of the front brakes.

Road Performance

Pro: Acceleration/torque: The V6 powerplant is a road burner with a fair amount of torque once it gets up to speed (0–100 km/h: 7.8 sec.). **Transmission:** The manual transmission and clutch work very well, and the 4-speed Overdrive automatic shifts smoothly most of the time. **Routine handling:** Nimble handling, and the steady, soft ride doesn't deteriorate as passenger load increases. Overall, a less jittery ride than previous versions. **Emergency handling:** Very good. The 626 is sure-footed, responds well to sudden corrections, and has little body roll or front-end plow when cornering under speed. **Steering:** Power steering is a bit light, but very accurate and predictable. **Braking:** Good braking (100–0 km/h: 119 ft.).

Con: The standard 2.0L 4-cylinder engine is smooth and peppy for urban duties, but it's at a disadvantage when pressed into more demanding service, like passing other vehicles on the highway or merging with fast-moving traffic. It works best with the manual gearbox. Equipped with the V6, power is channeled just a bit less smoothly than what you'd find with the Toyota Camry or Honda Accord. **Transmission:** Downshifts are sometimes jerky. Handling is also not quite as crisp and responsive as the Toyota and Honda competitors.

Comfort/Convenience

Pro: Standard equipment: Many standard performance and convenience features. **Driving position:** The front seats are exceptionally comfortable, and there's lots of head and leg room for tall drivers. **Controls and displays:** Well-positioned gauges and instruments. **Climate control:** Heating and ventilation are above reproach. **Entry/exit:** Easy as pie. **Interior space/comfort F/R:** The rear seat will hold two adults easily and comfortably. **Cargo space:** The hatchback version has a versatile cargo area and lots of handy storage bins. **Trunk/liftover:** Large trunk can be easily expanded through the use of the sedan's locking, folding rear seatbacks. **Quietness:** Body rigidity has been increased, making the car more comfortable and preventing many of the creaks and groans common to all small cars.

Con: The driver's seat may be too low for some. Excessive road noise in the passenger compartment.

COST				
List Price (negotiable)	**Residual Values** (months)			
	24	36	48	60
626 DX: $20,140 (16%)	$16,000	$12,000	$10,000	$8000

TECHNICAL DATA

Powertrain (front-drive)
Engines: 2.0L 4-cyl. (125 hp)
• 2.5L V6 (170 hp)
Transmissions: 5-speed man.
• 4-speed auto.
Dimensions
Passengers: 5
Height/length/width:
55.1/186.8/69.6 in.

Head room F/R: 39.2/37 in.
Leg room F/R: 43.6/34.6 in.
Wheelbase: 105.1 in.
Cargo capacity: 14.2 cu. ft.
Towing capacity: 2,000 lbs.
Fuel tank: 60L/reg.
Weight: 3,100 lbs.

SAFETY FEATURES

	Std.	Opt.
Anti-lock brakes	❏	■
Seatbelt pretensioners	—	—
Integrated child safety seat	—	—
Airbag cut-off switch	—	—
Depowered airbags	■	❏
Side airbags	—	—
Traction control	❏	■
Visibility (front/rear)	*****	*****
Crash protection D/P	****	*****
Crash protection (side) D/P	***	***
HLDI injury claims	Average	

Millenia

Millenia

RATING: Above Average. **Strong points:** Lots of power (S version), good handling and braking, comfortable ride, and sophisticated mechanical components. **Weak points:** Limited interior room and difficult rear seat access.

NEW FOR '99: No significant changes.

GENERAL COMMENTS: Despite its late entry into the luxury market—Lexus and Infiniti have had years to fortify their position—Millenia has been a hit, with surprisingly strong first-year sales.

Smaller than the Mazda 929, the front-drive Millenia carries the same 2.5L 170-hp V6 used by the 626. An optional 2.3L Miller-Cycle "S" 6-cylinder engine, although smaller than the base powerplant, still manages to pump out 210 horsepower. Both engines use a standard 4-speed automatic transmission.

As with all luxury cars, the Millenia comes with a wide array of standard features that would normally cost thousands of dollars more. Although billed as a five-passenger car, the middle occupant in the rear seat would be cramped and have to sit on a hump—a problem with which 929 owners are familiar.

Cost analysis/alternatives: Get the '99 model for the discounted MSRP. From a performance standpoint, the Camry V6, with its less complicated powertrain, outruns the Millenia; and the redesigned 626 gives you practically all the same features for less money. Other cars worth considering are the BMW 540i and 740i, Infiniti I30, Lexus ES 300, Mercedes-Benz E420, and Volvo S70 and S90 series. **Recommended options:** Traction control. The 4-Seasons Package is a must for leather seat heating. Get the dealer to change the limited spare tire for a full-service tire that can easily fit in the trunk well. Be wary of the sunroof option on the sedan if you're a tall driver; it takes away much-needed head room. **Rebates:** Instead of rebates, Mazda has announced hefty price cuts of $2,450 for the base model and over $5,000 on the Miller version. **Destination charge:** $600. **Depreciation:** Slower than average. **Insurance cost:** Higher than average. **Parts supply/cost:** Parts are frequently back-ordered and CAA says that Mazda parts are more expensive than parts for most other automakers. **Annual maintenance cost:** Average. **Warranty:** Bumper-to-bumper 3 years/80,000 km; powertrain 5 years/100,000 km; rust perforation 5 years/unlimited km. **Supplementary warranty:** Not necessary. **Highway/city fuel economy:** 8.3–12.3L/100 km with either engine.

Quality/Reliability/Safety

Pro: Quality control: Assembly and component quality are high. **Reliability:** No serious reliability problems noted. **Warranty performance:** Acceptable. **Owner-reported problems:** Nothing of any significance. **Service bulletin problems:** Nothing published, yet. **NHTSA safety complaints/safety:** No safety-related incidents have been recorded.

Con: Some complaints of poor servicing affecting reliability.

Road Performance

Pro: Acceleration/torque: The 170-hp V6 engine provides plenty of power in most driving situations, but the supercharged version is a real road burner (0–100 km/h: 8.3 sec.) that provides gobs of mid-range torque. **Routine handling:** Fun to drive due to the Millenia's crisp handling and comfortable ride, which doesn't deteriorate as passenger load increases. **Emergency handling:** Very good. Electronic traction control performs flawlessly. **Steering:** Smooth, precise steering. **Braking:** Relatively short braking distance without any fading after successive application (100–0 km/h: 130 ft.).

Con: Transmission: The Miller Cycle engine is a bit slow to get up to speed.

Comfort/Convenience

Pro: Standard equipment: Plenty of standard amenities. Great sound system. Firm, comfortable driver's seat has lots of control for height and tilt. **Climate control:** Works well with little noise. **Trunk/liftover:** Spacious trunk has a low liftover. **Quietness:** Very little engine or road noise intrudes into the interior. **Cargo space:** Above average storage space in the passenger compartment.

Con: Bland exterior styling. **Driving position:** Tall drivers may find head and leg room a bit limited. Insufficient thigh support with the bucket seats. **Controls and displays:** Controls aren't sufficiently lit. Radio controls aren't user-friendly. Erratic temperature control can't keep a consistent setting. **Entry/exit:** Narrow rear doors complicate rear seat access. **Interior space/comfort F/R:** Millenia's small interior offers less front head room and rear leg room than the 929 it replaced. Rear seating isn't very comfortable for three.

COST

List Price (negotiable)	Residual Values (months)			
	24	36	48	60
Base Millenia: $36,535 (28%)	$28,000	$22,000	$18,000	$14,000

TECHNICAL DATA

Powertrain (front-drive)
Engines: 2.5L V6 (170 hp)
2.3L V6 (210 hp)
Transmission: 4-speed auto.
Dimensions
Passengers: 5
Height/length/width:
54.9/189.8/69.7 in.

Head room F/R: 37.9/36.5 in.
Leg room F/R: 43.3/34.1 in.
Wheelbase: 108.3 in.
Cargo capacity: 13.3 cu. ft.
Towing capacity: 2,000 lbs.
Fuel tank: 68L/reg.
Weight: 3,400 lbs.

SAFETY FEATURES

	Std.	Opt.
Anti-lock brakes	■	❑
Seatbelt pretensioners	—	—
Integrated child safety seat	—	—
Airbag cut-off switch	—	—
Depowered airbags	■	❑
Side airbags	—	—
Traction control	❑	■
Visibility (front/rear)	*****	*****
Crash protection D/P	****	*****
Crash protection (side) D/P	N/A	
HLDI injury claims	Low	

MX-5 (Miata)

Miata

RATING: Recommended. Now that the RX-7s have been dropped, the Miata is Mazda's best roadster. **Strong points:** Good powertrain setup, exceptional handling, impressive braking, and a high resale value. **Weak points:** Limited passenger and cargo room, a firm ride, and an uncertain future.

NEW FOR '99: There was no '98 model, so everything is theoretically new.

GENERAL COMMENTS: The Miata is a stubby, rear-drive, two-seater sports car that combines new technology with old British roadster styling reminiscent of the Triumph, Austin-Healy, and Lotus Elan.

This is a fun car to drive, costing much less than other vehicles in its class. Built on a shortened 323 platform, the Miata is shorter than all other sports cars except the Porsche 911 (although it's almost 8 inches longer than the old Honda CRX). The 1.8L twin-cam 4-cylinder engine, borrowed from the Protegé, is coupled to a 5-speed manual gearbox, and the rear suspension is a copy of the RX-7's.

Cost analysis/alternatives: Other cars worth considering are the Ford Mustang, GM Camaro and Firebird, Honda Prelude, Nissan 240SX, and Toyota Celica. **Recommended options:** Anti-lock brakes, power steering, and a limited-slip differential. **Rebates:** $2,000–$3,500 on the '98s (which are really re-designated '97s); $1,500 on the '99s. **Destination charge:** $300. **Depreciation:** Much slower than average. **Insurance cost:** Higher than average. **Parts supply/cost:** Parts are easy to find, but CAA says that they cost more than average. **Annual maintenance cost:** Less than average. **Warranty:** Bumper-to-bumper 3 years/80,000 km; powertrain 5 years/100,000 km; rust perforation 5 years/unlimited km. **Supplementary warranty:** Not needed. **Highway/city fuel economy:** 7.4–10.2L/100 km.

Quality/Reliability/Safety

Pro: Quality control: Excellent workmanship and exceptional quality. **Reliability:** Nothing reported that would take these cars out of service. **Warranty performance:** Average, although a lot depends on dealer servicing. **Service bulletin problems:** Nothing published of any significance. **NHTSA safety complaints/safety:** Well-designed head restraints; if you must carry an infant, the Miata has a factory-installed airbag cutoff switch.

Con: Owner-reported problems: Owners complain that dealer servicing is still sub-par. Oil filter is hard to reach, replacement batteries are hard to find, and dirt and debris can clog up side door sill holes, allowing water to collect and corrosion to occur. Ask the dealer to drill larger drain holes. **Safety:** Shoulder belts may chafe your neck; seatbelt's low anchor causes the belt to pull down against your shoulder.

Road Performance

Pro: Acceleration/torque: Brisk acceleration with a good amount of low-end torque (0–100 km/h: 8.5 sec.). **Transmission:** Easy, precise throws with the manual and smooth, quiet shifting with the automatic. **Routine handling:** Lightness and 50/50 weight distribution make it an easy car to toss around corners without tossing your cookies. **Emergency handling:** No surprises. Performs emergency manoeuvres predictably and almost as quickly as the Porsche Boxster. Exceptionally responsive, with minimal body roll; the rigid chassis gives the car a solid feeling. **Steering:** Steering is crisp and predictable. **Braking:** Impressive braking performance on dry pavement with little brake fading after successive stops (100–0 km/h: 102 ft.).

Con: A 6-speed gearbox would be helpful in keep the noise level down. Although the ride is a bit choppy, it's not as harsh as previous versions. The rear end tends to swing out when cornering under speed.

Comfort/Convenience

Pro: Standard equipment: The base model is well equipped. The round dash air vents heighten the sports car image, giving the cockpit a 1960s British roadster allure. The convertible top is easily lowered from inside or outside of the car, and the optional hardtop is quite practical and easy to install. An innovative wind block flips up behind the rear seats. **Controls and displays:** Gauges are simple to comprehend and well-positioned. **Climate control:** Efficient, quiet heating and defrosting system is easy to adjust. **Entry/exit:** Not difficult once you get used to stepping down into your Miata. **Cargo space:** Storage areas include a relatively large locking glove compartment and centre console bin (with cupholder), net pouches behind the seats, and small map pockets in each door. **Trunk:** A low liftover makes for easy loading.

Con: Driving position: The steering wheel is set too close to the driver, isn't height-adjustable, and blocks your view of the ignition switch and power mirror control. Seats are set too low for short drivers. Unusually small inside door releases are mounted too far back to be accessed comfortably With the top in place, rear visibility is obstructed by the wide rear panels, the small rear window, and small side view mirrors. Small bucket seats give marginal lateral support and could use a bit more padding. **Interior space/comfort F/R:** Interior is a bit small for tall occupants, who must sit bolt upright when pushing their seat all the way back. Insufficient lower back and thigh support. Inadequate head and leg room for tall adults if you have large thighs, you may need a month at Weight Watchers to fit them between the steering wheel and seat cushion. **Cargo space:** Storage space for large objects is practically nonexistent; there's almost no room behind the rear seats. **Trunk/liftover:** Trunk is small and shallow. **Quietness:** Better get used to road, tire, and engine noise that increases as the Miata picks up speed.

COST

List Price (negotiable)	Residual Values (months)			
	24	36	48	60
Base Miata: $26,025 (21%)	$18,000	$15,000	$12,000	$10,000

TECHNICAL DATA

Powertrain (rear-drive)
Engine: 1.8L 4-cyl. (140 hp)
Transmissions: 5-speed man.
• 4-speed auto.
Dimensions
Passengers: 2
Height/length/width:
48.2/155.4/65.9 in.

Head room: 37.1 in.
Leg room: 42.7 in.
Wheelbase: 89.2 in.
Cargo capacity: 13.6 cu. ft.
Towing capacity: N/A
Fuel tank: 45L/reg.
Weight: 2,300 lbs.

SAFETY FEATURES

	Std.	Opt.
Anti-lock brakes	❏	■
Seatbelt pretensioners	—	—
Integrated child safety seat	—	—
Airbag cut-off switch	■	❏
Depowered airbags	■	❏
Side airbags	—	—
Traction control	❏	■
Visibility (front/rear)	*****	*
Crash protection D/P	****	***
Crash protection (side) D/P	N/A	
HLDI injury claims	Average	

MPV

MPV

RATING: Below Average. Outclassed by Chrysler, Ford, and Nissan. **Strong points:** Comfortable ride and easy handling, good driver's position, responsive steering. **Weak points:** Slow acceleration and braking, lots of interior wind noise and tire drumming, and less than impressive dealer servicing and head office support.

NEW FOR '99: No significant changes; next year it adopts front drive and will feature twin sliding doors. Rumour has it that Ford, which owns a quarter of Mazda, will force Mazda to drop the MPV and sell a re-badged Windstar, instead.

GENERAL COMMENTS: Mazda's only minivan quickly became a bestseller when it first came on the market, but during the past few years its popularity has fallen off. The competition is building better handling and more versatile minivans and selling them for less. The MPV offers seating for eight and easily handles a 4x8 sheet of plywood. In rear-drive mode, when equipped with the towing package, it can tow up to 4,300 pounds (1,935 kg).

  The MPV's innards are borrowed from the 929 luxury sedan, so it's not surprising that it handles quite well, although not as well as some of the front-drive competition. Overall, the MPV is a more expensive and less reliable challenger to the Chrysler Caravan and Ford Villager and Windstar.

Cost analysis/alternatives: Get the cheapest '98 or '99 model; they're practically identical. When buying the '98, however, try to get a better-quality second-series version made in March 1998 or later. Other mini-vans worth considering are the Chrysler Caravan/Voyager, Honda Odyssey, Mercury Villager/Nissan Quest, and the Toyota Sienna. **Recommended options:** Power seat adjustment, windows and door locks, and a rear AC/heater. **Rebates:** $2,000–$3,500 to clear out the

1998 models. **Destination charge and PDI:** $900. **Depreciation:** Worse than average. **Insurance cost:** Higher than average. **Annual maintenance cost:** Much higher than average. **Parts supply/cost:** Parts are often backordered due to the weak dealer network outside major centres. According to CAA, Mazda parts cost more than average. **Warranty:** Bumper-to-bumper 3 years/80,000 km; powertrain 5 years/100,000 km; rust perforation 5 years/unlimited mileage. **Supplementary warranty:** An extended warranty is worth having, particularly now that Mazda's head office support has been dramatically downsized. **Highway/city fuel economy:** *2WD*: 10.2–14.3L/100 km; *4WD*: 12.1–16.6L/100 km.

Quality/Reliability/Safety

Pro: Quality control: High-quality workmanship and rugged construction. **Service bulletin problems:** Nothing important.

Con: Warranty performance: Inadequate base warranty. Servicing has deteriorated a great deal over the past few years. **Reliability:** Early MPV models experienced expensive transmission failures due to inadequate cooling, and some ABS malfunctions caused by water infiltration. Rear-wheel ABS compares poorly with 4-wheel ABS performance. **Owner-reported problems:** Owners have complained about excessive oil consumption, premature front brake wear, AC leaks, and paint discolouration and peeling. **NHTSA safety complaints/safety:** AC failure; rough idle; driver-side airbag failed to deploy; the electric rear windows were opened while cruising, causing the change in air pressure to make the vehicle shake violently.

Road Performance

Pro: Acceleration/torque: Slow acceleration (0–100 km/h: 11.6 sec.). The base 6-cylinder engine, borrowed from the 929, provides adequate power in all gear ranges, considering the MPV's heft. Rear-drive setup makes for easy load carrying and trailer towing. **Transmission:** The versatile 4X4 Multi-Mode System goes from 2WD to 4WD at the touch of a button on the column shifter. Another button locks up the centre differential when needed to drive in deep snow or mud. Also performs well on dry pavement. Overdrive can be locked out at the touch of a switch. **Routine handling:** Car-like performance. Tracks well and has quick, precise steering response.

Con: Automatic transmission sometimes shifts roughly. The automatic 4-speed gearbox takes its toll on fuel economy. Low ground clearance limits off-road excursions. **Emergency handling:** This minivan's highway performance doesn't inspire confidence, especially on wet roads. (*Consumer Reports* recommends that the all-wheel drive be engaged all the time for safe driving.) The rear end tends to swing out when cornering under speed. **Braking:** Unacceptable braking is characterized by long stops (100–0 km/h: 143 ft.) and loss of directional control, unusual for a vehicle with ABS on all four wheels.

Comfort/Convenience

Pro: Standard equipment: Lots of standard features, including tilt steering and 4-wheel ABS. **Driving position:** Driver sits comfortably high with excellent fore and aft visibility. **Controls and displays:** Instrumentation on the car-like dash is easy to read, and all controls are within easy reach. **Climate control:** Excellent heating/defrosting/ventilation system. **Entry/exit:** Easy entry/exit up front. Centre bench seat flips forward to become a table. **Interior space/comfort F/R:** The comfortable, plush interior seats seven or eight and offers many storage areas. Front seats have lots of rearward travel to maximize leg room. Third row seats are roomier than the second row, but leg room is more restricted. Rear door windows roll all the way down. **Cargo space:** Adequate. The swing-out side door is easier to operate and less complicated to service than a sliding door. **Trunk/liftover:** Easy to load or unload.

Con: Interior space/comfort F/R: The MPV is less roomy than some other minivans, mainly because of thick walls and a non-removable middle seat that rob the interior of space. The 2-3-3 seating package is an attempt to squeeze eight people into a space adequate for only seven. Limited access and leg room for rear seat passengers. Swing-out side door hampers access in tight places. **Cargo space:** Cargo room is sacrificed with the hard-to-remove third seat in place. **Quietness:** Excessive engine, wind, and road noise.

COST				
List Price (very negotiable)	**Residual Values** (months)			
	24	36	48	60
Base: $25,199 (21%)	$18,000	$13,000	$11,000	$9000

TECHNICAL DATA	
Powertrain (rear-drive)	Height/length/width:
in. Engine: 3.0L V6 (155 hp)	68.9/183.5/71.9 in.
Wheelbase: 110 in.	Leg room F: 40.4/R1: 33.4/R2: 34.2
Transmission:	Head room F: 40/R1: 39.7/R2: 36.9 in.
• 4-speed auto.	Cargo capacity: 11.1 cu. ft.
Dimensions	Towing capacity: 3,000 lbs.
Passengers: 8	Fuel tank: 74L/reg.
	Weight: 3,800 lbs.

SAFETY FEATURES		
	Std.	**Opt.**
Anti-lock brakes	■	❑
Seatbelt pretensioners	—	—
Integrated child safety seat	—	—

Airbag cut-off switch	—	—
Depowered airbags	■	❑
Side airbags	—	—
Traction control	—	—
Visibility (front/rear)	*****	*****
Crash protection D/P	****	****
Crash protection (side) D/P	N/A	
HLDI injury claims	High	

NISSAN

Nissan sales have been steady but not impressive. Of Nissan's six models—three cars and three trucks—the Quest is the only one that returns this year with major changes. Slumping Nissan sales have improved slightly going into the fall sales period, due mainly to the all-new Infiniti G20. The automaker has expanded its position in the mid-size family sedan market with the Altima, a compact that fits in between the Sentra and Maxima. It's also making inroads into the minivan niche with its Quest, a co-venture with Mercury. Unfortunately, the company is saddled with a debt of about 3 trillion yen ($37.2 billion), a larger debt load than that of the U.S. Big Three combined. This debt hasn't been reduced much by Nissan's unsuccessful attempt to buy market share by offering rebates and free air conditioning and automatic transmissions. The company has also been hurt by the devaluation of the Mexican peso. It can't afford to expand beyond its Tennessee plant, which is already running at full capacity.

Nissan intends to gain market share and increase profits by taking four simple steps: cut the number of variations per model; slow down the model-change race to better amortize development costs; standardize parts so that 55 percent will be interchangeable; and offer innovative six-year leasing plans to bolster sales and service.

The 1999 models return this year relatively unchanged; again, this year, Nissan is standing pat on prices, pushing its comprehensive warranty, and using innovative long-term leasing programs to regain market share.

Sentra, 200SX ('98)

Sentra

RATING: Average, primarily for city commuting. **Strong points:** Cheap to buy and run, acceptable ride and handling, and good quality control. 2.0L-equipped versions provide much better acceleration, handling, and ride. **Weak points:** Base engine is sluggish, poor braking without ABS, poor high-speed handling, limited rear passenger room, and excessive engine, tire, and road noise.

NEW FOR '99: Except for the GXE's sportier front end, upgraded remote keyless entry, and additional standard features, the Sentra returns unchanged this year. A 2.0L 140-hp SE model will be added by year's end. The 200SX has been dropped.

GENERAL COMMENTS: Nissan redesigned the Sentra and decided to market a two-door version of the car as the sporty 200SX, which is more expensive and comes loaded with many features that are optional on the Sentra, or simply not available. Three body styles are offered: a two-door coupe, a three-door hatchback, and a four-door sedan. Unlike many bare-bones economy cars, entry-level Sentras offer solid, bare-bones, but dependable motoring at little cost. The 200SX was sold as the Sentra coupe in the U.S.; it sits on the Sentra sedan's wheelbase and is a bit wider than the smaller Canadian coupe. All base models are powered by an anemic 1.6L 115-hp 16-valve 4-cylinder engine. A sporty new SE model carries the same lively 2.0L 4-banger that powers the 200SX SE-R.

Cost analysis/alternatives: Either a '98 or identical '99 will do, but the discontinued '98s are the most susceptible to deep discounting. Keep in mind that the base price is very negotiable. Other worthwhile cars to consider are the Ford Escort, GM Cavalier and Sunfire, Honda Civic, Mazda Protegé, and Toyota Tercel. Fully equipped Sentras can often be bought for less than many other Japanese subcompacts, making them particularly good buys. **Recommended options:** Spend extra money for anti-lock brakes and better-grade, quieter tires. **Rebates:** $2,000 to clear out the leftover '98s. **Depreciation:** Average. **Insurance cost:** Average. **Parts supply/cost:** Inexpensive parts can be found practically anywhere. **Annual maintenance cost:** Less than average. Uncluttered under-hood layout makes servicing easy. **Warranty:** Bumper-to-bumper 3 years/80,000 km; powertrain 5 years/100,000 km; rust perforation 5 years/unlimited km. **Supplementary warranty:** Not needed. **Highway/ city fuel economy:** 6–8.5L/100 km with a manual transmission, and about a half-litre more with an automatic.

Quality/Reliability/Safety

Pro: Quality control: Sentras are almost trouble-free. First-class body assembly. **Reliability:** Overall reliability is better than average. **Service bulletin problems:** Nothing published, yet. **Warranty performance:** Average.

Con: Owner-reported problems: Some reports of 1.6L engine cylinder head and gasket failures. Clutch, exhaust system, and fuel system problems are fairly common after the first three years. Front brakes aren't very durable either. **NHTSA safety complaints/safety:** Airbag failed to deploy; ABS brake failure. Some '98 models have been recalled to prevent premature windshield wiper failure.

Road Performance

Pro: Acceleration/torque: The 2.0L 4-cylinder provides plenty of power for all driving situations. **Transmission:** Both manual and automatic transmissions shift very smoothly under normal circumstances. **Routine handling:** Good manoeuvrability around town. Firm but well-mannered ride on most roads. **Steering:** The steering is direct and predictable.

Con: The base 1.5L is woefully inadequate for highway driving. Engine surges in stop-and-go traffic. Full-throttle shifting is jerky at times. **Emergency handling:** High-speed handling is a bit sloppy, and emergency handling is sluggish. Very sensitive to side winds. Standard tires perform poorly while cornering. **Braking:** Unacceptably long braking distances (100–0 km/h: 147 ft.).

Comfort/Convenience

Pro: Driving position: Spartan, though acceptable instruments and controls. Seats a bit thinly padded. Hard to see through the rear quarter panels. **Controls and displays:** Easy-to-read dash gauges and convenient controls. Neatly finished interior. **Climate control:** Efficient and uncomplicated heating, defrosting, and ventilation. **Cargo space:** Average for this size car. **Trunk/liftover:** Spacious trunk has a low liftover.

Con: Standard equipment: Just the bare necessities, in keeping with this car's entry-level pretensions. Antiquated, boxy styling; the 200SX's spoiler looks cheap and silly. Rear vision is partially blocked by the rear pillars on the coupe. **Entry/exit:** Small rear door make access a bit difficult. **Interior space/comfort F/R:** Don't believe Nissan's claim of five-passenger seating: the four-door sedan only accommodates four people comfortably. The front driver's seat is set a bit too low. Rear seating is uncomfortable, especially with the coupe. All seats could use extra padding. **Entry/exit:** It's a chore getting in and out of the rear seat on two-door models. **Quietness:** Excessive road and engine noise in the passenger compartment.

COST

List Price (negotiable)	Residual Values (months)			
	24	**36**	**48**	**60**
Base Sentra: $14,998 (12%)	$11,000	$9000	$7500	$6500
'98 200SX: $17,598 (14%)	$13,000	$10,500	$9000	$8000

TECHNICAL DATA

Powertrain (front-drive)
Engines: 1.6L 4-cyl. (115 hp)
• 2.0L 4-cyl. (140 hp)
Transmissions: 5-speed man.
• 4-speed auto.
Dimensions
Passengers: 5
Height/length/width:
54.5/170.1/66.6 in.

Head room F/R: 39.1/36.5 in.
Leg room F/R: 42.3/32.4 in.
Wheelbase: 99.8 in.
Cargo capacity: 10.7 cu. ft.
Towing capacity: 1,000 lbs.
Fuel tank: 50L/reg.
Weight: 2,450 lbs.

SAFETY FEATURES

	Std.	Opt.
Anti-lock brakes	❑	■
Seatbelt pretensioners	—	—
Integrated child safety seat	—	—
Airbag cut-off switch	—	—
Depowered airbags	■	❑
Side airbags	—	—
Traction control	—	—
Visibility (front/rear)	*****	*****
'98 200SX	*****	*
Crash protection D/P	***	****
'98 200SX	*****	****
Crash protection (side) D/P	***	***
HLDI injury claims	High	

Altima

Altima

RATING: Average. **Strong points:** Handles well, good braking, reliable, and better than average craftsmanship. **Weak points:** Sluggish acceleration, unacceptable automatic transmission performance, limited rear seat room.

NEW FOR '99: Insignificant changes in trim level. Power driver seat standard on the SE.

GENERAL COMMENTS: Nissan's latest midsize sedan, this yuppie-mobile is a four-door, front-drive, 4-cylinder aimed at Chrysler's LH series and GM's best-selling Cavalier/Sunfire. The engine is a spinoff of the 240SX 16-valve 2.4L 4-banger that delivers 150 hp.

Cost analysis/alternatives: Either a '98 or identical '99 will do; choose whichever is cheapest. Although the SE gives the sportiest performance, the less-expensive GXE is the better deal. Other cars worth considering are the Honda Accord, Mazda 626, and Toyota Camry. **Recommended options:** Nissan tends to option-load its Altimas, forcing you to take a number of unwanted, unnecessary optional features along with the one you want. Forget the optional automatic transmission; it's not refined enough for pleasurable shifting. **Rebates:** $2,000 to clear out the leftover '98s. **Destination charge:** $500. **Depreciation:** A bit slower than average. **Insurance cost:** Higher than average. **Parts supply/cost:** Parts are easy to find, but CAA says that dealer prices can be steep. Independent suppliers often sell them at discount prices. **Annual maintenance cost:** Less than average. Uncluttered underhood layout makes servicing easy. **Warranty:** Bumper-to-bumper 3 years/80,000 km; powertrain 5 years/100,000 km; rust perforation 5 years/unlimited km. **Supplementary warranty:** Not needed. **Highway/city fuel economy:** 7.1–9.9L/100 km with the manual transmission and 8–11.5L/100 km with an automatic.

Quality/Reliability/Safety

Pro: Quality control: Good body assembly and powertrain components. **Reliability:** No reliability problems have been reported. **Warranty performance:** Average. Nissan staffers aren't particularly generous in handling premature brake wear complaints. **Service bulletin problems:** Nothing published, yet.

Con: Owner-reported problems: Minor electrical glitches and excessive brake wear, noise, and pulsations. **NHTSA safety complaints/safety:** Fire ignited in fuse box area; malfunctioning power door locks re-lock doors; rear seatbelts malfunction; front passenger shoulder/lapbelt won't pull out of seatbelt assembly; airbags failed to deploy; the driver hit a telephone pole head-on and neither airbag deployed; tiny horn buttons may be hard to locate in an emergency. Please note that Nissan has recalled the '98 Altima to correct malfunctioning rear seatbelt buckles.

Road Performance

Pro: Routine handling: Much improved, thanks to this year's suspension upgrade. Good manoeuvrability around town, and highway cruising is less jarring. **Emergency handling:** The Altima's sporty handling is way overrated, but it does handle sudden corrections quite well, if with just a bit too much body roll. **Steering:** Responsive, with good road feedback. **Braking:** Better than average (100–0 km/h: 120 ft.).

Con: Acceleration/torque: Slow acceleration (0–100 km/h: 9.8 sec.). Engine performance is smoother this year, but it's still noisy and rough-running. The 4-banger has insufficient top-end torque and gets buzzier the more it's pushed. This car cries out for a V6 like the one used in the Maxima. **Transmission:** The automatic transmission hesitates, and then shifts abruptly. The 5-speed manual transmission is sloppy. The more softly sprung suspension results in poor body control when passing over highway humps and dips.

Comfort/Convenience

Pro: Standard equipment: Fairly well-appointed. Infiniti J30 styling. **Controls and displays:** A major improvement. User-friendly controls, and instruments are easy to read and understand. **Interior space/ Comfort F/R:** Comfortable, supportive seats. Up front, there's good all-round head room and leg room. **Climate control:** Good heating, defrosting, and ventilation. **Cargo space:** Acceptable. Trunk pass-through allows for storage of long items. **Trunk/liftover:** Average size with a low sill to facilitate loading.

Con: Driving position: Not easy to get used to. Drivers may find that the pedals are set too close and the steering wheel is too far away. Rear roof pillars and high-tail styling obstruct rear/side visibility. **Interior space/comfort F/R:** The small cabin seats only four, with limited rear leg room. Although Nissan enlarged the interior, rear space hasn't been improved. **Entry/exit:** Rear seat access is difficult to master due to the slanted roof pillars, inward-curving door frames, and narrow clearance. **Quietness:** Too much engine, road, and tire noise intrudes into the passenger compartment. Trunk loading is made difficult by the wide bumper shelf; trunk lid hinges can damage cargo.

COST

List Price (very negotiable)	Residual Values (months)			
	24	36	48	60
Altima XE: $19,895(15%)	$14,000	$11,000	$9000	$7500

TECHNICAL DATA

Powertrain (front-drive)
Engine: 2.4L 4-cyl. (150 hp)
Transmissions: 5-speed man.
• 4-speed auto.
Dimensions
Passengers: 5
Height/length/width:
55.9/183.5/69 in.

Head room F/R: 39.4/37.7 in.
Leg room F/R: 42/33.9 in.
Wheelbase: 103.1 in.
Cargo capacity: 14 cu. ft.
Towing capacity: N/A
Fuel tank: 60L/reg.
Weight: 3,050 lbs.

SAFETY FEATURES

	Std.	Opt.
Anti-lock brakes	❏	■
Seatbelt pretensioners	—	—
Integrated child safety seat	—	—
Airbag cut-off switch	—	—
Depowered airbags	■	❏
Side airbags	—	—
Traction control	—	—
Visibility (front/rear)	*****	*****
Crash protection D/P	***	**
Crash protection (side) D/P	***	***
HLDI injury claims	High	

240SX ('98)

240SX

RATING: Above Average. **Strong points:** Sporty steering and handling, firm but comfortable ride, and better than average quality control. **Weak points:** Excessive engine noise and limited rear passenger and cargo room.

NEW FOR '99: Discontinued; there won't be a '99 model year.

GENERAL COMMENTS: This rear-drive sporty coupe has moved away from its sports car heritage toward what Nissan describes as a luxury sports coupe. Translation: you can get some standard luxury features to compensate for the engine's limited power range when compared to the cheaper Mustang and Camaro rear-drives.

Cost analysis/alternatives: The '98 model is a bargain if the price drops low enough; try for a 20 percent discount. Other cars worth considering are the '98 Eagle Talon, Ford Mustang, GM Camaro and Firebird, Honda Prelude, Mazda Miata, and Toyota Celica. **Recommended options:** Anti-lock brakes and theft deterrent system. **Rebates:** $2,000 to clear out the leftover '98s. **Destination charge:** $500. **Depreciation:** Slower than average. **Insurance cost:** Higher than average. **Parts supply/cost:** No problem finding reasonably priced parts. **Annual maintenance cost:** Lower than average. **Warranty:** Bumper-to-bumper 3 years/80,000 km; powertrain 5 years/100,000 km; rust perforation 5 years/unlimited km. **Supplementary warranty:** Not needed. **Highway/city fuel economy:** 7.8–10.6L/100 km.

Quality/Reliability/Safety

Pro: Quality control: Much better than average; excellent fit and finish. **Reliability:** Nothing reported that would take these cars out of service.

Warranty performance: Owners report that their claims are handled in a fair and efficient manner. **Service bulletin problems:** Nothing published, yet. **NHTSA safety complaints/safety:** No incidents recorded.

Con: Owner-reported problems: Reports of numerous electrical problems causing hard-to-diagnose powertrain, AC, and radio malfunctions.

Road Performance

Pro: Acceleration/torque: Brisk acceleration. **Transmission:** The 5-speed manual transmission shifts with minimal effort. **Routine handling:** Exceptional handling and a surprisingly comfortable ride that's not a kidney-pounder and doesn't deteriorate as the roadway roughens or passengers are added. **Emergency handling:** Emergency manoeuvres are a breeze. There's little body roll, lots of control, and sudden corrections don't throw the car off track. Hard acceleration produces no torque steer, which is more characteristic of front-drives. **Steering:** Steering is direct, predictable, and transmits lots of road feel.

Con: Engine loses torque in the higher gear ranges, producing an unimpressive 0–100 km/h acceleration time of 8.5 seconds. It also runs roughly when hitting the 2,500–3,500 rpm range. The automatic transmission compromises the 240SX's sportiness. Rear-drive layout makes the car hard to control on icy, wet roads because the rear end tends to suddenly swing out upon hard acceleration. **Braking:** Not impressive (100–0 km/h: 137 ft.).

Comfort/Convenience

Pro: Standard equipment: Well-appointed interior is comfortable, with elegance nicely complementing sportiness. **Driving position:** Very good. Intimate cockpit has everything within easy reach. Large windows and thin side pillars give the driver an excellent view of the road. **Controls and displays:** Wrap-around dash houses easily read and accessed instruments and controls. Comfortable front seats, with plenty of head and leg room. **Climate control:** Efficient, quiet, and uncomplicated. **Trunk/liftover:** Low trunk liftover facilitates loading.

Con: Entry/exit: It's nearly impossible to climb in or out of the rear seat. **Interior space/comfort F/R:** Rear seating is an oxymoron; it's a torture chamber for the average-sized adult. **Cargo space:** Very limited. **Trunk/liftover:** Extremely small trunk barely holds a bag of groceries. **Quietness:** Engine is noisy when pushed, and too much road noise invades the interior.

COST				
List Price (very negotiable)	**Residual Values** (months)			
	24	36	48	60
Base '98 240SX: $26,698 (22%)	$16,000	$13,000	$11,000	$9000

TECHNICAL DATA

Powertrain (rear-drive)
Engine: 2.4L 4-cyl. (155 hp)
Transmissions: 5-speed man.
• 4-speed auto.
Dimensions
Passengers: 5
Height/length/width:
51/177.2/68.1 in.

Head room F/R: 38.3/34.3 in.
Leg room F/R: 42.6/20.9 in.
Wheelbase: 99.4 in.
Cargo capacity: 8.6 cu. ft.
Towing capacity: N/A
Fuel tank: 65L/premium
Weight: 2,800 lbs.

SAFETY FEATURES

	Std.	Opt.
Anti-lock brakes	❑	■
Seatbelt pretensioners	—	—
Integrated child safety seat	—	—
Airbag cut-off switch	—	—
Depowered airbags	■	❑
Side airbags	—	—
Traction control	—	—
Visibility (front/rear)	*****	*****
Crash protection D/P	***	****
Crash protection (side) D/P	N/A	
HLDI injury claims	High	

Maxima

Maxima

RATING: Recommended. A high-quality, reasonably priced luxury sedan that's hidden by all the Infiniti hype. **Strong points:** Impressive powertrain performance, comfortable ride, pleasant handling, and above average reliability. **Weak points:** Delayed, jerky downshifts with the automatic transmission, cramped rear seating, poor fuel economy, and missing some standard safety and convenience features like ABS and side airbags.

NEW FOR '99: Anti-theft system with an ignition cut-off. Standard traction control on models with automatic transmission and ABS. Debut of an ES (EuroSport) model that includes alloy wheels, ABS, traction control (with automatic), anti-theft system, and keyless remote entry.

GENERAL COMMENTS: The front-wheel drive Maxima soldiers on as Nissan's luxury flagship, one step removed from the briefly discontinued and recently resuscitated Infiniti G20. The 190-hp 24-valve DOHC V6 is a real dazzler. With its impressive array of standard features, the Maxima becomes a full-fledged member of what Nissan calls the "executive sports" luxury sedan class that includes the base Infiniti and Lexus models, as well as European entries like the Volvo 900/S90, Audis, and smaller BMWs. In fact, the Maxima "borrowed" its aerodynamic shape from BMW's 5-series.

There's not much risk involved in buying a Maxima; it's a pleasure to drive and much cheaper than most of the competition.

Cost analysis/alternatives: Get the '99 model for the upgrades; consider a '98 model only if the price is cut 15 percent or more. Other cars worthy of consideration are the BMW 3-series; Ford Taurus and Sable, Crown Victoria, and Grand Marquis; Lexus ES 300; Mazda Millenia; Toyota Camry and Avalon; and Volvo S70 and S90 series. **Recommended options:** Side airbags, anti-lock brakes and the form-fitting SE seats. The optional sonar suspension found on the GXE is an unnecessary gadget; it will give the average mechanic nightmares. Be wary of the sunroof option (it eats up head room) and don't buy the optional instrument panel: it's distracting, confusing, and more suitable to a video arcade than a luxury automobile. **Rebates:** $2,000 to clear out the leftover '98s. **Destination charge:** $500. **Depreciation:** Average. **Insurance cost:** Higher than average. **Parts supply/cost:** Reasonably priced parts aren't hard to find from dealers or independent suppliers. **Annual maintenance cost:** Less than average. **Warranty:** Bumper-to-bumper 3 years/80,000 km; powertrain 5 years/100,000 km; rust perforation 5 years/unlimited km. **Supplementary warranty:** Not needed. **Highway/city fuel economy:** 8.2–10.9L/100 km.

Quality/Reliability/Safety

Pro: Quality control: Outstanding. **Reliability:** Maximas have always had an impressive reliability history. **Warranty performance:** Acceptable most of the time, although the company's claims handlers can be rather obtuse in interpreting Nissan's warranty obligations to Maxima owners. (I'm reminded of the ongoing battle that some customers are waging in order to get the company to pay for exhaust manifold components.) **Service bulletin problems:** Nothing published, yet.

Con: Owner-reported problems: Scattered reports of automatic-transmission and electrical-system malfunctions, as well as paint defects (paint chips easily). **NHTSA safety complaints/safety:** While driving the front wheels locked up, causing extensive undercarriage damage; the trunk lid and latch are hazardous when raised.

Road Performance

Pro: Acceleration/torque: The powerful and smooth standard V6 engine provides substantial power without excessive noise (0–100 km/h: 8.7 sec.). **Transmission:** The smooth-shifting automatic transmission has an Auto position that switches the transmission from normal to power mode when accelerating. It also has a switch to let you lock out fourth gear to assist in trailer towing and to prevent frequent gear changes over hilly terrain. The standard 5-speed manual gearbox has a good shift linkage. **Routine handling:** Very good, with lots of control. The ride is fairly firm but comfortable, due to the refined suspension that handles rough roads well if the car is lightly loaded. **Emergency handling:** A bit slow, but well controlled. **Steering:** Accurate and predictable. **Braking:** Acceptable braking without ABS (100–0 km/h: 131 ft.).

Con: Engine loses much of its torque after reaching 100 km/h. Delayed, jerky, automatic transmission downshifts. The power steering doesn't transmit road feel very well.

Comfort/Convenience

Pro: Impressive theft-deterrent system sounds an alarm, flashes the lights, and disables the car if the vehicle is disturbed. The system is automatically armed whenever the Maxima's doors are locked with a key. **Driving position:** Very good. Firm, supportive, and comfortable front seating, plenty of head and leg room, and good all-around visibility. **Controls and displays:** Although some controls are a bit fussy, the dashboard is designed well, with easily read analogue gauges that don't wash out in sunlight. **Climate control:** Efficient and quiet. **Entry/exit:** Easy front and rear access. **Cargo space:** Lots of little storage bins for odds and ends. **Trunk/liftover:** Trunk has a low liftover to facilitate loading. **Quietness:** Much improved this year, with little wind and road noise invading the passenger compartment.

Con: Rear visibility is blocked by rear-side pillars. **Standard equipment:** Disappointing. High-tech luxury interior with emphasis on electronic gadgets. Many safety and convenience features that are standard on other luxury cars are missing from the Maxima. **Interior space/ comfort F/R:** Only two adults will fit comfortably in the rear. Low, flat seats give inadequate thigh support, and obtrusive side wing bolsters push passengers into the middle. Head restraints in the rear are too low for average-sized adults. **Trunk/liftover:** The trunk isn't very deep.

COST

List Price (negotiable)	Residual Values (months)			
	24	**36**	**48**	**60**
Maxima GXE: $28,598 (23%)	$23,000	$18,000	$15,000	$13,000

TECHNICAL DATA

Powertrain (rear-drive)
Engines: 3.0L V6 (190 hp)
Transmissions: 5-speed man.
• 4-speed auto.
Dimensions
Passengers: 5
Height/length/width:
55.7/187.7/69.7 in.

Head room F/R: 40.1/37.4 in.
Leg room F/R: 43.9/34.3 in.
Wheelbase: 106.3 in.
Cargo capacity: 14.5 cu. ft.
Towing capacity: N/A
Fuel tank: 70L/reg.
Weight: 3,050 lbs.

SAFETY FEATURES

	Std.	Opt.
Anti-lock brakes	❏	■
Seatbelt pretensioners	—	—
Integrated child safety seat	—	—
Airbag cut-off switch	—	—
Depowered airbags	■	❏
Side airbags	❏	■
Traction control	■	■
Visibility (front/rear)	*****	*****
Crash protection D/P	****	**
Crash protection (side) D/P	****	***
HLDI injury claims	Average	

SUBARU

Subaru's overall product lineup for 1999 reinforces the company's return to its four-wheel drive roots with emphasis put on its Legacy and Impreza 4X4 lineup as Outbacks. (Half of all Legacys sold are Outbacks.) Two years ago, the Legacy came out with its 2.5L GT all-wheel drive sporting sedan and wagon, and this year the Impreza and Legacy line get additional muscle with their own 2.5L SOHC engine that squeezes out a bit more performance from what is admittedly a limited range of engines. This year, Subaru will continue to tap the sport-utility craze through lower prices and by offering a greater variety of AWD vehicles. Other refinements for 1999: a minor facelift and smoother shifting manual and automatic transmissions.

Are Subarus good buys? Devotees will insist that there's no other car as versatile, and the manufacturer is justifiably proud of the high J. D. Power owner satisfaction rating earned in the U.S. Canadian owners, on the other hand, are not all that satisfied with the company's weak dealer network and spotty servicing.

A word of warning: *Consumer Reports* says that the Outback upgrade isn't worth the extra thousands you'll pay. They point out that Subaru's ads are misleading when they show Paul Hogan zipping around off-road. They also say that handling isn't as competent as that of the regular Legacy (something to do with the higher centre of gravity, no doubt).

Of course, most Subaru owners could care less about the Outback's off-road prowess; only 5 percent will ever use their Subaru for that purpose. The other 95 percent just like knowing they have the option of going wherever they please, whenever they please.

Impreza

Impreza

RATING: Above Average. If you don't need the AWD capability, you're wasting your money. **Strong points:** One of the most refined and reliable AWD drivetrains you'll find. Standard ABS (Outback Sport, 2.5 RS), acceleration (2.5 RS) excellent handling, lots of storage space, and better than average quality control. **Weak points:** 2.2L engine has little reserve power for highway cruising; both engines are rough-running and noisy; limited rear seat room; difficult entry/exit, and very dealer-dependent for parts and servicing.

NEW FOR '99: New, torquier engines and a minor facelift.

GENERAL COMMENTS: The full-time four-wheel drive Impreza is essentially a shorter Legacy with additional convenience features and a bit more interior room than the discontinued Loyale. It comes as a two-door coupe, a four-door sedan, a wagon that resembles the old American Motors Pacer and, *surprise,* an Outback Sport wagon also powered by the 2.2L engine and dressed more aggressively in GT cladding.

The base engine is a peppy 2.2L 110-hp 4-cylinder, but the optional 2.5L powerplant provides an extra dose of power for highway passing and additional torque when traversing rough or hazardous terrain. Buyers may choose either a 5-speed manual or a 4-speed automatic transmission.

Cost analysis/alternatives: Get the '99 model for the engine and body upgrades. Sorry, but I can't think of a single 4X4 wagon competitor in this price range I could recommend. Front-drives worth looking at: Ford Escort, Honda Civic, Mazda Protegé, and the Toyota Corolla. **Recommended options:** Anti-lock brakes. The RS version's safety and performance upgrades are well worth the extra cost. **Rebates:** $500–$1,000 rebates to clear out the '98 models; $500 for the '99s. Matching dealer incentives are also applicable. **Destination charge:** $500. **Depreciation:** Slower than average. **Insurance cost:** Higher than average. **Parts supply/cost:** Parts aren't easy to find and can be costly. **Annual maintenance cost:** Higher than average. Mediocre, expensive servicing is hard to overcome because independent garages can't service key 4X4 powertrain components. **Warranty:** Bumper-to-bumper 3 years/60,000 km; powertrain 5 years/100,000 km; rust perforation 5 years/unlimited km. **Supplementary warranty:** A good idea. **Highway/city fuel economy:** 7.3–9.8L/100 km with the 2.2L engine.

Quality/Reliability/Safety

Pro: Quality control: Better than average. Above average quality mechanical components. **Reliability:** Powertrain components should be durable, and there should be few mechanical problems that would take these Subarus out of service. **Warranty performance:** Base warranty is fairly applied, but servicing quality is spotty. Subaru warranty claims processing can be slow at times. **Service bulletin problems:** Nothing significant. **Safety:** Huge, fold-away side mirrors.

Con: Body panel and trim fit and finish is inconsistent. **Owner-reported problems:** Poor engine idling, frequent cold weather stalling, manual transmission malfunctions, premature exhaust system rust-out and brake wear, minor electrical short circuits, catalytic converter failures, and paint peeling. **NHTSA safety complaints:** Driver burned from airbag deployment.

Road Performance

Pro: The 2.5L is the engine of choice. It's smooth and powerful with lots of low-end torque if you really need to go off-roading. The 2.2L engine is quite peppy with a manual gearbox when travelling over level terrain or darting in and out of city traffic. **Transmission:** The automatic transmission shifts smoothly. The all-wheel drive system is a boon for people who often need extra traction, and it works well with either a manual or automatic transmission. The manual transmission's "hill holder" clutch prevents the car from rolling backwards when starting out. **Routine handling:** Smooth and nimble. Hurtles through corners effortlessly with a flat, solid stance and plenty of grip. **Emergency handling:** Better than some sport-utilities. Tight cornering at highway speeds is done with minimal body lean and no loss of control. **Steering:** Precise and predictable. Average braking (100–0 km/h: 133 ft.).

Con: Acceleration/torque: The 2.2L lacks sufficient mid-range torque to traverse hilly terrain without straining. When harnessed to an automatic transmission, it quickly loses steam. Uncomfortable ride with a full load. Larger tires would improve handling. Non-assisted steering requires maximum effort when parking. **Braking:** Barely adequate with the L models. Non-ABS braking may lead to loss of directional stability that causes the car to spin out of control.

Comfort/Convenience

Pro: Standard equipment: Well-appointed base models have a nice array of standard safety and convenience features. **Driving position:** Very good. Comfortable front seat and plenty of head and leg room. **Controls and displays:** Clear and simple dashboard and gauges. Very firm and supportive front seats. Versatile hatchback design. **Trunk/liftover:** Trunk has a low liftover.

Con: The coupes' narrow rear window and large rear pillars hinders rear visibility. Radio has awkward to access, poorly marked, tiny buttons. **Climate control:** The heater is insufficient and air distribution is inadequate. **Entry/exit:** Small door restricts rear access. **Interior space/comfort F/R:** Front shoulder belts are uncomfortable and rear seatbelts are hard to buckle up. Rear seating is uncomfortable and limited to two small passengers. Tight rear leg room. **Cargo space:** Not exceptional. Even though the Wagon has extra storage capacity, overall capacity is a bit limited. **Trunk/liftover:** Small trunk. **Quietness:** This is not a quiet car. The clutch pedal and the dash click, the engine roars, and the fan whirs.

COST				
List Price (negotiable)	**Residual Values** (months)			
	24	36	48	60
Impreza Brighton: $17,795 (18%)	$13,000	$10,000	$8500	$6500

TECHNICAL DATA	
Powertrain (AWD)	Head room F/R: 39.2/37.4 in.
Engines: 2.2L 4-cyl. (137 hp)	Leg room F/R: 43.1/32.4 in.
• 2.5L 4-cyl. (165 hp)	Wheelbase: 99.2 in.
Transmissions: 5-speed man.	Cargo capacity: 25 cu. ft.
• 4-speed auto.	Towing capacity: 1,500 lbs.
Dimensions (Outback Sport)	Fuel tank: 50L/reg.
Passengers: 5	Weight: 2,900 lbs.

Height/length/width:
60/172.2/67.1 in.

SAFETY FEATURES

	Std.	Opt.
Anti-lock brakes	❑	■
Seatbelt pretensioners	—	—
Integrated child safety seat	—	—
Airbag cut-off switch	—	—
Depowered airbags	—	—
Side airbags	—	—
Traction control	—	—
Visibility (front/rear)	*****	*****
Crash protection D/P	****	****
Crash protection (side) D/P	N/A	
HLDI injury claims	High	

Legacy

Legacy

RATING: Above Average. The AWD is what this car is all about. Without it, the Legacy is just a nice, middle-of-the-road wagon. **Strong points:** A refined and reliable AWD system; standard ABS (except for the Brighton); a pleasant ride on both regular Legacys and Outbacks; handles easily; and has few factory-related defects. **Weak points:** Rough-running noisy engines, cramped back seat, and very dealer-dependent for parts and servicing.

NEW FOR '99: A new Legacy Sport utility Sedan, an enhanced 2.5L SOHC opposed-four engine, a minor facelift, and transmission refinements.

GENERAL COMMENTS: A competent, full-time 4X4 performer for drivers who want to move up in size, comfort, and features, this front-drive and AWD compact represents a clean break with the past. Available as a four-door sedan or five-door wagon, the Legacy is clean and conventionally styled, with even a hint of the Acura Legend in the rear end.

Owners who prize Subaru's rugged reliability and distinctive styling may find the Legacy too "modern." Nowhere is there any sign of the excessive reliance upon chrome moulding and oddball styling that has turned off buyers in the past. Another plus is that the Legacy's interior dimensions are similar to the Accord's—the benchmark for comfortable four-door sedans.

The mechanical components are modern as well—a standard 137-hp 2.2L 16-valve 4-banger hooked to a standard 5-speed or optional 4-speed gearbox and an optional 165-hp, 2.5L 4-cylinder. Wagons are about 600 pounds (270 kg) heavier, but they accentuate high performance with all-wheel drive, anti-lock brakes, a firmer suspension, 15-inch aluminum wheels, and top-quality tires.

Legacy Outback

The Legacy Outback is a marketing coup that stretches the definition of sport-utility by simply customizing the AWD Legacy wagon to give it more of an outdoorsy flair. American Motors tried the same marketing approach with the Eagle several decades ago and failed miserably. Of course, it didn't have the combination of all-wheel drive, four-wheel ABS, dual airbags, heavy-duty suspension, cargo area power outlet, air conditioning, and cruise control all wrapped up in a sporty compact.

As a wagon the Outback performs adequately, though it's a bit cramped. As a sport-utility it's a classic case of style over substance.

Another Legacy spin-off, the Forester, was launched last summer. It's a cross between a wagon and a sport-utility. Built on the Legacy's platform, the Forester uses the Legacy Outback's 2.5L, 165-hp Boxer engine. This year, it also gets an improved 2.5L engine, revised 5-speed manual transmission, and new optional 4-speed automatic.

Cost analysis/alternatives: Get the '99 model for the upgrades. I still can't think of a single 4X4 wagon in this price range I could recommend. Front-drives worth considering: Honda Accord, Toyota Camry, and VW Passat. **Recommended options:** ABS. **Rebates:** $750–$1,250 rebates to clear out the '98 models; $500–$750 for the '99s. Matching dealer incentives are also applicable. **Destination charge:** $500. **Depreciation:** About average. **Insurance cost:** Higher than average. **Parts supply/cost:** Parts aren't easily found and can be costly. **Annual maintenance cost:** Average. **Warranty:** Bumper-to-bumper 3 years/60,000 km; powertrain 5 years/100,000 km; rust perforation 5 years/unlimited km. **Supplementary warranty:** A good idea. **Highway/city fuel economy:** 7–10.5L/100 km with the base model and either transmission; 8–11L/100 km with the 2.5L engine.

Quality/Reliability/Safety

Pro: Quality control: Better than average, though powertrain defects have begun cropping up. Above average body assembly and finish.

Reliability: No major problems reported that would affect reliability. **Service bulletin problems:** Nothing important.

Con: Engine and transmission problems are beginning to show up. One owner of a '98 Legacy Outback has replaced his engine twice, at 800 km and 4,000 km. There are several reports of the transmission jumping out of first gear, or using first gear to slow down or to descend a steep grade. **Warranty performance:** Servicing quality is spotty and Subaru warranty claims processing can be slow at times due to the company's top-down management style. **Owner-reported problems:** The above-mentioned powertrain deficiencies and minor electrical, fuel system, and automatic transmission problems are common. Owners report that the front brakes require more attention than average. Premature surface rust and exhaust system rust-out are common. Servicing can be awkward because of the crowded engine compartment, particularly on turbocharged versions. Small horn buttons may be hard to find in an emergency. **NHTSA safety complaints/safety:** Igniter failure allowed unburned gasoline to flow into catalytic converter and resulted in chronic stalling; ABS brake failure; cruise control failed to disengage when brake pedal depressed; fuel sloshes in fuel tank due to the absence of baffles; during a collision, airbags deployed but failed to inflate. All 1998–99 Legacys have been recalled to replace the oil filter, which can crack and spray oil on hot surfaces.

Road Performance

Pro: Acceleration/torque: With the base 2.2L engine acceleration is average but more than adequate for most conditions when coupled to the 5-speed manual transaxle. The 2.5L engine is much peppier, but it also needs the manual gearbox to really strut its stuff (0–100 km/h: 9.7 sec.). **Transmission:** The electronically controlled automatic has a power mode and a manual button that holds the lower gears a bit longer to reduce irritating gear hunting. Manual transmission throws are short and precise. **Routine handling:** Fairly soft and comfortable ride isn't affected, and control isn't compromised, as passenger load is increased. **Steering:** Acceptable steering response and predictable handling. **Braking:** A bit better than average (100–0 km/h: 126 ft.).

Con: The 2.2L engine isn't as fast off the mark as is the Camry or Accord, and it doesn't give acceptable performance when hooked to an automatic transmission. Both engines are noisy and rough-running. Steering is a bit heavy at times. **Emergency handling:** Rear end tends to swing out when the Legacy takes corners under speed.

Comfort/Convenience

Pro: Standard equipment: Well-appointed. **Driving position:** Low but comfortable driving position, with plenty of head and leg room. Good fore and aft visibility. The left footrest prevents cramping. Adjustable driver's seat on the deluxe model. **Controls and displays:** Well designed, sweeping dashboard (similar to the Accord's) and control layout. Easy-to-read analog gauges. **Entry/exit:** Front and rear access is acceptable, but narrow doors don't leave much space for feet. **Interior space/comfort F/R:** Seating for four adults offers good head and leg room up front and good rear leg room. Comfortable cloth-covered seats with plenty of side and shoulder support. **Climate control:** Excellent climate control system that's both efficient and quiet. **Cargo space:** Better than average cargo capacity. **Trunk/liftover:** The cavernous trunk is expandable with the split rear seatbacks.

Con: Not much rear head, hip, and shoulder room. Power window and lock switches aren't easily accessible and the low-mounted stereo controls can't be easily adjusted. Limited-service spare tire. **Quietness:** Excessive drivetrain whine.

COST

List Price (firm)	Residual Values (months)			
	24	36	48	60
Legacy Brighton:				
$20,495 (20%)	$14,000	$11,000	$9000	$7500

TECHNICAL DATA

Powertrain (AWD)
Engines: 2.2L 4-cyl. (135 hp)
• 2.5L 4-cyl. (165 hp)
Transmissions: 5-speed man.
• 4-speed auto.
Dimensions
Passengers: 5
Height/length/width:
55.3/180.9/67.5 in.

Head room F/R: 37.2/36.5 in.
Leg room F/R: 43.3/34.6 in.
Wheelbase: 103.5 in.
Cargo capacity: 13 cu. ft.
Towing capacity: 1,500 lbs.
Fuel tank: 60L/reg.
Weight: 2,400 lbs.

SAFETY FEATURES

	Std.	Opt.
Anti-lock brakes	❑	■
Seatbelt pretensioners	—	—
Integrated child safety seat	—	—
Airbag cut-off switch	—	—
Depowered airbags	—	—
Side airbags	—	—
Traction control	—	—
Visibility (front/rear)	*****	*****
Crash protection D/P	****	****
Crash protection (side) D/P	***	N/A
HLDI injury claims	Low	

SUZUKI

Suzuki's sales have been less than stellar over the past several years, although the Esteem (especially the wagon version), launched in 1997, has been well received. Having made its reputation by building quality motorcycles and personal watercraft, Suzuki has been making very good entry-level small cars and sport-utility vehicles for over a decade. But most buyers aren't familiar with the company's products because they're mostly sold under GM's name. In fact, the company makes only three mainstream vehicles: the Swift (GM's Metro twin), the Esteem, and the 4X4 Sidekick—a vehicle sold by General Motors of Canada as the Tracker. Incidentally, the Swift is rated in the General Motors section, since it's practically identical to the Chevrolet Metro and Pontiac Firefly.

Chastened by the poor reputation garnered by its first 4X4, the Samurai (which captured the hearts and smiles of the young and trendy set and then made all the newspaper headlines when *Consumer Reports* showed it rolling over in low-speed turns), Suzuki has quietly gone about revamping its small model lineup.

Suzuki's Sidekick, Tracker, Swift, and Esteem have sold quite well, although its latest entry, the X-90 4X4, has met with mixed results, and as a result has been dropped for 1999.

Vitara

Vitara

RATING: Not Recommended; we'll have a better idea next year as to the Vitara's overall reliability.

GENERAL COMMENTS: The Vitara is longer, wider, taller and handles much better (read less tippy) than the Sidekick it replaces. It's essentially an entry-level version of the Grand Vitara, carrying a smaller 2.0L

127-hp 4-cylinder engine and less standard equipment.
Presenting a more solid appearance, a more refined interior, and less noise and vibration than both the Sidekick and Tracker, the Vitara is manufactured at Suzuki's CAMI factory in Ingersoll, Ontario, where Sidekicks and Chevrolet Tracker sport-utilities are currently built. The four-door Sidekick will be dropped in December as the four-door Vitara takes over, awaiting the arrival of the 2-door version and a convertible early in 1999. Prices haven't been disclosed.

Grand Vitara

RATING: Not Recommended during its first model year.

GENERAL COMMENTS: Suzuki's top-line entry, the Grand Vitara is wider, longer, and taller, and gives a more supple ride than the Sidekick Sport it replaces. It comes with a competent, though not very powerful, 24-valve, 2.5L 155-hp V6 powerplant coveted by GM for its Tracker. In fact, GM is reportedly seething after having been turned down in its request for a V6-equipped Tracker. A full-sized spare is standard as well as four-wheel ABS on any "+" model.

Selling for $22,995, the Grand Vitara is a versatile truck-base, body-on-frame sport-utility that may not provide as much car like handling as the Honda CR-V and Toyota RAV4, but neither Honda nor Toyota can offer V6 power and shift-on-the-fly capability. Furthermore, its plastic lower body and wheel-well covers will be effective in warding off rust and parking-lot dents. Inside, there's plenty of head room, arm room, and leg room, but like the RAV4, the interior is somewhat narrow—hips and thighs are pressed uncomfortably against the armrests. The rear seats and seatbacks fold flat, adding to cargo capacity, and there are plenty of small trays, bins, and compartments in which to store things.

Esteem

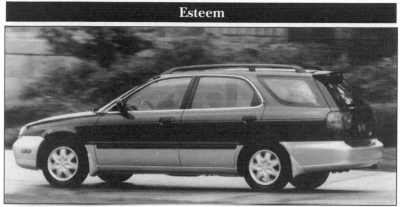

Esteem

RATING: Average. **Strong points:** Nice handling, plenty of cargo room (wagon), good fuel economy, and better than average quality control. **Weak points:** Weak, noisy engine, poor rear visibility, poor braking and ride, and excessive engine, road and wind noise.

NEW FOR '99: Both the sedan and wagon get redesigned front ends; the GL gets a standard tachometer, and the GLX comes with standard cruise control and optional ABS ($800). A bigger 1.8L engine (taken from the Sidekick Sport) will give the wagon a 25-hp boost when it's phased in by mid-1999.

GENERAL COMMENTS: The Esteem, Suzuki's largest car, is a small four-door sedan that's a step up from the Swift. Smaller than the Honda Civic and Dodge Neon, it has a fairly spacious interior, offering comparable or better rear accommodation for two full-sized adults than most cars in its class.

Both the base GL and upscale GLX come loaded with standard features that cost extra on other models. The GL, for example, comes with power steering, rear-window defroster, remote trunk and fuel filler door releases, tinted glass, and a fold-down rear seat (great for extra cargo space). GLX shoppers can look forward to standard ABS, power windows and door locks, and a host of other interior refinements.

Cost analysis/alternatives: Get the '99 model for the upgrades. Other cars worth considering are the GM Metro and Firefly, Honda Civic, Hyundai Accent, Nissan Sentra, and Toyota Tercel. **Recommended options:** Think twice about adding an automatic transmission; it shifts harshly and cuts fuel economy. Ditch the 13-inch tires for ones that are larger. **Rebates:** $500 and $300 rebates on the '98 and '99 models. **Depreciation:** Slower than average. **Insurance cost:** Average. **Parts supply/cost:** According to CAA, Suzuki parts are reasonably priced and not that hard to find. **Annual maintenance cost:** Average. Servicing can be done by any independent garage, and maintenance is made simple by an uncluttered under-hood layout. **Warranty:** Bumper-to-bumper 3 years/80,000 km; rust perforation 5 years/unlimited km. **Supplementary warranty:** A good idea. **Highway/city fuel economy:** 5.7–7.7L/100 km.

Quality/Reliability/Safety

Pro: Quality control: Better than average. Nevertheless, body panels and trim look flimsy, and wind and water leaks may be a problem. **Reliability:** Many of the mechanical components have been used on Suzuki's other models with few reliability problems reported. **Warranty performance:** Average. **Service bulletin problems:** Nothing published, yet. **NHTSA safety complaints/safety:** No safety incidents recorded.

Con: Owner-reported problems: Problems include noisy front metallic brake pads, wind and water intrusion into the passenger compartment, and fragile body panels and trim items.

Road Performance

Pro: Transmission: Both the manual and automatic gearbox perform flawlessly. **Routine handling:** Better than average, thanks to the Esteem's four-wheel independent suspension, which gives just the right balance between a comfortable ride and no-surprise handling. **Emergency handling:** Average. **Steering:** Predictable and precise.

Con: Acceleration/torque: Not very fast (0–100 km/h: 9.9 sec.); the 98-hp 4-cylinder engine could use a bit more grunt. Small tires compromise handling. Power steering doesn't transmit much road feedback. **Braking:** Terrible braking for a car this light (100–0 km/h: 149 ft.).

Comfort/Convenience

Pro: Standard equipment: Many standard features that would cost extra on other small cars. **Driving position:** Very comfortable. Everything's within reach and there's plenty of head and leg room. Wagon version provides a panoramic view of the road and surrounding environment. **Controls and displays:** Nicely laid-out instruments and controls. **Climate control:** Efficient, quiet-running heater, defroster, and AC. **Interior space/comfort F/R:** Roomy cabin has lots of front and rear head room and leg room for four adults. Despite sitting on a small wheelbase, the interior space beats out most of the competition, including that of the Honda Civic. **Cargo space:** Fairly good with the sedan; exceptional with the wagon's rear seats folded. **Trunk/liftover:** Average trunk space; a low sill makes for easier loading.

Con: Boring, bland styling. Vinyl upholstery. **Entry/exit:** Narrow rear doors complicate rear seat access. **Quietness:** Excessive wind, road, and engine noise.

COST

List Price (negotiable)	Residual Values (months)			
	24	**36**	**48**	**60**
Esteem GL: $13,995 (11%)	$8000	$6500	$5000	$4000

TECHNICAL DATA

Powertrain (front-drive)
Engines: 1.6L 4-cyl. (98 hp)
Transmissions: 5-speed man.
• 4-speed auto.
Dimensions
Passengers: 4
Height/length/width:
53.9/165.2/66.5 in.

Head room F/R: 39.1/37.2 in.
Leg room F/R: 42.3/34.1 in.
Wheelbase: 97.6 in.
Cargo capacity: 12 cu. ft.
Towing capacity: N/A
Fuel tank: 51L/reg.
Weight: 2,200 lbs.

SAFETY FEATURES

	Std.	Opt.
Anti-lock brakes	❏	■
Seatbelt pretensioners	—	—
Integrated child safety seat	—	—
Airbag cut-off switch	—	—
Depowered airbags	■	❏
Side airbags	—	—
Traction control	—	—
Visibility (front/rear)	*****	*****
Crash protection D/P	N/A	
Crash protection (side) D/P	N/A	
HLDI injury claims	N/A	

TOYOTA

There's no longer much difference between Toyota, Honda, and Nissan when it comes to the overall reliability and durability of their products. True, Toyotas hold up very well over the years, but Nissan has more competitive prices, and Honda is on the cutting edge of new technology relating to fuel economy and performance. Nevertheless, Toyotas are especially forgiving of owner neglect and cost very little to service at independent garages. Also, the company's warranty performance is outstanding in that customers are treated generously even after the warranty has expired. But the kicker for most buyers is the high resale value for most Toyotas; it's not unusual to see a five-year-old sedan selling for almost half its original selling price.

As for customer dissatisfaction with arrogant and ill-informed salespeople and service managers—a *Lemon-Aid* criticism for the last few years—the company has taken remedial steps that have apparently improved relations with its dealers and their customers both in the showroom and service bay. Now, when you call Toyota's customer relations staff, you can rest assured that your claim will be handled more professionally and competently than in the past. Hopefully, this trend will continue.

Believe it or not, there *are* some generic problems with Toyotas, but they're all mostly minor glitches affecting the front brakes, electrical system, AC, and accessories like the sound system and trim items. One serious problem that's recently cropped up may cost Toyota some big bucks, however. The California Air Resources Board has determined that the entire lineup of 1996–98 Toyota and Lexus models have defective emissions control hardware that requires the replacement of the OBD-II computer (at $250 U.S. a car). This problem has an impact on Canadians because the faulty equipment can cause driveability problems and create emissions that exceed provincial norms. Toyota has until January 1, 1999, to initiate a voluntary fix or face a mandatory recall.

Apart from launching a new Camry-based coupe (called the Solara) last summer, and gearing up for the debut of its full-sized Tundra pickup next spring, Toyota won't make many significant changes to most of its model lineup this year. The only exceptions are the Sienna's optional fourth door, the Celica and 4Runner's powertrain upgrade and restyled front and rear bumpers and grill, and seatbelt pretensioners added to the Tacoma pickup seatbelts. Vehicles that have been axed this year are the: Paseo, Tercel, Supra, Celica ST and GT, and T100 pickup.

Tercel ('98)

Tercel

RATING: Average. Acceptable only for city commuting. A competent, reliable, but poorly performing subcompact. **Strong points:** Cheap to run, good manoeuvrability in city traffic, excellent quality control. **Weak points:** Unacceptably weak, noisy engine, poor emergency handling, bare-bones, cheap-looking interior, and an uncertain future.

NEW FOR '99: The Tercel has been dropped from the Canadian market; it's a carried-over model in the States.

GENERAL COMMENTS: The entry-level, front-drive Tercel represented the best of what the subcompact car market had to offer when it was introduced in Canada in 1979. Since then the competition has caught up and passed the Tercel in terms of standard features and overall performance. Tercels are available as either two- or four-door sedans.

The main disadvantages of a Tercel are its high price and lack of comfort and convenience features. The base model is in chronically short supply and, for the price, one has to settle for a spartan interior and a rudimentary 4-speed manual transmission. In general, though, a Tercel performs decently, has room for four people and their luggage, and is likely to be more dependable than most cars.

Cost analysis/alternatives: If you are offered a leftover '98 Tercel, make sure it's discounted at least 20 percent. Other cars worth considering are the Ford Escort, Honda Civic, Hyundai Accent, Mazda Protegé, Nissan Sentra, Toyota Corolla, and VW Golf. **Recommended options:** The 60/40 split seatback on the DX version. Cloth upholstery instead of vinyl and anti-lock brakes. **Rebates:** Not likely; look for a hefty discount, instead. **Destination charge:** $300. **Depreciation:** Slower than average. **Insurance cost:** Average. **Parts supply/cost:** Parts are relatively inexpensive and easily found. **Annual maintenance cost:** Less than average. Owners have to replace the timing chain every 100,000 km and this pushes up maintenance costs. **Warranty:** Bumper-to-bumper 3 years/60,000 km; powertrain 5 years/100,000 km; rust perforation 5 years/unlimited km. **Supplementary warranty:** Not necessary. **Highway/city fuel economy:** 5.5–7.2L/100 km.

Quality/Reliability/Safety

Pro: Quality control: Toyota is the benchmark for quality control. **Reliability:** No major mechanical or body problems have been reported, and the Tercel's redesign two years ago hasn't yet affected reliability. **Warranty performance:** Exceptionally fair and efficient. Few warranty disputes end up in court. A large dealer network assures quick servicing. **Service bulletin problems:** No defects reported.

Con: Owner-reported problems: Tercel front brakes wear out very quickly and the exhaust system is rust-prone. Lately there's been a sharp rise in complaints concerning excessive rusting and paint chipping on body panels. **NHTSA safety complaints/safety:** Airbag failed to deploy.

Road Performance

Pro: The 1.5L 4-cylinder engine provides plenty of power in the lower gear ranges, primarily because of the car's light weight. **Transmission:** Well-matched, smooth-shifting manual and 4-speed automatic transaxles. **Routine handling:** Handling on smooth roads is quite acceptable for a car in this class.

Con: Acceleration/torque: Highway passing takes a lot of patience and nerve with the automatic transmission (0–100 km/h: 13.4 sec.). The automatic 3-speed shifts harshly and cuts fuel economy, but the better-performing 4-speed is found only with the Tercel's four-door variant. **Emergency handling:** Rough pavement makes this car dance all over the highway. Suspension bottoms out easily, and there's lots of body lean around corners. **Steering:** Manual steering is vague and takes lots of effort when cornering, but the power-assist over-corrects, giving little road feel. **Braking:** Exceptionally bad, with long stopping distances and loss of directional control (you can easily spin out): 100–0 km/h: 138 ft.

Comfort/Convenience

Pro: Driving position: The front seats are fairly comfortable and the driver has good visibility in front. **Controls and displays:** Well laid-out dashboard and controls. **Climate control:** Efficient, quiet heating and ventilation. **Trunk/liftover:** The sedan has a very large trunk, and long items are easily handled with the folding rear seatback. Low liftover.

Con: Standard equipment: Base model is very austere. The vinyl covering (on the basic hatchback) is slippery all the time and clammy in hot weather. The overly sensitive gas pedal requires a light touch, resulting in constant leg cramping. No side-window defogging vents. Rear roof pillars create an annoying blind spot. **Interior space/comfort F/R:** Forget about putting five passengers in this car—it's strictly a four-passenger subcompact, and if you have large hips or shoulders your discomfort index will soar. The back seat holds only two adults; it's unbelievably small and uncomfortable, with limited head and shoulder room, inadequate knee and foot room, and a low cushion that firms up uncomfortably in the middle. **Cargo space:** Average. Very small trunk with the coupe. **Entry/exit:** Difficult front and rear seat access caused by the small door openings and foot space. **Quietness:** Excessive road noise.

COST

List Price (negotiable)	Residual Values (months)			
	24	36	48	60
Tercel CE: $13,795 (10%)	$9000	$8000	$6500	$5000

TECHNICAL DATA

Powertrain (front-drive)
Engine: 1.5L 4-cyl. (93 hp)
Transmissions: 5-speed man.
• 3-speed auto.
• 4-speed auto.
Dimensions
Passengers: 5
Height/length/width:
53.2/161.8/64.8 in.

Head room F/R: 38.7/36.6 in.
Leg room F/R: 41.3/31.8 in.
Wheelbase: 93.7 in.
Cargo capacity: 9.3 cu. ft.
Towing capacity: N/A
Fuel tank: 45L/reg.
Weight: 1,950 lbs.

SAFETY FEATURES

	Std.	Opt.
Anti-lock brakes	❏	■
Seatbelt pretensioners	—	—
Integrated child safety seat	—	—
Airbag cut-off switch	—	—
Depowered airbags	■	❏
Side airbags	—	—
Traction control	—	—
Visibility (front/rear)	*****	**
Crash protection D/P	***	****
Crash protection (side) D/P	***	****
HLDI injury claims	High	

Corolla

Corolla

RATING: Recommended. **Strong points:** Good powertrain setup; pleasant ride, good raking, roomy interior and plenty of storage space; excellent quality control; and a high resale value. **Weak points:** Few standard features, optional side airbags and ABS, rear seats aren't for three adults, clumsy emergency handling, only hard-to-find stripped versions are reasonably priced.

NEW FOR '99: An AM/FM radio is standard on the base model.

GENERAL COMMENTS: The Corolla has long been Toyota's standard-bearer in the subcompact sedan class. Over the years, however, the car has grown in size, price, and refinement to the point where it can now be considered a small compact. All Corollas ride on a front-wheel-drive platform with independent suspension on all wheels. Four-wheel drive has been dropped as an option on the 4-door sedan.

Cost analysis/alternatives: The '98 and '99 models are identical; buy whichever one is cheapest. Other small cars that represent good investments are the Ford Escort, Honda Civic, Mazda Protegé, and Nissan Sentra. Other wagon choices: Ford's Escort and the Subaru Impreza LS. **Recommended options:** Side airbags, ABS, and the optional 4-speed automatic. Stay away from the 3-speed; it's mainly for rental agencies and driving schools. Also, consider the built-in rear child seat in the DX model, a rear wiper, and a full-sized spare tire for the wagon version (it has the storage space). **Rebates:** Not likely. **Destination charge:** $500. **Depreciation:** Slower than average. **Insurance cost:** Higher than average. **Parts supply/cost:** Parts are easily found, but CAA says they may carry a stiff price. **Annual maintenance cost:** Less than average. **Warranty:** Bumper-to-bumper 3 years/60,000 km; power-train 5 years/100,000 km; rust perforation 5 years/unlimited km.

Supplementary warranty: Not needed. **Highway/city fuel economy:** 6.5–8.5L/100 km with the 1.8L engine and a manual transmission; the 4-speed automatic uses only a half-litre more.

Quality/Reliability/Safety

Pro: Quality control: Outstanding. First-class component and assembly quality. **Reliability:** The Corolla is one of the most reliable cars sold. **Warranty performance:** Fair and generous in interpreting warranty obligations, even after the base warranty has expires. **Service bulletin problems:** No defects reported.

Con: Owner-reported problems: Premature exhaust system rusting, front brake wear, and electrical glitches are the more common problems. The front brakes need frequent servicing. **NHTSA safety complaints/safety:** When the vehicle was parked the parking brake was released and both airbags deployed; both airbags deployed right after driver turned on the ignition switch; airbags deployed after car passed over a bump in the road; faulty seatbelt wiring could cause a fire; sudden collapse of the rear axle. Crash ratings may not be applicable to this year's Corolla.

Road Performance

Pro: Acceleration/torque: Much-improved acceleration times with the new 1.8L engine. **Transmission:** Both manual and automatic transmissions shift smoothly. The automatic permits you to lock out fourth gear for towing or when climbing long grades. The manual transmission gives the Corolla extra pep. Light clutch. **Routine handling:** Better than average handling under normal driving conditions, thanks to this year's improvements; the ride is busy but comfortable for a small car. **Braking:** Better than average performance without ABS (100–0 km/h: 123 ft.).

Con: Emergency handling: A bit clumsy with some body roll, and sometimes the car plows straight ahead in hard cornering. Ride quality deteriorates as the load increases. **Steering:** Not much road feel. The sedan's ABS braking isn't impressive—too much weaving and veering to one side.

Comfort/Convenience

Pro: Standard equipment: Fairly well-equipped, with many past optional features standard this year. **Controls and displays:** The instrument panel and control layout are exceptionally user-friendly. **Entry/exit:** No problem. **Interior space/comfort F/R:** Comfortable front and rear seating. The rear seat will hold two comfortably in the sedan, and especially so in the wagon. **Climate control:** First-class heating, defrosting, and ventilation system. **Cargo space:** Spacious cargo area on the wagon

and a larger glove box this year. The rear seatback can be folded down.
Trunk/liftover: Large trunk on the sedan has a low sill for easy loading.
Quietness: Very little noise intrudes into the passenger compartment.

Con: DLX models don't have a deluxe interior. **Driving position:** In
models equipped with a sunroof, tall drivers may find the front head
room inadequate and thigh support lacking. Short drivers may have
trouble seeing over the wagon's hood. **Climate control:** Climate controls aren't user-friendly and there's no automatic shutoff for the rear
defroster. **Interior space/comfort F/R:** Tight rear seating and limited
rear foot room.

COST

List Price (very negotiable)	Residual Values (months)			
	24	**36**	**48**	**60**
Corolla: $16,095 (12%)	$12,000	$10,000	$8500	$7000

TECHNICAL DATA

Powertrain (front-drive)
Engine: 1.8L 4-cyl. (120 hp)
Transmissions: 5-speed man.
• 3-speed auto.
• 4-speed auto.
Dimensions
Passengers: 5
Height/length/width:
54.5/174/66.7 in.

Head room F/R: 39.3/36.9 in.
Leg room F/R: 42.5/33.2 in.
Wheelbase: 97 in.
Cargo capacity: 12.1 cu. ft.
Towing capacity: 1,000 lbs.
Fuel tank: 50L/reg.
Weight: 2,400 lbs. (est.)

SAFETY FEATURES

	Std.	Opt.
Anti-lock brakes	❑	■
Seatbelt pretensioners	■	❑
Integrated child safety seat	❑	■
Airbag cut-off switch	—	—
Depowered airbags	■	❑
Side airbags	❑	■
Traction control	—	—
Visibility (front/rear)	*****	*****
Crash protection D/P	****	****
Crash protection (side) D/P	***	***
HLDI injury claims	High	

Camry

Camry

RATING: Recommended. **Strong points:** Excellent powertrain setup (V6), pleasant ride, quiet interior, well-laid-out instrumentation and controls, legendary reliability, and a high resale value. **Weak points:** Suspension may be a bit too soft for some, limited rear visibility, little steering feedback, rear passengers could use additional head room, and annoying windshield reflections at night. *Solara:* Tricky entry/exit and trunk has a small opening and high sill.

NEW FOR '99: No significant changes.

GENERAL COMMENTS: The Camry is available only as a four-door sedan—gone are the coupe and station wagon variants. It's powered by a base 2.2L 133-hp 16-valve 4-cylinder engine (taken from the Celica), and an optional 3.0L 24-valve V6 that unleashes 194 horses. Either engine can be coupled to a 5-speed manual or an electronically controlled 4-speed automatic. The suspension features MacPherson struts up front, dual-link mounted struts at the rear, gas-pressurized shocks for better damping, and stabilizer bars in the front and rear. Control is further maintained through speed-sensing variable power steering.

No longer can we say that the Honda Accord or Ford Taurus offer little more than what a Camry CE provides for less. For example, all 4-cylinder Camrys still use rear drum brakes while most of the competition use disc brakes; variable intermittent wipers are found only on top-of-the-line Camrys while the competition spread them throughout their lineup; the Camry's MacPherson strut suspension is no match for the Accord's double-wishbone suspension at all four corners; and Camrys now have single-seal doors while the Accord uses double seals and the Taurus uses triple.

ABS is standard on all but the base 4-cylinder version, traction control is standard on all V6-equipped Camrys, rear seats have shoulder belts for the middle passenger, brighter low beam lights, optional heated mirrors, more cup holders, a sunglasses holder, and an additional power port in the centre console.

Camry Solara

The Solara's small, but it's not cheap. Built in Cambridge, Ontario, a base model Solara costs $26,245, but put in the Sienna and Lexus ES 300's V6 powerplant and you can expect to pay $29,815.

Introduced in the summer of 1998, the Solara is essentially, a longer, lower, bare-bones, 2-door Camry with a sportier powertrain and suspension. But don't let this put you off. Most new Toyota model offerings, like the Sienna, Avalon, and RAV4s, are Camry derivatives.

You have a choice of either a 4- or 6-cylinder powerplant. Unfortunately, if you choose the V6, you also get a gimmicky rear spoiler and a head room–robbing moonroof. The stiff body structure and suspension and tight steering makes for easy sports car-like handling with lots of road feel and few surprises. Anti-lock brakes are standard only with the V6 version; side airbags are optional. Other standard features: power windows, locks, and mirrors, air conditioning, tilt wheel, cruise control, foglights, dual illuminated vanity mirrors, and wood trim.

Cost analysis/alternatives: A 1999 model Camry would be your best bet if Toyota keeps the price down. If not, opt for a '98, if you can find one that's discounted. As far as the Solara is concerned, remember that first-year defects, although historically few, won't be ironed out until the middle of next year. Prices are at their highest during the fall, and most of the initial supply will be snapped up by leasing agencies and rental car firms, creating delays of 90 days or more for everyday buyers (make sure you have a *specific* delivery date spelled out in the contract along with a *protected* price, in case there's a price increase while you're waiting for delivery). Other cars worth considering are the Ford Taurus and Sable, Honda Accord, Lexus ES 300, and Nissan Maxima. **Recommended options:** The built-in child safety seat ($150). Stay away from the optional sunroof; it robs you of much-needed head room. Toyota's base radio and tape player are failure-prone; buy a better sound system from an independent supplier. **Rebates:** Not likely. **Destination charge:** $500. **Depreciation:** Slower than average. **Insurance cost:** Higher than average. **Parts supply/cost:** Parts are easily found, but CAA says they may be more expensive than for most other cars in this class (the alternator and ignition module, for example). **Annual maintenance cost:** Less than average. **Warranty:** Bumper-to-bumper 3 years/60,000 km; powertrain 5 years/100,000 km; rust perforation 5 years/unlimited km. **Supplementary warranty:** Not needed. **Highway/city fuel economy:** 7–10.4L/100 km with the 2.2L and manual transmission (an automatic burns up an additional litre); 8–12L/100 km with the 3.0L and an automatic transmission.

Quality/Reliability/Safety

Pro: Quality control: Exceptional. First-class body assembly and component quality. **Reliability:** The Camry's '97 redesign hasn't negatively affected its reliability or quality control. **Warranty performance:** Much better than average. Customers usually get a fair shake, even if the warranty has expired. **Service bulletin problems:** No defects reported.

Con: Owner-reported problems: Chronic braking problems even though pads and calipers are replaced repeatedly. **NHTSA safety complaints/safety:** Seatbelts are too tight on either side and tighten up uncomfortably with the slightest movement; vehicle tends to drift to the right at highway speeds; airbags failed to deploy; suspension bottoms out too easily, damaging the undercarriage; vehicle parked overnight has its rear window suddenly blow out; car rolled backwards after put into Park and ignition key was removed; excessive grinding noise and long stopping distances associated with ABS braking.

Road Performance

Pro: Acceleration/torque: Better than average (0–100 km/h: 8.7 sec. with the V6), with sufficient reserve torque for passing. Both the 4- and 6-cylinder powerplants are more powerful and offer better fuel economy than do previous years' engines. The smooth and flexible 2.2L 4-cylinder engine is best mated to the 5-speed manual transmission and should be relegated to city commuting, although it's surprisingly peppy in the lower gear ranges. This car shines on long drives, and for that you must have the exceptionally quiet-running 3.0L V6 mated to the smooth-shifting automatic gearbox with a dual-mode feature that allows the driver to choose either a power or economy setting. **Routine handling:** Nimble and predictable handling. Supple but steady ride on all but the worst roads. **Emergency handling:** Very good. Minimal body roll and front end plow. Responds well to sudden steering corrections. **Steering:** Precise and predictable. **Braking:** Better than average braking with the optional anti-lock brakes (100–0 km/h: 128 ft.).

Con: Neither the 4-banger nor the V6 are high-performance engines, but the Camry doesn't pretend to be a high-performance car. The torque converter disengages noisily when traversing hilly terrain. Overly compliant suspension makes for a busy ride when passing over bumps. Little road feel with power steering.

Comfort/Convenience

Pro: Standard equipment: Fully equipped. **Climate control:** Heater and climate controls are well-situated and easy to use, with large buttons and logical placement. Firm and supportive seats. **Entry/exit:** Front and rear seats are easily accessible. **Interior space/comfort F/R:** Large rear seats will easily seat three people. The wagon also comes with an optional rear-facing third seat that pops out of a recess in the trunk floor. **Controls and displays:** Well-designed instrument layout is both practical and attractive. **Climate control:** Efficient heating, defrosting, and ventilation. **Cargo space:** Better than average. Huge glove box and lots of little storage bins and door map pockets. Huge but narrow cargo area on the wagon. **Trunk/liftover:** Reasonably sized trunk has a low liftover sill and carries a full-size spare tire.

Con: Standard equipment: Squarish, angular, and conservatively styled, the Camry lacks distinctiveness. Rear taillights look to be the wrong size for the allocated space. Side-view mirrors don't spring back (if you clip your garage door, kiss your insurance deductible good-bye). You can get the manual transmission and V6, but only with the CE model. **Driving position:** The side-view mirrors can't be adjusted from inside unless you go for the power option. Front seat centre console armrest is set too far back to be comfortable. Limited over-the-shoulder visibility, worse with the Solara. **Entry/exit:** Difficult with the Solara's narrow rear passageway and the lack of a driver's seat slide-forward mechanism. **Interior space/comfort F/R:** Rear head room is still a bit tight for six-footers. **Cargo space:** Tall rear suspension towers cut into luggage space. Trunk hinges can damage cargo. **Quietness:** Noisy suspension transmits lots of shock absorber clunk and tire rumble into the passenger cabin.

COST

List Price (negotiable)	Residual Values (months)			
	24	36	48	60
Camry CE: $22,680 (16%)	$16,000	$14,000	$12,000	$10,000

TECHNICAL DATA

Powertrain (front-drive)
Engines: 2.2L 4-cyl. (133 hp)
• 3.0L V6 (194 hp)
Transmissions: 5-speed man.
• 4-speed auto.
Dimensions (Camry)
Passengers: 5
Height/length/width:
55.4/188.5/70.1 in.

Head room F/R: 38.7/37.6 in.
Leg room F/R: 43.5/35.6 in.
Wheelbase: 105.2 in.
Cargo capacity: 14.1 cu. ft.
Towing capacity: 2,000 lbs.
Fuel tank: 70L/reg.
Weight: 3,200 lbs.

SAFETY FEATURES

	Std.	Opt.
Anti-lock brakes	❑	■
Seatbelt pretensioners	—	—
Integrated child safety seat	❑	■
Airbag cut-off switch	—	—
Depowered airbags	■	❑
Side airbags	❑	■
Traction control	❑	■

Visibility (front/rear)	*****	*****
Crash protection D/P	****	*****
Crash protection (side) D/P	***	***
HLDI injury claims	N/A	

Avalon

Avalon

RATING: Above Average. Essentially an all-dressed Camry or an entry-level Lexus. **Strong points:** Standard ABS and side airbags, good powertrain performance, a roomy interior with plenty of storage space and easy access to comfortable rear seats. Exceptional reliability, quiet interior, and a high resale value. Sportier handling than the Camry. **Weak points:** Less interior room than most full-size domestic sedans, insufficient knee space in the middle seat, rear corner blind spots, and fuel-thirsty.

NEW FOR '99: Mostly a carried-over model, except for heated power mirrors.

GENERAL COMMENTS: Toyota's largest model, this near-luxury four-door offers more value, and reliability than do other cars in its class that cost thousands of dollars more. A front-engine, front-drive midsize sedan, based on a stretched Camry platform, the Avalon is similar in size to the Ford Taurus and bigger than the rear-drive Cressida it replaced.

Avalon offers a 200-hp version of the Camry's 3.0L V6 powerplant coupled to a 4-speed electronically controlled automatic transaxle. Base models give a nice array of standard comfort and convenience features, including air conditioning, power windows, power door locks, cruise control, and an AM/FM cassette sound system. Safety features include standard ABS and a three-point shoulder belt for the rear centre seat passenger.

The base price nudges the more expensive Camry, but when you start adding extras—ABS, for example—the Avalon's price is a bargain. For thousands less you could drive home in a comparably equipped Bonneville SSE, Eagle Vision TSi, or Oldsmobile Eighty Eight LSS, but you won't get Toyota's legendary quality or high resale value.

Cost analysis/alternatives: A second-series '98 would be the better buy, if you can find one. If you want a more driver-involved experience in a Toyota/Lexus, consider a Lexus ES 300 or GS 300. Other cars you may wish to look at: the Buick LeSabre, Ford Crown Victoria and Mercury Grand Marquis, Mazda Millenia, Nissan Maxima, and Toyota Camry V6. **Recommended options:** The engine immobilizing anti-theft system. **Rebates:** Not likely. **Destination charge:** $500. **Depreciation:** Slower than average. **Insurance cost:** Higher than average. **Parts supply/cost:** Parts are relatively inexpensive and easily found. **Annual maintenance cost:** Less than average. **Warranty:** Bumper-to-bumper 3 years/ 60,000 km; powertrain 5 years/100,000 km; rust perforation 5 years/ unlimited km. **Supplementary warranty:** Not needed. **Highway/city fuel economy:** 8–12L/100 km.

Quality/Reliability/Safety

Pro: Quality control: Top-quality powertrain and body components. Much-improved brake durability. **Reliability:** The Avalon uses conventional mechanical components employed on Toyota's other models, which explains why there are no major reliability or durability problems. **Warranty performance:** Better than average. Warranty claims are handled in a fair and professional manner. **Service bulletin problems:** Nothing important.

Con: Owner-reported problems: Owners report excessive wind noise intruding into the passenger compartment and some fragile trim items. **NHTSA safety complaints/safety:** Airbag deployed for no reason; transmission failure; fuel dampener and fuel pump failure caused fuel leak and fumes to enter interior; Bridgestone tire failure; upper steering knuckle broke.

Road Performance

Pro: Acceleration/torque: Brisk acceleration with the smooth, powerful, and quiet V6 engine; and there's plenty of torque for passing and traversing hilly terrain (0–100 km/h: 7.8 sec.). **Transmission:** The electronically controlled 4-speed automatic transmission is well matched to its power without any performance penalty. In fact, the powertrain setup is one of the smoothest, best-integrated combinations available. **Routine handling:** Better than average handling, thanks to the stiffened suspension. Ride quality is flawless, providing living-room comfort on virtually any kind of road. **Emergency handling:** Slow, but sure-footed. **Braking:** Better than average (100–0 km/h: 130 ft.).

Con: Steering: Power steering is over-assisted at all speeds, and the car has a tendency to oversteer. Tends to plow ahead when cornering at high speed.

Comfort/Convenience

Pro: Standard equipment: Loaded with standard safety and convenience features. **Driving position:** Plenty of room and comfortable, supportive seating. **Controls and displays:** Well-designed instrument layout is both practical and attractive, with controls that are both easy to see and well within reach (instruments are similar to the Camry's, with controls placed in all the familiar places). **Interior space/comfort F/R:** Roomier than the Camry; front and rear seats are exceptionally comfortable with plenty of thigh support. Large rear seat will easily seat three people. **Climate control:** Powerful climate control system—efficient heating, defrosting, and ventilation. User-friendly controls. **Entry/exit:** Easy access to both the front and rear seating areas. **Trunk/liftover:** Enormous trunk has a low liftover sill. **Quietness:** Lots of sound insulation makes for an interior that's quieter, generally speaking, than the Camry's.

Con: Bland styling, with a hint of Lexus' GS 300. Limited rear corner visibility. **Controls and displays:** Radio controls are busy, with lots of identical buttons that are difficult to operate while driving. The cup holders are flimsy, and the fuzzy headliner has a cheap appearance. Keyless entry sometimes opens the trunk inadvertently. **Interior space/comfort F/R:** Interior room equals that of a midsize car, well short of domestic full-size sedans. Middle seat passengers have their knees up to their chin. **Cargo space:** The Avalon doesn't have fold-down rear seats for trunk access and hauling long objects.

COST			
List Price (negotiable)	**Residual Values** (months)		
	24	36	48	60
Avalon XL: $36,605 (25%)	$25,000	$21,000	$17,000	$14,000

TECHNICAL DATA	
Powertrain (front-drive)	Head room F/R: 39.2/37.8 in.
Engine: 3.0L 4-cyl. (200 hp)	Leg room F/R: 44.2/38.3 in.
Transmission: 4-speed auto.	Wheelbase: 107.1 in.
Dimensions	Cargo capacity: 15.5 cu. ft.
Passengers: 5	Towing capacity: 2,000 lbs.
Height/length/width:	Fuel tank: 70L/reg.
55.9/190.2/70.3 in.	Weight: 3,300 lbs.

SAFETY FEATURES

	Std.	**Opt.**
Anti-lock brakes	■	❏
Seatbelt pretensioners	—	—
Integrated child safety seat	—	—
Airbag cut-off switch	—	—
Depowered airbags	■	❏
Side airbags	■	❏
Traction control	❏	■
Visibility (front/rear)	*****	***
Crash protection D/P	****	*****
Crash protection (side) D/P	*****	****
HLDI injury claims	Low	

Celica

Celica

RATING: Above Average. **Strong points:** Exceptionally well-matched engine and transmission, comfortable front seating, impressive reliability, and a high resale value. **Weak points:** Disappointing acceleration for a sports car, insufficient torque in the higher gear ranges, difficult rear seat access, cramped rear seating, and pricey.

NEW FOR '99: An engine upgrade; no more entry-level ST or GT coupe.

GENERAL COMMENTS: The front-wheel drive Celica offers benchmark reliability, good handling, and great fuel economy in an attractive sports car package. The GT and GTS have a firm suspension, well-equipped interior, ABS brakes, and a more sporting feel than do other versions. All handle competently and provide the kind of sporting performance expected from a car of this class. The extra performance in the higher-line versions does come at a price, but this isn't a problem given the high resale value and excellent reliability for which Celicas are known. Overall, it's one of the best choices in the sporty car field.

Cost analysis/alternatives: The '98 and '99 models are almost identical; buy whichever one is cheaper. The '98 Eagle Talon matches the Celica's features for thousands of dollars less. If you miss the GT version try the Acura Integra or Honda Prelude. Other cars worth considering are the Ford Mustang, GM Camaro and Firebird, Mazda Miata, and Toyota's '98 Supra. **Recommended options:** Go for the larger 2.2L engine. Opt for the '98 GT for high-performance thrills; the base '98 ST just doesn't have the grunt. **Rebates:** Expect sizeable mid-year rebates as the Celica nears the end of its days and the new Solara coupe is phased in. **Destination charge:** $500. **Depreciation:** Slower than average. **Insurance cost:** Higher than average. **Parts supply/cost:** Parts are relatively inexpensive and easily found. **Annual maintenance cost:** Less than average. **Warranty:** Bumper-to-bumper 3 years/60,000 km; powertrain 5 years/100,000 km; rust perforation 5 years/unlimited km. **Supplementary warranty:** Not necessary. **Highway/city fuel economy:** 6.5–8.5L/100 km with the 1.8L and manual transmission; about a half-litre more with an automatic. 7.5–10.5L/100 km with the 2.2L and manual transmission; an automatic actually uses a bit less fuel.

Quality/Reliability/Safety

Pro: Reliability: The Celica uses the same mechanical components that are employed on Toyota's other models, and this explains why there are no major reliability or durability problems. **Warranty performance:** Warranty claims are dealt with in an efficient, professional, and fair manner. **Service bulletin problems:** No defects reported. **Quality Control:** The best among automakers.

Con: Owner-reported problems: The front brakes are troublesome (see Toyota intro); some audio systems and trim items have also been failure-prone. **NHTSA safety complaints/safety:** Rear glass may shatter when lowering the convertible top.

Road Performance

Pro: The 2.2L powerplant coupled to the smooth-shifting 5-speed manual gearbox is the best choice for overall performance. **Routine handling:** Nimble and predictable handling in all conditions. Sportier handling on GT and GTS models makes for a firm but not uncomfortable ride. **Emergency handling:** Better than average. **Steering:** Responsive, predictable power steering also transmits plenty of road feel. **Braking:** Excellent performance (100–0 km/h: 120 ft.).

Con: Acceleration/torque: The base 1.8L engine is short on acceleration and power and is no match for many of its V6 and V8 competitors

(0–100 km/h: 10 sec.). **Transmission:** The 4-speed automatic is ill-suited to this kind of machine.

Comfort/Convenience

Pro: Standard equipment: Long on standard, innovative features. For example, the 10-speaker 200-watt "System 10" radio is one of the most advanced systems currently on the market. Restyled exterior resembles a Lexus coupe from the front and a Supra from the rear. **Driving position:** Very good. The driver's seat has a manual adjustment that's easy to use. **Controls and displays:** Complete and well-designed controls. **Climate control:** Works well and is easy to calibrate while driving. **Interior space/comfort F/R:** Basically a two-seater, front seats are particularly comfortable, especially on the GT and GTS. **Quietness:** Fairly quiet, well-insulated interior.

Con: Interior space/comfort F/R: Models equipped with the sunroof offer minimal head room for tall front-seat passengers. Limited outward vision. The high beltline and low seating position induce claustrophobia. **Entry/exit:** Very poor rear access forces you to practically crawl into the cramped back seat. **Cargo space:** Rather limited. **Trunk/liftover:** Small trunk has a high liftover. **Quietness:** Some road noise and transmission whine.

COST

List Price (negotiable)	Residual Values (months)			
	24	36	48	60
Celica GTS: $34,138 (20%)	$26,000	$23,000	$20,000	$17,000

TECHNICAL DATA

Powertrain (front-drive)
Engines: 1.8L 4-cyl. (105 hp)
• 2.2L 4-cyl. (130 hp)
Transmissions: 5-speed man.
• 4-speed auto.
Dimensions
Passengers: 4
Height/length/width:
51/174.2/68.9 in.

Head room F/R: 38.6/33.2 in.
Leg room F/R: 43.2/29.2 in.
Wheelbase: 99.9 in.
Cargo capacity: 16.3 cu. ft.
Towing capacity: N/A
Fuel tank: 60L/premium
Weight: 2,400 lbs.

SAFETY FEATURES

	Std.	Opt.
Anti-lock brakes	❑	■
Seatbelt pretensioners	—	—
Integrated child safety seat	—	—
Airbag cut-off switch	—	—
Depowered airbags	■	❑
Side airbags	—	—
Traction control	—	—

Visibility (front/rear)	**	***
Crash protection D/P	N/A	
Crash protection (side) D/P	N/A	
HLDI injury claims	High	

Supra ('98)

Supra

RATING: Average. **Strong points:** Excellent driveability, including acceleration, handling, steering, overall manoeuvrability, and braking. Exceptional quality control and a high trade-in value. **Weak points:** Poorly designed gear shift lever, kidney-pounding ride over rough roads, difficult rear seat access, cramped back seat, and insufficient storage space.

NEW FOR '99: The Supra has been dropped for 1999.

GENERAL COMMENTS: The rear-drive Supra comes with an in-line 6-cylinder engine that's available with or without turbocharging. The non-turbo base version uses the Lexus SC 300's 220-hp 3.0L 6-cylinder DOHC 24-valve powerplant, while the high-performance Supra Turbo produces an incredible 320 horsepower from the same in-line 6-cylinder. A unique, optional 4-speed automatic uses "fuzzy logic" to figure out which gear is best suited for each driving situation. Standard traction control with the engine upgrade.

Equipped in the tradition of large and powerful grand touring coupes, but with fewer gimmicky gadgets (AWD, four-wheel steering, etc.), the rear-drive Supra provides seating for four people, but only the two front passengers will be happy. The base price is very high, but you do get a lot for the money. There's very little about the Supra to criticize, aside from excesses in power and equipment—the same characteristics that make it popular. Those who can afford a Supra will get the renowned dependability of all Toyotas, and the assurance that they'll get their money back through the car's high resale value.

Cost analysis/alternatives: All you'll find is the '98 model; look for a 25 percent discount. Other cars worth considering are the '98 Eagle Talon, Ford Mustang, GM Corvette, Camaro, and Firebird. **Recommended options:** The automatic transmission. **Rebates:** Expect some heavy discounting. **Destination charge:** $500. **Depreciation:** Slower than average and likely to remain slow despite the Supra's discontinuation. **Insurance cost:** Much higher than average. **Parts supply/cost:** Parts are relatively inexpensive and easily found. Costs will rise, however, now that production has ceased. **Annual maintenance cost:** Costs are higher than on most other cars in this class because of the Supra's complex design. **Warranty:** Bumper-to-bumper 3 years/60,000 km; powertrain 5 years/100,000 km; rust perforation 5 years/unlimited km. **Supplementary warranty:** A good idea to guard against expected higher maintenance costs. **Highway/city fuel economy:** 8.9–14L/100 km with the manual 6-speed and about a litre less with the automatic in city driving.

Quality/Reliability/Safety

Pro: Quality control: Exceptional powertrain and assembly quality. **Reliability:** Quite good—a rare trait in most sports cars. **Warranty performance:** Very good. **Service bulletin problems:** Nothing significant. **NHTSA safety complaints/safety:** No safety-related problems have been reported.

Con: Owner-reported problems: Owners report frequent electrical glitches, problems with the brakes, and some instances of intercooler overheating.

Road Performance

Pro: Acceleration/torque: Brisk acceleration with lots of torque throughout all the gear ranges (0–100 km/h: 7 sec.). Smooth-shifting 5-speed manual and exceptionally responsive 6-speed. **Routine handling:** Very agile and sure-footed. Suspension absorbs small bumps without bouncing, making for a comfortable, though somewhat firm, ride. This year's stiffer body has eliminated many of the shakes and rattles present in previous versions. **Emergency handling:** Better than average. Minimal body lean and sudden corrections are handled quite well. **Steering:** The progressive, speed-sensitive power-steering system changes assist as road speed increases. This makes for precise and predictable steering, although some road feel is lost. **Braking:** Exceptional braking (100–0 km/h: 116 ft.).

Con: Transmission: The manual gear shift lever is too short and set too far back for easy, pleasurable shifting. As with most rear-drives, the rear end is a bit twitchy on slippery roads. What starts out as a firm ride becomes progressively unbearable as the roadway gets rougher.

Comfort/Convenience

Pro: Standard equipment: Fully loaded with standard safety and convenience features. **Controls and displays:** Excellent cockpit ergonomics. Very comfortable, supportive front seats should suit everyone (as long as you're not too short). **Climate control:** Remarkably efficient, quiet, and easy to adjust. The removable roof panels provide the strong body structure of a sedan with the open-air feeling of a convertible.

Con: Driving position: Low front seats make it hard to see out, and they don't have a power height adjustment. No telescoping steering wheel. Poor front and rear visibility. Some controls are a bit complicated. **Entry/exit:** Very difficult rear access. **Interior space/comfort F/R:** Comfortable seating only for two average-sized adults up front; the rear seat isn't suited for adults. **Cargo space:** Minimal. **Trunk/liftover:** Limited trunk room for bulky objects. **Quietness:** Despite the additional soundproofing added last year, there's still too much interior engine, wind, and road noise.

COST

List Price (negotiable)	Residual Values (months)			
	24	36	48	60
Supra $80,758 (30%)	$60,000	$50,000	$38,000	$28,000

TECHNICAL DATA

Powertrain (rear-drive)
Engines: 3.0L 6-cyl. (220 hp)
• 3.0L 6-cyl. (320 hp)
Transmissions: 4-speed man.
• 5-speed man
• 4-speed auto.
• 6-speed auto.
Dimensions
Passengers: 5

Height/length/width:
49.8/177.8/71.3 in.
Head room F/R: 37.6/32.9 in.
Leg room F/R: 44/23.9 in.
Wheelbase: 100.4 in.
Cargo capacity: 10.1 cu. ft.
Towing capacity: N/A
Fuel tank: 70L/reg.
Weight: 3,200 lbs.

SAFETY FEATURES

	Std.	Opt.
Anti-lock brakes	■	❏
Seatbelt pretensioners	—	—
Integrated child safety seat	—	—
Airbag cut-off switch	—	—
Depowered airbags	■	❏
Side airbags	—	—
Traction control	■	■
Visibility (front/rear)	*	*
Crash protection D/P	N/A	
Crash protection (side) D/P	N/A	
HLDI injury claims	N/A	

Sienna

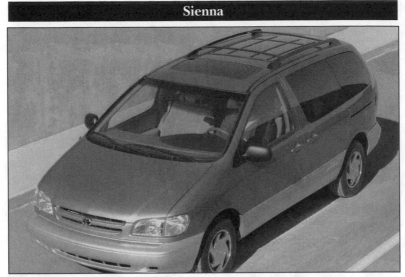

Sienna

RATING: Recommended. Move over, Windstar and Caravan—the Sienna and Honda Odyssey have got you beat as far as reliability is concerned. **Strong points:** Standard ABS and side airbags (LE, XLE), smooth V6 engine, a comfortable, stable ride, a fourth door, quiet interior, easy entry/exit, and better than average fit and finish reliability. **Weak points:** V6 performance compromised by AC and automatic transmission power drain; lacks the trailer-towing brawn of rear-drive minivans, no traction control, poor fuel economy (premium fuel), low-mounted radio hard to reach, third row seats lack a fore/aft adjustment to increase cargo space.

NEW FOR '99: An optional, passenger-side power sliding door.

GENERAL COMMENTS: Toyota's new Camry-based front-drive mini-van replaced the Previa last year. It's built in the same Kentucky assembly plant as the Camry (don't worry, quality control hasn't declined) and comes with lots of safety and convenience features that include side airbags, anti-lock brakes, and a low-tire-pressure warning system.

Sienna abandons the Previa's futuristic look in favour of a more conservative Chevrolet Venture styling. It seats seven, offers dual power sliding doors with optional remote controls and a V6 powerplant (an engine the Previa sorely needed). As with most minivans and vans, you can save money by buying the Sienna's cargo version, but you won't get as many features.

Cost analysis/alternatives: Get the '99 model for the upgrades. Interestingly, auto brokers tell me they are seeing heavy price-cutting by Toyota. Aim for a 10–15 percent discount. Other minivans worth considering are the Ford Windstar, Honda Odyssey, '98 Mercury Villager/Nissan Quest, and Chrysler Caravan/Voyager. **Recommended options:** Power windows and door locks and rear heater and AC unit. **Rebates:** Not likely. Toyota favours discounts, instead. **Destination charge:** $900 (est.). **Depreciation:** Much slower than average. **Insurance cost:** A bit higher than average. **Annual maintenance cost:** Like the Camry, much lower than average. **Parts supply/cost:** Excellent supply of reasonably priced parts taken from the Camry parts bin. Body panels are likely to be in short supply. **Warranty:** Bumper-to-bumper 3 years/60,000 km; powertrain 5 years/100,000 km; rust perforation 5 years/unlimited mileage. **Supplementary warranty:** An extended warranty is a wise decision during the Sienna's first year on the market. **Highway/city fuel economy:** 8.8–12.9L/100 km.

COST

List Price (negotiable)	Residual Values (months)			
	24	36	48	60
Sienna CE: $26,808 (18%)	$19,000	$16,000	$13,000	$11,000

TECHNICAL DATA

Powertrain (front)
Engine: 3.0L V6 (194 hp)
Transmission: 4-speed auto.
Passengers: 7
Dimensions (LE)
Height/length/width:
67.3/193.5/73.4 in.

Leg room F:41.9/R1: 36.6/R2: 34 in.
Head room F: 40.6/R1: 39.9/R2: 37.7 in.
Wheelbase: 114.2 in.
Cargo capacity: 131 cu. ft.
Towing capacity: N/A
Fuel tank: N/A
Weight: 3,759 lbs.

SAFETY FEATURES

	Std.	Opt.
Anti-lock brakes	■	❑
Seatbelt pretensioners	■	❑
Integrated child safety seat	❑	■
Airbag cut-off switch	—	—
Depowered airbags	■	❑
Side airbags	■	❑
Traction control	—	—
Visibility (front/rear)	*****	*****
Crash protection D/P	*****	*****
Crash protection (side) D/P	N/A	
HLDI injury claims	N/A	

European Vehicles

European hatchbacks, sedans and convertibles ("cabriolets") are back in favour with Canadian motorists. These cars are more fun and comfortable to drive than most American vehicles, they're loaded with high-tech gadgets, most have a relatively slow rate of depreciation, and during the past several years their prices have been more reasonable than those of the Japanese and American competition.

Volkswagen has managed to do relatively well as a result of both its comprehensive warranty and its adherence to the mid-price range, where Japanese imports are too pricey and American cars don't perform as well. Luxury car importers such as Audi and BMW have also made a remarkable comeback through price cuts and the launching of less expensive entry-level models (for example, Audi's A4 1.8T, a spin-off of the A4 2.8).

On the other hand, some European automakers have abandoned the U.S. and Canadian markets altogether, while others are barely hanging on. Fiat, Renault, and Peugeot were the first to turn tail, while Jaguar and Saab continue to struggle with losses that are draining GM and Ford's cash reserves.

Why? Because buyers are wary of European automakers' reputation for poor quality, high parts and servicing costs, and weak dealer networks. As heretical as it sounds, some of the luxury makes have indeed proved to be surprisingly problematic. One MIT report, for example, concludes that German automakers have gotten lazy and now fail to build quality into every step of the production process, as do Japanese manufacturers. Researchers found that these automakers instead waste time and money correcting mistakes at the end of the assembly line rather than preventing them at the beginning.

This conclusion is echoed by Canadian drivers. *Lemon-Aid* readers who own pricey European imports invariably tell me of nightmarish electrical glitches that run the gamut from the annoying to the life-threatening. Other problems noted by owners include premature brake wear and excessive brake noise, AC malfunctions, faulty computer modules leading to erratic shifting, poor driveability, hard starts, and frequent stalling.

Although the servicing problem is usually more acute with vehicles that are new on the market, it has long been the Achilles heel of European importers. Owners give them low ratings for mishandling complaints, inadequate service training, and hiring an insufficient number of service representatives—not to mention the abrasive, arrogant attitude typified by some automakers and dealers who bully customers because they have a virtual monopoly on servicing in their region. Look at their dealer networks and you'll see that most European automakers are crowded into Quebec and Ontario, leaving their eastern and western Canada customers to fend for themselves. This makes the chance of finding competent repairs somewhat akin to winning the lottery.

In light of all these shortcomings, why are European vehicles still so popular? Because they make driving so much fun and so comfortable that you quickly forget about Franz, Ingmar, and Luigi waiting for your return for servicing at Marquis de Sade Motors Inc.

AUDI

Audi sales plummeted in the '80s amid controversy over the 5000's reputation for sudden, unintended acceleration, poor reliability, and sky-high maintenance costs. But Audi refused to follow Fiat and Peugeot back to Europe and has staged a spectacular comeback in North America with well-built, moderately priced front-drive and AWD Quattro A sedans. Through a limited lineup of just three vehicles (the A4, A6, and A8), Audi has gained the reputation for making sure-footed, all-wheel drive luxury cars that are loaded with lots of high-tech bells and whistles. This year heralds the arrival of new Avant wagons, and lots of additional innovative safety and performance features.

As with most European makes, Audis excel in comfort and performance. But servicing remains problematic, especially now that VW/Audi has closed down its Canadian headquarters and runs its Canadian operations from the U.S. and Germany.

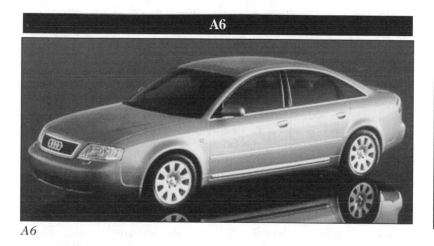

A6

A6

European vehicles

RATING: Above Average. **Strong points:** Standard ABS and side airbags, "smart" dual front airbags, superb handling, comfortable seating, plenty of passenger and cargo room (beats out both BMW and Mercedes in this area), easy front and rear access, and very good build quality. Avant wagon performs like a sporty sport-utility with side airbags and intense HID Xenon headlights. **Weak points:** Firm suspension can make for a jittery ride, some tire thumping and engine growling, low-mounted climate controls aren't user-friendly, outside mini-mirrors make side and rear vision a bit tricky, the wagon's two-place rear seat is rather small, door-mounted stowage compartments frequently open inadvertently, and servicing can be problematic.

NEW FOR '99: This year we'll see the addition of the Avant station wagon (launched last June) equipped with a 2.8L 200-hp V6 mated to a 5-speed Tiptronic transmission. New safety features include a larger right-side outside mirror, lockable head restraints on the front seats, "smart" front seatbelts, fasteners on the rear floor mats, a first-aid kit stowed in the armrest, and an upgraded tool kit. The restyled body carries an aluminum hood, weighs much less, and is 50 percent stiffer.

GENERAL COMMENTS: The $48,880 A6 is essentially a larger, fully equipped A4. It's a comfortable, spacious, front-drive or all-wheel drive luxury sedan or wagon that comes with standard dual front side airbags and ABS. It uses the same V6 powerplant and platform as its smaller sibling and exhibits similar driving characteristics. Its Tiptronic automatic transmission also has a manual gearshift capability.

Acceleration/torque: Much improved acceleration and more torque with this year's engine enhancement (0–100 km/h: 9.6 sec.). **Braking:** Better than average braking performance (100–0 km/h: 125 ft.). **Service bulletin problems:** Excessive brake squeal; inoperative power driver seat; front/rear door seals, friction noise. The screen in the air filter could shatter during a backfire, sending pieces into the air intake system—these cars were recalled for this problem.

Cost analysis/alternatives: Choose the '99 model for the safety upgrades. Other vehicles worth taking a look at: the BMW 328, Infiniti I30, Lexus ES 300, Mazda Millenia, Mercedes C-class, Toyota Avalon, and the Volvo C70 and S70. **Recommended options:** All-wheel drive. Think twice about getting the power moonroof if you're a tall driver. **Rebates:** Not likely. **Destination charge:** $600. **Depreciation:** Slower than average. Audi values no longer plummet when the base warranty expires and high repair costs have been brought under control. **Insurance cost:** Higher than average. **Parts supply/cost:** Very dealer-dependent and expensive. Independent suppliers carry few Audi parts. **Annual maintenance cost:** Low during the warranty period, then it climbs steadily. **Warranty:** Bumper-to-bumper 3 years/80,000 km; powertrain 3 years/80,000 km; rust perforation 10 years/unlimited km. **Supplementary warranty:** A prerequisite to Audi ownership, and it guarantees a good resale price. **Highway/city fuel economy:** 9.5–13.5L/100 km. Add another half-litre for the Quattro version.

A8

RATING: Above Average. **Strong points:** Well-appointed with many innovative safety features, good acceleration with the 4.2 version, exceptional handling, excellent build quality, and a smooth, quiet ride. **Weak points:** Horsepower compromised by the 3.7 model's heft, control layout (obtrusive centre console), fuel economy, and price. Servicing is relegated to large urban areas where most dealers are found.

NEW FOR '99: A new warm weather package that gives you rear window shades ("Hey dad, can I take the A8 out tonight?") and a solar sunroof that circulates cabin air while the car is parked (it's such a burden to open the windows). Other new features: a standard CD changer, a larger right-side outside mirror, a first-aid kit, and an upgraded tool kit. It will be replaced in 2001.

GENERAL COMMENTS: The $90,540 A8, Audi's all-aluminum luxury sedan, made its debut in 1997 and offers two models: an A8 3.7 and the A8 4.2 Quattro. Both A8s are set on an aluminum-alloy frame, and carry standard dual front airbags and 4-side airbags. The 3.7 model uses a 230-hp, 3.7L V8 engine mated to a 5-speed manual transmission; the 4.2 Quattro variant comes with a 300-hp, 4.2L V8 and permanently engaged four-wheel drive. These cars do everything well, but they aren't particularly fast when compared with the competition. Suggested alternatives: *A8 3.7:* BMW 7-series and Mercedes-Benz S-class or CL-class; *A8 4.2:* Lexus LS 400 and BMW 740iL.

A4

RATING: Recommended. **Strong points:** Standard side airbags, "smart" airbags, ABS, traction control (front-drive 2.8), optional AWD, powerful and smooth-running base engine, comfortable ride, exceptional handling, and much-improved build quality. **Weak points:** Not as fast as its rivals, plain, functional interior, an obtrusive centre console limits leg movements, limited rear seat room, climate controls mounted too low, some tire drumming and engine noise, and servicing remains Audi's Achilles heel.

NEW FOR '99: The 2.8 Avant wagon arrives. New safety features include a larger right-side outside mirror, lockable head restraints on the front seats, "smart" front seatbelts, a first-aid kit, and an upgraded tool kit. The 1.8 T Avant will have two new powertrain options—a Quattro 5-speed with automatic transmission with Tiptronic and a Quattro 5-speed manual transmission. The A4 will be replaced in the year 2000.

GENERAL COMMENTS: The A4 bills itself as Audi's family sport sedan and targets the BMW 3-series and Volvo S70 by featuring increased interior room (about 2 inches), standard multi-link suspension, upgraded automatic climate control, a light body, low-speed traction enhancement, an optional 5-speed automatic/manual transmission, and all-wheel drive for about an extra $2,000. Equipped with standard dual and side airbags, ABS, and a 150-hp 1.8L turbo or a 193-hp 2.8L V6 engine coupled to an electronic 4-speed automatic transmission, this entry-level four-door is reasonably powerful, easy to handle, and holds its value very well.

Cost analysis/alternatives: Get the '99 model for the upgrades. Other vehicles worth taking a look at: the BMW 328, Infiniti I30, Lexus ES 300, Mazda Millenia, Mercedes C-series, Toyota Avalon, and the Volvo C70 and S70. **Recommended options:** An automatic transmission and all-wheel drive. Think twice about getting the power moonroof if you're a tall driver. **Rebates:** Not likely. **Destination charge:** $500. **Depreciation:** Fairly slow. Audi values no longer nosedive when the base warranty expires and repair costs become the owner's responsibility. **Insurance cost:** Higher than average. **Parts supply/cost:** Often back-ordered and expensive. Forget about saving money by getting parts from an independent supplier; they carry few Audi parts. **Annual maintenance cost:** Low during the warranty period, then it jumps. **Warranty:** Bumper-to-bumper 3 years/80,000 km; powertrain 3 years/80,000 km; rust perforation 10 years/unlimited km. **Supplementary warranty:** Don't leave home without it. **Highway/city fuel economy:** 8.5–12.5L/100 km. Add another half-litre for the Quattro version.

Quality/Reliability/Safety

Pro: Quality control: Better than average. Overall quality control has improved markedly over the past several years, with fewer body, trim, accessory, brake, and electrical glitches than exhibited by previous models. **Reliability:** Nothing major. Electrical problems have taken these cars out of service for extended periods in the past. The jury is still out on the new 2.8L's long-term reliability. **Warranty performance:** Better than average over the past few years.

Con: Owner-reported problems: Long servicing delays and minor brake, electrical, and powertrain glitches. **Service bulletin problems:** Excessive brake squealing and front/rear door seals friction noise. **NHTSA safety complaints/safety:** *Quattro:* Total loss of power when coming to an intersection and depressing the accelerator pedal; the screen in the air filter could shatter during a backfire, sending pieces into the air intake system—a recall campaign covers this defect.

Road Performance

Pro: Acceleration/torque: Surprisingly, the base 1.8L engine provides gobs of low-end torque and accelerates better with the automatic transmission than with the manual gearbox. The turbocharger works well with no turbo delay or torque steer. The 2.8L V6 engine needs full throttle for adequate performance. Nevertheless, it provides respectable acceleration times and plenty of torque for passing and traversing hilly terrain (0–100 km/h: 8.7 sec.). **Transmission:** Both the manual and Tiptronic automatic transmission perform flawlessly. AWD is extended to entry-level models at a time when most automakers are dropping the option on passenger cars. **Routine handling:** Handling is exceptional, with no passenger discomfort. **Emergency handling:** Better than average. **Steering:** Crisp and predictable, with lots of road feedback. **Braking:** Impressive braking performance (100–0 km/h: 118 ft.).

Con: The A4's rivals provide better acceleration. The ride is a bit firm, and the car still exhibits some body roll and brake dive under extreme conditions. Braking is a bit twitchy at times.

Comfort/Convenience

Pro: Standard equipment: A nice array of functional, though not lavish, features. **Driving position:** Acceptable. Comfortable, firm seating and a telescopic steering column help you easily find the right driving position. Excellent visibility fore and aft. **Controls and displays:** Most major controls can be easily reached and the instrument layout is both practical and complete. **Climate control:** Efficient climate control system, although some of the controls take getting used to. **Entry/exit:** Easy front and rear access. **Interior space/comfort F/R:** Plenty of head room and interior space for passengers up front. **Cargo space:** Average cargo space for a vehicle this size. **Trunk/liftover:** Large trunk is easy to load and unload. **Quietness:** Exceptionally quiet interior.

Con: The wide centre console robs the driver of much-needed leg and knee room, and the optional power moonroof cuts head room by almost two inches. Rear passenger room is a bit limited. Radio and climate controls aren't intuitive; keep the owner's manual handy. Don't mistake Audi's automatic locking differential for traction control. It's not as effective.

COST				
List Price (negotiable)	**Residual Values** (months)			
	24	36	48	60
A4 1.8: $32,700 (23%)	$22,000	$18,000	$14,000	$12,000

TECHNICAL DATA	
Powertrain (front/AWD)	Leg room F/R: 41.3/33.5 in.
Engines: 1.8L 4 (150 hp)	Head room F/R: 38.2/36.8 in.
• 2.8L V6 (190 hp)	Wheelbase: 103 in.
Transmissions: 5-speed man.	Cargo capacity: 13.7 cu. ft.
• 5-speed auto.	Towing capacity: 2,000 lbs.
Dimensions	Fuel tank: 62L/reg.
Passengers: 5	Weight: 3,000 lbs.
Height/length/width:	
55.8/178/68.2 in.	

SAFETY FEATURES		
	Std.	**Opt.**
Anti-lock brakes	■	❑
Seatbelt pretensioners	■	❑
Integrated child safety seat	❑	■
Airbag cut-off switch	—	—
Depowered airbags	—	—
Side airbags	■	❑
Traction control	❑	■
Visibility (front/rear)	*****	*****
Crash protection D/P	****	*****
Crash protection (side) D/P	N/A	
HLDI injury claims	Low	

BMW

BMW continues to build well-appointed cars that excel at handling and driving comfort. Its vehicles have excellent road manners, depreciate slowly, and have a cachet that only lots of money can buy. Unfortunately, they also have limited interior room (except for the high-end models) and are difficult and expensive to service. But these drawbacks haven't discouraged BMW's loyal following of young professionals and people who want something prestigious but not priced entirely beyond reach. Tapping this growing popularity, over the past several decades BMW has brought out a larger and much more expensive line of sedans known as the 3.0, the Bavaria and, since 1976, different combinations of the 5-series, 6-series, 7-series, and 8-series.

All BMWs have improved technically and aesthetically over the years. Even so, they still lag behind the Japanese competition in terms of interior comfort and high-tech components. And, as with Audi, servicing has always been problematic with Bimmers. Nevertheless, there are three good reasons for buying one of these German cars: high-performance road handling, prestige value, and a low rate of depreciation. Keep in mind, though, that there are plenty of other cars that cost less, offer more interior room (Passat and Audi come to mind), and are safer, more reliable, and better performing. So if you're buying a BMW, remember that the entry-level versions of these little status symbols are more show than go. The larger, better-performing high-end models are more expensive and don't give you the same standard features as do many Japanese imports. Also, be prepared to endure some poor servicing, body and trim glitches, and brake, electrical, and accessory problems.

Z3

RATING: Recommended. You may wish to reconsider the restyled M coupe, called "perky and quirky" by some, and said to handle "like a go-kart" by BMW officials (faint praise, indeed). **Strong points:** Attractively styled (M and Z3 coupes excepted), standard traction control, impressive acceleration (V6), excellent handling, exceptional braking, and top quality fit and finish. **Weak points:** Mediocre acceleration (4-cylinder and automatic transmission), excessive engine, road, and wind noise filters through the soft top, difficult rear access, and limited rear leg room.

NEW FOR '99: A new M coupe and Z3 coupe 2.8. A 2.3L V6 replaces the four-banger and the 193-hp 2.8L V6 carried over from last year is also improved. The M version gets a 240-hp 3.2L V6.

GENERAL COMMENTS: BMW's Z3 is an attractive, rear-drive, $43,900 roadster made with parts cobbled together from the automaker's other cars. Its modern interior, head-turning body, and affordable base price makes the Z3 a tough competitor in a market niche heretofore monopolized by the cheaper and less distinctive Mazda Miata. It too offers the 1.9L 4-cylinder and an optional 2.8 V6 borrowed from the 3-series and coupled to either a 5-speed manual or 4-speed automatic transmission. The M version comes with a high-performance 3.2L, 240-hp 6-cylinder powerplant.

On the plus side are the Z3's excellent handling and braking, a firm ride, and its uniquely German styling. Safety features include smart airbags and three-point seatbelts with pretensioners. The base 1.9L 4-banger is slower than the 2.8L inline six, but it's more fuel efficient. Unlike some other convertibles, the Z3 has few body rattles and groans, the climate system works well, and lowering the top, assisted by an electric motor, is a breeze. Resale value remains high, primarily because the

Z3 is so new to the market and is still relatively rare in Canada.

Some of the Z3's less impressive features: Acceleration is about a half a second slower than the Miata and braking performance is about 20 feet longer than what the Miata can do. Furthermore, the tail can slide out suddenly during hard cornering and the transmission won't upshift when cold.

The small interior also has its minuses. For example: six footers will find the seats don't retract far enough and the low windshield blocks their view of overhead traffic lights, and other drivers may have difficulty seeing over the nonadjustable steering wheel. Visibility is further hampered by side mirrors that are set too far back on the doors and by the plastic rear window, which is easily damaged and lacks a defroster. As with many convertibles, there's plenty of noise that intrudes into the interior at highway speeds, and storage capacity is limited to a small glove compartment and mini storage bins.

Other deficiencies mostly concern poor ergonomics, a surprising oversight for a German-engineered car. Examples are: inside door handles are located too far back on the doors, getting the spare tire from under the vehicle is a chore, and shoulder belts that are uncomfortable.

Suggested alternatives: Mazda Miata, Mercedes-Benz SLK230, and Porsche Boxster.

5-Series

5-Series

RATING: Above Average. **Strong points:** Standard side airbags, ABS, and Head Protection System, engine and transmission are well-matched for maximum performance and comfort (540i), excellent handling and braking, top-quality construction, and a high resale value. **Weak points:** Poor low-speed acceleration (528i), rear seat discomfort, limited storage/trunk space, uses only high-octane fuel, and sells for full list price.

NEW FOR '99: Optional rear side airbags. The M5 will be replaced next summer by an improved version housing a more powerful 4.5L 410-hp V8.

GENERAL COMMENTS: Representing BMW's "mid-range" line, the 5-series is more conservatively styled, with a longer, wider, and taller body. It offers a quieter and more spacious interior; uses a lighter, all-aluminum suspension and chassis; and features rack-and-pinion steering, standard traction control, ABS, and six airbags to protect the chest, head, and side. Power is supplied by a 190-hp 2.8L 6-cylinder and a 282-hp, 32-valve 4.4L V8 engine.

The 528i ($57,200) soldiers on with its in-line 6-cylinder engine, while the 540i ($72,900) comes with a standard automatic transmission and a lusty 4.4L V8 powerplant. The wagon's engine puts out seven more horsepower than does the in-line 6-cylinder motor, and uses a more sophisticated automatic transmission that has a torquier first gear. Kings of the sporty luxury car hill are the $62,900 M3 coupe and its identically priced sedan variant.

These medium-sized sedans have proven to be fairly reliable in the short term, although accident repair costs for the 525i's and 535i's are much higher than average. Featuring a modern, rounded body, they offer an impressive package that combines great performance (except for some excessive body roll in turns and a jittery ride with the tighter sport suspension) and good comfort. Although touted as five-seaters, only four adults can be accommodated in comfort. All 5-series models are pre-wired for an alarm system and remote telephone controls and offer a number of trim and electronic upgrades. The M5's standard features include a 3.73:1 axle (for better fuel economy) and Servotronic power steering.

Acceleration/torque: The base engine provides better than average acceleration, but the V8 is a real road burner with power to spare (0–100 km/h: 6.1 sec.). **Braking:** Exceptional braking (100–0 km/h: 124 ft.), particularly for a vehicle that weighs almost 4,000 lbs. **Service bulletin problems:** Transmission won't upshift when cold; faulty fuel level sensor causes inaccurate fuel tank readings; tilt wheel fails to operate with driver's door open. **NHTSA safety complaints/safety:** *528:* Sudden brake failure; ABS failed to engage; intermittent steering loss. *540:* Side door airbag deployed as the ignition was turned on; short drivers feel threatened by airbag's location. Redesigned for the 1997 model year, BMW 5-series models have front and side airbags for both driver and right front passenger, plus dual-locking shoulder belts. The front airbags are designed to deploy at higher crash speeds when occupants are belted than when they're unbelted. Belts in the front seat have tensioners that activate in a crash to reduce belt slack. Sensors in the seat and belt deactivate the airbags and belt pretensioner on the passenger side if no occupant is riding in this seat. The middle back seat has a lap/shoulder belt.

The '98 528i has been recalled for failing to start or starting while in Drive or Reverse. All '98 5-series models have been recalled for the prevention of pinion shaft failures.

Cost analysis/alternatives: The '98 and '99 models are practically identical; buy the one that saves you the most money. Other cars worth considering are the Acura RL, Lexus GS 300 or 400, and the Mercedes' E-Class models. **Recommended options:** None; the Bimmer comes fairly loaded. **Rebates:** Not likely. **Destination charge:** $525. **Depreciation:** Average. **Insurance cost:** Higher than average. **Parts supply/cost:** Not easily found, and they're costly. **Annual maintenance cost:** Average until the warranty expires, then costs start to rise. **Warranty:** Bumper-to-bumper 4 years/80,000 km; powertrain 4 years/80,000 km; rust perforation 6 years/unlimited km. **Supplementary warranty:** A wise investment. **Highway/city fuel economy:** *528i:* 7.9–11.9L/100 km; *540i:* 8.9–13.4L/100 km.

740iL, 750iL

7-series

RATING: Above Average. **Strong points:** Standard side airbags, ABS, traction control, quick acceleration, comfortable ride, easy handling, excellent braking, user-friendly and luxurious interior, plenty of passenger room, well-appointed, better than average quality control, and a high resale value. **Weak points:** Poor fuel economy and control layout, and limited trunk space. Poor dashboard design, limited head room and trunk space, pricey, and rapid depreciation.

NEW FOR '99: Minor exterior changes; the 7-series will be replaced in the year 2000.

GENERAL COMMENTS: These large sedans are indulgence on wheels, with a large, aerodynamic body, two powerful engines (a base V8 and a high-performance 322-hp 5.4L V12), a key-controlled remote unlocking system, a revamped interior with improved steering wheel controls, quad headlights under glass, side-impact airbags, and a 5-speed automatic transaxle.

The 740iL sells for a little over (but who's counting?) $93,900, while this year's 750iL, with its longer body and V12 engine, will set you back a cool $137,900. It comes with an electronically adjustable steering column, an electronic damping control system, and a number of trim and electronic upgrades. Only the S-Class Mercedes-Benz can rival the solidity, performance, and comfort of these luxury touring cars. The sophisticated electronics found on the 7-series have caused owners a few problems, the AC is noisy, and the in-dash navigation system and climate/audio/cell phone display and controls aren't user-friendly.

Acceleration/torque: Better than average acceleration with the base 4.4L, but the optional V12 is a pocket rocket (0–100 km/h: 7 sec.) that handles 4,300 lbs. as if it were nothing. **Braking:** First-class braking that produces unbelievably short stopping distances (100–0 km/h: 118 ft.) for a car of this heft. **Service bulletin problems:** Transmission won't upshift when cold; tilt wheel fails to operate with driver's door open. **NHTSA safety complaints/safety:** *735:* The jack rolls when trying to change a tire. *740:* When vehicle goes over a bump or dip the suspension bottoms out, cracking the differential wheel housing area; while parked the windshield started cracking on the driver and passenger side and spread outward; airbag failed to deploy.

Cost analysis/alternatives: You don't need a '99 model, if you can get a much cheaper '98. Other vehicles worth looking at: Infiniti Q45, Lexus LS 400, and Mercedes-Benz S-Class and CL-Class. **Recommended options:** None; these cars come fully loaded. **Rebates:** Not in the near future. **Destination charge:** $725. **Depreciation:** Faster than average. **Parts supply/cost:** Parts are fairly expensive and dealer-dependent. **Annual maintenance cost:** Higher than average when the warranty expires. **Warranty:** Bumper-to-bumper 4 years/80,000 km; powertrain 4 years/80,000 km; rust perforation 6 years/unlimited km. **Supplementary warranty:** A good idea. **Highway/city fuel economy:** *740i:* 9.2–13.9L/100 km. *750iL:* 10.9–16.2L/100 km.

3-Series

3-Series

RATING: Recommended. **Strong points:** Standard traction control, ABS, and side airbags, good acceleration (except for the 318ti), excellent handling, impressive braking, top-notch quality control. **Weak points:** Limited rear seat room and cargo area, tricky entry/exit, even on sedans, and excessive tire noise.

NEW FOR '99: Standard side airbags for the 318ti. BMW is phasing in redesigned 1999 model year sedans as the 323i and the 328i, equipped with lighter more-powerful (three more horses) 193-hp 6-cylinder engines and likely to be priced similarly to last year's 4-cylinder offerings. Furthermore, all '99 models get a new 5-speed automatic transmission, more responsive steering, a stiffer suspension and more rigid chassis, larger brakes to improve braking performance, side airbags, and head airbags on the sedans. Looking like a small 5 series, the 3 series offerings present a larger interior with emphasis on more back seat room (still cramped seating, in my opinion).

GENERAL COMMENTS: Combining power, performance, and aerodynamic styling, the entry-level 318ti returns this year accompanied by a convertible and a high-performance coupe. The 318ti is cheaper because it comes only as a hatchback, is 8.8 inches shorter overall, carries a smaller fuel tank and limited-service spare tire, uses a cheaper rear suspension, and offers a no-frills dashboard and instruments.

With BMW's recent styling changes and increased exterior and interior dimensions, the 323i and 328i have come to resemble their more expensive big brothers. The 2.8L 4-valves-per-cylinder 193-hp in-line 6-cylinder engine is borrowed from the 525i. The less expensive 318i is powered by a 16-valve DOHC in-line 4-cylinder with 138 horsepower. Its convertible twin is a budget version of the 328 convertible. It has a manual top and a smaller 1.9L engine. A BMW 320i is available only in Canada. Its 150-hp, small 6-cylinder powerplant is the first Canadian application of BMW's optional 5-speed automatic. The 320i comes only as a sedan.

Cost analysis/alternatives: Get the '99 models for the upgrades and additional room; don't look twice at the less refined '98s, even if they are discounted. Other cars worth considering are the Audi A4, Lexus ES 300, and Mercedes-Benz C-Class and SLK. **Recommended options:** If you buy the 325i convertible, invest $1,500 in the rollover protection system that pops up from behind the rear seat. **Rebates:** Not likely. **Destination charge:** $500. **Depreciation:** Slower than average. **Insurance cost:** Higher than average. **Parts supply/cost:** Parts are less expensive than for other cars in this class, and even other BMW models, according to CAA. Unfortunately they aren't easily found outside of the dealer network, where they're often back-ordered. **Annual maintenance cost:** Average, until the warranty runs out; then Fritz and Heinrich start sharing your pay cheque. **Warranty:** Bumper-to-bumper 4 years/80,000 km; powertrain 4 years/80,000 km; rust perforation 6 years/unlimited km. **Supplementary warranty:** A prerequisite to Bimmer ownership. **Highway/city fuel economy:** *318ti:* 7.5–11L/100 km. *Base 323:* 8–12L/100 km.

Quality/Reliability/Safety

Pro: Quality control: Better than average. Body assembly and workmanship have improved lately. **Reliability:** No serious reliability problems have been reported. **Warranty performance:** Average. BMW usually resolves disputes through individual "goodwill" settlements. **Safety:** All 3-series models are pre-wired for an alarm system and use a Coded Driveaway Protection system that won't allow the car to start unless the ignition key matches the ignition switch code, which changes each time the car is started. Automatic seatbelt tensioners draw up slack for maximum collision protection.

Con: Parts are scarce outside major metropolitan areas, and independent mechanics are rare. **Owner-reported problems:** Brakes, electrical system, and some body trim and accessories are the most failure-prone components. **Service bulletin problems:** Transmission won't upshift when cold (see bulletin on following page). **NHTSA safety complaints/safety:** *318:* Sudden acceleration; gas and brake pedals are so close together, driver can easily confuse the two; airbag safety light keeps going off. *328i:* When pulling out of a parking space with both feet on the brake pedal, vehicle started moving forward; vehicle lurches forward in Drive as well as in Reverse; water leaks into the vehicle from all doors in rainy weather; bent aluminum wheels cause the vehicle to shake at cruising speed.

Group 24
Automatic Transmission
Bulletin Number
24 04 97
Woodcliff Lake, NJ
November 1997
Product Engineering
SUBJECT:
Transmission does not Upshift when Cold
MODEL:
E31, E32, E34, E36, E38, E39
Situation:
Customer may complain of the following:
• Transmission does not want to upshift during the first few minutes of driving following a cold engine start.
• Transmission upshifts at a higher road speed or higher RPM for the first few minutes of driving following a cold engine start.
• Transmission hangs in lower gear during the first few minutes of driving following a cold engine start.
Explanation:
In order to reduce vehicle emissions immediately following a cold engine start, the engine will operate in a "warm-up" cycle until the engine operating temperature is reached. The purpose of the "warm-up" cycle is to allow the engine and catalytic converter to reach operating temperature more quickly. In order to get the engine to its operating temperature more quickly the transmission will shift at higher engine/road speeds during this time period. During the "warm-up" cycle the transmission shift points are similar to the shift points used in the "Sport" program. As a benefit to our environment, no changes to this feature are available.
NOTE:
The length of the engine "warm-up" cycle is engine temperature dependent and will therefore be extended at lower ambient temperatures. Customers should be advised accordingly.

Road Performance

Pro: Acceleration/torque: Impressive off-the-line acceleration with the 1.9L 4-cylinder engine, and a manual transmission oriented toward driving enthusiasts. Responsive optional 2.8L in-line 6-cylinder engine and transmissions are the essence of harmonious cooperation. The 3.0L 6-cylinder motor is a real tire-burner. **Transmission:** Light and precise gear shifting with easy clutch and shift action. **Routine handling:** Competent and predictable handling on dry surfaces. **Emergency handling:** No-surprise suspension and steering makes for crisp high-speed and emergency handling. **Steering:** Exceptionally accurate and sensitive. Lots of road feedback. **Braking:** Incredibly short stopping distances with the 318ti (100–0 km/h: 107 ft.), and the 328i does almost as well (100–0 km/h: 120 ft.).

Con: The 318i's acceleration is embarrassingly slow with an automatic transmission. Traction is notoriously poor on slippery surfaces. A throttle-shift delay takes getting used to for smooth takeoffs ('98s only). The ride is firm and occasionally uncomfortable on rough roads.

Comfort/Convenience

Pro: Driving position: Comfortable driving position enhanced by firm, supportive seats, nice ergonomics, and good all-around visibility. **Controls and displays:** Excellent control layout and design, though it could use additional gauges. Wiper action automatically drops from constant to intermittent when you slow down or stop. All power windows have an express down and up. **Climate control:** The 325i's additional room and separate driver and passenger climate controls make for a more hospitable interior. **Entry/exit:** Acceptable, but tight. The four-door model offers marginally improved access to the rear seat. **Interior space/comfort F/R:** Plenty of space and comfort for four occupants—not five, as BMW would like you to believe. **Trunk/liftover:** Trunk has a low liftover for easy loading. **Quietness:** A rigid body design keeps rattles and clunks to a minimum.

Con: Standard equipment: Bland styling and very austere interior. Interior plastics look tacky. **Controls and displays:** Confusing switches on the dual climate-control system. **Interior space/comfort F/R:** Limited head room when equipped with a sunroof. Centre console cuts into driver's leg and knee room. Seats are too firm for some. Rear seating is comfortable only for two adults. **Cargo space:** At a premium. **Trunk/liftover:** Limited trunk space. Noisy high-performance tires.

COST

List Price (firm)	Residual Values (months)			
	24	**36**	**48**	**60**
318ti: $27,800 (24%)	$22,000	$18,000	$15,000	$12,000

TECHNICAL DATA

Powertrain (rear-drive)
Engines: 1.9L 4-cyl. (138 hp)
• 2.5L 6 (168–170 hp)
• 2.8L V6. (190–193 hp)
• 3.2L V6. (240 hp)
Transmissions: 5-speed man.
• 4-speed auto.
Dimensions ('98 328i)
Passengers: 5

Height/length/width:
  54.8/174.5/66.9 in.
Head room F/R: 37.2/36.7 in.
Leg room F/R: 41/34 in.
Wheelbase: 106.3 in.
Cargo capacity: 10.3 cu. ft.
Towing capacity: 1,000 lbs.
Fuel tank: 62L/premium
Weight: 3,100 lbs.

SAFETY FEATURES

	Std.	Opt.
Anti-lock brakes	■	❏
Seatbelt pretensioners	■	❏
Integrated child safety seat	—	—
Airbag cut-off switch	—	—
Depowered airbags	■	❏
Side airbags	■	❏
Traction control	■	❏
Visibility (front/rear)	*****	*****
Crash protection D/P	N/A	
Crash protection (side) D/P	N/A	
HLDI injury claims	Average	

LADA

Russia's car industry remains in deep trouble. However, the devaluation of the ruble has allowed Lada to further decrease its prices and successfully get rid of its excess production. Presently, Lada and GM are discussing a joint venture production plant in Russia, as other Russian automakers have done with Fiat and Renault.

While bigger and richer European automakers have turned tail and abandoned the Canadian market when their sales declined, Lada has weathered a second Russian revolution, near-bankruptcy, and a Not Recommended label from *Lemon-Aid*—all in the 20 odd years since these primitive econoboxes first hit our shores.

Initially no more than a Russian-built Fiat 124, sales were good in the late 1970s when the Canadian public began to turn away from gas-guzzling land yachts and embraced inexpensive economy cars—no matter what their origin. In its zeal to promote inexpensive economy cars, even the APA briefly put the Lada on its recommended list.

Quality-control problems and Lada's refusal to honour warranty claims in the mid-'80s gave these low-priced and low-tech cars an unsavoury reputation and made them the butt of cheap jokes ("Hey, you wanna double your Lada's trade-in value? Fill up the gas tank! Yuk, Yuk."). Buyers deserted Lada showrooms in droves.

Lada has never recovered from all the bad publicity, despite having considerably improved its cars' overall quality control and its own warranty performance. Many Lada dealerships have gone bankrupt or changed their franchises over the years, leaving a weak support system for parts and servicing.

The company is barely holding on by its fingertips, selling just two vehicles—the Samara and the Niva 4X4. It sold just 11 cars last August for an eight-month total of 198 vehicles, as compared with 893 units sold through August of 1997.

Lada Canada says that it plans to expand its base to 120 dealers and sell 12,000 to 14,000 units annually through aggressive pricing within the next few years. Sure—and Sheila Copps will "kill" the GST.

Samara, Sagona

Samara

RATING: Not Recommended. **Strong points:** Cheap to buy and cheap to maintain, not likely to be stolen, an excellent teaching tool for young would-be mechanics. **Weak points:** Primitive in the extreme, no airbags, ABS, traction control, or seatbelt pre-tensioners, cheap construction, rapid depreciation, and unreliable.

NEW FOR '99: Nothing significant.

GENERAL COMMENTS: Launched in 1989, the first 1.3L three-door Lada hatchback sold for $15,000 in the Soviet Union and $5,595 in Canada. The 1999 Lada lineup includes a base Samara retailing for $8,395, and a $10,225–$11,690 1.5L 66-hp four-door Samara/Sagona equipped with fuel injection made by General Motors. Base hatchbacks are likely the cheapest cars available in Canada; they come "loaded" with standard intermittent wipers, dual mirrors, folding rear seatbacks, a rear defroster, and a rear window washer and wiper. The "sporty" Sagona sedan's high-tech, high-performance add-ons include upgraded upholstery, a tachometer, spoiler, side skirts, and chrome exhaust.

The Samara is modern—for the '70s. It doesn't offer the sleek, aerodynamic body of today's cars, or their mechanical sophistication. The design is (for lack of a better term) utilitarian, with a large rear seating area and trunk.

Cost analysis/alternatives: The 1999 Samaras are virtually identical to the '98 versions, but these cars are priced so low it's unlikely that buying an earlier model will save you what the extra year's depreciation will cost. (And you might find it too costly to keep the car long enough to amortize its early depreciation losses.) Other cars worth considering are the Ford Escort or '98 Tracer, Hyundai Accent, and Suzuki Swift. **Recommended options:** None. Stay away from the AC option; the powertrain can't support the extra load. **Rebates:** Not likely. **Destination charge:** $300. **Depreciation:** Faster than average. If the past is any guide, the Samara is a poor investment. Ladas all depreciate very quickly, because no one wants to buy a used one. **Insurance cost:** Less than average. **Parts supply/cost:** Parts are found only within the dealer network, but CAA says they cost much less than average. **Annual maintenance cost:** Average. **Warranty:** Bumper-to-bumper 3 years/72,000 km; powertrain 3 years/72,000 km; rust perforation 5 years/unlimited km (optional). **Supplementary warranty:** A must-have. **Highway/city fuel economy:** 5.4–7.9L/100 km.

Quality/Reliability/Safety

Pro: Quality control: The quality of mechanical and body components is generally poor, but not as poor as in the past. **Reliability:** Average. Most of Lada's quality-control deficiencies don't sideline the car. **Warranty performance:** Average. There have been few customer complaints concerning warranty servicing. **NHTSA safety complaints/ safety:** The U.S. government doesn't concern itself with Lada safety complaints or crash testing because Ladas aren't sold in the United States. Interestingly, the Canadian government hasn't crash-tested these cars either. No airbags. **Service bulletin problems:** Nothing published.

Con: Owner-reported problems: Expect fuel and electrical system failures and premature brake wear. The body is sloppily assembled and highly vulnerable to premature rusting and paint peeling.

Road Performance

Pro: Quicker throttle response with the addition of GM fuel injection system (imagine how bad it was before).

Con: Acceleration/torque: Glacial acceleration in the 0–100 km/h range is about 14 seconds. In terms of performance, the car is predictably unpredictable. The 1.5L engine is often hard to start, and noisy when revved. Once started, it tends to stumble and stall. Even the hard starting is unpredictable, with drivers endlessly cranking the starter on warm days but having the engine start right up at -35 degrees. **Braking:** Not impressive, with considerable fading after successive stops. **Transmission:** The 5-speed manual transmission—the only one offered—has a vague and somewhat balky shifter that's oriented more toward saving fuel than easy shifting. The shift linkage is imprecise, and clutch takeup is far from smooth. **Routine handling:** The ride is always busy and uncomfortable on secondary roads. **Emergency handling:** Not good. The body leans heavily in cornering and excessive torque steer causes the car to jerk unexpectedly to the right and even to lift up the inside right wheel when negotiating curves under heavy throttle. **Steering:** Steering is imprecise and slow. **Braking:** Barely adequate.

Comfort/Convenience

Pro: Driving position: Acceptable. **Controls and displays:** Primitive, but easy to adjust and understand. **Entry/exit:** Average. **Interior space/comfort F/R:** Roomy interior will hold four adults in comfort. **Cargo space:** Lots of little storage areas. **Trunk/liftover:** Average-sized with a low liftover.

Con: Side pillars compromise rear visibility. **Standard equipment:** Fairly bare-bones, but there *is* a tire pump and toolbox in the trunk. Poor-quality radio. **Climate control:** Very slow and weak. **Quietness:** Excessive road, wind, and engine noise.

COST				
List Price (firm)	**Residual Values** (months)			
	24	**36**	**48**	**60**
Base 3d: $8395 (9%)	$4500	$4000	$3500	$2800

TECHNICAL DATA	
Powertrain (rear-drive)	Wheelbase: 97 in.
Engine: 1.5L 4-cyl. (69 hp)	Cargo capacity (L): 300
Transmission: 5-speed man.	Towing capacity: N/A
Dimensions (Samara)	Fuel tank: 43L/reg.
Passengers: 5	Weight: 2,083 lbs.
Height/length/width:	
55.2/158.1/70 in.	

SAFETY FEATURES		
	Std.	**Opt.**
Anti-lock brakes	—	—
Seatbelt pretensioners	—	—
Integrated child safety seat	—	—
Airbag cut-off switch	—	—
Depowered airbags	—	—
Side airbags	—	—
Traction control	—	—
Visibility (front/rear)	*****	**
Crash protection D/P	N/A	
Crash protection (side) D/P	N/A	
HLDI Injury claims	N/A	

MERCEDES-BENZ

You can't lose money buying a Mercedes-Benz if you keep it long enough. The German automaker has long made it a point to design and engineer cars at the forefront of technology and safety, and to clothe them in conservative, though attractive, garb.

In an attempt to respond to critics' charges that its cars were priced out of most buyers' reach and that its styling was antiquated, Mercedes tried out its own new aero look about six years ago with the entry-level 190 ("baby Benz") series. It was a flop.

But the aero look was retained, and is now what makes these luxury imports distinctive. More realistic prices in the past several years, and a revamped model lineup full of high-tech safety and convenience features, have brought the company back to profitability. During the past few years, Mercedes has introduced three new models (SLK, CLK, and M-Class), enhanced or revised its existing model lineup, and dropped the hot-rod C36 and SL320. Its revised model lineup looks like this: C-Class, E-Class, S-/CL-Class, SL, SLK, CLK, and the ML320 sport-utility.

C-Class, CLK, SLK

C-Class

RATING: Recommended. **Strong points:** Standard "smart" airbags, side airbags, traction control (optional on the C230), "Brake Assist," and ABS. Good powertrain match-up enhanced with this year's supercharger. Comfortable ride, easy handling, good braking, excellent quality control, innovative anti-theft system, and a high resale value. **Weak points:** Limited rear seat and cargo room, small, oddly shaped trunk, tight entry/exit, a choppy ride, some tire thumping, engine, and wind noise.

NEW FOR '99: The C230 gets a supercharger, taken from the SLK roadster, boosting output from 148 to 185 hp, and is re-designated the

C230 Kompressor. Other changes include standard leather seating and an optional sport package.

GENERAL COMMENTS: Entry-level sedans are accompanied by a coupe companion, the CLK320. The C230 uses a supercharged 4-banger, while the C280 comes with a V6. A limited-production AMG-modified C43 carrying a high-performance 302-hp 4.3L V8 is also available this year. The CLK320, styled a bit like the larger E-Class, is equipped with a 3.2L version of the C280 6-cylinder powerplant. A V8 CLK430 coupe and a CLK230 convertible will make their debut later in the model run.

CLK
The $57,750 CLK 320 is a stylish, four-passenger roomy coupe that's both practical and well-appointed, with technically advanced features that enhance high performance and comfort. Standard safety features include front and side airbags, a BabySmart sensor that disconnects the passenger airbag when a special child seat is in place, and a "smart" passenger airbag that won't deploy if no one is seated, cutting repair costs. An innovative brake assist feature is tied into the anti-lock brake system to provide an extra boost upon hard braking.

In addition to a high degree of comfort and safety, the CLK carries a 215-hp V6 engine that posts a 0–100 km/h time of less than 7 seconds—with an automatic 5-speed transmission. The multi-link suspension and optional Electronic Stability Program (ESP) allow for high-speed, sure-footed cornering in quiet comfort. The CLK320 convertible debuts this fall along with the 275-hp 4.3L V8-equipped CLK430.

SLK230
Taking its cue from BMW's 318ti and Audi's new 1.8t, Mercedes-Benz has launched its own $57,550 entry-level SLK230 ("simple luxury that's kind to your wallet"), a rear-drive roadster that's almost half the cost of M-B's other roadsters. In addition to a great price, there are a number of amenities one would expect to find only with a far costlier SL, including a one-button full-power top, roll-over protection, side airbags, ABS, and traction control. Add to this a 191-hp 2.3L supercharged in-line four hooked to a 5-speed automatic transmission pulling only 3,000 pounds, and you can expect swift performance and superb handling. This year, the SLK230 Kompressor roadster gets an optional 5-speed manual transmission and sport package that features bigger wheels and tires.

Cost analysis/alternatives: Get an upgraded '99 model. Other cars worth considering are the Audi A4, BMW 3-series, Volvo C70, S70, or V70. Rivals to the CLK and the SLK230 would be: the BMW Z3, Chevrolet Corvette, Mazda Miata (OK, I *am* reaching a bit here), and other models in the Mercedes-Benz SL-Class stable. **Recommended options:** Seriously consider the traction control option. **Rebates:** Not likely. **Destination charge:** $600. **Depreciation:** Average. **Insurance cost:** Higher than average. **Parts supply/cost:** Limited availability, but CAA says parts aren't that expensive. **Annual maintenance cost:** Less than average. **Warranty:** Bumper-to-bumper 4 years/80,000 km; powertrain 4 years/80,000 km; rust perforation 5 years/unlimited km. **Supplementary warranty:** Not needed. **Highway/city fuel economy:** 8–11L/100 km with the 2.3L; 8–10.5L/100 km with the 2.8L V6. No information available on the 4.3L.

Quality/Reliability/Safety

Pro: Quality control: Above average. **Reliability:** Major components that would affect reliability are relatively trouble-free. **Service bulletin problems:** Internal service bulletins don't show any factory-related defects that require correction. **Safety:** Standard three-point seatbelts, side airbags, and anti-theft alarm (thieves just adore these cars; they steal the badges from the grille and rear panel, and there are a dozen thieves for each Blaupunkt radio).

Con: NHTSA safety complaints: *280:* Sudden acceleration while in Reverse; incredibly complex mechanical and electronic systems.

Road Performance

Pro: Acceleration/torque: The supercharged 2.3L engine is quite competent in handling most driving chores with plenty of low-end torque. And speaking of grunt, the 2.8L powerplant is a real powerhouse in this small car. Although its power is used most effectively when coupled to a 5-speed manual transmission, its performance with the 5-speed automatic is quite acceptable. **Transmission:** Smooth and quiet shifting. **Routine handling:** Exemplary. The C-Class combines superb handling with enhanced passenger comfort. **Emergency handling:** Excellent. Hard cornering produces very little body roll and sudden corrections don't compromise handling or comfort. **Steering:** Quick, precise, and predictable. **Braking:** First-class braking that produces incredibly short stopping distances (100–0 km/h: 106 ft.) for a car of this heft.

Con: The ride is a bit choppier than what you would find with the E-class.

Comfort/Convenience

Pro: Standard equipment: These cars are lavishly equipped with safety, convenience, and high-performance features. **Driving position:** Very good, with everything within easy reach. **Controls and displays:** Well laid-out displays and complete instrumentation. **Climate control:** Efficient, quiet, and innovative. Large buttons calibrate the system; a "rest" setting circulates warm air with the engine off. **Entry/exit:** Easy access to the front seats. **Interior space/comfort F/R:** Has as much room up front as the E-Class sedan. Comfortable, supportive front and rear seats. **Cargo space:** Average. **Trunk/liftover:** Average-sized trunk has a low liftover. **Quietness:** Better than most cars.

Con: CLK's wide rear roof pillars obstruct visibility. Rear seat is a squeeze for three adults and access is a bit tricky. The coupe's rear seat is configured for two adults only. Some road noise intrudes into the passenger compartment.

COST				
List Price (firm)	**Residual Values** (months)			
	24	**36**	**48**	**60**
C230 Kompressor:				
$37,950 (30%)	$27,000	$22,000	$18,000	$15,000

TECHNICAL DATA

Powertrain (rear-drive)
Engines: 2.3L 4-cyl. (185 hp)
• 2.8L V6 (194 hp)
• 3.2L V6 (215 hp)
• 4.3L V8 (302 hp)
Transmissions: 4-speed auto.
Dimensions ('98 C230)
Passengers: 5
Height/length/width:
56.1/177.4/67.7 in.

Head room F/R: 37.2/37 in.
Leg room F/R: 41.5/32.8 in.
Wheelbase: 105.9 in.
Cargo capacity: 11.5 cu. ft.
Towing capacity: 2,000 lbs.
Fuel tank: 62L/premium
Weight: 3,200 lbs.

SAFETY FEATURES

	Std.	Opt.
Anti-lock brakes	■	❑
Seatbelt pretensioners	■	❑
Integrated child safety seat	—	—
Airbag cut-off switch	—	—
Depowered airbags	■	❑
Side airbags	■	❑
Traction control	❑	■
Visibility (front/rear)	*****	**
Crash protection D/P	****	****
Crash protection (side) D/P	***	****
HLDI injury claims	Low	

E-Class

E-Class

RATING: Recommended. **Strong points:** Standard "smart" airbags, side airbags, traction control, "Brake Assist," and ABS. Excellent engine and transmission combo, easy handling, good braking, comfortable ride, roomy interior, innovative anti-theft system, excellent quality control, and a high trade-in value. **Weak points:** A surprisingly small trunk, poor fuel economy (E430), and tall drivers may be bothered by the knee bolsters.

NEW FOR '99: A new 215-hp V6 engine with more torque and two less horses than last year's in-line six. The E300 gets a new 174-hp turbo diesel, a revised V8 for the E430, a station wagon variant that will arrive later in the year, three-point seatbelts for all passengers, optional all-wheel drive, and standard traction control.

GENERAL COMMENTS: Most of the midsize E-Class sedans offer in-line 6-cylinder engines, but a V8 powerplant is offered on the E300D ($59,950) with its 134-hp 3.0L turbodiesel, the E320 ($66,750) with a 217-hp 3.2L, and the E440 ($74,250) with its 275-hp 4.2L V8.

Redesigned twice in the past seven years, the E-Class is considered to be the state of the art in German auto technology. These cars do everything well, and manage to hold five people in relative comfort. They're first class in combining performance, road manners, and comfort. True, they're not the best riding, handling, or accelerating cars available, but they're able to perform each of these tasks almost as well as the best cars in each specific area without sacrificing some other important element in the driving equation.

The E-Class continues to offer standard traction control that prevents wheelspin upon acceleration. Another interesting feature is the remarkably smooth and quiet base 24-valve 217-hp high-performance version of the in-line 6-cylinder engine that powers the 300 series.

Mercedes E class models have front and side airbags for both driver and right front passenger, plus dual-locking shoulder belts. The front airbags are designed to deploy at higher crash speeds when occupants are belted than when they're unbelted. Belts in the front seat have tensioners that activate in a crash to reduce belt slack. Sensors in the seat and belt deactivate the airbags and belt pretensioner on the passenger side if no occupant is riding in this seat. The middle back seat has a lap/shoulder belt. Energy-absorbing padding between the footwell and floor carpet is designed to reduce the forces on drivers' legs in serious frontal crashes.

All these safety and luxury features have their price, though. If you'd like to drive one of these cars but are of an economical frame of mind, choose a leftover 280; it offers everything the E320 does but for much less. The E300CE is a coupe version, appealing to a sportier crowd, while the E300TE is the station wagon variant. Both the 300E sedan and 300TE station wagon carry the 4Matic all-wheel drive.

Acceleration/torque: Better than average acceleration with the base engine, but the 4.2L V8's performance is dazzling (0–100 km/h: 8 sec.). **Braking:** You won't find better braking with any other car in this class (100–0 km/h: 114 ft.). **Service bulletin problems:** Nothing reported. **NHTSA safety complaints/safety:** *320:* Vehicle pulls hard to the right when driven at any speed; blurred images from rear view mirror and rear windshield; bumpers crack from minor impacts.

Cost analysis/alternatives: Get the '99 model for the upgraded engines. Other cars worth considering are the BMW 5-series, Lexus GS 300 or 400, Volvo S90 and V90. **Recommended options:** None. **Rebates:** Not likely. **Destination charge:** $500. **Depreciation:** Slower than average. **Insurance cost:** Higher than average. **Parts supply/cost:** Hard to find outside of the dealer network, but CAA reports that parts aren't expensive. **Annual maintenance cost:** Less than average. **Warranty:** Bumper-to-bumper 4 years/80,000 km; powertrain 4 years/80,000 km; rust perforation 5 years/unlimited km. **Supplementary warranty:** Not needed. **Highway/city fuel economy:** 7.9–12.4L/100 km with most of the gasoline engines; 7–9.5L/100 km with the 3.2L V6 diesel powerplant.

SL-Class

SL-Class

RATING: Recommended. **Strong points:** Standard "smart" airbags, side airbags, traction control, "Brake Assist," and ABS. Good powertrain match-up, excellent structural rigidity, comfortable ride, easy handling, good braking, impressive quality control, innovative anti-theft system, and a high resale value. **Weak points:** Limited cargo room. Tall drivers may find leg and head room a bit tight. Large rear blind spots with top up. Convertible rear window is plastic. Pricey.

NEW FOR '99: The SL500 gets a new 305-hp, 5.0L V8—a three-valve-per-cylinder, 16-spark-plug engine that's much lighter than the previous 315-hp V8. Both the SL500 and the SL600 get restyled instrument panels, steering wheels, and shifter consoles.

GENERAL COMMENTS: The oldest design in the Mercedes lineup (first launched in 1990), these SL-Class cars are the Mercedes-Benz flagships. They range from the entry-level $87,950 S320 and $101,900 S420 to the mid-range $117,900 S500 and include the most expensive Mercedes of all, the $176,600 S600. Designed to incorporate a more aerodynamic, flowing style with understated power, the base powerplant is a 3.2L 228-hp 6-cylinder engine. The S420 is essentially a S320 equipped with a 4.2L 275-hp V8 engine. The S600 returns with a standard 6.0L 389-hp V12 engine with a top speed of 150 mph (240 km/h).

Reliability and durability have never been a problem with any of these models, although the new electronic wizardry has had some initial glitches. All SL-Class models feature sound-insulating double-pane side windows. All Mercedes cars have very high resale values, but the SL320 does especially well.

Acceleration/torque: Amazingly fast, considering that the V8 powerplant has to propel 4,700 lbs. (0–100 km/h: 7.2 sec.). **Braking:** Much better than average (100–0 km/h: 120 ft.).

Cost analysis/alternatives: Get the '99 models for their upgrades. Other cars worth considering are the Lexus SC 300 and SC 400 and '98 Lincoln Mark VIII. **Recommended options:** None. **Rebates:** Not likely. **Destination charge:** $450. **Depreciation:** Much slower than average. **Insurance cost:** Higher than average. **Annual maintenance cost:** Average. **Warranty:** Bumper-to-bumper 4 years/80,000 km; powertrain 4 years/80,000 km; rust perforation 5 years/unlimited km. **Supplementary warranty:** Not needed. **Highway/city fuel economy:** 8–14L/100 km with the 3.2L L6 DOHC; 8–11.5L/100 km with the 3.5L L6 SOHC turbo diesel; 11–15.5L/100 km with the 4.2L V8 DOHC.

VOLKSWAGEN

Like most European cars, Volkswagens are practical, and offer excellent handling and great fuel economy without sacrificing interior comfort. While overall reliability isn't spectacular, the entry-level models are reasonably priced. And they're not all that difficult to service at independent garages, which have grown increasingly popular as owners flee more expensive and harder to find dealerships. Although VW parts are fairly expensive, independent repair agencies usually have no trouble finding them.

The only continuing concern is how the closure of its Canadian headquarters will affect Volkswagen's supply of new vehicles, its warranty administration, and parts availability. In a recent Canadian Federation of Automobile Dealer Associations dealer survey, done before VW relocated, VW dealers blasted Volkswagen management as being insensitive to their concerns. VW's move to the U.S. reinforces that impression.

This year, Volkswagen brings back a restyled and re-powered EuroVan, turbocharges its New Beetle, launches a Passat wagon—sized between the Audi A4 Avant and the bigger Audi A6 Avant—and upgrades the engine on the Golf, Jetta, and Cabrio.

New Beetle

New Beetle

RATING: Average, though overpriced. **Strong points:** Standard side airbags, easy handling, sure-footed, comfortable, though firm, ride, impressive braking, most instruments and controls are user-friendly, comfortable and supportive front seats with plenty of head room and leg room, cargo area can be expanded by folding down the rear seats, and top-quality mechanical components and workmanship. **Weak points:** Base engine runs out of steam around 100 km/h, diesel engine lacks pep and produces lot of noise and vibration, delayed shifts from Park to Drive, easily buffeted by crosswinds, optional ABS, high-mounted side mirrors and large front roof pillars obstruct front visibility, quirky styling makes it appear the car is running backwards, limited rear leg and head room, difficult rear entry/exit, excessive engine noise, awkward to access radio buttons and door panel-mounted power switches, skimpy interior storage and trunk space.

NEW FOR '99: An optional 1.8L 150-hp turbocharged 4-cylinder engine (borrowed from the Passat GLS), leather seats, a power-assisted glass sunroof, alloy wheels, and, believe it or not, a speed-activated rear spoiler.

GENERAL COMMENTS: Volkswagen's New Beetle is a retro phenomenon that never would have been as popular as it is if VW hadn't milked to death the public's nostalgia for the old Beetle that was discontinued in 1977.

Why so much emotion for an ugly German import that never had a functioning heater, was declared "Small on Safety" by Ralph Nader and his Center for Auto Safety, and carried a puny 48-hp engine? The simple answer is that it was cheap, and represented the first car most of us could afford as we went through school, got our first job, and dreamed of getting a better car. Time has taken the edge off of the memories of the hardship the Beetle made us endure—like having to scrape the inside windshield with our nails as our breath froze—and left us with the cozy feeling that the car wasn't that bad, after all.

But it was.

Now VW has resurrected the Beetle and produced a competent front engine, front-drive, compact car—set on the chassis and running gear of the Golf hatchback—that's much safer than its predecessor, but oddly enough is still afflicted by many of the same deficiencies we learned to hate with the original.

Again, the 115-hp base engine is underwhelming when you get it up to cruising speed, there's still not much room for rear passengers, engine noise is disconcerting, front visibility is hindered by the car's quirky design, and storage capacity is at a premium.

On the other hand, a more powerful optional turbocharged engine is on the way, the heater works fine, steering, handling, and braking are quite good, and the interior is not as spartan or tacky as it once was.

Conclusion: The New Beetle is an expensive $20,000+ trip down memory lane. Personally, I don't think it's worth it—with or without its speed-activated spoiler and dash-mounted bud vase.

Cost analysis/alternatives: Get a second-series '99 model with the optional engine. Other cars worth considering are the Honda Civic, Mazda Protegé, Nissan Sentra, Toyota Corolla, and VW Cabrio. **Recommended options:** Anti-lock brakes. **Rebates:** Look for some substantial price cuts next year as the originality wears off. **Destination charge:** $525. **Depreciation:** Much slower than average, especially during the first two years. **Insurance cost:** Higher than average. **Parts supply/cost:** Not hard to find since they're taken from the Golf/Jetta parts bin, but CAA says they may be more expensive than parts for most other cars in this class. **Annual maintenance cost:** Less than average during the first three years, then expect repair costs start to climb dramatically. **Warranty:** Bumper-to-bumper 2 years/40,000 km; powertrain 5 years/80,000 km; rust perforation 6 years/unlimited km. **Supplementary warranty:** A good idea. **Highway/city fuel economy:** N/A.

Golf, Jetta, Cabrio

Golf

RATING: Recommended. **Strong points:** Superb all-around front-drive performers that offer power to spare with the manual shifter (GTI VR6, GLX), first-class handling, a comfortable ride, and good fuel economy, all for a reasonable base price. Standard ABS (GTI, GLX), side airbags, and anti-theft system. **Weak points:** Powerful V6 produces excessive torque steer, imprecise manual shifter, harsh automatic transmission downshifts, difficult entry/exit, and limited rear leg room.

NEW FOR '99: At year's end, a redesigned Jetta will debut with junior-Passat features; the Golf and GTI will follow next year with similar changes. All three will offer an upgraded 115-hp 2.0L standard 4-cylinder engine, while the GTI VR6 and Jetta GLX will be equipped with a similarly upgraded 172-hp, 2.8L V6. A turbocharged diesel will also equip some Golfs. VW says its new 4-banger has a lower overall height, smoother, quieter operation, a quicker response to the throttle, and a torque peak that's reached earlier for more passing and merging grunt.

The Cabrio misses out on the fourth-generation redesign and is restyled, instead, to resemble the new Golf with new sheet metal and a reworked, more user-friendly interior.

This trio get other new standard features that include side airbags, ABS with disc brakes, and a premium sound system.

GENERAL COMMENTS: Reasonably priced, practical, and fun to drive. That pretty well sums up the main reasons why these VWs continue to be so popular. Yet they offer much more, including lots of front interior room, a peppier engine than what you'll find in most cars this size, responsive handling, great fuel economy, and better than average reliability over the first three years.

The Jetta is a more expensive Golf with a trunk (interestingly, Jettas outsell Golfs 5 to 1), and the Cabrio is a much more expensive Golf without a roof. The Golf GTI V6 is a sporty performer that comes with lots of standard equipment, including air conditioning, an upgraded sound system, and a split folding rear seat. Jettas offer standard cruise control, power mirrors, and alloy wheels.

Three engines are available: a 115-hp 2.0L base 4-cylinder, a 90-hp turbo diesel variant, and a 172-hp 2.8L V6 borrowed from the Corrado and Passat. A manual 5-speed transmission is also offered as a standard feature, along with an optional 4-speed automatic. Power steering is optional on base-level models.

Although the entry-level Golf's engine is no tire burner, it's well mated to the base manual transmission and handles most driving conditions with ease. From the standpoint of driveability and purchase price, the Jetta is an overlooked bargain.

Cost analysis/alternatives: Get a second-series '99 model for the engine and safety upgrades. I wouldn't even consider last year's less-refined models, no matter how much they're discounted (on the other hand, if they were free...). Other cars worth considering are the Honda Civic, Mazda Protegé, Nissan Sentra, and Toyota Corolla. Cabrio shoppers might also want to test-drive a convertible Chevrolet Cavalier or Sunfire. **Rebates:** Not likely, but look for some substantial price-cuts next year. **Recommended options:** Stay away from the electric sunroof; it costs a bundle to repair and offers not much more than the well-designed manual sunroof. Plus, you lose too much head room. **Destination charge:** $525. **Depreciation:** Slower than average, especially the Jetta and all Cabriolet versions. **Insurance cost:** Higher than average. **Parts supply/cost:** Not hard to find, but CAA says that parts are more expensive than most other cars in this class. **Annual maintenance cost:** Less than average during the first three years, then repair costs start to climb dramatically. **Warranty:** Bumper-to-bumper 2 years/40,000 km; power-train 5 years/80,000 km; rust perforation 6 years/unlimited km. **Supplementary warranty:** A good idea. **Highway/city fuel economy:** 6–7.5L/100 km with the 1.9L SOHC diesel; 7–10L/100 km with the 2.0L; and 9–13L/100 km with the 2.8L V6.

Quality/Reliability/Safety

Pro: Quality control: Better than average. Major components are relatively trouble-free. **Reliability:** Good overall reliability (that's why so many are used as taxis) during the first few years. **Warranty performance:** Slow but fair treatment of warranty claims. **Safety:** Standard three-point seatbelts and anti-theft alarm (thieves just adore these cars).

Con: Now made in Mexico, the quality control on these vehicles isn't comparable to German workmanship. Apparently, reliability deteriorates about the same time as the warranty expires. **NHTSA safety complaints:** *Golf:* uncomfortable driver's seat creates excessive fatigue on long trips; horn can't be located when wheel is turned; improper lug nuts allow wheel to separate from the car. *Jetta:* Airbag warning light comes on for no apparent reason; ABS failure; driver's seat faulty wiring caused a fire; passenger-side airbag deployed seconds after impact; exhaust pipe extends underneath the bumper, revealing raw edge of pipe; car hit the curb and airbag deployed, hitting driver's head and killing him; adhesive that secures the brake light in the rear window can melt due to sunlight; passive restraints failed, allowing driver to hit the windshield even though the airbag deployed; vehicle was hit from all sides and neither airbag deployed; when vehicle is driven at speeds over 35 mph (57 km/h), tachometer registers 4,700 rpm before downshifting; gear console gives an inaccurate gear reading. *GTI:* Corner front wheel hit curb at 10 mph (16 km/h) and was severely damaged. **Owner-reported problems:** The brakes and the electrical, fuel, and exhaust systems are especially troublesome. Owners report that doors are poorly hung, rattles are omnipresent, and dashboard controls and interior and exterior trim items aren't very durable. Paint defects and premature rusting have been common. **Service bulletin problems:** Clutch pedal may not fully return; cruise control will not function; unpleasant AC odours can be eliminated by following Volkswagen's instructions outlined in DSB #97-01. The correction is covered by VW's base warranty (see bulletin below).

Group: 87
Number: 97-01
Date: Oct. 23, 1997
Subject:
Musty Odor from Heating and Ventilation System
Model(s):
All with A/C   All
Condition
Unpleasant "musty" odor from Heating and Ventilation system.
Odor mainly occurs after vehicle has been sitting (unused) at least 5 hours and within 20 to 60 seconds after vehicle is first started.
This odor may be caused by residual condensate in and around evaporator mixing with airborne pollutants. This forms the growth of bacteria and or fungi.
Note:
Condensate is a normal condition in all A/C systems.
This odor can be eliminated by destroying the bacterial and or mold growth using a product called Airsept(R).
Service
Prior to performing Airsept(R) procedure:
• Condensate drain(s) in bottom of plenum chamber must be open and free of any debris.
• Bulkhead must be seated (no leaks/water ingress into passenger compartment) --> Technical Bulletin Group 51 Number 93-02 dated November 15, 1993.
• Evaporator water drain valve (behind bulkhead insulation) must open freely.

Road Performance

Pro: Acceleration/torque: All gas engines posted excellent acceleration times with plenty of torque. The standard 2.0L 4-cylinder engine is acceptable for city driving and leisurely highway cruising with the manual gearbox, thanks mainly to the car's light weight and improved fuel injection. I would still wait for the upgrade variant due later this year. The V6 is the prerequisite engine for performance thrills (0–100 km/h: 8 sec.). **Routine handling:** Excellent handling. Ride quality is less firm than with previous models. **Emergency handling:** Acceptable, despite the softer suspension creating additional body roll. **Steering:** Precise and predictable steering. **Braking:** Acceptable (100–0 km/h: 130 ft.).

Con: The base 4-cylinder engine provides sluggish acceleration when hooked to an automatic transmission. Excessive torque steer with the V6. Diesel engines equipped with cruise control can't handle small hills terribly well, and usually drop 10 to 15 km/h. **Transmission:** Manual 5-speed transmission is imprecise and requires long lever throws to change gear. Harsh automatic transmission downshifts at full throttle. The soft suspension produces lots of body roll when cornering under power.

Comfort/Convenience

Pro: Standard equipment: Adequate. Although you don't get a lot of lavish standard features, the essentials are all there. **Driving position:** Excellent driving position. Comfortable and versatile front bucket seats help to make driving a pleasure. Front seat head room is adequate for most drivers, even with a sunroof. Ergonomics are impressive. **Controls and displays:** The dash is well laid-out and gauges are easy to read. Most controls are easy to find and use. **Climate control:** Generally works well and is easy to adjust. However, some owners have complained that heating is barely sufficient. Check this out on the dealer's lot before accepting delivery. **Interior space/comfort F/R:** Although the interior is very austere, it's well finished and fairly spacious up front. The rear seats include headrests. **Cargo space:** The Golf's hatchback design is a bit more versatile for diverse cargo. **Trunk/liftover:** Spacious trunk has a low liftover.

Con: Quietness: Despite additional sound deadening, the '98 model's 2.0L engine is fairly noisy and tends to produce excessive vibrations; with any luck, this year's improvements will correct these problems. **Entry/exit:** A bit tricky. The front seats are too firm for some and the low-profile tires make small bumps unusually harsh. The rear seats are too narrow and there's not enough knee room. Radio and power window buttons are too small. The lack of a centre console cuts down on storage space. The Cabriolet's trunk is too small. The odd way the trunk opens compromises loading.

COST				
List Price (firm)	**Residual Values** (months)			
	24	**36**	**48**	**60**
Base Golf: $15,610 (13%)	$11,000	$9000	$6000	$4500

TECHNICAL DATA	
Powertrain (front-drive)	Height/length/width:
Engines: 2.0L 4-cyl. (115 hp)	56.2/160.4/66.7 in.
• 1.9L 4-cyl. diesel (90 hp)	Head room F/R: 37.6/37.4 in.
• 2.8L V6 (172 hp)	Leg room F/R: 42.3/31.5 in.

Transmissions: 5-speed man.	Wheelbase: 97.4 in.
• 4-speed auto.	Cargo capacity: 17 cu. ft.
Dimensions (GTI VR6)	Towing capacity: 1,000 lbs.
Passengers: 5	Fuel tank: 55L/reg.
	Weight: 2,800 lbs.

SAFETY FEATURES

	Std.	Opt.
Anti-lock brakes	❏	■
Seatbelt pretensioners	■	❏
Integrated child safety seat	—	—
Airbag cut-off switch	—	—
Depowered airbags	—	—
Side airbags	■	❏
Traction control	—	—
Visibility (front/rear)	*****	*****
Crash protection D/P	***	***
Crash protection (side) D/P	N/A	
HLDI injury claims	Average	

Passat

Passat

RATING: Recommended. **Strong points:** Well-appointed, with standard side airbags, traction control, and ABS. Refined road manners, plenty of passenger and cargo room, exceptional driving comfort, and top-quality construction and mechanical components. **Weak points:** Mediocre acceleration (automatic transmission-equipped GLS 1.8T and TDI), rear corner blind spots, tire drumming, and poor fuel economy.

NEW FOR '99: A completely redesigned Passat was launched last summer as a '99 model and is carried this year practically unchanged. Later this year, a 2.8L 190-hp 30-valve V6-equipped wagon will debut, and a four-wheel drive Syncro system should be available on the V6 GLX models by mid-1999.

GENERAL COMMENTS: Volkswagen's largest front-drive compact, the Passat is an attractive midsize car that rides on the same platform as the Audi A4, giving it a three-inch larger wheelbase and more passenger room. It has a more stylish design than that of the Golf or Jetta, but still provides a comfortable, roomy interior and gives good all-round performance for highway and city driving. The car's large wheelbase and squat appearance give it a massive, solid feeling, while its aerodynamic styling makes it look sleek and clean. Most Passats come fully loaded with air conditioning, tinted glass, power-assisted disc brakes on all four wheels, front and rear stabilizer bars, full instrumentation, and even a roof rack with the wagon. Engine offerings include a new 150-hp 1.8L turbocharged in-line four, a 190-hp 2.8L V6, and a 90-hp 1.9L turbodiesel, all hooked to either a 5-speed manual or a 5-speed Tiptronic automatic transmission.

Cost analysis/alternatives: Get the second-series '99 models for the engine and 4X4 upgrades. Other cars worth considering are the BMW 3-series, Honda Accord, and Toyota Camry. **Recommended options:** The 2.8L V6 and a good anti-theft system. **Rebates:** Not likely. **Destination charge:** $500. **Depreciation:** Slower than average. **Insurance cost:** Higher than average. These cars are favourites with thieves—whether for radios, wheels, VW badges, or the entire car. **Parts supply/cost:** Not hard to find. Parts and service are much more expensive than average, reports CAA. **Annual maintenance cost:** Higher than average. **Warranty:** Bumper-to-bumper 2 years/40,000 km; powertrain 5 years/80,000 km; rust perforation 6 years/unlimited km. **Supplementary warranty:** A must-have. Maintenance costs are higher than average once the warranty expires, which is all the more reason to buy the optional warranty from VW. **Highway/city fuel economy:** 6–8L/100 km with the diesel engine, and 9–13L/100 km with the 2.8L.

Quality/Reliability/Safety

Pro: Warranty performance: Apparently good. VW officials have been particularly sensitive to Passat complaints, but their generosity could change at any moment. **Quality control:** So far so good. The new Passat uses mechanical parts and underpinnings borrowed from Audi, so overall reliability and problem areas should be similar to those of the Audi A4. **Reliability:** Predicted above average reliability during the first three years. **Service bulletin problems:** Nothing significant. **Safety:** Please note that the NHTSA crash ratings may not apply to the redesigned Passat.

Con: NHTSA safety complaints/safety: Rear window defroster power button failure, only works when held in the "on" position; steering wheel locked up when turning at 10 mph (16 km/h). **Owner-reported problems:** Nothing reported on the new Passat. On last year's version: problems with the automatic transmission, steering, front brakes, MacPherson struts, and the fuel and electrical systems. Interior trim and controls are fragile. The screen in the air filter could shatter during a backfire, sending pieces into the air intake system; a safety recall will cover the costs of fixing this defect.

Road Performance

Pro: Acceleration/torque: Decent acceleration with the base 1.8L turbocharged engine, unless saddled with an automatic transmission. Better acceleration times with more torque can be wrung from the V6 (0–100 km/h: 7.9 sec.). Diesel power is relatively quick and quiet. **Transmission:** Smooth and quiet shifting with the automatic gearbox. The Synchro 4X4 shifts effortlessly into gear. **Routine handling:** Suspension is firm but not unpleasant and handling is superior to most of the competition. **Emergency handling:** Better than average. **Steering:** Quick, precise, and predictable.

Con: Forget about last year's wimpy base 115-hp 2.0L 4-cylinder motor. **Braking:** Less than impressive (100–0 km/h: 141 ft.).

Comfort/Convenience

Pro: Standard equipment: This is VW's most luxurious car, so it comes fairly well-appointed. Heated outside mirror. **Driving position:** Very good. Comfortable seating and good fore and aft visibility. Fairly good dashboard layout. **Controls and displays:** User-friendly instrument panel. **Climate control:** Efficient and quiet operation. Includes a dust-and-pollen filter. **Entry/exit:** Relatively easy front and rear access. **Interior space/comfort F/R:** Spacious interior seats four in comfort, as long as the rear passengers aren't too tall. All seats are supportive and comfortable. **Trunk/liftover:** Large and accessible trunk has an innovative latch and low liftover. **Cargo space:** Average for the sedan. Many small storage spaces. **Quietness:** Additional sound-deadening material keeps interior noise to a minimum.

Con: Rear visibility is compromised by the styling of the rear pillars. Limited rear head room. Excessive tire noise.

COST				
List Price (firm)	**Residual Values** (months)			
	24	36	48	60
Passat GLS 1.8:				
$29,100 (23%)	$21,000	$17,000	$14,000	$11,000

TECHNICAL DATA	
Powertrain (front-drive)	Head room F/R: 39.7/37.8 in.
Engines: 1.8L 4-cyl. (150 hp)	Leg room F/R: 41.5/35.3 in.
• 2.8L V6 (190 hp)	Wheelbase: 106.4 in.
Transmissions: 5-speed man.	Cargo capacity: 15 cu. ft.
• 3-speed auto.	Towing capacity: 1,000 lbs.

Dimensions	Fuel tank: 47L/reg.
Passengers: 5	Weight: 3,250 lbs.
Height/length/width:	
57.4/184.1/68.5 in.	

SAFETY FEATURES

	Std.	Opt.
Anti-lock brakes	■	❑
Seatbelt pretensioners	—	—
Integrated child safety seat	—	—
Airbag cut-off switch	—	—
Depowered airbags	—	—
Side airbags	■	❑
Traction control	—	—
Visibility (front/rear)	*****	**
Crash protection D/P	****	****
Crash protection (side) D/P	N/A	
HLDI injury claims	N/A	

EuroVan

EuroVan

RATING: Not Recommended. Outclassed by the competition. **Strong points:** Standard ABS, lots of convenience features. **Weak points:** Expensive retail price, doubtful reliability.

NEW FOR '99: Significantly improved with a revamped seven-passenger interior, a restyled front end, and the inclusion of a torquier 2.8L 140-hp VR6 powerplant.

GENERAL COMMENTS: Introduced to North Americans in the late 1950s, VW's rear-engine Microbus was the first North American mini-van. During the 1960s it was considered to be both car and home by the so-called hippie generation. The Westfalia Camper version came later, and appealed mostly to retirees wanting to "rough it" in comfort. After an absence of several years, the front-drive EuroVan will return to dealer showrooms by year's end and will be available in two trim levels: GLS and MV. The Camper van is converted by Winnebago and features a pop-up roof, two beds, a battery-powered refrigerator, and a propane stove. There's a closet, kitchen sink, dining tables, and mosquito netting for the rear hatch—all for about $49,815. The camper gear adds about 1,000 pounds (450 kg) to the EuroVan's 3,950 lb. (1,778 kg) curb weight, bringing it just shy of 5,000 lbs. (2,250 kg).

Cost analysis/alternatives: The 1999 EuroVan is substantially improved this year, and is the only model worth buying. An inflated base price makes customized domestic full-sized vans, or more powerful V6-equipped minivans, better buys. If you're looking for a minivan people-hauler, consider the Ford Windstar, Honda Odyssey, Chrysler Caravan and Voyager, Nissan Quest, and Toyota Sienna. On the other hand, if it's a van/camper combo you want, look for a GM or Ford rear-drive, full-sized van and modify it as you wish at an independent conversion shop. **Recommended options:** Power mirrors and door locks. **Rebates:** Expect some substantial price cuts by the middle of next year. **Destination charge:** $800. **Depreciation:** Slower than average. **Insurance cost:** Higher than average. **Annual maintenance cost:** Predicted to be much higher than average. **Parts supply/cost:** Parts are often back-ordered; they're much more expensive than for other cars in this class, reports CAA. **Warranty:** Bumper-to-bumper 2 years/40,000 km; powertrain 5 years/80,000 km; rust perforation 6 years/unlimited km. **Supplementary warranty:** Essential, considering VW's precarious position in Canada and the EuroVan's past servicing history. Try to get VW's optional 10-year warranty protection, if it's still offered. **Highway/city fuel economy:** Figures aren't yet available.

VOLVO

In the past Volvo distinguished itself from the rest of the automotive pack through its much-vaunted standard safety features, crashworthiness, and engineering that emphasized function over style. But unfortunately these noteworthy features were eclipsed by bland styling, ponderous highway performance, inconsistent quality control that compromised long-term reliability and drove up ownership costs, and chancy servicing by a small dealer network.

Well, you can forget about bland styling and mediocre highway performance. Volvo's latest models are rounder, sleeker, and more attractively styled than anything the Swedish automaker has put out in the past three decades. In addition to the new C70 high-performance luxury coupe, Volvo has copied Subaru's successful marketing strategy and brought out an AWD wagon variation of its popular 850/S70/S80.

As far as quality control and dealer servicing are concerned, Volvo has improved service and warranty relations through accelerated service training programs and by allowing its dealers to carry out most warranty and extra-warranty repairs without obtaining prior authorization from the company.

For 1999, Volvo has axed the S90, launched the S80 sedan, T6, and C70 convertible, and brought back the S70 and V70 relatively unchanged.

S80

RATING: Not Recommended during its first year on the market.

NEW FOR '99: First model year, selling for $49,995 (S80) and $45,995 (S80 T6).

GENERAL COMMENTS: Volvo has replaced the rear-drive S90 sedan with the front-drive S80, equipped with a twin-cam 2.9L straight-six engine that generates 20 additional horses for a total of 201. Selling for about $5,000 more, the S80 T6 employs two turbochargers to boost the 2.8L engine's power to 268 horses and mate it to a 4-speed automatic transmission equipped with a Geartronic manual-shift feature.

Both models are well equipped with safety and convenience features that includes standard ABS, front side airbags and Inflatable Cushion side airbags that extend from the front to the rear roof pillars, seatbelt pretensioners, traction control, a "WHIPS" seatback and head restraint whiplash protection system, and an optional Dynamic Stability and Traction Control System.

C70

RATING: Recommended.

GENERAL COMMENTS: A $54,695 luxury coupe based on the 850 (pardon, S70) platform, and marketed as a high performance Volvo—last May, a convertible version made its debut. It has just one engine, a 235-horsepower in-line 5-cylinder turbocharged powerplant that's hooked to either a 5-speed manual or a 4-speed automatic transaxle. The C70 has comfortable seating for four. Volvo has made rear-seat access easier with a power folding mechanism that works well, but takes both skill and patience to master.

Acceleration is impressive, despite the fact that the car feels underpowered until the turbo kicks in around 1,500 rpm—a feature that drivers will find more frustrating with a manual shifter than with an automatic.

Safety features include dual driver/passenger airbags, side airbags, ABS, traction control, and a platform designed to give maximum passenger protection in a collision.

S70, V70

S70

RATING: Recommended. **Strong points:** Practical to the extreme, with plenty of power; good handling; lots of carrying capacity; and many standard safety features. **Weak points:** Limited rear visibility, excessive engine, wind, and road noise, fuel-thirsty (turbo models), and soaring base prices with little room for negotiating.

NEW FOR '99: These cars are carried over without any significant changes.

GENERAL COMMENTS: There are three variants of the S70 and V70: base, GLT, and T5. The base sedan uses a 2.4L 24-valve 168-hp 5-cylinder engine hooked to a front-drive powertrain. Wagons use the same base powerplant, hooked to a 5-speed manual or optional 4-speed electronic automatic. GLTs have a torquier, turbo variant of the same powerplant that boosts horsepower to 190.

The T5 "sports" sedan is a rounder, sportier-looking successor to the 850R model. It delivers honest, predictable performance but comes up a bit short on the "sport" side. Volvo's base turbo boosts horsepower to 222, but its new T5R variant uses an upgraded turbocharger that boosts power to 236 horses—for up to seven seconds.

Cost analysis/alternatives: Get either a second-series '98 or a '99 model; they're practically identical. Don't be surprised, though, if a '98 is hard to find. Other cars worth considering are the Acura TL, Audi A4, or the Infiniti I30. A fully equipped '98 Taurus or Sable wagon (with an extended warranty, of course) could save you over $10,000, perform almost as well, and would be easier to service at independent garages. Other wagons you may wish to consider: the BMW 5-series Touring, Audi S6, and Mercedes-Benz E-class wagon. **Recommended**

options: Integrated child safety seats, seat heaters, and a full-sized spare tire. The optional turbo's traction control and additional 22 horses aren't worth the extra cost. **Rebates:** Are you kidding? These cars are so hot, dealers are refusing to budge from the MSRP and some are tacking on unwarranted "administrative" fees and inflated PDI/destination charges. **Destination charge:** $700. **Depreciation:** Slower than average. **Insurance cost:** Higher than average. **Parts supply/cost:** Parts are highly dealer-dependent. Volvos are well serviced by the small dealer body, and parts aren't hard to find. **Annual maintenance cost:** Average. Higher than average predicted after the fourth year. **Warranty:** Bumper-to-bumper 4 years/80,000 km; powertrain 4 years/80,000 km; rust perforation 8 years/unlimited km. **Supplementary warranty:** A toss-up. This latest generation of Volvos hasn't shown any reliability weakness yet, but it's still too early to tell how they'll perform on a long-term basis. If you plan on keeping your Volvo longer than the standard warranty, the extra protection would make your trade-in easier to sell at a higher price. **Highway/city fuel economy:** 7.5–11.9L/100 km with the 2.4L; 8.4–12.3L/100 km with the turbocharged engine. AWD versions get about the same gas mileage.

Quality/Reliability/Safety

Pro: Reliability: No serious reliability problems have been encountered. **Warranty performance:** Much better than average. Many warranty claims are settled through "goodwill" on a case-by-case basis. **Service bulletin problems:** Nothing important. **Safety:** Standard side-impact airbags and standard traction control with the T5R version are a nice touch. Other safety features include rear head restraints, reinforced anti-roll bars, front and rear crumple zones, a practical, roof-mounted interior cargo net that protects passengers from being hit by objects stored in the rear, and rear three-point seatbelts.

Con: Body assembly and paint quality are better than average, but they can't match the Japanese competition. **NHTSA safety complaints:** *S70:* Car suddenly accelerated and brakes locked up at the same time; airbags failed to deploy; a piece of the vacuum brake system came loose, causing an increase in the engine rpms and locking up the brakes; dashboard causes excessive windshield glare which makes for serious eyestrain. *V70:* Fuel odour in vehicle after a fill-up; shoulder portion of the rear seatbelt won't retract; passenger exited rear door and exhaust pipe burned his leg. **Owner-reported problems:** Problem areas are limited to the front brakes, electrical system, and minor body faults. Some servicing delays decried.

Road Performance

Acceleration/torque: Plenty of high-range power with the base engine, especially with a manual gearbox. With an automatic transmission, the normally aspirated base engine has a 0-to-100 km/h time of 9.5

seconds. No turbo lag. The 190-hp engine posted better than average acceleration times (0–100 km/h: 8.8 sec.) with plenty of torque. **Transmission:** Smooth and quiet automatic and manual gearboxes. **Routine handling:** Nimble handling doesn't sacrifice passenger comfort. **Emergency handling:** Better than average, with minimal body roll and good control. **Steering:** Predictable, rapid steering response. Handles sudden steering corrections very well. **Braking:** Excellent braking performance (100–0 km/h: 115 ft.) on dry or wet pavement.

Con: Moderate torque steer when accelerating. Both the wagon and the sedan's soft ride deteriorates progressively as the road gets rougher and passenger weight is added.

Comfort/Convenience

Pro: Standard equipment: Lots of standard safety and performance features. **Driving position:** Excellent driving position and plenty of seat adjustments to accommodate almost any size of driver. **Controls and displays:** Everything is in plain sight, accessible and intuitive. **Entry/exit:** Easy front and rear access. **Interior space/comfort F/R:** Passenger space, seating comfort, and trunk and cargo space are unmatched by the competition. **Climate control:** Excellent. The system operates flawlessly and is simple to comprehend. **Cargo space:** The wagon's rear seatbacks fold flat and the seat cushion can be removed for additional cargo space. **Trunk/liftover:** Spacious trunk has a low liftover.

Con: Three rear head restraints limit rear visibility. **Quietness:** Excessive engine noise upon acceleration, as well as some wind and tire noise at highway speeds.

COST				
List Price (firm)	**Residual Values** (months)			
	24	**36**	**48**	**60**
Base S70: $34,995 (26%)	$25,000	$20,000	$15,000	$13,000

TECHNICAL DATA	
Powertrain (front-drive/AWD)	Height/length/width:
Engines: 2.4L 5-cyl. (168 hp)	56.2/185.9/69.3 in.
• 2.5L 5-cyl. turbo (190 hp)	Head room F/R: 39.1/37.9 in.
• 2.5L 5-cyl. turbo (236 hp)	Leg room F/R: 41.4/35.2 in.
Transmissions: 5-speed man.	Wheelbase: 104.3 in.
• 4-speed auto.	Cargo capacity: 37.1 cu. ft.
Dimensions (Wagon)	Towing capacity: 2,000 lbs.
Passengers: 5–7	Fuel tank: 73L/reg.
	Weight: 3,750

SAFETY FEATURES

	Std.	Opt.
Anti-lock brakes	■	❏
Seatbelt pretensioners	■	❏
Integrated child safety seat	❏	■
Airbag cut-off switch	—	—
Depowered airbags	■	❏
Side airbags	❏	■
Traction control	❏	■
Visibility (front/rear)	*****	***
Crash protection D/P	*****	*****
Crash protection D/P (side)	****	N/A
HLDI injury claims	Low	

S80

S80

RATING: Recommended. **Strong points:** Good engine and transmission match-up, comfortable ride, and many standard safety features. **Weak points:** Driving position not for everyone, ride comfort deteriorates as load is increased, fuel-thirsty, and high base prices proffered by dealers who won't negotiate.

NEW FOR '99: Volvo has replaced the rear-drive '98 S90 sedan with the front-drive '99 S80 and equipped it with a 2.9L straight-six engine that puts out 21 additional horses. Selling for about $5,000 more, the S80 T6 will employ two turbochargers to boost the 2.8L engine's power to 268 horses and mate it to a 4-speed automatic transmission, equipped with a Geartronic manual-shift feature.

GENERAL COMMENTS: Slightly larger than a Ford Taurus, the S80 front-drive sedans and wagons are practically identical in offering exceptional roominess, superb handling, and loads of standard safety and convenience features. Both versions are capable of carrying five people in comfort, and the wagon variant provides lots of cargo space.

Cost analysis/alternatives: Of course the only models worth buying are the upgraded '99 versions. Other cars worth considering are the BMW 5-series or Lexus GS 300 and 400. **Recommended options:** Built-in child safety seats and seat heaters. **Rebates:** Not likely. Get ready for some real sticker shock. These cars are so hot, dealers are refusing to budge from the MSRP and some are tacking on unwarranted "administrative" fees and inflated PDI/destination charges. **Destination charge:** $700. **Depreciation:** Average. **Insurance cost:** Higher than average. **Parts supply/cost:** Parts availability is very dealer-dependent; a high-volume dealer is your best bet. Volvos are well served by the small dealer body, and parts aren't generally hard to find. **Annual maintenance cost:** Average during the warranty period; expected to rise when the warranty expires. **Warranty:** Bumper-to-bumper 4 years/80,000 km; powertrain 4 years/80,000 km; rust perforation 8 years/unlimited km. **Supplementary warranty:** You can go either way with this option. This latest generation of Volvos hasn't shown any major reliability weaknesses yet, but it's still too early to tell how they'll perform on a long-term basis. If you plan on keeping your Volvo longer than the standard warranty, the extra protection would make your trade-in easier to sell at a higher price. **Highway/city fuel economy:** 8.3–13.3L/100 km with the 2.9L 6-cylinder.

Quality/Reliability/Safety

Pro: Quality control: Nothing that would sideline these cars for an extended period of time. Body assembly and finish is comparable to the Japanese competition. **Warranty performance:** Better than average. Volvo staffers have been fair and professional in handling warranty claims. **NHTSA safety complaints/safety:** Nothing recorded. Lots of standard safety features.

Con: Owner-reported problems: Failure-prone air conditioning, brakes, and electrical and fuel systems. Parts shortages and delivery delays are commonplace. **Service bulletin problems:** Unpleasant AC odours can be eliminated by installing a blower fan control module. This problem can be traced back to the 1988 900 series and its correction is covered by the base warranty (see bulletin on following page).

```
SECTION
8
GROUP
87
NO.
955
DATE
Sept. 1997
RE:
Odor from evaporator 700/900/S90/V90 1988-
REFERENCE:
TP 8701201, SECTION 8(87) CLIMATE UNITS: 700/900 1992-
TP 3701201, SECTION 3(37) WIRING REPAIRS, AND REPLACEMENT OF CABLE TERMINALS; 850900 TP 3502201, SECTION
3(35-39) LIGHTING, INSTRUMENTATION AND OTHER ELECTRICAL EQUIPMENT; 700/900 1982-
SERVICE BULLETIN 87-948, EVAPORATOR ODOR TREATMENT
This Service Bulletin replaces earlier Service Bulletin 87-965 from September 1996, which should be discarded.
Odor from evaporator, installation of blower fan control module
Under humid conditions the ECC unit can cause an unpleasant odor on start-up, especially when the temperature outside is
high. This Odor often disappears when humidity levels drops. The Odor can be caused by dirt or micro-organisms in the evap-
orator. A control module can be installed to eliminate the recurrence of the Odor. This starts the blower fan and airs resid-
ual dampness out of the evaporator.
It the compressor has been running more than 4 minutes and the ignition is then turned off for 50 minutes, the control mod-
ule starts the blower fan automatically and runs an airing out cycle at max. Blower speed for approximately 5 minutes.
Special tools needed: Wiring repair kit, P/N 9814235-9
```

Volvo says this fix is covered by its base warranty.

Road Performance

Acceleration/torque: The 2.9L 181-hp 6-cylinder puts out plenty of low-end and mid-range torque that meets all driving conditions with a minimum of strain or engine noise (0–100 km/h: 9.2 sec.). **Transmission:** Smooth and quiet automatic transmission. **Routine handling:** Acceptable handling prioritizes passenger comfort. **Emergency handling:** Very good. The multi-link rear suspension and front engine placement make for crisp handling. **Steering:** Good steering response, although road feel is a bit muted. **Braking:** Better than average. Braking is short and straight with minimal fading after successive brake application (100–0 km/h: 120 ft.).

Con: Some torque steer upon acceleration. Comfort and handling degrades as passenger/cargo load increases.

Comfort/Convenience

Pro: Very good driving position for most. User-friendly cockpit and better than average all-around visibility. **Controls and displays:** Well laid-out dash and analogue gauges are easy to read. Controls are within easy reach. **Climate control:** Climate control system is efficient, quiet, and unobtrusive. **Entry/exit:** Easy front and rear access. **Interior space/comfort F/R:** Front and rear seats are supportive and comfortable. Three passengers can sit in the rear in comfort. **Cargo space:** Plenty of cargo space. **Trunk/liftover:** Spacious trunk has a low liftover. **Quietness:** Whisper quiet.

Con: Standard equipment: Bland exterior and interior styling. **Driving position:** Short-statured drivers may find it necessary to lower the seat in order to extend the leg room to reach the accelerator comfortably. This makes it difficult to see over the steering wheel.

COST

List Price (firm)	Residual Values (months)			
	24	**36**	**48**	**60**
S80: $49,995 (30%)	$36,000	$30,000	$24,000	$20,000

TECHNICAL DATA

Powertrain (rear-drive)
Engine: 3.0L 6-cyl. (181)
Transmission: 4-speed auto.
Dimensions (S90)
Passengers: 5
Height/length/width:
56.6/191.8/68.9 in.

Head room F/R: 37.4/36.9 in.
Leg room F/R: 41/34.7 in.
Wheelbase: 109.1 in.
Cargo capacity: 16.6 cu. ft.
Towing capacity: 2,000 lbs.
Fuel tank: 73L/reg.
Weight: 3,500

SAFETY FEATURES

	Std.	Opt.
Anti-lock brakes	■	❑
Seatbelt pretensioners	■	❑
Integrated child safety seat	❑	■
Airbag cut-off switch	—	—
Depowered airbags	■	❑
Side airbags	■	❑
Traction control	■	❑
Visibility (front/rear)	*****	*****
Crash protection D/P	N/A	
Crash protection (side) D/P	N/A	
HLDI injury claims	Low	

Appendix I
1999 MODEL INDEX WITH PRICES

Part Three listed the strengths and weaknesses of individual models; now let's compare costs and see how prices can be cut by using rebates and the seasons to your advantage.

Most of the automakers' '98 prices have been carried over to the '99 models until new prices are announced in late fall. Then, we can expect GM, Ford, and Chrysler's new cars and minivans to cost only a bit more than the '98s, due to GM's desperate efforts to regain market share. Asian imports, on the other hand, will likely cost the same or less this year compared to last because of the added profit margin created by the devalued yen. Hyundai, the South Korean automaker, will likely offer the most attractive prices and dealer incentives in an attempt to recover from poor sales, labour strikes, and its own devalued currency.

European importers, though, are on a roll and aren't likely to offer any bargains going into the '99 model year. Apart from Jaguar and Saab, whose pricing policies follow closely Ford and GM and whose sales have been less than spectacular, European automakers will probably announce modest price increases throughout the model year.

MSRP Is Just the Beginning

The MSRP is the manufacturer's suggested retail price. It may or may not be posted on the vehicle's window, since there's no law that requires it. Nevertheless, it is used in most newspaper ads and TV commercials as a national benchmark to entice customers into dealers showrooms.

Jot down the MSRP wherever you find it and use the figure only as a starting point for negotiating a final price. Don't be surprised if the dealer says this guide's MSRP prices are too low. Simply ask for proof of when and by how much the MSRP was raised (a letter is sent by the automaker each time there is a price increase). You can always get the latest MSRP figures, transportation costs, and predelivery inspection (PDI) fees from the auto manufacturers' PR staff or independent car brokers.

Japanese carmakers give their dealers less generous markups within the MSRP than American manufacturers, while Europeans (except Jaguar and Sabb) give a bit more, but rarely offer customers rebates or dealers incentives to clear out leftover stock. Dealer profit from PDI and transportation fees, in addition to the 1–3% holdback allowance, represent additional profit areas that aren't counted in the MSRP markup.

Remember, the automakers make huge profits on each and every vehicle they sell. In some cases, their gross profit per vehicle will almost reach 30%.

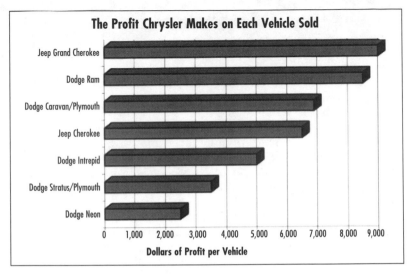

The Profit Chrysler Makes on Each Vehicle Sold

Dollars of Profit per Vehicle

Usually, one can expect to pay the full MSRP for any model bought between September and December. This year, however, GM kick-started a dealer incentive and customer rebate war in September to stanch its hemorrhaging sales. Ford and Chrysler have matched GM's programs and have pledged to continue to do so well into the new year. This means winter (January through March) shoppers can easily knock 5–10% off the MSRP. As you get into the late summer and early fall, a 2–3% price increase in the MSRP will probably be followed by additional rebates on leftover models that more than make up for the MSRP boost.

Company/Model	1998 ($)	Page #
ACURA		
1.6EL	$18,800	305
1.6EL Sport	$20,500	305
1.6EL Premium	$22,500	305
2.3CL	$30,000	306
3.0CL	$34,000	306
2.5TL	$35,000	308
3.2TL	$42,000	308
Integra GS	$25,500	311
GS-R	$27,300	311
Type R	$30,000	311
3.5RL	$55,000	309
NSX	$138,000	314
AUDI		.
Audi		
A4 1.8	$32,700	424
Quattro	$35,450	424
A4 2.8	$38,800	424
Quattro	$41,550	424
A6	$48,880	421
Quattro	$51,630	421
A8 Quattro	$90,540	423
BMW		
318ti	$27,800	433
318iS	$33,300	433
318iL	$49,900	433
323i	$34,900	433
323iC	$49,900	433
323iS	$39,900	433
328i	$44,900	433
328iC	$58,900	433
328iS	$49,900	433
M3 Coupe	$62,900	427
M Roadster	$61,900	427
Z3 2.3	$43,900	428
Z3 2.8	$52,900	428
528i	$57,200	429
540i	$72,900	429
740iL	$93,900	431
750iL	$137,900	431
Buick		
Century Custom	$25,199	253
Limited	$26,099	253

Company/Model	1998 ($)	Page #
LeSabre Custom	$28,845	262
Limited	$31,775	262
Park Avenue	$41,060	271
Ultra	$46,805	271
Regal LS	$28,845	253
GS	$31,775	253
Riviera	$44,125	267
CADILLAC		
Catera	$42,310	274
DeVille	$49,910	277
d'Elegance	$54,815	277
Concours	$57,490	277
Eldorado	$52,120	280
Touring Coupe	$55,370	280
Seville SLS	$59,195	280
STS	$63,080	280
CHEVROLET		
Astro CL	$22,660	296
CL AWD	$26,165	296
Camaro	$23,100	284
Convertible	$30,105	284
Z28	$28,670	284
Convertible	$37,100	284
Cavalier Coupe	$15,365	243
LS 4d	$18,575	243
Z24	$20,095	243
Convertible	26,450	243
Corvette HT	$50,165	288
Coupe	$52,870	288
Convertible	$59,850	288
Lumina	$22,329	259
LS	$23,749	259
LTZ	$25,270	259
Malibu	$20,895	250
LS	$24,045	250
Metro	$10,690	235
Metro Sedan	$11,680	235
Monte Carlo	$24,715	259
Z34	$26,145	259
Venture SW	$24,625	291
Venture LW	$26,930	291

Company/ Model	1998 ($)	Page #
CHRYSLER		
300M	$38,995	164
Cirrus LXI	$24,765	177
Concorde LX	$26,815	180
LXi	$31,015	180
Intrepid	$24,395	180
ES	$29,015	180
Sebring LX	$21,650	171
LXI	$26,810	171
JX	$27,530	171
JXi	$34,095	171
Town & Country	$42,915	185
AWD	$46,135	185
DODGE		
Avenger	$19,180	171
ES	$22,045	171
Caravan	$20,405	185
SE	$25,770	185
LE	$30,335	185
Grand Caravan	$23,310	185
SE	$29,135	185
LE	$31,345	185
ES	$34,035	185
SE AWD	$34,085	185
Neon Coupe EX	$15,870	167
4d	$15,975	167
Sport Coupe	$16,955	167
4d	$17,155	167
Stratus	$19,505	177
ES	$22,570	177
Viper R/T 10	$90,610	166
Roadster	$94,380	166
FORD		
Contour LX	$17,595	199
SE	$19,965	199
SVT	$28,195	199
Crown Victoria	$33,695	211
LX	$35,195	211
Escort LX	$14,895	196
SE	$16,395	196
SE Wagon	$16,395	196
ZX2	$15,895	196
Mustang	$22,595	203

Company/ Model	1998 ($)	Page #
GT	$26,995	203
Convertible	$33,595	203
Cobra	$36,095	203
Convertible	$39,495	203
Taurus LX	$23,295	206
SE	$23,995	206
SE Wagon	$24,495	206
SHO	$37,795	206
Windstar	$24,295	225
LX	$31,595	225
SEL	$35,995	225
GMC		
Safari SLX	$22,660	296
AWD	$26,900	296
HONDA		
Accord DX 4d	$22,000	319
EX	$26,800	319
V6	$30,800	319
LX	$23,800	319
EX 2d	$26,800	319
V6	$30,800	319
LX 2d	$23,800	319
Civic CX HB	$14,000	315
EX 4d	$17,000	315
LX 4d	$15,700	315
DX Coupe	$15,900	315
Si	$18,300	315
Prelude	$27,600	323
SH	$31,300	323
Odyssey	$29,800	326
HYUNDAI		
Accent L	$11,565	330
GL 4d	$12,995	330
GSi	$13,495	330
Elantra GL	$14,595	333
Wagon	$15,595	333
GLS	$17,695	333
Wagon	$18,845	333
Sonata GL	$19,495	336
GLS	$23,595	336
Tiburon	$17,595	340
FX	$19,495	340

Company/ Model	1998 ($)	Page #
INFINITI		
G20	$32,950	343
G20T	$34,050	343
I30	$41,350	344
I30t	$43,950	344
Q45	$66,500	347
Q45t	$69,000	347
JAGUAR		
Vanden Plas	$89,900	231
XJ8	$76,900	231
XJR	$92,900	231
XK8	$91,900	231
Convertible	$99,900	231
LADA		
Samara	$8,395	438
Sagona	$11,690	438
LEXUS		
ES300	$44,236	351
GS300	$59,220	353
GS400	$67,360	353
LS400	$78,300	355
LINCOLN		
Continental	$52,795	215
'98 Mark VIII	$53,695	218
Town Car Ex.	$50,895	211
Signature	$52,295	211
Cartier	$54,195	211
MAZDA		
626 DX	$20,140	361
ES	$29,215	361
LX	$22,575	361
Millenia	$36,535	364
Miller	$39,595	364
MPV	$25,199	370
LX	$29,635	370
4X4	$32,355	370
MX-5 (Miata)	$26,025	367
Protegé DX	$14,870	357
LX	$17,195	357

Company/ Model	1998 ($)	Page #
Mercedes-Benz		
C230E	$43,850	441
C230 Special	$37,950	441
C280 Sport	$45,650	441
C43	$75,700	441
CL500	$122,900	441
CL600	$161,800	441
CLK 320	$57,750	441
Convertible	$67,750	441
CLK 430	$68,750	441
E300 D	$59,950	445
E320	$66,750	445
4Matic	$71,500	445
Wagon	$67,250	445
E440	$74,250	445
ML320 Classic	$47,550	441
ML320 Elegance	$53,500	441
S320	$87,950	447
S420	$101,900	447
S500	$117,900	447
S600	$176,600	447
SL500	$115,900	447
SL600	$185,750	447
SLK 230	$57,550	441
MERCURY		
Cougar	$19,995	194
V6	$21,795	194
Grand Marquis GS	$33,695	211
LS	$35,195	211
Mystique GS	$17,995	199
LS	$20,995	199
Sable GS	$24,395	206
LS	$25,095	206
Wagon	$25,595	206
'98 Villager GS	$23,995	220
LS	$32,145	220
Nautica	$33,045	220
NISSAN		
'98 200SE	$17,598	376
'98 240SX	$26,698	380
SE	$28,698	380
LE	$31,639	380
Altima GLE	$27,998	377

Company/ Model	1998 ($)	Page #
GXE	$21,998	377
SE	$25,398	377
XE	$19,895	377
Maxima ES	$31,298	382
GLE	$37,548	382
GXE	$28,598	382
SE	$36,748	382
Quest GXE	$30,898	220
Sentra	$14,998	374
GXE	$19,448	374
XE	$16,798	374

OLDSMOBILE		
88 LS	$28,705	262
LSS	$32,515	262
Alero GL	$22,295	234
2d	$23,295	234
GX	$20,995	234
2d	$20,995	234
Aurora	$46,190	267
Intrigue GL	$28,779	253
GLS	$31,839	253
GX	$27,199	253
Silhouette GL	$29,890	291
Silhouette GLS	$34,045	291
Silhouette GS	$29,855	291

PLYMOUTH		
Breeze	$19,505	177
Neon 2d	$16,175	167
4d	$15,975	167
Prowler	$55,500	165
Voyager	$20,405	185
SE	$25,770	185
Expresso	$29,070	162
LE	$30,335	162
Grand Voyager	$23,310	185
LE AWD	$36,710	185

PONTIAC		
Bonneville SE	$29,000	262
SLE	$29,780	262
SSE	$35,170	262
SSEi	$36,685	262
Firebird	$24,865	284

Company/ Model	1998 ($)	Page #
Convertible	$33,265	284
Formula	$30,430	284
Firefly	$10,690	235
4d	$11,680	235
Grand Am GT	$25,895	247
SE	$21,795	247
Grand Prix GT	$27,489	247
SE	$25,399	247
Sunfire SE 2d	$15,165	243
4d	$16,135	243
GT	$25,895	243
Convertible	$27,565	243
Trans Sport SW	$27,265	291
Trans Sport LW	$28,365	291

SAAB		
9-3 HB	$33,200	300
Convertible	$50,650	300
9-5	$39,800	301
SE	$49,990	301

SATURN		
Saturn SC1	$15,493	239
SC2	$18,768	239
SL	$13,488	239
SL1	$14,398	239
SL2	$17,183	239
SW1	$16,118	239
SW2 Sport	$20,348	239

SUBARU		
Impreza Brighton	$17,795	386
Wagon	$20,495	386
SE Wagon	$22,795	386
Outback Sport	$24,995	386
2.5RS Coupe	$26,395	386
TS	$21,995	386
Legacy L	$25,995	389
GT	$29,995	389
GT Wagon	$30,995	389
Outback Sport	$24,995	389
Outback	$30,695	389
Limited	$34,295	389

Company/ Model	1998 ($)	Page #
SUZUKI		
Esteem GL	$13,995	395
GLX	$17,195	395
GL Wagon	$14,695	395
GLX Wagon	$18,495	395
Grand Vitara JX	$22,995	394
Grand Vitara JLX	$26,495	394
Swift	$11,495	393
TOYOTA		
Avalon XL	$36,605	409
Avalon XLS	$42,615	409
Camry CE	$22,680	405
LE	$27,070	405
CE V6	$28,435	405
XLE V6	$31,425	405
Solara SE	$26,245	405
V6	$30,515	405
Celica GT-S	$34,138	412
Corolla CE	$17,705	402
VE	$16,095	402
LE	$20,070	402
Sienna CE 4d	$26,808	418
Sienna LE 4d	$29,558	418
'98 Supra Turbo	$80,758	415
'98 TercelCE	$13,795	399
4d	$14,630	399
VOLKSWAGEN		
New Beetle	$19,940	449
TDI	$21,685	449
EuroVan GLS	$43,940	487
Camper	$49,815	487
MV	$46,200	487
Golf	$15,610	451
Convertible	$25,300	451
GLS	$30,070	451
GL	$16,765	451
GL Diesel	$16,665	451
GTi	$20,525	451
VR6	$26,465	451
Jetta GL	$18,085	451
TDI	$19,945	451
Wolfsburg	$21,325	451

Company/ Model	1998 ($)	Page #
Passat GLS	$29,100	455
Wagon	$29,900	455
V6	$32,750	455
Wagon	$33,550	455
GLX	$41,050	455
Wagon	$41,850	455
VOLVO		
C70	$54,695	461
S70	$34,995	462
Convertible	$58,795	462
S70 GLT	$41,995	462
S70 T5	$43,995	462
V70	$36,295	462
V70 GLT	$43,295	462
V70 T5	$45,295	462
V70 AWD	$45,495	462
V70 AWD XC	$48,995	462
V70 AWD R	$55,595	462
S80	$49,995	465
S80 T	$45,995	465

Appendix II
HARNESSING THE HYPE

How much will he take off? What are the monthly payments? How much time do I have to decide?

These are just a few of the questions that come to mind after you've had your session with the dealer's sales agent and are about to go home to mull over which dealership offers the best deal.

Use the following worksheet to keep all the figures in order and as a handy reference point to help you make a counter-offer. Make sure that each sales agent agrees with your notes before you leave the showroom. By the way, don't hesitate to show your figures to the other dealers to see if they'll beat the lowest offer.

DEALER PRICE REPORT

Dealership: _____

Salesperson: _____

Phone/fax: _____

Vehicle: _____   _____   _____
          Year   Brand   Model

Optional Equipment

Item	Dealer Price	Agreed Price
_____	$_____	$ _____
_____	$_____	$ _____
_____	$_____	$ _____
_____	$_____	$ _____
_____	$_____	$ _____
_____	$_____	$ _____
_____	$_____	$ _____
	Cost of Options:	$ _____

Manufacturer's suggested price (MSRP):_____ $ _____
Dealer's price: _____ $ _____
Destination charge/predelivery inspection:____ $ _____
Rebates/incentives:_____ $ _____
Price negotiated with dealer:_____ $ _____
Trade-in allowance:_____ $ _____

Appendix III
TEST-DRIVE REPORT

Use the form below to evaluate up to three vehicles that you're interested in purchasing. Rank each category by a score of 1 to 10.

0	1–2	3–4	5–6	7–8	9–10
No data	Poor	Fair	Average	Good	Excellent

	#1	#2	#3

Safety Features (Yes/No)
Overall crashworthiness
Frontal crashworthiness
Offset crashworthiness
Side crashworthiness
Side airbags
Depowered airbags
Passenger-side airbag disabler
Anti-lock brakes
Traction control
Seatbelt pretensioners
Integrated child safety seats
Childproof door locks
Anti-theft ignition/fuel cut off

Entry/Exit (1 to 10)
Step-up height (i.e., low/high)
Door width (i.e., too narrow)
Rear seat accesss

Seating Comfort (1 to 10)
Seats firm and supportive
Ease of seat adjustment
Seatbelt comfort

Interior Convenience (1 to 10)
Head/leg room
Seats fold/remove: ease of use
Efficient heating/defrosting/AC
Centre console (cupholders, etc.)
Glove box: size, depth
Door pockets for maps, etc.
Tinted windshield
Easy-access spare tire storage

Dashboard/Controls (1 to 10)
Gauges: size, ease of use
Steering wheel height
Transfer case button: location, ease of use
Turn signals, horn: location, ease of use
Windshield wipers: location, ease of use
High beam switch: location, ease of use
Power windows/locks: location, ease of use
Climate control system controls: ease of use
Sound system: volume, clarity

Visibility (1 to 10)
Forward vision
Rearward vision
Mirrors

Cargo Space (1 to 10)
Size (with rear seat up)
Size (with rear seat folded/removed)
Trunk capacity
Payload
Opening size
Liftover

Engine (1 to 10)
Ignition (i.e., easy or hard start)
Acceleration
Noise
Smoothness

Transmission (1 to 10)
Smooth shifting in all gear ranges
Clutch pedal: position, height

Handling/Ride (1 to 10)
Responsive steering
Road feel
Stable ride/cornering at speed

Braking (1 to 10)
Stopping distance/ABS performance
Front-end plow
Brake pedal: position/height

	#1	#2	#3

Noise (1 to 10)
Road/wind noise
Exhaust system noise
Squeaks/rattles

Style/Finish (1 to 10)
Pleasing lines
Overall assembly (welds, paint)
Interior finish (quality of components)

Total Points	#1	#2	#3

Appendix IV
1997–99 MODEL NHTSA CRASH-TEST SUMMARY

The following cars and minivans have been crash-tested by the U.S. government to determine how well they protect the driver and passenger from injury in a 57 km/h frontal or side collision.

Crash results from one model year can be extrapolated to another, as long as the model hasn't been substantially reworked, as was the Chrysler minivan in 1996 when it got an additional side door. To stay on top of the latest ratings, access the NHTSA web site at: *http://www.nhtsa.dot.gov/ncap/*.

ND=Incomplete Data

1997 MINI-CARS

Vehicle	Safety Rating			
	driver	passenger	driver side	passenger side
Geo Metro 2d	****	****	ND	ND
Suzuki Swift 2d	****	****	ND	ND

1997 SUBCOMPACTS

Vehicle	Safety Rating			
	driver	passenger	driver side	passenger side
Ford Aspire 4d	****	****	ND	ND
Honda Civic 2d	****	****	ND	ND
Honda Civic 4d	****	*****	***	***
Hyundai Accent 4d	***	****	ND	ND
Mazda Miata 2d	****	***	ND	ND
Mazda Protegé 4d	***	ND	ND	ND
Nissan Sentra 4d	****	****	ND	ND
Saturn SL2 4d	****	****	***	***
Toyota Paseo 2d	****	****	ND	ND
Toyota Tercel 4d	****	****	***	****

1997 COMPACTS

Vehicle	Safety Rating			
	driver	passenger	driver side	passenger side
Buick Skylark 4d	*****	****	*	***
Chev. Cavalier 4d	****	****	*	**
Chrysler Sebring 2d	*****	*****	ND	ND
Dodge Avenger 2d	*****	*****	ND	ND
Dodge Neon 4d	****	****	ND	ND
Eagle Talon 2d	****	****	ND	ND
Ford Escort 4d	***	****	***	***
Ford Probe 2d	*****	****	ND	ND
Geo Prizm 4d	****	****	***	***
Honda Accord 4d	****	***	**	***
Hyundai Elantra 4d	***	***	ND	ND
Hyundai Sonata	***	****	*	**
Infiniti I30 4d	****	***	****	***
Mazda 626 DX 4d	****	*****	**	***
Mazda MX6 2d	*****	****	ND	ND
Mercury Tracer 4d	****	****	***	***
Nissan 200SX 2d	*****	****	ND	ND
Nissan 240 SX 2d	***	****	ND	ND
Nissan Altima 4d	****	****	ND	ND
Nissan Maxima 4d	****	***	ND	ND
Olds. Achieva 4d	*****	****	*	***
Plymouth Neon 4d	***	****	ND	ND
Pontiac Gr. AM 2d	*****	****	*	***
Pontiac Sunfire 4d	****	****	*	**
Subaru Impreza 4d	****	****	ND	ND
Subaru Legacy 4d	****	****	ND	ND
Toyota Corolla 4d	****	****	***	***
Volkswagen Golf 4d	***	***	ND	ND
Volkswagen Jetta 4d	***	***	ND	ND

1997 MEDIUM

Vehicle	Safety Rating			
	driver	passenger	driver side	passenger side
Acura TL 4d	****	****	ND	ND
Audi A4 4d	****	*****	ND	ND

1997 MEDIUM cont.

Audi A6 4d	*****	*****	ND	ND
BMW 328i 4d	****	****	ND	ND
Buick LeSabre 4d	****	****	ND	ND
Chev. Camaro 2d	*****	*****	***	****
Chev. Lumina 4d	*****	****	****	***
Chev. Camaro 2d	*****	*****	***	****
Chev. Malibu 4d	****	****	*	***
Chry. Cirrus 4d	***	ND	***	**
Chry. Concorde 4d	****	****	****	***
Chry. Sebring Cvt.	****	****	ND	ND
Dodge Intrepid 4d	****	****	****	***
Dodge Stratus 4d	***	ND	***	**
Eagle Vision 4d	****	****	****	***
Ford Contour 4d	*****	****	***	****
Ford Mustang Cvt.	*****	*****	ND	ND
Ford Mustang 2d	****	****	ND	ND
Ford Taurus 4d	****	****	***	***
Ford T-bird 2d	*****	*****	***	*
Mazda Millenia 4d	****	*****	D	ND
Merc.-Benz C230 4d	****	****	ND	ND
Merc. Cougar 2d	*****	*****	***	*
Merc. Mystique 4d	*****	****	***	****
Merc. Sable 4d	****	****	***	***
Olds. Cutlass 4d	****	****	*	***
Plymouth Breeze 4d	***	ND	***	**
Pont. Firebird 2d	*****	*****	***	****
Pont. Gr. Prix 4d	****	****	ND	ND
Saab 900 4d	****	****	ND	ND
Toyota Avalon 4d	****	*****	ND	ND
Toyota Camry 4d	****	*****	***	***
VW Passat 4d	****	****	ND	ND
Volvo 850 4d	*****	****	****	ND

1997 LARGE

Vehicle		Safety Rating		
	driver	passenger	driver side	passenger side
Cadillac DeVille 4d	****	****	****	****
Chrysler LHS 4d	****	****	ND	ND
Ford Crown Vic. 4d	*****	*****	****	****
Lexus GS 300 4d	***	***	ND	ND
Lincoln Cont. 4d	****	*****	ND	ND
Lincoln T. Car 4d	****	*****	ND	ND
Merc. Gr. Marq. 4d	*****	*****	****	****
Olds. Aurora 4d	***	***	ND	ND
Pontiac Bonn. 4d	*****	***	ND	ND
Volvo 960 4d	****	****	ND	ND

1997 MINIVANS

Vehicle		Safety Rating		
	driver	passenger	driver side	passenger side
Chevrolet Astro	***	***	ND	ND
Chevrolet Venture	****	****	ND	ND
Chrysler T. & C.	****	*****	ND	ND
Chrysler T. & C. LX	***	****	ND	ND
Dodge Caravan	****	*****	ND	ND
Dodge Gr. Caravan	***	****	ND	ND
Dodge Ram Van	***	****	ND	ND
Ford Aerostar	****	***	ND	ND
Ford Econoline	***	****	ND	ND
Ford Windstar	*****	*****	ND	ND
GMC Safari	***	***	ND	ND
Mazda MPV	****	****	ND	ND
Mercury Villager	****	***	ND	ND
Nissan Quest	****	***	ND	ND
Olds. Silhouette	****	****	ND	ND
Plymouth Voyager	****	*****	ND	ND
Plymouth Gr. Voy.	***	****	ND	ND
Pontiac Trans Sport	****	****	ND	ND
Toyota Previa	****	***	ND	ND

1998 SUBCOMPACTS

Vehicle	Safety Rating			
	driver	passenger	driver side	passenger side
Ford Escort 4d	***	***	***	***
Honda Civic 2d	****	****	**	***
Honda Civic 4d	****	****	***	***
Hyundai Accent 4d	***	****	ND	ND
Mazda Protegé 4d	***	ND	ND	ND
Mercury Tracer 4d	***	***	***	***
Nissan Sentra 4d	***	****	***	***
Saturn SL2 4d	*****	****	***	***
Toyota Corolla 4d	****	****	***	***
Toyota Tercel 4d	ND	ND	***	****

1998 COMPACTS

Vehicle	Safety Rating			
	driver	passenger	driver side	passenger side
Buick Skylark	ND	D	*	***
Chev. Cavalier 2d	***	****	*	**
Chev. Cavalier 4d	****	****	*	***
Dodge Neon 4d	***	****	**	***
Eagle Talon 2d	ND	ND	*	ND
Ford Contour 4d	*****	****	***	****
Ford Escort ZX2 2d	ND	ND	***	***
Hyundai Elantra 4d	***	***	***	*
Hyundai Sonata 4d	***	****	*	**
Mazda 626 DX 4d	ND	ND	***	***
Merc. Mystique 4d	*****	****	***	****
Nissan Altima 4d	***	**	***	***
Olds. Achieva 4d	ND	ND	*	***
Plymouth Neon 4d	***	****	**	***
Pontiac Gr. Am 4d	ND	ND	*	***
Pontiac Sunfire 2d	***	****	*	**
Pontiac Sunfire 4d	****	****	*	***
Subaru Legacy 4d	****	****	***	ND
VW Jetta III 4d	ND	ND	***	**

1998 MEDIUM

Vehicle	Safety Rating			
	driver	passenger	driver side	passenger side
Acura TL 4d	****	****	ND	ND
Buick Century 4d	ND	ND	***	***
Buick LeSabre 4d	****	****	ND	ND
Buick Regal 4d	ND	ND	***	***
Chev. Camaro 2d	****	*****	***	****
Chev. Lumina 4d	****	*****	****	***
Chev. Malibu 4d	****	****	*	***
Chrysler Cirrus 4d	***	****	***	**
Dodge Stratus 4d	***	****	***	**
Ford Mustang 2d	*****	****	***	***
Ford Taurus 4d	****	****	***	***
Honda Accord 2d	****	****	ND	ND
Honda Accord 4d	****	****	****	****
Infiniti I30 4d	****	****	ND	ND
Lexus ES 300 4d	****	****	*****	****
Merc.-Benz C230 4d	****	****	***	****
Mercury Sable 4d	****	****	***	***
Nissan Maxima 4d	****	****	****	***
Olds. Cutlass 4d	****	****	*	***
Olds. Intrigue 4d	****	***	***	*
Plymouth Breeze 4d	***	****	***	**
Pontiac Firebird 2d	****	*****	***	****
Saab 900 4d	****	****	ND	ND
Toyota Avalon 4d	****	*****	***	***
Toyota Camry 4d	****	*****	***	***
Volvo S70 4d	*****	*****	****	ND

1998 LARGE

Vehicle	Safety Rating			
	driver	passenger	driver side	passenger side
Audi A8 4d	*****	*****	ND	ND
Cadillac DeVille 4d	****	****	****	****
Ford Crown Vic. 4d	*****	*****	****	****
Merc. Gr. Marq. 4d	*****	*****	****	****

1998 LARGE cont.

	driver	passenger	driver side	passenger side
Olds. Aurora 4d	***	***	ND	ND
Pontiac Bonn. 4d	*****	***	***	**
Volvo S90	****	****	ND	ND

1998 MINIVANS

Vehicle	Safety Rating			
	driver	passenger	driver side	passenger side
Chevrolet Astro	***	***	ND	ND
Chev. Venture	****	***	ND	ND
Chrysler T. & C.	***	***	ND	ND
Chrysler T. & C. (l.)	***	***	ND	ND
Dodge Caravan	***	***	ND	ND
Dodge Gr. Caravan	***	***	ND	ND
Ford Windstar	*****	*****	ND	ND
GMC Safari 2X4	***	***	ND	ND
Mazda MPV	****	****	ND	ND
Olds. Silhouette	****	***	ND	ND
Plymouth Voyager	***	***	ND	ND
Plymouth G. Voyager	***	***	ND	ND
Pont. Trans Sport	****	***	ND	ND
Toyota Sienna	*****	*****	ND	ND

1999 SUBCOMPACTS

Vehicle	Safety Rating			
	driver	passenger	driver side	passenger side
Ford Escort 4d	***	***	***	***
Honda Civic 2d	****	****	**	***
Honda Civic 4d	ND	ND	***	***
Hyundai Accent 4d	***	****	ND	ND
Nissan Sentra 4d	***	****	***	***
Saturn SL2 4d	ND	ND	***	***
Toyota Corolla 4d	****	****	***	***

1999 COMPACTS

Vehicle	Safety Rating			
	driver	passenger	driver side	passenger side
Chev. Cavalier 2d	***	****	*	**
Chev. Cavalier 4d	****	****	*	***
Dodge Neon 4d	***	****	**	***
Ford Contour 4d	ND	ND	***	****
Ford Escort ZX2 2d	ND	ND	*	****
Mazda 626 DX 4d	ND	ND	***	***
Merc. Mystique 4d	ND	ND	***	****
Nissan Altima 4d	ND	ND	***	***
Plymouth Neon 4d	***	****	**	***
Pontiac Sunfire 2d	***	***	*	**
Pontiac Sunfire 4d	****	****	*	***
Subaru Legacy 4d	****	****	***	ND
VW Jetta III 4d	ND	ND	***	**

1999 MEDIUM

Vehicle	Safety Rating			
	driver	passenger	driver side	passenger side
Buick Century 4d	ND	ND	***	***
Buick LeSabre 4d	****	****	***	***
Buick Regal 4d	ND	ND	***	***
Chev. Camaro 2d	****	*****	***	****
Chev. Lumina 4d	ND	ND	****	***
Chev. Malibu 4d	****	****	*	***
Chrysler Cirrus 4d	***	****	***	**
Dodge Stratus 4d	***	****	***	**
Ford Mustang 2d	ND	ND	***	***
Ford Taurus 4d	*****	*****	***	***
Honda Accord 2d	****	****	ND	ND
Honda Accord 4d	****	****	****	****
Lexus ES 300 4d	****	****	*****	****
Mercedes-Benz C230 4d	ND	ND	***	****
Merc. Sable 4d	*****	*****	***	***
Nissan Maxima 4d	ND	ND	****	***

1999 MEDIUM cont.

	driver	passenger	driver side	passenger side
Olds. Cutlass 4d	****	****	*	***
Olds. Intrigue 4d	ND	ND	***	*
Plymouth Breeze 4d	***	****	***	**
Pontiac Firebird 2d	****	*****	***	****
Toyota Avalon 4d	****	*****	*****	****
Toyota Camry 4d	****	*****	***	***
Volvo S70 4d	*****	*****	****	ND

1999 LARGE

Vehicle	Safety Rating			
	driver	passenger	driver side	passenger side
Audi A8 4d	*****	*****	ND	ND
Cadillac DeVille 4d	****	****	****	****
Ford Crown Vic. 4d	*****	*****	****	****
Merc. Gr. Marq. 4d	*****	*****	****	****
Olds. Aurora 4d	***	***	ND	ND
Pontiac Bonneville SSE 4d	*****	***	***	**

1999 MINIVANS

Vehicle	Safety Rating			
	driver	passenger	driver side	passenger side
Mazda MPV	****	****	ND	ND
Toyota Sienna	*****	*****	ND	ND

Appendix V
TWENTY-TWO BEST INTERNET
GRIPE SITES

1. Chrysler Owner Review Committee (*RAR17@chrysler.com*)
Set up almost a year ago, this Review Committee is still paying off customer claims that had been refused when presented through Chrysler's regular channels. I wish Ford had the good sense to create a similar mechanism for its aggrieved customers.

No, you won't read about Chrysler's newest consumer complaint committee in your owner's manual or see it touted anywhere at your local dealership. Chrysler's Review Committee was set up in February 1998 in response to the bad publicity and threats of court action coming from *Lemon-Aid* and about 600 Chrysler owners who helped form Chrysler Lemon Owners Groups (CLOGs) in British Columbia and New Brunswick. These groups submitted the names of irate owners to Chrysler and have succeeded in getting sizeable refunds for brake, transmission, and paint repairs.

If you have had any of these problems and want "goodwill" repairs or a refund for repairs already carried out, go through Chrysler's regular customer relations hot line. If you're not satisfied by the response you get, phone, fax, or email Mr. Bob Renaud, Vice President Parts, Service, and Engineering, at: tel. 519-973-2300, fax 519-561-7005, email *RAR17@chrysler.com*. He set up the Review Committee to take a hard look at all claims, including those that were previously rejected. Up to now, I can say he has kept his word and treated most consumer complaints diligently and professionally.

Three suggestions if you plan to contact the Review Committee: send Chrysler copies of all your repair bills or independent garage estimates, don't accept a refusal based on the fact that you're not the first owner, and finally, don't let Chrysler turn your claim down because the repairs were carried out by an independent repair facility.

If you wish to reach the co-chairs of CLOG (B.C.), contact Dean Tkatachow at: tel. 604-325-0921, fax 604-325-5207; or Patricia Wong at: tel. 604-657-2298, fax 604-255-1831, email *underdog@Lynx.bc.ca*.

2. Chrysler Products' Problem Web Page (*http://www.wam.umd.edu/~gluckman/Chrysler/*)
I'm not trying to bludgeon Chrysler, but it just happens that the company has had the uncanny ability to so anger its customers that they are motivated to set up web sites, form protest groups and organize demonstrations. (Are you listening, Ford?)

This page was designed to be a resource for Chrysler owners who have had problems in dealing with Chrysler, including issues with peeling paint, transmission failure, the Chrysler installed Bendix-10 ABS, and other maladies. There is also an interesting Dodge Durango web site that can be accessed from here (*http://www.baylor.edu/~ Jimmy_Stuart/dinfo.htm*).

3. Ford Paint Delamination/Peeling (*http://www.ihs2000.com/~peel*)
Everything you should know about the cause and treatment of Ford paint delamination. Useful links to other sites and tips on dealing with Ford and GM paint problems.

4. GM Paint Delamination/Peeling
Unfortunately, there's no longer a single web site that relates to the above GM problem. (One awesome site existed for two years and then was taken down. A GM payoff? Who knows?) Nevertheless, there are many sites where the problem is discussed. Simply access Alta Vista or any other browser and type in "GM paint delamination" or "GM peeling paint."

5. Ford Contour/Mystique Gripe Site (*http://www.contour.org/FAQ/*)
Similar to the Nissan site, except that it provides a more comprehensive listing of major problems affecting the Ford and Mercury Contour and Mystique.

6. Jeep Paint Delamination/Peeling (*http://www.goofball.com/badpaint/*)
Jeep paint and other body defects are covered. Useful links to other sites.

7. Nissan Gripe Site (*http://129.22.253.156/index.html*)
For dissatisfied owners of most Nissan vehicles, this site is particularly helpful in providing useful links to groups and government agencies who will take your complaint. It also covers in detail what it calls Nissan's "silent recall" of defective engines.

8. Sport-utility Gripes, Blasts, Whines, and Guilt Trips (The Roadhog Info Trough: *http//www.suv.org*; Sport Utility Vehicle Anti-Fan Club: *http//www.howard.net/ban-suvs.htm*; The Ultimate Poseur SUV Page: *http//www.poseur.4x4.org* or link from the Anti-Fan Club, above)
These anti-SUV sites believe that sport-utilities and trucks are safety and environmental hazards, in addition to being just plain annoying. You'll find lots of important info and links on the environmental and safety downsides of sport-utility, truck, and van ownership, but keep in mind that much of it is one-sided and some info is outdated. The Friends of the Earth's "Roadhog" site is a hoot to browse if only because of its Internet survey list of 22 questions and reponses that show most respondants don't care much about those policies our Corolla-Prizm-hugging activists hold dear.

9. "Lemon Aid or How to Get Carmakers to Call You and Beg for Mercy" (*http://www.saabnet.com/aas/1997.W26/1344522661.26426.html*)
Although not affiliated with the *Lemon-Aid* car guides, this site contains

a hilarious listing of tactics to use in getting auto manufacturers to return your calls, listen to your complaints, and give you compensation. For example, here's how you're advised to deal with the automaker's customer relations rep:

...This is what you should do. DENY THAT YOUR CAR HAS ANY PROBLEMS, and try to sell the car to the person who answered the phone. They will absolutely hate this. When you see that you are going nowhere with this, then ask the customer service rep to go around the office to take up a collection to pay for the car. Say outrageous things; take my word for it, they will remember your name! Alternatively, demand to know the telephone number of the rep's mother. When the rep asks you why you want his/her mother's telephone number, say you have a piece of metal to sell and you feel that his/her mother deserves it...

10. Canadian Law Resources on the Internet (*http://mindlink.net/drew_ jackson/mdj.html*)
If you have to take a dealer or automaker to court and need a lawyer or additional jurisprudence, this is an excellent site to find legal aid. Lots of case summaries, articles, and links to Canadian lawyers and experts. There are a number of discussion groups where lawyers will field your questions for (gasp!) free.

11. Trujillo vs. Volvo (*http://www.law.emory.edu/1circuit/mar98/97-1792. 01a.html*).
This U.S.-initiated lawsuit provides an interesting, though lengthy, dissertation on the safety hazards that airbags pose and why automakers are ultimately responsible for the injuries and deaths caused by their deployment.

12. Lemon-Aid Feedback (*lemonaid@earthlink.net*)
Comments and critiques are welcome, particularly if you have an experience to relate that can help other *Lemon-Aid* readers.

13. U.S. NHTSA (*http://www.nhtsa.dot.gov/cars/problems/*)
Run by the Big Daddy of federal-government auto-safety regulators, the National Highway Traffic Safety Administration, this site has a comprehensive database covering owner complaints, recall campaigns, defect investigations initiated by the department, and automaker service bulletins that may be helpful. Best of all, this data is easily accessed by typing in your vehicle's year, make, and model. Additionally, there's lots of pro and con information and updates relative to ABS, airbags, child safety seats, and frontal-side crash tests.

14. Transport Canada (*http://www.tc.gc.ca/vehiclerecalls/intro_e.htm*)
"We are presently enhancing the recall system in order to provide a searchable database. While this system is being developed, safety recalls

will not be available on the Internet."

Yep, that's been the message for the last eight months (March–November). Hopefully, by the time you read this, Transport Canada's Road Safety Branch will have a more user-friendly database up and running. As things stand now, Transport staffers give recall info only for the last three years and owner complaints aren't listed.

This site is a useful guide to university accident research teams, with plenty of links to provincial transport bureaucrats, auto clubs, and other safety organizations. It churns out lots of "establishment" auto safety info that promotes the traditional namby-pamby dialectic.

15. Insurance Institute for Highway Safety (*http://www.hwysafety.org/*)
A dazzling site that's long on crash photos and graphs that show which vehicles are the most crashworthy. Lots of safety info that eschews the traditional "nut behind the wheel" rhetoric. (Let owners deactivate their airbags if they feel at risk and beware of driving schools: they don't make kids better drivers.)

16. Royal Bank (*http://www.royalbank.com/personalfinances.html*)
If you want to challenge the dealer's estimate of your trade-in, or simply find out how much any used vehicle is worth, this Royal Bank site has the figures.

17. Alldata Service Bulletins (*http://www.alldata.com/consumer/TSB/yr.html*)
Automotive recalls and technical service bulletins are listed by year, make, model, and engine option. Select a year then a manufacturer to see a summary list of recalls and technical service bulletins for your car or truck. The only drawback is that you can't see the contents of individual bulletins.

18. Automobile News Groups
These news groups are compilations of email raves and gripes and cover all makes and models. They fall into four distinct areas: *rec.autos.makers. chrysler* (you can add any automaker's name at the end); *rec.autos.tech*; *rec.autos.driving*; and *rec.autos.misc*. The following news group bulletin board is particularly helpful to owners with minivan and van problems: *http://www.he.net/~brumley/family/vanboard.html.*

19. The Auto Channel (*http://www.theautochannel.com*)
This web site gives you comprehensive information useful in choosing a new or used vehicle, filing a claim for compensation, or linking up with other owners. Lots of background info on ABS defects and paint delamination/peeling with an update as to where the paint class actions are before the courts.

20. CompuServe Auto Forum or Consumer Forum
Here you will find owner gripes and service manager responses backed by a useful library. Simply go online and type "GOCARS."

21. Automobile Protection Association (*http://www.apa.ca/apa-services.html*)

The APA is a Canadian non-profit auto industry watchdog that works for improved legislation, industry sales practices, and automobile safety. It mediates complaints and provides lawyers for its members.

For $25, plus provincial and federal sales tax, the APA will mail or fax you the dealer's cost or invoice price for any vehicle you are considering buying. It will also provide any information on rebates and interest rate promotions. No credit card or email requests are taken, but the Invoice Request Form can be printed from the group's web site and mailed to the association with the $25 fee.

22. Center for Auto Safety http: (*http://www.autosafety.org/*)

Consumers Union and Ralph Nader founded the Center for Auto Safety (CAS) in 1970 to provide consumers a voice for auto safety and quality in Washington and to help lemon owners fight back across the country. CAS has a small budget but a big impact on the auto industry. It collects complaints and provides a lawyer referral service for its members.

Appendix VI
SURVEY AND BULLETIN SEARCH

Rate Your Vehicle

The information found in this book has been garnered from motorists' responses to surveys like the one on the facing page. Your answers to this survey will help us to protect others from sales scams and bad products. Include any photographs (especially of paint defects), diagrams, contracts, or work orders that expose a defect or dishonest practice. If you order a bulletin summary, your survey comments will also help me to zero in on bulletins that may be useful to you.

I pull the computer bulletin summaries myself (it keeps me in touch with readers like yourself), and usually have them faxed back within a few days. Sorry, I can only process Visa cards.

Phil Edmonston
lemonaid@earthlink.net

Cut Repair Costs • Fight Fraud and Incompetence With...

Lemon-Aid's $15 Bulletin Summary

If you plan to buy a vehicle, have just bought one, or want to know everything about your present vehicle before the warranty expires, you need a bulletin summary computer print-out. Nothing gives you a stronger argument with a service manager or mechanic than pulling out a confidential dealer service bulletin (DSB) that says a failure is factory-related or is covered by an extended warranty.

Fill out the form on the next page. You'll receive an exhaustive summary of DSBs (published in the U.S.) that concern your 1982–87 vehicle.

Bulletins show repair shortcuts, labour time, lists of upgraded parts, probable defects, recall campaigns, and secret warranties. With your order, we'll also give you your vehicle's present wholesale and retail value.

Order by fax or mail. There's no difference in price, although fax is much quicker. Set your fax to receive. The fax will be sent in the evening.

- FAX (Visa only): 954-563-2448 (24 hours a day).
- MAIL: Make your cheque out to "Lemon-Aid DSB,"
  2805 E. Oakland Park Blvd., Suite 211, Ft. Lauderdale, FL 33306

LEMON-AID SURVEY/DSB SUMMARY REQUEST

❏ I don't need a summary; my survey comments are below.

❏ Please fax/mail me a DSB summary for my car ($15 Cdn fee enclosed) and an estimate of its worth.

Fax #_____ Tel.# _____

VISA (ONLY) # _____

(will be used once and then destroyed)

Signature: _____

Name: _____

Address: _____

Province: _____Postal code:_____

MY VEHICLE'S PROFILE

Make:_____ Model: _____

Year:_____Engine (litres): ____Mileage: _____

GENERAL COMMENTS
(Include a photo, diagram, or bill)

Safety: _____

Reliability: _____

_____

Performance: _____

_____

JOY OF OWNERSHIP
(Recommended ⑤, Above Average ④, Average ③,
Below Average ❷, Not Recommended ❶)

Overall Reliability

Air conditioning	Ignition system
Automatic transmission	Rust resistance
Body integrity	Steering
Braking system	Suspension
Electrical system	**Dealer service**
Engine	**Maintenance**
Exhaust/converter	**Parts availability**
Fuel system	**Repair costs**